MANAGEMENT
Challenges in the 21st Century

MANADGEMENT
Challenges in the 21st Century

Pamela S. Lewis
University of Central Florida

Stephen H. Goodman
University of Central Florida

Patricia M. Fandt
University of Washington—Tacoma

West Publishing Company

Minneapolis/St. Paul   New York   Los Angeles   San Francisco

PRODUCTION CREDITS

Copyediting: Patricia Lewis
Text design: Robyn Loughran
Dummy: David Farr, Imagesmythe
Photo research: Kim Moss
Artwork: Randy Miyake
Composition: Parkwood Composition Services, Inc.
Index: Barbara Farabaugh
Cover image: "On the Points," Wassily Kandinsky, Musee National d'Art Moderne, Paris, France. Giraudon/Art Resource, NY. © 1995 Artists Rights Society (ARS), New York/ADAGP, Paris.

Text and photo credits follow index.

WEST'S COMMITMENT TO THE ENVIRONMENT

In 1906, West Publishing Company began recycling materials left over from the production of books. This began a tradition of efficient and responsible use of resources. Today, up to 95 percent of our legal books and 70 percent of our college and school texts are printed on recycled, acid-free stock. West also recycles nearly 22 million pounds of scrap paper annually—the equivalent of 181,717 trees. Since the 1960s, West has devised ways to capture and recycle waste inks, solvents, oils, and vapors created in the printing process. We also recycle plastics of all kinds, wood, glass, corrugated cardboard, and batteries, and have eliminated the use of Styrofoam book packaging. We at West are proud of the longevity and the scope of our commitment to the environment.

Production, Prepress, Printing and Binding by West Publishing Company.

British Library Cataloguing-in-Publication Data. A catalogue record for this book is available from the British Library.

COPYRIGHT ©1995   By WEST PUBLISHING COMPANY
610 Opperman Drive
P.O. Box 64526
St. Paul, MN 55164-0526

Printed in the United States of America

02 01 00 99 98 97 96 95   8 7 6 5 4 3 2

Library of Congress Cataloging-in-Publication Data

Lewis, Pamela S.
    Management : challenges in the 21st century / Pamela S. Lewis, Stephen H. Goodman, Patricia M. Fandt.
      p.   cm.
    Includes bibliographical references and index.
    ISBN 0-314-04568-6 (Student Hardcover Edition)
    ISBN 0-314-04708-5 (Student Softcover Edition)
    ISBN 0-314-04569-4 (Annotated Instructor's Edition)
    1. Management. I. Goodman, Stephen H. II. Fandt, Patricia M.
III. Title.
HD31.L388 1994
658—dc20

94-22667
CIP

To Terry, Ashley, Patrick, and Mom—for your unwavering love and support.
PSL

To Cynthia and Whitney—for the joy you bring into my life each day.
SHG

To Jim—for your confidence in me and support of all my projects; and to my students, who challenge me to be a more effective educator.
PMF

ABOUT THE AUTHORS

PAMELA S. LEWIS

Pamela Lewis is an Associate Professor of Management and Chair of the Department of Management at the University of Central Florida. She completed her Ph.D at the University of Tennessee in the area of Strategic Management and International Business. She teaches courses in management, strategic planning, and international management, and has won a number of teaching awards for her efforts. She played a leadership role in the development and implementation of Business Education 2000 (BE2000), an undergraduate business curriculum that has gained national recognition as an innovative, competency-based approach to business education. She has published numerous articles in the areas of entrepreneurship, organization theory, strategy, and international management. She is active in executive development and has conducted numerous seminars in strategic planning and international business for both domestic and international audiences.

STEPHEN H. GOODMAN

Stephen H. Goodman is an Associate Professor of Management at the University of Central Florida. He received his Ph.D in Business Administration from Pennsylvania State University, where he specialized in operations management and operations research. Prior to his doctoral study he received a B.S. in Aeronautical Engineering and an M.B.A., also from Penn State. During his more than 20 years in academia, he has taught, researched, and published primarily in production planning and control. He has also served as a coauthor of a textbook in the field of production/operations management. Currently he has a major teaching and research focus in quality management. He is an active member of the Decision Sciences Institute (DSI) and the American Production and Inventory Control Society (APICS), having held offices in each, engaged in journal review activities, and conducted professional training classes. He has achieved the distinction of Certified Fellow in Production and Inventory Management (CFPIM) from APICS.

PATRICIA M. FANDT

Patricia Fandt is an Associate Professor and Director of the Business Administration Program at the University of Washington Tacoma. She acquired more than 12 years of professional experience in sales and management prior to being awarded her Ph.D in Organizational Behavior from Texas A&M University. During her academic career, she has taught, researched, and published primarily in the areas of team development, management skill assessment, decision making, impression management, and classroom/training techniques for enhancing learning and student performance. She is the author of *Management Skills: Practice and Experience.* She is an active member of the Academy of Management, Southern Management Association, and the Organizational Behavior Teaching Society. She serves as an officer for the Southern Management Association and the Management Education & Development Division of the Academy of Management.

CONTENTS IN BRIEF

CONTENTS

6   Effective Managerial Decision Making   179

7 Decision-Making Tools and Techniques   209

10 Managing Human Resources   317

PART IV   LEADERSHIP CHALLENGES IN THE 21ST CENTURY   385

13 Understanding Leadership in a Dynamic Environment   423

14 Effectively Managing Individual and Group Behavior   457

15 Motivating Organizational Members   491

PART V   CONTROL CHALLENGES IN THE 21ST CENTURY   525

16 Organizational Control in a Complex Business Environment   527

17 Productivity and Quality in Operations   561

18 Information Technology and Control   597

PREFACE

You are about to begin studying one of the most important and interesting disciplines of business—the field of management. What an exciting time to be a student of management! Times are changing and so are the functions and roles of the manager. Tomorrow's managers must be prepared to meet the challenges of a highly dynamic and rapidly changing business environment. Our overriding objective in developing this book was to capture the excitement and challenge of management in the business environment of the twenty-first century.

Change is coming from all directions—quality management has radically changed the way many organizations do business; the global marketplace has redefined the competitive structure of many industries; and the increasing predominance of entrepreneurial and service-based organizations has altered the structure of our economy. Diversity in the workforce has become the rule rather than the exception; organizations are being restructured and redesigned to be lean, flexible, and adaptable to change; and managers in all areas and at all levels of the organization are expected to be proactive, team-oriented, and focused on results. Succeeding as a manager in the organization of today and tomorrow requires a special set of management skills and competencies.

Management: Challenges in the 21st Century is a book that will peak your excitement about the field of management. With almost every turn of the page, you will be exposed to the new challenges and contemporary issues that today's managers must continually address. Global competition, emphasis on quality, gender, ethnic, and racial diversity in the workforce, and entrepreneurial initiatives are just a few of the issues that you, and other contemporary managers, will confront.

Management: Challenges in the 21st Century provides comprehensive coverage of traditional management theory and has a special focus on meeting the challenges inherent in the dynamic, global environment of business. The application orientation of the book provides you with an opportunity to apply the material you learn and to understand a wide variety of real-world management situations. In short, the book is designed to help you to develop an understanding of the field of management and to develop the competencies and skills that will enable you to succeed in the business environment of the future.

FEATURES OF THE BOOK

This book includes a number of features designed to prepare students to be managers in the year 2000. These features focus on: (1) meeting the challenges inherent in a dynamic, rapidly changing business environment, (2) developing the competencies and skills that managers will need in the future, and (3) responding to the contemporary management trends that will affect both organizations and managers in the twenty-first century.

- *Meeting the Challenge.* The underlying, integrating theme that forms the foundation of this book is meeting the challenge. Contemporary managers will be continually challenged to respond to opportunities and threats that arise in the dynamic, global environment of business. Further, tomorrow's managers will be challenged to excel in everything they do. As competitive pressures continue to escalate and consumers across the globe demand increasing levels of quality, managers must strive for excellence in all facets of their organizations. Our focus in this book is on meeting these challenges as they affect the functions of management and the roles and activities of the manager.

- *Competencies and Skills.* Beyond our theme of meeting the challenge, we have developed this book with an emphasis on the competencies and skills needed by contemporary managers. Students of management must be prepared to translate theory into practice as they move into the work place. To do so, they will need to fully develop their skills in such important areas as teamwork, critical thinking, problem solving, communication, and adapting to change. Only managers who possess strong skills in these areas will succeed in the organization of the future. As you learn about management, you will have the opportunity to develop and practice management skills through problem-solving exercises, case discussions, self-assessment instruments and other experiential learning aids that are applicable to managers in a wide variety of roles.

    This text bridges the gap between management theory and practice by using an interdisciplinary, applied approach to the material in the text. Because managers come from all areas of an organization (e.g., production departments, finance and accounting departments, sales and marketing departments, etc.), it is important to understand how the concepts of management are applied in the various functional areas of an organization. Further, an interdisciplinary approach to the study of management is essential given the blurring of the lines separating the traditional functions of business (e.g., management, marketing, finance, etc.) and the increasing predominance of interfunctional work teams within contemporary organizations.

    In addition, it is essential that student understand how management theories and tools are applied in real organizations. We provide examples of organizations of all sizes and types that have implemented contemporary management concepts to achieve success within their industries. For example, we examine IBM's efforts to reorganize to improve its competitiveness, NationsBank's strategy for growth through acquisition, and Ford Motor Company's efforts to survive and prosper in the global marketplace through quality management programs.

    To further the objective of building the competencies and skills of students of management, this text can be used in conjunction with *Management Skills: Practice and Experience* by Patricia M. Fandt. *Management Skills* is organized into nine skills modules on: interpersonal, leadership, written communication, oral communication, perception, organizing and planning, decision-making, decisiveness, and flexibility—that can be packaged individually or grouped in any way to support the primary text.

- *Contemporary Management Trends.* Finally, we have identified and highlighted several contemporary management trends that present challenges for organizations and managers today. They include global management, entrepreneurship, service management, quality, team-based management, ethics, and cultural diversity. These topics are discussed in light of their impact on modern management practices, and numerous examples of how they are affecting contemporary organizations are provided. Rather than adding a separate chapter on each of these trends, we introduce them very early in the text and then integrate the topics into each and every chapter of the book. For example, rather than being treated as an isolated topic in a separate chapter, the globalization of the economy and business environment is discussed in each chapter to show how it affects all of the functions of management. This approach provides a more streamlined and integrative perspective of how contemporary management practices are affected by important societal, business, and organizational trends.

Organization of the Book

Like most management texts, this book is organized around the four primary functions of management—planning, organizing, leading, and controlling. The overall structure of the text departs from the traditional format in one important way, however. Rather than closing with chapters on special topics (i.e., global management, entrepreneurship, and ethics), this book introduces that material early on and then integrates and highlights it in each subsequent chapter. This approach allows for both a more streamlined structure and more effective and focused treatment of contemporary managerial challenges.

Part I of the text addresses the basic concepts of management, the roles of the manager, and the changing nature of both the contemporary organization and the contemporary manager. The contemporary management trends discussed above are introduced, and a foundation is laid for examining how these trends affect management theory and practice. In addition, the history of management thought is reviewed, and the topics of social responsibility and ethics are addressed in light of their increasing importance in modern organizations.

Part II explores the managerial function of planning. This section examines the basic principles of the planning process, as well as planning from a strategic perspective. Strategy is examined as a tool for responding to challenges in today's highly competitive, global business environment and for achieving quality in every aspect of an organization's operations. Further, decision making is addressed as a key managerial responsibility, and a number of tools and techniques for decision making are presented.

Part III of the text focuses on the organizing function of management. More specifically, this section addresses the fundamental principles of organizing, as well as the models of organizational design that are appropriate for contemporary, team-oriented organizations. Issues of organizational culture, change, and human resource management are also addressed in this section. Particular emphasis is placed upon organizing to improve flexibility, facilitate change, utilize team management, and respond to the challenges of a diverse and heterogeneous work environment.

Part IV explores the managerial function of leadership. This section focuses on factors that influence the behavior of people. Separate chapters examine individual and group behavior, what motivates members of the workforce, the nature of leadership, and communicating with others. Special attention is given to developing a leadership style that empowers the members of diverse organizations to excel in everything they do and to work as a team to achieve the goals and objectives of the organization.

Part V of the book examines the management function of control. The foundation principles of control are addressed, and specific attention is given to productivity, quality control, and information systems control. Control is presented as a principal tool for achieving quality in the products, services, and processes of the organization, as well as a tool for developing a competitive advantage based on enhanced productivity, increased efficiency, and superior quality.

Pedagogical Elements of the Book

Consistent with our application-oriented approach to the presentation of contemporary management trends, we have included the following elements, which are designed to help you become a more effective manager:

- *Video Supplements.* Throughout the text, company examples are used to illustrate certain management principles. Some of the companies discussed in these examples have been highlighted in video supplements. The primary purpose of these videos is to illustrate how specific management theories are applied in practice. The video approach brings a management situation to life by giving you a first-hand view of how management principles apply in the real world of business. For example, students will see how managers have restored the profitability of their companies by adapting their strategy to changing business conditions, improved the performance of their organization by implementing comprehensive quality management programs, and built new businesses through entrepreneurial management practices.

- *Chapter Overview.* Each chapter opens with an executive summary that describes the general content of the chapter. This opening summary highlights the primary topics and concepts to be covered in the chapter and explains why the information is important to the manager of the future.

- *Learning Objectives.* Each chapter contains a well-defined set of learning objectives. These objectives focus on the specific topics that will be covered in the chapter and provide a checklist of important points discussed in the chapter. The learning objectives are directly tied to the chapter summary.

- *Managerial Incident/Resolution.* Each chapter contains a Managerial Incident that details a real-life organizational problem or situation that is related to the content of the chapter. This incident is referred to often as the chapter unfolds. At the close of the chapter, a Management Resolution describes how the problem was solved or the situation was addressed using the management concepts discussed in the chapter. The Managerial Incident/Resolution allows the student to see how the concepts and theories presented in each chapter can be and are applied to real-world business situations and in real-world companies such as Motorola, PepsiCo, and Boeing. For example, you will see how business problems can be resolved through improving the decision-making process, developing a cohesive and quality-oriented organizational culture, and fostering teamwork throughout the organization.

- *Chapter Summary.* Each chapter closes with a summary of the major points presented in the chapter. This overview of the chapter contents provides students with an overall perspective of the topics covered. The summary is organized so that it is directly tied to the learning objectives at the beginning of the chapter.

- *Review/Discussion Questions.* A set of review and discussion questions is provided at the end of each chapter. The review questions relate directly to the content of the chapter. The discussion questions are application-oriented in that they require students to respond to real-world situations or issues using the knowledge gained from the chapter. For example, students will be asked to evaluate the effect of new and evolving management practices on various organizations such as their university, church, or a business for which they work. In addition, these questions have been designed to enhance students' critical thinking, communication, and teamwork skills.

- *Ethics: Take a Stand.* An ethical dilemma is presented at the end of each chapter. The dilemma relates to the material presented in the chapter Students will evaluate various alternative courses of action in terms of their ethical implications and select a course of action that is both ethical and meets the objectives of the organization. The Ethics: Take a Stand feature highlights the increasing importance of making managerial decisions that are founded on strong individual and organizational ethics.

- *Thinking Critically: Debate the Issue.* Each chapter contains a debate topic related to the content of the chapter. Students are asked to work in teams to develop arguments to support a particular position. The instructor selects two teams to present their findings to the class in a debate format. This exercise helps students to develop critical thinking skills, teamwork skills, and oral communication skills. For example, students are asked to debate the advantages and disadvantages of differing globalization strategies, using the grapevine to enhance organizational communication, and team-based organizational systems.

- *Chapter Video Cases.* Each chapter concludes with a video case that presents a real organization that uses contemporary management practices. Many of these video cases were produced specifically for use in this book. For example, we examine the social responsibility strategy of Union Camp, the strategic planning efforts of the Minnesota Twins, and the quality improvement efforts of Lanier. Other video cases include Northern Telcom, Southwest Airlines, and AT&T. Through these videos, management challenges come alive, and students see how real managers address organizational problems and opportunities.

- *End-of-Chapter Cases.* In addition to the video case at the close of each chapter, a second case outlines a fictitious situation that provides an opportunity for students to apply the concepts and tools presented in the chapter. These cases are designed to help students develop their analytical thinking skills and to apply the knowledge they gained from the chapter to resolve problems or address situations that often occur in contemporary organizations. The cases can be used as homework assignments, for group discussion, or for in-class discussion.

- *Experiential Exercises.* A structured experiential exercise is provided at the close of each chapter. These exercises can be used in either large or small class environments and are designed get students directly involved in the learning process by requiring them to apply management theory to real-world situations. Many of these exercises involve "self-assessment" and will help students gain a greater understanding of their own strengths and weaknesses in terms of their management competencies and skills. For example, students will evaluate the service quality of an organization with which they are familiar, assess the organizational culture of a present or former employer, and evaluate their ability to work in and lead a team. The primary purpose of these exercises is to help students develop the skills they will need to succeed in the business environment of the future.

- *Highlighted Examples.* Throughout the book, organizations that provide examples of contemporary management practices are highlighted. These highlighted examples are designed to profile real companies that are confronting management challenges and responding in proactive and innovative ways. Some of these examples are supplemented by video segments. The highlighted examples include:

- *Managing for Excellence.* Companies that have achieved excellence through their management practices are featured in Managing for Excellence. Of particular interest are those organizations that have adopted a quality orientation in everything they do. Companies profiled in Managing for Excellence include Compaq Computer, Federal Express, and Microsoft.

- *Global Perspective.* Organizations that have pursued international business strategies and compete effectively in the global marketplace are profiled in Global Perspective. The focus of these examples is on how management practices must be adapted to cope with the complexities of the international business area. Profiled companies include Sony, General Motors, and Corning.

- *Service Challenge.* Service Challenge highlights the activities of efficiently managed service organizations such as American Express, Wal-Mart, and AT&T. The examples focus on management challenges that are unique to service organizations and require special attention by managers.

- *Entrepreneurial Approach.* Businesses, both large and small, that have succeeded as a function of their entrepreneurial approach to management are profiled in Entrepreneurial Approach. These examples highlight the importance of innovative and creative management in today's rapidly changing business environment. Companies described in Entrepreneurial Approach include Gateway Computers, 3M, and Federal Express, as well as several smaller organizations.

- *Meeting the Challenge.* Meeting the Challenge provides an opportunity for students to practice the management principles that they have studied. The purpose of this feature is to allow students to apply management concepts in responding effectively to specific management challenges. For example, students will be given the opportunity to use self-assessment instruments to describe their own personal management styles and organizational assessment instruments to evaluate organizations with which they are familiar. In addition, in some cases they'll be asked to apply step-by-step prescriptive tools to specific management situations. This is a skill-building feature that is designed to prepare managers of the future to cope with the challenges they will face.

- *Cohesion Case—IBAX.* Each of the five major parts of the book (i.e., Introduction, Planning, Organizing, Leading, and Controlling) concludes with a comprehensive and integrated cohesion case that is supplemented by video. The company is IBAX—a joint venture between IBM and Baxter. In 1990, the company was losing $25 million, customer satisfaction was very poor, and employee morale was extremely low. Over the next three years, under the leadership of CEO Jeff Goodman, IBAX's profitability was restored, customer satisfaction was greatly improved, and employee morale skyrocketed. The case that closes each part shows how the contemporary management concepts, tools, and techniques described in that section facilitated the IBAX turnaround. The cases are supplemented by 7–12 minute videos that show IBAX's real-life executives, managers, and team members reflecting on how the change came about. This powerful story.

The video ties the concepts together, clearly illustrating how modern management practices led to success for one highly troubled firm.

Supplement Package

A professor's job is demanding. Because professors' jobs demand a lot, we expect professors to demand a lot from the publisher and the authors of *Management*. Both the textbook and the accompanying ancillary materials have been developed to help instructors excel when performing their vital teaching function.

The extensive learning support package with *Management* includes an annotated instructor's edition of the book, an instructor's resource manual, a test bank and computerized test bank, more than 250 color acetates, advanced instructional modules, and an electronic presentation software program. Furthermore, there is a comprehensive multimedia program. Videotapes, a videodisc, and other multimedia ancillary materials provide the means to bring the contemporary world of management to the classroom. For students, there is a study guide, a reader of current articles reflecting the themes of the book, a notetaking guide, and simulation software. Highlights of the ancillary package follow below.

Annotated Instructor's Edition

Prepared by P. C. Smith of the University of Tulsa, an outstanding set of annotations provides lecture enhancements for instructors. The annotations include the following:

- Discussion Considerations that suggest additional topics for discussion.
- Alternative Examples of current topics related to the text discussion.
- Points to Emphasize in discussing text concepts.
- Integrations that pinpoint where to use key supplements, such as transparencies and advanced instructional modules.
- Video Integrations that suggest what videos to use for specific discussions.

Instructor's Resource Manual

The instructor's resource manual for *Management* was prepared by Constance Campbell of Georgia Southern University and provides important information for each chapter. The manual is also available on disk for those instructors who prefer to work from disk. Each chapter of the manual includes the following information:

- Learning Objectives for each chapter.
- A detailed outline of the chapter material, including appropriate points at which to use the transparency support material.
- An Extended Outline with narratives under each major point to flesh out the discussion and show alternative examples and issues to bring forward.
- Detailed responses to the review questions, discussion questions, Ethics: Take a Stand exercises, cases, video cases, and experiential exercises.
- Additional Cases with suggested answers are also included in the manual for those instructors who wish to supplement the case material included in the text.

Test Bank

Special attention was given to the preparation of the test bank because it is one of the most important ancillary materials. Ned D. Young of Sinclair Community College prepared an excellent set of testing materials. The test bank contains over 3,500 multiple choice, true/false, matching, case, and essay questions. The questions have been categorized according to Bloom's taxonomy for cognitive complexity. The questions are classified as recall, comprehension, or application. Furthermore, difficulty rankings allow the instructor to know in advance if students are likely to find a question easy, medium, or hard.

Westest, the computerized version of the test bank, provides instructors with a convenient means of generating tests. The menu-driven testing package has many user-oriented features, including the ability to edit and add exam questions, scramble questions within sections of the exam, and merge questions. Westest is available for DOS, Windows, or the Macintosh. Call-in testing is also available.

Astound Presentation Software

Astound is a state-of-the-art presentation graphics program for Microsoft Windows or the Macintosh. This integrated program allows instructors to retrieve and work with any of the transparencies that accompany the book. Images can easily be edited, added, or deleted. Other features of the system include the following:

- The instructor can present transparencies electronically in the classroom.
- Transparencies from the program can be printed in one or four colors.
- The instructor can edit and change any of the material included in the transparency set, or add new material as needed.
- The instructor can animate and show a slide show with transition effects.

Multimedia Program

Video materials bring an excitement to management in a way that nothing else can. *Management* provides the professor with both videotapes and a videodisc. The comprehensive video program is described below.

Part I: Video Cases   The video cases are much like regular end-of-chapter cases but with an accompanying video segment that portrays some element of the case. The Minnesota Twins baseball club, IBAX, Union Camp Company, First Bank, Lanier Worldwide, and Price Club/Costco are among the organizations that allowed us to produce video case materials exclusively for this textbook. Each of the video cases in the book is based on real businesses.

Part II: The Video Lecture Support Series   For each chapter, we have integrated video segments on some of the most important and timely issues in management today. Each chapter includes several in-text video segments illustrating important concepts found in the text. This includes videos on international topics, total quality management, ethics, small businesses, and entrepreneurship. The video program also includes an integrated video case that presents management issues in the healthcare systems industry, through IBAX. This exciting video tracks the people and their management strategies in this highly dynamic industry. IBAX clearly illustrates that management is not an isolated business activity. Each video segment shows management decisions and explores how these decisions must be integrated with other functional areas of the corporation, such as finance, human resources, operations, etc. Each IBAX segment was custom-produced for exclusive use with this book.

The Videodisc

The videodisc is an innovative teaching tool that marks management education's entrance into the 21st century. It allows the instructor to combine the best elements of several media into a single presentation system. The videodisc allows for animated exhibits, video clips, special effects, and many visual features that can make management come alive in the classroom. This innovative supplement will make a big impact in the classroom and will help you better communicate the principles of management to your students.

Management On-Line

Professors will never be out of touch with the changing environment of management with free access to West Publishing and the Internet. You'll receive frequent updates to information in the text, additional annotations for use in lectures, suggested readings, and more through West's electronic bulletin board.

Advanced Instructional Modules

The advanced instructional modules are seven self-contained units on current "hot" topics in management. The objective of each module is to provide instructors with two comprehensive lectures beyond what is discussed in the book. Along with two complete lectures, each module contains student learning objectives, outlines of the lectures, transparency masters to supplement the lectures, and test questions covering the module's content. The modules average 50 pages each and are available in a separate printed supplement for the instructor. The subjects and authors of the modules are listed below:

- *Understanding the Management Challenges of Business Ethics and Corporate Responsibility,* Patricia M. Fandt, University of Washington—Tacoma
- *Total Quality Management,* Stephen H. Goodman, University of Central Florida
- *International Management,* Pamela S. Lewis, University of Central Florida
- *Diversity,* by Barbara Parker, Seattle University
- *Services,* William J. Quain, University of Central Florida
- *Entrepreneurship and Innovation,* Ben Arbaugh, University of Wisconsin Oshkosh
- *Teamwork,* William Callarman, University of Central Florida

Transparency Masters

More than 400 transparency masters, consisting of materials taken from the book and from non-text sources, are provided with *Management.* All were created using Astound presentation graphics and are available on Astound for optical editing. This comprehensive package was prepared by P. C. Smith of the University of Tulsa.

Transparency Acetates

More than 150 full-color transparency acetates are provided with *Management.* The transparencies were selected from the book and also from materials that do not appear in the book.

Multimedia Manual

Instructors will find suggestions and instructions on how to use the videos and videodisc that accompany *Management* in the multimedia manual. It also includes topics on classroom use, questions for discussion, and other helpful material. The manual was prepared by John Hall of the University of Florida, who also directed the content of the video and videodisc programs.

Student Study Guide

The extended study guide for *Management* was written by George Carnahan of Northern Michigan University. For each chapter, this comprehensive guide includes learning objectives with detailed descriptions; a chapter outline; multiple choice and agree or disagree questions with answers; exercises; and a chapter summary.

Student Notetaking Guide

This unique bound supplement includes selected copies of the transparency masters for students to take notes during lectures. Detailed outlines are also provided for each chapter of the book.

Insights: Readings in Management

A readings book is available for those faculty who wish to supplement text assignments with articles from the current business press. This soft cover book contains multiple selections from academic and popular press sources that discuss contemporary issues and trends in management.

Management Skills: Practice and Experience

Written by Patricia M. Fandt, this is for those instructors who emphasize skill development in the classroom. This integrated book consists of nine modules: interpersonal skills, leadership, written communication, oral communication, perception, organizing and planning, decision making, decisiveness, and flexibility. The modules are designed to provide theory, exercises, and assessment to assist students in developing these important skills. Each module can be custom-bound for flexibility, and each has its own professionally developed video.

The Complete Manager: A Management Simulation

This professionally produced package involves students as the President of a hypothetical multi-million dollar company, giving them the chance to make decisions on problems that real world managers face every day. The simulation is easy to run and requires no experience with computers.

ACKNOWLEDGMENTS

A book such as this does not come to fruition solely at the hands of the authors. Many individuals have had significant involvement with this project, and their contributions must not go unrecognized. These major contributors include colleagues at the University of Central Florida College of Business, colleagues at other educational institutions, members of the project development team at West Publishing, and personnel at IBAX. In addition to the material support provided by these groups, we must also acknowledge the moral support provided by our families.

We are quite fortunate to have received tremendous support from many of our colleagues at the University of Central Florida. In particular, we would like to thank Dean Richard Huseman for his continual support and encouragement to develop the highest-quality product possible. His commitment to delivering a highly innovative, competency-based undergraduate curriculum at the University of Central Florida (BE2000) has inspired us to focus the book on developing competencies that are critical to business success. We are also very grateful to Professor John Hatfield who has performed an enormous service for us by pretesting the materials in a classroom setting. We would also like to single out Professor Foard Jones for his valuable contributions to the Human Resource Management chapter. In addition, we would be remiss if we did not acknowledge the timely advice, valuable input, and general support that we received from countless other colleagues and friends at the University of Central Florida.

The Department of Management at the University of Central Florida is very fortunate to have three exceptionally committed and hardworking administrative assistants—Ann Houser, Zulema Sequel, and Janice Pasquine. We are grateful for their support throughout this project. Not only did they perform clerical services for us, but they were willing to do whatever was necessary to deliver a high-quality product within the deadlines we faced.

A number of graduate students at the University of Central Florida served as research assistants on this project. Debbie Camilleri, Leslie Connelly, Robbin Cooper, Amy Eller, and Frank Schumacher did considerable legwork as we built the base of empirical and applied research on which this book is founded. We are very thankful for their efforts and appreciate the contributions they have made to this book.

Many reviewers made insightful comments and valuable suggestions on the preliminary drafts of this book. Although criticism is sometimes a bitter pill to swallow, we can now look back and agree that the reviewer comments led to modifications that greatly strengthened the final product. We would like to express our gratitude to each of the following reviewers:

Royce Abrahamson, Southwest Texas State University
Jeffrey Bailey, University of Idaho
Edward Bewayo, Montclair State University
Allen Bluedorn, University of Missouri
Peggy Brewer, Eastern Kentucky University
Deborah Brown, Santa Fe Community College
George Carnahan, Northern Michigan University
James F. Cashman, University of Alabama
Daniel S. Cochran, Mississippi State University
Roy Cook, Fort Lewis College
John Cotton, Marquette University
Marian Crawford, University of Arkansas, Little Rock
Carol Danehower, Memphis State University
Arthur Darrow, Bowling Green State University
Richard V. Dick, Missouri Western State University
Kenneth K. Eastman, Oklahoma State University
Stanley W. Elsca, Kansas State University
Roy Farris, Southeast Missouri State University
Jan Feldbauer, Austin Community College
Diane Ferry, University of Delaware
Robert A. Figler, University of Akron
George Foegen, Metro State College
Sonia Goltz, University of Notre Dame
Richard Grover, University of Southern Maine
Ted Halatin, Southwest Texas State University
John Hall, University of Florida
Dorothy Heide, California State University, Fullerton
Marvin Hill, Northern Illinois University
Phyllis Holland, Valdosta State College
John Jackson, University of Wyoming
Dewey Johnson, California State University, Fresno
Forest Jourden, University of Illinois, Champaign
Marvin Karlins, University of South Florida
Robert E. Kemper, Northern Arizona University
Russell Kent, Georgia Southern University
David G. Kuhn, Florida State University
James M. Lahiff, University of Georgia
Lars Erik Larson, University of Wisconsin, Whitewater
Esther Long, University of West Florida

Barbara Marting, University of Southern Indiana
Dan McAllister, University of Nevada, Las Vegas
James McElroy, Iowa State University
Joseph Michlitsch, Southern Illinois University
Edward J. Morrison, University of Colorado, Boulder
Diana Page, University of West Florida
Allayne Pizzolatto, Nicholls State University
Paul Preston, University of Texas, San Antonio
Richard Randall, Nassau Community College
Bill Ryan, Florida Atlantic University
Jerry D. Scott, Southeastern Oklahoma State University
Dawn Sheffler, Central Michigan University
Jane Siebler, Oregon State University
Mary Thibodeaux, University of North Texas
Ronald Vickroy, University of Pittsburgh at Johnstown
John Villareal, California State University
John Wallace, Marshall University
Deborah Wells, Creighton University
Carolyn Wiley, University of Tennessee, Chattanooga
Mimi Will, Foothill College
Jack Wimer, Baylor University
Lou J. Workman, Utah State University
Robert J. Paul, Kansas State University

In addition to these manuscript reviewers, other colleagues have contributed greatly by developing several of the high-quality, comprehensive supplements that support this book. These individuals, and their contributions for which we are so grateful, include:

Instructor's Manual	Constance Campbell, Georgia Southern University
Study Guide	George Carnahan, Northern Michigan University
Test Bank and Computerized Testing	Ned D. Young, Sinclair Community College
Transparency Masters	P. C. Smith, University of Tulsa
Videos	John Hall, University of Florida
Annotated Instructor's Edition	P. C. Smith, University of Tulsa
Advanced Instructional Modules	Diversity, Barbara Parker, Seattle University Services, William J. Quain, University of Central Florida
	Teamwork, William Callarman, University of Central Florida
	Entrepreneurship and Innovation, Ben Arbaugh, University of Wisconsin, Oshkosh

A project of this magnitude is never undertaken without a great deal of commitment on the part of the author team. However, it is important to acknowledge someone who was equally committed to the project—our executive editor, Rick Leyh. It is doubtful that we would have undertaken such an immense project with another editor. Rick's commitment to quality, attention to detail, never-ending enthusiasm for the project, and encouragement to continue throughout the long process of writing this book were directly responsible for this project reaching completion. His pushing and prodding to make each draft a significant improvement over the prior one has resulted in a product in which we take great pride.

In addition to Rick, a number of other individuals at West made valuable contributions to this project. They include Jessica Evans, our developmental editor, who played a critical role in linking the huge network of contributors to this project; Sandy Gangelhoff, our production editor, who not only tolerated our continual changes to the manuscript as it moved through production, but actually encouraged us to change whatever was necessary to make this product the very best possible; and Stephanie Johnson, our media editor, whose creative energy and vision for the video program and the IBAX cohesion case were key to making them a success.

It is our belief that the IBAX cohesion case adds an important dimension to the book. IBAX provided us with an opportunity to follow and detail the turnaround of a company and to tie that turnaround to contemporary management practices. The cooperation and candor of IBAX's managers in the video interviews were greatly appreciated. In particular, we'd like to thank Jeff Goodman for giving rise to the story and taking the time to share it with us, as well as with many students of management.

Finally, we'd like to thank our families for their support throughout this project. Their tolerance of our absence from many family activities, their understanding of the time commitment a project like this requires, and their continual encouragement to push on enabled us to endure the lone nights and Lost weekends that made it possible for us to complete this book. For that support and commitment, we will always be grateful.

Meeting the Challenges of the 21st Century

PART I

Management and Managers: Yesterday, Today, and Tomorrow

CHAPTER 1

▼ CHAPTER OVERVIEW

Managers today confront extraordinary challenges that their predecessors rarely faced. These challenges include escalating global competition, an unprecedented demand for quality and value on the part of the consumers, and an ever pressing need to radically change the way their organizations function. More importantly, tomorrow's managers will face an even more demanding business environment. To meet the challenges of the business environment of today and tomorrow, managers must be flexible, proactive, and focused on quality in everything they do.

In this chapter, we examine the manager of yesterday, today, and tomorrow. Our primary focus is on the manager's job and how it will change as a result of changes in the business environment. We explore the competencies that tomorrow's managers must possess if they are to achieve success.

▼ LEARNING OBJECTIVES

When you have finished studying this chapter, you should be able to:

Define the concept of management within an organizational context and as a process.

Identify the roles played by managers.

Describe how managers spend their time.

Discuss the responsibilities of functional and general managers.

Describe the three levels of managers in terms of the skills they need and the activities in which they are involved.

Describe the environmental trends that are affecting the way organizations operate and managers do their jobs.

Identify and discuss the organizational changes that are affecting managers' jobs.

Describe the manager of tomorrow in terms of both managerial style and the competencies that will be necessary for success.

MANAGERIAL INCIDENT

IBAX: A COMPANY IN NEED OF LEADERSHIP

IBAX is a provider of information services software to the health care industry. The company, created in 1989, is a partnership between IBM and Baxter. For IBM, the venture provided entry into the software side of the computer business. For Baxter, the partnership with IBM provided much needed credibility in a computer-related business.

IBAX got off to a very rocky start and posted a loss of millions of dollars in its two years of existence. The market for health care information systems was extremely competitive, and gaining market share proved more difficult than originally thought. In addition, the health care industry was experiencing significant change due to a continuing stream of technological improvements and an uncertain regulatory environment. The company seemed to lack an identity of its own, and the absence of a strong organizational culture made it difficult to build a team of people who were committed to achieving the organization's goals. Quality was not the first priority, and a customer orientation was lacking throughout the organization. Finally, and perhaps most importantly, IBAX lacked strong leadership and, as a result, couldn't seem to correct its problems.

That was the situation when Jeff Goodman assumed the role of chief executive officer of IBAX in early 1991. Goodman knew that he faced many challenges in turning IBAX around, but he was committed to doing whatever was necessary to make this venture a success.[1] ▼

INTRODUCTION

The situation Jeff Goodman faced was not an enviable one. How could he take a company that was struggling to survive to a position of leadership? Improving technology, escalating demands for quality and value, and growing pressures from government regulation had created a business environment characterized by rapid and dramatic change. IBAX's ability to survive and prosper would depend upon the abilities of Jeff Goodman and his management team to adapt to this environment.

Unfortunately, IBAX's predicament is not uncommon. Today, organizations of all sizes and types are operating in a business environment that is more competitive and changing more rapidly than ever before. As a result, contemporary managers are facing extraordinary challenges and are being forced to rethink the way they manage their operations. Yesterday's management styles, practices, and processes may simply be ineffective given the very different challenges that the manager of today faces and the manager of tomorrow will confront.

The purpose of this book is to introduce students to the field of management. Management, as a discipline, has been greatly affected by the significant environmental and organizational changes that have occurred in recent years. We will explore the effect of these changes on the contemporary manager and learn how managers can achieve success in the highly dynamic business environment of the twenty-first century.

In this chapter we define and discuss the concept of management. Further, we examine the research that describes the roles managers play, the way they spend their time, and the skills they need to be successful. Finally, we examine how environmental and organizational change is affecting the manager's job, in terms of the competencies that are necessary to be a successful manager in the twenty-first century.

MANAGEMENT AND WHY WE STUDY IT ▬▬▬▬▬

Everything that we will address in the subsequent chapters of this book relates to managing the organization and the job of the manager. Consequently, it is important to develop a clear understanding of the concept of management at the outset. Let's look at a definition of management, the organizational context in which management occurs, and the process of management from a functional perspective.

MANAGEMENT DEFINED

Management has been defined in many ways. Mary Parker Follett, an early management scholar, offered what has come to be known as the classic definition when she described management as "the art of getting things done through people."[2] Although this definition captures the human dimension of management, a more comprehensive definition is needed.

For the purposes of this book, **management** is defined as the process of administering and coordinating resources effectively, efficiently, and in an effort to achieve the goals of the organization. **Effectiveness** is achieved when the organization pursues appropriate goals. **Efficiency** is achieved by using the fewest inputs (e.g., people, money) to generate a given output. In other words, effectiveness means "doing the right things" and efficiency means "doing things right."[3]

Managing for success requires a focus on achieving superior performance in every aspect of an organization's activities by all the individuals and groups within the organization. Achieving excellence has become a priority for many organizations as they face the challenges of a more competitive business environment. Tom Peters and Robert Waterman originally drew attention to the concept of excellence in their classic book *In Search of Excellence,* where they profiled some of America's best-run companies.[4] Based on their study of these organizations, Peters and Waterman identified eight characteristics of well-managed organizations (see Table 1.1). Many of today's managers regard these attributes as indicators of organizational excellence and success.

Management
The process of administering and coordinating resources effectively and efficiently and in an effort to achieve the goals of the organization.

Effectiveness
Pursuing the appropriate goals—doing the right things.

Efficiency
Using the fewest inputs to generate a given output—doing things right.

THE ORGANIZATIONAL CONTEXT OF MANAGEMENT

Management, as we have defined it, occurs within an organizational context. The management processes, tools, and techniques that we will examine and discuss in this book are those appropriate for managers who work in organizations. But what is an organization?

An **organization** is a group of individuals who work together toward common goals. Organizations can be for-profit, such as the business organizations with which we are all familiar (e.g., Chrysler, Pizza Hut, J. C. Penney), or not-for-profit, such as churches, fraternities, and public universities. Whether they are for-profit or not-for-profit, organizations have one characteristic in common: they are made up of people. The efforts of these people must be coordinated if the organization is to accomplish its goals.

Organization
A group of individuals who work together toward common goals.

THE PROCESS OF MANAGEMENT

Four major functions are associated with the process of management: (1) planning, (2) organizing, (3) leading, and (4) controlling. Figure 1.1 illustrates these functions and shows how they relate to the goals of the organization. These four functions form the foundation of this book. Although each is examined

▼ **TABLE 1.1**   Characteristics of Excellent Organizations

- **A bias for action,** favoring "doing" over "planning."
- **Simple form and lean staff,** that is, a small number of staff relative to production or line employees, few levels in the hierarchy, and a relatively simple structure.
- **Close to the customers,** with customer needs, goals, and satisfaction considered as important as any other factor (including profit.)
- **Productivity through people,** for all employees, and a focus on improving productivity by increasing people's desire and authority to make such improvements and then recognizing their contributions.
- **Encouragement of entrepreneurship,** by expecting managers to act as innovators and giving them the authority to do so.
- **Focus on key business values,** to provide clear and focused organizational goals and a strong and shared culture.
- **Emphasis on what the organization does best,** and on building on strengths, rather than on branching out into new areas that the organization has few resources for dealing with.
- **Controls that are, in a sense, both "tight" and, at the same time, "loose,"** that is, very clearly defined limits but with great freedom and autonomy within those limits.

SOURCE: Selected excerpt from *In Search of Excellence: Lessons from America's Best-Run Companies* by Thomas J. Peters and Robert H. Waterman, Jr. Copyright © 1982 by Thomas J. Peters and Robert H. Waterman, Jr. Reprinted by permission of HarperCollins Publishers, Inc.

in detail in a separate part of the book (planning in Part II, organizing in Part III, leading in Part IV, and controlling in Part V), a brief introduction of these functions is appropriate here.

Planning

Planning
Setting goals and defining the actions necessary to achieve those goals.

Managers at all levels of the organizational hierarchy must engage in **planning.** Planning involves setting goals and defining the actions necessary to achieve those goals. While top management establishes overall goals and strategy, managers throughout the hierarchy must develop operational plans for their work groups that contribute to the efforts of the organization as a whole. All managers must develop goals that are in alignment with and supportive of the

▼ **FIGURE 1.1**
The Functions of Management

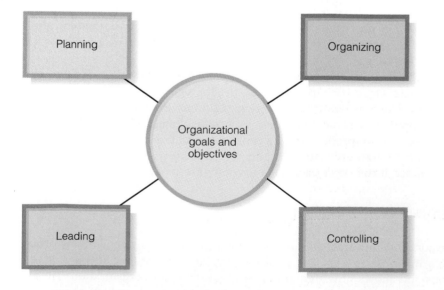

overall strategy of the organization. In addition, they must develop a plan for administering and coordinating the resources for which they are responsible so that the goals of their work group can be achieved.

Organizing

The managerial function of **organizing** involves determining the tasks to be done, who will do them, and how those tasks will be managed and coordinated. Managers must organize the members of their work group and organization so that information, resources, and tasks flow logically and efficiently through the organization. Issues of organizational culture and human resource management are also key to this function. Most importantly, the organization must be structured in light of its strategic and operational goals and so that it can be responsive to changes in the business environment.

Leading

Managers must also be capable of **leading** the members of their work group toward the accomplishment of the organization's goals. To be effective leaders, managers must understand the dynamics of individual and group behavior, be able to motivate their employees, and be effective communicators. In today's business environment, effective leaders must also be visionary—capable of envisioning the future, sharing that vision, and empowering their employees to make the vision a reality. Only through effective leadership can the goals of the organization be achieved.

Controlling

Managers must monitor the performance of their organizations, as well as their progress in implementing strategic and operational plans. **Controlling** requires identifying deviations between planned and actual results. When an organization is not performing as planned, managers must take corrective action. Such actions may involve pursuing the original plan more aggressively or adjusting the plan to the existing situation. Control is an important function in the managerial process because it provides a method for ensuring that the organization is moving toward the achievement of its goals.

With the four functions of management in mind, let's move on to examine the manager. **Managers** are the people who plan, organize, lead, and control the activities of the organization so that its goals can be achieved. Over the years researchers have examined managers in detail to find out who they are and what they do. These studies can help us develop a general understanding of managers.

Organizing
Determining the tasks that must be done, who will do them, and how those tasks will be managed and coordinated.

Staffing, Hiring & Rewarding

Leading
Motivating and directing the members of the organization so that they contribute to the achievement of goals of the organization.

Controlling
Monitoring the performance of the organization, identifying deviations between planned and actual results, and taking corrective action when necessary.

Managers
Organizational members who are responsible for planning, organizing, leading, and controlling the activities of the organization so that its goals can be achieved.

WHAT WE KNOW ABOUT MANAGERS

Regardless of your particular career interest, you may someday become a manager. Accountants become managers, sales people become managers, and so do computer scientists and engineers. Some musicians are managers, as are some actors. In fact, even professors become managers. If you are successful in your chosen career and have administrative and leadership skills, you may be called upon to manage others.

Much of the research of the 1970s and 1980s focused on who managers are and what they do.[5] More specifically, many studies examined the roles managers play, the skills they need, and how they spend their time.[6] Others examined how roles, skills, and time allocation vary according to managerial level and scope of responsibility.[7] The next paragraphs examine some of the more enlightening research on the subject of managers.

MANAGERIAL ROLES

According to a widely referenced study by Henry Mintzberg, managers serve three primary roles: interpersonal, informational, and decision making.[8] Figure 1.2 illustrates Mintzberg's theory of managerial roles, and the following discussion describes each role in greater detail.[9]

Interpersonal Roles

Interpersonal roles
The manager's responsibility for managing relationships with organizational members and other constituents.

The first set of roles identified by Mintzberg are **interpersonal roles.** These roles, which arise directly from the manager's formal authority base, involve relationships with organizational members and other constituents. The three interpersonal roles played by the manager are figurehead, leader, and liaison.

As the heads of organizational units, managers must perform certain duties that are primarily ceremonial in nature. For example, managers may have to make an appearance at community functions, attend social events, or host luncheons for important customers. In doing so, managers fulfill their role as *figureheads.*

Because managers are largely responsible for the success or failure of their organizational units, they must also play the role of *leaders* within their work groups. In this capacity, managers work with and through their employees to ensure that the organization's goals are met.

Finally, managers must also serve as organizational *liaisons.* They act as liaisons both in working with individuals and work groups within the organization and in developing favorable relationships with outside constituents. Managers must be politically sensitive to important organizational issues so that they can develop relationships and networks both within and beyond their organizations.

Informational Roles

Informational roles
The manager's responsibility for gathering and dissseminating information to the stakeholders of the organization.

The second set of managerial roles identified by Mintzberg are informational roles. In their **informational roles,** managers are responsible for ensuring that the people with whom they work have sufficient information to do their jobs effectively. By the very nature of managerial responsibilities, managers become the communication centers of their units and are a communication source for other work groups within the organization. People throughout the organization depend upon the management structure and the managers themselves to provide access to or to disseminate the information they need to do their job.

▼ **FIGURE 1.2**
The Roles of the Manager

SOURCE: Henry Mintzberg, "The Manager's Job: Folklore and Fact," *Harvard Business Review* (March–April 1990): 49–61.

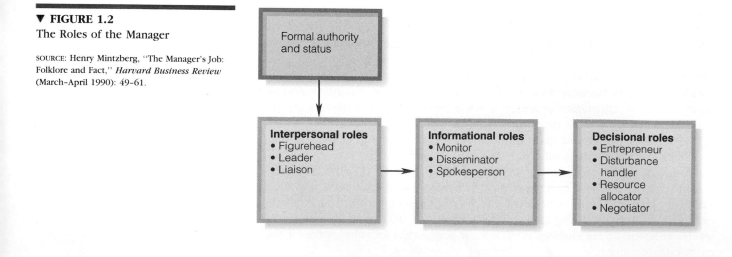

Formal authority and status

Interpersonal roles
• Figurehead
• Leader
• Liaison

Informational roles
• Monitor
• Disseminator
• Spokesperson

Decisional roles
• Entrepreneur
• Disturbance handler
• Resource allocator
• Negotiator

One of the informational roles that a manager must assume is that of monitor. As *monitors*, managers continually scan the internal and external environments of their organizations for useful information. Managers seek out information from their subordinates and liaison contacts and may receive unsolicited information from their network of personal contacts. From this information, managers identify potential opportunities and threats for their work groups and organizations.

In their role as *disseminators*, managers share and distribute much of the information that they receive as information monitors. As disseminators, managers pass important information on to the members of their work group. Depending on the nature of the information, managers may also withhold information from work group members. Most importantly, managers must ensure that their employees have the information necessary to perform their duties efficiently and effectively.

The final informational role played by managers is that of *spokesperson*. Managers must often communicate information to individuals outside their units and their organizations. For example, directors and shareholders must be advised about the financial performance and strategic direction of the organization; consumer groups must be assured that the organization is fulfilling its social obligations; and government officials must be satisfied that the organization is abiding by the law.[10] Lawrence Rawls, the former chief executive officer of Exxon, was acting in a spokesperson role when he personally delivered a message to the American public about the *Exxon Valdez* oil spill in Alaska.

▼ This manager is serving in an informational role as he provides information to shareholders at this Philadelphia Electric Company shareholder meeting.

Decisional Roles

Finally, managers also play the role of decision maker. In their **decisional roles,** managers process information and reach conclusions. Information in and of itself is nearly meaningless if it is not used to make organizational decisions. Managers make those decisions. They commit their work groups to courses of action and allocate resources so that the group's plans can be implemented.

Decisional roles
The manager's responsibility for processing information and reaching conclusions.

One of the decisional roles played by managers is that of *entrepreneur*. Recall that in the monitor role, managers scan the internal and external environments of the organization for changes that may present opportunities. As an entrepreneur, the manager initiates projects that capitalize on opportunities that have been identified. This may involve developing new products, services, or processes.

A second decisional role that managers play is that of a *disturbance handler*. Regardless of how well an organization is managed, things do not always run smoothly. Managers must cope with conflict and resolve problems as they arise. This may involve dealing with an irate customer, negotiating with an uncooperative supplier, or intervening in a dispute between employees.

As a *resource allocator*, the manager determines which projects will receive organizational resources. Although we tend to think primarily in terms of financial or equipment resources, other types of important resources are allocated to projects as well. Consider, for example, the manager's time. When managers choose to spend their time on a particular project, they are allocating a resource. Information is also an important resource. By providing access to certain information, managers can influence the success of a project.

The final decisional role played by the manager is that of *negotiator*. Studies of managerial work at all levels have found that managers spend a good portion of their time negotiating. Managers may negotiate with employees, suppliers, customers, or other work groups. Regardless of the work group, the manager is responsible for all negotiations necessary to ensure that the group is making progress toward achieving the goals of the organization.

SCOPE AND LEVELS OF MANAGERS

We have looked at the various roles that managers play within the organization. To this point, however, we have not distinguished among types of managers. Is it true that all managers are alike? No, it is not. Managers often differ with regard to both the scope of their responsibilities and their level within the vertical structure of the organization.

Scope of Responsibility

The nature of the manager's job will depend on the scope of his or her responsibilities. Some managers have functional responsibilities, whereas others have general management responsibilities.

Functional managers

Managers who are responsible for managing a work unit that is grouped based on function served.

Functional managers are responsible for a work group that is segmented according to function. For example, a manager of an accounting department is a functional manager. So is the manager of a production department, a research and development department, and a marketing department. Work groups segmented by function tend to be relatively homogeneous. Members of the group often have similar backgrounds and training and perform similar tasks. Functional managers often have backgrounds similar to the people they manage. Their technical skills are usually quite strong as they are typically promoted from within the ranks of the work group. The greatest challenge for these managers lies in developing an understanding of the interrelationship between their work groups and the other work units within the organization. Equally important, functional managers must convey information back to their work groups and ensure that the members of their unit understand the group's role within the organization as a whole.

General managers

Managers who are responsible for managing several different departments that are responsible for different tasks.

In contrast to functional managers, **general managers** manage several different departments that are responsible for different tasks. For example, the manager of a supermarket is responsible for managing all the departments within her store. The produce manager, grocery manager, bakery manager, and floral manager all report to the general manager. Because general managers manage diverse departments, their technical skills may not be as strong as the skills of the people they manage. The manager of the supermarket, for example, may not know the difference between a chrysanthemum and a violet or have the faintest idea how croissants are made. Whatever general managers lack in technical skills, however, they make up for in communication skills. General managers must coordinate and integrate the work of diverse groups of people. They are responsible for ensuring that all the discrete parts of their organizations function together effectively so that the overall goals of the organization can be achieved.

Levels of Management

Managers exist at various levels in the organizational hierarchy. A small organization may have only one layer of management, whereas a large organization may have several. Consider, for example, the number of levels of management in a single-unit family restaurant versus a large restaurant chain such as Chili's. While the small family restaurant may have only one level of management (the owner), Chili's has several layers, such as general store managers, area directors, and regional directors.

In general, relatively large organizations have three levels of managers: first-line managers, middle managers, and top managers. Figure 1.3 illustrates

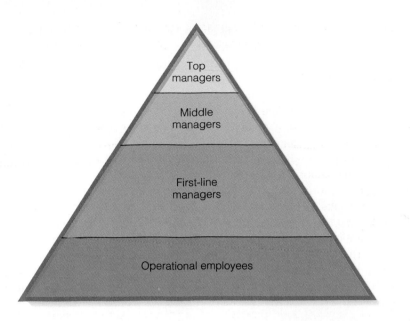

these managerial levels, as well as the "operatives," or the individuals who are not in the managerial ranks, but who actually deliver the product or service of the organization. The pyramid shape of the figure reflects the number of managers at each level. Most organizations have more first-line managers than middle managers, and more middle managers than top managers. As we will see later in this chapter, however, the trend of the 1990s has been to reduce the number of employees in organizations in an effort to improve efficiency. The net effect of such downsizing has been a significant reduction in the number of middle managers within many corporate structures.

The skills required of managers at different levels of the organizational hierarchy vary just as their job responsibilities vary. In other words, managers at different levels have different job responsibilities and therefore require different skills. The skills necessary for first-line managers to be effective are not the same as the skills needed by middle or top-level managers, just as the skills needed by middle managers differ from those needed by top-level managers.

While managers at each level must generally possess planning, organizing, leading, and controlling skills, certain job-specific skills are more important at one level than at another. Figure 1.4 illustrates three broad types of managerial skills that vary in importance according to the level of management. As we

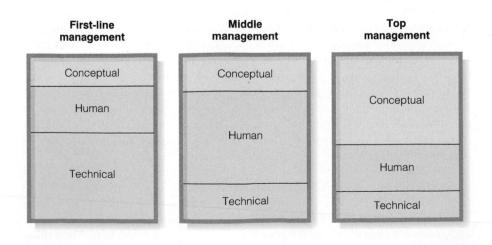

▼ This production quality control supervisor at Hewlett Packard provides an example of a first-line manager. It is his responsibility to ensure that the employees on his production line do their work efficiently and effectively.

Technical skills
The ability to utilize tools, techniques, and procedures that are specific to a particular field.

Human skills
The ability to work effectively with others.

will discuss, technical skills are likely to be most important for first-line managers, human skills for middle managers, and conceptual skills for top-level managers. Nevertheless, it is important to note that managers at all levels use these skills to some degree, and human skills, in particular, are very important at all three levels of the management hierarchy.[11]

Just as skills vary across levels of management, so do the activities in which managers are involved. A recent study of over a thousand managers examined the extent to which managers at each level engaged in certain basic activities such as managing individual performance, instructing subordinates, planning and allocating resources, coordinating interdependent groups, managing group performance, monitoring the business environment, and representing one's staff. The results of the study suggest that managers at different levels of the organizational hierarchy are involved in these activities to varying degrees.

As we examine the levels of management in more detail, we will look at the skills that are required of managers at each level, as well as the activities in which they are involved. By doing so, we can gain a better understanding of how managers' jobs vary according to their positions within the organization.

First-Line Managers: One to One with Subordinates   First-line managers supervise the individuals who are directly responsible for producing the organization's product or delivering its service. They carry titles such as production supervisor, line manager, section chief, or account manager. First-line managers are often promoted from the ranks based on their ability to deliver the product or service of the organization, as well as their ability to manage others who do the same. The primary objective of first-line managers is to ensure that the products or services of their organization are delivered to the customer on a day-to-day basis.

Technical skills are most important for first-line managers. **Technical skills** enable managers to use their knowledge of the tools, techniques, and procedures that are specific to their particular field. These skills are usually trainable and can be taught to other members of the work group where necessary. Surgeons, secretaries, computer programmers, and auto workers use technical skills every day.

First-line managers are most involved in two of the basic activities listed earlier—managing individual performance and instructing subordinates. *Managing individual performance* involves motivating and disciplining subordinates, monitoring performance, providing feedback, and improving communications. *Instructing subordinates* includes training, coaching, and instructing employees on how to do their jobs. Both of these activities become less important as managers rise in the managerial ranks.

Middle Managers: Linking Groups   Middle managers supervise first-line managers or staff departments. They carry titles such as department head, product manager, or marketing manager. Middle managers may come from the ranks of first-line managers in a particular department or from other areas of the organization. These managers are typically selected because they have a strong understanding of the overall strategy of the organization and a commitment to ensuring that it is implemented well. The primary objective of most middle managers is to allocate resources effectively and manage the work group so that the overall goals of the organization can be achieved.

Middle managers must possess strong human skills, commonly known as interpersonal or people skills. **Human skills** involve the ability to work effectively with members of one's work group, as well as with other work groups within the organization. Within the work group, middle managers must manage group dynamics, encourage cooperation, and resolve conflicts. They must listen to the opinions of others and be tolerant of differing beliefs and viewpoints. Further, they should create a work environment where members of the work group can express themselves freely, offer ideas, and participate in the planning activities of the unit. When interacting with outside work groups, middle managers serve as liaisons, communicating the needs and issues of their work group to other members of the organization and conveying information from other work groups back to their units. Fulfilling these responsibilities requires the constant use of human skills.[13] Managers who do not possess these skills are unlikely to be effective middle managers.

Consistent with their linking function, middle managers are most involved in three basic activities—planning and allocating resources, coordinating interdependent groups, and managing group performance. The importance of these three activities rises sharply as one moves from first-line to middle management, but interestingly, it declines slightly for the top management group.

Planning and allocating resources involves setting target dates for project completion, estimating resource requirements, determining where resources should be spent, interpreting the implications of overall organizational strategy for the activities of the work group, and developing evaluation criteria to measure the group's performance. *Coordinating interdependent work groups* includes reviewing the work and plans of the manager's unit, as well as other work groups, and setting priorities for activities. This may also require persuading others to provide the information or resources needed by the manager's group. Finally, in *managing group performance,* managers must define areas of responsibility for managerial personnel, monitor the performance of group members, and provide feedback on their performance.

Top Managers: An Eye on the Outside   Top managers provide the strategic direction for the organization. They carry titles such as chief executive officer (CEO), president, chief operations officer, chief financial officer, and executive vice president.

Occasionally, top-level managers work their way up the organizational hierarchy from the first-line management level. Ron Magruder, president of Olive Garden Restaurants, a subsidiary of General Mills Restaurants, is an excellent example of such a manager. Magruder started as a manager trainee with Red Lobster Restaurants (another subsidiary of General Mills Restaurants) and worked his way up to his present position over 20 years with the company. More often, however, CEOs of large organizations come with management experience gained from many other organizations. For example, when Lou Gerstner was hired as CEO of IBM, he came with many years experience with several organizations, including American Express and RJR Nabisco.

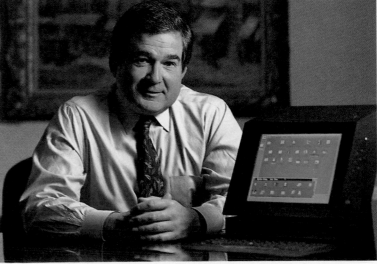

▼ Lou Gerstner, the newest CEO of IBM, will face many managerial challenges as he attempts to restore IBM's leadership position in the rapidly changing computer industry.

Regardless of their background, top-level managers should be selected because they have a vision for the organization and the leadership skills necessary to guide the organization toward reaching that vision. Top managers must set the strategic direction of the organization in light of organizational resources, assets, and skills and the opportunities and threats that exist in the external environment. This was the primary challenge that Jeff Goodman faced when he took the helm of IBAX. A strategic vision was essential if this firm was to survive and prosper.

Conceptual skills
The ability to analyze complex situations and respond effectively to the challenges faced by the organization.

Top-level managers need to have strong conceptual skills if they are to be effective. **Conceptual skills** enable managers to process a tremendous amount of information about both the internal and the external environment of the organization and to determine the implications of that information. Conceptual skills also enable top-level managers to look at their organization as a whole and understand how separate work groups and departments relate to and affect each other. Finally, strong conceptual skills enable top managers to develop a distinctive personality or culture for the organization.

Research indicates that top managers are much more heavily involved in one particular management activity than are their first-line and middle manager counterparts—monitoring the business environment. Though this activity ranks lowest in importance for both first-line and middle managers, it is extremely important at the executive level. *Monitoring the business environment* involves scanning the external environment for sales, business, economic, and social trends that might affect the organization. In addition, it involves developing and maintaining relationships with outside constituents of the organization. It is important to note that while historical research has suggested that this activity is important only at the top level of the organization, that may change in the future. Later in the chapter, we will examine some changes in the business arena that suggest that monitoring the environment will become an important activity at all levels of the organization.

It is interesting to note that one managerial activity was considered equally important by all three levels of managers—representing staff. From the lower to the upper ranks of management, managers felt that this was an important responsibility. Representing staff is consistent with the spokesperson role outlined by Mintzberg for it involves communicating on behalf of one's work group with other work groups and helping subordinates to interact with other groups. In essence, this activity requires managers to be ambassadors for their units.

All managers must have technical, human, and conceptual skills if they are to be successful. Further, most managers are responsible, to some degree, for all of the managerial activities discussed here. As we have seen, and as is illustrated in Table 1.2, each level of management requires a slightly different mix of skills and involves a somewhat different set of activities (see Table 1.2). Further, since managers will be involved in different activities at various levels of the organization, they need to develop new skills as they move up the corporate ladder.

We have examined a number of research studies that have focused on managers—who they are, what they do, and how they spend their time. At this point, it is important to examine some environmental and organizational trends

▼ **TABLE 1.2**   Levels of Management and Associated Skills and Activities

MANAGEMENT LEVEL	SKILLS	ACTIVITIES
First-line	Technical	Managing individual performance Instructing subordinates Representing staff
Middle	Human	Planning and allocating resources Coordinating interdependent groups Managing group performance Representing staff
Top/executive	Conceptual	Monitoring the business environment Representing staff

that are influencing the job of the manager. Contemporary management theory has begun to recognize the accelerating rate of change in today's business environment and the significant impact of such change on the manager's job. Accordingly, we turn our attention to a review of the changes that are occurring and their effect on the job of the manager of tomorrow.

MANAGING IN THE TWENTY-FIRST CENTURY

Virtually everyone would agree that we live in a dynamic and rapidly changing world. While some might argue that change is nothing new, others would suggest that we are now experiencing hyperchange. **Hyperchange** involves changes that come more quickly, are more dramatic, complex, and unpredictable, and have a more significant impact on the way organizations are managed than the changes of the past.[14] Further, and most importantly, the success both of an organization and of individual managers is often dependent upon their ability to respond to hyperchange.

Hyperchange
A condition of rapid, dramatic, complex, and unpredictable change that has a significant effect on the ways in which organizations are managed.

Recognizing change is insufficient—responding proactively is essential. For example, as early as the 1970s, top management at McDonald's recognized the trend away from eating red meat and high-fat foods. Nevertheless, they continued to focus almost exclusively on hamburgers and to fry their french fries in animal fat. Similarly, the three major U.S. car manufacturers knew that the American public wanted smaller, more fuel-efficient automobiles, yet they continued to turn out large, gas-guzzling cars. And although Xerox recognized that demand for the low-end copiers produced by its Japanese competitors was rising, it continued to market only high-end products.

In each of these cases, managers realized that changes were occurring, but failed to react proactively. And in all of these cases, they responded only when the competition forced them to do so. Increasing competition from Wendy's and other restaurants that offered healthy food alternatives finally drove McDonald's to respond to consumers' growing health consciousness. Foreign competition forced U.S. automobile manufacturers to respond to the needs of the consumer. And competition from both domestic and Japanese organizations caused Xerox to open its eyes to the changing marketplace.

Though all of these companies were slow to respond to change, there are also numerous examples of organizations that have capitalized on current trends. Managing for Excellence illustrates how Ted Waitt, CEO of Gateway 2000, recognized an increasing demand for value in the computer industry and forged an enviable market position by charging consumers "fewer bucks for the bang."[15] This company gained significant market share at a time when Compaq, a long-time leader in the industry, was under fire for failing to offer a low-cost product alternative, and IBM was struggling to make a profit.

Change will continue at a relatively rapid rate.[16] Though the 1980s were called the "White Knuckle Decade," most believe that the changes experienced in that period will pale in comparison to what will be seen in the future. Competition is brutal and is coming from sources unimaginable 20 years ago. Advances in transportation, communication, and information technology have made it possible to do business across the globe with a level of efficiency that has redefined the competitive structure of many industries. Further, companies can't win with just the lowest price or the highest quality anymore—they have to have both. We are living in a radically different world, and it calls for different methods of management. Achieving organizational success will be extremely challenging in the business environment of the future.

Tomorrow's managers must be prepared to cope with change if they are to be effective. Let's take a look at some of the changes, both environmental

MANAGING FOR EXCELLENCE

MORE BANG FOR LESS BUCKS AT GATEWAY COMPUTER

Ted Waitt went from being a small-town boy to the owner of a $600 million a year computer company. His road to success began when he quit college as a sophomore to work in a friend's computer retailing business. He and his future partner started a club network to find computer software and add-on devices for a particular personal computer marketed by Texas Instruments. They charged members $20 for newsletters that cataloged products and add-on devices that they had located. Club members could order these items from Waitt and his partner for slightly above cost. As their membership grew, the partners began to negotiate with manufacturers to develop the products they wanted.

Eventually, Waitt had saturated his original market niche. At that point, he began to build complete personal computers. When no bank would loan him the additional $10,000 he needed to get his new company off the ground, he asked his grandmother for assistance. She put up the collateral and Waitt's new company, Gateway, was born.

Because computer buyers hate to sink thousands of dollars into a machine that will be obsolete in a few years, Waitt focuses on giving his customers more bang for the buck by keeping prices as low as possible. Gateway is an assembly operation only. Mike Hammond, the cofounder of the company, selects components for personal computers from many different companies and searches for the lowest prices amongst suppliers. Gateway limits its sales strictly to phone orders and does not use retail outlets. This gives Waitt the flexibility to cut prices immediately without upsetting dealers. Gateway has also kept costs low by locating in South Dakota, one of the cheapest areas in the country to run a business.

Waitt has employed a well-orchestrated strategy that has made him the envy of many of his competitors. As a result, Gateway is positioned to play a leadership role in the personal computer industry for many years to come.

and organizational, that will influence the job of the manager and how organizations will function in the future.

ENVIRONMENTAL TRENDS

Many changes have affected and will continue to affect the modern business environment.[17] The next paragraphs describe four of the most pervasive developments. These four deserve special emphasis because of the far-reaching and profound effect they will have on managers and organizations. Because each of these trends will be addressed in greater detail throughout the book, here we will only briefly consider how they will effect the ways in which organizations are managed.

Globalization of the Marketplace

One need only glance at the recent trends in international trade and foreign direct investment to recognize that the global marketplace is growing in size and economic importance. Most organizations today are involved, in some way, in the international business environment. The level of involvement varies dramatically from company to company, however. Some organizations maintain relatively simple import or export relationships with foreign suppliers or customers. A more significant commitment may involve a contractual, franchising, or licensing agreement with a foreign company. If a firm has an equity investment in foreign assets, it may be involved in a partnership or a strategic alliance with an organization from another nation. At the far end of the continuum of international business involvement would be the organization that owns and operates foreign subsidiaries.

Organizations that are involved in the international business arena often face unique managerial challenges.[18] The global business environment is more complex than the domestic environment, and organizations operating in the international marketplace face a much broader set of environmental forces. Capitalizing on today's global opportunities demands managerial skills that were not required of yesterday's manager.[19] For example, decisions about where to locate a plant to minimize labor and transportation costs, how to coordinate production schedules across national borders, and how to disseminate new technology on a global basis are far more common today than in the past. Further, many organizations are finding that they must partner with other firms to maintain their competitiveness worldwide. The recognition of the need to "cooperate to compete" has led to many global partnerships that require very special international management skills.[20]

Not only has the evolution of the world marketplace forced many organizations to radically change the way they operate, but it will continue to influence the way industries will be structured and companies will function for many years to come. Consequently, we have focused on issues of global management throughout this book.

Increasing Predominance of Entrepreneurial Firms

Large organizations have long been credited with being the cornerstone of the U.S. economy. While few would argue against the economic benefits of these organizations, the performance results experienced by such companies in recent years has been less than impressive. Over the last several years, sales growth has been relatively stagnant in Fortune 500 companies. Further, literally hundreds of thousands of jobs have been eliminated in these same organizations over the same time period.[21]

That's the bad news. Here's the good news. Although estimates vary widely, entrepreneurship is believed to be responsible for the creation of 40–80 percent of all new jobs in the United States. In fact, millions of new jobs are created annually from business start-ups alone.[22] The role of the entrepreneurial company in fostering the vitality of the domestic and world economy is indisputable.

The spirit of the entrepreneur has entered the mainstream of American management philosophy, and entrepreneurial companies are influencing the business environment in many ways. Consider the following:

▼ Mary Kay Ash provides an excellent example of an entrepreneur who overcame significant obstacles to develop a highly successful cosmetic company—Mary Kay Cosmetics.

- Entrepreneurial firms are responsible for a disproportionate number of new products, services, and processes. And those new products, services, and processes are coming faster than ever before. Consider, for example, that gunpowder took 200 years to move from the laboratory to artillery. Today, the equivalent innovation would travel the same path in only a few months.

- Entrepreneurial activities place pressure on large, bureaucratic firms to be more innovative and proactive. In fact, some would suggest that entrepreneurship represents a key solution to problems in product and service quality, poor productivity, and the declining competitiveness of American industry.

- Entrepreneurship provides opportunities for minorities and others who may face barriers in traditional corporate environments. Both immigrants

ENTREPRENEURIAL APPROACH

JUBILATIONS, INC.: IT HASN'T BEEN A PIECE OF CAKE

Tamara S. Craddock, of Columbus, Mississippi, found that a quality product was far from the only ingredient she needed to make her cheesecake bakery, Jubilations, Inc., grow. In fact, her toughest challenge initially was securing financing for her new business. She had baked for profit from her own kitchen for six years, and each year profits had increased. But when she wanted to open a facility outside her home, three local banks denied her loan application. But she was tenacious and finally found an individual who would co-sign her note at a bank and invest in the business.

Locating suppliers willing to sell to a small new enterprise was challenging as well. A dairy wanted to sell butter in railroad boxcar loads. Container companies wanted to sell only in lots of 10,000. But, after much research and searching, she finally located the appropriate suppliers. Finding brokers to represent her was also difficult. Craddock says most reputable brokers prefer to handle name brands that sell themselves.

But she worked very hard to find customers. She called on hotel and restaurant owners, chefs, and store owners, serving them cheesecake. She managed to place cakes in owner-operated groceries, hoping the track record she established there would help her sell to chains. She even advertised for mail-order customers. In one four-week stretch she drove a rented, 18-foot freezer truck to sales shows in Alabama, Florida, and Louisiana, as well as in her own state. In an effort to gain exposure, Craddock handed out up to 2,000 sample bites a day.

Sales have doubled in the past three years. Craddock gives much of the credit to her products. Her cheesecakes contain only first-quality ingredients, come in more than 30 flavors and two sizes, and are unsliced or presliced. She also gives much credit to her four employees, whom she calls together regularly for idea sessions and rewards when appropriate. For example, an employee who thought up a recipe improvement that saved money got a $100 bill. Craddock says she wants to maintain a jubilant working atmosphere in keeping with her company's name.

and women have benefited greatly from entrepreneurial activities. In fact, Entrepreneurial Approach describes how one woman put her talents to work to achieve success in the bakery business.[23]

While the benefits of entrepreneurship are widely recognized, a number of criticisms have been leveled at entrepreneurship in general. Some argue that continuous innovation can cause the premature obsolescence of many products and processes. This forces many organizations to invest heavily in research and development in order to imitate others' innovations. In addition, some critics argue that an economic system that facilitates small entrepreneurial companies at the expense of large established firms weakens the global competitiveness of the nation. This problem is particularly acute in industries where success is dependent upon size and economies of scale.

Despite these arguments, entrepreneurs and entrepreneurially spirited companies will continue to create pressures for change in organizations of all sizes and types. In fact, innovation, proactiveness, and flexibility will become a prerequisite for success in most industries. Managers must be prepared to respond quickly to changing customer demands and to be proactive with regard to product, service, or process innovation. For that reason, we have highlighted entrepreneurial management practices throughout the book.

Growth in Service-Based Organizations

Though the U.S. manufacturing sector will never be insignificant, the fastest-growing segment of our economy is the service sector.[24] Nearly 80 percent of U.S. jobs and 60 percent of gross domestic product come from the performance of services rather than the production of goods.[25] The United States spends $2.4 trillion on services annually, roughly double the amount spent in Japan (the world's second largest services consumer).[26] Further, a glance at Fortune's 1994 list of the 100 largest U.S. service corporations would find some of the world's most respected companies, including American Express, Walt Disney, and Wal-Mart. Table 1.3 lists the ten largest and the ten most profitable service companies in the United States.

The shift to a service-based economy has created challenges for many managers. The manufacturing environment requires certain tools, techniques, and managerial practices that may be inappropriate for service organizations.[27] Employees, customers, and managers play dramatically different roles in service firms than in manufacturing firms. As a result, many managers have had to change their approach, and redefine relevant performance measures.

If service organizations are going to prosper in the long term, they must develop and maintain management systems that are suited to their unique and special needs.[28] In a recent article in *Harvard Business Review,* Leonard Schlesinger and James Heskett proposed a new model of service management that:

- values investments in people as much as investments in machines;
- uses technology to support the efforts of men and women on the front line, not just to monitor or replace them;
- makes recruitment and training as crucial for salesclerks and housekeepers as for managers and senior executives;
- links compensation to performance for employees at every level, not just for those at the top.[29]

The message is clear—frontline workers are the key to success in service organizations. Whereas the old model fails to adequately recognize the importance of recruiting, selecting, and supporting the people who deliver the service to the customer, the new model puts the service delivery employee at the forefront of the management system. The potential benefits of such a system are profound, and senior managers at firms that have adopted such an approach to service management (e.g., retail company Dayton Hudson and

▼ **TABLE 1.3**   Fortune 500 Service Corporations

THE TEN LARGEST U.S. SERVICE CORPORATIONS (RANKED BY 1993 SALES)	THE TEN MOST PROFITABLE* SERVICE CORPORATIONS
1. American Telephone and Telegraph (telecommunications)	1. U.S. Healthcare
2. Fleming (wholesale)	2. GAP
3. SuperValu Stores (wholesale)	3. Tele-Communications
4. MCI Communications (telecommunications)	4. Home Depot
5. McKesson (wholesale)	5. Leucadia National
6. Sprint (telecommunications)	6. Washington Federal S & L
7. Sysco (wholesale)	7. Walt Disney
8. WMX Technologies (waste)	8. First financial Management
9. Walt Disney (theme parks)	9. Computor Assoc. Intl.
10. Electronic Data Systems (computing)	10. Olsten

*As measured by total return to investors for the last ten years (1983–93).

SOURCE: "Fortune Service 500," *Fortune,* (May 30, 1994), pp. 200+. © 1994 Time Inc. All rights reserved.

hotel chain Fairfield Inn) have found that service delivery can be the cornerstone of a competitive strategy. As we study the fundamental principles of management, we will apply those principles to service organizations throughout the text.

Focus on Quality

Everywhere you turn today, you hear about quality. In fact, quality has been touted as one of the principal solutions to the decline in competitiveness experienced by many U.S. firms in the last decade. But what exactly is quality?

Quality is a term that is used to describe a product or service. A quality product or service is one that meets the customers' needs and provides the value that they want and expect. **Quality management** is a formal approach to management where the overriding priority of the organization is to deliver a quality product or service and to work toward excellence and continuous improvement in everything it does.

Many organizations today face increased competitive pressures from both domestic and foreign sources. As these organizations strive to develop or maintain a competitive advantage within their industries, quality management becomes essential.[30] By improving quality, an organization may achieve benefits such as reduced costs, increased sales, and better customer satisfaction.[31] The promise of such benefits has encouraged many organizations to invest millions of dollars in training and development and new equipment and facilities in an effort to improve their competitiveness.

Quality has become, and will continue to be, a key competitive determinant for most companies. As Robert Stempel said, during his tenure as chair of General Motors, "The worldwide quality revolution has permanently changed the way we all do business. Where once quality was limited to technical issues, it is now a dynamic, perpetual improvement process involving people in all aspects of the business."[32] Quality is a fundamental business strategy for many organizations, and few businesses, if any, will survive without a quality orientation. Jeff Goodman certainly found this to be true in the health care information systems industry. In fact, as we will see in the Managerial Resolution at the close of this chapter, Goodman credits the turnaround at IBAX largely to its new quality orientation.

Not only is improving quality vital to increasing the profitability of corporations around the world, it is vital to improving the competitiveness of nations. A quality orientation enables organizations to compete in global markets and to capture a share of the worldwide demand for their products. U.S. corporations originally looked to the principles of quality management as a means of combating the increasingly competitive and quality-oriented organizations from Japan. Today, firms from around the globe are looking to quality management as a cure for overall sluggish performance. Global Perspective describes how American Express employed a quality management program to improve its competitiveness on a worldwide basis.[33]

Providing the highest-quality product or service has become the managerial challenge of the 1990s and will likely continue to be a key competitive challenge long into the future.[34] As you study management and work your way through this book, you will find that we have focused on quality management all along the way.

The four environmental trends outlined here have had a significant impact on the business environment of today and will continue to influence the business environment of the future. Related to these environmental changes are a number of fundamental changes that are occurring within organizations. The nature of the workplace is changing dramatically, and these changes will also have significant implications for the manager of the future.

Quality management
A formal approach to management where the overriding priority of the organization is to deliver a quality product or service and to work toward excellence and continuous improvement in all areas of the organization.

AMERICAN EXPRESS: THE WORLD OVER

Service organizations are always interested in measuring the quality of their service. One such organization, American Express, has developed a system to measure service quality on a worldwide basis. This company, which is widely recognized as a pioneer in improving service quality, has earned its reputation by developing a tracking system that gauges service to business customers and individual credit card holders. In just the first three years of using this tracking system, American Express improved the quality of its service delivery by 78 percent and reduced the average cost of each transaction by 21 percent.

Key to the tracking system is the ''service tracking report.'' This monthly document compiles statistics on the performance of American Express business units throughout the world, measured against more than 100 service quality factors. Many of these relate to cardmember concerns, but the report also evaluates how quickly the company reimburses service providers and meets their needs in other ways.

American Express has operations in more than 30 countries. Each national unit prepares a monthly performance report that includes suggested strategies for improvement. It also sets its own performance standards based on the economy, laws, culture, and customer expectations in that country.

When the reports arrive at headquarters, they are consolidated into a master document, and copies are sent to the firm's top managers worldwide. Through this mechanism, business units can share solutions to common problems, even though they are separated geographically.

In addition to tracking service performance, the company continually studies the satisfaction of individual cardmembers through ''transaction-based surveys.'' After customer representatives clear up a billing problem or other complaint, American Express mails a survey to the customer to find out if the representative was courteous, competent, and knowledgeable, how satisfied the client was with the overall service, and whether the customer was confident that the representative handled the request properly.

American Express has set the standard for service quality—a standard that many service organizations are looking to match.

ORGANIZATIONAL CHANGES

Contemporary organizations are experiencing a number of important changes that revolve around achieving excellence.[35] The inflexible, authoritarian rulers of the past are being replaced by charismatic, visionary leaders. Similarly, you'll find far fewer middle managers who provide little added value to their companies. In their place are self-managed work teams with a focus on quality and bottom-line results. The relative homogeneity that once characterized the management teams of most U.S. organizations has vanished as the U.S. workforce has become more heterogeneous and culturally diverse. Finally, the rigid, vertically integrated corporate structures that were predominant in American corporations over the last several decades are increasingly being abandoned for streamlined, flexible structures that permit greater adaptability to change. While these topics will be discussed in detail elsewhere in the book, let's examine each briefly here.

The Changing Chief Executive Officer

Over the last several decades, most public organizations have grown significantly. With that growth came a larger and more fragmented shareholder base. As the relative power of individual shareholders began to decline, the model for chief executive officers became that of "professional managers"—in theory, accountable to everyone, but in actuality, accountable to no one. Such managers built self-sufficient hierarchies with explicit chains of command. The command-control military model of management was often characteristic of these World War II generation managers.[36] But today things have changed—dramatically.

Everywhere you turn you find an announcement of another CEO resignation.[37] Prominent and once successful CEOs who have resigned in the last several years include James Robinson from American Express,[38] John Akers from IBM,[39] and Paul Lego from Westinghouse Electric, to name just a few. One can point to a number of reasons why many CEOs are experiencing trouble. The most recent recession (1990–1992) has taken a toll on many companies, as has the increasingly brutal global competition many industries are experiencing. Further, institutional shareholders wield greater power today and have begun to take a more activist stance, demanding greater accountability from CEOs. But another more fundamental reason for the fall of these mighty CEOs may be that times are changing. The leadership style of yesterday is simply not appropriate for today's business environment.[40]

Today's CEOs can't be afraid of change—they have to love it and be eager to influence its course. They have to be willing to shake things up and make what some might see as radical decisions to ensure the competitive strength of their organizations. They must be willing to abandon the tall hierarchy in favor of flatter, more flexible, participatory designs, encourage dialogue and tolerate dissenting opinions and views, and instill a team-oriented culture that makes quality the first priority.[41] CEOs who embrace this new form of leadership will be those who prosper in the highly volatile business environment of the future, and therefore, we will focus on this style of management throughout the book.

From Middle Managers to Self-Managed Teams

One of the most pervasive trends in American corporations in the last decade has been to "right-size" corporate structures. What does that mean? It means that companies of all sizes and types have reduced their employee base in an effort to streamline their operations and achieve greater productivity.[42]

The hardest-hit segment of the organization has been the middle manager. Although middle managers make up only about 5 percent of the total workforce, they accounted for approximately 22 percent of the total layoffs in 1992.[43] Why have middle managers become so dispensable?

Employees at all levels of the organization are being held accountable for their value-added contribution to the firm. And given the changing times, many middle managers simply can not be justified based on that criterion. Computers are swiftly altering the way we communicate. With the increasing power of information technology, the informational role of the manager is less critical today. Employees throughout the organization have ready access to the information necessary to do their jobs effectively.

But how are organizations coping with fewer middle managers? Many companies are replacing their traditional hierarchies with self-managed teams (SMTs). **Self-managed teams** are groups of employees who work together toward the achievement of preestablished goals and objectives. Many companies today use SMTs to reduce middle management costs and foster teamwork throughout the organization. In most cases, the team-oriented culture that results leads to better organizational performance.[44]

Self-managed teams
Groups of employees that work together toward the achievement of self-determined goals and objectives.

▼ Self-managed teams, like the one illustrated here, must work together to set goals for the group and develop and implement the plans necessary to meet those goals.

In the future, the middle management function will be performed by managers who are prepared to be team leaders for SMTs. Their primary responsibility will be to empower others to do whatever is needed to achieve the goals of the team. This new breed of middle manager may carry the title of coach, facilitator, sponsor, or team leader rather than manager.

There are numerous examples of organizations that have moved toward a team-oriented work environment. Nabisco, Citicorp, Chrysler, General Foods, GE, and Honeywell are just a few of the organizations that have made the shift. Xerox first used a team approach to evaluate and improve an uncompetitive work area. The team ended up saving the company $3.7 million. Based on that experience, Xerox looked for and found many other ways to use SMTs to improve its productivity and competitiveness.[45]

Although the implementation of an SMT work environment has not been problem-free for all organizations, today's competitive business arena will encourage many organizations to consider its use.[46] In fact, SMTs may dominate the organizational design of companies in the future. Consequently, we will focus on this team-oriented approach to management as we work our way through this book.

Increasing Diversity in the Workplace

Closely connected to the globalization of business has been the globalization of the labor market. Just as goods and services flow relatively freely across national boundaries, so do human resources. The result is increased diversity of the population base in this country (and in others as well) and increased diversity in the workplace.[47] **Diversity** refers to the heterogeneity of the workforce. No longer is the workplace comprised only of individuals who are very similar to one another (i.e., white males); now it includes individuals of both genders,[48] as well as people of various races, nationalities, and ethnic backgrounds.

Diversity presents new challenges for businesses and managers. As we will see in subsequent chapters, organizational success often requires strong organizational culture and group cohesiveness. Achieving this may be more difficult when the work place includes people with different backgrounds, from different nations, or with different cultural frames of reference. Men, women,

Diversity
The heterogeneity of the work force in terms of gender, race, nationality, and ethnicity.

Caucasians, Hispanics, African Americans, and others with diverse racial, national, and ethnic backgrounds often have very different perceptions about the same situations. As a consequence, it may be more difficult for diverse groups to reach a consensus on common goals and on the methods for achieving those goals.

Many organizations today have established training programs to help employees develop an appreciation for diversity and to foster cooperation among culturally diverse groups. These programs focus on valuing, perhaps even celebrating, diversity and the breadth of thought and experience that results from diverse work groups. Issues of diversity will continue to influence the activities of organizations and the behavior of managers long into the future. Consequently, this topic is discussed in much greater detail throughout the book.

A New Organizational Model

For decades organizations have aspired to be large. Growth was considered to be synonymous with success, and the "bigger is better" syndrome governed the strategic decision making of most firms. Some of the largest and most successful companies of the past (e.g., IBM, General Motors) used this model very successfully for decades. Today, however, the model presents problems for many companies. Maintaining flexibility and responding quickly to change are often impossible in large, complex organizations.[49] Being lean and flexible has now become preferable to being big for many organizations.[50] This is particularly true for organizations that operate within rapidly changing industries.

Further, while an organization may be able to develop superior skills in certain core areas of its business, maximizing effectiveness over a broad range of business activities is becoming increasingly difficult. As a result, a number of successful organizations today have adopted an alternative organizational model that offers advantages over the traditional model.[51] While this new model goes by a number of names—the modular corporation, the virtual corporation, and the network corporation, to name a few—the concept is similar.[52] The strategy is to focus on core business activities and outsource other business functions to organizations that can perform those functions more effectively and efficiently. For example, an organization may outsource the production function, marketing function, distribution function, or all three. The central organization simply coordinates the activities of others so that the product reaches the ultimate consumer in the most efficient manner possible.

Success with this model requires an ability to develop a set of relationships with organizations that can fulfill business functions that are best outsourced. Consider, for example, the strategies of Dell Computer and Chrysler as compared to IBM and General Motors. Dell and Chrysler are gaining market share from their more established and heavily integrated counterparts. Why? Because they have a competitive advantage—flexibility and efficiency. This competitive advantage is made possible by a set of relationships with other organizations that perform many business functions for the core organization.

The modular corporation is not a fad, but rather a streamlined organizational model that fits the rapidly changing environment of today and tomorrow. It provides maximum flexibility and efficiency because partnerships and relationships with other firms can be created and disbanded as needed. In addition, this model allows companies to direct their capital and other critical resources toward developing a core competency that provides a competitive advantage. As Donald Beall, CEO of Rockwell International recently commented, "Without a doubt, focusing on a core competency—and outsourcing the rest—is a major trend of the 1990s."

The environmental and organizational changes we have just described will undoubtedly affect the job of the manager. Accordingly, let's examine the impact of these changes on the contemporary manager.

THE CONTEMPORARY MANAGER

What effect will these changes have on the managers of tomorrow? Will they depend on the same set of skills and competencies as managers of the past or will there be new requirements for managerial success? As we begin our study of management, it is helpful to identify the characteristics of managers who will be successful in the future.[53]

THE NEW MANAGER PROFILE

Successful managers will have a different managerial style in the future.[54] Managers will no longer think of themselves as the "boss," but will view themselves as sponsors, team leaders, or internal consultants. The chain of command will be less relevant as managers seek out whomever they need to get the job done. They will work within a fluid organizational structure, involve others in decision making, and share information freely. They will develop their cross-functional skills so they can be more flexible. And, perhaps most importantly, these new managers will demand results, not just long hours, from their work teams. Table 1.4 lists the key characteristics of the old and new managers.[55]

COMPETENCIES OF TOMORROW'S MANAGERS

This profile implies that the new managers will require certain competencies to be successful.[56] As you study about management and business, you must try to develop these competencies.[57] In effect, the manager of tomorrow must be all of the following:

- *The great communicator.* Communication skills can make or break a career, as well as an organization. A good leader spends more time speaking—informing, persuading, and inspiring—than doing anything else. Though speaking is essential, listening may be the key managerial talent of the 1990s. Your ability to understand and apply the techniques of busi-

▼ **TABLE 1.4**   Old Versus New Manager Profile

Which kind are you?	
OLD MANAGER	NEW MANAGER
■ Thinks of self as a manager or boss	■ Thinks of self as a sponsor, team leader, or internal consultant
■ Follows the chain of command	■ Deals with anyone necessary to get the job done
■ Works within a set organizational structure	■ Changes organizational structures in response to market changes
■ Makes most decisions alone	■ Invites others to join in decision making.
■ Hoards information	■ Shares information
■ Tries to master one major discipline, such as marketing or finance	■ Tries to master a broad array of managerial disciplines
■ Demands long hours	■ Demands results

SOURCE: Brian Dumaine, "The New Non-Manager Managers," *Fortune*, February 22, 1993, 80–84. © 1993 Time Inc. All rights reserved.

▼ Today's managers must be qualified to use the latest technology to do their work. Information technology will be key to enhancing productivity, efficiency, and quality in the future.

ness does not occur in a vacuum. Solutions are hardly ever simple. It is imperative that you learn to read with comprehension, listen intently, question effectively, and write persuasively.

● *The team player.* Managers of the future must be capable of functioning effectively both as team members and as team leaders. Whether these are work teams within the organization or partnerships and team efforts between organizations (e.g., the modular corporation), managers will require strong team management skills. Productivity and effectiveness can be greatly enhanced when people work together toward common goals. Team leaders are responsible for ensuring that individual team members are selected appropriately, trained well, encouraged to contribute in meaningful ways to the group effort, and rewarded equitably for their contributions.

● *The technology master.* The Information Age is now! As Tom Peters notes in his book *Thriving on Chaos,* "Technology is . . . a wild card affecting every aspect of doing business."[58] Almost every business, large and small, has come to view the new technologies of the 1990s as key technologies for the next century. Certainly, managers of the future must be proficient in information technology. Business has transformed from manufacturing products to managing information, and managers must be capable of making this transition as well. Organizations have exceptionally high expectations of their desktop computers—and the people who use them.

● *The problem solver.* The ability to solve problems is essential for the contemporary manager. The problem solver does not confuse opinions with arguments or association with causality. She can both evaluate arguments and construct them. The ability to think incisively, evaluate evidence judiciously, recognize hidden assumptions, and follow lines of reasoning to the sometimes tortuous end is an essential competency for the successful manager.

● *The foreign ambassador.* As was suggested earlier, the global marketplace has become an economic reality. Though the United States continues to be a dominant player, its relative position in the world economy has declined in comparison to Germany and Japan. Maintaining a strong international position will require managers who are prepared to function effectively in a global environment. These managers must appreciate cultural diversity, understand the complexities of the global environment, and be willing to adapt their skills and strategies to cope with international business challenges.

- *The change maker.* Managers of the future must be capable of adapting to change when appropriate and creating change when necessary. Effective managers cannot be threatened by change, but rather must embrace change and desire to influence its course.[59] In fact, tomorrow's managers will be the architects of change to the extent that they respond proactively to environmental trends, look for new ways to meet the needs of their customers, and explore methods of increasing the efficiency and effectiveness of their organization.

- *The twenty-first-century leader.* In the highly competitive business environment of today and tomorrow, managers can't wield total control from the top of a pyramid; nor can they control the action from the sidelines. Rather, they must empower the individual employees of the organization to do whatever is necessary to achieve its goals and work with them to ensure that they have the resources to get the job done.

Meeting the Challenge provides a questionnaire that will help assess your readiness to be a manager in the year 2000. It evaluates your management orientation with regard to being a team player. If you find that your orientation is to work independently or to be highly competitive with others in your work group, you may want to focus on building your teamwork skills as you continue your education.

MANAGERIAL IMPLICATIONS ━━━━━━━━━━━━━━━━

The managers of the future must be better, brighter and have more energy, enthusiasm, and insight than the managers of the past. The flatter, leaner structures that characterize today's organizations leave fewer avenues for promotion.[60] As a result, only the very best will make their way up the corporate ladder. The jobs of tomorrow's managers will be increasingly demanding and challenging, but will be rewarding for those who perform well.

To be an effective manager in tomorrow's business environment, you must:

- Keep abreast of changing conditions that affect the organization.
- Develop an understanding of the major environmental trends that are affecting organizations across the globe.
- Be flexible and adaptable to organizational changes, as well as proactive in initiating change when appropriate.
- Understand the changing role of the manager within the corporate structure.
- Make the most of your education and develop the skills and competencies necessary for managerial success.
- Focus on excellence and quality in everything you do.

As you read this book and study the field of management, you must focus on learning how to be an effective manager. Only through a conscious effort to develop your managerial talent can you hope to prosper as a leader in the business environment of tomorrow.

MEETING THE CHALLENGE

ARE YOU READY TO MANAGE IN THE YEAR 2000?

Use the following scale to rate the frequency with which you perform the behaviors described below. Place the number (1–7) in the blank preceding the statement.

Rarely	Irregularly	Occasionally	Usually	Frequently	Almost Always	Consistently
1	2	3	4	5	6	7

____ 1. In dealing with others, my major concern is getting what I want; what happens to others is not very important to me.

____ 2. If I had to choose between working hard on some task and working very little but still doing more than other persons, I would prefer the latter.

____ 3. I am not satisfied with a relationship or business arrangement unless the other people in it are satisfied too.

____ 4. I like it best if my peers and I are about equally successful.

____ 5. In doing my work, I tend to set my own standards; I'm not very concerned with how others do their work.

____ 6. It is exciting to pit my abilities, skills, and intelligence against those of others.

____ 7. If I were to receive a larger reward than another person, even though we both did the same work, I would be quite unhappy.

____ 8. If I were to receive a bigger raise than my co-workers, I would feel uncomfortable.

Transfer your answers to the scoring form below and total the four columns. Circle your highest score.

Column A	Column B	Column C	Column D
Question 1 ____	Question 2 ____	Question 3 ____	Question 4 ____
Question 5 ____	Question 6 ____	Question 7 ____	Question 8 ____
Total ____	Total ____	Total ____	Total ____

If your highest score was for column A, you are considered an *individualist.* You are mainly concerned with your own outcomes and have little interest in those of others. If your highest score was for column B, you are probably a *competitor.* Your main concern is being better than others, overcoming them in competitive situations. If your highest score was for column C, you are a *cooperator.* You prefer to maximize the other person's outcomes as well as your own. If you highest score was for column D, you are an *equalizer.* You prefer to minimize differences between yourself and others. Of course, you may well show a mixed pattern. In any case, examine your answers to these questions carefully—they may reveal much about your management orientation. Managers in the future need to be oriented toward working with, not against, others.

SOURCE: Robert A. Varon and Paul B. Paulus, *Understanding Human Relations: A Practical Guide to People at Work,* 312–13. Copyright © 1991 by Allyn and Bacon. Adapted by permission.

When Jeff Goodman joined IBAX in 1990, the company was millions of dollars in the red. By the close of 1993, the company posted a profit of $2.1 million. What happened to cause such a turnaround? Many say it was strong leadership and a focus on doing things differently.

In three years, Goodman reduced the company's staff from 750 to 580—which included slashing management ranks from 100 to 60. By cutting these salaries and eliminating unnecessary travel and consultants' fees, Goodman cut $20 million from IBAX's operating expenses.

Then Goodman really went to work. He decided IBAX could grow best if it was freed from its monolithic structure. Instead, Goodman created six self-running companies within the corporation. Each has its own leaders, who have formed employee teams to handle operations. A look at IBAX's hiring process shows just how deep-rooted the teamwork concept is. Goodman and other top executives don't hire people for openings. That's left up to the rank and file—the other team members. Goodman thinks they're best suited to determine whether a position needs to be filled, create job descriptions, interview candidates, and hire them if they fit in.

Goodman also focused the company's attention on quality. Continuous improvements in product and service quality became the driving force behind decision making at IBAX. In fact, Goodman's relentless pursuit of quality earned him comparisons to a pit bull. But such dogged traits produced results—both customer satisfaction and sales began to grow.

IBAX is a contemporary organization that has responded to its changing environment by implementing modern management practices such as team building and a quality orientation.[61] The cohesion case that appears at the close of each part of this book provides a more detailed description of how IBAX's performance was improved dramatically through effective planning, organizing, leading, and controlling. You can follow the IBAX story as you move through the book and learn more about effective management practices. ▼

MANAGERIAL INCIDENT RESOLUTION

SUMMARY

- Management is defined as the process of administering and coordinating resources effectively, efficiently, and in an effort to achieve the goals of the organization. Management typically occurs in an organizational setting. Organizations are comprised of a group of individuals who work together toward common goals. The process of management involves four primary functions: planning, organizing, leading, and controlling.

- Henry Mintzberg identified three primary roles played by managers—interpersonal roles, informational roles, and decisional roles. In their interpersonal roles, managers act as figureheads, leaders, and liaisons. In their informational roles, managers serve as monitors, disseminators, and spokespeople. Finally, managers in their decisional roles function as entrepreneurs, disturbance handlers, resource allocators, and negotiators.

- Managers' scope of responsibility varies depending on whether they are functional or general managers. Functional managers are responsible for a work group that is segmented according to function. General managers oversee several different departments that are responsible for different tasks. Functional managers typically have strong technical skills, whereas general managers require strong human skills.

- Most large organizations have three levels of managers: first-line, middle, and top managers. These managers differ both in terms of the skills they require and the way they spend their time.

- Four environmental trends will continue to have a significant effect on the way organizations operate and managers do their jobs. These trends are (1) the globalization of business, (2) the increasing predominance of entrepreneurial firms, (3) the growth of service-based organizations, and (4) the focus on quality management.

- A number of important organizational changes are occurring today. The autocratic and inflexible CEOs of the past are being replaced by charismatic, visionary leaders. Team leaders of self-managed teams are replacing traditional middle managers in many corporate structures. Further, culturally diverse work groups have become the norm rather than the exception. Finally, the large, complex corporate structures of the past are being replaced by streamlined, flexible structures that depend on outsourcing to achieve efficiency.

- The managers of tomorrow will be quite different from the managers of yesterday. They will be more team-oriented, participatory, flexible, and focused on results. Further, they must be strong communicators, team players, masters of technology, problem solvers, foreign ambassadors, change makers, and leaders.

KEY TERMS

Management (p. 5)	Controlling (p. 7)	Technical skills (p. 12)
Efficiency (p. 5)	Managers (p. 7)	Human skills (p. 12)
Effectiveness (p. 5)	Interpersonal roles (p. 8)	Conceptual skills (p. 14)
Organization (p. 5)	Informational roles (p. 8)	Hyperchange (p. 15)
Planning (p. 6)	Decisional roles (p. 9)	Quality management (p. 20)
Organizing (p. 7)	Functional managers (p. 10)	Self-managed teams (p. 22)
Leading (p. 7)	General managers (p. 10)	Diversity (p. 23)

REVIEW QUESTIONS

1. Define the concept of management within an organizational context. What are the functions of management and why are they important?

2. Describe the roles of the manager as outlined by Mintzberg.

3. Describe the responsibilities of the functional manager. Describe the responsibilities of the general manager. How do the skills needed by each type of manager differ?

4. Distinguish among the three levels of managers in terms of the skills they need and the activities in which they are involved.

5. What are the four environmental trends that are affecting organizations today? Explain how each of these trends may affect the job of the contemporary manager.

6. Identify and discuss the organizational changes that are occurring today. What is the anticipated impact of these changes on the job of the contemporary manager?

7. Describe the manager of tomorrow in terms of both managerial style and the competencies that will be necessary for success.

DISCUSSION QUESTIONS

Improving Critical Thinking

1. How is the increasing diversity of this nation influencing the student body at your university? Is the university administration taking proactive steps to ensure diversity on your campus? Do they maintain programs to ensure that diversity is celebrated rather than simply tolerated? Brainstorm on additional ways in which your university could encourage and support diversity on your campus.

2. Review the business curriculum at your university.

In what ways is it designed to support the development of the managerial style that will be needed by the manager of the future? What could you do outside the classroom to further develop this profile?

Enhancing Communication Skills

3. What can you do to ensure that you develop the competencies you need to succeed? Write a one-page summary of your plan to develop these competencies.

4. Identify a company that you feel has a quality orientation and one that you feel does not. Compare and contrast these organizations. Present your assessment to the class orally.

Building Teamwork

5. We have concluded that the contemporary manager is somewhat different than the manager of the past. If Mintzberg were to conduct his research on managerial roles today, how would you expect his results to differ? With a small group of your fellow students, formulate a response that can be presented to the class.

6. As organizations continue to downsize and the ranks of middle managers are reduced, how might the responsibilities of both top-level managers and first-line managers change? Form a student team to respond to this question.

ETHICS: TAKE A STAND

Bob Wise is the Vice President of Operations for Work Station, a national distributor of office supplies. Bob has just come from a meeting with store managers where he listened to the ideas and philosophies of the company's management team. One manager, Sally Mims, made a particularly good impression on Bob. Sally, a recent MBA graduate from the local university, was the most creative and proactive of the managers on Bob's team. Her employee group is the most cohesive and has won virtually all of the sales and promotion contests held by the company for the last year. Further, and not surprisingly, Sally's store consistently outperformed stores in similar market areas.

As Bob walked back to his office, he thought about the other managers on his team. Most of the store managers were older men, over the age of 50. All of them had been with the company for over 10 years, many had a complacent attitude about their work, and most of the managers seemed to be very resistant to change. Although the company had held numerous management development workshops over the last several years, the managers resisted attending. Even when they did attend, they seemed to gain very little from the experience. They almost ridiculed the team approach to management, preferring to rely on authoritarian relationships with their subordinates to get the performance they desired—even though that approach did not seem to be working.

As Bob contemplated the situation, two alternative courses of action came to mind. Perhaps what his managers needed was more extensive training. Maybe he should find a two- or three-week management development program that would help the older managers see the light. Though such a program would be expensive, it might be the only way to instill some creativity into the company's current management team. Bob was doubtful that the training would help many of the managers, however.

As Bob looked for another alternative, he could not help thinking about how impressive Sally Mims had been in the store managers' meeting. Her MBA training and her youthful enthusiasm were definite advantages in this business. "If only we had a management team comprised of managers like Sally," Bob thought. As this image formed in his mind, Bob began to think of ways to build such a team. It would require terminating many of the current managers, but to the extent that they could be replaced by younger, more effective managers, the company could reap great benefits. From a cost perspective, this alternative was quite attractive as the younger employees would come in at lower salaries and could be given less expensive benefit packages.

Though the second alternative seemed to have much greater long-range potential for the company, Bob was concerned about the impact of terminating his present management team. Where would they go? Could they get other jobs? Would it be fair to treat people who had given 10 years of their lives to the company in such a way?

For Discussion:
1. Do you think it is ethical to replace managers with ten years' seniority with younger, less expensive managers? Why or why not?
2. What are the advantages and disadvantages of each of the alternatives that Bob identified?
3. Which alternative would you choose if you were Bob? Why?

THINKING CRITICALLY
Debate the Issue

PROTECTIONISM VERSUS FREE MARKETS

As this chapter explained, the world is fast becoming a global marketplace. As this transpires, many continue to argue the benefits of free market economies versus independent market economies that do not encourage free trade and follow protectionism policies.

Form teams with four to five students on each team. Half of the teams should prepare to argue the benefits of free markets, while the other teams should prepare to argue the benefits of protectionist policies. This will require significant research into the topic of world trade. Your instructor will select two teams to present their findings to the class in a debate format.

VIDEO CASE

Northern Telecom

Northern Telecom, Ltd., incorporated under the laws of Canada in 1914, is a large designer and manufacturer of fully digital telecommunications equipment. The company operates 42 manufacturing plants in eight countries, including the United States and Canada. Wireless Systems Plant, a subsidiary of Northern Telecom, is located in Calgary, Alberta, Canada. This facility has discarded the traditional corporate management structure and adopted the concept of self-directed teams (also known as self-managed teams).

Central to the operations at Wireless Systems are the auto insertion teams. These self-directed teams come up with ideas to correct problems and address cost issues at the operator level. The philosophy behind the teams is that when you are this close to the process, you can focus on opportunities for improvement that may have been overlooked by those who see only the big picture. The team approach provides the framework to act on these ideas without having to rely on management to solve problems.

Managers had to change their views on management and learn how to function as part of the team.

Even the compensation system had to be adapted to support the team concept. With the old management method, people were unaware of the actual progress or quality of the products they were manufacturing. There was no direct day-to-day feedback. Now, an operator can go directly to a controller to ask a question, and the controller will respond openly and willingly. Information sharing is a key part of feedback, and at Wireless Systems charts are an essential part of the distribution of information.

Team members rotate functions and self-delegate responsibilities. But learning to reach agreement as a team takes time. Interpersonal skills training is often necessary to assist team members in communicating. Open communication is essential, and peer appraisals let all team members know where they stand with the rest of the team, before they hear it from their managers.

The reasoning at Wireless Systems is that rules should serve people, rather than people serving rules. This plant is one big team with one big purpose. Even modest savings and detail improvements contributed by teams (toward zero defects) add up. As Mike Garrett, manufacturing manager, says, ''the only way to remain viable is to be the most cost effective, quality product, delivered on time to the customer,'' and with self-directed teams Wireless Systems Plant is achieving this goal.

For Discussion

1. Why did Wireless Systems Plant shift away from the old management methods to self-directed teams? What was involved in changing from its traditional system to self-directed teams?

2. What steps did the company take to assure that the self-directed teams would be successful?

3. How did management at Wireless view the self-directed teams? Was management's attitude positive or negative? Did it change over time? How about the workers' attitude?

CASE

A Day in the Life of Becky Johnson

Becky Johnson is the operations manager for ABE Manufacturing Company. She arrives at work every day at 7:30 A.M. Today, she must prepare for a meeting that is scheduled for 8:00 A.M. The meeting lasts one hour, and the managers attending discuss budget problems that have resulted from an increase in a supplier's prices. The group decides that Becky will call the supplier to negotiate a better price. If a lower price cannot be negotiated, ABE will drop this supplier and seek out another.

At 9:30 A.M. Becky goes back to her office where four phone messages (one personal, three business) are waiting for her. She only has time to return two business calls. She makes an appointment for next week with one of the callers. At 10:10 A.M. she writes a letter to another important supplier and takes a phone call from the marketing department about a current product's safety record. At 10:40 A.M. she holds a meeting with office personnel to talk about new office procedures that will speed up the process of ordering raw materials. She stresses how important it is to keep improving inventory management. She mentions some minor problems that, if corrected, could improve productivity, but also commends everyone on what a great job they are doing otherwise. At 11:30 A.M. she goes to the production floor to meet with floor supervisors and workers.

At 12:10 P.M. Becky goes to a well-deserved lunch and bumps into fellow managers from several other departments. During lunch the manager from the marketing department discusses several potential product ideas for ABE. Several of the managers, including Becky, set up a time when they can meet formally to discuss these ideas.

At 1:00 P.M. Becky returns from lunch to discover three new messages. She only has time to return two phone calls, including one from earlier in the morning. Afterward, she prepares for a meeting with her boss that is scheduled for 2:00 P.M. During this meeting the boss talks to Becky and other managers about ways to reduce inventory levels. The meeting lasts until 3:30 P.M.

Since Becky likes to make sure all of her employees understand company policies and procedures, she goes back to her office and writes a brief report about the inventory improvement meeting for their review. Later, on the way down the hall to get a drink, Becky sees the marketing manager and they continue their conversation about the new product ideas. She then proceeds to the production floor to talk to the production employees and supervisors. She asks specifically if they've had any problems with components or raw materials.

Finally, at 4:45 P.M. Becky returns to her office to make a couple of final phone calls. One call is an inquiry to a manager in another division. Becky asks if he has experienced any difficulty with a certain piece of equipment that has been a real problem spot for one of Becky's production lines. At 5:30 P.M. Becky Johnson decides to go home.

For Discussion:

1. At what points in the day was Becky acting in (1) interpersonal roles, (2) informational roles, (3) decisional roles?

2. In what activities (as outlined in the chapter) did Becky engage throughout the day?

3. Did Becky spend her time appropriately? How might she have adjusted her management style to be more effective?

EXPERIENTIAL EXERCISE 1.1

What Is Excellence?

Purpose: The purpose of this exercise is to identify the characteristics of "excellent" organizations and to see if the class can come up with a common set of characteristics that people agree are associated with sustained high performance in organizations.

Step 1. For 10 minutes, have each class member make a list of characteristics of "excellence."

Step 2. Form small groups of four or five people. Each group will review the individual lists of each of its members. After discussion a group list should be developed. If most of the members disagree with a particular characteristic, it should be deleted from the list. Display the final group list on the chalkboard or flip-chart.

Step 3. Reassemble the class to discuss the group lists. Make a new combined list of those characteristics identified by several groups.

Step 4. Discuss how the combined class list compares to the set of eight factors identified by Peters and Waterman in Table 1.1

For Discussion:

1. Were the original individual lists very different or fairly similar? Why?

2. How easy or difficult was it for groups to agree on a list? Why?

3. Did the class list resemble the Peters and Waterman list? Why?

SOURCE: "Managing for Excellence," in *Experiencing Management,* ed. Marshall Sashkin and William C. Morris (1987).

NOTES

1. Based on an interview with Jeff Goodman, CEO of IBAX, and Gene Yasuda, "IBAX's Goodman Gets to the Heart of Problems," *Orlando Sentinel,* January 17, 1994.

2. Mary Parker Follet, "Dynamic Administration," in *Dynamic Administration: The Collected Papers of Mary Parker Follett,* ed. H. Metcalf and L. F. Urwick (New York: Harper & Row, 1942).

3. Peter F. Drucker, *The Effective Executive* (New York: Harper & Row, 1967).

4. Thomas J. Peters and Robert H. Waterman Jr., *In Search of Excellence: Lessons from America's Best-Run Companies* (New York: Harper & Row, 1982).

5. See, for example, Colin P. Hales, "What Do Managers Do? A Critical Review of the Evidence," *Journal of Management Studies* 23 (1986): 88-113; Cynthia M. Pavett and Alan W. Lau, "Managerial Work: The Influence of Hierarchical Level and Functional Specialty," *Academy of Management Journal* 26 (1983): 170-77; Hugh Willmott, "Images and Ideals of Managerial Work: A Critical Examination of Conceptual and Empirical Accounts," *Journal of Management Studies* 21 (1984): 349-68; and Hugh Willmott, "Studying Managerial Work: A Critique and a Proposal," *Journal of Management Studies* 24 (1987): 249-70.

6. Allen I. Kraut, Patricia R. Pedigo, D. Douglas McKenna, and Marvin D. Dunnette, "The Role of the Manager: What's Really Important in Different Management Jobs," *Academy of Management Executive* 3 (1989): 286-93.

7. Pavett and Lau, "Managerial Work."

8. Henry Mintzberg, "The Manager's Job: Folklore and Fact," *Harvard Business Review* (September-October 1974): 91.

9. Henry Mintzberg, "The Manager's Job: Folklore and Fact," *Harvard Business Review* (July-August 1974): 49-61.

10. Ibid.

11. Robert L. Katz, "Skills of an Effective Administrator," *Harvard Business Review* (September-October 1974): 91.

12. Kraut, Pedigo, McKenna, and Dunnette, "The Role of the Manager."

13. Katz, "Skills of an Effective Administrator," 92.

14. George Land, *Grow or Die: The Unifying Principle of Transformation* (New York: Random House, 1973).

15. Andrew Kupfer, "The Champ of Cheap Clones," *Fortune,* September 23, 1991, 115-20.

16. Walter Kiechel III, "How We Will Work in the Year 2000," *Fortune,* May 17, 1993, 38-52.

17. John Huey, "IS Impossible," *Fortune,* September 23, 1991, 135-40.

18. Peter F. Drucker, "Behind Japan's Success," *Harvard Business Review* (January-February 1981): 83-90; and Emily Thornton "50 Fateful Years: From Enemy to Friend to _____?" *Fortune,* December 16, 1991, 126-34.

19. Emily Thornton, "Japan's Struggle to Be Creative," *Fortune,* April 19, 1993, 129-34.

20. John W. Slocum Jr. and David Lei, "Global Strategic Alliances: Payoffs and Pitfalls," *Organizational Dynamics* (1990): 44-61.

21. Edmund Faltermayer, "Poised for a Comeback," *Fortune,* April 19, 1993, 174-76+; and Fortune 500, *Fortune,* April 18, 1994, 210+.

22. Ibid.

23. Adapted from "Jubilations Inc.," *Strengthening America's Competitiveness: The Blue Chip Enterprise Initiative* (Warner Books on behalf of Connecticut Mutual Life Insurance Company and the U.S. Chamber of Commerce, 1991), 22.

24. Myron Magnet, "Good News for the Service Economy," *Fortune*, May 3, 1993, 46-52.

25. Ron Zemke, "The Emerging Art of Service Management," *Training*, January 1992, 37-42.

26. Rosabeth Moss Kanter, "From the Editor," *Harvard Business Review* (September-October 1991): 8-9.

27. Martha E. Mangelsdorf, "Making It: Service Firms Have a Lot to Learn from U.S. Manufacturing Companies These Days," *Inc.*, October 1991, 20-24.

28. Kate Bertrand, "In Service, Perception Counts," *Business Marketing*, April 1989, 44-51; Zemke, "The Emerging Art of Service Management"; and Gail Foster, "What Service Firms Can Learn from Manufacturing," *Across the Board*, March 1992, 55.

29. Ibid.

30. Peter F. Drucker, "The New Productivity Challenge," *Harvard Business Review* (November-December 1991): 69-79.

31. Brian M. Cook, "Quality: The Pioneers Survey the Landscape," *Industry Week*, October 21, 1993, 68-73; and Philip B. Crosby, "The Next Effort," *Management Review*, 1992, 64.

32. "International Quality Study: The Definitive Study of the Best International Quality Management Practices," A Joint Project of Ernst & Young and American Quality Foundation, 1991, 1.

33. Robert Titetelman, "Image vs. Reality at American Express," *Institutional Investor*, February 1992, 36-47; and Bertrand, In Service, Perception Counts, 44+.

34. Rahul Jacob, "TQM: More than a Dying Fad?" *Fortune*, October 18, 1993, 66-72.

35. Thomas A. Stewart, "The Search for the Organization of Tomorrow," *Fortune*, May 18, 1992, 92-98.

36. John A. Byrne, "Requiem for Yesterday's CEO: Old-Style Execs Who Can't Adapt Are Losing Their Hold," *Business Week*, February 15, 1993, 32-33.

37. Thomas A. Stewart, "The King Is Dead," *Fortune*, January 11, 1993, 34-41.

38. Bill Saporito, "The Toppling of King James III," *Fortune*, January 11, 1993, 42-43.

39. Carol Loomis, "King John Wears an Uneasy Crown," *Fortune*, January 11, 1993, 44-45.

40. Ibid.

41. Rahul Jacob, "Thriving in a Lame Economy," *Fortune*, October 5, 1992, 44-54.

42. Louis S. Richman, "When Will the Layoffs End?" *Fortune*, September 20, 1993, 54-56; and Jaclyn Fierman, "When Will You Get a Raise?" *Fortune*, July 12, 1993, 34-36.

43. Stratford Sherman, "A Brave New Darwinian Workplace," *Fortune*, January 25, 1993, 50-56.

44. David Barry, "Managing the Bossless Team: Lessons in Distributed Leadership," *Organizational Dynamics*, Winter 1992, 31-47.

45. Paul Chance, "Great Experiments in Team Chemistry," *Across the Board*, May 1989, 18-25.

46. Barry, "Managing the Bossless Team."

47. William B. Johnstone, "Global Work Force 2000: The New World Labor Market," *Harvard Business Review* (March-April 1991): 115-29.

48. Nancy J. Perry, "More Women Are Executive VPs," *Fortune*, July 12, 1993, 16.

49. Thomas A. Stewart, "Brace for Japan's Hot New Strategy," *Fortune*, September 21, 1992, 62-74.

50. Louis Kraar, "How Americans Win in Asia," *Fortune*, October 7, 1991, 133-60.

51. Raymond E. Miles and Charles C. Snow, "Organizations: New Concepts for New Forms," *California Management Review* 28 (1986): 62-73.

52. Shawn Tully, "The Modular Corporation," *Fortune*, February 8, 1993, 106-14; John Byrne, "The Virtual Corporation," *Business Week*, February 8, 1993, 98-103; Miles and Snow, "Organizations: New Concepts for New Forms," 62-71.

53. Thornton, "Japan's Struggle to Be Creative."

54. Bernard Keys and Thomas Case, "How to Become an Influential Manager," *Academy of Management Executive* 4 (1990): 38-49.

55. Brian Dumaine, "The New Non-Manager Managers," *Fortune*, February 22, 1993, 80-84.

56. See, for example, Kenneth C. Green and Daniel T. Seymour, *Who's Going To Run General Motors* (Princeton, N.J.: Peterson's Guides, 1991).

57. Lawrence R. Dorsky, "Producing Managers Right the First Time," *Quality Progress*, February 1992, 37-41.

58. Tom Peters, *Thriving on Chaos: Handbook for a Management Revolution* (New York, NY: Random House, 1988).

59. Walter Kiechel III, "Facing up to Denial," *Fortune*, October 18, 1993, 163-66.

60. Jaclyn Fierman, "Beating the Midlife Career Crisis," *Fortune*, September 6, 1993, 52-62.

61. Yasuda, "IBAX's Goodman Gets to the Heart of Problems."

Evolution of Management Thought

CHAPTER 2

▼ CHAPTER OVERVIEW

The concept of management and the basic management functions are not new phenomena. Throughout recorded history, activities have been conducted that most certainly would have required careful attention to the management functions. Without management it is doubtful that the massive stone fortifications stretching across northern England and northern China would ever have been erected. The Great Pyramids of Egypt and other wonders of the ancient world would not have advanced beyond a vision in a dreamer's mind without management. Endeavors such as these require planning, organizing, leading, and controlling. Not only was management important in the past, but it continues to be important in the present, both in the erection of modern-day edifices and monuments and in the conduct of business and industry around the globe. Management will continue to be important as long as humans survive on earth.

Despite management's lengthy tenure, formal theories on management only began to emerge during the past one hundred years or so. In this chapter we will examine the historical evolution of management theories and philosophies and the factors that helped influence their development. This historical tour will explore the five major schools of management thought that have emerged over the years. Our trip through time will reveal that the degree of support for and use of these different perspectives have shifted, as times, conditions, and situations have changed. Components of each of these schools of thought still exist in current management thinking, however. Furthermore, they are likely to continue, perhaps in different degrees, to influence management thought in the future. If we understand the managerial philosophies of the past and present, we will be better equipped to be successful managers in the future.

▼ LEARNING OBJECTIVES

When you have finished studying this chapter, you should be able to:

Describe the major influences on the development of management thought.

Identify the five major perspectives of management thought that have evolved over the years.

Describe the different subfields that exist in the classical perspective of management and discuss the central focus of each.

- Describe the theories of the major contributors to the behavioral perspective of management.
- Identify the major events that gave rise to the emergence of the quantitative perspective of management.
- Describe the structure of the building blocks of systems analysis.
- Discuss the nature of the contingency perspective of management.
- Discuss the future issues that will affect the further development of management thought.

MANAGERIAL INCIDENT

THE OLD MANAGEMENT PRACTICES LOSE THEIR EFFECTIVENESS AT HARLEY-DAVIDSON

Harley-Davidson, an 80-year-old U.S. motorcycle manufacturer, experienced a rather dramatic reversal of its fortunes during the late 1970s and early 1980s. Although Harley once held a dominant position in the U.S. motorcycle market, its market share slipped to less than 4 percent in the late 1970s. Honda, Kawasaki, and Yamaha motorcycles had come roaring in from Japan, offering not only lower prices but also higher-quality, state-of-the-art machines. Unable to compete with the Japanese imports on quality and price, Harley tried to prove in court that the Japanese were dumping their cycles in the United States at prices below cost to gain market share.

When it was revealed in court that the Japanese manufacturers' operating costs were 30 percent lower than Harley's, President Vaughn Beals realized that he would have to turn his attention inward to reverse Harley's downslide. Harley had been laboring under an outmoded production technology and a rather tall, cumbersome hierarchy in its organizational structure. Opinions of employees were seldom solicited—instead, employees were simply viewed as the muscle to carry out their prescribed job duties. The outmoded technology, organizational structure, and use of personnel all contributed to production inefficiencies and problems that resulted in motorcycles that were inferior in quality and price. Management style, organizational structure, and production technology were just a few of the areas that would require change if Harley were to survive.[1] ▼

INTRODUCTION

Harley-Davidson was beginning to realize that the management style, organizational structure, and production technologies that had worked in the past were not going to be successful in the future. As businesses and industries became more competitive in the global marketplace and the demand for quality increased, Harley found itself in an ever worsening position. In fact, if its management philosophy did not change, the long-term survival of the company was in doubt.

As we saw in Chapter 1, changes are occurring that are causing managers to revise their managerial styles and become more creative in their thinking. But change is nothing new—all that is new are the types of change. Management thinking has evolved throughout the centuries to deal with the ever changing environment. In this chapter we examine the evolution in management thought by describing several management theories and philosophies that have emerged over the years. The majority of the evolutionary changes and new perspectives of management have occurred since the nineteenth century, when the pace of change quickened as the Industrial Revolution transformed agricultural societies into industrial societies. Today, management thinking continues to evolve to meet the challenges raised by rapid and dramatic societal changes, and these factors will undoubtedly continue to influence future management developments. Before examining the historical developments in management thinking, let's first identify those factors that have influenced the evolution of modern management thought.

ENVIRONMENTAL FACTORS INFLUENCING MANAGEMENT THOUGHT

Through the years many environmental factors have caused management theorists and management practitioners to alter their views on what constitutes a good approach to management. These environmental factors can be conveniently categorized as economic, political, social, technological, and global influences. We will examine each of these influences in turn and the effects they have had on the evolution of management thought.

ECONOMIC INFLUENCES

Economic influences relate to the availability, production, and distribution of resources within a society. With the advent of industrialization, the goal of most manufacturing organizations was to find the most profitable way to provide products for newly emerging markets. They needed a variety of resources to achieve this objective. Some resources were material and some were human, but in each case, they tended to become scarcer over time.

When there was a seemingly endless expanse of virgin forests, loggers didn't think twice about clear-cutting a mountainside. Coal reserves were once stripped away with no thought of depletion. Flaring off (burning in the atmosphere) surplus natural gas was once a common practice. But, as resources became scarce, it became increasingly important that they be managed effectively. Time and circumstances dictate that supplies will not always be unlimited: through gradual depletion over time, resources can run out, and disruptions of supplies can occur due to temporary, but immediate circumstances. Witness the OPEC oil embargo of the 1970s and the ripple effect it had on the oil industry, petrochemical industry, and countless related industries. Or, consider the sudden and dramatic impact of Hurricane Andrew on south Florida in 1992. Manufacturers and distributors of construction materials had to quickly rethink their manufacturing and distribution strategies so they could act in a socially responsible manner. Businesses engaged in the retail sale of these commodities also found it necessary to manage their resources differently. For example, Home Depot closely monitored the track of the storm so it would be able to move such items as emergency generators and building materials into affected areas. In short, scarcity makes it necessary for resources to be allocated among competing users.

POLITICAL INFLUENCES

Political influences relate to the impact of political institutions on individuals and organizations. At a basic level are the various civil and criminal laws that influence individual and organizational behavior. In addition, the political system has bestowed various rights upon individuals and organizations, including the right to life and liberty, contract rights, an property rights, among others, and these also have an impact. Finally, government regulations are yet another source of political influence.

Political forces have influenced management thinking in a variety of ways. For example, over the years increasing concern for individual rights has forced management to adapt to a shorter work week for employees, provide a safe work environment, and make increasing contributions to employees' welfare. Regulations against monopolies have caused restructuring and reorganization in some organizations. Increased environmental regulation has caused many changes in many organizations. Deregulation of banking and trucking has had a dramatic influence on organizations in these industries. In short, evolving laws, rules, and regulations have tended to transform the way many organizations conduct business, necessitating changes in their management philosophies and styles over the years.

SOCIAL INFLUENCES

Social influences relate to the aspects of a culture that influence interpersonal relationships. The needs, values, and standards of behavior among people help to form the social contract of the culture. The social contract embodies unwritten rules and perceptions that govern interpersonal relationships, as well as the relationships between people and organizations. Management needs to be familiar with these perceptions if it is to act effectively. The ethnic, racial, and gender composition of today's workforce is becoming increasingly diverse. Recognizing and satisfying the varying needs and values of this diverse workforce present a challenge to management.

Throughout modern business history, management thinking and practice have been shaped, in part, by work stoppages, labor insurrections, and strikes by mine workers, auto workers, teamsters, and many others. Most of these

▼ Labor insurrections, such as this 1931 strike by coal miners, led to improved working conditions and welfare for workers.

incidents were precipitated not just by demands for more pay, but by safety concerns, welfare issues, and other social considerations.

Although these examples of social influence have a negative flavor, this need not always be the case. In recent years the social contract of our culture has been changing. Workers have become more vocal in their desire to be treated as more than just muscle to do the job. They are insisting on using their mental abilities as well as their physical skills. As we will see throughout this book, these changes have led to some of the contemporary approaches that empower workers, giving them decision-making authority and responsibility for their activities. This approach has had a positive impact on organizations that have tried it.[2] Empowered workers often exhibit pride of ownership for their work and a dedication to quality and excellence in all that they do. In the resolution to the opening Managerial Incident, we will see that changing its view of the workforce was one of the factors that helped Harley-Davidson survive.

TECHNOLOGICAL INFLUENCES

Technological influences relate to the advances and refinements in any of the devices that are used in conjunction with conducting business. As was noted in Chapter 1, advances in transportation, communication, and information technology have made it possible to conduct business on a global basis. Managers in the global economy must be alert to all opportunities for improvement. They must stay abreast of the new technology so they can make intelligent, informed decisions. The stakes are high because these decisions affect both the human and the technical aspects of operations. Whether an organization adopts the new technology may determine whether it retains its competitive edge.[3]

Managers are seeing constant innovations in communications and information exchange capabilities, including voice mail, electronic mail, fax machines, and electronic data interchange. In addition, you are probably very familiar with the dramatic improvements that have occurred in cellular telephones in the past few years. Early "portable" cellular telephones were not very portable and required separate battery packs carried over the shoulder in briefcase-sized satchels. Motorola, one of the premier innovators in this technology, now has battery-powered units that can fit into a shirt pocket. These will no doubt shrink even more as technological innovations continue. Similarly, advances in transportation are rapidly "shrinking" the globe. Factories of the future will incorporate such technologies as computer-aided design (CAD), computer-aided manufacturing (CAM), computer-integrated manufacturing (CIM), computerized numerically controlled machines (CNCM), automated storage and retrieval systems (AS/RS), and flexible manufacturing systems (FMS). Innovations such as these are transforming workers' job responsibilities and, consequently, the way in which they should be managed.[4]

GLOBAL INFLUENCES

Global influences relate to the pressures to improve quality, productivity, and costs as organizations attempt to compete in the worldwide marketplace. The international, or global, dimension of the organization's environment has had the most profound impact on management thinking in recent years. In the world of business, national boundaries are quickly disappearing. Global competition has begun to affect all businesses. For example, U.S. automakers can no longer claim this country as their exclusive domain. Foreign competitors

▼ Computer-aided design (CAD) allows this engineer to design an automobile engine part without the need for conventional drafting instruments and paper.

continually penetrate the U.S. market with high-quality, low-priced cars. To survive, U.S. automakers have found it necessary to compete on the same quality and price dimensions as their foreign competitors and to seek foreign markets of their own.[5]

Motorcycle manufacturers have had a similar experience. The opening Managerial Incident described the desperate plight of Harley-Davidson as the Japanese imports were beating them in both quality and price. The resolution describes how quality became a central theme in Harley's drive to become competitive again.

Similar examples in electronics and other industries could be cited. In all cases increasing global competition has caused organizations to focus on using all the skills and capabilities of their workers in an effort to improve quality, productivity, and costs. Contemporary and future perspectives on management have been and will continue to be influenced most heavily by the global dimension of the environment.[6]

SCHOOLS OF MANAGEMENT THOUGHT

Beginning in the late nineteenth century, and continuing through the twentieth century, managers and scholars have developed theoretical frameworks to describe what they believed to be good management practice. Their efforts have led to five different perspectives on management: the classical perspective, the behavioral perspective, the quantitative perspective, the systems perspective, and the contingency perspective. Each perspective is based on different assumptions about organizational objectives and human behavior. To help place these perspectives in their proper chronological sequence, Figure 2.1 displays them along a historical time line.

▼ FIGURE 2.1
Chronological Development of
Management Perspectives

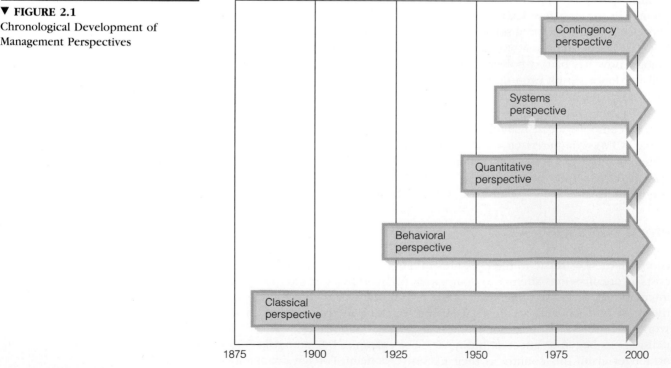

You might wonder why it is important to study the historical development of management thought. In general, studying history allows us to learn about mistakes made in the past so that they can be avoided in the future. Furthermore, it allows us to learn of past successes so that they can be repeated in the appropriate future situation. This certainly applies to the study of management history.

In addition, as Figure 2.1 shows, all these perspectives continue to influence managers' thinking, although opinions differ as to how influential each is. Consequently, it is important that future managers become familiar with the basic concepts of each school of thought. The following sections examine these major perspectives on management thought in more detail.

CLASSICAL PERSPECTIVE

The oldest of the "formal" viewpoints of management emerged during the late nineteenth and early twentieth centuries and has come to be known as the **classical perspective.** The classical perspective had its roots in the management experiences that were occurring in the rapidly expanding manufacturing organizations that typified U.S. and European industrialization. Early contributions were made by management practitioners and theorists from several corners of the world.

The classical perspective consists of three main subfields; (1) scientific management, (2) administrative management, and (3) bureaucratic management.[7] As we will see, the scientific management subfield focuses on the productivity of the individual worker, administrative management focuses on the functions of management, and bureaucratic management focuses on the overall organizational system. Nevertheless, as Figure 2.2 illustrates, these three subfields also contain some overlapping elements and components.

Classical perspective
The oldest formal viewpoints of management, it includes the scientific management approach, the administrative management approach, and the bureaucratic management approach.

▼ FIGURE 2.2
Subfields of the Classical Perspective on Management

Classical perspective

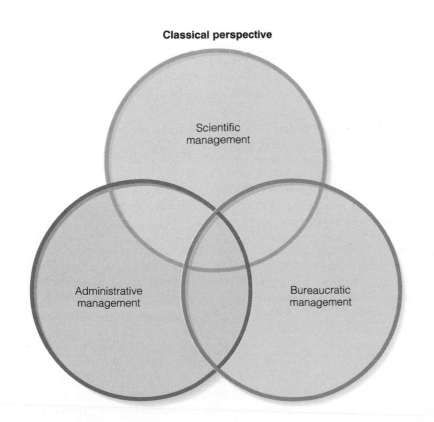

Scientific management

Administrative management

Bureaucratic management

Scientific management
Focuses on the productivity of the individual worker.

Scientific Management

Scientific management focuses on the productivity of the individual worker. As nineteenth-century society became more industrialized, businesses had difficulty improving productivity. Frederick Winslow Taylor (1856–1915), an American mechanical engineer, suggested that the primary problem lay in poor management practices. While employed at the Midvale Steel Company in Philadelphia, Pennsylvania, Taylor began experimenting with management procedures, practices, and methods that focused on worker/machine relationships in manufacturing plants. He contended that management would have to change, and that the manner of change should be determined by scientific study. Taylor's observations led him to formulate opinions in the areas of task performance, supervision, and motivation.[8]

Task Performance   Taylor was convinced that there was an ideal way to perform each separate work task, and he attempted to define those optimal procedures through systematic study. His celebrated "science of shoveling" refers to his observations and experiments on the best way for workers to perform this manual task during the manufacture of pig iron. Taylor experimented with different shovel sizes and designs to find the one that was most comfortable. He varied the size of the load scooped up onto the shovel to find the least fatiguing amount. He experimented with different combinations of work time and rest intervals in an attempt to improve worker recovery rate. Ranges of physical motion on the part of the workers were also examined. Based upon Taylor's suggestions, Midvale was able to reduce the number of shovelers needed from 600 to 140, while at the same time more than tripling the average daily worker output.[9]

These types of observations and measurements are examples of time and motion studies. Time and motion studies identify and measure a worker's physical movements while the worker performs a task, and then analyze the results to determine the best way of performing that task. In the attempt to find the best way of performing each task, scientific management incorporates several basic expectations of management, which include the following:

▼ Frederick W. Taylor, among the earliest of the management theorists, is acknowledged to be the "father of scientific management."

- *Development of work standards.* Standard methods should be developed for performing each job within the organization.
- *Selection of workers.* Workers with the appropriate abilities should be selected for each job.
- *Training of workers.* Workers should be trained in the standard methods.
- *Support of workers.* Workers should be supported by having their work planned for them.

Taylor's scientific management contributions went well beyond determining the one best way of performing a task. He also maintained rather strong convictions about supervision and motivation.[10]

Supervision   In the area of supervision, Taylor felt that a single supervisor could not be an expert at all tasks. This was because most supervisors were promoted to their positions after demonstrating high levels of skill in performing a particular function within the organization. Consequently, each first-level supervisor should be responsible only for workers who perform a common function familiar to the supervisor, such as machine operator, material handler, or inspector. Each supervisor's area of expertise would become an area of authority. Since in Taylor's era these supervisors were referred to as foremen, Taylor called this concept functional foremanship. Several foremen would be assigned to each work area, with each having a separate responsibility for such duties as planning, production scheduling, time and motion studies, material handling, and so forth.

Motivation   In the area of motivation, Taylor felt that money was the way to motivate workers to their fullest capabilities. He advocated a piecework system, where workers' pay was tied to their output. Workers who met a standard level of production were paid at a standard wage rate. Workers whose production exceeded the standard were paid at a higher rate for all of their production output. Taylor felt that such financial incentives would induce workers to produce more so that they might earn more money. He also felt that management should use financial incentives judiciously. If the increased employee earnings were not accompanied by higher profits generated by the productivity increases, then the incentives should not be used.

While Frederick Taylor is generally acknowledged to be the father of scientific management, the husband and wife team of Frank and Lillian Gilbreth also made some pioneering contributions to the field.[11] Frank Gilbreth specialized in time and motion studies to determine the most efficient way to perform tasks.[12] In one of his more notable studies, Gilbreth used the new medium of motion pictures to examine the work of bricklayers. He was able to change that task's structure in a way that reduced the number of motions from 18 to 5, resulting in a productivity increase of more than 200 percent. Contemporary industrial engineers still use Frank Gilbreth's methods to design jobs for the greatest efficiency.

Lillian Gilbreth concentrated her efforts on the human aspects of industrial engineering. She was a strong proponent of better working conditions as a means of improving efficiency and productivity. She favored standard days with scheduled lunch breaks and rest periods for workers. She also worked for the removal of unsafe working conditions and the abolition of child labor. The Gilbreths' time and motion experiments attracted quite a bit of notoriety. In fact, their application of time and motion studies and efficiency practices to their twelve children was eventually chronicled in the long-running Broadway play and subsequent motion picture *Cheaper by the Dozen.*

While Taylor and the Gilbreths with their focus on the productivity of the individual worker dominated the scientific management subfield of the classical perspective, their views were not embraced by all classical thinkers. Others focused on the functions of management or the overall organizational structure, as will be seen in the next two sections.

Administrative Management

Administrative management focuses on the managers and the functions they perform. This approach to management is most closely identified with Henri Fayol (1841–1925), a French mining engineer, whose major views emerged in the early twentieth century.[13] Fayol made his mark when he revitalized a floundering mining company and turned it into a financial success. He later attributed his success as a manager to the methods he employed rather than to his personal attributes. Fayol was the first to recognize that successful managers had to understand the basic managerial functions. He identified these functions as planning, organizing, commanding (leading), coordinating, and controlling. He also contended that successful managers needed to apply certain principles of management to these functions. Fayol developed a set of 14 general principles of management, which are listed in Table 2.1.[14]

Some of Fayol's principles are quite compatible with the views of scientific management. For example, the object of Fayol's principle on the division of work is to produce more and better work with the same amount of effort. Taylor was attempting the same thing with his shoveling experiments. Fayol's order principle stating that everything and everyone should be in their proper place is consistent with the orderly objective of time and motion studies.

Some of Fayol's classical theories and principles may not seem compatible with contemporary management as described in Chapter 1. For example, his

Administrative management
Focuses on the managers and the functions they perform.

Fayol: French Minor

▼ **TABLE 2.1**   Fayol's General Principles of Management

1. *Division of work.* By dividing the work into smaller elements and assigning specific elements to specific workers, the work can be performed more efficiently and more productively.

2. *Authority and responsibility.* Authority is necessary to carry out managerial responsibilities. Managers have the authority to give orders so that work will be accomplished.

3. *Discipline.* To ensure the smooth operation of the business, it is essential that members of the organization respect the rules that govern it.

4. *Unity of command.* To avoid conflicting instructions and confusion, each employee should receive orders from only one superior.

5. *Unity of direction.* Similar activities within an organization should be coordinated under and directed by only one manager.

6. *Subordination of individual interest to the common good.* The goals of the overall organization should take precedence over the interests of individual employees.

7. *Remuneration of personnel.* Financial compensation for work done should be fair both to the employees and to the organization.

8. *Centralization.* Power and authority should be concentrated at upper levels of the organization with managers maintaining final responsibility. However, managers should give their subordinates enough authority to perform their jobs properly.

9. *Scalar chain.* A single, uninterrupted chain of authority should extend from the top level to the lowest position in the organization.

10. *Order.* Materials should be in the right place at the right time, and workers should be assigned to the jobs best suited to them.

11. *Equity.* Managers should display friendliness and fairness toward their subordinates.

12. *Stability of personnel tenure.* High rates of employee turnover are inefficient and should be avoided.

13. *Initiative.* Subordinates should be given the freedom to take initiative in carrying out their work.

14. *Esprit de corps.* Team spirit and harmony should be promoted among workers to create a sense of organizational unity.

SOURCE: Based on C. George, Jr., *The History of Management Thought* © 1968, p. 109. Adapted by permission of Prentice Hall, Englewood Cliffs, New Jersey.

principle of centralization of power and authority at upper levels of the organization is contrary to the contemporary management view of allowing front-line workers more autonomy and authority for making and carrying out decisions. Furthermore, contemporary managers rarely demand that the goals of the overall organization take precedence over the interests of individual employees. Contemporary management thinking views employees as a valuable resource whose interests must be considered. Therefore, considerable importance is placed on satisfying the wants, needs, and desires of individual workers.

Despite the apparent incompatibility between some of Fayol's principles and the philosophies of contemporary management, several of his principles continue to be embraced by today's managers. His managerial functions of planning, organizing, leading, and controlling are routinely used in modern organizations. In fact, these functions form the framework for the organization of the material in this textbook. In addition, Fayol's principles on subordinate initiative, harmony, and team spirit are particularly applicable to the modern trend toward encouraging creativity and teamwork in the workplace.

Whereas scientific management focuses on the productivity of the individual worker and administrative management focuses on the functions of the manager, bureaucratic management, the final subfield of classical management, shifts its focus to the overall organizational system.[15]

Bureaucratic Management

Bureaucratic management focuses on the overall organizational system and is based upon firm rules, policies, and procedures; a fixed hierarchy; and a clear division of labor. Max Weber (1864–1920), a German sociologist and historian, is most closely associated with bureaucratic management.[16] Weber had observed that many nineteenth-century European organizations were managed on a very personal basis. Employees often displayed more loyalty to individuals than to the mission of the organization. As a consequence, resources were often used to satisfy individual desires rather than the organization's goals.

To counter this dysfunctional consequence, Weber envisioned a system of management that would be based upon impersonal and rational behavior.[17] Management of this sort is called a bureaucracy, and it has the following characteristics:

- *Division of labor.* All duties are divided into simpler, more specialized tasks so that the organization can use personnel and resources more efficiently.
- *Hierarchy of authority.* The organization has a pyramid-shaped hierarchical structure that ranks job positions according to the amount of power and authority each possesses. Power and authority increase at each higher level, and each lower-level position is under the direct control of one higher-level position, as in Figure 2.3.
- *Rules and procedures.* A comprehensive set of rules and procedures that provides the guidelines for performing all organizational duties should be clearly stated. Employees should strictly adhere to these formal rules.
- *Impersonality.* Personal favoritism should be avoided in the operation of the organization. The specified duties of an employee should dictate behavior. The rules and procedures should be impersonally and uniformly applied to all employees.

Bureaucratic management
Focuses on the overall organizational system.

▼ **FIGURE 2.3**
Bureaucratic Hierarchical Power Structure

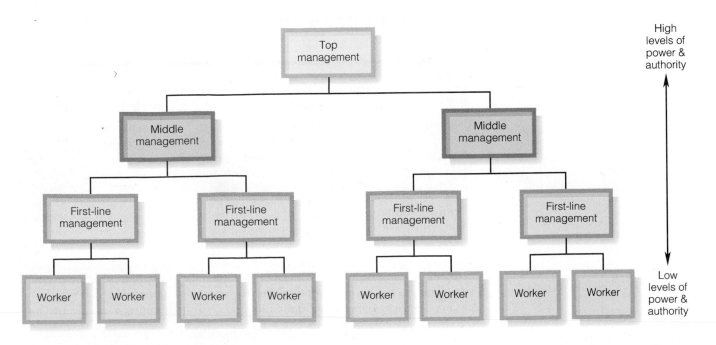

● *Employee selection and promotion.* All employees should be selected on the basis of technical competence, and should be promoted based upon their job-related performance.[18]

Weber believed that an organization exhibiting these characteristics would be more efficient and adaptable to change, for such a system would be able to maintain continuity. Regardless of the individual personalities who might enter or leave the system over the years, the formal rules, structure, and written records would allow the organization to continue to operate as it had in the past.

Weber believed there were three different types of authority: (1) traditional, (2) charismatic, and (3) rational-legal.[19] **Traditional authority** is based upon custom or tradition. **Charismatic authority** occurs when subordinates voluntarily comply with a leader because of her special personal qualities or abilities. **Rational-legal authority** is based upon a set of impersonal rules and regulations that apply to all employees. Superiors are obeyed because of the positions they hold within the organization. Table 2.2 briefly describes these three types of authority and provides examples of each.

The term "bureaucracy" has taken on a negative connotation today. In many cases negative opinions about a bureaucracy are fully justified, especially when its rules and regulations are imposed in an inflexible and unyielding manner. Who among us has not been frustrated by an encounter with the "bureaucratic red tape" of some government agency or university office? An inflexible and unyielding imposition of the rules and regulations is in direct conflict with the changing face of contemporary organizations as described in Chapter 1. There we noted that future managers will typically display a greater reliance on work teams that are empowered to use their creativity, self-motivation, and initiative to make decisions and solve problems as they work toward achieving the organization's goals.

Even though the trend is toward less bureaucracy, we should not be too quick to bury its basic tenets. Despite its associated rules and "red tape," it can still provide some effective control devices in organizations where many routine tasks must be performed. Low-level employees should be able to accomplish such work by simply following the rules. United Parcel Service (UPS) has become quite successful and efficient in the package delivery service. In fact, UPS can deliver packages more efficiently and cheaply than the U.S. Postal Service. The success of UPS is due in part to its bureaucratic structure. Rules,

Traditional authority
Subordinates comply with a leader because of custom or tradition.

Charismatic authority
Subordinates voluntarily comply with a leader because of her special personal qualities or abilities.

Rational-legal authority
Subordinates comply with a leader because of a set of impersonal rules and regulations that apply to all employees.

▼ **TABLE 2.2**   Weber's Three Authority Types

AUTHORITY TYPE	DESCRIPTION	EXAMPLES
Traditional	Subordinate obedience based upon custom or tradition.	Indian tribal chiefs, royalty (kings, queens, etc.)
Charismatic	Subordinate obedience based upon special personal qualities associated with certain social reformers, political leaders, religious leaders, or organizational leaders.	Martin Luther King, Jr., Cesar Chavez, Mahatma Gandhi, Billy Graham, Bill Gates (Microsoft), Mary Kay Ash (Mary Kay Cosmetics)
Rational-legal	Subordinate obedience based upon the position held by superiors within the organization.	Police officers, organizational executives, managers, and supervisors

regulations, policies, and procedures at UPS maintain a well-defined hierarchy of workers and a well-defined division of labor. Explicit policies exist for performance of each job, hiring, and promotion.[20]

Not all bureaucratic organizations can claim the success and efficiency of UPS, however. Sometimes the rules and red tape can be carried to an unhealthy extreme. When General Motors wanted to construct a truck assembly plant in Egypt, the proposal had to pass through many ministries and required a multitude of signatures to gain approval. As a result of this sea of red tape, more than three years elapsed before final approval was granted.[21]

The classical thinkers of the late nineteenth and early twentieth centuries made many valuable contributions to the theory and practice of management. However, their theories did not always achieve desirable results in the situations that were developing in the early twentieth century. Changes were occurring in the workplace that gave rise to new perspectives on management. As a result, the behavioral perspective of management, which represents a significant departure from classical thinking, emerged.

BEHAVIORAL PERSPECTIVE

During the first few decades of the twentieth century, the industrialized nations of the world were experiencing many social and cultural changes. Standards of living were rising, working conditions were improving, and the length of the average work week was declining. Although these improvements temporarily stopped during the Great Depression and World War II, they have continued during the rest of this century. One of the most profound changes was the newfound ability of workers to influence managerial decisions through the formation of powerful labor unions. Amid these changes, managers were increasingly finding that workers did not always exhibit behaviors that were consistent with what classical theorists had called rational behavior. Furthermore, effective managers were not always being true to the principles laid down by these traditionalists. Managers were being presented with more and more evidence that human behavior has a significant impact upon the actions of workers. Observations and evidence like this gave rise to the behavioral perspective of management, which recognizes the importance of human behavior patterns in shaping managerial style. The next sections describe the observations and research findings of several of the major contributors to this behavioral perspective.

Mary Parker Follett

In the first decades of the twentieth century, Mary Parker Follett, an early management scholar, made several significant contributions to the behavioral perspective of management. Follett's contributions were based upon her observations of managers as they performed their jobs. She concluded that a key to effective management was coordination. It was Follett's contention that managers needed to coordinate and harmonize group efforts rather than force and coerce people. She developed the following four principles of coordination to promote effective work groups:[22]

1. Coordination requires that people be in direct contact with one another.
2. Coordination is essential during the initial stages of any endeavor.
3. Coordination must address all factors in and phases of any endeavor.
4. Coordination is a continuous, ongoing process.

Follett believed that management is a continuous, dynamic process in which new situations and problems are likely to arise as the process is applied to solve a problem. She felt that the best decisions would be made by those people who were closest to the decision situation. Consequently, she thought that it was inappropriate for managers to insist that workers perform a task only in a specifically prescribed way. She argued that subordinates should be involved in the decision-making process whenever they are likely to be affected by the decision. Follett's beliefs that workers must be involved in solving problems and that management is a dynamic process rather than a static principle are certainly in contrast to the earlier views of Taylor, Fayol, and Weber, but are more consistent with contemporary management philosophy. Her views on coordination, teamwork, and employee decision making were put to good use by Veit, Inc., a manufacturer and wholesaler of garment-cleaning equipment described in Global Perspective.[23] In this illustration we can see how these factors contributed to Veit's international success.

Follett also made early contributions in the area of conflict management. She felt that managers could help to resolve interdepartmental conflict by communicating with one another and with the affected workers. She recognized that conflict could actually be a positive force in an organization, for, if managed properly, it could serve as an integrating factor that stimulates production efforts.[24]

Elton Mayo

Beginning in 1924, studies of several situational factors were being performed at the Western Electric Company's plant in Hawthorne, Illinois. One of these

GLOBAL PERSPECTIVE

VEIT, INC.: A PHENOMENAL TURN FOR THE BETTER

When Bill Watkins took over the controls of Veit, Inc., in the late 1980s, the Tucker, Georgia manufacturer and wholesaler of steam equipment for garment manufacturers, dry cleaners, and tailors was experiencing shrinking sales. Gunter and Reinhardt Veit, owner of both the Georgia company and a German company in the same field, brought Watkins in as a partner to oversee what they hoped would be a turnaround.

Veit's markets had been affected by both recession and the impact of foreign imports on U.S. garment manufacturers. Veit also suffered when key personnel left the company. To make matters worse, most current and potential customers had a negative opinion of the company.

Watkins began visiting customers and conducted a survey of both current and potential customers to determine what they wanted in the way of products and services. A procedure for handling customer complaints was established. The goal was to respond with a personal phone call within 24 hours. Watkins recognized that good performance had to start with good employees. Veit did extensive screening to fill the empty positions with people possessing the necessary skills. Recognizing the importance of teamwork, the company organized its employees into teams internally and worked externally to establish teamwork with its foreign affiliates in Germany and Singapore. Training assistance and management input were provided by the German affiliate. Watkins eventually tripled the number of distributors selling for Veit, expanding its markets to Central and South America.

Veit is now profitable. Sales have risen at double-digit rates, and the number of end users of its products has tripled to more than 1000. All in all, Veit, Inc., has experienced a remarkable turnaround.

experiments was designed to demonstrate that increased levels of lighting could improve productivity.[25] Test groups and control groups were formed. The test group was subjected to a variety of lighting conditions while the control group operated under constant lighting conditions. The results demonstrated that when illumination levels were increased, the productivity of the test group improved, as was expected. The experimenters were surprised, however, to find a similar increase in productivity when the test group's level of illumination was dramatically decreased. Equally puzzling was the fact that the control group's productivity also increased, even though its lighting conditions remained constant.

▼ Mechanism for recording each worker's output of assembled telephone relays during illumination studies at Western Electric's Hawthorne Works.

Elton Mayo, a Harvard professor and management consultant, was brought in to investigate these puzzling results. After reviewing the results of these and other newly designed experiments, Mayo and his colleagues explained the results by what has come to be known as the **Hawthorne effect.** Productivity increases were not being caused by a physical event but by a human behavior phenomenon. Workers in both groups perceived that special attention was being paid to them, causing them to develop a group pride, which in turn motivated them to improve their performance. The Hawthorne studies revealed that factors not specified by management may directly influence productivity and worker satisfaction. It was found, for example, that an informal group leader in a task group may have more power among group members than the formal supervisor. Although the Hawthorne studies were conducted between 1924 and 1933, they did not have much impact until the 1950s because of world events (the Great Depression and World War II).[26]

Hawthorne effect
Phenomenon where individual or group performance is influenced by human behavior factors.

It has been said that the Hawthorne studies "represent the transition from scientific management to the early human relations movement" and that they "brought to the forefront the concept of the organization as a social system, encompassing individuals, informal groups, and intergroup relationships, as well as formal structure."[27] In short, the Hawthorne studies added the human element to management thinking, an element that had been missing in the classical approaches to managerial thought.

Douglas McGregor

Douglas McGregor, whose background and training were in psychology, had a variety of experiences as a manager, consultant, and college president. McGregor was not totally satisfied with the assumptions about human behavior that were to be found in the classical perspective and the early contributions to the behavioral perspective. His experiences and background helped McGregor formulate his Theory X and Theory Y, which pose two contrasting sets of assumptions with which managers might view their subordinates. Table 2.3 provides a summary list of the assumptions inherent in these contrasting views.[28]

McGregor proposed that **Theory X** managers perceive that their subordinates have an inherent dislike of work and that they will avoid it if at all possible. This theory further suggests that subordinates will need to be coerced, directed, or threatened in order to get them to work toward the achievement of organizational goals. Finally, Theory X assumes that subordinates have little ambition, wish to avoid responsibility, and prefer to be directed. Managers who subscribe to this theory are likely to exercise an authoritarian style, telling people what to do and how to do it.

Theory X
Managers perceive that subordinates have an inherent dislike of work, and will avoid it if possible.

▼ **TABLE 2.3**   Comparison of Theory X and Theory Y Assumptions

FACTOR	THEORY X ASSUMPTIONS	THEORY Y ASSUMPTIONS
Employee attitude toward work	Employees dislike work and will avoid it if at all possible.	Employees enjoy work and will actively seek it.
Management view of direction	Employees must be directed, coerced, controlled, or threatened to get them to put forth adequate effort.	Employees are self-motivated and self-directed toward achieving organizational goals.
Employee view of direction	Employees wish to avoid responsibility; they prefer to be directed and told what to do and how to do it.	Employees seek responsibility; they wish to use their creativity, imagination, and ingenuity in performing their jobs.
Management style	Authoritarian style of management.	Participatory style of management.

Theory Y

Managers perceive that subordinates enjoy work, and will gain satisfaction from their jobs.

In contrast, **Theory Y** managers perceive that their subordinates enjoy work and that they will gain satisfaction from performing their jobs. Furthermore, this theory assumes that subordinates are self-motivated and self-directed toward achieving the organization's goals. Commitment to the organization's goals is a direct result of the personal satisfaction that they feel from a job well done. Finally, Theory Y assumes that subordinates will seek responsibility, display ambition, and use their imagination, creativity, and ingenuity when working toward the fulfillment of organizational goals. Managers who subscribe to Theory Y are likely to exercise a participatory style, consulting with subordinates, soliciting their opinions, and encouraging them to take part in decision making.[29] In Chapter 1 we looked at the ways management and managers are changing. The greater reliance on employees as decision makers, problem solvers, and team players is a strong endorsement for McGregor's Theory Y assumptions. Meeting the Challenge provides a self-assessment exercise that allows you to assess your own tendency toward Theory X or Theory Y assumptions. This exercise can be used to apply the theory to yourself and others with whom you work to assess your management styles.[30]

Chester Barnard

Chester Barnard studied economics at Harvard, and although he never completed the requirements for his degree, he had a very successful management career. He started in the statistical department of AT&T, and by 1927 he had become the president of New Jersey Bell. Barnard made two major contributions to management thought: one dealt with the functions of executives, and the other was his theory of authority. He felt that executives serve two primary functions. First, executives must establish and maintain a communications system among employees. Barnard regarded organizations as social systems that require employee cooperation and continual communication to remain effective. Second, executives are responsible for clearly formulating the purposes and objectives of the organization and for motivating employees to direct all their efforts toward attaining these objectives.

Barnard's other major contribution was his theory on authority. According to Barnard, authority flows from the ability of subordinates to accept or reject an order. His acceptance theory of authority suggests that employees will accept a superior's orders if they comprehend what is required, feel that the orders are consistent with organizational goals, and perceive a positive, per-

ASSESSING YOUR THEORY X AND THEORY Y TENDENCIES

The following table lists seven pairs of contrasting statements about natural characteristics attributed to people. For each of the paired characteristics, rate yourself from 0% to 100% depending upon how strongly the characteristic seems to apply to you (100% is most applicable, 0% is least applicable). The only restriction is that the total of your A and B responses should be 100% for each of the seven pairs of characteristics. Then total the percentages assigned in the A and B columns.

STATEMENT OF CHARACTERISTIC		A %	B %
1. A	Prefer play or rest to work	___	___
B	Enjoy meaningful work		
2. A	Need close supervision at work	___	___
B	Work best when working on own		
3. A	Need direction at work	___	___
B	Will direct self at work		
4. A	Avoid job responsibility	___	___
B	Seek job responsibility		
5. A	Have little ambition	___	___
B	Have considerable ambition		
6. A	Prefer security to opportunity	___	___
B	Prefer opportunity to security		
7. A	Lack imagination and creativity	___	___
B	Possess imagination and creativity		
	Totals:	___	___

Scoring: Your Theory X tendency is obtained by dividing the A column total by 7. Your Theory Y tendency is obtained by dividing the B column total by 7.

SOURCE: R. A. Varon and P. B. Paulus, *Understanding Human Relations: A Practical Guide to People at Work*, 312–13. Copyright © 1991 by Allyn and Bacon. Adapted by permission.

sonal benefit.[31] Many management scholars consider Barnard the father of the behavioral approach to management. In fact, many believe that his work laid the foundation for several contemporary approaches to management.

As we approach the mid-twentieth century on the time line of Figure 2.1, we begin to encounter new problem-solving and decision-making tools that gave rise to a quantitative perspective on management. As you will see, the quantitative school provided managers with sophisticated, new analytical tools and problem-solving techniques.

QUANTITATIVE PERSPECTIVE

The quantitative perspective had its roots in the scientific management approaches and is characterized by its use of mathematics, statistics, and other quantitative techniques for management decision making and problem solving. The most significant developments in this school of thought came during World War II, when military strategists had to contend with many monumentally complex problems, such as determining convoy routes, predicting enemy locations, planning invasion strategies, and providing troop logistical support.[32] Such massive and complicated problems required more sophisticated decision-making tools than were then available. To remedy this situation, the British and Americans assembled groups of mathematicians, physicists, and other scientists to develop techniques to solve these military problems. Because the problems often involved the movement of large amounts of materials and the efficient use of large numbers of people, the techniques they devised could be readily transferred from the military arena to the business arena.

The use of mathematical models and quantitative techniques to solve managerial problems is often referred to as operations research. This term comes from the names applied to the groups of scientists during World War II (operational research teams in Great Britain and operations research teams in the United States).[33] This approach is also referred to as management science in some circles. Regardless of the name, the quantitative perspective has four basic characteristics:

1. *Decision-making focus.* The primary focus of the quantitative approach is on problems or situations that require some direct action, or decision, on the part of management.

2. *Measurable criteria.* The decision-making process requires that the decision maker select some alternative course of action. To make a rational selection, the alternatives must be compared on the basis of some measurable criterion, or objective, such as profit, cost, return on investment, output rate, or reject level.

3. *Quantitative model.* To assess the likely impact of each alternative on the stated criteria, a quantitative model of the decision situation must be formulated. Quantitative models make use of mathematical symbols, equations, and formulas to represent properties and relationships of the decision situation.

4. *Computers.* Although many of the quantitative models can be solved manually, such a process is often time-consuming and costly. Consequently, computers are quite useful in the problem-solving process (and often necessary for extremely complex quantitative formulations).[34]

In the past few decades, computer sophistication has advanced tremendously. Computer hardware that fits in the palm of one's hand can outperform hardware that filled rooms a few decades ago. Similarly, a host of quantitative decision-making tools evolved in this century, including such tools as linear programming, network models, queuing (waiting line) models, game theory, inventory models, and statistical decision theory. Several of these are described in more detail in Chapter 7.

SYSTEMS PERSPECTIVE

An approach to problem solving that is closely aligned with the quantitative perspective is **systems analysis.** Because many of the wartime problems reflected exceedingly complex systems, the operations research teams often found it necessary to analyze them by breaking them into their constituent elements. Since any system is merely a collection of interrelated parts, identifying each of these parts and the nature of their interrelationships should simplify the model-building process. Systems can be viewed as a combination of three building blocks: inputs, outputs, and transformation processes. These blocks are connected by material and information flows.[35] Figure 2.4 illustrates the interaction of these blocks and flows.

Although a more thorough discussion of inputs, outputs, and transformation processes can be found in Chapter 17, the basic components of the systems model can be briefly introduced here. **Inputs** can vary greatly depending

Systems analysis
An approach to problem solving that is closely aligned with the quantitative perspective on management.

Inputs
Such diverse items as materials, workers, capital, land, equipment, customers, and information used in creating products and services.

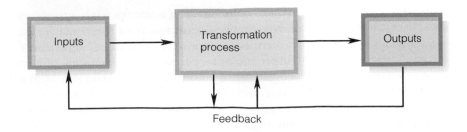

▼ **FIGURE 2.4**
Basic Structure of Systems

upon the nature of the system. Such diverse items as materials, workers, capital, land, equipment, customers, and information are potential inputs. **Outputs** typically reflect some physical commodity or some intangible service or information that is desired by the customers or users of the system. The **transformation process** is the mechanism by which inputs are converted to outputs. We usually think in terms of a physical transformation process, in which material inputs are reconfigured into some desired output. This scenario would be typical of a manufacturing system. Several other types of transformation processes are found in nonmanufacturing types of systems, however.[36] For example, in transportation/distribution systems such as Federal Express or Delta Airlines, the transformation process merely alters the location of the inputs, and not their form. In storage systems such as a U-Haul Storage Facility or a Bank of America Safety Deposit Box Division, the inputs change in the time dimension, but not in form or location. **Feedback** represents information about the status and performance of the system.

Systems are often further distinguished by whether or not they interact with the external environment. **Open systems** must interact with the external environment to survive. The interactions can be reflected in the exchange of material, energy, information, and so forth. **Closed systems** do not interact with the environment. In both the classical and early behavioral perspectives, systems were often thought of as closed. In fact, the quantitative perspective often uses a closed system assumption to simplify problem structures. Nevertheless, the difficulty of totally eliminating environmental interactions makes it hard to defend the concepts of open and closed systems in the absolute. Perhaps more appropriately, we might view systems as relatively open or relatively closed.[37] Thus, we might think of the production department of an organization as a relatively closed system. It can manufacture products in a continuous fashion while maintaining little interaction with the external environment. Meanwhile, the marketing department would be more appropriately viewed as an open system, for it must constantly interact with external customers to assess their wishes and desires. Long-run organizational survival requires that all organizations have some interaction with the external environment; therefore it is appropriate to think of contemporary business organizations as open systems.

Most complex systems are often viewed as a collection of interrelated subsystems. Because changes in any subsystem can affect other parts of the organization, it is crucial that the organization be managed as a coordinated entity. If decisions are made independently at the subsystem level, the organization as a whole will often achieve less than optimal performance. But, when all organizational subsystems work together, the organization can accomplish more than when the subsystems are working alone. This property where the whole is greater than the sum of its parts is referred to as **synergy.**

The Harley-Davidson Company described in the opening Managerial Incident was suffering from suboptimal performance as a result of lack of coordination between subsystems. Harley had been computing productivity

Outputs
The physical commodity, or intangible service or information that is desired by the customers or users of the system.

Transformation process
The mechanism by which inputs are converted to outputs.

Feedback
Information about the status and performance of the system.

Open systems
Systems that must interact with the external environment to survive.

Closed systems
Systems that do not interact with the environment.

Synergy
Phenomenon where an organization can accomplish more when its subsystems work together than it can accomplish when they work independently.

separately for each of its many work centers and departments. Each operations manager oversaw a different process and was separated from the next process by stockrooms full of inventory. Consequently, overall measures for an entire motorcycle were not meaningful for any one operations manager. One of Harley's eventual changes was a reorganization into product-focused cells, with a close connection in time between operations. As a result, improvements in any operations now show up clearly and directly in the new overall measures of performance for a whole motorcycle.[38]

Entropy
The tendency for systems to decay over time.

Another important property of systems is **entropy,** which refers to their tendency to decay over time. As is the case with living systems, organizations must continuously monitor their environments and adjust to economic, social, political, technological, and global changes. Survival and prosperity often require that new inputs be sought. A system that does not continually receive inputs from its environment will eventually die.

CONTINGENCY PERSPECTIVE

Contingency perspective
A view that proposes that there is no one best approach to management for all situations.

In the 1960s managers were becoming increasingly aware that the effectiveness of different management styles varied according to the situation. With this awareness came the emergence of the **contingency perspective,** which proposes that there is no one best approach to management. This perspective recognizes that any of the four previously discussed management perspectives might be used alone or in combination for different situations.[39] In the contingency perspective, managers are faced with the task of determining which managerial approach is likely to be most effective in a given situation. This requires managers to first identify the key contingencies, or variables, in the given organizational situation. For example, the approach used to manage a group of teenagers working in a fast-food restaurant would be quite different from the approach used to manage a medical research team trying to discover a cure for AIDS.

The young fast-food workers might best be managed in a classical, authoritative style. Bureaucratic rules and regulations might be put in place to guide all worker actions and behaviors. Scientific management principles would probably be used to define the best way to perform each work task. Variation from the prescribed method would not and probably should not be tolerated in this situation. This is not the time or place to experiment with different ways to fry the burgers or mix the shakes!

It is doubtful that the medical research team would succeed under this approach to management. The team is faced with a very complex, unstructured endeavor that will require the team members to bring together all of their unique problem-solving skills. Such a situation requires that the team be given the autonomy to try out different solutions, pursue different avenues, and take risks that would simply be out of the question for the teenaged burger flippers.

Because the contingency perspective proposes that managerial style is situation-specific, it has not yet developed to the point where it can dictate the preferred way to manage in all situations. A particularly important factor to consider in the contingency approach is the type of technology being used by the organization. In pioneering contingency studies conducted in the 1960s, Joan Woodward discovered that a particular managerial style was affected by the organization's technology. Woodward identified and described three different types of technology:

1. *Small-batch technology.* Organizations of this type exhibit job shop characteristics in which workers produce custom-made products in relatively small quantities.

▼ **TABLE 2.4**   Production Technology Examples

PRODUCTION TECHNOLOGY	EXAMPLES
Small-batch technology	Custom fabrication machine shop, manufacturer of neon advertising signs, print shop specializing in personal business cards, trophy engraving shop
Mass production technology	Manufacturer of automobiles, manufacturer of refrigerators, manufacturer of hair dryers, manufacturer of pencils
Continuous process technology	Oil refinery, flour mill, soft drink bottler, chemical processor

2. *Mass production technology.* Organizations of this type exhibit assembly line characteristics in which standardized parts and components are used to produce large volumes of standardized products.

3. *Continuous process technology.* Organizations of this type have a process in which the product flows continuously through the various stages of conversion.

The level of human interaction varies with each of these technology types. Small-batch technology tends to have the most human involvement (the most labor-intensive) due to the customized outputs. Mass production technology tends to have less human involvement due to the automated and robotic equipment that typifies assembly line operations. Continuous process technology has the lowest level of human involvement as the product flows through the stages of conversion. Consider, for example, how little "hands on" human involvement is needed in an Exxon oil refinery as crude oil flows through the various processing stages on its way to becoming gasoline. Examples of each of these production technologies appear in Table 2.4, and all three are discussed more thoroughly in Chapter 17.[40]

Some of Woodward's findings showed that bureaucratic management methods were most effective in organizations that were using mass production technology. Conversely, organizations using small-batch and continuous process technologies had little need for the formalized rules and communication systems of the bureaucratic style.[41] Continued studies of this type will fill in all the gaps and eventually provide more definitive guidelines as to which managerial style is desirable for a particular situation.

Other important factors to consider in defining the contingencies for each situation include environment, organizational size, and organizational culture.[42] For example, large organizations may find it necessary to use more structured and rigid rules, regulations, and policies to control organizational activities. On the other hand, smaller organizations may find that they can rely less on the formal structure and allow workers the autonomy to make decisions for the situations and problems that they encounter. In this example, the larger organization would undoubtedly tend toward a more bureaucratic management style, while the smaller organization would display a more behavioral orientation. As Figure 2.5 shows, parts of all of the management perspectives we have examined might be combined to form a contingency approach.

FUTURE ISSUES: DIVERSITY, GLOBALIZATION, AND QUALITY

As you might expect, the theories and ideas that have emerged thus far do not represent the end of the road in the evolution of management thought. Eco-

▼ FIGURE 2.5

Blending Components into a
Contingency Perspective

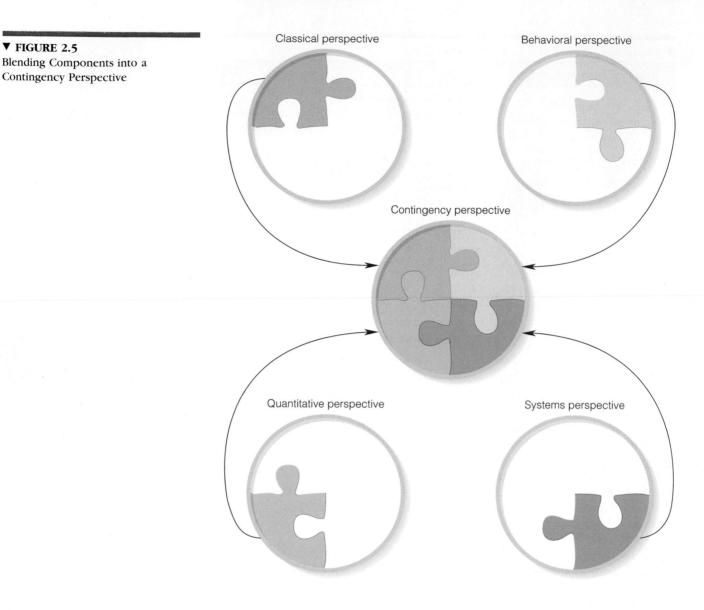

nomic, political, social, technological, and global forces that influence management thinking continue to change. A major trend in recent years has been
heightened concern for diversity within the workplace. As the workforce becomes more varied, the ranks of management need to exhibit a similar level
of diversity. Managing for Excellence illustrates how the Denny's Restaurant
chain has embraced the diversity concept to strengthen its image following
several recent incidents of negative publicity.[43]

Diversity within an organization can have an added side benefit. When
government contracts stipulate that minority suppliers must be used, businesses displaying cultural, ethnic, and gender diversity stand a better chance
of winning government business. This factor certainly was instrumental in the
success of Ferco Tech, described in Entrepreneurial Approach.[44] Ferco's success as an aircraft engine parts manufacturer was aided by its minority ownership, as well as by its commitment to quality, on-time delivery, and
competitive pricing.

In recent years Japanese management styles have received considerable
scrutiny due to the tremendous successes achieved by Japanese industries.
Most readers are surely aware of the degree to which the Japanese have taken
control of the global automobile and electronic markets. There are technical

DENNY'S EMBRACES DIVERSITY

In 1993 Denny's, a national chain of over 1500 restaurants, found itself at the center of some unfortunate incidents that were tarnishing its family-friendly image. On separate occasions at separate restaurants, there were allegations that black customers were asked to prepay for meals or were refused service. In addition, some current and former Denny's managers sued the company, claiming ethnic discrimination. Denny's top managers initially spent months defensively answering discrimination charges. But, in May 1994, Denny's agreed to pay close to $50 million in damages to mistreated black customers. In agreeing to the settlement, Jerome Richardson, chief executive of Flagstar (Denny's parent company), denied that Denny's ever had a policy or practice of discrimination against blacks. Richardson indicated that the company decided to settle the case because of the high cost of fighting the charges in court and because of the negative public perception of Denny's relationship with black customers.

Prior to the settlement, Denny's top managers began zealously embracing diversity. In the summer of 1993, Flagstar shook up the top management of Denny's, installing three executives considered to be particularly sensitive to workplace diversity. Two of these three executives are black. The company also agreed with the National Association for the Advancement of Colored People (NAACP) to hire more minority managers, award 53 minority-owned franchises by 1997, and steer more than $700 million in business to minority-owned suppliers. In May 1994, along with the damage settlement, Flagstar agreed to provide diversity training for employees and franchises, include more minorities in Denny's ads, and hire independent testers to conduct blind tests of how white and minority patrons are treated in hundreds of Denny's restaurants nationwide.

Ron Petty, Denny's new chief operating officer, summarized the company's new philosophy. "There are companies that bury their heads in the sand and say, 'I'm going to conduct my business the same way I've always conducted my business.' And there are enlightened companies that say 'There are opportunities outside of the way we've normally done business,'" Petty said. For Denny's, the new course will be one that embraces diversity.

reasons for much of this success, for it has been achieved in part because of a managerial philosophy that is committed to quality and a just-in-time operating philosophy (a concept that is treated in more detail in Chapter 17).[45]

The successes of the Japanese management style are not due entirely to the technical operating system, however. Many aspects of the Japanese management style follow the prescriptions for successful management in the twenty-first century that were discussed in Chapter 1. A focus on quality is certainly central to the Japanese style. It is somewhat ironic that the Japanese emphasis on quality was a result of the teachings of the noted American quality philosophers W. Edwards Deming and Joseph Juran. Another noted American, Armand Feigenbaum, originated the concept of total quality control, which was quickly adapted by the Japanese. Many American firms have now embraced the concept of quality and have been successful enough to win the coveted Malcolm Baldrige National Quality Award. Some of the more recognizable recent winners of this award include Motorola, Westinghouse, Xerox, Cadillac, IBM, and Federal Express.[46]

It would be difficult to dispute that the Japanese maintain a global focus. Although not as apparent to observers from abroad, their management style

ENTREPRENEURIAL APPROACH

FERCO TECH

When G. G. Fernandez started an aircraft engine parts manufacturing company in 1984, he knew he was trying to enter a capital-intensive industry on a shoestring. Aerospace manufacturing requires advanced machinery, computer technology, skilled labor, and the highest-quality assurance systems. Today Ferco Tech of Franklin, Ohio, is a $3.7 million business with 70 employees and long-range contracts with the U.S. Army, the Air Force, and large aircraft and engine builders.

Fernandez's key resource was a group of associates who were willing to work without compensation until the business got going. The management team—an accountant, an aerospace engineer, a production engineer, and Fernandez as group leader—pledged personal resources, including their homes, to raise the first $50,000 loan for operating capital. While the two engineers were installing the equipment and preparing quality assurance systems, Fernandez and his treasurer/controller were out making sales calls to introduce the new company. One thing Ferco had to offer was its status as a minority contractor, but its primary attraction was something else: dedication to accommodating the customer with quality, on-time delivery, and competitive pricing.

By the second year, the company could begin paying salaries to its executives. It has steadily developed capacity, and its sales have continued to grow—by 50 percent in the past three years. Ferco has been consistently profitable, and it has exercised its option to buy its leased facilities. Looking back to the company's beginnings, Fernandez says a prime reason for its success has been a reputation in the industry as a "customer's kingdom."

also incorporates the concept of workers as decision makers, problem solvers, and team players. These were all identified in Chapter 1 as keys to operating successfully in the twenty-first century. It should also be noted that the Japanese management style embraces aspects from several of the historically evolving management perspectives discussed in this chapter. There is a hint of bureaucratic management in the Japanese philosophy of life-long career commitment to employees. At the same time, the Japanese philosophy includes a strong behavioral component, for it recognizes the importance of workers as decision makers and problem solvers.

The Japanese management style spawned the development of Theory Z by William Ouchi, a contemporary management scholar.[47] **Theory Z** is a management approach that advocates trusting employees and making them feel like an intimate part of the organization. According to the theory, once a trusting relationship is established with workers, production will increase.

Many question whether the Japanese management style has developed and evolved to the point where it can be considered a major school of management thought. Perhaps the bigger question is whether we should be calling this style "Japanese management" or something else. Much of what we call the Japanese management philosophy originated in the Japanese automobile industry. However, these manufacturers readily admit that most of their technical innovations and ideas were borrowed from the methods used by U.S. automobile manufacturers in the heyday of Henry Ford. The Japanese simply refined these technical practices and principles, as they did the behavioral and classical components that form the total package. With this awareness, perhaps a name other than Japanese management would be more appropriate. Whatever the name, we must still ask whether this management style has evolved

Theory Z
Advocates that managers place trust in the employees and make them feel like an intimate part of the organization.

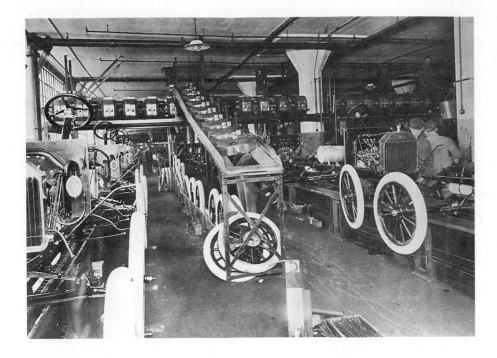

▼ Much of the Japanese manufacturing philosophy was adapted from the successes achieved in Ford's Model T assembly line.

to the point where it can be considered a major school of management thought. Probably not yet, for it still must stand the test of time. Nevertheless, in time this philosophy or another might be more thoroughly developed and added to the list of major management schools of thought. Any new philosophy that emerges will undoubtedly contain bits and pieces from prior theories, but these will most assuredly be combined with new elements that have evolved in response to political, economic, social, technological, and global influences. New eras present new problems and challenges, and new management styles arise to deal with them.

MANAGERIAL IMPLICATIONS

Over the years management theorists have developed several views on the best way to manage an organization. Each of these views is based on differing assumptions about organizational objectives and human behavior. To demonstrate quality in the management of an organization, it is important that managers use the appropriate management approach. Therefore, it is critical that tomorrow's manager be:

- Thoroughly schooled in the different management perspectives that have evolved over the years.
- Able to understand the various economic, political, social, technological, and global influences that have affected management thinking over the years, and will continue to shape future evolutionary changes in management thought.
- Capable of identifying and understanding such key variables as environment, production technology, organization culture, organization size, and international culture as they relate to his organization.
- Prepared to select elements from the various management perspectives that are appropriate for her situation.
- Adaptable to change, for future conditions and developments can quickly render his chosen approaches obsolete.

In this chapter we toured the major historical developments in the evolution of management thought. We saw the emergence of five major perspectives on management, and many subfields within those major classifications. This march through time has revealed that certain aspects of every one of these evolutionary views are still appropriate for use in both today's and tomorrow's organizations. The successful managers of tomorrow will be the ones who can blend together the appropriate components from the wide body of management theory.

MANAGERIAL INCIDENT RESOLUTION

THE OLD MANAGEMENT PRACTICES LOSE THEIR EFFECTIVENESS AT HARLEY-DAVIDSON

Many significant changes and improvements were made, and continue to be made, at Harley-Davidson. The result has been a complete reversal of fortunes. Both employee productivity and product quality have increased. Meanwhile, significant reductions in material costs, production costs, and inventory levels have been achieved. Perhaps most importantly, the company has been continuously profitable since beginning to implement these changes. There are many reasons for this dramatic turnaround. Some of them can be attributed to production technology changes, a topic that will be discussed further in Chapter 17. Much of the turnaround can also be attributed to changes in management philosophy.

Harley-Davidson replaced its tall vertical hierarchy with a flatter structure. Management revised its view of the workforce; it stopped assigning workers to narrowly defined jobs and no longer disregarded their opinions and expertise. This Theory X–like practice was replaced with a Theory Y–type attitude in which job descriptions were enlarged and workers were cross-trained to provide them with more flexibility, variety, and job security. Perhaps even more importantly, workers are continuing to be brought into the decision-making and problem-solving processes. Their opinions are valued; after all, they are the ones who are closest to the jobs.

Harley-Davidson was able to achieve some rather dramatic improvements as a result of these changes and some additional technology changes. Productivity increased by 30 percent, inventory has been reduced by 40 percent, the costs of scrap and rework have dropped by 60 percent, and machine setup time has gone down by 75 percent. All of these improvements helped to ensure that Harley-Davidson would continue to be a key player in the global motorcycle market.[48] ▼

SUMMARY

- As agricultural societies were transformed into industrial societies as a result of the Industrial Revolution, managerial thinking was impacted by a variety of economic, political, social, technological, and global influences. Such influences continue to affect the way in which managers function.

- In the past century five major perspectives of management thought have evolved: the classical, behavioral, quantitative, systems, and contingency perspectives. The classical perspective developed in the later part of the nineteenth and first part of the twentieth century. The behavioral perspective began to evolve in the early third of the twentieth century. Development of the quantitative perspective began in earnest during World War II. The systems perspective began to evolve in the 1950s, while the contingency perspective is the most recent, having begun in the 1960s.

- The classical perspective includes scientific management, administrative management, and bureaucratic management subfields, each of which has a different focus. Scientific management focuses on the improvement of individual worker productivity. Time and motion studies observe and measure a worker's physical movements in order to determine the best way of performing a task. The expectation in scientific management is that managers will develop standard methods for performing each job, select workers with the appropriate abilities for each job, train workers in standard methods, and support workers by planning their work. Scientific management proponents believe that financial incentives are the major motivating factor that will induce workers to produce more. Administrative management focuses on the managerial process and the functions of the manager. Fayol identified planning, organizing, leading, coordinating, and controlling as the basic managerial functions. Bureaucratic management has as its primary focus the overall structure of the organization. This subfield emphasizes the division of labor into specialized tasks, a hierarchy of authority in which power and authority increase at higher levels of the organization, a comprehensive set of rules and procedures for performing all organizational duties, a climate of impersonality in which personal favoritism is to be avoided, and an employee selection and promotion process that is based on technical competence and performance.

- The behavioral perspective of management had several major contributors. Mary Parker Follett emphasized the importance of coordination and harmony in group efforts. Elton Mayo recognized that the human element could play a significant role in determining worker behavior and output. Douglas McGregor proposed Theory X and Theory Y to explain employee attitudes and behavior. Chester Barnard examined the functions of executives. He contended that executives are responsible both for establishing and maintaining a communications system among employees and for clearly formulating the purposes and objectives of the organization and motivating employees toward attaining those objectives. Barnard also contributed an acceptance theory on authority, which was a new way of describing how subordinates accept or reject orders of their superiors.

- The major impetus for the emergence of the quantitative perspective of management was World War II and the many monumentally complex problems associated with the war effort. The quantitative perspective has a decision-making focus in which an alternative course of action must be selected as a solution to some problem. It requires the establishment of some measurable criteria so that alternatives can be compared prior to selection. Quantitative models are used to assess the impact of each alternative on the stated criteria, and computers are often quite helpful in the problem-solving process.

- The systems perspective takes a set of inputs and subjects them to some transformation process, thereby generating some type of output. Inputs, transformation processes, and outputs can be quite varied, but the basic structure remains the same. Throughout this process, feedback loops constantly filter information about the status and performance of the system.

- The contingency perspective of management suggests that there is no one best approach to management. It is a situational approach, for the proper managerial style is dependent upon the key variables, or contingencies, within the given situation.

- In the future, cultural, racial, and gender diversity will have a huge influence on management thinking. In addition, quality and globalization will have enormous impacts upon how businesses and industries are managed.

KEY TERMS

Classical perspective (p. 43)
Scientific management (p. 44)
Administrative management (p. 45)
Bureaucratic management (p. 47)
Traditional authority (p. 48)
Charismatic authority (p. 48)
Rational-legal authority (p. 48)

Hawthorne effect (p. 51)
Theory X (p. 51)
Theory Y (p. 52)
Systems analysis (p. 54)
Inputs (p. 54)
Outputs (p. 55)
Transformation process (p. 55)

Feedback (p. 55)
Open systems (p. 55)
Closed systems (p. 55)
Synergy (p. 55)
Entropy (p. 56)
Contingency perspective (p. 56)
Theory Z (p. 60)

REVIEW QUESTIONS

1. List and briefly describe the major factors that have influenced the evolution of management thought.
2. Identify the five major perspectives of management thought.
3. Briefly describe the main focus of scientific management and its basic expectations.
4. Briefly describe the purpose of time and motion studies.
5. What does the scientific management approach view as the major motivator for workers?
6. Briefly describe the main focus of administrative management.
7. Identify and briefly describe the basic managerial functions identified by Fayol.

8. Describe the Hawthorne effect and how it changed managerial thinking.
9. Discuss Follett's four principles of coordination.
10. Briefly describe the two functions of executives attributed to Barnard.
11. What is the acceptance theory of authority?
12. What event had the greatest impact on the evolution of the quantitative perspective of management?
13. Discuss the four basic characteristics of the quantitative perspective of management.
14. Discuss the systems concepts of synergy and entropy.
15. What is the main contention of the contingency perspective of management?

DISCUSSION QUESTIONS

Improving Critical Thinking

1. Reexamine Fayol's 14 general principles of management, identify which seem most appropriate for contemporary management situations, and discuss why you feel that way.
2. Some suggest that Japanese management is just the same old stuff in a new package, while others suggest that this style is a new and different departure. Provide arguments in support of both of these views.
3. Suppose you overheard one of your peers comment that "The contingency approach to management is a cop-out. They're just making it up as they go along!" What would you say to try to convince this

student that this approach is a valid way of dealing with unique and different situations?
4. Japanese management—wave of the future or passing fancy? What do you think, and why?

Enhancing Communication Skills

5. In your own life experiences, you probably have had some occasion to use aspects of the scientific management approach. Try to recall some physical task that you analyzed to determine the best or most efficient way to perform it. To enhance your oral communication skills, prepare a short (10–15 minute) presentation for the class in which you describe that task and the results of your analysis.

6. Based upon your observations of businesses with which you have interacted, try to identify one where employees seemed to fall into McGregor's Theory X category and one where they seemed to fit Theory Y. To enhance your written communication skills, write a short (1–2 page) essay describing these businesses and explaining why you classified them as falling into the Theory X or Theory Y category.

Building Teamwork

7. Have you ever been influenced by the Hawthorne effect? Try to recall some incident in which your performance was affected because you knew you were being watched. To refine your teamwork skills, meet with a small group of students who have been given this same assignment. Compare and discuss your experiences and then reach a consensus on the group's two most interesting experi-

ences with the Hawthorne effect. The group members whose experiences were judged the most interesting will act as spokespersons to describe these experiences to the rest of the class.

8. Try to recall from your own experiences an encounter that you had with a bureaucratic organization. Think about both the positive and negative aspects of that encounter. To refine your teamwork skills, meet with a small group of students who have been given this same assignment. Compare and discuss your experiences, and then reach a consensus on the two most severe cases of a bureaucratic response from the organization. The group members whose experiences were judged the most severe cases of a bureaucratic response will act as the spokespersons to describe these experiences to the rest of the class.

ETHICS: TAKE A STAND

In the continuing evolution of management thinking, much attention is currently being paid to what is called the "Japanese style of management," which is often associated with a just-in-time (JIT) operating philosophy. In a manufacturing environment, JIT proposes many departures from the traditional Western way of operating. In a high-volume, repetitive manufacturing environment, one of the traditional Western ways of thinking advocates a division of labor coupled with a highly specialized workforce. Worker responsibilities are often very narrowly defined, and each worker's skill expectations are quite specific. In fact, over the years union contracts have often evolved that specify precisely what a worker can and cannot be expected to do.

The emerging JIT philosophy holds that there is no room in such an environment for highly specialized workers. Instead, multiskilled, cross-trained workers are essential to make the system operate effectively. Often long-time, specialized workers find that they are out of their element in such situations and are in danger of being phased out.

For Discussion

1. Discuss the ethical issues and dilemmas when workers no longer fit the mold.

2. Discuss potential remedies for this problem.

BUREAUCRATIC MANAGEMENT—GOOD OR BAD?

THINKING CRITICALLY
Debate the Issue

Form teams of four or five students as directed by your instructor. Research the topic of bureaucratic management, identifying both its positive and its negative aspects. Look for situations where it works effectively and others where its seems to be ineffective. Prepare to debate either the pros or cons of this approach. When it is time to debate this issue in front of the class, your instructor will tell you which position you will take.

VIDEO CASE

Lincoln Electric Company

 Lincoln Electric Company of Cleveland, Ohio, is the world's leading manufacturer of welding machines, with sales in excess of $800 million. Despite being located in the heart of America's rust belt, this non-union Fortune 500 company has prospered, as have its employees. Lincoln can boast of the highest-paid factory workers in the world, with an average wage of over $45,000. Some workers have seen their annual wage exceed $85,000. Added to these wages are annual bonuses. In a recent year, $48 million in profit was divided among 2,650 employees. Workers were graded on such factors as attendance and cooperation; the highest-rated worker received a bonus of $37,000, while low-grade workers received only a few thousand dollars. In addition to the high wages, Lincoln is also proud of the fact that it does not lay off workers. Even when sales declined 40 percent between 1982 and 1983, no workers were laid off.

How is Lincoln able to achieve these results? It uses a system that ties workers' pay directly to their output. Lincoln uses this piecework pay system exclusively. Workers only get paid for good products manufactured. Workers receive no paid sick days or holidays. They are paid only when they produce. Many employees choose to work straight through their shifts, minimizing or eliminating lunch and rest breaks. They also often report to work when they are sick. In fact, to curb employees' enthusiasm for work, Lincoln has posted a sign at the employee entrance telling workers not to come to work more than 30 minutes early.

Although unions have fought against piecework for years, Lincoln Electric does not apologize for its system. Don Hastings, CEO of Lincoln, asserts that "to get paid for what you negotiate and not for what you produce does not make any sense." He contends that the recent emphasis on job satisfaction with happy workers exercising and singing company songs is baloney. Workers come to Lincoln to earn a good living, he says. Although many Lincoln workers may not be particularly fond of their jobs, they do like the money and want no part of unions or strikes.[49]

For Discussion

1. Critics of Lincoln's system contend that if it were used throughout American industry, it would throw us back into the nineteenth century, rivaling the worst days of the Industrial Revolution. Discuss the rationale that would lead to such a prediction.

2. Some people say that Lincoln Electric is behind the times, while others see it as ahead of the times. Provide support for each side of this argument.

CASE

DesignTech Products: Let's Find the Best Way

DesignTech Products is a small, privately owned manufacturer of specialty computer circuit boards. These boards are used in conjunction with computer-aided design software primarily for architectural and construction applications. DesignTech was founded by Rodman W. Spilling, a licensed architect by vocation and a computer tinkerer by avocation. Spilling was able to combine his knowledge of computer circuitry with his expertise in architecture to fabricate a "better mousetrap" in his home workshop. Realizing the vast potential of his improved circuit board, Spilling mortgaged his home, borrowed from his life insurance and his in-laws, and secured some bank loans in order to start DesignTech.

Since DesignTech's circuit boards had unique features for different customers, they could not be manufactured in a high-volume, assembly line fashion. Instead, Spilling designed small work pods, where individual workers were required to perform a variety of tasks to produce a board. For example, a single worker might select and install components and chips, wire circuits, and solder connections among other tasks. Spilling gave the workers complete autonomy to decide how they would perform these tasks.

Early operations of DesignTech did not go quite as Spilling had planned. He noticed that workers seemed to vary considerably in the way they performed these routine tasks; consequently, there was no way to predict the amount of time it would take to manufacture a specific circuit board. Many times Spilling would observe his workers and say to himself, "I wonder what would possess someone to do it that way.'' When he asked one of his workers why a particular procedure was used, the worker responded, "Well R.W. (as Spilling was referred to throughout the company), nobody ever sat us down and told us there was a perfect way."

For Discussion

1. Do you think that Spilling provided his workers with too much autonomy in selecting work procedures?

2. Review the principles of scientific management, and discuss how they might be used to improve the task performance of DesignTech's workers.

EXPERIENTIAL EXERCISE 2.1

To Which School Do You Subscribe?

Purpose: To give class members an opportunity to observe how each of the various schools of management thought affects individual and group behaviors.

Procedure: Prior to the experiential exercise described below, conduct a class in which the theories and ideas associated with each of the various schools of management thought are presented and discussed. Before dismissing the class, perform Steps 1, 2, and 3 of the following procedure. Then, in a subsequent class meeting, perform Steps 4 and 5.

Step 1   Divide the class into small groups of approximately three to five students per group. Be sure that at least five groups are formed. Depending upon the class size, it may be necessary to vary from this guideline.

Step 2   Randomly assign each of the groups to a particular school of management thought. If more than five groups were formed, more than one group will be assigned to a particular school of thought. This is perfectly acceptable. The assignments of groups to schools of thought are to be secret. Groups must not divulge to other groups which school of management thought they were assigned.

Step 3   Instruct each group to design a brief skit that shows a manager in a work situation engaging in the type of behavior that their school of management thought would predict or advocate. Inform the groups that these skits are to be presented before the entire class in the next class session.

Step 4   In the following class meeting, the skits will be presented before the entire class. Class members are to guess which school of management thought was represented in each skit.

Step 5   After the skits have been presented and student guesses made, the class will conclude with a discussion that might include the following issues:

● What are the similarities and differences among the schools of management thought?
● Does any one school of management thought seem more appropriate for use by contemporary managers in today's business organizations?
● Would certain types of organizations be more likely to subscribe to a particular school of management thought?
● Are any of the schools completely out of date and no longer appropriate for use by contemporary managers?

EXPERIENTIAL EXERCISE 2.2

Fayol's Principles versus Woodward's Technology Types: How Do They Fit?

Purpose: To assess how well each of Fayol's 14 principles fits with Woodward's three technology types.

Procedure: Follow these steps:

Step 1   Construct a matrix containing 14 rows and three columns. Label each of the rows with one of Fayol's principles and each of the columns with one of Woodward's technology types.

Step 2   Place a rating between 1 and 10 in each of the cells of the matrix. The rating in a cell is to be your subjective assessment of how well the principle identified by the row fits or applies to the technology type identified by the column. A rating of 1 indicates the least applicable (or worst fit), and a rating of 10 indicates the most applicable (or best fit). Since your ratings for a principle might vary for different companies in the same technology type, try to make each rating an average of your observations, experiences, or knowledge of different companies in each technology type.

Step 3 With the aid of your instructor, assemble the ratings from your classmates who have had this same assignment. Compute a class mean rating for each cell of the matrix.

NOTES

1. Based on R. Willis, "Harley-Davidson Comes Roaring Back," *Management Review,* March 1986, 20–27; J. Van, "Message to American Companies: Rebuild from Scratch," *Orlando Sentinel,* December 8, 1991, F1+; D. Hutchins, "Having a Hard Time with Just-in-Time," *Fortune,* June 9, 1986, 64–66; J. A. Conway, "Harley Back in Gear," *Forbes,* April 20, 1987, 8; J. A. Saathoff, "Maintaining Excellence through Challenge," *Target,* Spring 1989, 13–20; M. A. Vonderembse, and G. P. White, *Operations Management: Concepts, Methods and Strategies,* 2d ed. (St. Paul, Minn.: West Publishing Company, 1991), 476; L. J. Krajewski, and L. P. Ritzman, *Operations Management: Strategy and Analysis,* 3d ed. (Reading, Mass.: Addison-Wesley, 1993), 696; and J. R. Evans, *Applied Production and Operations Management,* 4th ed. (St. Paul, Minn.: West Publishing Company, 1993), 719.

2. J. A. Conger, "Leadership: The Art of Empowering Others," *Academy of Management Executive,* 3 (1989): 17–24.

3. Krajewski and Ritzman, *Operations Management,* 216–21.

4. J. R. Evans, D. R. Anderson, D. J. Sweeney, and T. A. Williams, *Applied Production and Operations Management,* 3d ed. (St. Paul, Minn.: West Publishing Company, 1990), 423–28.

5. J. Evans and W. Lindsay, *Production/Operations Management: A Focus on Quality* (St. Paul, Minn.: West Publishing Company, 1993).

6. B. Brocka and M. S. Brocka, *Quality Management* (Homewood, Ill.: Business One Irwin, 1992), 18.

7. D. Wren, *Evolution of Management Thought,* 2d ed. (New York: Wiley, 1979).

8. F. W. Taylor, *Scientific Management (New York: Harper & Row, 1947).*

9. C. Wrege and A. G. Peroni, "Taylor's Pig-Tale: A Historical Analysis of Frederick W. Taylor's Pig-Iron Experiments," *Academy of Management Journal* 17 (March 1974): 6–27.

10. C. Wrege and A. M. Stotka, "Cooke Creates a Classic: The Story behind F. W. Taylor's Principles of Scientific Management," *Academy of Management Review* 3 (October 1978): 736–49.

11. Wren, *Evolution of Management Thought.*

12. F. B. Gilbreth, *Principles of Scientific Management* (New York: Van Nostrand, 1911).

13. H. Fayol, *Industrial and General Administration* (New York: Sir Isaac Pitman and Sons, 1930).

14. C. George Jr., *The History of Management Thought* (Englewood Cliffs, N.J.: Prentice-Hall, 1968).

15. J. F. Mee, "Pioneers of Management," *Advanced Management—Office Executive* (October 1962): 26–29.

16. M. Weber, *General Economic History,* trans. F. H. Knight (London: Allen & Unwin, 1927).

17. Wren, *Evolution of Management Thought.*

18. M. Weber, *The Theory of Social and Economic Organizations,* ed. and trans. A. M. Henderson and T. Parsons (New York: Free Press, 1947).

19. Ibid.

20. R. W. King, "UPS Isn't About to Be Left Holding the Parcel," *Business Week,* February 13, 1989; and K. Labich, "Big Changes at Big Brown," *Fortune,* January 18, 1988.

21. D. Ignatius, "The Egyptian Bureaucracy Galls Both the Public and Foreign Investors," *Wall Street Journal,* March 24, 1983.

22. M. P. Follett, *Creative Experience* (London: Longmans, Green, 1934).

23. Adapted from Veit, Inc., *Real-World Lessons for America's Small Businesses: Insights from the Blue Chip Initiative* (Published by *Nation's Business* on behalf of Connecticut Mutual Life Insurance Company and the U.S. Chamber of Commerce, 1993), 74–75.

24. M. P. Follett, "Dynamic Administration," in *Dynamic Administration: The Collected Papers of Mary Parker Follett,* ed. H. Metcalf and L. F. Urwick (New York: Harper & Row, 1942).

25. H. M. Parson, "What Happened at Hawthorne?" *Science* 183 (1974): 922–32.

26. J. A. Sonnenfeld, "Shedding Light on the Hawthorne Studies," *Journal of Occupational Behavior* 6 (1985): 111–30.

27. F. Kast and J. Rosenzweig, *Organization and Management: A Systems and Contingency Approach* (New York: McGraw-Hill, 1979).

28. D. McGregor, *The Human Side of Enterprise* (New York: McGraw-Hill, 1960), 33–58.

29. Ibid.

30. R. A. Baron and P. B. Paulus, *Understanding Human Relations: A Practical Guide to People at Work* (Needham Heights, Mass.: Allyn & Bacon 1991), 312–13.

31. C. Barnard, *The Functions of the Executive* (Cambridge, Mass.: Harvard University Press, 1938).

32. B. Render and R. M. Stair Jr., *Introduction to Management Science* (Boston: Allyn & Bacon, 1992).

33. L. Austin and J. Burns, *Management Science* (New York: Macmillan, 1985).

34. T. Cook and R. Russell, *Introduction to Management Science* (Englewood Cliffs, N.J.: Prentice-Hall,1985), 6–20.

35. K. Boulding, "General Systems Theory—The Skeleton of Science," *Management Science* 2 (April 1956): 197–208.

36. Krajewski and Ritzman, *Operations Management*, 3–4.

37. Kast and Rosenzweig, *Organization and Management: A Systems and Contingency Approach,* 102.

38. J. A. Saathoff, "Maintaining Excellence through Challenge," *Target,* Spring 1989, 13–20.

39. F. Luthans, "The Contingency Theory of Management: A Path out of the Jungle," *Business Horizons* 16 (June 1973): 62–72.

40. J. Woodward, *Industrial Organizations: Theory and Practice,* 2d ed. (London: Oxford University Press, 1980).

41. Ibid.

42. F. Kast and J. Rosenzweig, *Contingency Views of Organizations and Management* (Chicago: Science Research Associates, 1973).

43. "Denny's Advocates Diversity," *Orlando Sentinel,* October 12, 1993, C-5.

44. Adapted from "Ferco Tech," in *Real-World Lessons for America's Small Businesses: Insights from the Blue Chip Enterprise Initiative* (*Nation's Business* on behalf of Connecticut Mutual Life Insurance Company and the U.S. Chamber of Commerce, 1992), 68–69.

45. Vonderembse and White, *Operations Management.*

46. Evans and Lindsay, *Production/Operations Management,* 152.

47. W. Ouchi, *Theory Z: How American Business Can Meet the Japanese Challenge* (Reading, Mass.: Addison-Wesley, 1981).

48. Based on Willis, "Harley-Davidson Comes Roaring Back"; J. Van, "Message to American Companies: Rebuild from Scratch," *Orlando Sentinel,* December 9, 1991, F1+; Hutchins, "Having a Hard Time with Just-in-Time," Conway, "Harley Back in Gear"; Saathoff, "Maintaining Excellence through Challenge"; Vonderembse and White, *Operations Management,* 476; Krajewski and Ritzman, *Operations Management,* 696; and Evans, *Applied Production and Operations Management,* 719.

49. Lincoln Electric, CBS "60 Minutes," November 8, 1992, produced by Rome Hartman, reported by Leslie Stahl. Manufactured and distributed by Ambrose Video Publishing, Inc.

Social Responsibility and Ethics

CHAPTER 3

▼ CHAPTER OVERVIEW

Corporate social responsibility and business ethics have been the focus of a great deal of attention in recent years. Organizations are increasingly being held accountable for the contributions they make to society, as well as for the degree to which their individual members adhere to an appropriate code of ethical conduct. Further, managers of the future will be expected to address important social issues proactively and to maintain a high standard of ethical behavior if they are to succeed within the corporate environment.

This chapter begins with a discussion of the stakeholder view of the firm. With that view in mind, we will explore the concept of social responsibility, examine three perspectives of social responsibility, and consider four strategies for approaching social issues. In addition, recommendations for developing a socially responsive position are offered. The topic of business ethics can be approached in several ways. Here we will consider values and the role they play in shaping one's ethical behavior. Approaches for addressing ethical dilemmas are discussed as well. Our examination of ethics concludes with a discussion of ways to encourage and support ethical behavior in a corporate environment. Implications for tomorrow's managers are also discussed.

▼ LEARNING OBJECTIVES

*When you have finished studying this chapter,
you should be able to:*

- Discuss the stakeholder view of the firm.
- Describe the concept of corporate social responsibility and the primary premises upon which it is based.
- Distinguish among the three perspectives of corporate social responsibility.
- Identify and evaluate different strategies for responding to social issues.
- Discuss the ten commandments of social responsibility.
- Explain what values are and how they form the basis of an individual's ethical behavior.
- Distinguish between terminal and instrumental values.
- Identify and discuss the differences in the utility, human rights, and justice approaches to ethical dilemmas.

- Explain the methods used by an organization to encourage ethical business behavior.
- Describe the different approaches used in ethics training programs.
- Discuss what is meant by whistleblowing in monitoring ethical behavior.

MANAGERIAL INCIDENT

MARTIN MARIETTA

MARTIN MARIETTA: ALLEGATIONS OF FRAUD

Martin Marietta is a major defense contractor for the U.S. government. Headquartered in Baltimore, Maryland, this company designs, manufactures, integrates, and operates systems and products in leading edge technologies, including aerospace, electronics, information management, materials, and energy.

In 1991, Martin Marietta found itself in a very difficult situation. The company was the target of some damaging allegations of fraud and corruption. More specifically, the U.S. Department of Justice had launched an investigation of Melvyn R. Paisley, the Navy Assistant Secretary for Research and Engineering, on charges that he had accepted bribes in exchange for providing sensitive information to Martin Marietta. The company's Naval Systems Division had suffered a rather steady financial decline during the early to mid-1980s, and it was speculated that the desire to improve the division's performance was a driving force behind Martin Marietta's alleged involvement in the scandal.

As the investigation unfolded, the name of Thomas G. Pownall, a board member and former chairman of the board for Martin Marietta, surfaced as the corporate official involved in the scandal. Pownall allegedly was involved in establishing an account that was used to pay for repairs on a home owned by Paisley just weeks before Paisley named Martin Marietta as the principal contractor for a $500 million top secret Navy program. The notoriety this incident brought to Martin Marietta was clearly unwanted and, presumably, undeserved. Martin Marietta needed to respond to the accusations that were being made so that its image could be preserved.[1] ▼

INTRODUCTION

Management at Martin Marietta was facing a very difficult situation. The integrity of the company was being challenged by the U.S. government and, perhaps more importantly, by other segments of society. Regardless of whether Martin Marietta and the accused official were guilty of misconduct, the allegations against the company were potentially very damaging to the image of the firm.

Unfortunately, such situations are far too common in today's business environment. Many respectable organizations have faced allegations of socially irresponsible or illegal behavior. Such accusations can have serious consequences for an organization's image in its local community, the financial community, and society overall. Consequently, managers must take care to act responsibly and ethically with regard to issues that affect the general welfare of society.

As we examine corporate social responsibility and ethics, you will see examples that illustrate the benefits of responsible and ethical behavior, as well as others that illustrate the negative consequences of irresponsible or unethical behavior. First, however, it is important to answer a very important question. To whom is business responsible? Is it the stockholders of the company? The customers? The employees? Answering such questions requires an understanding of the stakeholder view of the firm.

ORGANIZATIONAL STAKEHOLDERS IN A GLOBAL ENVIRONMENT

Central to the issues of corporate social responsibility and ethics is the concept of stakeholders. **Stakeholders** are all those who are affected by or can affect the activities of the firm.[2] While it has long been accepted that a corporation must be responsible to its stockholders, contemporary social responsibility theory maintains that a corporation has obligations to all of its stakeholders. This perspective broadens the scope of the business's obligations beyond a relatively narrow group of shareholders to a much broader set of constituents that includes such groups as government, consumers, owners, employees, and communities throughout the globe.[3]

Figure 3.1 illustrates the many and varied constituent groups that can be stakeholders in a given organization. The primary stakeholders of a firm are those who have a formal, official, or contractual relationship with the organization. They include owners (stockholders), employees, customers, and suppliers. Peripheral to this group are the secondary stakeholders, who include other societal groups that are affected by the activities of the firm. Consider, for example, who might represent primary and secondary stakeholders for your college or university. As a student, are you a primary or secondary stakeholder? What about the employers in your community? Are they primary or secondary stakeholders?

As organizations become involved in the international business arena, they often find that their stakeholder base becomes wider and more diverse. Organizations that must cope with stakeholders from across the globe face special challenges that require a heightened sensitivity to and awareness of economic, political, and social differences among groups. For example, international firms must be responsive to customers with very different needs, owners with varied expectations, and employees with distinct, and perhaps dissimilar, motivations. Dealing effectively with such groups requires a focus on understanding the

Stakeholders
People who are affected by or can affect the activities of the firm.

▼ FIGURE 3.1
The Stakeholder View of the Firm

SOURCE: A. Carroll, *Business & Society: Ethics and Stakeholder Management* (Cincinnati: Southwestern Publishing, 1989), 60.

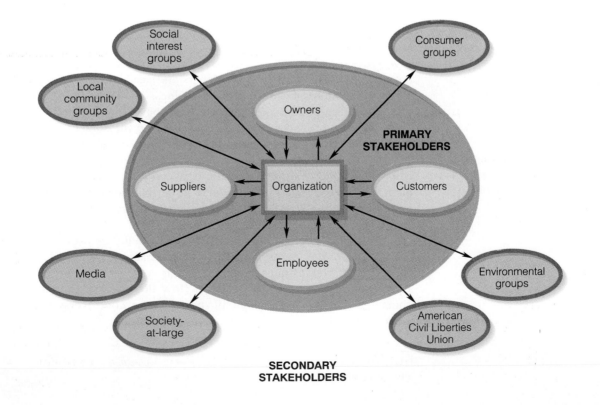

▼ Shareholders represent a very important stakeholder group for many large organizations. This group of RCA shareholders meet regularly to learn more about the management of the organization.

global nature of stakeholders and on developing strategies that recognize and respond to such differences.

With the stakeholder view of the organization in mind, we will move on to examine the concepts of social responsibility and ethics. Although these two topics are integrally related, they can and should be addressed independently. Corporate social responsibility is an organizational issue that relates to the obligation of business to society. In contrast, ethical issues are most relevant at an individual level, for ethics is maintained by people, not organizations. Nevertheless, both are important topics that have significant implications for the long-term success of any organization.

SOCIAL RESPONSIBILITY

Few issues have been the subject of more heated debate than corporate social responsibility. For decades practitioners and academics have argued over the nature and extent of the obligations business has to society. Perspectives on the issue of corporate social responsibility have varied dramatically over the years, and even today achieving a consensus on the subject is difficult.

What is corporate social responsibility?* It is a complex concept that resists precise definition. In a very general sense, **corporate social responsibility** can be thought of as the interaction between business and the social environment in which it exists. Most would agree that being "socially responsible" means acting in a way that is acceptable to society and that all organizations should act in a socially responsible manner.

The debate over corporate social responsibility focuses on the nature of socially responsible behavior. Does being socially responsible mean that the corporation's actions must not harm society, or does it mean that the corporation's actions should benefit society? How does one determine "harm" and "benefit"? These issues are at the heart of the controversy over corporate social responsibility.

Corporate social responsibility
The interaction between business and the social enviornment in which it exists.

_____

*The terms *corporate social responsibility* and *social responsibility* will be used interchangeably.

To gain a better understanding of corporate social responsibility, we will first examine the two basic premises of the concept. Then, with these premises in mind, we will explore three perspectives of corporate social responsibility that exist today, as well as a model for evaluating corporate social behavior.

THE PREMISES OF THE SOCIAL RESPONSIBILITY DEBATE

Many would argue that the controversy over the responsibility of business was inevitable, given the moral and ethical challenges that corporate America has faced over the last several decades. You don't need to look far to find examples of organizations that have acted "irresponsibly" in the eyes of some segment of society. Whether it involved a violation of worker safety regulations, insufficient attention to product safety for consumers, or the relocation of a plant (and numerous jobs) to a foreign country with lower labor costs, corporate America has been besieged with accusations of social irresponsibility in recent years.[4]

The discussion of social responsibility began over 35 years ago when H. R. Bowen proposed that businesses and managers have an obligation to "pursue those policies, to make those decisions, or to follow those lines of action that are desirable in terms of the objectives and values of our society."[5] This simple proposition inspired the modern debate about social responsibility.

Bowen's assertions rest on two fundamental premises, **social contract** and **moral agent,** which can be summarized as follows:

- *Social contract.* Business exists at the pleasure of society, and as a result, it must comply with the guidelines established by society. An implied set of rights and obligations is inherent in social policy and assumed by business. This set of rights and obligations can be thought of as a social contract between business and society.
- *Moral agent.* Business must act in a way that is perceived as moral. In other words, business has an obligation to act honorably and to reflect and enforce values that are consistent with those of society. Further, business can be held accountable as a moral agency.

These two premises have provided the foundation for the concept of social responsibility, but they have also served as targets for critics of the concept. In fact, there are several perspectives on social responsibility which differ mainly in their view of these two premises. Let's examine these perspectives in greater detail.

THREE PERSPECTIVES OF SOCIAL RESPONSIBILITY

Three primary perspectives of corporate social responsibility have emerged over the years: (1) economic responsibility, (2) public responsibility, and (3) social responsiveness.[6] Table 3.1 outlines the primary tenets of these perspectives. Each perspective views Bowen's two premises somewhat differently and, consequently, offers a different view of the concept of corporate social responsibility.[7]

Economic Responsibility
Although many hold the economic responsibility perspective, one of its most outspoken proponents is Milton Friedman. Friedman maintains that the only social responsibility of business is to maximize profits within the "rules of the game." In his opinion, the only constituents to which business is responsible are the stockholders, and it is the firm's responsibility to maximize the wealth

Social contract
An implied set of rights and obligations that are inherent in social policy and assumed by business.

Moral agent
A business' obligation to act honorably and to reflect and enforce values that are consistent with those of society.

▼ **TABLE 3.1**   Three Perspectives of Social Responsibility

PERSPECTIVE	BASIC TENETS
Economic responsibility	• The responsibility of business is to make a profit within the "rules of the game." • Organizations cannot be moral agents. Only individuals can serve as moral agents.
Public responsibility	• Business should act in a way that is consistent with society's view of responsible behavior, as well as with established laws and policy.
Social responsiveness	• Business should proactively seek to contribute to society in a positive way. • Organizations should develop an internal environment that encourages and supports ethical behavior at an individual level.

SOURCE: L. Wartick and P. L. Cochran, "The Evolution of the Corporate Social Performance Model," *Academy of Management Review* 10 (1985): 764.

of this constituent group. This is the only social contract to which business should be committed. If socially responsible behavior on the part of the corporation serves to reduce the financial return to the stockholders, the managers of the business have undermined the market mechanism for allocating resources and have violated the social contract of business as it should be in a free market society.

Proponents of the economic responsibility perspective also argue that corporations cannot be moral agents. Only individuals can serve as moral agents. When individuals choose to direct their own assets or resources toward the public good, that behavior is appropriate and to the benefit of society. When they begin to direct corporate resources toward that end, however, they have violated their commitment to the owners (i.e., stockholders) of those assets or resources.

Critics of the economic responsibility perspective argue that many of today's business organizations are not merely economic institutions and to view them as such is both unrealistic and naive. Many large corporations wield significant political power and have tremendous influence on a wide variety of public policies and regulations across the globe. Further, the activities of many corporations are essential to realizing important social goals such as equal opportunity, environmental protection, and increased global competitiveness in critical industries. Viewing the modern corporation as simply an economic institution is myopic and ignores the reality of the worldwide evolution of business.[8] Figure 3.2 illustrates, in a somewhat humorous way, how decisions that are economically desirable can be very negative from a social welfare perspective, reinforcing the view that business has a significant impact on society.[9]

Public Responsibility

The public responsibility perspective represents an alternative view of social responsibility. Focusing almost exclusively on the social contract premise, proponents of public responsibility argue that business should act in ways that are consistent with public policy. Rather than viewing public policy as simply the laws and regulations with which business must comply, supporters of this philosophy define public policy very broadly as "the broad pattern of social direction reflected in public opinion, emerging issues, formal legal require-

▼ **FIGURE 3.2**
Economic Consequences versus Social
Consequences

SOURCE: "A CEO Forum: What Corporate Social
Responsibility Means to Me," *Business and Society Review* (1989).

ments and enforcement or implementation practices."[10] In other words, public policy refers to the overall perceptions and expectations of the public with regard to the interaction between business and society.

Critics of the public responsibility position argue that it lacks clarity. If public responsibility means adhering to existing public policy, which is traditionally considered to be the laws and regulations of the legal system, then this perspective differs little from the economic perspective. Like the economic perspective, this view would imply only that business should comply with the "rules of the game." If, however, a broader view of public policy is assumed, the public responsibility perspective differs little from the traditional view of social responsibility and Bowen's concept of social contract. Consequently, critics of the public responsibility position argue that it does not reflect a unique philosophy and that, unless it is defined more clearly, it is redundant to other perspectives.

Social Responsiveness

The third perspective of social responsibility is that of social responsiveness. Proponents of this perspective argue that corporate social responsibility should not be simply an obligation on the part of business to meet the minimum expectations of society. Viewing social responsibility in this way suggests that it is a burden. Rather, modern corporations should proactively seek to act in ways that improve the welfare of society. Social responsiveness implies a proactive and tangible effort to contribute to the well-being of society.

The social responsiveness perspective also recognizes the moral agency aspect of corporate social responsibility. While proponents of this perspective agree with the economic responsibility proponents that morality is an individual rather than an organizational obligation, they maintain that the organization is responsible for creating and maintaining an environment where moral behavior on the part of individual organizational members is encouraged and supported.

Although many have endorsed the social responsiveness perspective, it has also sparked some legitimate questions. Most pervasive, perhaps, has been the question of how much social responsiveness is enough. The perspective fails to define the extent to which an organization should proactively attempt to benefit society. At what point do the efforts of the organization come at the expense of profitability?

Critics of this perspective also argue that it ignores issues of social irresponsibility. Acting irresponsibly is often of greater consequence than failing to act responsively. Consider, for example, how Exxon's irresponsible behavior during the *Valdez* oil spill affected the environment. Further, consider how Martin Marietta's alleged irresponsible behavior may have affected both its primary and secondary stakeholders. Irresponsible behavior by organizations can have far-reaching and long-term effects.

Evaluating the social behavior of organizations can be quite difficult given the diversity of perspectives regarding social responsibility. The following section describes one framework for evaluating the extent to which organizations demonstrate socially responsible behavior.

THE FOUR FACES OF SOCIAL RESPONSIBILITY

In a very general sense, an organization's social behavior can be categorized according to two dimensions—legality and responsibility. As illustrated in Figure 3.3, four combinations of legal and responsible behaviors are possible: (1) legal/responsible, (2) legal/irresponsible, (3) illegal/responsible, and (4) illegal/irresponsible.[11]

Although one would hope that all organizations would operate in a legal and responsible manner, the evidence suggests otherwise. In fact, there are far too many examples of firms that have behaved in an illegal or irresponsible way. Why would a company choose to behave illegally and irresponsibly? Let's consider a situation where that might happen.

A manufacturing company has been notified of a new pollution regulation that will affect one of its plants. The cost of complying with the regulation is $1.2 million while the fine for failing to comply is $25,000. The likelihood of being caught in noncompliance is 10 percent, and even if the organization is caught, there will be little publicity. Although noncompliance would be both illegal and irresponsible, a cost-benefit analysis might suggest that the organization not comply with the regulation. Is this an appropriate decision? Absolutely not. Yet some companies facing such a situation might make that choice. When the penalty associated with breaking the law is less costly than complying with the law, an organization may make an inappropriate decision.

Consider the other two quadrants in the model. Can you think of examples of organizations that have acted legally, but irresponsibly? Illegally, but re-

▼ **FIGURE 3.3**
The Four Faces of Social Responsibility

SOURCE: D. R. Dalton and R. A. Cosier, "The Four Faces of Social Responsibility," *Business Horizons*, May/June 1982, 19–27.

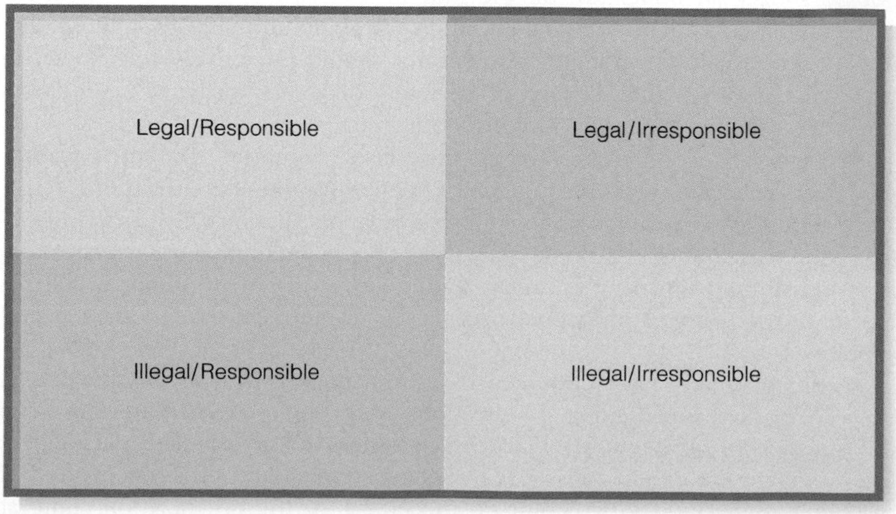

| Legal/Responsible | Legal/Irresponsible |
| Illegal/Responsible | Illegal/Irresponsible |

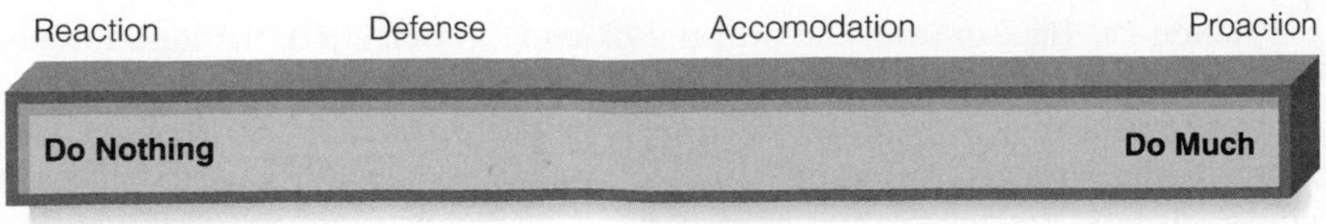

Reaction	Defense	Accomodation	Proaction

Do Nothing ———————————————————————— **Do Much**

▼ **FIGURE 3.4**
Social Responsibility Strategies

SOURCE: A. Carroll, "A Three-Dimensional Conceptual Model of Corporate Performance," *Academy of Management Review* 4 (1979): 497–505.

sponsibly? Under what conditions might an organization choose to act in such ways? Would it be appropriate to act in such a way given the circumstances you have outlined? How might such situations be avoided?

Organizations will typically behave in ways that are consistent with their overall strategy for responding to social issues. Social responsibility strategies may range from doing nothing to making an attempt to benefit society in very tangible ways. The following section identifies four different strategies for social responsibility and examines reasons why an organization might choose a particular strategy.

SOCIAL RESPONSIBILITY STRATEGIES

As we know, organizations take widely different approaches to corporate social responsibility. Some organizations do little more than operate to ensure profitability for their stockholders while others maintain very aggressive and proactive social responsiveness agendas.

Figure 3.4 illustrates a continuum of social responsibility strategies that range from "do nothing" to "do much." Four distinct strategies can be identified along this continuum: reaction, defense, accommodation, and proaction. They vary according to the organization's tendency to be socially responsible or responsive.[12]

Reaction
An organization that assumes a reaction stance simply fails to act in a socially responsible manner. Consider, for example, the classic case of Manville Corporation.[13] Over 40 years ago, the medical department of Manville Corporation (then known as Johns Manville) discovered evidence to suggest that asbestos inhalation causes a debilitating, and often fatal, lung disease. Rather than looking for ways to provide safer work conditions for company employees, the firm chose to conceal the evidence.

Why? That's hard to say. But there is evidence to suggest that the company was more concerned about profitability than about the health and safety of its employees. Presumably, top executives at Manville thought it would be less costly to pay workers' compensation claims than to develop safer working conditions.

Manville's irresponsibility did not go without notice, however. Eventually, as a result of litigation, the company was forced to pay a $2.6 billion settlement, which forced a reorganization that left the company on very shaky ground. Was shareholder wealth maximized by the irresponsibility of Manville's leaders? Obviously not. The stockholders of the firm lost a substantial amount of money as a result of the company's reactive social responsibility strategy.

Defense
Organizations that pursue a defense strategy respond to social challenges only when it is necessary to defend their current position. Consider, for example, the three major automobile manufacturers in this country. How did they react to the social issues of air pollution, vehicle safety, and gas shortages in the 1970s?

When Dr. Haagan-Smit, the prophet of smog, proclaimed that automobiles were the major contributor to U.S. smog, domestic car manufacturers argued that the problem was really a function of poorly maintained vehicles. When Ralph Nader brought the issue of vehicle safety to the foreground of social consciousness, the automakers argued that bad drivers were the problem, not unsafe cars. And when the oil crisis struck and consumers demanded more fuel-efficient automobiles, car manufacturers continued to give them new models of the same gas hogs of the past.[14]

Can we call this social responsiveness? Hardly. The U.S. car manufacturers' strategy was one of defense. Not until the Japanese automakers stepped up with solutions to these social issues, and the U.S. automakers begin to see the effect of their complacency on the bottom line, did they begin to act in a socially responsible manner. They were forced to respond to the needs of society (and their customers) as a result of pressures from foreign competitors.

Accommodation

Corporations with an accommodation strategy of corporate social responsibility readily adapt their behaviors to comply with public policy and regulation where necessary and, more importantly, attempt to be responsive to public expectations.[15]

Bank of America, for example, has always readily disclosed information required by law. This policy has not differentiated the company from its competitors, however, because virtually every financial services company meets the minimum requirements of disclosure regulation. In contrast to many of its competitors, Bank of America has pioneered a code for voluntary disclosure of bank information requested by its customers or by any other member of the public. This policy of "ask and you shall receive" is an example of an accommodative strategy of social responsibility.[16]

Proaction

Organizations that assume a proaction strategy with regard to corporate social responsibility subscribe to the notion of social responsiveness. They do not operate solely in terms of profit; nor do they consider compliance with public policy, regardless of how it is defined, to be sufficient. These organizations proactively seek to improve the welfare of society.

Although many organizations have gone above and beyond the call of duty to address important social issues (see Table 3.2 for some examples), General Electric stands out as one organization that has aggressively worked to contribute to society in the area of education. General Electric's CEO, Jack Welch, considers it the responsibility of business to "teach and lead" students who represent the future of this country. Several GE plants have developed volunteer programs that support mentoring relationships between GE employees and local high school students. As a result of these programs, several high schools have dramatically increased the number of their students who go on to college.[17]

Another example of a proactive organization is Ben & Jerry's Homemade, Inc. As this company's mission statement demonstrates (see Table 3.3), social responsibility is a core organizational value. Ben & Jerry's has been recognized nationally for its focus on employees, the community in which it operates, and society as a whole.[18]

Which strategy is the best? Should all organizations assume a proaction strategy with respect to corporate social responsibility? Not necessarily. There are, however, some basic social responsibility principles to which all organizations should prescribe.

▼ **TABLE 3.2**   Examples of Proactive Social Responsiveness

- *Honda.* Voted #1 by *Consumer Reports* for its safety-oriented self-propelled lawnmowers. It beat its competitors to the market with the mower even before safety legislation was passed.
- *Pennsylvania Power & Light Company.* Set up a citizen advisory board to discuss company issues that affect the general public.
- *Xerox Corporation.* Allows employees with at least three years of company service to take a one-year leave of absence to participate in a community service project. Employees receive normal pay and raises from Xerox and are promised a comparable job when they return.
- *3M Company.* Initiated an environmental protection program called "Pollution Prevention Pays." As part of the program, 3M set a goal of reducing its air, land, and water releases 90% by the year 2000. So far it has been successful in cutting pollutants by more than 500,000 tons since 1975. The National Wildlife Federation's Corporate Conservation Council gave 3M an Environmental Achievement Award in recognition of its progress to date.
- *Kaiser Aluminum.* Agreed to an affirmative-action plan that would place more racial minorities in craftwork positions.
- *GE Plastics.* At GE company conferences, employees teamed up to discuss ways of renovating old community buildings in San Diego.
- *Merck & Company.* Spent millions of dollars to develop Mectizan, a drug that prevents river blindness, a disease found mostly in West Africa. The company also distributed the drug free of charge in all countries where river blindness is found.
- *Gulf Power Company.* Pensacola, Florida-based Gulf Power Company helped find and fund a new home for wildlife when the original site of a wildlife sanctuary was sold. The company helped recruit its employees to volunteer and also donated money to the effort.
- *Kraft General Foods.* Now uses recycled plastic for its salad dressing bottles, making it the first company to use recycled plastics in food containers other than soft drink bottles.
- *Rubbermaid.* Came out with a litterless lunch box called the "Sidekick." It features plastic sandwich, drink, and snack containers and means that plastic wrap, cans, and milk cartons will no longer be necessary to pack a lunch. The box has developed a strong market share and become the rage among grade-schoolers.
- *Monsanto.* Chair and CEO Richard J. Mahoney pledged that the company would be environmentally responsible by reducing emissions, eliminating waste, working for sustainable agriculture, and managing corporate land to benefit nature.
- *Eastman Kodak.* Encourages its 100,000 employees to volunteer in local community programs by allowing them to take time off from work (up to 40 hours a year) with pay to volunteer for public service. The time does not offset vacation or sick leave and is typically used for volunteering at churches, schools, shelters, and environmental organizations.

SOURCES: "Corporations Going Green," *Business Ethics,* March/April, 1992, 10.; D. Bihler, "The Final Frontier," *Business Ethics,* March/April, 1992, 31; and "On Company Time: The New Volunteerism," *Business Ethics,* March/April, 1992, 33.

SOCIAL RESPONSIBILITY PRINCIPLES FOR THE YEAR 2000

All evidence points to a growing emphasis on social responsibility in the future.[19] This may be, in part, a result of the increasing concern for quality in

▼ **TABLE 3.3**   Ben and Jerry's Homemade, Inc., Statement of Mission

Ben and Jerry's is dedicated to the creation and demonstration of a new corporate concept of linked prosperity. Our mission consists of three interrelated parts:

- *Product mission.* To make, distribute and sell the finest-quality all-natural ice cream and related products in a wide variety of innovative flavors made from Vermont dairy products.

- *Social mission.* To operate the company in a way that actively recognizes the central role that business plays in the structure of society by initiating innovative ways to improve the quality of life of a broad community: local, national and international.

- *Economic mission.* To operate the company on a sound financial basis of profitable growth, increasing value for our shareholders and creating career opportunities and financial rewards for our employees.

Underlying the mission of Ben & Jerry's is the determination to seek new and creative ways of addressing all three parts, while holding a deep respect for individuals, inside and outside the company, and for the communities of which they are a part.

SOURCE: J. J. Laabs, "Ben & Jerry's Caring Capitalism," *Personnel Journal* (November 1992): 50–57.

many organizations. While achieving quality clearly requires a focus on meeting the needs of customers, it may also require increased concern for meeting the needs of all stakeholders of the organization. In fact, organizations that strive to respond effectively to the expectations and needs of all of their stakeholders may have a competitive edge over others in their industry.

As corporations and managers look for ways to fulfill their obligations to society, they should keep the following Ten Commandments in mind:[20]

- *Commandment I: Thou Shall Take Corrective Action before It Is Required.* Compliance with self-imposed standards is almost always preferable to compliance with standards that are imposed by outside constituencies. Organizations should continually look for ways to improve product safety and reliability before they are forced to do so by lawsuits, regulatory bodies, or competition (see Table 3.2 for an example of how Honda demonstrated this commandment).

- *Commandment II: Thou Shall Work with Affected Constituents to Resolve Mutual Problems.* Organizations should not make decisions that have significant social implications in isolation. Instead, they should work with those involved to try to find mutually acceptable solutions. For example, many organizations that have considered closing plants have found that discussing the issues with plant employees has led to alternative solutions (e.g., cost-cutting measures, employee stock option plans, and the like) that have been preferable for all parties involved.

- *Commandment III: Thou Shall Work to Establish Industrywide Standards and Self-Regulation.* Companies and industries can preserve their freedom to conduct business as they see fit by behaving responsibly before a regulatory body forces them to do so. Although developing industrywide standards requires cooperation and coordination among the players in the industry, the effort is well worth the price if it can avert ill-conceived regulations.[21] Always remember that regulations developed by those who know less about the industry than the major players do are likely to be less effective than self-developed policy.

- *Commandment IV: Thou Shall Publicly Admit Your Mistakes.* Few things are worse for a company's image than being caught trying to cover up socially irresponsible behavior. It is far better to admit mistakes as soon as they are discovered, make restitution as expediently as possible, and establish control systems to ensure that such mistakes never happen again. If, for example, it turned out that Martin Marietta was involved in the scandal described in the Managerial Incident, top executives would be well advised to confront the issue head-on by openly acknowledging the problem and implementing systems to avoid such problems in the future.[22]

- *Commandment V: Thou Shall Get Involved in Appropriate Social Programs.* Most organizations that are truly concerned about their responsibility to society become involved in one or more social programs. Where possible, organizations should look for programs that have a need for some special talent or skill that they possess, so that the benefits of their contribution are magnified.

- *Commandment VI: Thou Shall Help Correct Environmental Problems.* Regardless of the industry in which a firm operates, there are always opportunities to address environmental issues in a proactive manner. At a minimum, doing so can help a company build a favorable image in its community, and in many cases, it can even lead to significant cost savings. Managing for Excellence describes how a number of computer companies are working with the Environmental Protection Agency to provide energy-efficient computer systems that reduce power consumption.[23]

- *Commandment VII: Thou Shall Monitor the Changing Social Environment.* Like other components of the external environment, the social environment is ever changing. Socially responsible organizations should monitor these changes and act proactively to address social trends as they occur. For example, the increasing diversity of the workforce requires organizations to make an aggressive effort to ensure that people of different racial, ethnic, and cultural backgrounds are given equal opportunities for advancement. Being on the "cutting edge" of social responsiveness will enhance the image of the organization and provide greater benefits for those affected by such trends.

- *Commandment VIII: Thou Shall Establish and Enforce a Corporate Code of Conduct.* Every business organization should establish a code of conduct that governs the actions of the organization, as well as the behavior of its individual members. This code of conduct should be distributed throughout the organization and should be used as a guide for decision making and action by all individuals and groups in the organization.

- *Commandment IX: Thou Shall Take Needed Public Stands on Social Issues.* Organizations should never ignore social issues or refrain from taking a position. Clearly, many organizations would prefer to avoid controversial issues, but it is important that they stand up for what is right, whether the issue is discrimination, unsafe products, or disregard for the environment. It is important to take a stand.

- *Commandment X: Thou Shall Strive to Make Profits on an Ongoing Basis.* Ignoring the need to make profits is one of the most severe acts of irresponsibility. An organization cannot provide jobs and employ workers if it is not in a position to make consistent profits. To fail to recognize the importance of profitability is to threaten the livelihood of the employees of the organization.

Managers today must act in a socially responsible fashion. Their actions will be in vain, however, if the individual members of the organization do not have strong ethical values. In the next section of the chapter, we will examine more closely how ethics influences the behavior of individuals in the organization.

MANAGING FOR EXCELLENCE

PARTNERSHIPS FOR ENVIRONMENTAL SOLUTIONS

The world's environmental problems are real, immediate, and long term in their effect. Business and government must face them with creative thinking, definitive action, and total commitment. The Energy Star Computers program of the Environmental Protection Agency (EPA) is a partnership effort with the computer industry to promote the introduction of energy-efficient personal computers, monitors, and printers and reduce air pollution caused by power generation.

The program was introduced on Earth Day 1993, when computer equipment capable of going into an energy-saving sleep mode when sitting idle earned itself an EPA "Energy Star." President Clinton has mandated that the largest PC buyer in the world, the U.S. government, is committed to purchasing only Energy Star-compliant computers. Nearly 300 computer manufacturing companies, including Apple, Canon, Digital Equipment Corporation (DEC), Hewlett-Packard, and IBM, have embraced the concept. Now more than 75 companies offer products or even entire product lines that carry the Energy Star label.

The fact that many Energy Star computers cost no more than their energy-wasting counterparts adds to their appeal. They are easy to spot since the Energy Star program allows the manufacturers of these computers to display its logo on computers that draw no more than 30 watts of power when not in use and go to full power at the touch of a key. This allows the energy-conscious computer user to conserve energy automatically and effortlessly.

The EPA's Brian Johnson estimates that 26 billion kilowatts of energy could be saved by the year 2000. This amount of electricity could power Maine, New Hampshire, and Vermont for a year. The earth could be spared 20 million tons of carbon dioxide, the primary greenhouse gas, plus 140,000 tons of sulfur dioxide and 75,000 tons of nitrogen oxides.

This is a good example how an entire industry has become more responsive to environmental concerns. But the breakthrough was not so much in technology as in the EPA's promise to promote the end-result. In fact, the government spent little at its end and gave no money to the cooperating companies. But this hasn't stopped some manufacturers, notably Apple, Hewlett-Packard, and IBM, from going well beyond Energy Star in greening their PC.

ETHICS

Ethics is everyone's business, from top management to employees at all levels of the organization. One of management's most important challenges is to conduct business ethically while achieving high levels of economic performance. Why ethical problems arise in business and what can be done about them are some of the issues that will be addressed in this section.

UNDERSTANDING BUSINESS ETHICS

Should you pay a bribe to obtain a business contract in a foreign country? Is it acceptable to allow your company to dispose of hazardous waste in an unsafe fashion? Can you withhold information that might discourage a job candidate from joining your organization? Is it appropriate to conduct personal business on company time? These are just a few examples of ethical and moral dilemmas you may face as a manager.

In recent years, increasing attention has been focused on ethics in business due in large part to media coverage of a number of unethical actions.[24] For example, computer hackers were once regarded as youthful pranksters who broke into computer networks to play harmless games and prove their programming skills. No longer is this game considered harmless or ethical. In the past few years, a new wave of hackers has been on the loose creating viruses that have dangerous consequences and encourage unethical behavior. The *Legion of Doom,* for example, is a group of over 20 hackers who were able to disrupt the 911 service in nine states. In response, the Secret Service started "Operation Sun Devil," which has been aggressively tracking down unethical and illegal hackers across the country.[25]

Ethics reflects established customs and morals and fundamental human relationships that may vary throughout the world. Often ethical issues are controversial because they raise emotional questions of right and wrong behaviors. For our purposes, we will define **ethical behavior** as behavior that is morally accepted as "good" and "right" as opposed to "bad" or "wrong" in a particular setting. Right behavior is considered ethical behavior, while wrong behavior is considered unethical. In the business world, however, the difference between right and wrong behavior is not always clear. Although many unethical behaviors are illegal, some may be within the limits of the law.

Corporate executives are concerned with business ethics because they want to be perceived as "good" by resolving conflicts in values and analyzing the impact of decisions on organizational members. In many cases, the goal is to avoid illegal or unethical corporate behavior leading to adverse governmental or societal reactions, such as warnings, recalls, injunctions, monetary or criminal penalties, adverse public opinion, or loss of contracts.[26]

Foundations of Ethics

Although ethical behavior in business does reflect social and cultural factors, it is also highly personal and is shaped by an individual's own values and experiences. In your daily life, you face situations where you can make ethical or unethical decisions. You make your choices based on what you have learned from parents, family, teachers, peers, friends, and so forth. In addition, your ethics are also determined by your values.

Values are the relatively permanent and deeply held preferences of individuals or groups; they are the basis upon which attitudes and personal choices are formed. Values are among the most stable and enduring characteristics of individuals. Much of what we are is a product of the basic values we have developed throughout our lives. An organization, too, has a value system, usually referred to as its organizational culture. We will discuss organizational culture in more detail in Chapter 11.

To better understand the role of values as the foundation for ethical behavior, let's look at a basic values framework. Rokeach developed a values framework and identified two general types of values: instrumental values and terminal values.[27] **Instrumental values,** also called means-oriented values, prescribe desirable standards of conduct or methods for attaining an end. Examples of instrumental values include ambition, courage, honesty, and imagination. **Terminal values,** also called ends-oriented values, prescribe desirable ends or goals for the individual and reflect what a person is ultimately striving to achieve. Terminal values are either personal (peace of mind) or social (world peace). Examples of terminal values are a comfortable life, family security, self-respect, and a sense of accomplishment.

Different groups of people tend to hold different values. For example, business school students and professors tend to rate ambition, capability, responsibility, and freedom higher than people in general do. They tend to place

Ethics
The established customs, morals, and fundamental human relationships that exist throughout the world.

Ethical behavior
Behavior which is morally accepted as good or right as opposed to bad or wrong.

Values *what you believe in.*
Relatively permanent and deeply held preferences upon which individuals form attitudes and personal choices.

Instrumental values
Standards of conduct or methods for attaining an end.

Terminal values
Goals an individual will ultimately strive to achieve.

less importance than the general public on concern for others, helpfulness, aesthetics, cultural values, and overcoming social injustice.[28]

In most cases, the ethical standards and social responsibility of an organization or business reflect the personal values and ideals of the organization's founders or dominant managers. Over the years, those values and ideals become institutionalized and become integral to the organization's culture. For example, Thomas Watson's personal values and ethics formed the basis of IBM's culture. At Johnson & Johnson, the culture is based on the ideals of General Robert Wood Johnson. At Hewlett-Packard, the values reflect the personality and beliefs of Bill Hewlett and David Packard. At General Motors, Alfred Sloan was credited with being the moral voice of the culture. In each case, these individuals were the source of their organization's experiences, values, and principles. They were the behavioral role models for the organization's ethical behavior and commitment to social responsibility.

An organization's culture and the practices of its senior managers can influence the ethical behavior, not only of its employees, but also of other individuals and entities associated with the organization. Therefore, the challenge facing an organization is how to successfully develop, sustain, review, and adapt its ethical standards and its commitment to socially responsible behavior.

Business Ethics

Business ethics

The application of general ethics to business behavior.

Business ethics is not a special set of ethical rules that differ from ethics in general. **Business ethics** is the application of the general ethical rules to business behavior. If a society deems dishonesty to be unethical and immoral, then anyone in business who is dishonest with employees, customers, creditors, stockholders, or competition is acting unethically and immorally.

Businesses pay attention to ethics because the public expects a business to exhibit high levels of ethical performance and social responsibility. Many ethical rules operate to protect society against various types of harm, and business is expected to observe these ethical principles. High ethical standards also protect the individuals who work in an organization. Employees resent invasions of privacy, being ordered to do something against their personal convictions, or working under hazardous conditions. Businesses that treat their

▼ Many organizations use ethics training programs to gain a strategic advantage, increase employee awareness of ethics in business decision making, and help employees be more attentive to ethical issues to which they may be exposed. This ethics class focuses on interaction and employee involvement of important issues.

employees with dignity and integrity reap many rewards in the form of high morale and improved productivity. People feel good about working for an ethical company because they know they are protected along with the general public.

Pressures to Perform

In the past few years, the negative and questionable ethical practices of many public figures and corporations have attracted considerable media attention. White-collar crimes such as insider trading and money laundering appear to be on the increase. A recent *Business Week* article noted that white-collar crime drains billions of dollars a year from corporations and governments. This cost is ultimately borne by consumers and taxpayers. The rise in unethical behavior is blamed on the current emphasis on materialism as well as on economic and competitive pressures to perform.[29]

Jack Eckerd, founder and past president of the Eckerd Drug Corporation, is a strong believer that pressure to perform does not have to be a negative experience for the organization. Eckerd teaches managers how to turn ethics and values into greater sales and higher profits. For example, Eckerd describes a day in 1971 when he was walking through one of his Eckerd Drugstores and spotted a couple of youngsters sitting on the floor reading *Playboy* and *Hustler* magazines. Recalling the experience 22 years later, Eckerd still insists that the behavior made him mad. His anger did not abate the next day when he opened a letter from a concerned grandmother who was not thrilled with the contents of a provocative paperback book her 14-year-old grandson had purchased at Eckerd. Within 48 hours, the book and the magazines were off the racks at Eckerd, even though an Eckerd vice president warned that the company would lose $3 million in sales. As it turned out, sales were up 43 percent the next year.[30] Eckerd argues that strong corporate ethics are effective strategies for survival and profitability in a highly competitive arena. He insists that it is not possible to separate values and profits.

Many strategic management decisions, such as investment in human resources, modernization, product and service developments, marketing, environmental issues, and executive salaries, involve ethical questions. Managers must continually decide between maximizing the economic performance of the organization (as indicated by revenues, costs, profits, and so forth) or improving its social performance (as indicated by obligations to customers, employees, suppliers, and others). Most ethical tradeoffs are conflicts between these two desirable ends—economic versus social performance.[31] Making effective decisions in such situations is not merely a matter of choosing between right and wrong, or between good and bad. Most of the alternatives are not so clear-cut. Individuals who manage these ethical tradeoffs effectively have a clear sense of their own values and the values of their organization. They have developed their own internal set of universal, comprehensive, and consistent principles upon which to base their decisions.

MANAGERIAL GUIDELINES FOR ETHICAL DILEMMAS

An **ethical dilemma** is a situation in which a person must decide whether or not to do something that, although beneficial to oneself or the organization or both, may be considered unethical. Ethical dilemmas are common in the workplace. Research, in fact, suggests that managers encounter such dilemmas in their working relationships with superiors, subordinates, customers, competitors, suppliers, and regulators. Common issues underlying the dilemmas include honesty in communications and contracts, gifts and entertainment, kickbacks, pricing practices, and employee terminations.

Ethical dilemma
A situation in which an individual must decide whether or not to take action which may be considered unethical.

Organizations need a set of guidelines for thinking about ethical dilemmas. These guidelines can help managers and employees identify the nature of the ethical problem and decide which course of action is the most likely to produce the most ethical results. The following three approaches—utility, human rights, and justice—provide managerial guidelines for handling ethical dilemmas.

Utility Approach

Utility approach
A situation in which decisions are based on an evaluation of the overall amount of good that will result.

The **utility approach** emphasizes the overall amount of good that can be produced by an action or a decision. It judges actions, plans, and policies by their consequences. The primary objective of this approach is to provide the greatest good for the greatest number of people. It is often referred to as a cost-benefit analysis because it compares the costs and benefits of a decision, a policy, or an action. These costs and benefits can be economic (expressed in dollars), social (the effect on society at large), or human (usually a psychological or emotional impact). This type of results-oriented ethical reasoning tries to determine whether the overall outcome produces more good than harm—more utility or usefulness than negative results. The utility approach supports the ethical issues of profit maximization, self-interest, rewards based on abilities and achievements, sacrifice and hard work, and competition.[32]

The main drawback to the utility approach is the difficulty of accurately measuring both costs and benefits. For example, some things, such as goods produced, sales, payrolls, and profits, can be measured in monetary terms. Other items, such as employee morale, psychological satisfactions, and the worth of human life, do not easily lend themselves to monetary measurement. Another limitation of the utility approach is that the majority may override the rights of those in the minority.

Despite these limitations, cost-benefit analysis is widely used in business. If benefits (earnings) exceed costs, the organization makes a profit and is considered to be an economic success. Because this method uses economic and financial outcomes, managers sometimes rely on it to decide important ethical questions without being fully aware of its limitations or the availability of other approaches that may improve the ethical quality of decisions. One of these alternative approaches is the impact of the decisions on human rights.

Human Rights Approach

Human rights approach
A situation in which decisions are made in light of the moral entitlements of human beings.

Human rights is a second method for handling ethical dilemmas. The **human rights approach** to ethics holds that human beings have certain moral entitlements that should be respected in all decisions. These entitlements guarantee an individual's most fundamental personal rights (life, freedom, health, privacy, and property, for example). These have been spelled out in such documents as the U.S. Bill of Rights and the United Nations Declaration of Human Rights.[33] A right means that a person or group is entitled to something or is entitled to be treated in a certain way. The most basic human rights are those claims or entitlements that enable a person to survive, make free choices, and realize his or her potential as a human being. Denying those rights to other persons and groups or failing to protect their rights is considered to be unethical. Respecting others, even those with whom we disagree or whom we dislike, is the essence of human rights, provided that others do the same for us.

The human rights approach to ethical dilemmas holds that individuals are to be treated as valuable ends in themselves simply because they are human beings. Using others for your own purposes is unethical if, at the same time, you deny them their rights to their own goals and purposes. For example, an organization that denies a group of women employees an opportunity to bid for all jobs for which they are qualified is depriving them of some of their rights.

The main limitation on using the human rights approach as a basis for ethical decisions is the difficulty of balancing conflicting rights. For example, using a polygraph test to evaluate an employee's honesty to protect the organization's financial responsibilities may be at odds with the employee's right to privacy. Many difficult decisions have involved minorities and women who are competing with white males for the right to hold jobs in business and government. Rights also clash when U.S. multinational corporations move production to a foreign nation, causing job losses at home while creating new jobs abroad. In such cases, whose job rights should be protected?

The degree to which human rights are protected and promoted is an important ethical benchmark for judging the behavior of individuals and organizations. Most people would agree that the denial of a person's fundamental rights to life, freedom, privacy, growth, and human dignity is generally unethical. By defining the human condition and pointing the way to a realization of human potentialities, such rights become a kind of common denominator setting forth the essential conditions for ethical actions and decisions.

Justice Approach

A third method of ethical decision making concerns justice. Under the **justice approach,** decisions are based on an equitable, fair, and impartial distribution of benefits (rewards) and costs among individuals and groups. Justice is essentially a condition characterized by an equitable distribution of the benefits and burdens of working together. It exists when benefits and burdens are distributed equitably and according to some accepted rule. For society as a whole, social justice means that a society's income and wealth are distributed among the people in fair proportions.

A common question is "Is it fair or just?" For example, employees want to know if pay scales are fair; consumers are interested in fair prices when they shop. When new tax laws are proposed, there is much debate about their fairness—where will the burden fall, and will all taxpayers pay their fair share? Using the justice approach, the organization considers who pays the costs and who gets the benefits. If the shares seem fair, then the action is probably just.

Determining what is just and unjust can be an explosive issue if the stakes are high. Since distributive rules usually grant privileges to some groups based on tradition and custom, sharp inequalities between groups can generate social tensions and clamorous demands for a change to a fairer system.

As with the utilitarian approach, a major limitation of the justice approach is the difficulty of measuring benefits and costs precisely. Another limitation is that many of society's benefits and burdens are intangible, emotional, and psychological. People unfairly deprived of life's opportunities may not willingly accept their condition. Few people, even those who are relatively well off, are ever entirely satisfied with their share of society's wealth. For these reasons, the use of the justice approach can be tricky. Although everyone is intensely interested in being treated fairly, many are skeptical that justice will ever be fully realized. In spite of these drawbacks, the justice approach to ethical dilemmas can still be applied in many business situations. Meeting the Challenge provides an opportunity for you to apply these decision-making approaches to several ethical dilemmas. How would you respond to these situations?

FOSTERING IMPROVED BUSINESS ETHICS

In recent years, many well-publicized and questionable business practices have brought business ethics to the forefront of concerns in the business community. Until the late 1980s, business ethics was little more than an obscure debate among some scholars. In the wake of many questionable events, however, businesses, business leaders, and academic institutions have placed

Justice approach
A situation in which decisions are based on an equitable, fair, and impartial distribution of benefits and costs among individuals and groups.

greater emphasis on developing ethical standards and fostering an appreciation for adherence to ethical business behavior.[34] Unfortunately, many of these efforts have proved to be more image than substance. Part of the problem is that the sudden push for ethical standards has focused on addressing clear-cut ethical issues of good versus bad and right versus wrong. No one would question that pollution is bad, embezzlement is wrong, and honoring product warranties is right. But the advocates of business ethics have discovered that the real ethical issues are not black and white, but gray and complex with no obvious solutions that enable everyone to win.

To foster improved business ethics in an organization, action must be directed at five levels: the international, societal, association, organizational, and individual levels. The most fundamental effort is directed at the individual.

Agreements among nations help to foster ethical behavior at the international level. Laws at the societal level help shape ethical behavior. At the association level, groups of similar businesses can join together and establish codes of ethics for their industry or profession and provide a mechanism for monitoring and disciplining members who violate the code. For example, the Florida Bar Association is attempting to help lawyers improve their ethics by developing an ethics school. Lawyers accused of minor misconduct and brought up before the bar association on charges will soon have a choice—a reprimand by the bar—or two or three days in a classroom with an ethics expert. Classes in the new Florida ethics school will cover such topics as professionalism, ethical codes, courtroom etiquette, and dealings with clients. Ethics school will be available only for first-time offenders. It is not intended for lawyers accused of criminal offenses such as skimming clients' trust funds, misrepresentation, or other major infractions. With complaints on lawyer misconduct in Florida now totaling about 8000 annually, the school should be well attended when it opens in 1994. Can the ethics school really reduce the number of misconduct complaints and teach lawyers to behave in a more ethical manner? Thomas Ervin, who headed the committee that came up with the ethics school concept, thinks that it is a step in the right direction.[35]

At the organizational level, improving business ethics requires managers who can model the expected ethical behavior, set realistic goals for workers, and encourage ethical behavior by providing an organizational environment that rewards such behavior and punishes violators.

At the individual level, the challenge to organizations is to develop employees' awareness of business ethics (see Table 3.4) as well as to help them confront complex ethical issues. Employees find it helpful when their organi-

▼ **TABLE 3.4**   Developing Employee Awareness of Ethics

1. Enabling the ethical component of a decision to be recognized.
2. Legitimizing the consideration of ethics as part of decision making.
3. Avoiding variability in decision making caused by lack of awareness of rules or norms.
4. Avoiding ambivalence in decision making caused by an organizational reward system that psychologically pulls a person in opposite directions.
5. Avoiding ambivalence in decision making caused by confusion as to who is responsible for misdeeds, particularly when the employee has received an order from a superior.
6. Providing decision-making frameworks for analyzing ethical choices and helping employees to apply such frameworks.

SOURCE: S. J. Harrington, "What Corporate America Is Teaching about Ethics," *Academy of Management Executive* 5 (1991): 21-29.

ARTHUR ANDERSEN & COMPANY

This video is part of a training program for employees at Arthur Andersen, a "Big Six" public accounting firm. If any professionals must have high ethical standards, certainly public accountants would be high on the list. After all, they certify the financial records of firms people invest in. The video presents five situations that highlight specific ethical issues in the workplace. As you watch the five vignettes, think about how you might react.

- *Vignette 1: The High Bid Dilemma.* A young assistant to the purchasing agent finds himself facing the "reality" of business when his boss, the company purchasing manager, prefers a high bid for bronze facing. The assistant recommends Metaltech, the low bidder, but the purchasing manager prefers Spin Cast Systems because the president of Spin Cast is a former fraternity brother and friend. The purchasing manager's advice: "If you take care of your suppliers, they'll take care of you."

- *Vignette 2: A Compensation Issue.* Discrimination is the source of contention when Sandy and Brenda start talking. Brenda, an African American, tells Sandy that she has discovered she is paid less than another secretary who started at the same time and has the same responsibilities. Brenda becomes annoyed when Sandy tries to find a logical reason for the difference in pay. Brenda's comment: "They expect me to be just the same as everyone else. Why can't they pay me the same?"

- *Vignette 3: Sexual Harassment.* Sexual harassment is against the law. Two types of conditions are classified as sexual harassment: (1) quid pro quo, or you do this and I'll do that; and (2) a hostile work environment. Shelly has a difficult time escaping the advances of Bill, who is described as "a very friendly fellow." She does not believe he treats other women the way he treats her and that she is being sexually harassed. She confides in Ginny, a co-worker, and asks, "What am I to do?"

- *Vignette 4: Competition or Revenge?* Is it fair to kick a person who is down and out? Phil, George, and Jean seem to think so. They resent the fact that Jack, a former co-worker who now works for another company, may be calling on their customers and cutting into their established business. To address the problem, Jean offers to spread false rumors about Jack. George tells him: "Survival is the name of the game."

- *Vignette 5: Creative Expense Reporting.* Jim and Ken are having a discussion about Jim's expense report. Jim lost his receipts and has filled out his expense report using ballpark figures, some of them debatable and some clearly not business expenses. Ken is not sure that what Jim is doing is appropriate, but Jim's comment is, "What's the difference?"[55]

SOURCE: Adapted with permission of Arthur Andersen & Co., SC.

zation publicly announces what it believes in and expects in terms of employee behavior.[36] Ultimately, though, ethical business behavior comes from the individual, not the organization.[37]

In the next section, we examine two of the most common ways in which organizations foster ethical behavior—creating codes of conduct and developing ethics training programs. In general, such actions must reflect relevant employee concerns and must be tailored to specific needs and value statements.

Codes of Ethics

Code of ethics
The general value system, principles, and specific rules that a company follows.

A code of ethics describes the general value system, ethical principles, and specific ethical rules that a company tries to apply. It can be an effective way to encourage ethical business behavior and raise an organization's standards of ethical performance. Whether called a code of ethics, a credo, declaration of business principles, statement of core values, or something similar, the number of these documents is growing rapidly. In response to the ethical problems that have been arising in the United States, companies and professional societies are publishing codes of conduct and then implementing these codes through ethics training programs. These companies have determined that maintaining an ethical organization can be a strategic advantage.[38] Over the past decade, most major U.S. corporations, including more than 300 of the Fortune 500 companies, have developed a code of ethics.[39]

Typically, a code of ethics covers a wide range of issues and potential problem areas that an organization and its members may encounter. It is a set of carefully articulated statements of ethical principles rooted in the organization's goals, objectives, organizational history, and traditions. A code contains explicit statements and precepts intended to guide both the organization and its employees in their professional behavior. A code helps employees know what is expected in ethical terms when they face an uncertain situation. It becomes the basis for establishing continuity and uniformity in managerial action and can be a unifying force that holds the organization together so that its employees can act in a cohesive and socially responsible manner.

▼ A code of ethics usually covers a wide range of issues and potential problem areas that an organization and organizational members may encounter. Employees are working to develop a code based on the organization's ethical principles rooted in its goals, objectives, organizational history, and traditions.

As we saw in the Managerial Incident at the beginning of the chapter, Martin Marietta found itself in a very difficult ethical situation. To preserve its image, Martin Marietta developed the code of ethics, or credo, that is shown in Table 3.5. The credo reveals both the company's statement of unifying principles and its code of ethics and standards of conduct.

An organization's code of ethics can serve several purposes. First, it creates employee awareness that ethical issues need to be considered in making business decisions. Second, it demonstrates that the organization is fully committed to stating its standards and to incorporating them into daily activities. Third, a code can contribute to transforming an "us-them" relationship between the organization and its employees into an "us-us" relationship.[40] Nevertheless, a code's impact on employee behavior is weakened if the code's purpose is primarily to make the company look good or if it is intended to give the company's top executives a legal defense when illegal or unethical acts are committed by lower-ranking employees.

One defense contracting corporation has recognized significant benefits from its new code of ethics. When it was suspended from government contracting for unethical conduct throughout the organization, it was required to develop, implement, and enforce a rigorous code of ethics. The president of the corporation immediately contacted a private ethics resource center for help in developing an ethics program. An ethics center was established where employees could seek advice as well as report improper conduct. This new

▼ **TABLE 3.5** Martin Marietta Credo

STATEMENT OF UNIFYING PRINCIPLES	CODE OF ETHICS AND STANDARDS OF CONDUCT
In our daily activities we bear important obligations to our country, our customers, our owners, our communities, and to one another. We carry out these obligations guided by certain unifying principles: • Our foundation is INTEGRITY. We conduct our business in an open and forthright manner in strict compliance with applicable laws, rules, and regulations so that we are correctly perceived to be an ethical organization of dedicated and competent individuals of high integrity and credibility producing quality products and services that contribute significantly to our communications and to our nation. • Our strength is our PEOPLE. The collective talents of our employees comprise our most important asset. Therefore, we provide an organization and operating environment that attracts, nurtures, stimulates, and rewards employee professionalism and creativity, providing a safe workplace and an opportunity for hands-on accomplishment, a criterion highly regarded for promotion and growth. • Our style is TEAMWORK. As pioneers and leaders in technology advancement, from design and systems development to manufacturing, testing, and operational integration, the corporation emphasizes teamwork, recognizing within that framework the critical contribution of the individual. Providing a workplace environment that effectively balances and stimulates the individual and the team is our hallmark. • Our goal is EXCELLENCE. Excellence in the form of quality is a shared attribute of the customers and markets we serve and the products we build. Attention to detail and performance are stressed in every line and staff function from the factory floor through the highest levels of management, resulting in a total dedication to mission success.	Martin Marietta Corporation believes in the highest ethical standards. We demonstrate these beliefs through our commitments—commitments we are dedicated to fulfill. • To our EMPLOYEES we are committed to just management and equality for all, providing a safe and healthy workplace, and respecting the dignity and privacy due all human beings. • To our CUSTOMERS we are committed to produce reliable products and services at a fair price that are delivered on time and within budget. • To the COMMUNITIES in which we live we are committed to be responsible neighbors, reflecting all aspects of good citizenship. • To our SHAREHOLDERS we are committed to pursuing sound growth and earnings objectives and to exercising prudence in the use of our assets and resources. • To our SUPPLIERS we are committed to fair competition and the sense of responsibility required of a good customer.

focus on ethics has transformed the organization from a national villain to a model for others to follow.[41]

A code of ethics can resemble a set of regulations (Our employees will not . . .), aspirations (Our employees should . . .), or factual statements (Our organization is committed to . . .), but all effective codes appear to share at least three characteristics:

1. They generally govern activities that cannot be supervised closely enough to assure compliance.
2. They ask more of employees than would otherwise be expected.
3. They can serve the long-term interest of the organization.

In addition, the most effective codes of ethics are those drawn up with the cooperation and participation of employees, as the profile of Nynex in Service Challenge illustrates.[42]

SERVICE CHALLENGE

Nynex Corporation: Doing the Right Thing

Several incidents of inappropriate employee behavior and charges of overbilling and use of incorrect rates by the Federal Communications Commission led Graydon R. Wood, vice president for ethics and business conduct at Nynex, to take action. As a service organization, Nynex, (the New York–based Baby Bell phone company) couldn't afford to alienate its customers with unethical behavior.

Wood's first action was to launch a full-blown ethics program that included a written code of ethical conduct and formal training procedures. An Ethics Policy Committee was created to draft the code of ethics. Then Wood went on the road, visiting Nynex facilities where lower-level managers edited and improved upon the code by focusing on relevant day-to-day issues. The final code was circulated to all Nynex managers. The guidelines include an outline of company ethical standards, a question-and-answer section, a reference guide, and company standards on subjects ranging from political contributions and sexual harassment to relations with government officials and outside employment.

Supporting the code of ethics is a strong training program that helps to make the code relevant to organizational areas, such as purchasing and personnel. Nynex is striving to put all of its managers through a full-day seminar dealing with proper conduct in matters of money, law, and treatment of employees.

To further reinforce its ethics policies, Nynex has established a "whistleblowers" hotline for its 90,000 workers. Within a year of its inception, the hotline had received more than 1200 calls. About 12 percent of the calls dealt with allegations of wrongdoing while the rest were fairly evenly divided between requests for information and personnel issues.

Nynex's ethics department will continue to focus on education, communication, and enforcement. While Wood contends that the company has a long way to go, the strides it has already made paint a bright picture for the ethical future of Nynex.

Johnson & Johnson has taken a unique approach to discussing and revising its code of ethics. It holds meetings where new employees are challenged to explore whether the company ethics code is still valid. In this way employees can discuss the code in a nonthreatening, nonlecturing way and have an opportunity to bring up specific situations or cases.[43] These challenge sessions also acquaint employees with official company policy on ethical issues and show how those policies can be translated into the specifics of everyday decision making.

Given the rapid changes in the marketplace, some organizations have recognized that statements of ethical standards and socially responsible behavior have to be dynamic and provide a degree of flexibility. These organizations have found that a simple creed or policy statement is a more practical guideline for determining ethical practices and behaviors. McDonnell-Douglas Corporation governs its ethical practices with the simple creed that its employees are "honest and trustworthy in all relationships." J. C. Penney's simply adopted the Golden Rule: "Do unto others as you would have them do unto you." Such statements serve more as a general reference point or an anchor that provides an ethical and socially responsible perspective while allowing flexibility of action in dealing with a wide variety of situations. Under these types of statements, individual managers or employees bear much of the responsibility for defining the ethical standards that they exercise within the prevailing corporate culture.

Ethical statements and social responsibility policies are not sufficient by themselves to cause people to behave in a socially responsible manner. A 20-page policy statement by General Dynamics failed to prevent a widespread lapse in ethical conduct involving government contracts. The real challenge for top management is to create an environment that sustains, promotes, and develops ethical behavior and a commitment to social responsibility. The effort must begin at the highest levels of the organization. Unless top management, beginning with the CEO, provides leadership, commitment, and role modeling, no organization can hope to attain high ethical standards or consistently behave in a socially responsible manner. Top management must also ensure that the organization's expectations of ethical behavior and social responsibility are clearly conveyed to its employees and to all parties involved with the organization, that is, the stakeholders. This requires extensive communication among all parties and the establishment of systems within the organization to reinforce ethical behavior.[44]

Reinforcing Ethical Behavior

Insider trading, Defense Department favoritism to suppliers, fraudulent billing practices—these are just a few of the issues recently raised by the news media and stockholders. In response, companies and professional societies are beginning to develop methods to integrate ethical behavior into their organizational culture through positive reinforcement.

Several methods have been successfully used to reinforce ethical behavior in the organization. An assessment of individual ethical commitments and behaviors can be incorporated into the performance appraisal system. Another possibility is to use ethical audits. **Ethical audits** measure specific compliance with ethical standards and determine how successful the organization and its employees have been in achieving established ethical goals. Finally, extensive ethics training programs can be developed. Since most organizations train their employees in accounting methods, marketing techniques, safety procedures,

Ethical audits
Methods by which compliance with ethical standards is measured.

▼ A team of employees works together to develop an ethical audit that measures the organization's specific compliance with ethical standards and how well the organization and its employee have done in achieving established goals of social responsibility.

and technical systems, there is no reason why training in ethics can't be provided as well.

The goals of ethics training vary widely from organization to organization. Some of the most prominent reasons include avoiding adverse publicity, potential lawsuits, illegal behavior, and monetary and criminal penalties. Many organizations also use ethics training to gain a strategic advantage, increase employee awareness of ethics in business decision making, and help employees be more attentive to ethical issues to which they may be exposed.[45]

Ethics training programs have been shown to help employees avoid rationalizations often used to legitimize unethical behavior. Among the rationalizations often advanced to justify organizational misconduct are believing that: (1) the activity is not really illegal or immoral, (2) it is in the individual's or the corporation's best interest, (3) it will never be found out, or (4) the company will condone it because it helps the company.

Ethics training programs can help managers clarify their ethical framework and practice self-discipline when making decisions in difficult circumstances. Allied Corporation, Martin Marietta, Arthur Andersen, McDonnell-Douglas, Hershey Foods, Pitney Bowes, and General Dynamics are among the prominent companies with training programs for managers, supervisors, and anyone else likely to encounter an ethical question at work.[46] As we see in Managing for Excellence 3.2, Martin Marietta has even developed an ethics game called *Gray Matters* to help foster an improved ethical environment by reinforcing ethical behavior.[47]

The content and approach of ethics training programs may differ depending on the organization's goals. Case studies, often specific to the business functions of the organization's audience, are the most widely used approach. Other popular approaches include presenting the rules or guidelines for deciding ethical issues (such as the Golden Rule or the utilitarian approach), using cognitive approaches that attempt to develop higher levels of ethical understanding, or developing a checklist such as the one shown in Table 3.6 to aid managers in making ethical decisions.[48]

The training approach at Boeing Corporation, where more than 145,000 employees have been exposed to the ethics value program, is a customized in-house program tailored to meet the organization's ethics goals. First, a division general manager delivers a message emphasizing ethical business practices. Next, employees receive a company-created pamphlet entitled Business Conduct Guidelines, which stresses policies on ethics and standards of conduct and compliance. Hypothetical situations are presented, and a business

▼ **TABLE 3.6**   Checklist for Managers to Use When Facing Ethical Dilemmas

1. Recognize and clarify the dilemma.
2. Get all possible facts.
3. List all your options.
4. Test each option by asking, "Is it legal? Is it right? Is it beneficial?"
5. Make your decision.
6. Double-check your decision by asking, "How would I feel if my family found out about this? How would I feel if my decision was printed in the local paper?"
7. Take action.

SOURCE: Developed in part from A. L. Otten, "Ethics on the Job: Companies Alert Employees to Potential Dilemmas," *Wall Street Journal*, July 14, 1986, 17.

GRAY MATTERS: ETHICS BECOMES A GAME TO PLAY

While many organizations are trying to emphasize the importance of business ethics through seminars and corporate policies, the Martin Marietta Corporation has treated the issue as a game—literally! Martin Marietta has developed a board game called *Gray Matters*, designed to teach participants how to handle ethical challenges and dilemmas that occur daily in every type of business. In addition to encouraging discussions at proper procedures, the game stimulates employees' imaginations and gets them to consider the ethical consequences of their business decisions and actions.

Gray Matters consists of a series of minicases, each with a different scenario, its own options, and rewards and penalties corresponding to those options. Each minicase is played in about 10 minutes, and the entire game takes from one to two hours to complete. Martin Marietta contends that answers to life are never all black or all white, so most of the cases in Gray Matters do not have completely right or completely wrong answers but rather alternatives in varying shades of "correctness." Players must pick the answer that they can best justify based on company policies as well as their experiences, education, ethical training, and beliefs. Competition adds spice to the game, which can be played by individuals or by a larger group divided into teams.

The game is designed to create controversy for participants, and the solutions don't necessarily appeal to everyone. The idea is to generate discussion among the players about the rationale behind the most appropriate responses. Gray Matters includes policies from more than one company to encourage the participants to consider multiple approaches to ethical dilemmas. The resulting group discussions help to inform employees about Martin Marietta's values and standards on business ethics and conduct. Through the discussions, participants also learn the proper procedure(s) for dealing with ethical concerns that can arise in their day-to-day job responsibilities.

Martin Marietta has experienced such success with Gray Matters that other corporations have asked to use the game to augment their own ethics training programs. Employee participants agree that applying company standards to hypothetical situations is a more effective way to strengthen their ethical skills than listening passively to a speech or reading an abstract set of ethical principles.

ethics adviser in each division leads discussions. The training also stresses the procedures for discussing or reporting unethical behavior or infractions.

Whistleblowing

One method of monitoring the ethical conviction of the organization and its top management is to observe its approach to professional dissent or, as it is more commonly called, whistleblowing. Whistleblowing occurs when an insider reports alleged organizational misconduct to the public. A **whistleblower** is someone who exposes organizational wrongdoing in order to preserve ethical standards and protect against wasteful, harmful, or illegal acts.

Whistleblowing is becoming a staple on the front pages. An employee—or, more often, a former employee—of a big corporation goes public with charges that the company has been playing dirty. Next step: a lawsuit that sets out the details of the misconduct and charges that the whistleblower was at best ignored and at worst harassed, demoted, or fired.

Whistleblower
Someone who exposes organizational misconduct or wrongdoing to the public.

Doubtless, some whistleblower suits are brought by employees with an ax to grind. Others may be in search of a big payoff. For example, under the False Claims Act, whistleblowers can receive up to 25 percent of any money recovered by the government. Christopher M. Urda, for instance, was awarded $7.5 million in July 1992 for providing evidence that his employer, then a unit of Singer Corporation, bilked the Pentagon out of $77 million in the 1980s.[49]

Generally, employees are not free to speak out against their employer because there is a public interest in allowing organizations to operate without harassment from insiders. Organizations face countless ethical issues and internal conflicts in their daily operations. Choices must be made where there are many opinions. Mistakes are made, and waste does occur, but usually corrective action is taken.

Although whistleblowing typically exposes unethical practices, how it is done and how it is handled may also be ethically questionable. The costs of whistleblowing are high for both the company and the whistleblower. The company "gets a black eye" whether it wins or loses, which can create considerable internal conflict. The company spends much time and money defending itself and may damage general employee morale by seeming to be unsympathetic to legitimate concerns expressed by employees. The whistleblower also suffers. Many times whistleblowers are subject to retaliatory action by disgruntled employers and often are blackballed for not being team players. Even if the whistleblower wins, the costs can be high for legal expenses, mental anguish, ostracism by former co-workers, and damage to a career.

To avoid the costs for both the company and the employee, many companies have become more receptive to employee complaints. Some organizations have established regular procedures for professional dissent, such as hotlines that employees can use to report dangerous or questionable company practices or the use of ombudsmen who can act as neutral judges and negotiators when supervisors and employees disagree over a policy or practice. Confidential questionnaires are another device to encourage potential whistleblowers to report their concerns before they become a big issue. In these ways, progressive companies attempt to lessen the tensions between the company and its employees and maintain the confidence and trust between them.

Table 3.7 shows a model whistleblower policy recently developed by the Conference Board.[50] The policy can work in the real world if managers emphasize that ethics are more than fancy policy. Managers should ask employees whether they have confidence in the company's ethics system and make them believe that exposing internal wrongdoing is part of their job. Whistleblowers who raise real issues should be rewarded.[51] Whatever technique is used, it should permit individuals to expose unethical practices or lapses in socially responsible behavior without disrupting the organization.

▼ **TABLE 3.7**   A Model Whistleblower Policy

- *Shout it from the rooftops.* Aggressively publicize a reporting policy that encourages employees to bring forward valid complaints of wrongdoing.
- *Face the fear factor.* Defuse fear by directing complaints to someone outside the whistleblower's chain of command.
- *Get right on it.* An independent group, either inside or outside the company, should investigate the company immediately.
- *Go public.* Show employees that complaints are taken seriously by publicizing the outcome of investigations whenever possible.

SOURCE: L. Driscoll, "A Better Way to Handle Whistle-Blowers: Let Them Speak," 36. Reprinted from July 27, 1992, issue of *Business Week* by special permission, copyright © 1992 by McGraw-Hill, Inc.

MANAGERIAL IMPLICATIONS

Two approaches to addressing ethical issues have been identified—one proactive and one responsive. First, a manager can intervene to end unethical organizational practices by working against the persons and organizations behaving unethically. Second, the manager can initiate ethical organizational change by working with others and the organization. These approaches are not mutually exclusive. Depending on the individual, the organization, the relationships, and the situation, either or both approaches may be appropriate for addressing ethical issues.[52]

Achieving social responsibility and business ethics at an organizational level is a challenge that tomorrow's managers will face.[53] This challenge can be met when managers:

- Explore ways in which the organization can be more socially responsive.
- Recognize the effect of the organization's actions on its stakeholders.
- Create an environment in which employees commit to behaving in socially responsive and ethical ways.
- Make sure that a code of ethics is put in place and followed.
- Ensure that a whistleblowing and an ethical concerns procedure is established for internal problem-solving.
- Involve line and staff employees in the identification of ethical issues to help them gain understanding and resolve issues.
- Determine the link between departments and issues impacting the company, and make them known to employees in the departments.
- Integrate ethical decision making into the performance appraisal process.
- Publicize, in employee communications and elsewhere, executive priorities and efforts related to ethical issues.

By following these guidelines, managers will be taking a major step toward achieving a high level of social responsibility in the organization and increasing employee awareness of ethical issues.

In this chapter we have explored the issues of social responsibility and business ethics. Managers of the future will be expected to address important social issues proactively and to maintain a high standard of ethical behavior.

MARTIN MARIETTA: ALLEGATIONS OF FRAUD

Martin Marietta appears to have weathered the negative press from the "Ill Wind" investigation fairly well. The company's current CEO, Norman Augustine, has denied any knowledge of fraud related to the securing of the Navy contract. Thomas Pownall, however, has resigned from Martin Marietta's board. Yet Augustine has indicated that he will continue to support Pownall until such time as there is clear evidence of misconduct on his part. Further, Augustine continues to emphasize Martin Marietta's "commitment to the highest standard of ethical conduct in its service to the nation, its customers, its shareowners and communities."[54] ▼

**MANAGERIAL INCIDENT
RESOLUTION**

SUMMARY

- The concepts of social responsibility and ethics require an understanding of the stakeholder view of the organization. Whereas the traditional view of socially responsible behavior considers only the stockholders, contemporary theory recognizes a much broader group of constituents—stakeholders. Stakeholders include any individual or group that is affected by or can affect the organization.

- Corporate social responsibility has been the subject of much controversy and debate over the last several decades. Although the concept defies precise definition, in a very general sense, social responsibility refers to the interaction between business and the social environment in which it exists. The concept of social responsibility rests on two premises—social contract and moral agent.

- Three perspectives of corporate social responsibility have significant support from both practitioners and academics. The economic responsibility perspective suggests that the only social responsibility of business is to maximize profits within the "rules of the game." The public responsibility perspective argues that business has an obligation to act in a way that is consistent with society's overall expectations of business. Social responsiveness supporters suggest that it is the responsibility of business to act proactively to improve the welfare of society.

- There are four distinct strategies for responding to social issues. These strategies, which span a continuum ranging from "do nothing" to "do much," are: (1) reaction, (2) defense, (3) accommodation, and (4) proaction. Although none of these strategies is appropriate for all organizations, the accommodation or proaction strategic approaches to social responsibility are appropriate in most cases.

- As organizations consider a strategy for social responsibility, a number of "commandments" should be considered. In general, these commandments suggest that organizations should be observant of social issues, honest with their constituents, cooperative with stakeholders with regard to social concerns, and proactive in their efforts to fulfill their obligation to society.

- Values are the relatively permanent and deeply held desires of individuals or groups. They are the bases upon which attitudes and personal preferences are patterned. Values are among the most stable and enduring characteristics of individuals and form the foundation of an individual's ethical behavior.

- Instrumental, or means-oriented, values describe desirable standards of conduct or methods for attaining an end. Terminal, or ends-oriented, values describe desirable ends or goals for the individual and reflect what a person is ultimately striving to achieve.

- The utility approach emphasizes the overall amount of good that can be produced by an action or a decision. The human rights approach holds that decisions should be consistent with fundamental rights and privileges such as those of life, freedom, health, privacy, and property. Under the justice approach, decisions are based on an equitable, fair, and impartial distribution of benefits (rewards) and costs among individuals and groups.

- Organizations often develop codes of ethics along with training programs to encourage and reinforce ethical business behavior. A code of ethics describes the organization's general value system, its ethical principles, and the specific ethical rules that it tries to apply.

- Several different approaches can be used in ethics training programs. These approaches include case studies, the presentation of rules or guidelines for deciding ethical issues, and cognitive approaches that attempt to develop higher levels of ethical understanding

● A whistleblower is someone who exposes organizational wrongdoing in order to preserve ethical standards and protect against wasteful, harmful, or illegal acts.

KEY TERMS

Stakeholders (p. 73)
Corporate social responsibility (p. 74)
Social contract (p. 75)
Moral agent (p. 75)
Ethics (p. 85)

Ethical behavior (p. 85)
Values (p. 85)
Instrumental values (p. 85)
Terminal values (p. 85)
Business ethics (p. 86)
Ethical dilemma (p. 87)

Utility approach (p. 88)
Human rights approach (p. 88)
Justice approach (p. 89)
Code of ethics (p. 92)
Ethical audits (p. 95)
Whistleblower (p. 97)

REVIEW QUESTIONS

1. Describe the stakeholder view of the organization. How does the stakeholder view differ from the stockholder view, and what are the implications of these differences for the concept of corporate social responsibility?

2. Define the concept of corporate social responsibility. What are the two premises advanced by Bowen in his original definition of social responsibility and the three resulting perspectives?

3. Evaluate the four different strategies for social responsibility. Describe how these strategies differ and give an example of a company that has pursued each strategy.

4. What are the ten commandments of social responsibility? Which perspective of social responsibility (see question 2) is most consistent with these commandments?

5. Explain why ethical behavior is considered to be individualistic.

6. What are values? Why are they the basis of an individual's ethical behavior?

7. Distinguish between terminal and instrumental values. Give an example of each.

8. Describe the utility, human rights, and justice approaches to ethical dilemmas, and explain how they differ.

9. Describe the different goals an organization can have for developing a code of ethics.

10. What are the common approaches used in ethics training programs?

11. Explain what is meant by whistleblowing.

DISCUSSION QUESTIONS

Improving Critical Thinking

1. Consider the implications of self-regulation versus government-imposed regulation (refer to Commandments I and III). Why is it preferable for an industry to be self-regulated?

2. Describe an ethical dilemma you have experienced at work or as part of a business or social organization. What was your response? If you faced a similar dilemma now, would your response differ?

Enhancing Communication Skills

3. Select an organization with which you are familiar or that you are interested in researching. Evaluate the social responsibility strategy of that company with regard to the following social issues: (1) environmental protection, (2) worker health and safety, and (3) product safety. Has this company been in a reaction, defensive, accommodation, or proaction mode with regard to these social issues? Make an oral presentation of your findings to the class.

4. Using current business periodicals or newspapers, find an example of an organization that has faced an ethical problem. How did it solve the problem? Did the organization have a code of ethics? What actions did it take to resolve the problem? Write a summary of your findings as a way to demonstrate your understanding of the issue and practice your written communication skills.

5. Examine the policy your college or university has for handling academic dishonesty. How appropriate is the policy? Would you suggest any changes?

Write up your suggestions and discuss them with a small group or your class.

Building Teamwork

6. In small groups, or as directed by your instructor, select a company that is considering relocating its major manufacturing plant from a domestic site to a country with lower labor costs. What are the social considerations that are most relevant for this company? Evaluate how this decision would be viewed by proponents of each of the three perspectives of social responsibility (economic responsibility, public responsibility, and social responsiveness).

7. As part of a small group, develop a code of ethics for an organization to which one or more of you belong, such as a fraternity, sorority, business association, or your college. What are the key issues that need to be addressed? Share your code with the class and the organization.

8. As part of a small group, develop an outline of an ethics training program for an organization for which one or more of you belong, such as a fraternity, sorority, or business association. What is the most appropriate approach? What key issues will you include?

ETHICS: TAKE A STAND

ABC Architecture has just received a commission to design an office building for a large multinational account that it has been trying to win for many years. ABC could potentially make a substantial profit on the project as well as expand its influence into international circles. The only drawback is that the multinational customer is a developer doing business in China. The developer believes in human rights and equality and has assured ABC that it supports the Chinese dissidents and their efforts for reform.

Nevertheless, ABC cannot be assured that all the tenants of the building will advance these values. The partners/owners of ABC feel strongly about fundamental human rights, but they also recognize that if they don't provide these services, someone else will. ABC's partners/owners must soon decide whether to accept the commission.

For Discussion:

1. Divide the class into two groups. One group should take a stand to accept the commission; the second group should take a stand against accepting the commission.

2. The members of each group should prepare arguments to support their position.

3. As a class, discuss the pros and cons of each viewpoint.

4. Take a poll to determine which side presented the more convincing arguments.

THINKING CRITICALLY
Debate the Issue

ECONOMIC RESPONSIBILITY VERSUS SOCIAL RESPONSIVENESS

Form teams with four to five students on each team. Half of the teams should prepare to argue the economic responsibility perspective of social responsibility. The other half of the teams should prepare to argue the social responsiveness perspective. Where possible, do some research to identify organizations that have behaved in ways prescribed by these perspectives and describe the outcomes of their behaviors. Your instructor will select two teams to present their findings to the class in a debate format.

VIDEO CASE

Union Camp

 Union Camp Corporation, headquartered in Wayne, New Jersey, is a leading manufacturer of paper, packaging, chemicals, and wood products. The company has many divisions both domestic and overseas. Some of its domestic products include paper, building products, chemicals, and flavors and fragrances. Overseas, the company operates corrugated container plants, chemical plants, and flavor and fragrance facilities.

Union Camp continually invests to upgrade and modernize its facilities so that it can produce high-quality products as efficiently as possible. At the same time, the company is concerned about environmental issues on a number of fronts. Consider the following actions of Union Camp:

- *Clean water.* During the 1980s and 1990s, Union Camp scientists developed and patented the industry's latest environmental advance—elemental chlorine-free ozone bleaching—which drastically reduces water use and pollution. The researchers say, with a gleam in their eyes, that this is just an intermediate step toward the pollution-free process of the future.

- *Clean air.* America's paper industry has spent more than $4 billion since 1970 to reduce atmospheric emissions. Union Camp has participated in this process and continues to spend heavily on research and manufacturing equipment aimed at clearing the air. Because Union Camp's Eastover mill has the tightest odor collection system in the world, the EPA studied the mill to establish industry-wide standards.

- *Renewable, growing forests.* Union Camp's Forest Resources Group includes field professionals and scientists who work on Union Camp's 1.6 million acres in the southeastern United States. Their work enables the company to use this renewable resource for mul-

tiple purposes. In cooperation with state and federal agencies and environmental groups, Union Camp protects endangered plant and animal species on its land. Union Camp's land-use ethic demonstrates that a forest can provide clean air and water and abundant wildlife while producing the wood and paper products we all need.

- *The power to produce.* Union Camp was one of the first companies in the United States to join the EPA's Green Lights program. With a net investment of $120,000, its plant in Wayne, New Jersey, reduced its energy consumption significantly, saving 1.4 million kilowatt-hours per year worth about $100,000.

- *Recycling* More than 55 percent of the fiber used in paper comes from waste materials. Nearly 60 percent of all corrugated containers are recycled. Creative customer relationships allow Union Camp to reuse other material wastes as well. For example, printers recover the solvent and ship it back to Union Camp, saving 15 million pounds of solvent per year.

Union Camp is committed to being socially responsible. It employs about 100 people—scientists, engineers, and technicians—whose main job is to monitor, research, and improve the company's environmental performance. Further, every employee at Union Camp receives in-depth training and frequent communication regarding environmental issues. The company's special ethic is evident in its attitude of caring for its communities.

For Discussion

1. Evaluate Union Camp's responsiveness to its stakeholders. Which of the four social responsibility strategies is this company following?

2. What are the advantages of Union Camp's position on social responsibility? Are there any disadvantages?

CASE

U.S. Amalgamated Steel, Inc.

U.S. Amalgamated Steel, Inc., located outside Athens, Georgia, is one of the largest manufacturers of rolled steel products in the United States. These products are used by a wide variety of customers including the automobile, industrial machinery, household appliance, and storage and file cabinet industries.

U.S. Amalgamated Steel has been cited numerous times by the U.S. government for pollution violations and has been fined over $500,000 over the past seven years. Moreover, due to the recent U.S. economic slowdown and increased foreign competition, U.S. Amalgamated has been experiencing less demand for its products. As a result, this year the corporation will realize only 67 percent of last year's profits, and the company's economic forecasters are predicting minimal growth for next year.

The stockholders of U.S. Amalgamated are extremely concerned about the future of the company. The CEO and the board of directors have done extensive research and have determined that the firm has two options: it can remain in Georgia, or it can relocate overseas in an effort to take advantage of lower labor costs and less stringent pollution regulations.

If U.S. Amalgamated stays in Georgia, it will have to lay off 47 workers and reduce the wages of the remaining employees by 3 percent with no guarantee of raises or bonuses for the next three years. The chief financial officer has estimated that these measures would save the company $1.75 million over a three-year period. Due to increased U.S. pollution regulation and strong financial penalties for noncompliance, however, U.S. Amalgamated would have to spend an additional $550,000 to be retrofitted with technologically advanced smokestack scrubbers and other "clean air" equipment. Therefore, the overall net savings to the firm would be $1.2 million.

If U.S. Amalgamated relocates to Singapore, however, it would reduce its personnel by 289 employees.

This alternative would save the company $2.55 million in labor costs over the next three years. Additionally, the firm would save the $550,000 allocated for pollution equipment, but would have to spend approximately $1 million to transfer operations to Singapore. Thus, the net savings to U.S. Amalgamated would be about $2.1 million.

U.S. Amalgamated executives are very concerned about the implications of their decision. The company is one of the primary employers in Athens, Georgia, and frequently provides small production contracts to local businesses. More importantly, U.S. Amalgamated is one of only four firms remaining in the U.S. rolled steel industry.

For Discussion:

1. From a purely economic perspective, which option should U.S. Amalgamated Steel choose? Why?

2. From a public policy perspective, which alternative would be most appropriate for the firm? Why?

3. If the management of U.S. Amalgamated subscribes to the social responsiveness perspective of social responsibility, which alternative would they be likely to choose? Why?

EXPERIENTIAL EXERCISE 3.1

Observing and Reporting Unethical Behavior

For each of the following statements place an "O" on the line if you have observed someone doing this behavior. Place an "R" on the line if you reported this behavior within the organization.

O = Observed   R = Reported

_____ 1. Coming to work late and getting paid for it.

_____ 2. Leaving work early and getting paid for it.

_____ 3. Taking long breaks/lunches and getting paid for them.

_____ 4. Calling in sick when one is not ill.

_____ 5. Using the company copier/fax for personal use.

_____ 6. Using company postage for personal correspondence.

_____ 7. Taking company supplies or merchandise for personal use at home.

_____ 8. Accepting gifts, meals, or trips from customers/suppliers in exchange for giving them business.

_____ 9. Filing for reimbursements or for other expenses that were not actually incurred.

_____ 10. Using the company car for personal business.

_____ 11. A student copying a friend's homework assignments.

_____ 12. A student cheating on an exam.

_____ 13. A student passing off a term paper as his or her own work.

Complete the following questions either individually or in small groups as directed by your instructor.

1. From items 1–10, select the three behaviors that you consider the most unethical. Who is harmed and who benefits by these unethical behaviors?

2. Who is harmed and who benefits from the unethical behaviors in items 11–13? Who is responsible for changing these behaviors? Develop a realistic plan to accomplish this goal.

3. If you observed unethical behavior but didn't report it, why didn't you? If you did report the behavior, why did you? What was the result?

4. What other behaviors that you consider unethical have you observed or reported?

EXPERIENTIAL EXERCISE 3.2

What Good Is an Honor System?

Working in a small group of three to five individuals, read the following scenario and then answer the questions that follow. Try to come to a consensus with your group members about your responses. Report your answers to your instructor or to the whole class.

I went to a small liberal arts college where they had a very strict honor system. For example, if you saw another student cheating, you were supposed to turn that student in to the authorities. In reality, some students did cheat, but only rarely did other students report the problem. There seemed to be several reasons for this: (1) it was a hassle to get involved because you had to go to meetings, fill out forms, and answer numerous questions; (2) nobody wanted to be considered a "tattletale"; and (3) even if you were sure the person had cheated, you had to have very specific evidence to support the charge.

Ten years later, I am out of college and law school and practice law with a large firm. We have an honor system here, too, but bringing a complaint against another professional is difficult: (1) it takes time and energy to get involved; (2) no one trusts or likes a person who turns in a peer; and (3) evidence to support a complaint is often poor or difficult to obtain.

For Discussion

1. What are the ethical dilemmas students face while going to college? What examples can you provide from your own or others' experience to support this?

2. Discuss the ethical dilemmas lawyers face in performing their jobs. Give some specific examples (consider recent news reports or stories from current television shows).

3. Discuss ethical dilemmas faced by other professional groups such as accountants, professors, engineers, and psychologists.

4. Discuss the pros and cons of an honor system.

SOURCE: Adapted from G. Manning and K. Curtis, "The Honor System," in *Ethics at Work: Fire in a Dark World* (Cincinnati: Southwestern Publishing, 1988).

NOTES

1. Based on R. Howe and S. Perlstein, "Ex-Chief of Martin Marietta Probed," *Washington Post,* June 18, 1991, A1; J. D. Morrocco, "Ill Wind Probe Shifts to Corporate Official Following Paisley's Guilty Plea," *Aviation Week and Space Technology,* June 1991, 27–35; and S. Perlstein, "Marietta Chief: Charges Damage Firm's Standing," *Washington Post,* June 25, 1992, C8.

2. A. B. Carroll, *Business & Society: Ethics and Stakeholder Management* (Cincinnati: Southwestern Publishing, 1989).

3. Ibid., 60.

4. T. R. Mitchell and W. G. Scott, "America's Problems and Needed Reforms: Confronting the Ethic of Personal Advantage," *Academy of Management Executive* 4 (1990): 23–33.

5. H. R. Bowen, *Social Responsibilities of the Businessman* (New York: Harper & Row, 1953), 6.

6. Most of this discussion comes from S. L. Wartick and P. L. Cochran, "The Evolution of the Corporate Social Performance Model," *Academy of Management Review* 10 (1985): 758–69.

7. Carroll, *Business & Society,* 60.

8. C. Grant, "Friedman Fallacies," *Journal of Business Ethics* 10 (1991): 907–14.

9. "A CEO Forum: What Corporate Social Responsibility Means to Me," *Business and Society Review* (1989).

10. L. E. Preston and J. E. Post, "Private Management and Public Policy," *California Management Review* 23 (1991): 57.

11. D. R. Dalton and R. A. Cosier, "The Four Faces of Social Responsibility," *Business Horizons,* May/June 1982, 19–27.

12. Carroll, *Business & Society,* 60.

13. S. W. Gellerman, "Why 'Good' Managers Make Bad Ethical Choices," *Harvard Business Review* (July/August 1986): 85–90.

14. L. Alexander and W. F. Matthews, "The Ten Commandments of Corporate Social Responsibility," *Business and Society Review* 50 (1984): 62–66.

15. S. Vyakarnam, "Social Responsibility: What Leading Companies Do," *Long Range Planning* 25 (1992): 59–67.

16. Alexander and Matthews, "The Ten Commandments of Corporate Social Responsibility," 62–66.

17. "A CEO Forum: What Corporate Social Responsibility Means to Me," *Business and Society Review* 22 (1992): 88–89; "Corporations Going Green," *Business Ethics,* March/April 1992, 100; D. Bihler, "The Final Frontier," *Business Ethics,* March/April 1992, 31; "On Company Time: The New Volunteerism," *Business Ethics,* March/April 1992, 33.

18. J. J. Laabs, "Ben & Jerry's Caring Capitalism," *Personnel Journal* (November 1992): 50–57.

19. L. Reynolds, "A New Social Agenda for the New Age," *Management Review* (January 1993): 39–41.

20. Ibid.

21. R. N. Sanyal and J. S. Neves, "The Valdez Principles: Implications for Corporate Social Responsibility," *Journal of Business Ethics* 10 (1991): 883–90.

22. Howe and Perlstein, "Ex-Chief of Martin Marietta Probed"; Morrocco, "Ill Wind Probe Shifts to Corporate Official Following Paisley's Guilty Plea"; and Perlstein, "Marietta Chief: Charges Damage Firm's Standing."

23. K. S. Betts, "The Coming of Green Computers," *The Environmental Magazine,* April 1994, 28–35.

24. T. R. Mitchell and W. G. Scott, "America's Problems and Needed Reforms: Confronting the Ethic of Personal Advantage," *Academy of Management Executive* 4 (1990): 23–33.

25. J. Rothfeder and E. I. Schwartz, "Computer Anarchism Calls Tough Response," *Business Week,* August 6, 1992, 72.

26. S. J. Harrington, "What Corporate America Is Teaching about Ethics," *Academy of Management Executive* 5 (1991): 21–29.

27. M. Rokeach, *The Nature of Human Values* (New York: Free Press, 1973).

28. G. F. Cavanaugh, *American Business Values in Transition* (Englewood Cliffs, N.J.: Prentice-Hall, 1980).

29. K. Andrews, "Ethics in Practice," *Harvard Business Review* (September/October 1989): 99–104.

30. D. Marlow, "Ethics, Values Still Have Spot in Corporate America," *Orlando Sentinel,* September 5, 1993, F-1.

31. L. T. Hosmer, *The Ethics of Management* (Homewood, Ill.: Irwin, 1987).

32. R. Perloff, "Self-interest and Personal Responsibility Redux," *American Psychologist* 42 (1987): 3–11.

33. M. Velasquez, D. Moberg, and G. Cavanagh, "Organizational Statesmanship and Dirty Politics: Ethical Guidelines for the Organizational Politician," *Organizational Dynamics* (Autumn 1993): 65–80.

34. B. Hager, "What's Behind Business' Sudden Fervor for Ethics," *Business Week,* September 23, 1991, 65.

35. Adapted from "Can I Charge for Having Ethics?" *Business Week,* July 13, 1992, 38.

36. D. Fritzsche and H. Becker, "Linking Management Behavior to Ethical Philosophy—An Empirical Investigation," *Academy of Management Journal* 27 (1984): 166–75.

37. Harrington, "What Corporate America Is Teaching about Ethics."

38. Ibid.

39. M. Davis, "Working with Your Organization's Code of Ethics," *Management Solutions,* June 1988, 9–11.

40. S. Modic, "Corporate Ethics: From Commandments to Commitment," *Industry Week,* December 1987, 33–36.

41. S. E. Sonnesyn, "A Question of Ethics," *Training & Development Journal* 45 (1991): 36–37.

42. "Crime Stoppers: Tougher Penalties Put Ethics on the Front Burner at Nynex," *Business Ethics,* March/April 1992, 18; and Hager, "What's Behind Business' Sudden Fervor for Ethics."

43. J. A. Byrne, "Businesses Are Signing Up for Ethics 101," *Business Week,* February 15, 1988, 56–57.

44. J. Huey, "Finding New Heroes for a New Era," *Fortune,* January 25, 1993, 62–69.

45. Center for Business Ethics at Bentley College, "Are Corporations Institutionalizing Ethics?" *Journal of Business Ethics* 5 (1986): 86–91.

46. Hager, "What's Behind Business' Sudden Fervor for Ethics."

47. "Gray Matters: The Ethics Game," Martin Marietta Corporation, 1992.

48. A. L. Otten, "Ethics on the Job: Companies Alert Employees to Potential Dilemmas," *Wall Street Journal,* July 14, 1986, 17.

49. L. Driscoll, "A Better Way to Handle Whistle-Blowers: Let Them Speak," *Business Week,* July 27, 1992, 36.

50. Ibid.

51. Ibid.

52. R. P. Nielsen, "Changing Unethical Organizational Behavior," *Academy of Management Executive* 3 (1989): 123–30.

53. Huey, "Finding New Heroes for a New Era."

54. This incident was developed from Howe and Perlstein, "Ex-Chief of Martin Marietta Probed"; Morrocco, "Ill Wind Probe Shifts to Corporate Official Following Paisley's Guilty Plea," and Perlstein, "Marietta Chief: Charges Damage Firm's Standing."

IBAX: A COMPANY IN NEED OF LEADERSHIP

As you will recall from the Managerial Incident/Resolution in Chapter 1, IBAX is a vendor of health care information systems software. The company began in 1983 as the Systems Division of Baxter Health Care Corporation, the world's largest supplier of hospital products. Over the first six years of its existence, Baxter's Systems Division grew through the acquisition of a number of small information systems companies. However, the division suffered from quality, customer satisfaction, and productivity problems that resulted in poor financial performance.

In 1990, Baxter reached an agreement with IBM to spin off the Systems Division and create a new company—IBAX. For IBM, the venture provided entry into the software side of the computer business. For Baxter, the partnership with IBM provided much needed credibility in a computer-related business. There was great fanfare associated with the partnering of IBM and Baxter. Virtually everyone agreed that two highly successful companies like these would surely be able to make a mark in the health care information systems industry. Employees, customers, and even the trade press were tremendously enthusiastic about the future of the company.

Despite the favorable projections, IBAX got off to a very rocky start. Although the company was projected to break-even in the first year of the partnership, it lost $11 million. The losses were a result of the same quality, customer satisfaction, and productivity problems that had plagued Baxter's Systems Division and had not been corrected since the formation of the partnership. As it became apparent that no significant improvements had been made in product quality or customer service, the trade press began to criticize the company harshly.

By late 1990, the principals in the partnership knew that a turnaround was imperative. The challenge was to find someone who could make that happen. In January of 1991, IBM and Baxter hired Jeff Goodman as the CEO of IBAX. Goodman, with a University of Virginia MBA, a General Electric background, and the successful turnaround of two other companies under his belt, had developed a reputation for his ability to turn poorly performing companies into highly efficient and effective organizations. The partners gave Goodman his marching orders—improve product quality, enhance customer satisfaction, and fix the financial profile of the company.

THE ASSESSMENT

As Goodman took the helm at IBAX, he assessed the management challenges he faced. Some of those challenges related to marketing issues, others to organizational and employee issues, and still others to financial issues. The paragraphs that follow describe what Goodman found when he evaluated IBAX at the beginning of 1991.

MARKETING ISSUES

In order to understand the marketing issues that were most relevant to turning IBAX around, you must understand the company's product line, its market position, and its efforts of the sales force.

The Products

IBAX's software products are designed to provide high-quality, cost-effective methods of managing financial information, patient accounting information, and clinical information for its primary target market; hospitals located in the United States. The company maintains three core product lines:

- Series 3000. This software product serves hospitals of 100 beds or less. This product is a cost-effective information systems software package for small hospitals.
- Series 4000. This product is targeted at hospitals having 100-600 beds. The Series 4000 is appropriate for higher-capacity institutions that have unique requirements because of the breadth of services they offer.
- Series 5000. This product is targeted at major medical centers and teaching institutions. The Series 5000 software can be customized to meet the needs of larger health care institutions.

The Series 3000, 4000, and 5000 products provide three sources of revenue—software sales, installation and customization services, and on-going software maintenance and support.

Unfortunately, there were significant problems with each of the core product lines. The customer base for the Series 3000 was eroding as a result of the changing nature of the hospital industry. Increasingly, small hospitals were unable to compete effectively because of size limitations. These institutions were being merged with or acquired by larger hospitals. The installed base for this product had declined from a high of 285 to 220 hospitals by early 1991.

The Series 4000 was the subject of a myriad of contract disputes between client hospitals and IBAX. The IBAX sales force had made commitments to the customers regarding such things as the disk capacity used by the system, response time, and the availability of product upgrades and add-ons. Unfortunately, such commitments had not been discussed with the developers of the products and were impossible to meet. The Series 4000 customers were angry about the unfulfilled promises of the sales force.

The company maintained a "hot list" of 15 very large hospitals using the Series 5000 that were problem accounts. Because the IBM and Baxter names were so vulnerable in these hospitals, Goodman was instructed to do whatever it took to fix the problems quickly. In fact, he was required to report on the status of those accounts monthly to the IBAX partnership committee.

Beyond the core product lines, IBAX develops and markets department-based information systems to support functions such as pharmacy management, billing operations, and operating room scheduling. In addition, it markets products that network physician offices to hospitals. The sales in these areas were not as significant as in the three primary product lines. Fortunately, neither were the problems.

Market Position

Interestingly, an assessment of IBAX's market position alone did not reflect the reality of the company's problems. As of 1991, the company had a 12 percent market share of the installed base in the United States. In other words, 600 of the 5,000 domestic hospitals used IBAX products. IBAX was, in fact, the market leader in the product segments in which it competed.

More relevant, however, was the fact the IBAX's market position was declining. The eroding base for the Series 3000, coupled with the company's problems with product quality and customer service, was resulting in a deteriorating customer base. Even those who still used IBAX products were hesitant to purchase add-on products because of their dissatisfaction with the company as a whole.

Sales Force

The morale of the sales force at IBAX was very poor. They were, as one IBAX employee said, "being hammered by the customers, the IBM and Baxter partners, and the trade press." The customers were perpetually unhappy because the products did not meet their expectations and did not perform as promised. Baxter blamed IBAX for giving the company a bad reputation in the hospitals it served; IBM thought IBAX's sales efforts were "amateurish" and were impeding IBM's efforts to secure hardware sales in hospitals. The trade press was continually criticizing the company and its products. Needless to say, the IBAX sales force was discouraged and was described as "wandering around leaderless, making very little progress in the field."

ORGANIZATIONAL AND EMPLOYEE ISSUES

From an organizational and employee perspective, IBAX was in a very poor position. As noted earlier, the company had developed through the acquisition of a number of small information systems software companies. As a result, it was geographically dispersed. Corporate headquarters was in Long Island, New York. There was a big operating facility in Orlando, Florida, a service center in Ohio, another business unit in Rhode Island, one in Illinois, and a major project staff in California. Employees in these various locations felt little need to cooperate with employees elsewhere in the organization. Consequently, it was difficult to develop and implement consistent product, marketing and financial strategies.

Even more detrimental than IBAX's geographic fragmentation was the fact that there was no homogeneous culture within the company. Employee commitment to the company was very weak and there were no evolved corporate values.

Morale was extremely low and the employees were described as "generally miserable." The management style at IBAX was authoritative and directive. Employees felt disfranchised as they were not involved in decision making and had little influence over what happened within the organization. The structure of the company was highly bureaucratic, and company policies and procedures were rigid and inflexible.

Intra-organizational communication at IBAX was so poor that the employees didn't even know how badly the company was performing. Some described their relationship with customers as "adversarial," and many employees didn't seem to understand why such a relationship was detrimental. The company had few performance standards and made little effort to hold employees accountable for their efforts.

Operationally, the company was very inefficient. The company had 750 employees and was well on its way to growing to 800. In an industry where labor costs represent a high proportion of total costs (60 percent), IBAX was heavily overstaffed. The sales of the company were simply not high enough to justify an employee base of that size.

Finally, there was a general void in the senior-level management team. Within two months after Goodman's arrival, the only senior staff at IBAX were

Goodman, an attorney and a human resource executive. Although the deficiency presented an immediate problem in that many functions were devoid of leadership, Goodman would have an opportunity to build an entirely new management team.

FINANCIAL ISSUES

The IBAX partnership was formed with an initial capital base of $80 million. It was a 50/50 partnership in that both IBM and Baxter contributed $40 million in a combination of assets and cash to the partnership. There was no debt in the initial capital structure and there was approximately $20 million in cash. Further, no losses were projected, and IBAX was forecasted to break even during the first year.

As we know, IBAX did not break even in the first year of the partnership. In fact, the company had operating losses in excess of $11 million in 1989 and $14 million in 1990. A total of $40 million was borrowed from the parent companies to support cash flow losses of approximately $30 million per year for the first two years of the partnership. It was clear that the company could not continue as a viable entity unless its financial position greatly improved.

AFTER THE ASSESSMENT

Goodman's assessment of IBAX's current position was discouraging. The partners had been very clear in their expectations—he was to improve product quality, resolve the customer satisfaction problems, and fix the financial position of the company. Goodman suspected, however, that the partners had greatly underestimated the problems at IBAX. IBAX was ill-prepared to compete effectively in the highly competitive health care information systems industry.

As Goodman sat at his desk and contemplated the situation, he realized that he'd need a plan. That plan would have to include: (1) building a new team at the executive level, (2) educating the employees as to the severity of the company's problems, (3) improving productivity and efficiency at the operating level, (4) establishing and communicating standards for quality and performance, and (5) developing an organizational culture that provided employee empowerment, a focus on quality and a commitment to do whatever necessary to meet the needs of the customer.

As you work your way through this book, you will learn about the modern management tools and techniques that were used to turn IBAX around. By watching the video that accompanies this case, you will have the opportunity to meet the senior-level executives and employees who were responsible for the turnaround. They will explain how they applied contemporary management theories and practices to resolve the problems faced by IBAX. The IBAX story provides a unique opportunity to observe a company that avoided failure and achieved success through innovative and effective management.

For Discussion:
1. Why do you think IBAX performed so poorly before Goodman's arrival?
2. Why do you think Goodman felt that he had a realistic chance of turning the company around?
3. If you were Goodman, what is the first thing you would do to begin the turnaround?

PLANNING CHALLENGES IN THE 21ST CENTURY

PART II

Planning in the Contemporary Organization

CHAPTER 4

▼ CHAPTER OVERVIEW

Planning is one of the most important responsibilities of managers today. Plans provide a foundation for coordinating and directing the activities of the organization so that goals can be achieved. Through planning, managers prepare their organizations to achieve success in both the long term and the short term. Given the highly competitive nature of the business environment today, effective planning has never been more important.

In this chapter, we focus on planning in the contemporary organization. The planning function is explored, and special attention is given to understanding the planning process at both the strategic and the operational levels. We will also examine methods for encouraging, supporting, and rewarding effective planning.

▼ LEARNING OBJECTIVES

When you have finished studying this chapter, you should be able to:

- Describe the managerial function of planning and explain why managers should plan.
- Discuss three approaches for initiating the planning process.
- Define strategic planning and describe the three levels of strategic planning.
- Identify the four stages of the strategic planning process.
- Discuss how quality can be achieved through strategic planning.
- Define operational planning and distinguish between standing and single-use plans.
- Describe a management by objective program and discuss the advantages and disadvantages of this system of planning.
- Define contingency planning and identify the circumstances under which contingency planning would be appropriate.
- Describe the common barriers to effective planning and explain ways to reduce these barriers.
- Discuss how tomorrow's managers can achieve success through planning.

MANAGERIAL INCIDENT

NationsBank®

NATIONSBANK: PLANNING FOR GROWTH THROUGH ACQUISITION

Over the last decade, the market for financial services has changed dramatically. Regulatory changes within the banking industry have created a new competitive environment, and extensive merger activity between banking institutions has reduced the number of competitors in this industry. As these changes have occurred, many banking institutions have developed new plans for the future.

NationsBank (formerly NCNB) is one financial institution that has responded to the changes in the banking industry by developing new plans. The company realized that the consolidation of the banking industry provided opportunities to grow through the acquisition of smaller competitors. One of its first targets for acquisition was Citizen's & Southern (C&S), an Atlanta-based banking institution. The merger would nearly double NationsBank's branch units and employees. Managing this merger and ensuring a successful transition for the employees and customers of both firms required a detailed and well-developed plan. This was the challenge facing the managers of NationsBank.[1] ▼

INTRODUCTION

NationsBank faced the challenge of merging its operations with those of C&S. The success of the merger would depend upon the development of a plan providing directions for consolidating the two banking institutions. Without such a plan, the merger would be problematic at the least, and perhaps even a failure.

Planning provides a foundation for all organizational activities. Through planning, managers coordinate organizational activities so that the goals of the organization can be achieved. Organizational success is dependent upon the ability of managers to develop a plan that brings together, in a logical way, the diverse set of tasks that occur within the organization. In its simplest form, planning involves understanding where you are, knowing where you want to go, and devising the means to get there.

In this chapter, we explore the managerial function of planning. We begin by addressing a number of important questions about the nature of planning. With that information as a foundation, we discuss the two primary types of planning that occur within organizations—strategic and operational planning. Next, the concept of contingency planning is explored. The chapter concludes with a discussion of the barriers to planning, methods for overcoming those barriers, and the planning implications for tomorrow's managers.

MANAGERIAL PLANNING

Planning is an essential, but potentially complex, managerial function. To gain a better understanding of the planning function, let's start by answering a few key questions—what is planning, why should managers plan, and where should the planning process begin?

WHAT IS PLANNING?

Planning is the process of outlining the activities that are necessary to achieve the goals of the organization. Through planning, managers determine how

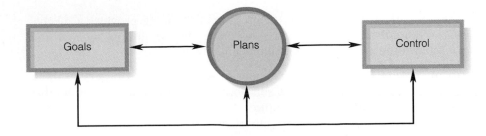

▼ FIGURE 4.1
Planning as a Linking Mechanism

organizational resources are to be allocated and how the activities of the organization will be assigned to individuals and work groups. The output of the planning process is the plan. A **plan** is a blueprint for action; it prescribes the activities necessary for the organization to realize its goals.[2]

The purpose of planning is simple—to ensure that the organization is both effective and efficient in its activities. In the broad sense, an organization must develop a plan that ensures that the appropriate products and services are offered to its customers. More specifically, planning gives guidance and direction to the members of the organization as to their role in delivering those products and services.[3]

Critical to understanding the planning process is an understanding of the relationships among goals, plans, and controls (see Figure 4.1). In general, **goals** represent the desired position of the organization. From the highest-level goal of maximizing shareholder wealth down to the goals of first-line operating managers, these targets for achievement are important determinants of the plans that an organization will develop. Plans establish the means for achieving the organization's goals. Through planning, managers outline the activities necessary to ensure that the goals of the organization are achieved. **Controls** monitor the extent to which goals have been achieved and ensure that the organization is moving in the direction suggested by its plans. Goals, plans, and controls are inextricably intertwined and must be well integrated if the planning process is to be successful.[4]

Plans
Blueprints for action that prescribes the activities necessary for the organization to realize its goals.

Goals
The results that an organization seeks to achieve.

Controls
The mechanisms used to monitor the organization's performance relative to its goals and plans.

WHY SHOULD MANAGERS PLAN?

Planning is a critical managerial function for any organization that strives for success. In fact, it has often been said that "failing to plan is planning to fail." Yet most experienced managers recognize that there are both benefits and costs to planning.

Benefits of Planning
Theoretically, planning leads to superior performance for the organization. From a very general perspective, the planning process offers four primary benefits: (1) better coordination, (2) a focus on forward thinking, (3) a participatory work environment, and (4) more effective control systems.

Better Coordination Planning provides a much needed foundation for the coordination of a broad range of organizational activities. Most organizations are comprised of multiple work groups, each of which is responsible for contributing to the accomplishment of the goals of the organization. A plan helps both to define the responsibilities of these work groups and to coordinate their activities. Without such a mechanism for coordination, it would be difficult to direct the efforts of organizational members and groups toward common organizational goals.

Consider, for example, how many departments at NationsBank and C&S would be involved in the merger of these two organizations—operations, information systems, personnel, and many others. Planning provides a mechanism for coordinating the activities of these diverse groups so that the organizations can merge their operations effectively.

Focus on Forward Thinking   The planning function forces managers to think ahead and consider resource needs and potential opportunities or threats that the organization may face in the future. While the identification of organizational problems and solutions is an important by-product of the planning process, its overriding focus should be on preparing the organization to perform more effectively and efficiently in the future than in the past.

Florida Power & Light uses planning to anticipate and respond to the changing needs of its customers. Through forward thinking and a focus on ensuring success in the long term, this company has earned a reputation for being a premier utility company that is highly responsive to change.

Participatory Work Environment   The successful development and implementation of organizational plans require the participation of a wide range of organizational members. As a consequence, a more participatory work environment typically evolves. Participatory work environments provide two important benefits to the organization.

First, the organization benefits from having access to a broad base of expertise and knowledge in developing its plans. This is particularly true in organizations with diverse groups of employees. Planning that is participatory usually leads to a more fully developed plan that reflects the multiple, diverse, and sometimes contradictory issues faced by the organization.

Second, organizational members are more likely to "buy in" to a plan that they have helped to develop. Employees who have participated in the planning process will typically be more committed to and supportive of their organization and its goals than those who have not been involved.[5] As you will recall from our discussion of IBAX in Chapter 1, involving the employees in the planning process of that organization was key to setting the company on the right track.

More Effective Control Systems   As we will discuss later, an organization's plan provides a foundation for control. The implementation of the activities prescribed by the plan can be evaluated, and progress toward the achievement of performance objectives can be monitored. A plan provides a mechanism for ensuring that the organization is moving in the right direction and making progress toward achieving its goals.[6]

Costs of Planning

Despite these benefits, planning also entails costs. These costs can be significant and may discourage managers from planning.

Management Time   Done properly, the planning process requires a substantial amount of managerial time and energy. Managers must work with their employees to evaluate existing resources, identify opportunities to improve the operations of the work group, and establish organizational goals. Some work groups may find that planning requires an assessment of external information related to the products, prices, and strategies of competing firms. The collection, analysis, and interpretation of such information can be very costly.

As an illustration, consider the time, energy, and travel expenses that went into the Marriott Corporation's plan to enter the economy segment of the hotel industry. A team of researchers spent six months traveling the country, checking into economy hotels, and gathering information on pricing structures, brands of shampoo and soap, types of decor and soundproofing, and quality of personnel. Although the cost of acquiring this information was significant,

FORTE INDUSTRIES: CATCHING UP WITH YOURSELF

The notable success of Forte Industries, a distributor of material-handling equipment based in Cincinnati, presented the company with a severe challenge. It had expanded so rapidly from its beginnings in 1980 that it was outgrowing its own resources. Its technical expertise was being stretched by new opportunities in large, automated conveyor systems; some formerly effective managers were not up to handling the problems of dynamic growth; and several key outside suppliers were unable to meet the demands of the larger projects Forte was ready to take on.

Eugene A. Forte, the president and owner, could foresee stagnating sales, depressed cash flow and profitability, increasing employee turnover, and declining supplier quality and deliveries. Future growth was threatened by "inexperienced personnel mishandling prime opportunities."

As Forte admits, his first attempt at a solution was "painfully unsuccessful." To solve the problem of personnel underperformance, he tried motivational techniques like unscheduled pay increases and performance bonuses and a highly visible recognition program. He could see some individual improvement, but overall results were inadequate. To solve the problem of supplier quality, he sought out new suppliers. Again, success was marginal.

Rethinking the situation, Forte soon embarked on what would prove to be the solution to his problem. The key was developing a systematic expansion plan. He took a comprehensive six-month strategic planning course at the Greater Cincinnati Chamber of Commerce "to formalize the idea I had been cultivating." His plan built on the company's strengths. It must stick to its financial controls, including detailed job costing "from the time we get the order to the time we get paid." To those strengths would be added as much internal automation through computerization as possible to increase productivity. The company was restructured into four operating divisions. Marketing techniques and quality management were refined. Additional management talent was hired.

Results so far are gratifying. Profitability overall and per job has increased, and monthly and quarterly fluctuations have been greatly reduced. Quality and consistency have improved. Market penetration, by pursuing existing "corridors of business" and new accounts, is at an all-time high. Furthermore, this expansion has been financed internally—without borrowing.

---

it enabled Marriott to develop an effective plan for entering the market with its chain of economy hotels—Fairfield Inns.[7]

Delay in Decision Making   Another potential cost of planning is that it may delay decision making. Some managers argue that planning directs the focus toward *evaluating* rather than *doing*. This can delay the organization's response to changes in the industry, marketplace, or internal operations. The delay can be particularly detrimental when an organization's success is dependent upon its ability to respond to change quickly.[8]

When you weigh the potential benefits of planning against the potential costs, it is clear that planning pays. There are many examples of firms that have been on the brink of failure that have recovered through the development and implementation of an effective plan. Consider the experience of the company profiled in Entrepreneurial Approach.[9] The performance of Forte Industries was declining rapidly when Eugene Forte, president of the company, took a six-month course on strategic planning and developed a plan that restored the profitability of his firm.

Managers plan because planning leads to better performance. In today's highly competitive business environment, planning can help managers cope with the challenges they face. For example, many organizations have found that achieving quality through effective planning is key to ensuring their competitiveness.[10] As we saw in Chapter 1, quality doesn't just happen—it requires planning from the top of the organization down to the front line. With the spotlight on quality in nearly every industry across the globe, effective planning has become critical for success.

WHERE DOES PLANNING START?

Assuming that organizations should plan, the question then becomes "who should initiate the planning process?" Planning is carried out at various levels of the organization and for various departments, work groups, and individuals at each level. Although a broad range of organizational members should be involved in the planning process, the process must be initiated and coordinated at some specific point in the organizational hierarchy. At what organizational level should planning begin?

Traditionally, there have been two basic approaches to planning depending on where in the organizational hierarchy the planning function is initiated—the top-down approach and the bottom-up approach. Table 4.1 illustrates some of the differences between these two approaches. Today, however, many organizations take a more integrated approach that combines aspects of both top-down and bottom-up planning.

With a top-down planning approach, planning efforts begin with the board of directors and the top executives of the organization. They determine the general direction of the organization and establish a master plan to achieve its overall goals. The master plan establishes the parameters within which the work groups of the organization develop their plans. Managers develop plans for their work groups based on what their units must accomplish to support the master plan.

In contrast, with a bottom-up planning approach, planning is initiated at the lowest levels of the organizational hierarchy—with those individuals who are most directly involved in the delivery of the organization's products and services and who are closest to the customers or suppliers of the organization. The managers and employees at the operational level of the organization begin the planning process by estimating sales potential, describing needed product and service modifications or new product and service developments, and identifying potential problems or opportunities in the supply of input resources. As these plans move up through the organization, they are developed further, refined, and evaluated for accurateness and feasibility. Finally, the board of directors and top-level executives bring together all the plans of the organization's work groups to develop a cohesive and well-integrated master plan that establishes the overall direction of the organization.[11]

Both the top-down and bottom-up approaches to planning have advantages and disadvantages. The primary advantage of top-down planning is that the top managers, who presumably are most knowledgeable about the organization as a whole, drive the development of the plan. Although one might argue that the people at the lowest level of the organization know the most about how the organization actually operates, top-level management has a

▼ **TABLE 4.1**   Top-Down versus Bottom-Up Planning

	TOP-DOWN	BOTTOM-UP
Level at which initiated	Board of directors, top executive level	Individuals closest to product, service, or customer
Role of organizational units	As the plan moves down the hierarchy, units determine actions that will support the plan	Units develop their own goals and plans. As these plans move up the hierarchy, they are evaluated and adjusted for accuracy and feasibility
Specificity of plan	Begins as broad, becomes more specific as it moves down the hierarchy	Begins as very fragmented and specific, becomes cohesive and integrated
Advantages	Plans are driven by top management who are most knowledgeable about all factors affecting the organization	Those closest to customers, suppliers, and operating systems provide focus of plans
Disadvantages	Top managers are often far removed from the "front line"	Lower level managers may lack understanding of all factors affecting the organization
Appropriateness	When the organization's success is dependent on quick response to external pressure and threats	When an organization's success is dependent on its ability to respond quickly to changes in operational systems

more comprehensive understanding of the wide variety of internal and external factors that affect the overall success of the organization.

Yet having those closest to the operating system, customers, and suppliers provide the focus for the planning process also offers advantages. These individuals may have a better understanding of the competitive and operational challenges faced by the organization than would the board of directors and top executives who are far removed from the front line of the organization.

Which approach is better? The answer to that question depends on the specific circumstances facing the organization. Where success is largely a function of the organization's ability to respond quickly and effectively to changes in its operating system, customer focus, or supplier relationships, bottom-up planning may be more appropriate. When success is dependent upon the ability to make high-level organizational changes in response to more general external threats and pressures (e.g., industry consolidation via mergers and acquisitions, changes in the regulatory environment, or demographic trends), a top-down planning approach may be more appropriate. For example, a pharmaceutical company such as Eli-Lilly, which must respond to Food and Drug Administration (FDA) directives and other regulatory issues, might benefit from a top-down approach. In contrast, a computer firm like Hewlett Packard may find that a bottom-up planning approach supports its efforts to be sensitive to the technological needs of its customers in designing new products.

Further, and perhaps most importantly, these planning modes are not mutually exclusive. Many organizations use a bottom-up approach to formulate plans in one area (i.e., marketing) but develop plans in other areas (i.e., finance) from a top-down perspective. In fact, by being flexible, managers can capitalize on the benefits of both approaches.

Now that we have sketched out the managerial function of planning in general, let's examine the two primary types of planning that occur in most organizations—strategic and operational planning.

STRATEGIC VERSUS OPERATIONAL PLANNING

In general, most organizations engage in both strategic and operational planning. Although strategic and operational planning differ in a number of ways, they are also interrelated. Let's explore both of these important planning processes.

STRATEGIC PLANNING

Strategic planning
The process by which an organization makes decisions and takes actions to enhance its long-run performance.

Strategic plans
Plans that identify the markets in which an organization competes, as well as the ways in which it competes in those markets.

Competitive advantage
Any aspect of an organization that distinguishes it from its competitors in a positive way.

Planning that is strategic in nature focuses on enhancing the competitive position and overall performance of the organization in the long term.[12] In other words, **strategic planning** is the process by which an organization makes decisions and takes actions that affect its long-run performance. A strategic plan is the output of the strategic planning process. **Strategic plans** define both the markets in which the organization competes and the way in which it competes in those markets.[13]

The purpose of strategic planning is to move the organization from where it is to where it wants to be and, in the process, to develop and maintain a sustainable competitive advantage within the industries in which it competes.[14] A **competitive advantage** is any aspect of an organization's operations that distinguishes it from its competitors in a positive way.[15] For example, most would point to IBM's reputation for quality and service as being a key competitive advantage (despite the company's recent performance problems), while Gateway Computer's competitive advantage rests on its ability to provide IBM-compatible computers differentiated on the basis of price. Apple Computer has distinguished itself through its innovative and user-friendly system designs, while a reputation for technologically advanced scientific computing equipment has given Hewlett Packard its competitive edge. Through their strategies, each of these firms has developed a distinct competitive advantage and leadership position in the computer industry.[16]

You don't have to look far to find an organization that attributes its success to its strategy.[17] Similarly, there are numerous examples of companies that would attribute their failure or the failure of a given product, service, or project to the absence of an effective strategic plan.[18] Managing for Excellence illustrates how K Mart's strategy enabled it to achieve a leadership position in the discount retail industry while its one-time strong competitor, W. T. Grant, failed because it lacked an effective strategic plan.[19]

Levels of Strategic Planning

Strategic planning occurs at three primary levels within the organization: the corporate, business, and functional levels.[20] Each level can be distinguished by the focus of the strategic planning process, the participants in the process, the specificity of the strategy, and the time horizon of the plan. Table 4.2 summarizes the key differences in these three levels of strategic planning, and the discussion that follows elaborates on each.

K Mart versus W. T. Grant: Strategic Focus versus Strategic Chaos

K Mart, which began in the early 1960s, was an extension of S. S. Kresge Company's "five and ten" variety stores. Sebastian Kresge founded the original company in 1899 and developed it into a successful concept that continued into the 1950s.

As large supermarkets and shopping centers began to draw customers away from the variety stores, Kresge Company developed K Mart, which was essentially a large-scale version of the original Kresge. The company's strategic plan targeted low- and middle-income families and emphasized low prices. The plan was so successful that both store units and total sales grew by leaps and bounds. By 1976, K Mart had become the second largest general merchandise retailer in the United States, and it continues to be successful today.

W. T. Grant's story is dramatically different. Once a market leader in the discount retail industry, this firm's lack of strategic focus and operational control eventually led to its demise. While many analysts placed most of the blame for Grant's failure on an expansion plan that was overly aggressive and ill-conceived, company insiders tell a different story. Some believe that Grant simply failed to define a strategy for dealing with changing industry conditions. Torn between competing for the K Mart customer or the Wards/Penney's customer, Grant failed to target either consumer group effectively. This lack of strategic focus, coupled with extremely poor operational controls, left Grant in a weakened position that eventually led to bankruptcy. The end result—over $400 million in bad debts and 80,000 people out of work.

Corporate Strategic Planning   Strategic planning that occurs at the corporate level of the organization focuses on developing corporate strategy. **Corporate strategy** addresses the question, "what business should we be in?" and is most relevant for organizations that operate in multiple lines of business. Corporate strategic planning involves assessing the organization's portfolio of businesses to determine if an appropriate mix exists.[21] The objective is to develop a mix of business units that meet the long-term growth and profitability goals of the organization.

For example, consider General Cinema Corporation. This company has four business units: Harcourt Brace & Company (publishing), Neiman Marcus Group (specialty retail), Insurance Group (insurance), and General Cinema

Corporate strategy
Decisions and actions that define the portfolio of business units that an organization maintains.

▼ **TABLE 4.2**   Levels of Strategic Planning

	FOCUS	SPECIFICITY	PARTICIPANTS	TIME HORIZON
Corporate Strategy	To develop a mix of business units that meets the company's long-term growth and profitability goals	• Broad • General	• Board of directors • Top-level executives	5–10 years
Business Strategy	To develop and maintain a distinctive competitive advantage that will ensure long-term profitability	• More specific than the corporate strategy	• Top-level executives • Managers within the business unit	1–5 years
Functional Strategy	To develop action plans that ensure that corporate and business strategies are implemented	• Very specific	• Middle-level managers • Lower-level managers	1–2 years

(movie theaters). Each of these units contributes in some way to the overall goals of the corporation. At the corporate level, managers must determine if this particular mix of businesses positions the organization well for long-term success.

Diversification is often at the core of corporate strategy.[22] Diversification occurs when an organization chooses to add a new business unit to its portfolio of businesses. A company may pursue a strategy of diversification if it wishes to reduce its dependence on its existing business units or to capitalize on its core competencies by expanding into another business. Anheuser-Busch, for example, embarked on a fairly aggressive strategy of diversification into food products (Eagle Snacks) and theme parks (Busch Gardens and Sea World) in an effort to reduce the company's dependence on the highly threatened and slow-growing alcoholic beverage industry. In contrast, Xerox made a corporate decision to diversify into the office products industry in an effort to capitalize on its name recognition in the copier business. For both firms, diversifying was a desirable option, although for very different reasons.

Because corporate strategy defines the very nature of the organization, it is formulated by the organization's board of directors and top-level executives. In developing their strategic plans, however, these individuals rely, to a great extent, on information provided by middle- and lower-level managers.

Corporate strategy is relatively broad and general in nature and may extend as far as 5 to 10 years into the future. For example, a firm like Apple, which operates a single business unit, may need to diversity its portfolio as the computer industry begins to mature. By developing or acquiring a business unit in a higher-growth industry, Apple could ensure strong corporate growth despite the maturing computer market. Although this aspect of Apple's strategic plan might be established in 1994, it would not be intended for implementation until the growth rate in the computer industry begins to slow—most likely some time after the year 2000.

Business Strategic Planning   The product of the strategic planning process at the business level is business strategy. **Business strategy** defines how each business unit in the organization's corporate portfolio will operate in its market arena. Strategy formulated at this level addresses the question, "how do we compete in our existing lines of business?" The primary focus of business strategic planning is to develop and maintain a distinct competitive advantage that will ensure long-term profitability.

Consider the various business strategies that must be developed for Anheuser-Busch's portfolio of businesses. One of the company's earliest efforts to diversify resulted in the development of Eagle Snacks. Business strategy that would ensure the success of Eagle Snacks in the highly competitive snack food industry had to be developed. More recently, Anheuser-Busch acquired Sea World. This business unit will also require a well-developed business strategy to ensure its long-term success. And we must not forget Anheuser-Busch's main line of business—beer. Anheuser-Busch International (the beer segment) will also require an effective strategy to maintain and build its market share in an industry that is intensely competitive.[23]

Business strategy should be formulated by those individuals who are most familiar with the operations of the business unit. Consequently, the board of directors and corporate executives are typically not involved with strategy formulation at the business level. Instead, this responsibility lies with the top-level executives and managers within the specific business units. For example, the CEO and top management teams at Eagle Snacks, Sea World, and Anheuser-Busch International will be most instrumental in formulating business strategy for their respective units.

Business strategy
Defines how each business unit in the firm's corporate portfolio will operate in its market arena.

▼ Anheuser-Busch's acquisition of SeaWorld represented a corporate level diversification strategy for the company. In addition, business level strategy must now be formulated to ensure SeaWorld's long-term success.

▼ **TABLE 4.3**   Examples of Functional Strategies

Human resource strategies:
- Recruit for management positions.
- Design commission structure.
- Develop training program.
- Design benefit package.

Marketing strategies:
- Develop market research study.
- Identify additional distribution channels.
- Create promotional program.
- Evaluate pricing structure.

Finance strategies:
- Secure debt financing.
- Evaluate capital structure.
- Initiate and manage budget process.
- Review and revise credit policies.

Operations strategies:
- Evaluate robotics system.
- Redesign quality-control processes.
- Locate alternative sources of supply.
- Develop inventory management system.

Business strategy is more specific than corporate strategy and spans a more limited time frame (1–5 years). For example, given the improvements in artificial intelligence technology in recent years, Hewlett Packard may pursue a business-level strategy aimed at developing new products based on that technology. This strategy would position Hewlett Packard to capitalize on potential market opportunities over the next several years.

Functional Strategic Planning   Functional strategic planning leads to the development of functional strategy. **Functional strategy** specifies the operations, research and development, financial, human resource management, and marketing activities necessary to implement the organization's corporate and business strategies. Table 4.3 lists some of the areas where functional planning occurs and gives examples of functional strategies in each area.

Strategy formulation at the functional level addresses the question, "how do we implement our corporate and business strategies?" While an organization's corporate and business strategies address *what* should be done, functional strategy focuses on *how* things will get done. In other words, corporate and business strategies deal with "doing the right thing" while functional strategy deals with "doing things right."

Consider, for example, the functional strategies necessary to implement Hewlett Packard's product development strategy described above. The research and development department would have to prepare product specifications and prototypes, the operations department would have to design a production system to manufacture the product, and the marketing department would have to develop a pricing, promotion, and distribution plan to bring the product to market. Each of these activities represents functional strategy.

Functional strategy
Specifies the operations, research and development, financial, human resource management, and marketing activities necessary to implement the organization's corporate and business strategies.

▼ At the functional level, strategy involves first-line managers and operational employees. This production
supervisor works with an employee
to ensure that product quality is at
the level specified in the company's
strategic plan.

Strategic analysis
An assessment of the internal and external conditions of the firm.

Strategy formulation
The establishment of strategic goals
for the organization and the development of corporate and business level
strategies.

Strategy implementation
The actions required to ensure that
the corporate and business level strategy of the organization is put into
place.

Functional strategic planning is carried out by middle- and lower-level managers, who develop functional strategy to ensure that their units are supporting
the corporate and business strategies of the organization. Strategic planning at
the functional level is more specific than corporate and business strategic planning, and functional strategies typically span a shorter time frame, usually one
or two years at most.

Having examined the three primary levels of strategic planning, we turn our
attention to the actual process of strategic planning. As you will see, a well-
defined model is available to guide the process of strategic planning in virtually
all organizations that choose to develop and implement strategic plans.

Strategic Planning as a Process

Strategic planning can be thought of as a process.[24] Figure 4.2 illustrates a
process-driven strategic planning model that is simple, straightforward, and
applicable to a wide variety of organizational situations. While the level of
sophistication and formality of the strategic planning process will differ among
organizations, the process itself should be the same across all organizations.[25]

As Figure 4.2 indicates, the strategic planning process is carried out in four
stages. Recall that the overall purpose of strategy is to get the organization
from where it is to where it should be. Each stage of the strategic planning
process makes some contribution to that overall purpose.[26]

During the first stage of the process, **strategic analysis,** the internal and
external conditions faced by the organization are evaluated. The information
gathered during strategic analysis serves as a foundation for the formulation of
the organization's strategic plan. Based on this information, the strategic direction of the firm is determined during the second, or strategy formulation,
stage of the process. The intent of **strategy formulation** is to establish strategic goals for the organization and to develop corporate and business strategies that will bridge the gap between the current position of the organization
and its desired position. **Strategy implementation** involves doing whatever
is necessary to ensure that the strategy of the organization is put into place at
all levels. Functional strategies are developed during the strategy implemen-

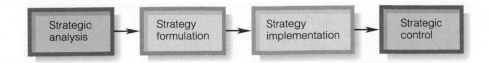

▼ **FIGURE 4.2**
The Process of Strategic Planning

tation stage. The final stage of the strategic planning process, **strategic control,** is designed to monitor the organization's progress toward implementing its plans and achieving its goals. Strategic control mechanisms identify deviations between actual and planned results so that managers can make the adjustments necessary to ensure that organizational goals can be achieved in the long term.[27]

Strategic control
The methods by which the performance of the organization is monitored.

Achieving Quality through Strategic Planning

As the competitive environment of most industries continues to globalize and intensify, many organizations are searching for ways to achieve and maintain a competitive advantage. Increasingly, they are looking toward quality improvement as a means of establishing such an advantage.[28] As you will recall from Chapter 1, improving quality can lead to reduced costs, increased sales, and greater customer satisfaction.[29] Providing the highest-quality product or service has become the strategic challenge of the 1990s and will continue to be a key determinant of competitive success long into the future.[30]

Achieving quality has become a primary objective of the strategic planning process in many organizations. In fact, total quality management programs have become an integral part of the strategic plans of many companies. The term **total quality management (TQM)** is widely used to describe organizational efforts to enhance product, service, process, and operational quality. As C. Jackson Grayson, a national expert in the area of quality, suggests, TQM stands for:

Total quality management (TQM)
A systematic approach for enhancing products, services, processes, and operational quality control.

- *Total.* Managing all people, functions, customers, and suppliers.
- *Quality.* Meaning not just products, but processes, reliability, and quality of work life.
- *Management.* Meaning senior management strategy, goals setting, organizational structure, compensation, and profits.[31]

TQM does not stand alone as an organizational activity; it is not simply an additive to the customer service function; and it does not involve a discrete set of organizational members.[32] Rather, TQM is an unwavering strategic commitment to enhancing the quality of an organization's output through continuous improvement by all members of the organization.[33] Further, quality-oriented strategies are appropriate for organizations of all sizes and types and in all kinds of industries.[34]

So how does a focus on quality affect the strategic planning process? Customer satisfaction becomes a driving force for the strategic plan. Strategic analysis focuses on identifying the needs and expectations of the customer, and the strategy formulation process is driven by a commitment to meet those needs and exceed customer expectations.[35] Strategy implementation focuses on empowering employees to do whatever is necessary to ensure customer satisfaction, and control mechanisms focus on ensuring that the products, services, processes, and operations of the organization are continuously improved.[36] Table 4.4 illustrates a detailed plan for achieving TQM.[37]

Strategic planning is the focus of the next chapter, which will explore the activities associated with each stage of the strategic planning process in much greater detail. For now, let's turn our attention to the second type of planning—operational planning.

▼ **TABLE 4.4**   Developing a Plan for Total Quality Management

Establish a foundation:
- Set strategic objectives.
- Define a vision statement.

Build an infrastructure:
- Establish a TQM council.
- Appoint a TQM executive.
- Establish subordinate support committees.

Educate the workforce:
- Conduct employee surveys.
- Hold executive workshops.
- Train management.
- Train other personnel.

Initiate process improvement:
- Identify candidate processes.
- Establish benchmarks.

Establish communication channels:
- Publish letters to employees.
- Establish other TQM media techniques.

Establish control system:
- Identify quantifiable indicators of quality improvement.
- Monitor indicators.

SOURCE: Adapted from A. C. Fenwick, "Five Easy Lessons," *Quality Progress*, December 1991, 63–66. © 1991 American Society for Quality Control. Reprinted with permission.

OPERATIONAL PLANNING

Operational planning
The process of determining the day to day activities that are necessary to achieve the long-term goals of the organization.

Operational plans
An outline of the tactical activities necessary to support and implement the strategic plans of the organization.

Operational planning focuses on determining the day-to-day activities that are necessary to achieve the long-term goals of the organization. **Operational plans** outline the tactical activities that must occur to support and implement the strategic initiatives of the organization. Operational plans are more specific than strategic plans, address shorter-term issues, and are formulated by the mid- and lower-level managers who are responsible for the work groups in the organization.

Consider, for example, the comprehensive operational plans that were necessary to support Walt Disney Company's strategy to enter the European market with a new theme park—Euro Disneyland. From site location to construction to food service, from human resource management to marketing, operational plans had to be formulated, coordinated, and implemented. In fact, Global Perspective illustrates how the planning of just one department, human resource management, was essential to the opening of Euro Disneyland.[38]

In general, plans can be categorized as standing or single-use plans depending on whether they address recurring issues or are specific to a given set of circumstances. Most organizations maintain both standing and single-use plans, as both are applicable to a broad range of organizational situations.

While standing and single-use plans are usually developed for work groups within the organization, operational planning can also occur for individual organizational members. This individualized planning is called management by objectives.

GLOBAL
PERSPECTIVE

THE EURO DISNEYLAND PLAN TO HIRE 12,000 CAST MEMBERS

In the fall of 1991, the human resource department of Euro Disneyland began a recruiting process that took over a year to plan and implement. Euro Disneyland, a $4.4 billion theme park that opened east of Paris in the summer of 1992, developed its plan based on its recruiting experiences at other parks and in light of the unique employment market in France.

The company calculated that in order to hire the 12,000 employees it needed to open the park, it would have to attract approximately 120,000 applicants. One of the first things the human resource managers at Euro Disney learned was that Disney theme parks were not well known in France. To lure prospective employees, Disney launched an extensive advertising campaign that was intended to educate the French about the company's theme parks. The process of educating future workers continued as they waited in line to be interviewed. At the Disney casting center, applicants watched a 5½-minute video of Disney employees performing various jobs at the company's California theme park. Then applicants gathered in a theater to view a 15-minute video. The video stressed the importance of reliable transportation, appearance standards, and the necessity of working holidays and weekends. At the end of this video, applicants had an opportunity to leave if they were no longer interested in the job. Those who stayed went through a seven-minute interview. Based on the results of that interview, the best candidates were invited to explore employment opportunities at Disney further.

Through its well developed recruiting plan, Euro Disney was able to attract the employees necessary to open the park. It was a managerial challenge that required extensive planning and careful execution.

Standing Plans

Standing plans are designed to deal with organizational issues or problems that recur frequently. By using standing plans, management avoids the need to "reinvent the wheel" every time a particular situation arises. In addition, such plans ensure that recurring situations are handled consistently over time. This may be particularly important for an organization with a highly diverse workforce. Individuals from different cultural and social backgrounds may react to certain situations differently. Standing plans ensure that such situations will be handled in prescribed ways. Standing plans can, however, limit employees' flexibility and make it difficult to respond to the needs of the customer. For this reason, managers should carefully consider how standing plans can be used most effectively before they are designed and implemented.

Standing plans include (1) policies, (2) procedures, and (3) rules. Each provides guidance in a different way.

Policies   **Policies** are general guidelines that govern how certain organizational situations will be addressed. Policies provide guidance to managers who must make decisions about circumstances that occur frequently within the organization. Most organizational units will establish policies to provide direction for decision making.

For example, human resource management departments maintain policies that govern sick leave, vacation leave, and benefit options. Production departments establish policies for procurement, inventory management, and quality

Standing plans
Plans that deal with organizational issues and problems that recur frequently.

Policies
General guidelines for decision making within the organization.

Procedures
Instructions on how to complete recurring tasks.

Rules
Detailed and specific regulations for action.

Single-use plans
Plans which address specific organizational situations that typically do not recur.

control. A university's administration maintains policies about admittance to certain academic programs, grade appeals, and permissible course waivers or substitutions. These policies provide a framework for decision making that eliminates the need to evaluate the specific circumstances surrounding each individual case.

Procedures   **Procedures** are a second type of standing plan. Procedures are more specific and action-oriented than policies and are designed to give explicit instructions on how to complete a recurring task. Most companies maintain some sort of procedures manual to provide guidance for certain recurring activities. Many use a Standard Operating Procedures (SOPs) manual to outline the basic operating methods of the organization.

Most units of the organization will have procedures as well as policies. For example, human resource management departments develop procedures for filing benefit claims, documenting the reasons for sick leave, and requesting vacation time. Production departments establish procedures for identifying and evaluating suppliers and ordering supplies, operating a given inventory management system, and identifying and implementing specific quality-control criteria. A university will maintain specific procedures for registering for admittance to certain programs, appealing grades, and applying for course waivers and/or substitutions.

Rules   **Rules** are the strictest type of standing plan found in organizations. Rules are not intended to serve as guidelines for making organizational decisions; instead, they provide detailed and specific regulations for action.

For example, a human resource management department may have rules governing the number of sick days an employee may take with pay, the months in which vacation time can be scheduled, and the length of time an organizational member must be employed before qualifying for benefits. The production department may have rules governing the percentage of supplies that can be purchased from a single supplier, the method in which inventory must be accounted for, and the way in which products of substandard quality are handled. A university may have rules to govern the minimum grade point average necessary for admission to a given academic program, the period in which a grade can be appealed after a course is completed, and the specific courses that may be substituted for one another.

Meeting the Challenge provides an opportunity for you to evaluate and develop standing plans for an organization with which you are familiar. Based on this exercise, you should see the potential value of establishing standing plans to cope with recurring organizational situations.

Single-Use Plans

Single-use plans are developed to address a specific organizational situation. Such plans are typically used only once either because the specific situation to which they apply does not recur. For example, NationsBank's merger with C&S is an example of an event that would require a very detailed and specialized plan of action. Such a plan would be a single-use plan. Once the plan has been implemented, it would be of little use to NationsBank. In the event that NationsBank acquires another bank at some future date, it is unlikely that the specifics of that acquisition (i.e., number and location of branches, personnel, operating policies, and so forth) would be similar enough to the C&S acquisition to justify the use of the current plan.

There are three primary types of single-use plans: (1) programs, (2) projects, and (3) budgets. Each offers a different degree of comprehensiveness and detail. Programs are the most comprehensive plans; projects have a nar-

EVALUATING STANDING PLANS

Choose an organization with which you are familiar. This can be a company for whom you work or have worked, a social organization with which you are associated (i.e., church, sorority, fraternity), or even your university. Identify three policies, procedures and rules that exist within that organization. Evaluate the purpose and effect of each.

Would you change the plan in some way? If so, indicate your proposed change and explain the effect that you feel it would have on the functioning of the organization. A format like the following can be used to summarize your assessment.

	Policy	Purpose	Effect	Proposed Change	Effect
1.					
2.					
3.					

	Procedure	Purpose	Effect	Proposed Change	Effect
1.					
2.					
3.					

	Rule	Purpose	Effect	Proposed Change	Effect
1.					
2.					
3.					

rower scope and, in fact, are often undertaken as a part of a program; budgets are developed to support programs or projects.

Programs **Programs** are single-use plans that govern a relatively comprehensive set of activities that are designed to accomplish a particular set of goals. Such plans outline the major steps and specific actions necessary to implement the activities prescribed by the program. The timing and sequencing of the efforts of individuals and units are also articulated in the plan.

The Walt Disney Company's recruiting program, described in Global Perspective, was designed to support the company's goals of growth through entry into the European market. In contrast, a firm that operates in an industry that has been subject to declining demand or increasing competition, might develop a retrenchment program to adapt to new industry conditions. For example, USAir recently undertook a cost-reduction program designed to improve the firm's competitive position within the airline industry.[39]

Projects **Projects** direct the efforts of individuals or work groups toward the achievement of specific, well-defined goals. Projects are typically less comprehensive and narrower in focus than programs and usually have predetermined

Programs
Single-use plans that govern a comprehensive set of activities designed to accomplish a particular set of goals.

Projects
Single-use plans that direct the efforts of individuals or work groups toward the achievement of a specific goal.

▼ As competition in the airline industry has intensified over the last several years, many airline companies have implemented cost reduction programs. USAir was one airline that developed a detailed plan for reducing costs and improving their competitiveness. Interestingly, the employees of the company acquired 51% ownership of the firm shortly after the benefits of the cost reduction began to be realized.

Budgets
Single-use plans that specify how financial resources should be allocated.

Management by objectives (MBO)
A method for developing individualized plans which guide the activities of individual members of an organization.

target dates for completion. Many projects are designed to collect and analyze information for decision-making purposes or to support more comprehensive planning efforts, such as a program.

For example, a marketing manager for Euro Disneyland Resort might be asked to develop an advertising campaign to attract job applicants. This project has a narrow scope and would be undertaken to support The Walt Disney Company's efforts to recruit the necessary human resources to open its new theme park. Similarly, public relations specialists at USAir might undertake a project to communicate the details of the proposed cutback to the employees, stockholders, and the general public in an understandable and informative manner.[40] This could require the development of informational seminars and packets for the employees, letters of explanation for the stockholders, and press releases for the general public.

Budgets   Budgets are the final form of single-use plans. **Budgets** are often undertaken as a part of other planning efforts because they specify the financial resource requirements associated with other plans (i.e., programs and projects). In addition, budgets serve as a mechanism for controlling the financial aspects of implementing the plan.[41]

Disney has a large budget to support its efforts to recruit personnel for its European theme park. USAir will undoubtedly establish a budget for outplacement services for individuals who lose their jobs as a result of the cost-reduction program. These budgets will both support the specific planning initiatives of these organizations and serve as a means of controlling the implementation of their plans.

Although all the types of standing and single-use plans discussed here can be used for very specialized planning purposes, they are often interrelated. For example, projects are often subcomponents of more comprehensive programs or are undertaken in an effort to develop or implement policies, procedures, and rules. In fact, most organizations will engage in all of these forms of planning over time.

Management by Objectives

A special planning technique, **management by objectives (MBO),** provides a method for developing personalized plans that guide the activities of individual members of the organization. The MBO approach to planning helps managers balance conflicting demands by focusing the attention of the manager and the employee on the tasks to be completed and the performance to be achieved at an individual level.[42]

MBO Process   Figure 4.3 outlines the primary steps in an MBO program. As the figure illustrates, MBO programs are circular and self-renewing in nature. The process begins when employees, in conjunction with their managers, establish a set of goals that serve as the foundation for the development of their work plans. Once a set of mutually agreeable goals has been determined, criteria for assessing work performance are identified. Next, employees formulate and implement the action plans necessary to achieve their goals and review their progress with their managers on an intermittent basis. At the end of the

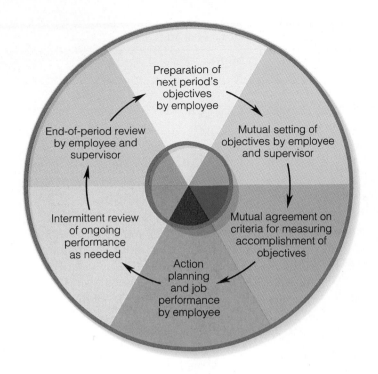

▼ FIGURE 4.3
Management by Objectives: the Cycle

SOURCE: K. Davis and J. Newstrom, *Human Behavior at Work: Organizational Behavior,* (New York: McGraw-Hill, 1989), 209. Reproduced with permission of McGraw-Hill.

MBO period, the performance of the employees is compared to the goals established at the beginning of the period. Performance rewards should be based on the extent to which the goals have been achieved. Once the MBO cycle is complete, employees begin formulating goals to drive the next MBO planning period.[43]

Benefits of MBO   As originally conceived, MBO programs provide three primary benefits:

- MBO programs provide a foundation for a more integrated and system-oriented approach to planning. Establishing goals and action plans for individual employees forces managers to examine how the activities of each individual in their work group contribute to the achievement of the overall goals of the group. As an MBO system works its way up the hierarchy of the organization, it provides a mechanism for ensuring systemwide coordination of work efforts.

- The MBO approach to planning requires communication between employees and their managers since they must agree on the performance goals outlined in the plan. This increased communication often serves to build stronger relationships between employees and managers.

- MBO systems lead to more participatory work environments where employees feel they have a voice and can have input into how their jobs should be designed and what their performance targets should be. Further, employees gain a greater understanding of their organization when they are forced to plan their activities in line with the organization's overall goals.[44]

In addition to these general benefits, MBO systems offer the more specific advantages listed in Table 4.5.[45] These benefits include such things as higher

▼ MBO programs require close interaction between managers and their subordinates. Here, a manager discusses potential goals with one of her employees.

▼ **TABLE 4.5**   Advantages and Disadvantages of MBO Systems

ADVANTAGES

- Results in better overall management and the achievement of higher performance levels.
- Provides an effective overall planning system.
- Forces managers to establish priorities and measurable targets or standards of performance.
- Clarifies the specific role, responsibilities, and authority of personnel.
- Encourages the participation of individual employees and managers in establishing objectives.
- Facilitates the process of control.
- Provides a golden opportunity for career development for managers and employees.
- Lets individuals know what is expected of them.
- Provides a more objective and tangible basis for performance appraisal and salary decisions.
- Improves communications within the organization.
- Helps identify promotable managers and employees.
- Facilitates the organization's ability to change.
- Increases motivation and commitment of employees.

DISADVANTAGES

- Requires time and commitment of top management. May divert their activities away from other important activities.
- May require excessive paperwork, thus complicating administrative processes.
- May create a tendency to focus on short-term versus long-term planning.
- Can be difficult to establish and operationalize.

SOURCE: Adapted from J. Gordon, *Management and Organizational Behavior* (Boston: Allyn & Bacon, 1990), 129–32.

overall performance levels, prioritized goals, and greater opportunities for career development for both managers and employees.[46]

Disadvantages of MBO   At the same time, however, a number of disadvantages are associated with the use of MBO systems (see Table 4.5). These systems require the time and commitment of management and, as a result, may divert attention away from other important activities. Many systems require excessive paperwork that complicates the administrative processes within the organization. Further, some argue that MBO programs focus attention on short-run problems rather than on issues that are relevant to the long-term success of the organization. Finally, goals may be difficult to establish and operationalize in some cases. As a consequence, MBO systems may not be suitable for all job designs.[47]

In addition, the increasing diversity of the workforce has created new challenges for those involved in MBO programs. While MBO systems work quite well for many employees from the United States, people from other cultures may not adapt well to this type of planning. The MBO concept is predicated on employees' desire to be reasonably independent and their willingness to work toward predetermined goals—both of which are relatively common characteristics of workers in the United States. In many other cultures, however, such attitudes toward work are not common. MBO programs may be far less effective when used with individuals from such cultures.[48]

Consequently, managers must be sensitive to the diversity of their work teams and may need to modify the MBO concept to suit different individuals.

In general, MBO systems are considered an effective tool. Although they can be cumbersome if implemented throughout every unit of an organization, these programs can be beneficial to the planning process when used selectively. Monsanto is an example of a firm that has embraced the MBO approach to planning. Corporate executives credit this system for the high level of commitment of Monsanto employees to the overall plans and strategy of the firm.[49]

THE RELATIONSHIP BETWEEN STRATEGIC AND OPERATIONAL PLANNING

Thus far, our examination of strategic and operational planning has highlighted their differences. Despite these differences, however, strategic and operational plans cannot be developed in isolation. In fact, both types of plans must be developed from an integrative perspective. Regardless of whether the organization uses a top-down or a bottom-up planning approach, in the end it must develop a single, well-integrated master plan. The operational plans of the various work units within the organizational system must be supportive of the organization's overall strategic plan.

Whenever the strategic and operational plans of an organization are inconsistent, problems are certain to result. Friendly Restaurants, profiled in Managing for Excellence on the next page, found out the hard way that a failure to integrate strategic and operational planning can lead to significant problems. When Hershey Foods acquired Friendly, the parent company applied its manufacturing mentality to the new subsidiary. Such a mentality was inconsistent with the service nature of Friendly's business. As a consequence, Friendly suffered severe operational problems that resulted in a significant loss of market share.[50]

CONTINGENCY PLANNING FOR CHANGING ENVIRONMENTS ━━━━━

Contingency planning is an approach that has become very popular in today's rapidly changing business environment. Organizations that face strategic or operating conditions that are subject to significant change may choose to employ a contingency approach in their planning process. This approach is particularly useful when the organization's effectiveness is highly dependent on a particular set of business conditions.

Contingency planning requires the development of two or more plans, each of which is based on a different set of strategic or operating conditions that could occur. The plan that is implemented is determined by the specific circumstances that come to pass.[51] For example, while an organization may plan to begin production at a new plant facility in June 1997, managers should develop a contingency plan that ensures uninterrupted production in the event that the plant opening is delayed for some reason.

NationsBank intends to achieve its growth objectives through the acquisition of other banking institutions—in this case, C&S. However, C&S was not particularly keen on the idea of being acquired, and there was a chance that the merger would not occur. While NationsBank's primary plan to achieve its growth objectives included the C&S acquisition, the company would have been well advised to develop one or more contingency plans in the event that the acquisition did not occur. Plan B might have focused on the acquisition of another banking institution—First Union Bank, for example. Plan C might have been designed to achieve NationsBank's growth objectives through the development of internal operating units.

Contingency planning
Development of two or more plans based on different strategic operating conditions.

MANAGING FOR EXCELLENCE

FRIENDLY: A MISMATCHED STRATEGIC AND OPERATIONAL STRATEGY

The Blake brothers began Friendly Restaurants in 1935 in Wilbraham, Massachusetts. From one small unit, Friendly's company-owned restaurants grew to over 700 by the late 1970s. They were a powerful contender in the coffee shop segment of the restaurant industry.

In 1979, the family-owned Friendly was sold to Hershey Foods Corporation. In the late 1970s, candy sales had become flat, and shortages in the cocoa bean crop had squeezed Hershey's margins. Hershey was looking for new opportunities for growth. Following the lead of other food manufacturers, Hershey purchased Friendly as part of a corporate strategy to diversify operations. Corporate executives at Hershey believed that their new acquisition would provide a growth vehicle for the company as the restaurant market was not yet saturated.

The fit between Hershey and Friendly was not a good one, however. Hershey's profit goals for Friendly were based on its manufacturing standards rather than on the margins that were typical for the restaurant industry. The parent company was unwilling to accept restaurant returns on investment and demanded that Friendly cut its costs to achieve a better margin.

Strategic plans were imposed on Friendly by Hershey's top management, and developing operational plans to support those strategic plans required decisions that seriously compromised the business. The extreme cost-cutting measures that were necessary to meet the parent company's goals for profitability began to have a cumulative effect on the restaurants. Buildings, equipment, and grounds were not maintained, labor and food costs were squeezed, and training and development expenditures were eliminated almost entirely. After seven years of unreasonable goals and poor planning by Hershey, Friendly was literally falling apart.

In 1988, Hershey announced its plans to sell its Friendly Restaurant chain to Tennessee Restaurant Corporation (TRC). Things changed for Friendly when TRC bought the company. Donald N. Smith, the CEO of TRC, "has made a career out of reacting to food companies' inability to effectively run restaurants." Friendly was a prime target for Smith, and he has implemented a plan to restore the company's profitability in the 1990s.

Briggs-Weaver, a Dallas-based industrial distribution firm, develops formalized contingency plans based on bottom-up forecasts of sales. According to Briggs's president, Rob Mellor, "If our sales drop by more than 10 percent, a contingency plan automatically goes into effect." While Mellor also notes (gratefully) that the company has never had to put a contingency plan into action, developing such plans ensures that the company is ready to cope with changing demands for its services.[52]

FACILITATING THE PLANNING PROCESS

Presuming that one accepts the proposition that planning is a critical organizational activity, it is important to examine ways to facilitate the planning process. While most managers would admit that they need to plan, many would also admit that they do much less planning than they should. This situation is a result of a number of barriers to planning.

BARRIERS TO EFFECTIVE PLANNING

Why do some managers fail to plan effectively? There are a number of potential causes—all of which may be overcome by developing an organizational culture that encourages and supports the planning process. Doing so, however, requires a clear understanding of the main reasons why managers fail to plan effectively.

Demands on the Manager's Time

Some managers may simply be too busy "putting out fires" to take the time to plan properly. Managers often feel as though they face a continual stream of problems from the time they arrive at work until they leave. Although this constant troubleshooting may seem to leave few opportunities for planning, the hectic nature of the manager's day in itself suggests that planning is very much needed. Through better planning (e.g., policies, rules, and the like), managers can develop operational systems that are more effective and less problematic and demanding of their time.

Ambiguous and Uncertain Operating Environments

Environmental complexity and volatility are another commonly cited reason for not planning. Managers who are uncomfortable with ambiguity may find it difficult and frustrating to plan under conditions of uncertainty. Yet, while it may be difficult to develop plans under such circumstances, effective managers make an effort to do so. Organizations that operate in rapidly changing and complex environments often find that planning provides a mechanism for coping with such conditions.

Resistance to Change

Finally, managers may hesitate to plan because they are resistant to change. Organizational members may associate planning with a need to change the way they do their job. Their hesitancy to change may discourage them from initiating the planning process.[53] Given the current focus on quality and continuous improvement, resistance to change can have very detrimental results for the organization in the long term.

OVERCOMING THE BARRIERS TO PLANNING

As discussed previously, achieving success through planning requires the participation of a broad range of organizational members. Consequently, organizations must develop and maintain a culture that encourages planning and rewards those who plan effectively. To do so, managers must involve employees in decision-making processes, tolerate a diversity of views, and encourage strategic thinking.

Involve Employees in Decision Making

Employee involvement in the planning process is essential for its success. Regardless of whether a top-down or bottom-up approach is utilized, input from all levels of the organization is essential to the success of the organization's planning system. Managers should solicit the opinions and views of their employees when formulating plans, and they should maintain an open door policy that encourages individual organizational members to initiate communication about the planning efforts of the unit and the firm. Discouraging employees from sharing information that might be very important to the planning process (see Figure 4.4) will result in less effective organizational plans.[54]

▼ FIGURE 4.4
Encouraging Open Communication

SOURCE: J. Rosenzweig, F. Kast, and T. R. Mitchell, *The Frank and Ernest Manager* (Los Altos, Calif.: Crisp Publications, 1991). Reprinted by permission of NEA, Inc.

Tolerate a Diversity of Views

Managers who are intolerant of a diversity of views within their unit eliminate one of the primary benefits associated with a participatory planning system. Diverse views and perspectives lead to a broader assessment and evaluation of organizational problems and opportunities. In fact, this is one of the primary benefits of maintaining a diverse workforce. Organizations that encourage a wide range of different ideas and views are more likely to produce plans that are comprehensive and fully developed.

Encourage Strategic Thinking

Developing an organizational culture that encourages strategic and results-oriented thinking will lead to more effective planning. Thinking is a skill and, as is the case with most skills, it can be developed through training and practice.[55] Employees should be provided with the training necessary to develop strategic thinking skills and given the opportunity to practice those skills in their work environment. Further, individuals should be rewarded for thinking strategically when developing their plans.[56]

MANAGERIAL IMPLICATIONS

Tomorrow's manager will face many challenges in developing effective strategic and operational plans. Planning has become increasingly difficult as the pace of change in the business environment has accelerated. While change makes the planning process more difficult, it also makes planning more critical. Managers of the future must be forward thinking and focused on achieving the goals of their work groups and their organizations through effective planning.

The ultimate objective of the planning process is the development of good plans. Plans are good if they can be implemented successfully and result in the accomplishment of the goals for which they were designed. Managers are more likely to develop good plans when they:

- Recognize and communicate the importance of planning in achieving organizational success.
- Understand and appreciate the relationship between strategic and operational planning.
- Involve those responsible for implementing the plan in the planning process.
- Remove the barriers to planning at the work group and individual level.
- Reward those who think strategically and follow through with operational planning.
- Look to contingency planning as a means of maintaining flexibility in rapidly changing business environments.

In this chapter, we have examined the managerial function of planning. Our focus, at both the strategic and operational levels, has been on achieving organizational success through planning. The process of strategic planning is examined in much greater detail in the next chapter where we discuss strategy as a tool for achieving competitive success in the twenty-first century.

NATIONSBANKS: PLANNING FOR GROWTH THROUGH ACQUISITION

MANAGERIAL INCIDENT RESOLUTION

NationsBank®

For two years, Bennett A. Brown, chairman of Citizens & Southern Corporation, rejected the hostile takeover threats from NationsBank chairman Hugh L. McColl, Jr. In 1991, however, when C&S Corporation was struck by heavy loan losses, Brown finally decided to listen to McColl's merger deal.

This merger added 1000 C&S branches located in Texas, Virginia, and Georgia to NationsBank's existing operations, making a total of 1900 banking branches from Maryland to Florida. By eliminating duplicate branches, NationsBank would save over $130 million in overhead costs, and consolidating the two companies' corporate headquarters would result in another $150 million savings. By bringing together NationsBank's back-office expertise and C&S's knowledge of special receivable lending, the merged bank was stronger than many of its competitors.

NationsBank is now the fourth largest bank holding company in the United States and the second largest holder of total assets. Without proper planning, this merger would surely have failed. Furthermore, by implementing periodic reevaluations of its strategic and operational plans, NationsBank can continue to grow and prosper as a major banking institution.[57] ▼

SUMMARY

- Planning is an important managerial function through which managers outline the activities necessary to achieve the goals of the organization. The purpose of planning is to ensure organizational effectiveness and efficiency in both the short term and the long term.

- Traditionally, organizations used either a top-down or a bottom-up approach to planning. Most organizations today plan from an integrative perspective, using a top-down approach in some areas of the organization and a bottom-up approach in others.

- Strategic planning is the process by which an organization makes decisions and takes actions that affect its long-run performance. Strategy is the output of the strategic planning process. Corporate, business, and functional strategies vary with respect to focus, specificity, time horizon, and the participants in the planning process.

- The strategic planning process consists of four primary stages: (1) strategic analysis, (2) strategy formulation, (3) strategy implementation, and (4) strategic control. Each stage of the process contributes, in some way, to the achievement of the strategic goals of the organization.

- Many organizations today are striving to achieve quality through strategic planning. Planning for quality requires a commitment to meeting customer needs and exceeding customer expectations, a willingness to empower employees, and a focus on continuous improvement in every aspect of the organization's operations.

- Operational planning determines the day-to-day activities that are necessary to achieve the long-term goals of the organization. Standing plans, which include policies, procedures, and rules, are developed to address issues that recur frequently in the organization. Single-use plans address a specific issue or problem that the organization experiences only once. Single-use plans include programs, projects, and budgets.

- Management by objectives (MBO) is a specialized approach to operational planning that occurs at the level of the individual organizational member. While MBO systems can be time-consuming and complex, employing this approach to plan the work activities of individual employees can be beneficial.

- Contingency planning involves the development of a set of plans that are designed for the varied strategic or operating conditions that the firm might face. Contingency planning is most appropriate for organizations that operate in environments that are subject to frequent or significant change.

- The three common barriers to planning are demands on the manager's time, ambiguous and uncertain environmental conditions, and resistance to change. Overcoming the barriers to planning requires the development of an organizational culture that supports and encourages planning.

- The highly competitive, rapidly changing nature of the business environment will create many planning challenges for tomorrow's managers. Managers of the future must not only develop their own planning skills but must also create a work environment in which effective planning is encouraged and rewarded.

KEY TERMS

Planning (p. 114)
Plan (p. 115)
Goals (p. 115)
Controls (p. 115)
Strategic planning (p. 120)
Strategic plans (p. 120)
Competitive advantage (p. 120)
Corporate strategy (p. 121)
Business strategy (p. 122)

Functional strategy (p. 123)
Strategic analysis (p. 124)
Strategy formulation (p. 124)
Strategy implementation (p. 124)
Strategic control (p. 125)
Total quality management (p. 125)
Operational planning (p. 126)
Operational plans (p. 126)
Standing plans (p. 127)

Policies (p. 127)
Procedures (p. 128)
Rules (p. 128)
Single-use plans (p. 128)
Programs (p. 129)
Projects (p. 129)
Budgets (p. 130)
Management by objectives (p. 130)
Contingency planning (p. 133)

REVIEW QUESTIONS

1. Describe the managerial function of planning, explaining what it is, why managers should do it, and where it should begin.

2. Define strategic planning. What are the three levels at which strategy is formulated, and how do they differ in terms of (a) focus, (b) participants, (c) specificity, and (d) time horizon?

3. Describe the process of strategic planning.

4. Why and how are firms seeking to achieve quality through strategic planning?

5. What is operational planning and how does it differ from strategic planning? Identify and describe standing and single-use plans.

6. Describe an MBO program. What are the advantages and disadvantages of this type of planning?

7. What is contingency planning? Under what circum-

stances would it be most appropriate to use a contingency approach to planning?

8. What are the common barriers to planning? What might a manager do to reduce the barriers to planning?

9. How can tomorrow's manager achieve excellence through planning?

DISCUSSION QUESTIONS

Improving Critical Thinking

1. Evaluate the benefits of an MBO as an employer and as an employee. Would you want to participate in an MBO program? Why or why not?

2. As an employee of an organization, would you prefer a top-down or bottom-up approach to planning? What would you consider to be the advantages and disadvantages of each from an employee's perspective?

Enhancing Communication Skills

3. Consider an organization with which you have been fairly closely affiliated as an employee or a member (e.g., a business, church, sorority, and the like). Describe the planning system of this organization. Was it effective? If not, why? What might the managers of the organization have done to ensure better planning? To improve your oral communication skills, present your analysis of this situation to the class.

4. How might the planning process for a new business venture differ from the process in an established business? How would it differ for small versus large businesses? To practice your written communication skills, prepare a one-page written summary of your response.

Building Teamwork Skills

5. We know that planning occurs at the strategic and operational levels. Is it more important to plan at one level than at the other? Why or why not? Discuss this question in teams of four to five students and develop a position that you can present to the class.

6. Evaluate some of the standing plans at your university or college that directly affect you as a student. Are the policies, procedures, or rules that you identified meant to benefit or hinder the student? Why do you think that the administration at your school feels that it is necessary to have well-defined standing plans? What would happen if none of the plans that you identified existed? Form teams of four to five students, answer the preceding questions, and present your responses to the class.

ETHICS: TAKE A STAND

Smart Toy Company is a subsidiary of a large corporation that owns a number of diversified businesses. The company, which employs about 500 workers, manufactures high-quality toys for preschool children. Smart Toy prides itself on its safety and employee satisfaction records. The company values the opinions of its workers and encourages a participatory planning process.

Recently, Smart Toy's market share has fallen dramatically as a result of the increasing demand for high-tech toys such as video games and remote-control cars. The effect of this loss in market share has been a significant reduction in the profitability of the subsidiary. Corporate headquarters has expressed its displeasure at the current situation at Smart Toy and has given the company six months to reverse the decline in profitability. If profitability cannot be restored within this time frame, the subsidiary will be shut down, and the employees will lose their jobs.

While Smart Toy's management feels that they can turn the business around within the next two years, the six-month time frame presents a significant problem. To achieve the profitability goals set by the parent company within the next six months, costs would have to be reduced significantly. To do so, the company would have to buy lower quality materials, reduce its quality-control efforts, and eliminate its production safety programs. Top management is very concerned about the impact of such decisions on the quality and safety of Smart Toy's products, as well as on the safety of production employees. Yet the only other alternative is to allow the company to be dissolved.

For Discussion:

1. How do you feel about the demands corporate headquarters has imposed on Smart Toy Company?
2. Which of the two alternatives outlined above would you chose?
3. How might you address the issues presented in the case using planning techniques?

THINKING CRITICALLY
Debate the Issue

TOP-DOWN VERSUS BOTTOM-UP PLANNING

As was mentioned in the chapter, planning can begin at the top of the organization and flow downward or start at the bottom of the organization and move upward. Certain advantages and disadvantages are associated with each method.

Form teams of four to five students as directed by your instructor. Half of the teams should prepare to argue the benefits of top-down planning, while the other teams should prepare to argue the benefits of bottom-up planning. Draw from the experiences of real managers with whom you are familiar when developing your arguments. Your instructor will choose two teams to present their findings to the class in a debate format.

VIDEO CASE

Tenneco's Planning and Leadership Conference

By 1991, the members of the board of directors at Tenneco—a conglomerate involved in gas pipelines, tractors, and other businesses, and one of the 50 largest manufacturers in the United States—recognized the need for major change. Losses that year totaled $732 million on sales of $14 billion. In September 1991, 49-year-old Mike Walsh was tapped as CEO of the Houston-based company.

Walsh brought a diverse background to the job: Stanford running back, White House fellow, Yale Law graduate, public defender, and U.S. attorney. Walsh was 37 years old when he entered corporate life, first as executive vice president of operations at Cummins Engine and then as CEO of Union Pacific Rail Road. In his first full year as CEO, Tenneco posted $1.3 billion in losses; in 1993, the company's net earnings were $426 million.

This turnaround was accomplished at no small cost. Walsh cut Tenneco's workforce from 89,000 to 75,000 employees and sold company assets. More importantly, he instituted a rigorous planning program throughout the organization. In his meeting with Tenneco's top 300 managers on December 11, 1992,

Walsh outlined specific goals, strategies, and support processes for the company.

Emphasizing the need for all employees at Tenneco to set and achieve their goals, Walsh highlighted three basic conditions facing the company. First, Tenneco faces a scissors curve, with increasing price and ongoing cost pressures. Second, these price and cost pressures exist in a no-growth environment. Finally, although technology is important to Tenneco, technology alone will not provide the company with a competitive advantage.

Walsh went on to discuss Tenneco's need for a strategy emphasizing operating cost leadership through quality initiatives and strong action plans, with an unrelenting focus on results.

For Discussion:

1. What planning approach was used at Tenneco? Why was this approach used?
2. What aspects of Walsh's plan deal with strategic planning and which with operational planning?
3. What is the role of quality in Walsh's plans for Tenneco?

CASE

Morgan Chemical

When Kenneth J. Morgan began peddling his industrial-strength cleanser to local businesses, he was 26 years old and full of dreams and ambitions that seemed far-fetched by most standards. However, the young entrepreneur from Ann Arbor, Michigan, eventually proved everyone wrong. From its meager beginnings, the company he founded grew to have more than $45 million in sales and operating facilities across the nation. Morgan's products now include an entire line of industrial cleansers primarily for hotels, restaurants, office buildings, and recreation centers. Amazingly, the company has remained more than 80 percent family owned throughout its history.

Now Bob Morgan is sitting in his Detroit headquarters looking out over the bay and thinking about how successful and well-focused his grandfather, Kenneth Morgan, had been. Even though Bob has earned an MBA from Northwestern, at 31 years of age he knows that filling his grandfather's shoes will be difficult. Unfortunately, Morgan Chemical has been without skilled leadership since his grandfather's death almost seven years ago. Providing a new direction is Bob's first priority as a fledgling CEO.

As Bob attempts to develop a plan for the company, he finds the complexity of his task overwhelming. Morgan has 23 sales offices in the United States and manufacturing plants in three different states. In addition to the need to institute more formalized planning, the company faces several serious problems. The North Carolina plant has had to shut down production because of a misunderstanding with the local labor union. The industry is entering the mature stage of the life cycle, and many of Morgan's larger competitors are beginning to merge to achieve better economies of scale. In addition, much of Bob's information about the internal operations of the firm is unreliable due to an ineffective and out-of-date management information system. Profits and sales have been declining over the last three years, and it has been more than five years since the company introduced a new product.

Bob doesn't know where to begin. How can he develop a plan that will put Morgan Chemical back on track?

For Discussion

1. How is the changing environment posing problems for Morgan Chemical? Do the changes present greater planning difficulties for Bob? Why or why not?

2. Would a top-down or bottom-up approach be better in this case? Why?

3. How would you advise Bob to begin developing a system for planning?

EXPERIENTIAL EXERCISE 4.1

Consider your own career plan. Have you developed a plan for your education and career? If you haven't developed a plan, consider the following questions in developing your plan. If you have, use your plan to respond to these questions.

1. What are your goals and objectives?

2. What must you do to achieve those goals and objectives?
   a. What resources will you require?
   b. What actions must you take?

3. What control mechanisms can you put in place to monitor your progress in achieving your plan?

4. What could happen to derail your plans? Do you have contingency plans that address those factors?

NOTES

1. "Why Hugh McColl Is Courting an Atlanta Belle," *Business Week,* April 17, 1989, 19–20; and "Super Banker: NCNB's Hugh McColl Is out to Make History with His Bid for C&S/Sovran," *Business Week,* July 15, 1991, 116–20.

2. A. P. DeGeus, "Planning as Learning," *Harvard Business Review* (March/April 1988): 70–74.

3. P. F. Drucker, *Managing for Results* (New York: Harper

& Row, 1964); and *The Effective Executive* (New York: Harper & Row, 1967).

4. C. Perrow, "The Analysis of Goals in Complex Organizations," *American Sociological Review* 26 (1961): 854.

5. J. A. Pearce II and W. A. Randolph, "Improving Strategy Formulation Pedagogies by Recognizing Behavioral Aspects," *Exchange,* December 1980, 7–10.

6. R. Michaels, "Planning: An Effective Management Tool or

Corporate Pastime?" *Journal of Marketing Management* (Spring 1986): 259.

7. B. Dumaine, "Corporate Spies Snoop to Conquer," *Fortune,* November 7, 1988, 68-76.

8. T. J. Peters and T. H. Waterman, *In Search of Excellence: Lessons from America's Best Run Companies* (New York: Harper & Row, 1982).

9. Adapted from "Forte Industries," in *Strengthening America's Competitiveness: The Blue Chip Enterprise Initiative* (published by Warner Books on behalf of Connecticut Mutual Life Insurance Company and the U.S. Chamber of Commerce, 1991), 171.

10. B. M. Cook, "Quality: The Pioneers Survey the Landscape," *Industry Week,* October 21, 1993, 68-73; P. B. Crosby, "The Next Effort," *Management Review,* February 1992, Vol. 81, No. 2, 64; and R. Jacob, "TQM: More Than a Dying Fad?" *Fortune,* October 18, 1992, 66-72.

11. W. H. Brickner and D. M. Cope, *The Planning Process* (Massachusetts: Winthrop Publishers, 1977): 52-56.

12. R. Evered, "So What Is Strategy," *Long Range Planning* 16 (1983): 57-72.

13. M. Leontiades, "The Confusing Words of Business Policy," *Academy of Management Review* 7 (1982): 45-48.

14. A. Ginsberg, "Operationalizing Organizational Strategy: Toward an Integrative Framework," *Academy of Management Review,* Vol. 9, No. 3, 1984, pp. 548-557.

15. C. C. Snow and L. G. Hrebiniak, "Strategy, Distinctive Competence and Organizational Performance," *Administrative Science Quarterly* 25 (1980): 317-36.

16. D. A. Aaker, "How to Select a Business Strategy," *California Management Review* (Spring 1984): 167-75.

17. S. S. Thune and R. J. House, "Where Long-Range Planning Pays Off," *Business Horizons* 14 (1970): 81-87; L. C. Rhyne, "The Relationship of Strategic Planning to Financial Performance," *Strategic Management Journal* (1986): 423-36; Z. A. Malik and D. W. Karger, "Does Long-Range Planning Improve Company Performance?" *Management Review* 64 (1975): 27-31; and R. Rumelt, *Strategy, Structure, and Economic Performance* (Boston: Graduate School of Business Administration, Harvard University, 1974).

18. A. D. Chandler, *Strategy and Structure: Chapters in the History of the American Industrial Enterprise* (Cambridge, Mass: MIT Press, 1962).

19. J. Little and L. Alexander, "K-Mart Stores: Where America Shops and Saves," in *Selected Cases in Strategic Management* (New York: McGraw-Hill, 1990), 227-31; "Investigating the Collapse of W. T. Grant," *Business Week,* July 19, 1976, 60-62; and "How W. T. Grant Lost $175 Million Last Year," *Business Week,* February 24, 1975, 74-76.

20. S. C. Wheelwright, "Strategy, Management, and Strategic Planning Approaches," *Interfaces* 14 (1984): 19-33.

21. M. Porter, "From Competitive Advantage to Corporate Strategy," *Harvard Business Review,* May-June 1987, pp. 43-59.

22. H. Ansoff, "Critique of Henry Mintzberg's 'The Design School: Reconsidering the Basic Premises of Strategic Management,' " *Strategic Management Journal,* Vol. 12, February 1991, pp. 449-61.

23. Anheuser-Busch Companies Annual Report, 1991.

24. H. Mintzberg, "Crafting Strategy," *Harvard Business Review,* July-August 1987, pp. 66-75.

25. R. Evered, "So What Is Strategy?" *Long Range Planning,* 1983, 16, pp. 57-72.

26. S. R. Baldwin and M. McConnell, "Strategic Planning: Process and Plan Go Hand in Hand," *Management Solution* (June 1988): 29-37.

27. M. Goold and J. Quinn, "The Paradox of Strategic Control, *Strategic Management Journal,* 11, 1990, 43-57.

28. *International Quality Study: The Definitive Study of the Best International Quality Management Practices* (A Joint Project of Ernst & Young and American Quality Foundation, 1991): 1.

29. Crosby, "The Next Effort."

30. K. Bertrand, "In Service, Perception Counts," *Business Marketing,* April 1989, 44+.

31. B. M. Cook, "Quality: The Pioneers Survey the Landscape," *Industryweek,* October 21, 1991, 68-73.

32. Jacob, "TQM: More Than a Dying Fad?"

33. L. L. Axline, "TQM: A Look in the Mirror," *Management Review,* July 1991, Vol. 80, No. 7, 64.

34. M. Barrier, "Small Firms Put Quality First," *Nation's Business,* May 1992, 22-32.

35. J. M. Juran, "Acing the Quality Quiz," *Across the Board,* July/August 1992, 58.

36. D. A. Garvin, "How the Baldridge Award Really Works," *Harvard Business Review* (November/December 1991): 80-93.

37. A. C. Fenwick, "Five Easy Lessons," *Quality Progress,* December 1991, 63-66.

38. V. Vaughn, "Disney Begins Massive Hiring Task," *Orlando Sentinel,* October 20, 1991, D-1.

39. S. Hagstrom, "U.S. Air Rebuilds," *Orlando Sentinel,* October 15, 1991, C-1; and C. P. Fotos, "USAir Is Building on Strengths to Survive in Fierce Market," *Aviation Week and Space Technology,* June 1, 1992, 33-36.

40. Ibid.

41. P. Drucker, *The Practice of Management* (New York: Harper, 1954).

42. K. Davis and J. Newstrom, *Human Behavior at Work in Organizational Behavior* (New York: McGraw-Hill, 1989): 209.

43. J. L. Mendelson, "Goal Setting: An Important Management Tool," in *Executive Skills: A Management by Objectives Approach* (Dubuque, Iowa: Brown, 1980).

44. Ibid.

45. J. Gordon, *Management and Organizational Behavior* (Boston: Allyn & Bacon, 1990): 129-32.

46. W. B. Werther and W. Heinz, "Refining MBO through Ne-

gotiations," in *Executive Skills: A Management by Objectives Approach* (Dubuque, Iowa: Brown, 1980).

47. J. N. Kondrasuk, "Studies in MBO Effectiveness," *Academy of Management Review* 6 (1981): 419-30.

48. G. Hofstede, "Motivation, Leadership, and Organization: Do American Theories Apply Abroad?" *Organizational Dynamics* (Summer 1980): 55.

49. A. S. Smith and A. P. Houser, *Personnel Management* (Reading, Mass: Addison-Wesley, 1986).

50. H. Dawley, "Friendly Makeover Completed: Company Moves Ailing Chain in New Direction—Maybe," *Restaurant Business,* April 10, 1992, 36.

51. D. D. McConkey, "Planning for Uncertainty," *Business Horizons,* January/February 1987, 40-43.

52. D. Harper, "Planning: One Step at a Time," *International Distribution,* June 1986, 37-42.

53. L. V. Gerstner, "Can Strategic Planning Payoff?" in *Perspectives on Strategic Marketing Management* (Boston: Allyn & Bacon, 1980).

54. J. Rosenzweig, F. Kast, and T. R. Mitchell, *The Frank and Ernest Manager* (Los Altos, Calif.: Crisp Publications, 1991).

55. See, for example, E. DeBono, *Six Thinking Hats* (Boston: Little Brown, 1985); and K. Albrecht, *Brain Power: Learn to Improve Your Thinking Skills* (Englewood Cliffs, N.J.: Prentice-Hall, 1990).

56. J. Martin, "Business Planning: The Gap between Theory and Practice," *Long Range Planning* 48 (1979).

57. "Why Hugh McColl Is Courting an Atlanta Belle"; and "Super Banker: NCNB's Hugh McColl Is out to Make History with His Bid for C&S/Sovran."

Strategic Planning in a Global Environment

CHAPTER 5

▼ CHAPTER OVERVIEW

The development of effective strategy is essential for survival in today's business world. Organizations don't just happen to be successful—rather they develop and implement strategies that are designed to ensure their long-term success. Through strategic planning, managers initiate the actions necessary to get the organization from where it is to where it wants to be. Developing a sustainable competitive advantage is the primary purpose of the strategic planning process.

This chapter examines strategic planning as a managerial process. This process involves four primary activities: (1) strategic analysis, (2) strategy formulation, (3) strategy implementation, and (4) strategic control. Special emphasis is given to strategic planning and strategy as a competitive tool for contemporary organizations operating in an increasingly competitive global environment.

▼ LEARNING OBJECTIVES

When you have finished studying this chapter,
you should be able to:

- Define strategic planning and describe its purpose and benefits.
- Explain the process of strategic planning.
- Describe strategic analysis as a part of the strategic planning process.
- Discuss how strategy is formulated at the corporate and business levels.
- Describe strategy in terms of grand strategy, generic strategy, and international strategy.
- Explain the role of strategy implementation in the strategic planning process, as well as the importance of functional strategy and the theory of "fit."
- Describe strategic control systems.
- Discuss how tomorrow's manager can achieve success through strategic planning.

MANAGERIAL INCIDENT

RCA: THE CHALLENGE OF RESPONDING TO ENVIRONMENTAL CHANGE

From the 1940s to the 1960s, the television division of RCA maintained a leadership position in the U.S. market. This position began to erode in the late 1960s, however, when a new type of competitor entered the market—foreign manufacturers.

As the largest single market in the world and an affluent society that maintained very liberal trade policies, the United States had become a very attractive market. Consequently, many foreign firms began to target the United States as a major market for their products. As foreign televisions flowed into the United States, RCA and other U.S. manufacturers began to experience tremendous competitive pressures.

The environment had changed—cheaper foreign imports had transformed the television industry. Product differentiation was difficult to achieve in an industry where all the competitors' products had the same characteristics. The greatest rewards went to the manufacturers who maintained the lowest costs and offered the lowest price.

Unfortunately, RCA was not strategically positioned to compete on the basis of low cost and low price. The company had two alternatives: (1) find a way to differentiate its products sufficiently to justify a higher price, or (2) reduce its cost structure significantly and compete on the basis of price. This was RCA's strategic dilemma.[1] ▼

INTRODUCTION

RCA faced an important strategic challenge. Meeting that challenge could make the difference between prosperity and demise for the company. If the managers at RCA failed to respond effectively to escalating foreign competition, the company might fail. But if they could develop a strategy that would provide RCA with a competitive edge in its marketplace, the company could prosper. The key seemed to lie in the development and implementation of effective competitive strategy.

Organizational strategy has been a topic of great interest for academics and practitioners for the last several decades. In fact, few managerial topics have received more attention in recent years than strategic planning. Effective strategic planning has been touted as a key solution to the reactive behavior that has characterized many U.S. corporations during the last several decades.

In this chapter, we examine the process of strategic planning, as well as the result of that process—the strategic plan. Special attention is given to each of the stages of the strategic planning process, which are strategic analysis, strategy formulation, strategy implementation, and strategic control. We will also see how strategy can serve as a tool for meeting the challenges of the twenty-first century.

Strategic planning
The process by which an organization makes decisions and takes action to enhance its long-run performance.

Strategic plan
A plan that identifies the markets in which an organization competes, as well as the ways in which it competes in those markets.

THE IMPORTANCE OF STRATEGIC PLANNING

As you may recall from Chapter 4, **strategic planning** is the process by which an organization makes decisions and takes actions that affect its long-run performance. A **strategic plan** is the output of the strategic planning process.[2] An organization's strategic plan provides direction by defining its strategic approach to business.[3] Central to the concept of strategic planning is the notion

A STRATEGY FOR VISION OF DREAMZ

Vision of Dreamz, founded in November 1992, is a company sponsored by Junior Achievement, funded by McDonnell Douglas, and created and managed by high school students from Long Beach, California. The students involved in this program were "at risk" kids, who normally don't participate in Junior Achievement. But this was a special project. The purpose of the program was to have teenagers develop a strategic plan for a minicorporation that they would create and operate. For the Vision of Dreamz' team, that included such activities as electing officers, selling stock for $1.00 per share, making and marketing a product, paying wages and taxes, and distributing dividends.

The founders of Vision of Dreamz, Nicole Woods and Jesse Richardson, discovered a great way to make money, keep costs down, produce a quality product, and promote teamwork. When they started their business, these business concepts were like a foreign language, but Nicole, Jesse, and the 11 other participants came to appreciate those concepts as they learned that making money in a creative and honest way can be more fun than getting into trouble.

Vision of Dreamz made teddy bears. The company bought teddy bears for $2.95, decorated them with $1.00's worth of ribbons, lace, and other ornaments, and sold them for $8.50 at Valentine's Day and Christmas. The company's managers made a number of strategic decisions that boosted profits considerably. For example, rather than giving employees raises, the managers decided to increase sales commissions from 10 percent to 25 percent. They also increased their returns by leveraging the company. Instead of selling 100 shares of stock, they sold only 53 shares and then borrowed $300 from their corporate partner, McDonnell Douglas. When it came time to liquidate the company after 12 weeks, stockholders had earned a 224 percent return on their original $1.00 investment. The team repaid the McDonnell Douglas loan in full and donated $40 to the church where they met every Thursday night.

Profits were not the only reward for their strategic planning efforts. Ultimately, the most rewarding payoff for the students who created Vision of Dreamz was a boost in self-esteem and self-reliance. In fact, Jesse's grades went from F's to B's, and he is now considering a career in the clothing industry. Nicole plans to open a booth at a flea market in Long Beach where she will continue to pursue her "vision of dreams."

of competitive advantage. As we noted in Chapter 4, the purpose of strategic planning is to move the organization from where it is to where it wants to be and, in the process, to develop a sustainable competitive advantage in its industry. Through strategic planning, managers develop strategies for achieving a competitive advantage over other organizations in their industry.

Strategic planning is essential for organizations of all sizes and types and in industries across the globe. In this chapter, we examine how strategic planning has affected the performance of many organizations, both large and small. In fact, Entrepreneurial Approach describes how even the smallest venture can benefit from strategic planning.[4]

THE BENEFITS OF STRATEGIC PLANNING

Strategic planning requires a great deal of managerial time, energy, and commitment. To justify the associated costs, strategic planning must also produce tangible benefits.[5] Research suggests that the benefits of strategic planning are both economic and behavioral.[6]

From an economic perspective, a number of studies suggest that organizations that plan strategically outperform those that do not. Researchers have examined organizations in such industries as petroleum, food, drug, steel, chemical, and machinery and have focused on a variety of financial measures including return on investment, return on equity, and earnings per share. Their findings suggest that there are financial benefits associated with strategic planning.

The process of strategic planning can also produce behavioral benefits. Since effective planning requires the involvement of a broad base of organizational members, the benefits associated with participatory management are typically associated with strategic planning. These include:

- An increased likelihood of identifying organizational and environmental conditions that may create problems in the long run.
- Better decisions as a result of the group decision-making process.
- More successful implementation of the organization's strategy because organizational members who participated in the planning process understand the plan and are more willing to change.[7]

Given the potential benefits of strategic planning and the potential costs of the failure to plan, most organizations recognize that strategic planning is essential. In fact, many organizations stress that being a strategist is an important part of being a manager.[8]

STRATEGIC PLANNING AS A PROCESS

Figure 5.1 illustrates a model of the strategic planning process that was introduced in Chapter 4. This model is simple, straightforward, and applicable to a wide variety of organizational situations. It includes: (1) strategic analysis, (2) strategy formulation, (3) strategy implementation, and (4) strategic control. As the feedback lines in the model indicate, the strategic planning process is interactive and self-renewing. The four stages are interrelated, and the process continues as changes in the business environment and the organization create a need for revised strategic plans.[9]

Each stage of the strategic planning process raises an important question that must be addressed when developing a strategic plan:

- Strategic analysis asks, "What is the current position of the organization?"
- Strategy formulation asks, "Where does the organization want to be?"
- Strategy implementation asks, "How can the organization get to where it wants to be?"

▼ **FIGURE 5.1**
The Process of Strategic Planning

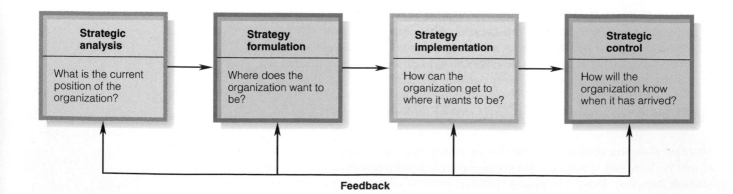

Strategic analysis	Strategy formulation	Strategy implementation	Strategic control
What is the current position of the organization?	Where does the organization want to be?	How can the organization get to where it wants to be?	How will the organization know when it has arrived?

Feedback

▼ Front line workers are important internal resources for many firms—resources that must be evaluated as part of an internal analysis. Service organizations, like this hotel, will find that these employees are critical to their long-term success.

● Strategic control asks, "How will the organization know when it has arrived?"

By working through the strategic planning process and answering each question, a comprehensive strategic plan can be developed.

The strategic planning process is the focus of the remainder of this chapter. The specific activities associated with each stage of the process are discussed in the following sections.

STRATEGIC ANALYSIS: ASSESSMENT WITHIN A GLOBAL ENVIRONMENT

The first stage of the strategic planning process is strategic analysis. The purpose of strategic analysis is to evaluate the present situation of the organization.[10] Until you understand the current position of the organization, it is impossible to determine where it could and should be.[11] Strategic analysis requires two primary activities: (1) internal analysis and (2) environmental analysis.

CONDUCTING AN INTERNAL ANALYSIS

Strategic analysis requires a thorough evaluation of the internal operations of the organization. The purpose of internal analysis is to identify the organizational assets, resources, skills, and processes that represent either strengths or weaknesses. Strengths are aspects of the organization's operations that represent potential competitive advantages or distinctive competencies,[12] while weaknesses are areas that are in need of improvement.

Several areas of the organization's operations should be examined in an internal analysis. Key areas to be assessed include the marketing, financial, research and development, production operations, and general management capabilities. These areas are typically evaluated in terms of the extent to which they foster a quality orientation and support the competitive advantage sought by the organization. Table 5.1 lists a number of other variables that should be evaluated when conducting an internal analysis.[13]

▼ **TABLE 5.1**   Internal Organizational Factors

MARKETING CAPABILITIES	FINANCIAL CAPABILITIES	GENERAL MANAGEMENT CAPABILITIES	R & D CAPABILITIES	PRODUCTION AND OPERATIONS CAPABILITIES
Product mix	Liquidity	Employee relations	Basic and applied product research competencies	Purchasing system
Market share position	Leverage	Organizational structure	Process research competencies	Capacity (plant & equipment)
Market research capabilities	Efficiency/asset utilization	Compensation system	Physical facilities (i.e., laboratory)	Location of facilities
Distribution systems	Profitability	Rules, policies, and procedures	Organization of R & D unit	Inventory management system
Sales organizations	Earnings per share	Quality of top management	Communication within the organization	Maintenance system
Customer goodwill and brand loyalty	Trend analysis	Planning capabilities	Quality of technological forecasting	Use of economies of scale
Promotion strategies			Success ratio of new product innovations to products brought to market	Use of modern technologies (i.e., robotics)
Pricing strategies				

SOURCE: J. Montanari, C. Morgan, and J. Bracker, *Strategic Management: A Choice Approach* (Chicago: Dryden Press, 1990), 81-85.

Consider RCA's situation as described in the Managerial Incident at the beginning of this chapter. RCA lost its leadership position in the television industry largely as a result of a key internal weakness—the company's operating system was less efficient than that of its foreign competitors. These inefficiencies resulted in a higher cost structure for the company and higher prices for consumers. This aspect of RCA's internal environment represented a strategic weakness that, if not corrected, would result in lost sales and an unfavorable long-term outlook for the firm.

One of the most important aspects of an organization's internal environment is its human resources. In fact, some management scholars suggest that the only thing that truly distinguishes one organization from another is its people. The human resources of the organization, from top management down to front-line workers, are what determine the ability of the organization to achieve a competitive advantage in its industry.

The increasing diversity of the U.S. workforce presents a potential strategic advantage for many organizations. To the extent that managers are prepared to capitalize on the breadth of thought and experience that is inherent in a diverse workforce, they can formulate more creative strategies and plans. To do so, however, organizations must consciously attempt to recruit individuals of both genders, varying nationalities, and differing racial and ethnic backgrounds and then must involve them in the planning process.

EVALUATING THE EXTERNAL ENVIRONMENT

The second area to be assessed in a strategic analysis is the external environment of the organization. The purpose of an external analysis is to identify those aspects of the environment that represent either an opportunity or a

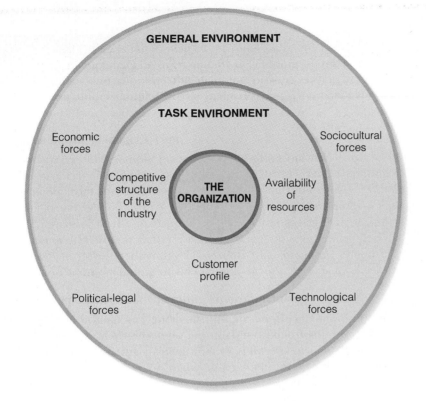

▼ **FIGURE 5.2**

Dimensions of the Global External Environment

threat. Opportunities are those environmental trends on which the organization can capitalize and improve its competitive position. External threats are conditions that jeopardize the organization's ability to prosper in the long term.

Figure 5.2 illustrates the primary dimensions of a global external environment. The external environment is divided into two major components—the general environment and the task environment. The **general environment** includes environmental forces that are beyond the influence of the organization and over which it has no control. Forces in the **task environment** are within the organization's operating environment, and it may influence them to some degree.

General Environment

The general component of an organization's external environment includes economic, sociocultural, technological, and political-legal factors. The analysis must consider the global dimensions of all of these factors as well as their domestic effects. Table 5.2 lists examples of trends in each of these areas that might affect an organization's strategic plans.[14]

Economic Environment   The economic component of the general environment is represented by the general state of both the domestic and the world economy. The health of the domestic economy is reflected by variables such as total gross domestic product (GDP), growth in the GDP, interest rates, the inflation rate, the consumer price index, and unemployment rates. Similar measures can be used to evaluate the world economy. World trade and foreign direct investment trends are also useful for that analysis.

Although a favorable economic climate generally represents opportunities for growth, this is not the case for all businesses. The alcoholic beverage industry, for example, has traditionally fared well during times of economic downturn. Mobile homes, bologna, and car repair services are other examples

General environment
Those environmental forces that are beyond a firm's influence and over which it has no control.

Task environment
Those environmental forces that are within the firm's operating environment and over which the firm has some degree of control.

▼ **TABLE 5.2**   Sample Issues in the General Environment

SOCIOCULTURAL	ECONOMIC	TECHNOLOGICAL	POLITICAL-LEGAL
Lifestyle changes	GNP trends	Total federal spending for R & D	Antitrust regulations
Career expectations	Interest rates	Total industry spending for R & D	Environmental protection laws
Consumer activism	Money supply	Focus of technological efforts	Tax laws
Rate of family formation	Inflation rates	Patent protection	Special incentives
Growth rate of population	Unemployment levels	New products	Foreign trade regulations
Regional shifts in population	Wage/price controls	New developments in technology transfer from lab to marketplace	Attitudes toward foreign companies
Life expectancies	Devaluation/revaluation	Productivity improvements through automation	Laws on hiring and promotion
Birth rates	Energy availability and cost		Stability of government
	Disposable and discretionary income		

SOURCE: T. Wheelen and J. D. Hunger, *Strategic Management* (Reading, Mass.: Addison-Wesley, 1990), 100.

of products and services that are in greater demand during poor economic times. Regardless of the direction of the effect, the economy is generally considered to be a strong determinant of the demand for goods and services. Consequently, forecasts of economic activity will influence the strategic plans of most organizations.

Sociocultural Environment   The sociocultural component of the general environment is represented by the attitudes, behavior patterns, and lifestyles of the individuals who ultimately purchase the products or services of the organization. In addition, the analysis must also consider demographic conditions and trends. As these aspects of the sociocultural environment change, so must the strategy of organizations that are affected by such changes.

Although some sociocultural trends cross national boundaries (e.g., the popularity of jeans among young people), not all developments occur on a global basis. In fact, many aspects of the sociocultural environment are specific to certain nations or groups of nations. Consequently, organizations that operate internationally often must cope with multiple heterogeneous sociocultural environments and therefore must develop strategies to deal with different environmental conditions.

One of the most important sociocultural trends in this country (and others) in the last several decades has been the increasing number of women entering the workforce. Consider, for example, the effect of this trend on the demand for such products and services as convenience appliances, professional apparel, child care, and housekeeping services. Further, many businesses have adapted their products and services to respond to the slightly different needs of the female business consumer. For example, briefcases now come in sleeker and lighter designs, women's shoes can be purchased in more sensible styles, and room accommodations with special services for female patrons are available at a number of hotel chains.

Technological Environment   Technological forces are the third component of the general environment. They include changes in technology that affect the way organizations operate or the products and services they provide. To keep abreast of technological trends, many organizations engage in "technology forecasting." Such forecasts identify trends in technology that require adaptation on the part of the organization.

The success of many organizations is dependent upon their ability to identify and respond to technological changes. IBM, General Motors, and Federal

KAO CORPORATIONS: TOTAL FLEXIBILITY

Watch out U.S. cosmetic and soap manufacturers, here comes Kao Corporation. Kao is the largest soap and cosmetic manufacturer in Japan and the sixth largest in the world. Kao has achieved its position, in part, through its innovative manufacturing methods. But the company also attributes much of its success to a massive computer information system that serves as a powerful competitive weapon.

One computer system links sales, marketing, production, purchasing, shipping, accounting, research and development, cash registers from retailers around the globe, and thousands of portable computers used by Kao salespeople. The company's information is so complete that its accountants can produce a "year-end closing statement by noon of the first day of the new year."

Thanks to this information system, managers can see sales and production figures on a daily basis. This information enables Kao and its wholesalers to predict future demand and deliver orders to its 280,000 customers, worldwide, within 24 hours. Computer linkages allow factories to know what to produce because changes in consumer demand are detected immediately. The computer systems also provide information on what products are not selling. Managers also know when a competitor is running a sale and can adjust their prices accordingly.

When companies bring out new products, they usually test-market the items first. Often months pass before management receives adequate feedback about the success or failure of the products. Kao's managers have that information in two weeks through a test-market operation called Echo System, which brings point-of-sale information from 216 retailers together to gauge the success of a new product.

Kao's has risen to a leading position in Japan's highly competitive soap and cosmetics industry in only 10 years. By continuing its global strategy and maintaining flexibility through the use of its fast-paced information systems, Kao is well positioned to be the global market leader in the long term.

Express are just a few examples of firms that must keep abreast of technological changes if they hope to remain successful in the long term.

One of the most significant technological trends of the last several decades has been the increasing availability and affordability of management information systems. Through these systems, managers have access to information that can improve the way they operate and manage their businesses. The grocery store industry, for example, has been transformed by the introduction of scanner technology. Not only have scanners improved the efficiency of the grocery checkout process, but they also provide important inventory management information to support procurement and warehousing efforts. Grocery stores that do not take advantage of such technology are at a competitive disadvantage.

Global Perspective describes how Kao Corporation uses its information technology to help service its customers worldwide.[15] This company has used its management information system to build an enviable position in the global market for cosmetics and soap.

Political-Legal Environment   The final component of an organization's general environment is its political-legal environment. The political-legal environment includes the regulatory parameters within which the organization must operate. Tax policy, trade regulations, minimum wage legislation, and pollution standards are just a few examples of political-legal issues that can affect the strategic plans of an organization. Like the sociocultural environment, the political-legal environment often varies dramatically from nation to nation. As a consequence, organizations that operate internationally must develop a strategy for dealing with multiple political-legal systems.

The political-legal component of environment can have a significant effect on the strategic plans of many organizations. Consider, for example, how McDonald's and other fast-food restaurants would be affected by an increase in the minimum wage. These companies would likely look for ways to maximize the efficiency of their human resources. In addition, new pricing strategies might be necessary in light of increased labor costs.

Task Environment

In addition to general environmental issues, organizations must also be aware of trends in the task environment. Recall that these forces are within the organization's operating arena, and may be influenced, to some degree, by the organization. Critical task environmental variables include the competition in an industry, the profiles of the targeted customer base, and the availability of resources.

Competition   In assessing the competition in a given industry, it is important to evaluate both individual competitors and the way they interact. Where possible, competitors should be evaluated using a common set of characteristics. For example, each competitor might be assessed in light of its market share, marketing strategy, product mix, product quality, and financial strength. Such information provides managers with a better understanding of how their organization compares to its competitors, as well as with a general sense of the roles that each plays within the industry. One can rest assured that IBM, Compaq, Apple, and Hewlett Packard maintain sophisticated systems for tracking and evaluating the strategic moves of all the competitors in the computer industry.

Competitive analysis has become increasingly complex as more and more industries have globalized. Researching the strategies of foreign competitors is often difficult because many international firms are not subject to the same disclosure regulations as U.S. firms. Nevertheless, it is an essential aspect of the strategic planning process, and managers must commit the time and energy necessary to gain a clear understanding of their competitors both domestically and globally.

Customers   Customer profiles must also be assessed as part of the strategic analysis. At a time when the "customer is king" philosophy has been embraced by organizations across the globe, and a quality orientation has become essential to the success of most organizations, it is imperative to have an in-depth understanding of the characteristics, needs, and expectations of the organization's customers.

An organization's customer may be another firm in the production chain, or it may be the ultimate consumer. When an organization's customers are mainly industrial or wholesale clients, it needs information about the types of organizations that are using its products and services, their specific needs and expectations, their financial health, and the extent to which they are dependent upon the organization's products and services.

When an organization's customers are consumers, their demographic and psychographic characteristics, as well as their specific needs and expectations, are the most relevant dimensions for analysis. Relevant demographic characteristics include average age, income levels, gender, and marital status. Psy-

▼ Evaluating the needs of customers is an essential part of the strategic planning process. However, doing so is often more difficult today since customers often come from different parts of the world and may have very different tastes and desires. This man admires a garment being sold by a street vendor in an international location.

chographic characteristics relating to the consumer's lifestyle and personality may also be critical determinants of buying behavior.

Again, as with competitive analysis, the globalization of the marketplace has complicated the process of customer analysis. With customers spread across the globe, the relevant dimensions for analysis are more difficult to identify, evaluate, and predict. Therefore, managers in international organizations must take special care to ensure that they have a clear understanding of their customers in each national market served.

Resource Availability   Resource availability is the final component of the organization's task environment. The term "resource" can be applied to a broad range of inputs and may refer to raw materials, personnel, or capital. To the extent that high-quality, low-cost resources are available to the organization, opportunities exist to create marketable products or services. When any resource is constrained, the organization faces a threat to its operations. Thus, strategic plans will be affected by the availability of the resources, both domestically and globally, needed to produce goods and services.

Strategic analysis provides important information about the organization's existing situation. As we have seen, the purpose of this stage of the strategic planning process is to answer the question, "what is the current position of the organization?" By examining the internal and external environment of the organization, this question can be answered. Having addressed this question, it is time to move to the second stage of the strategic management process—the strategy formulation stage.

STRATEGY FORMULATION: ACHIEVING ▬▬▬▬▬▬ A COMPETITIVE ADVANTAGE

Once the strategic analysis is completed and the current position of the organization has been assessed, corporate and business strategy can be formulated. Recall that strategy formulation addresses the question, "where does the organization want to be?" Answering that question requires (1) establishing the mission of the organization, (2) setting strategic goals, (3) identifying strategic alternatives, and (4) evaluating and choosing the strategy that provides a competitive advantage and optimizes the performance of the organization in the long term.

ESTABLISHING AN ORGANIZATIONAL MISSION

Based on the information derived from the strategic analysis, an organizational mission can be developed. An **organizational mission** defines the reason(s) for which the organization exists and provides strategic direction for the members of the organization.[16] It is a statement of the overall purpose of the organization and describes the attributes that distinguish it from other organizations of its type.[17]

A mission statement should be more than words on a piece of paper. It should be a living, breathing document that provides both information and inspiration for the members of the organization. Such documents should reflect the strategic vision of the leaders of the organization with regard to what the organization is and what it can become. A mission statement provides focus for the organization by getting its members to work together in the pursuit of common goals.[18]

Although mission statements will vary greatly among firms, every mission statement should describe three primary aspects of the organization: (1) primary products or services, (2) distinctive competitive advantage(s), and

Organizational mission
The reasons for which the organization exists; and provides strategic direction for the members of the organization.

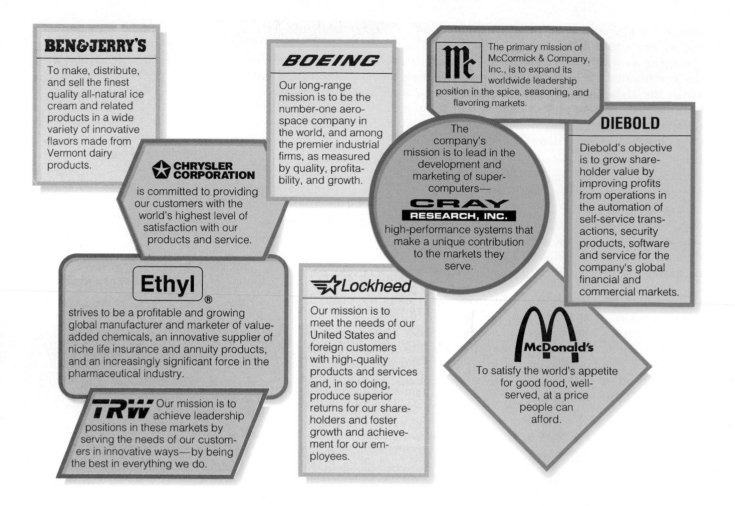

▼ FIGURE 5.3
Corporate Mission Statements

SOURCE: D. L. Calfee, "Get Your Mission Statement Working," *Management Review*, January 1993, 54-57.

(3) overall strategy for ensuring long-term success. This information serves as the foundation upon which corporate and business strategy is built. If, for example, the mission of your university is to meet the educational needs of individuals in your state by offering innovative programs in the arts, sciences, business, engineering, and health care, the strategy of the university should be developed to fulfill that mission.

Figure 5.3 contains the mission statements for a number of organizations.[19] Now that you have an understanding of how important a mission statement can be, evaluate a mission statement as explained in Meeting the Challenge.

STRATEGIC GOAL SETTING

Strategic goals
The results that an organization seeks to achieve in the long-term.

Once the mission of the organization has been developed, strategic goals can be established. **Strategic goals** are very broad statements of the results that an organization wishes to achieve in the long term. Such goals relate to the mission of the organization and specify the level of performance that it desires to achieve.

Most organizations establish their goals to reflect their perception of "success." In many organizations, managers look to profit as an indicator of success, and maximizing profit becomes their primary strategic goal. However, Peter Drucker, a prominent management theorist, warns against focusing solely on profit as a measure of success. He suggests that a preoccupation with profits alone can lead to short-term thinking and reactive management behavior.

MAKING A MISSION STATEMENT WORK

The following exercise can help you develop your skills at evaluating mission statements. Choose a mission statement to evaluate. You may want to use one of the missions in Figure 5.3 or the mission statement of an organization that you have worked for or work for now. Evaluate the mission statement by responding to each of the following questions. Use a scale of 1 (not at all) to 5 (to a high degree) to indicate how well the mission statement meets each of the criteria. Place the number that corresponds to your response on the line to the left of each statement.

To a High Degree		Somewhat		Not at All
5	4	3	2	1

_____ 1. To what degree does the mission statement discuss the organization's primary products or services?

_____ 2. To what degree does the mission statement consider the organization's competitive advantage(s)?

_____ 3. To what degree does the mission statement describe the attributes of the organization that distinguish it from others of its type?

_____ 4. To what degree does the mission statement reflect the strategic vision of the organization's leaders?

_____ 5. To what degree does the mission statement discuss the organization's overall strategy for long-term success?

_____   Total

Add the numbers to obtain the total score. Scores can range from a low of 5 to a high of 25. If the mission statement you examined scored lower than 20, how would you revise the statement so that it would meet the criteria of an effective mission?

Rather, success should be operationalized more broadly and should include such things as market standing, innovation, productivity, physical and financial resources, profitability, managerial performance and development, worker performance and attitudes, and public responsibility.[20]

Further, it is important to recognize that strategic success can vary greatly across organizations and between industries. Two organizations may measure and evaluate success in dramatically different ways. For example, a growth-oriented firm such as Blockbuster Video may stress market share gains, whereas an organization that operates in a mature, slow-growth industry, such as General Foods, may place its emphasis on maximizing bottom-line profitability.

Several characteristics are associated with effective strategic goals. Because the goals established during the planning process serve as a benchmark by which the organization will eventually evaluate its performance, it is important that they be: (1) specific, (2) measurable, (3) time linked, and (4) realistic, but challenging. Table 5.3 provides some guidance on how to develop goals that meet these criteria.

PART II   Planning Challenges in the 21st Century

▼ **TABLE 5.3**   Criteria for Effective Goals

Effective goals should meet the following criteria:

- *Specific goals* relate to a particular and easily defined performance area. For example, setting a goal of increasing productivity by 40 percent is not meaningful if "productivity" is not defined. Will productivity be measured by sales/employee? Sales/square foot? Cost/unit? Effective goals must be specific as to what will be evaluated.

- *Measurable goals* are usually expressed in quantitative terms. For example, increasing sales by 20 percent and reducing costs by 15 percent are examples of quantitative goals. Sometimes, however, it is necessary to express goals in qualitative terms. For example, an organization might establish a goal of being more socially responsive. While this goal cannot be expressed quantitatively, it is an important qualitative goal against which the organization will eventually evaluate its performance. Where possible, however, goals should be established in clearly measurable, quantitative terms.

- *Time-linked goals* are to be achieved within a specified time period. For example, an organization might establish a goal of increasing market share by 3 percent by 1998. Because the goal is time linked, it provides the organization with a deadline for achieving its target performance.

- *Realistic, but challenging goals* provide a challenge for those who must meet them, but the challenge should not be so great that the goal cannot be achieved. People don't strive to achieve goals that are set unrealistically high. On the other hand, a goal that is set too low is not motivating. Finding the balance between challenge and realism is important in setting goals.

IDENTIFYING STRATEGIC ALTERNATIVES

The third stage of the strategy formulation process involves identifying strategic alternatives. These alternatives should be developed in light of the strengths, weaknesses, opportunities, and threats facing the organization, its mission and its strategic goals. Strategic alternatives should focus on optimizing organizational performance in the long term.[21]

Strategy can be defined in a variety of ways. The following sections describe three ways to define strategic alternatives.

Grand Strategy

Many organizations define their strategic alternatives in terms of grand strategies. A **grand strategy** is a comprehensive, general approach for achieving the strategic goals of an organization.[22] Grand strategies which can be applied at both the corporate and business levels, fall into three broad categories: stability, growth, and retrenchment strategies.

Stability Strategies   Stability strategies are intended to ensure continuity in the operations and performance of the organization. At the corporate level, stability implies that the organization will remain in the same line(s) of business as it has in the past. No new businesses are added; no businesses are eliminated. The organization maintains a stable and unchanged corporate portfolio. Wendy's is an example of a firm that began as and continues to be a chain of fast food restaurants. It has pursued a strategy of stability from inception.

At the business level, stability strategies require very little, if any, change in the organization's product, service, or market focus. Organizations that pursue stability strategies continue to offer the same products and services to the same target markets as in the past. They may, however, attempt to capture a larger share of their existing market through market penetration.

Grand strategy
A comprehensive, general approach for achieving the strategic goals of an organization.

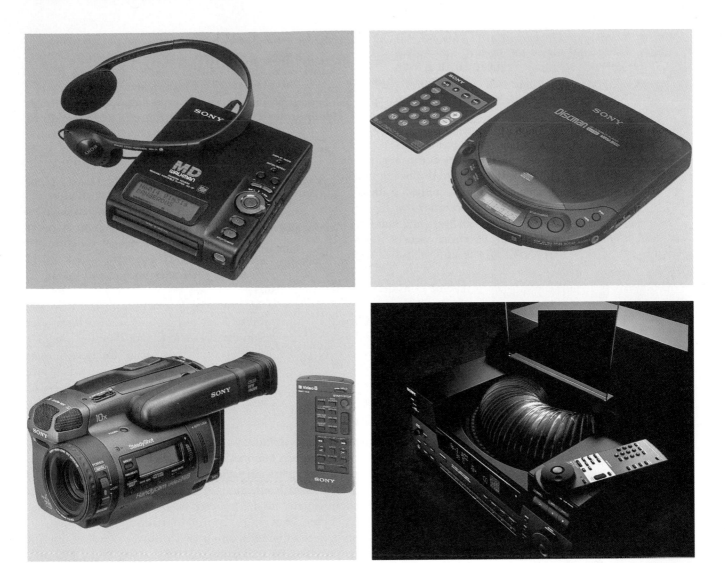

Growth Strategies   Growth strategies are designed to increase the sales and profits of the organization. At the corporate level, growth strategies imply the addition of one or more new businesses to the corporate portfolio. This may be accomplished by adding a business that has synergistic potential with an existing business unit or by adding a business that is unrelated to the firm's existing businesses. General Mills, for example, at one time pursued an aggressive strategy of growth at the corporate level. The company acquired and developed several businesses that were unrelated to its core food products business (e.g., Monet Jewelry, Talbots mail order) as well as several restaurants that were synergistically related (e.g., Red Lobster, Darryl's, and Casa Gallardo).

At the business level, growth strategies involve the development of new products for new or existing markets or the entry into new markets with existing products. The purpose of growth strategies is to increase the sales and profits of the organization in the long term and to position the organization as a market leader within its industry.

In many cases, growth strategies focus on being innovative, seeking out new opportunities, and taking risks. Such strategies are suitable for organizations that operate in dynamic, growing environments where creativity and organizational responsiveness are often more important than efficiency. Sony is an example of a firm that offers a steady stream of innovative product alter-

▼ Sony serves as an excellent example of an organization that has achieved growth through new product introductions. This company has distinguished itself as a leader in the electronic products industry through a focus on innovation, research and development, and product development.

▼ Food Lion is a company that has distinguished itself as a low cost leader in the grocery store industry. Though a focus on cost savings at the operational level, this organization has managed to keep prices low, while achieving a profit margin comparable to the industry average.

Generic strategies
The fundamental way in which an organization competes in the marketplace.

Cost leadership strategy
A strategy for competing on the basis of price.

natives—many of them displace the firm's existing products, but all contribute to the organization's growth in sales and profits.

Retrenchment Strategies   The purpose of retrenchment strategy is to reverse negative sales and profitability trends. At the corporate level, retrenchment often requires the elimination of one or more business units either through divestment (the sale of the unit as an ongoing concern) or through liquidation (the sale of assets of the business unit). The cash generated from the elimination of a business unit is often used to acquire other business units, build more promising units, or reduce corporate debt.

At the business level, retrenchment strategy focuses on streamlining the operations of the organization by reducing costs and assets. Such reductions may require plant closings, the sale of plant and equipment, spending cuts, or a reduction in the workforce of the organization. Further, new systems, processes, and procedures must be designed to support the new, leaner organization. If the retrenchment strategy is successful, stability or growth strategies may be considered in the long term.

To illustrate retrenchment, consider the classic example of Lee Iacocca's efforts to restore Chrysler to profitability. This turnaround was accomplished by cutting costs and assets, redesigning more efficient and effective organizational systems, and slowly rebuilding the company's image for quality automobiles. More recently, we have seen retrenchment efforts by one-time giants IBM, General Motors, and Sears. As we will see later, IBAX also used a retrenchment strategy to improve its industry position.

Generic Strategy

While no two strategies are exactly alike, the strategies of some organizations do have common characteristics. Michael Porter, a well-known Harvard professor of industrial economics, has identified three **generic strategies** that describe the strategy of most organizations.[23] Generic strategies reflect the primary way in which an organization competes in its market. They are commonly referred to as: (1) cost leadership, (2) differentiation, and (3) focus.

Porter defines the generic strategies along two primary dimensions—the competitive advantage provided by the strategy and the competitive scope of the strategy. Competitive advantage is achieved by offering customers superior value either through a lower price or through a differentiated product or service that justifies a higher price. Competitive scope refers to the breadth of the market targeted by the organization. Some organizations target their products and services to very broad markets, while others identify a relatively narrow segment of the market.

The matrix in Figure 5.4 identifies the three generic strategies based on competitive advantage and competitive scope.[24] As you will note, the focus strategy has been broken into two separate strategies depending on whether the competitive advantage sought is cost leadership or differentiation.

Cost Leadership   Organizations that pursue a **cost leadership strategy** compete on the basis of price. To do so, the organization must be highly efficient so that it can achieve a low-cost position in the industry. Costs may be minimized by maximizing capacity utilization, achieving size advantages (economies of scale), capitalizing on technology improvements, or employing a more experienced workforce.

Numerous organizations and products have succeeded based on cost leadership. Examples include Bic pens, Timex watches, Budget motels, and Food Lion grocery stores. Each has concentrated on maximizing the efficiency of its production/delivery system, achieving a lower cost structure than its compet-

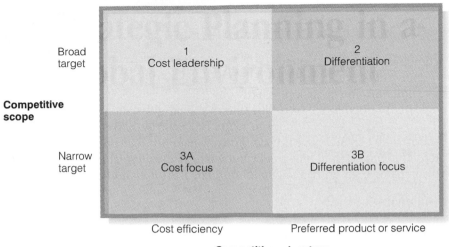

▼ **FIGURE 5.4**
Generic Strategies Matrix

SOURCE: Adapted from M. Porter, *Competitive Advantage: Creating and Sustaining Superior Performance* (New York: Free Press, 1985).

itors, and passing the benefit of lower costs on to the consumer in the form of lower prices.

Differentiation   Organizations that pursue a **differentiation strategy** compete by offering products or services that are differentiated from those of their competitors in some way. The company charges a higher price based on the differentiated product or service feature. Distinctive characteristics may include exceptional customer service, quality, dependability, availability, innovation, or image. Managing for Excellence describes how one company succeeded in a highly competitive industry by differentiating its products and services on the basis of quality.[25]

Many organizations pursue a differentiation strategy. Examples of products that have succeeded through such a strategy include Cross pens, Seiko watches, and Maytag appliances. Consider Volvo cars for a moment. What is the differentiating characteristic of these vehicles? Has this differentiation strategy been successful for Volvo?

Focus   The final generic strategy identified by Porter is a focus strategy. A **focus strategy** occurs when an organization targets a specific, narrow segment of the market and thereby avoids competing with other competitors that target a broader segment of the market. Further, companies that pursue a focus strategy may compete in their niche market with either a cost leadership or a differentiation strategy. Therefore, the focus strategy appears in two boxes of the matrix in Figure 5.4. If the market segment is very narrow and competition is extremely limited, however, neither competitive advantage may be necessary.

Examples of products that have succeeded based on a focus strategy include BMW motorcycles, A&W root beer, and White Castle hamburgers. A prime example of an organization that has used such a strategy within the grocery store industry is Fiesta Mart, a Texas-based grocery store chain that caters specifically to Hispanic consumers.

International Strategy

Organizations choose to engage in international business activity for a variety of reasons.[26] Many are trying to improve production efficiency by taking advantage of lower labor costs or better access to raw material. Others may be seeking new market opportunities. Regardless of the motive, an organization

Differentiation strategy
A strategy for competing by offering products or services that are differentiated from those of competitors.

Focus strategy
A strategy for competing by targeting a specific and narrow segment of the market.

MANAGING FOR EXCELLENCE

PHOTRONICS: THE GOAL IS "CUSTOMER DELIGHT"

It's not easy for a small manufacturer to compete with giants, but Photronics, Inc., of Brookfield, Connecticut, has been doing so successfully for years. Since its establishment in 1969, Photronics has become one of the world's leading microchip manufacturers, competing with such giants as Du Pont and Topan, a $7 billion Japanese company. Photronics uses sophisticated film images involving a technique called photomasking to reduce large computer chip circuits to microscopic size. The photomasking concept of creating microchips is similar to shrinking a photograph.

As an industry leader, Photronics had a number of strengths that provided certain competitive advantages. Photronics was recognized for its product leadership and total quality programs. The total quality programs created partnerships that resulted in a seamless interface between the company and its customers. The company's customers could find out the status of their products at any point in the production process. In addition, Photronics used its marketing function to assess the needs of its customers and then positioned its marketing representatives in offices across the United States and globally to satisfy these needs. Finally, Photronics had a premier human resources program that attracted first-rate scientific and manufacturing personnel.

To continue the company's success and to strengthen its position in the domestic market, the construction of a new manufacturing facility in California's Silicon Valley became necessary. Photronics redirected its financial policies to allow outside investors to purchase equity in the company. As a result, the company's initial stock offering in 1987 funded the construction of the California manufacturing facility. The success of the 1987 equity issue prompted Photronics to finance its global expansion efforts with additional stock offerings in 1990 and 1991.

Through a focus on differentiating its products and services on the basis of quality, Photronics has achieved excellent performance results. Photronics has a healthy balance sheet and has shown strong profits in 22 of the last 23 years. As a result of its commitment to excellence, Photronics has become the preferred supplier to three of Japan's largest microchip manufacturers—Toshiba, Mitsubishi, and Fujitsu.

that pursues an international strategy must make decisions about both its mode of entry into international markets and the focus of its strategy.

Mode of Entry An organization can enter an international market in several different ways. Each mode of entry offers certain advantages and disadvantages and requires a different level of commitment. Commitment may be thought of as a loss of flexibility to withdraw from a market. In other words, once a strategic decision has been made to enter a particular international market, the entry mode selected will determine how easily the organization can rescind its decision and cease operations in that market.

Entry modes, and the associated commitment, range from informal agreements with export management companies to contractual obligations with overseas licensees, contractors, or franchisors to actual investment in foreign assets via joint ventures or wholly owned subsidiaries. Obviously, the more attractive the market identified and the more experience the organization has

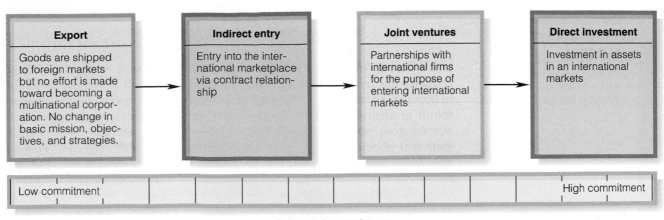

Degree of commitment

with international business activities, the more willing management may be to make a strong commitment to that market.

Figure 5.5 illustrates four different entry modes and the level of commitment associated with each. Many organizations have used these modes of entry to enter new markets and develop a global presence in their respective industries.[27]

Multidomestic versus Global Strategic Focus   A second dimension of international strategy relates to the focus of the strategy, which may be either multidomestic or global. An organization pursues a **multidomestic strategy** when it operates in multiple international markets and follows an independent strategy in each market. Essentially, the organization views each nation in which it operates as a distinct host country market. There is not a conscious attempt to transport products, services, technology, managerial skills, or other resources across national boundaries. Consequently, the organization recognizes few economies of scale or operating efficiencies associated with the integration of its overseas units. An international organization that pursues a multidomestic strategy can offer products or services tailored to meet differing market demands. Many cosmetic, food, and entertainment companies pursue multidomestic strategies.

With a **global strategy,** the organization pursues an integrated strategy in multiple national markets. National boundaries no longer define the firm's competitive spheres; competitive boundaries are represented simply by the world marketplace. Where possible, efficiency and standardization serve as the driving forces for strategy. Product differences are minimized. Transfer of resources, technology, and managerial skills is critical to the implementation of the strategy. IBM and Sony are examples of firms that have pursued a global strategy effectively. Both of these organizations market relatively standardized products to high-volume world markets.

EVALUATING AND CHOOSING STRATEGY

Designing strategy can be a very challenging task. When determining an optimal strategy for the organization, managers can draw upon a variety of tools and techniques to generate, evaluate, and choose between strategic alternatives. Among the most popular evaluation and decision-making techniques are portfolio assessment models and decision matrices.

Portfolio assessment models provide a mechanism for evaluating an organization's portfolio of businesses, products, or services. These models classify the organization's portfolio of holdings into categories based on certain im-

▼ FIGURE 5.5
International Strategies and Commitment

Multidomestic strategy
A strategy for competing in multiple international markets by tailoring products and services to meet the specific needs of each host country market.

Global strategy
A strategy for competing in multiple international markets with a standard line of products and services.

portant criteria (e.g., growth rate, competitive position). Based on that classification, the organization's portfolio is assessed as to the appropriateness of the mix of business units, products, or services. The optimal strategy for each business unit, product, or service may vary according to its position in the portfolio. Popular portfolio assessment models include the BCG growth-share matrix and the General Electric industry attractiveness/business strength matrix. Both of these portfolio assessment models are discussed in Chapter 7.

Decision matrices help managers choose between strategic alternatives. A decision matrix provides a method for evaluating alternative strategies according to the criteria that the organization's managers consider most important (contribution toward sales growth, market share growth, profitability, and the like). Managers rate strategic alternatives according to the established criteria and select the alternative that has the best overall rating. Chapter 7 also provides a detailed discussion of decision matrices that can be used to make strategic choices.

Once the strategy formulation stage of the strategic planning process is complete, it is time to begin implementing the strategy. Strategy implementation is a critical and complex component of the strategic planning process.

STRATEGY IMPLEMENTATION: FOCUSING ON RESULTS

The importance of strategy implementation should never be underestimated for the best formulated strategy is worthless if it cannot be implemented effectively. If an organization is to achieve the best results from its strategic planning efforts, it must ensure that its strategy is put into action.

Few managers find it difficult to formulate competitive strategy. When it comes time to execute the plan, however, many experience difficulty. Why is that so? Many managers simply underestimate and undermanage the strategy implementation process. Organizations that achieve strategic success commit a tremendous amount of time, energy, and effort to making sure that the strategy is implemented effectively.[28]

Recall that strategy implementation addresses the question, "how can the organization get to where it wants to be?" Answering that question requires two primary activities. First, functional strategy must be developed. Second, various aspects of the organizational system must be designed to ensure that the selected strategy can be institutionalized.[29]

FORMULATING FUNCTIONAL STRATEGY

Recall from Chapter 4 that functional strategy provides an action plan for strategy implementation at the level of the work group and individual. It operationalizes corporate and business strategy by defining the activities needed for implementation.

Depending on the specific strategy to be implemented, functional strategy may need to be formulated by a variety of work groups within the organization. Consider, for example, the functional strategies that would be necessary if Coca-Cola decided to develop a new line of fruit juices. The research and development department would have to develop a formula; the marketing department would have to conduct taste tests, develop promotional campaigns, and identify the appropriate distribution channels; and the production department would have to purchase new equipment and perhaps build new facilities to produce the fruit juice line. Table 5.4 outlines just a few of the functional strategies necessary to introduce a new line of fruit juices.

▼ **TABLE 5.4**   Examples of Functional Strategies Needed to Implement a New
                   Product Development Strategy

Marketing:

- Coordinate with R&D for formula development
- Conduct market research with consumers
- Develop a pricing strategy
- Design promotional materials
- Identify and negotiate with potential distributors
- Coordinate with Production as to product specifications
- Coordinate with Human Resources regarding personnel needs

Production:

- Identify suppliers of input materials
- Negotiate purchasing agreements
- Arrange for storage facilities for both raw materials and finished goods
- Design and/or purchase new production equipment
- Coordinate with Human Resources regarding personnel needs

Human Resources:

- Work with Production to assess human resource needs
- Work with Marketing to assess human resource needs
- Identify potential candidates for new positions
- Develop compensation and benefits packages for new employees
- Design and provide training for new employees

The most significant challenge lies in coordinating the activities of the various work groups that must work together to implement the strategy. The strategies must be consistent both within each functional area of the business (e.g., the marketing department) and between functional areas (e.g., the marketing department and the production department).[30] For example, if Coca-Cola's new fruit juice line is to be priced at a premium level, it must be promoted to buyers who desire a premium product and distributed through channels that reach those buyers. These marketing decisions must be consistent. Further, the production department must purchase high quality raw materials and produce a product that is worthy of a premium price. Without consistency within and between the work groups of the organization, the implementation process is sure to fail.

INSTITUTIONALIZING STRATEGY

While functional strategies are essential to the strategy implementation process, it is also important that the strategy be institutionalized within the organization. Institutionalizing strategy means that every member, work group, department, and division of the organization prescribes to and supports the organization's strategy with its plans and actions. Theory suggests that a "fit" must exist between the strategy of the organization and its structure, culture, and leadership if the strategy is to be institutionalized. Each of these topics will be examined in much greater detail in a subsequent chapter (organizational structure in Chapter 9, culture in Chapter 11, and leadership in Chapter 13), but here we will briefly discuss their relationship to strategy.

Organizational Structure

Organizational structure, most commonly associated with the organizational chart, defines the primary reporting relationships that exist within an organization.[31] The structure of an organization establishes its chain of command and its hierarchy of responsibility, authority, and accountability.[32]

Organizational structure
The primary reporting relationships that exist within an organization.

Departmentalization of organizational activities is the focus of the structuring process. Organizing work responsibilities into departments requires grouping individuals on the basis of the tasks they perform. If, for example, work units are structured so that all production tasks are grouped together, all marketing tasks are together, and all finance tasks are together, then the departments are organized on the basis of function. Similarly, if work units are structured so that all tasks related to serving the U.S. market are grouped together, all tasks for the European market are together, and all tasks for the Asian market are together, then organizational members are grouped according to the geographic market served.

Alfred Chandler, one of the earliest researchers in the area of strategy, originally advanced the idea that "structure follows strategy."[33] In essence, Chandler's findings indicate that an organization's strategy should influence its choice of organizational structure. For example, organizations that pursue growth through product development may benefit from a structure that is departmentalized by products. In contrast, those that pursue a geographic market development strategy may find an area-based structure to be most suitable. Furthermore, when an organization fails to change its structure in response to changes in its strategy, it will most likely experience operational problems that will eventually result in declining performance.[34] Since Chandler's classic research, a significant body of research has developed that suggests that organizations should develop structures that are appropriate for and supportive of their strategies. In fact, several studies have successfully linked a strategy-structure fit to superior financial performance.[35]

In Chapter 9, a number of organizational structures will be identified and discussed. In addition, we will examine the advantages and disadvantages of the different structures as well as their suitability for varying strategic conditions.

Organizational Culture

Organizational culture
An organization's system of shared beliefs and values.

The second organizational component that should be in alignment with an organization's strategy is organizational culture. **Organizational culture** refers to the system of shared beliefs and values that develops within an organization. It guides the behavior of and gives meaning to the members of the organization.[36]

Peters and Waterman's classic survey of America's best-managed companies has drawn attention to the contribution of organizational culture to strategic success. Peters and Waterman attributed the success of such firms as Procter & Gamble, General Electric, and 3M, in large part, to an organizational culture that supports their strategic initiatives.[37] Many organizations that wished to emulate the success of these companies began to look to changes in organizational culture as a means of doing so.

In an organization with an effective culture, employees are convinced that top management is committed to the implementation of its strategy. Further, employees believe that they will receive the support necessary to implement the plans of the organization. For example, 3M supports its "champions" of new product designs by removing bureaucratic impediments, giving them access to whatever resources they need, and providing executive support for their efforts. Individuals who champion new product concepts are confident that they will get the organizational support necessary to bring their ideas to fruition.[38]

Reward systems are also a critical component of the organization's culture. Employees must know not only that they will be supported, but that they will be rewarded for taking the actions necessary to implement the organization's strategy. While financial rewards will always be important to some degree, other types of rewards can be useful as well. For example, a manager of one of IBM's sales offices rented the Meadowlands Stadium, home of the New York Giants, to stage a special tribute to the salespeople in his office. He invited the family, friends, and colleagues of his sales personnel to attend the ceremony and had each salesperson run through the players' tunnel to be recognized for his or her outstanding sales achievements.

Developing a strong, pervasive organizational culture has become more challenging as the workforce in the United States has become more culturally diverse. As we mentioned in Chapter 1, people with different backgrounds, from different nations, or with different cultural frames of references often have very diverse views about organizations and how they should function. Reaching agreement can be more difficult among such groups—both in terms of establishing common goals and in determining methods for achieving those goals. Managers must be prepared to work harder and more creatively to ensure that a strong culture exists within culturally diverse organizations.

Organizational Leadership

Leadership is the third organizational component that should be in alignment with the strategy of the organization. If an organization is to implement its strategy effectively, it must have the appropriate leadership.[39] Without effective leadership, it is unlikely that the organization will realize the benefits of its selected strategy. This is particularly true when a quality orientation is a key aspect of its strategy.[40]

At the top of organization must be the visionary leader. Such leaders envision the future, communicate their vision to those around them, empower the people of the organization to make the vision happen, and reward them when it becomes a reality.[41] Bill Gates of Microsoft has often been described as a visionary leader. Gates saw an opportunity to redefine the market for personal computing operating systems and made that vision a reality with the introduction of Microsoft Windows. The effective implementation of that strategy has made Microsoft one of the most successful organizations in the United States.

Equally important to strategy implementation is effective leadership in the ranks of managers. In today's organizations, they may be team leaders, coaches, or champions rather than traditional middle managers, but the idea is the same. These individuals must do whatever is necessary to ensure that their work groups are making a contribution toward fulfilling the mission of the organization, achieving its goals, and implementing its strategy. Without effective leadership throughout the management ranks, strategy implementation can be very problematic. Leadership will be discussed in Chapter 13, where we will examine the relationship between leadership and strategy in greater detail.

It is essential for an organization to develop the systems necessary to support its strategy. Structure, culture, and leadership are among the aspects of an organization's system that are particularly relevant for effective strategy implementation. When a strategy is being implemented, it is also very important to monitor both the success of the implementation process and the effectiveness of the strategy. Strategic control provide the mechanism for doing just that.

STRATEGIC CONTROL: ENSURING QUALITY AND EFFECTIVENESS ━━━

The last stage of the strategic planning process is strategic control. Strategic control involves monitoring the implementation of the strategic plan and ensuring quality and effectiveness in terms of organizational performance. An effective control system identifies problems and signals the organization that a change may be needed.

Achieving strategic control in organizations that are heavily involved in the international marketplace can be particularly difficult. When operating units are in geographically dispersed locations, differences in time, language, and culture complicate the control process. Acquiring information is more difficult when the scope of the organization's operations is broad, and processing and interpreting information from such diverse sources can be challenging. Consequently, organizations that pursue international strategies must often maintain very sophisticated control systems.

In general, control mechanisms can be either feedforward or feedback controls. Let's examine what each involves.

FEEDFORWARD CONTROLS

Feedforward controls
Controls designed to identify changes in the external environment or the internal operations of the organization that may affect its ability to fulfill its mission and achieve its strategic goals.

Feedback controls
Controls that compare the actual performance of the organization to its planned performance.

Feedforward controls are designed to identify changes in the external environment or the internal operations of the organization that may affect its ability to fulfill its mission and meet its strategic goals. Premise controls are one of the most common feedforward controls. Premise controls are designed to identify changes in any condition, internal or external, upon which the strategy of the organization was based.

Consider, for example, a large construction company that plans to develop 500,000 acres of residential property over the next three years. By the end of the first year of the company's plan, the economy begins to deteriorate, and interest rates, inflation, and unemployment begin to rise. If premise controls are in place and are designed to detect changes in the economic conditions upon which the construction company's plan is based, the company will know to adapt its strategy to the changing economic conditions.

FEEDBACK CONTROLS

▼ Improvements in information technology have had a significant impact on the control systems of many organizations. Information regarding such things as sales trends, market share fluctuations, profitability, and productivity measures are more readily available today than ever before.

Feedback controls compare the actual performance of the organization to its planned performance. These controls usually target the goals established in the organization's strategic and operational plans. One of the primary benefits of feedback control is that it focuses the attention of managers on the results for which they are responsible in the organization's plan. This may discourage managers from spending too much time on situations and issues that are unrelated to the overall goals of the organization. Often feedback controls evaluate financial results, such as revenues, profitability, stock price, and budget variances. Other feedback controls monitor nonfinancial results such as customer relations, product and service quality, productivity, and employee turnover.

Organizations should maintain both feedforward and feedback controls. Relying on only one type of control could be a mistake because they focus on different issues that could affect the organization's plans. Just as organizations establish different goals and pursue different strategies, they should develop control systems to meet their specific strategic needs. An organization's control system must be in alignment with its strategic initiatives.[42]

For example, an organization pursuing a growth strategy is unlikely to develop the same control system as one that is pursuing a retrenchment strategy. The growth-oriented firm would monitor such variables as forecasts for demand, sales levels, sales growth, increases in market share, and brand awareness. In contrast, the organization pursuing retrenchment would monitor such variables as supply costs, productivity, sales per employee, sales to assets, gross and net margins, and other indicators of efficiency and bottom-line profitability.

The increasing availability and sophistication of information technology have had a tremendous impact on the ability of organizations to develop and maintain effective control systems. For example, tracking the sales of individual products in specific regions and at various price levels is much simpler given the information technology available today. Similarly, purchasing, inventory management, human resource management, and other operating activities are more easily monitored today. A well-designed management information system can provide accurate, timely information on a wide variety of activities to managers throughout the organization. Unfortunately, many organizations fail to utilize the information made available by management information systems to ensure effective strategic control.[43] Given the increasing competitiveness in most industries, however, many organizations are searching for ways to improve their strategic control processes. More effective use of information technology will provide a solution for many such organizations.

Strategic planning is a critical organizational activity that will affect the long-term performance of most organizations. We conclude by exploring the implications of strategic planning for the manager of tomorrow.

MANAGERIAL IMPLICATIONS ━━━━━━━━━━━━━━━━━━━━

At several points so far in this book, we have suggested that the business environment is in a state of constant change. These changes will present special challenges for those who must plan strategically. Table 5.5 presents today's frame of reference for developing strategy, as well as one person's view of the frame of reference for tomorrow's managers.[44]

While the future of the business environment remains uncertain, it is important for you, as a manager of the future, to recognize the changing nature of the environment and the implications of those changes for strategic planning. As you engage in strategic planning, you may want to keep the following tips in mind:

- Use a participatory approach to planning where possible.
- Recognize the importance of a thorough and accurate assessment of the current situation of the organization. A plan will be only as good as the analysis on which it is based.
- Make sure your mission statement is a working document that provides direction for the members of the organization.
- Strategic goals serve as targets for achievement. Make sure they are measurable, specific, and realistic.
- Strategy should be designed to provide the organization with a distinctive competitive advantage in the long term. Never lose sight of that imperative.
- Strategy is meaningless if it is not implemented well. Ensure that you plan for implementation all along the way.
- Never underestimate the importance of strategic control. It is the only means of ensuring that the company is on track.

▼ **TABLE 5.5**   A Frame of Reference for Tomorrow's Manager

TODAY'S FRAME OF REFERENCE	A NEW FRAME OF REFERENCE
Long-term future is predictable to some extent.	Long-term future is unknowable.
Visions and plans are central to strategic management.	Dynamic agendas of strategic issues are central to effective strategic management.
Vision—a single shared organizationwide intention. A picture of a future state.	Challenge—multiple aspirations, stretching and ambiguous. Arising out of current ill-structured and conflicting issues with long-term consequences.
Strongly shared cultures.	Contradictory countercultures.
Cohesive teams of managers operating in state of consensus.	Learning groups of managers, surfacing conflict, engaging in dialogue, publicly testing assertions.
Decision making as purely logical, analytical process.	Decision making as exploratory, experimental process based on intuition and reasoning by analogy.
Long-term control and development as the monitoring of progress against plan milestones. Constraints provided by rules, systems, and rational argument.	Control and development in open-ended situations as a political process. Constraints provided by need to build and sustain support. Control as self-policing learning.
Strategy as the realization of prior intent.	Strategy as spontaneously emerging from the chaos of challenge and contradiction, through a process of real-time learning and politics.
Top management drives and controls strategic direction.	Top management creates favorable conditions for complex learning and politics.
General mental models and prescriptions for many specific situations.	New mental models required for each new strategic situation.
Adaptive equilibrium with the environment.	Nonequilibrium, creative interaction with the environment.

SOURCE: R. Stacey, "Strategy as Order Emerging from Chaos," *Long Range Planning* 26 (February 1993): 10–17.

In this chapter, you have learned about the process of strategic planning. This process provides a strong foundation for the development and implementation of effective strategy. Although strategic planning creates many challenges for managers, it is essential for those organizations that strive to achieve excellence in the highly competitive business environment of today and tomorrow.

MANAGERIAL INCIDENT RESOLUTION

RCA: THE CHALLENGE OF RESPONDING TO ENVIRONMENTAL CHANGE

When RCA's corporate managers recognized that foreign imports had changed the competitive structure of their industry, they knew it was time to rethink the firm's strategic orientation. Faced with either differentiating their product to justify a higher price or reducing costs in an effort to be a low-cost/low-price leader, RCA chose the latter. While one of its U.S. competitors, Curtis Mathis, chose to pursue a product differentiation strategy (actually quite successfully), RCA's managers believed they had the potential to develop a global leadership position through a cost leadership strategy. This strategic decision required some significant changes in RCA's operating strategy.

To maximize the efficiency of its production process, RCA expanded its operations worldwide. Production facilities were located in geographic regions where resources were cheapest. Business units were established in such countries as Taiwan, Japan, Mexico, and Canada, and each specialized in a particular aspect of RCA's production process. Further, RCA's efforts to sell its products in the global market created the sales volume necessary to maximize economies of scale and minimize per unit costs.

Through its cost leadership strategy, RCA was able to prosper once again in the television industry—this time on a worldwide basis. RCA's television division remains strong today, but the company must continue to monitor the external environment so that it can develop effective responses to the environmental changes of tomorrow.[45] ▼

SUMMARY

- Strategic planning is the process by which an organization makes decisions and takes actions that affect its long-run performance. The purpose of strategic planning is to move the organization from where it is to where it wants to be. Both economic and behavioral benefits are associated with strategic planning.

- The strategic planning process consists of four primary stages: (1) strategic analysis, (2) strategy formulation, (3) strategy implementation, and (4) strategic control.

- Strategic analysis involves identifying the organization's internal strengths and weaknesses and external opportunities and threats, and assessing their strategic implications.

- Strategy formulation follows strategic analysis and results in the development of strategy at the corporate and/or business levels. Strategy formulation requires the development of an organizational mission, the determination of strategic goals, the identification of strategic alternatives, and the evaluation and selection of an appropriate strategy.

- Strategies can be thought of as grand strategies, generic strategies, or global strategies. Grand strategies include stability, growth, and retrenchment strategies. The three generic strategies that can be formulated are cost leadership, differentiation, and focus. Global strategy relates both to the mode of entry and to the scope of strategy.

- Strategy implementation puts the strategy of the organization into effect. It is the action phase of the strategic planning process. Strategy implementation requires two primary activities: (1) functional strategy must be developed, and (2) the organizational system must be designed to ensure effective implementation.

- Strategic control involves monitoring the organization's progress toward fulfilling its mission, achieving its strategic goals, and implementing its strategic plans. In general, control mechanisms can be either feedforward or feedback controls.

- The rapidly changing business environment creates many challenges for managers who must plan strategically. Managers of the future must remember the basic principles of strategic planning as they attempt to ensure the competitiveness of their organizations through the development of effective strategy.

KEY TERMS

Strategic planning (p. 146)
Strategic plan (p. 146)
General environment (p. 151)
Task environment (p. 151)
Organizational mission (p. 155)
Strategic goals (p. 156)

Grand strategy (p. 158)
Generic strategies (p. 160)
Cost leadership strategy (p. 160)
Differentiation strategy (p. 161)
Focus strategy (p. 161)
Multidomestic strategy (p. 163)

Global strategy (p. 163)
Organizational structure (p. 165)
Organizational culture (p. 166)
Feedforward controls (p. 168)
Feedback controls (p. 168)

REVIEW QUESTIONS

1. Why is it important for organizations to engage in strategic planning? What are the benefits of the strategic planning process?

2. What are the three organizational levels at which strategy must be formulated? How do they differ with respect to (a) focus, (b) participants, (c) specificity, and (d) time horizon?

3. Describe the process of strategic planning. How are the four stages of the process interrelated?

4. What is the purpose of strategic analysis?

5. What is involved in (a) developing an organizational mission, (b) assessing managerial values and attitudes, (c) identifying the strengths and weak-

nesses of the firm, and (d) identifying the opportunities and threats facing the organization?

6. What is grand strategy? What are the three broad categories of grand strategy?

7. What are the three generic strategies developed by Michael Porter? Give examples of organizations or products that have pursued each strategy.

8. What role does strategy implementation play in the strategic planning process?

9. What are functional strategies? What aspects of a firm's organizational system need to be in alignment with its strategy?

DISCUSSION QUESTIONS

Improving Critical Thinking

1. What are some of the changes in the business environment in the last 20 years that have increased the need for strategic planning for many businesses?

2. How has the emergence of a global marketplace complicated the process of strategic analysis for many organizations?

Enhancing Communication Skills

3. Consider an organization that you have worked for at some time or that you currently work for. Would you classify that organization as having a stability, growth, or retrenchment strategy? Do the organization's culture, leadership, and control system match its strategy? To improve your oral communication skills, prepare a brief presentation for the class.

4. Under what conditions might an organization choose to shift from a cost leadership strategy to a product differentiation strategy? Would this be a dif-

ficult adjustment for most organizations? To practice your written communication skills, write a one-page summary of your response.

Building Teamwork

5. Describe the effect each of the following would have on an organization.
   a. Ineffective implementation of a good strategy
   b. Effective implementation of a poor strategy
   c. Ineffective implementation of a poor strategy
   Discuss this with a group of four to five of your fellow students.

6. Form teams of four or five students. For each of the following strategies, identify an organization (beyond those cited in the text) that can be characterized as pursuing each strategy: (1) cost leadership, (2) differentiation, and (3) focus. Why did you choose these particular organizations? Be prepared to discuss your selections with the class.

National Clothiers is a U.S.-based manufacturer of women's apparel. The firm has been in business for over 40 years. For the first 35 years of its existence, National enjoyed stable growth in sales and profitability, but the last 5 years have been quite different. Sales growth has stagnated, and the company has experienced significant pressure on its bottom line. Most of the problem can be attributed to foreign competitors who can charge significantly lower prices due to their lower labor costs.

National Clothiers needs to formulate a strategy. Its strategic alternatives are quite limited, however. One option is to continue as is, but if National maintains its four plants in the United States, the higher labor costs will continue to depress profit margins. In the long term, profits will be too low to support new product development or plant expansion. The other option is to move its plants to Central America. Several Central American countries are anxious to attract U.S. manufacturers and are offering very favorable tax and trade options. Although costs would be incurred for the relocation, National's labor costs would drop by nearly 40 percent, and the effect on the firm's overall cost structure would be very positive.

As National's managers contemplate these alternatives, their minds keep turning to how relocation would affect their employees. Some of National's workers have been with the company since its inception, and the average length of employee tenure is over seven years. The company's four plants are located in fairly small towns, and National is the primary employer in each community. Shutting down these plants will not only affect National's employees, but will have a very negative effect on the economy of the community as a whole. What makes the situation even worse is that National has always prided itself on its commitment to its employees and its efforts to maintain a positive and productive corporate culture.

For Discussion

1. What are the pros and cons associated with the two strategic alternatives presented in the case?
2. Do you think that the second alternative presents any ethical issues? If so, what are they?
3. Which alternative would you choose and why?

MULTIDOMESTIC VERSUS GLOBAL STRATEGY

Form teams of four to five students per team. Half of the teams in the class should prepare to argue the benefits of multidomestic strategy, while the other half of the teams should prepare to argue the benefits of global strategy. Use the experiences of real companies in preparing your arguments. Your instructor will select two teams to present their findings to the class in a debate format.

VIDEO CASE

Minnesota Twins

 The Minnesota Twins are an American League baseball team based in Minneapolis, Minnesota. Although some might think that a major league baseball team would be very different from a typical business organization, that's just not so, especially when it comes to organizational planning. The Twins, like any other organization, consider strategic planning to be critical to their long-term success.

With regard to strategic analysis, the Twins face many internal and external issues. Internally, the organization must cope with fan relations, marketing issues (e.g., promotions, ticket sales), and limitations on their stadium, the Metrodome (e.g., seating, vendors, other tenants). One of the most important aspects of the internal organization is human resources. In baseball, this takes on tremendous significance since the quality of the product is so highly dependent on having strong human resources out on the field.

Externally, competition for the consumer's entertainment dollars presents challenges for a major league baseball team. Legal issues are also relevant because, like any other business organization, baseball teams have to deal with antitrust issues, tax regulations, and potential lawsuits regarding any number of issues. Technology has impacted the game in many ways as well. For example, computer networking now makes it easier to purchase tickets at kiosks throughout the city. All of these external environmental issues have a significant impact on the Twins' strategic plan.

The Twins have a formal mission statement that sets out the organization's reasons for existence, as well as its fundamental goals. While the most visible goal of the organization is to win on the field, it has other important goals related to total sales, profit, and other financial measures of success. Based on these goals, the Twins have pursued a growth strategy directed at attracting more fans to the games, as well as better media coverage.

Functional strategies are necessary at many levels of the organization. For example, the Promotions De-

partment has developed a number of strategies designed to increase attendance at the games. These strategies range from simply advertising games with strong competitors heavily to elaborate in-stadium giveaway plans to attract fans to less competitive games. Marketing efforts to attract more media coverage of the games are essential to implementing the Twins' strategy of growth as well. Strategies for recruiting players, assessing talent, building a strong roster, and enhancing player relations are also important at the functional level of the organization.

The management and players of the Minnesota Twins feel that, in the end, it is their organizational culture that sets them apart from other major league teams. The Twins take a great deal of pride in maintaining a culture that values hard work, having fun, playing the best game possible, and not carrying a briefcase to work. The Twins' culture is a function of their commitment to give 100 percent of their energy, effort, and enthusiasm to building a team that their fans can be proud of.

Through strategic planning, the Twins have charted a path for their future success. Time will tell if their strategies are effective.

For Discussion:

1. Develop a list of the external and internal issues that would likely affect the strategic plan of the Twins (some issues are mentioned in the case; others will need to be identified from your knowledge of major league baseball). Describe how these issues would affect their strategic plan.

2. What performance goals do you feel would be most important to the Twins?

3. Develop a comprehensive list of functional strategies that would be necessary to implement a strategy of growth and thereby meet the goals you identified in Question 2.

CASE

Fastener, Inc., Faces Competitive Pressures

Mr. Palladino leaned back in his chair and stared at the ceiling. What in the world could be going wrong with his company? Fasteners, Inc., had been in busi-

ness for nearly 10 years, and up until 2 years ago, the firm had commanded a strong market share in the fastener industry. Since then, however, the company had been experiencing declining sales and profits as a result of some competitive changes that had redefined the market for fasteners.

The industry had become driven by costs and price. Standardized fasteners had become the norm, and Fasteners, Inc., had no way to distinguish itself from its competitors. Further, the company had no cost advantage over its competitors; in fact, it seemed to have a slightly higher cost structure than its two biggest competitors. It was time for a new strategic plan.

As Mr Palladino considered his situation, he wondered where to begin. Obviously, he was going to have to rely on his top managers to help develop a new strategy. As he prepared to draft a memo notifying this group of a strategic planning meeting, he thought about the meeting agenda. He knew that he needed to organize the meeting so that the management group could make the most of their strategic planning time.

For Discussion

1. How might Mr. Palladino and his managers have avoided their current declining position?
2. Develop an agenda for Mr. Palladino's planning meeting. Where should the managers begin in their efforts to develop a new strategy for Fasteners, Inc.?

EXPERIENTIAL EXERCISE 5.1

Form a team with at least four other people. As a group, assume that you are the Executive Committee for the College of Business Administration at your university. Develop a strategic plan for your college through the year 2000. In doing so, address the following:

1. Develop a mission statement for the college.
2. Evaluate the dean's office with respect to its strategic orientation.
3. Identify the strengths and weaknesses of the college.
4. Identify the opportunities and threats facing the college.
5. Develop a mission statement for the college.
6. Develop a set of strategic alternatives.
7. Establish strategic goals for the college.
8. Select a strategy.
9. Develop implementation plans.

Make a presentation to the class of your analysis, your strategic decision, and your implementation plans. How does your plan compare to the plans of other groups in your class? How did the assumptions you made about the internal and external environment of the college affect your strategic plan?

NOTES

1. P. Wright, "The Strategic Options of Least-Cost, Differentiation and Niche," *Business Horizons*, March/April 1986, 21–26; "RCA: Will It Ever Be a Top Performer," *Business Week*, April 2, 1984, 52–62; and "No Brand Like an Old Brand," *Forbes*, June 11, 1990, 179–80.
2. R. Evered, "So What Is Strategy?" *Long Range Planning*, 16 (1983): 57–72; and A. Ginsberg, "Operationalizing Organizational Strategy: Toward an Integrative Framework," *Academy of Management Review* 9 (1984): 548–57.
3. M. Leontiades, "The Confusing Words of Business Policy," *Academy of Management Review*, 7 (1982): 45–48.
4. N. J. Perry, "Vision of Dreamz: Big Returns from the Basics," *Fortune*, April 19, 1993, 90.
5. M. Thankur and L. M. R. Calingo, "Strategic Thinking Is Hip, But Does It Make a Difference," *Business Horizons*, September/October, 1992, 47–54.
6. For example, see J. A. Pearce, E. B. Freeman, and R. B. Robinson, "The Tenuous Link between Formal Strategic Planning and Financial Performance," *Academy of Management Review*, 12 (1987): 658–75; S. Schoeffler, R. D. Buzzell, and D. F. Heany, "Impact of Strategic Planning on Profit Performance," *Harvard Business Review* (March/April 1974): 137–45; and D. M. Herold, "Long-Range Planning and Organizational Performance: A Cross-Valuation Study," *Academy of Management Journal* (March 1972): 91–102.
7. J. A. Pearce II and W. A. Randolph, "Improving Strategy Formulation Pedagogies by Recognizing Behavioral Aspects," *Exchange*, December 1980, 7–10.
8. H. H. Hinterhuber and W. Popp, "Are You a Strategist or Just a Manager?" *Harvard Business Review* (January/February 1992): 105–13.
9. S. R. Baldwin and M. McConnell, "Strategic Planning: Process and Plan Go Hand in Hand," *Management Solutions*, June 1988, 28–37.
10. P. J. H. Schoemaker, "How to Link Strategic Vision to Core Capabilities," *Sloan Management Review* (Fall 1992): 67–81.
11. H. Mintzberg, "Crafting Strategy," *Harvard Business Review* (July/August 1987): 66–75.

12. C. C. Snow and L. G. Hrebiniak, "Strategy, Distinctive Competence, and Organizational Performance," *Administrative Science Quarterly*, 25 (June 1980): 317-37.

13. J. Montanari, C. Morgan, and J. Bracker, *Strategic Management: A Choice Approach* (Chicago: Dryden Press, 1990), 81-85.

14. T. Wheelen and D. J. Hunger, *Strategic Management* (Reading, Mass.: Addison-Wesley, 1990), 100.

15. T. A. Stewart, "Brace for Japan's Hot New Strategy," *Fortune,* September 21, 1992, 62-74.

16. S. F. Stershirc, "Mission Statements Can Be a Field of Dreams," *Marketing News,* February 1, 1993, 7 + .

17. J. A. Pearce and F. David, "Corporate Mission Statements: The Bottom Line," *Academy of Management Executive,* 1 (1987): 109-16.

18. D. L. Calfee, "Get Your Mission Statement Working," *Management Review* (January 1993): 54-57.

19. Ibid.

20. R. B. Robinson, "Planned Patterns of Strategic Behavior and Their Relationship to Business-Unit Performance," *Strategic Management Journal,* 9 (1988): 43-60.

21. J. A. Pearce, K. Robbins, and R. Robinson, "The Impact of Grand Strategy and Planning Formality on Financial Performance," *Strategic Management Journal,* 8 (1987): 125-34.

22. Robinson, "Planned Patterns of Strategic Behavior."

23. Adapted from M. Porter, *Competitive Advantage: Creating and Sustaining Superior Performance* (New York: Free Press, 1985).

24. Ibid.

25. Adapted from "Photronics," in *Strengthening America's Competitiveness: The Blue Chip Enterprise Initiative* (published by Warner Books on behalf of Connecticut Mutual Life Insurance Company and the U.S. Chamber of Commerce, 1991), 86.

26. G. M. Feiger, "Managing the New Global Enterprise," *The McKinsey Quarterly* (Summer 1988): 25-38.

27. Ibid.

28. L. A. Huston, "Using Total Quality to Put Strategic Intent into Motion," *Conference Executive Summary* (September/October 1992): 21-23.

29. Ginsberg, "Operationalizing Organizational Strategy."

30. For example see R. Hayes and S. Wheelwright, *Restoring Our Competitive Edge: Competing through Manufacturing* (New York: John Wiley & Sons, 1984).

31. A. D. Chandler, *Strategy and Structure: Chapters in the History of the American Industrial Enterprise* (Cambridge, Mass.: MIT Press, 1962).

32. R. Rumelt, *Strategy, Structure, and Economic Performance* (Boston: Graduate School of Business Administration, Harvard University, 1974).

33. Chandler, *Strategy and Structure.*

34. For example, see C. Bartlett, "How Multinational Organizations Evolve," *Journal of Business Strategy* 3 (Summer 1982): 20-32; R. Drazin and P. Howard, "Strategy Implementation: A Technique for Organizational Design," *Columbia Journal of World Business* 19 (Summer 1984): 40-54; and J. R. Galbraith and R. K. Kazanjian, *Strategy Implementation: Structure Systems and Process* (St. Paul, Minn.: West Publishing Company, 1978).

35. For example, see D. Miller, "Configurations of Strategy and Structure: Towards a Synthesis," *Strategic Management Journal* 7 (1986): 233-49; D. Miller, "Strategy Making and Structure: Analysis and Implications for Performance," *Academy of Management Journal* 30 (1987): 7-32; and D. Miller, "Relating Porter's Business Strategies to Environment and Structure: Analysis and Performance Implications," *Academy of Management Journal* 31 (1988): 280-308.

36. J. S. Ott, *The Organizational Culture Perspective* (Monterey, Calif.: Brooks Cole, 1989).

37. T. J. Peters and R. H. Waterman, *In Search of Excellence* New York: Harper & Row, 1982).

38. 3M *1992 Annual Report;* and "Master of Innovation," *Business Week,* April 1990, 58-63.

39. A. K. Gupta and B. Govindarajan, "Business Unit Strategy, Management Characteristics, and Business Unit Effectiveness at Strategy Implementation," *Academy of Management Journal* 27 (March 1984): 25-41.

40. J. M. Juran, "Acing the Quality Quiz," *Across the Board* (July/August 1992), 58.

41. F. Westley and H. Mintzberg, "Visionary Leadership and Strategic Management," *Strategic Management Journal* (1989): 17-18.

42. P. Lorange and D. Murphy, "Considerations Implementing Strategic Control," *Journal of Business Strategy*, Vol. 4, Spring 1984, 27-35.

43. M. Goold and J. Quinn, "The Paradox of Strategic Controls," *Strategic Management Journal* 11 (1990): 43-57.

44. R. Stacey, "Strategy as Order Emerging from Chaos," *Long Range Planning* 26 (February 1993): 10-17.

45. P. Wright, "Strategic Options of Least-Cost, Differentiation, and Niche," *Readings in Strategic Management* (1990): 113-17.

Effective Managerial Decision Making

CHAPTER 6

▼ CHAPTER OVERVIEW

Consider all the decisions necessary to carry out any major effort—from launching a space satellite to marketing and producing a new line of automobiles. The managers responsible for these decisions rely on good decision-making skills.

A manager's responsibility as a decision maker is very important. While all managers are called upon to make decisions, the kinds of decisions that are required will vary with their level of authority and type of assignment. Poor decisions can be disastrous to a department and an organization. Good decisions help work to flow and enable the organization to achieve its goals.

This chapter introduces concepts and models that focus on the demands of managerial decision making. Managers may not always make the right decision, but they can use their knowledge of appropriate decision-making processes to increase the odds of success. Skill as a decision maker is a distinguishing characteristic of most successful managers.[1] We will explore how managers in organizations make decisions by taking you through the seven steps in the decision-making process and examining two commonly used models of decision behavior. Since managers are frequently involved with groups and teams, we focus on the participative model of group decision making by looking at techniques that managers can use to improve this process.

▼ LEARNING OBJECTIVES

When you have finished studying this chapter, you should be able to:

- Explain the steps in the decision-making process.
- Examine some of the ethical dilemmas managers face in decision making.
- Describe the rational-economic model of decision making.
- Discuss the behavioral decision model.
- Illustrate the participation model of decision making.
- Recognize the advantages and disadvantages of group decision making.
- Explain the various techniques used to improve group decision making.
- Discuss the implications of effective decision making for future managers.

AN ILL-FATED DECISION WATCHED BY MILLIONS

Millions of Americans watched the launch of the space shuttle *Challenger* that clear, cold January day in 1986. The explosion of the ill-fated space shuttle 74 seconds after launch took the lives of the seven crew members. For several weeks following the explosion, the public believed it was an inexplicable accident, caused by a freak hardware failure, that no one could reasonably have been expected to foresee. In the weeks to come, the world would discover that the *Challenger* tragedy was as much a failure of decision making as of technology.

As a commission investigated the *Challenger* loss, the general public wondered how NASA's managers could have allowed this to happen. Whatever pressure was on NASA to launch the shuttle, as good managers shouldn't they have made the decision based on technical information about the safety of the launch provided by trained rocket engineers?

The commission investigating the *Challenger* disaster found that NASA's managers did have sufficient information to be concerned about safety and therefore to cancel the launch. Several rocket engineers from Morton Thiokol, Inc., which supplied the booster rockets for the shuttle, had argued strenuously against a launch only hours before the shuttle was scheduled to lift off. The engineers' testimony was particularly embarrassing to Morton Thiokol because they described, in painstaking detail, how they had unanimously opposed the launch on the night before the disaster. But the engineers were overruled by their managers, and the decision to launch was made despite repeated warnings. Managers at NASA insisted on "proof of probable failure" before they would abort a launch. That decision made history.[2] ▼

INTRODUCTION

At NASA, managers were faced with a critical decision: whether or not to launch the space shuttle *Challenger*. The *Challenger* tragedy was as much a failure of decision making as of technology. But why and how was this unfortunate decision made? What got in the way of good critical thinking processes?

Some decisions, like those made by NASA's managers, are critical and can have a major impact on personal and organizational lives. Other decisions are more routine, but still require that we select an appropriate course of action.

This chapter introduces concepts and models that focus on the demands of managerial decision making. **Decision making** is the process through which managers identify and resolve problems and capitalize on opportunities. Here the focus is on how managers in organizations make decisions. First, we explore how individuals make decisions by examining the seven steps in the decision-making process, ethical dilemmas in decision making, and two models of decision behavior. Since managers are often involved with groups and teams, we discuss group considerations in decision making. Finally, we look at techniques that managers can use to improve group decision making and the implications of achieving excellence in the decision-making process.

Decision making
The process through which managers identify and resolve problems and capitalize on opportunities.

STEPS IN THE DECISION-MAKING PROCESS

Good decision making is important at all levels in the organization. It begins with a recognition or awareness of problems and opportunities and concludes with an assessment of the results of actions taken to solve those problems.

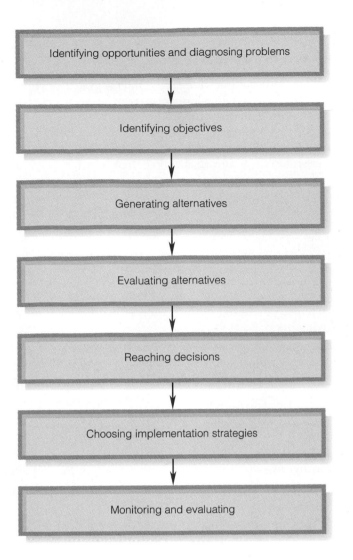

▼ **FIGURE 6.1**
Seven Steps in the Decision-Making Process

Before we begin to examine these steps in greater detail, think about how you make decisions. How skilled a decision maker are you?

Take a few minutes to complete the decision-making process questionnaire (DMPQ) in Meeting the Challenge. The DMPQ evaluates your current level of decision-making ability.[3] As we progress through the chapter, you will learn more about sharpening these skills that are an important part of most managerial experiences.

An effective decision-making process generally includes the seven steps shown in Figure 6.1. Although the figure shows the steps proceeding in a logical, sequential order, managerial decision making often unfolds in a quite disorderly and complex manner. Keep in mind that managers are influenced at each step in the decision-making process by their individual personalities, attitudes, and behaviors (as we will discuss in Chapter 14), ethics and values (as discussed in Chapter 3), and culture as we will discuss later in the chapter. First, though, we will briefly examine each of the seven steps in managerial decision making.

IDENTIFYING AND DIAGNOSING PROBLEMS

Decision makers must know where action is required. Consequently, the first step in the decision-making process is the clear identification of opportunities

MEETING THE CHALLENGE

ASSESSING YOUR DECISION-MAKING SKILLS

This decision-making process questionnaire (DMPQ) evaluates your current decision-making skills. These behaviors are part of most managerial experiences, but you will find that the questions are applicable to your own experience even if you are not yet a manager. If you do not have experience in a management-level position, consider a group you have worked with either in the classroom or in an organization such as a fraternity, sorority, club, church, or service group.

Use the following scale to rate the frequency with which you perform the behaviors described in each statement. Place the appropriate number (1–7) in the blank preceding the statement.

Rarely	Irregularly	Occasionally	Usually	Frequently	Almost Always	Consistently/ Always
1	2	3	4	5	6	7

_____ **1.** I review data about the performance of my work and/or my group's work.

_____ **2.** I seek outside information, such as articles in business magazines and newspapers, to help me evaluate my performance.

_____ **3.** When examining data, I allow for sufficient time to identify problems.

_____ **4.** Based on the data, I identify problem areas needing action.

_____ **5.** To generate alternative solutions, I review problems from different perspectives.

_____ **6.** I list many possible ways of reaching a solution for an identified problem.

_____ **7.** I research methods that have been used to solve similar problems.

_____ **8.** When generating alternative courses of action, I seek the opinions of others.

_____ **9.** I explicitly state the criteria I will use for judging alternative courses of action.

_____ **10.** I list both positive and negative aspects of alternative decisions.

or the diagnosis of problems that require a decision. Managers regularly review data related to their area or responsibility, including both outside information and reports and information from within the organization. Discrepancies between actual and desired conditions alert a manager to a potential opportunity or problem. Identifying opportunities and problems is not easy considering human behavior in organizations. The origins of a problem may be deeply rooted in an individual's past experience, in the complex structure of the organization, or some combination of individual and organizational factors. Therefore, a manager must pay particular attention to ensure that problems and opportunities are assessed as accurately as possible.

The assessment of opportunities and problems will be only as accurate as the information on which it is based. Therefore, managers put a premium on obtaining accurate, reliable information. Poor-quality or inaccurate information can waste time and lead a manager to miss the underlying causes of a situation.[4] This basic principle is well understood by U.S. business managers who

____ 11. I consider how possible decisions could affect others.

____ 12. I estimate the probabilities of the possible outcomes of each alternative.

____ 13. I study information about problems that require my decisions.

____ 14. I determine if I need additional data in light of my objectives and the urgency of the situation.

____ 15. To reach a decision, I rely on my judgment and experience as well as on the available data.

____ 16. I support my choices with facts.

____ 17. Before finally accepting a decision, I evaluate possible ways to implement it.

____ 18. I choose the simplest and least costly methods of putting my decisions into effect.

____ 19. I select resources and establish time frames as part of my implementation strategy.

____ 20. I choose implementation strategies that help achieve my objectives.

Enter your score for each category in the following table, and sum the five category scores to obtain your total score. Enter that total score in the space indicated. Scores can range from a low of 4 to a high of 28 in each skill category. Total scores can range from a low of 20 to a high of 140. Your instructor will have further information on your scores.

SKILL AREA	STATEMENTS	SCORE
Diagnosing the problem	1, 2, 3, 4	_____
Generating alternatives	5, 6, 7, 8	_____
Evaluating alternatives	9, 10, 11, 12	_____
Reaching decisions	13, 14, 15, 16	_____
Choosing implementation strategies	17, 18, 19, 20	_____
Total score		_____

spend millions of dollars each year on market research to identify trends in consumer preferences and buying decisions. Nevertheless, sometimes crucial information is overlooked. For example, in developing the new Coke, Coca-Cola conducted exhaustive taste tests, but failed to assess one crucial factor: brand loyalty. The unveiling of the new Coke, which was one of the most spectacular marketing flops of all time, is discussed further in Chapter 7.

Even when quality information is collected, it may be misinterpreted. Sometimes, misinterpretations accumulate over time as information is consistently misunderstood or problematic events are unrecognized.[5] Most major disasters or accidents turn out to have had long incubation periods in which warning signs were misunderstood or overlooked. Note how misinterpreted information contributed to the critical decision error that led to the *Challenger* disaster as described in the opening Managerial Incident.

To complicate matters further, even when managers have accurate information and interpret it correctly, factors beyond their control may affect the identification of opportunities and problems. Nevertheless, by insisting on high-quality information and interpreting it carefully, managers will improve their chances of making good decisions.

IDENTIFYING OBJECTIVES

Objectives
The desired results to be attained.

Objectives reflect the results the organization wants to attain. Both the quantity and quality of the desired results should be specified, for these aspects of the objectives will ultimately guide the decision maker in selecting the appropriate course of action. As the Managerial Incident makes clear, one of NASA's objectives was to launch the *Challenger* on schedule.

As you will recall from Chapters 4 and 5, objectives are often referred to as targets, standards, and ends. They may be measured along a variety of dimensions. For example, profit or cost objectives are measured in monetary units, productivity objectives may be measured in units of output per labor hour, and quality objectives may be measured in defects per million units produced.

Objectives can be expressed for long spans of time (years or decades) or for short spans of time (hours, days, or months). Long-range objectives usually direct much of the strategic decision making of the organization, while short-range objectives usually guide operational decision making. Regardless of the time frame, the objectives will guide the ensuing decision-making process.

GENERATING ALTERNATIVES

Once an opportunity has been identified or a problem diagnosed correctly, a manager develops various ways to achieve objectives and solve the problem. This step requires creativity and imagination. In generating alternatives, the manager must keep in mind the goals and objectives that he or she is trying to achieve. Ideally, several different alternatives will emerge. In this way, the manager increases the likelihood that many good alternative courses of action will be considered and evaluated.

▼ When generating alternatives, managers must rely on training, personal experience, education, and knowledge of the situation. This manager examines the various alternative courses of action before she makes a decision.

Managers may rely on their training, personal experience, education, and knowledge of the situation to generate alternatives. Viewing the problem from varying perspectives often requires input from other people such as peers, employees, supervisors, and groups within the organization. For example, consumer product companies such as Procter & Gamble often use customer focus groups to supply information that can be used in this stage of decision making.

The alternatives can be standard and obvious as well as innovative and unique. Standard solutions often include options that the organization has used in the past. Innovative approaches may be developed through such strategies as brainstorming, nominal group technique, and the delphi technique. These strategies, which encourage consideration of multiple alternatives, will be discussed in more detail later in the chapter as methods for enhancing group decision making.

EVALUATING ALTERNATIVES

The fourth step in the decision-making process involves determining the value or adequacy of the alternatives generated. Which solution is the "best"? Fundamental to this step is the ability to assess the value or relative advantages and disadvantages of each alternative under consideration. Predetermined decision criteria such as the quality desired, anticipated costs, benefits, uncertainties, and risks of the alternative may be used in the evaluation process. The result should be a ranking of the alternatives. For example, the manager might ask, Will this alternative help achieve our quality objective? What is the anticipated cost of this alternative? What are the uncertainties and risks associated with this alternative? We more thoroughly examine the tools used by managers to evaluate alternatives in Chapter 7.

REACHING DECISIONS

Decision making is commonly associated with making a final choice. Reaching the decision is really only one step in the process, however. Although choosing an alternative would seem to be a straightforward proposition—simply consider all the alternatives and select the one that best solves the problem—in reality, the choice is rarely clear-cut. Because the best decisions are often based on careful judgments, making a good decision involves carefully examining all the facts, determining whether sufficient information is available, and finally selecting the best alternative.[6]

CHOOSING IMPLEMENTATION STRATEGIES

The bridge between reaching a decision and evaluating the results is the implementation phase of the decision-making process. When decisions involve taking action or making changes, choosing ways to put these actions or changes into effect becomes an essential managerial task. The keys to effective implementation are (1) sensitivity to those who will be affected by the decision and (2) proper planning and consideration of the resources necessary to carry out the decision. Those who will be affected by the decision must understand the choice and why it was made; that is, the decision must be accepted and supported by the people who are responsible for its implementation. These needs can be met by involving employees in the early stages of the decision process so that they will be motivated and committed to its successful implementation.

According to recent research, senior executives frequently complain that middle and operating managers fail to take actions necessary to implement decisions. Implementation problems often occur as a result of poor understanding and commitment to the decisions by middle management.[7]

The planning process is a key to effective implementation. Without proper planning, the decision may not be accepted by others in the organization, cost overruns may occur, needed resources may not be available, and the objectives may not be accomplished on schedule. To plan properly for implementation, managers need to perform the following activities:

- Determine how things will look when the decision is fully operational.
- Draw up a chronological schedule of the activities and tasks that must be carried out to make the decision fully operational.
- List the resources and activities required to implement each activity or task.
- Estimate the time needed for each activity or task.
- Assign responsibility for each activity or task to specific individuals.

MONITORING AND EVALUATING

No decision-making process is complete until the impact of the decision has been evaluated. Managers must observe the impact of the decision as objectively as possible and take further corrective action if it becomes necessary. Quantifiable objectives can be established even before the solution to the problem is put into effect. For example, 3M recently began a five-year program dubbed Challenge '95 to increase quality control and reduce manufacturing costs by 35 percent. The company must constantly monitor its efforts to determine if it is making progress toward those goals.

Monitoring the decision is useful whether the feedback is positive or negative. Positive feedback indicates that the decision is working and that it should be continued and perhaps applied elsewhere in the organization. Negative feedback indicates either that the implementation requires more time, resources, effort, or planning than originally thought or that the decision was a poor one and needs to be reexamined.

The importance of assessing the success or failure of a decision cannot be overstated. Evaluation of past decisions as well as other information should drive future decision making as part of an ongoing decision-making feedback loop.

Thus far we have explored how managers in organizations make decisions by taking you through the seven steps in the decision-making process. The process starts when the organization recognizes a problem or becomes aware that an issue exists. The process concludes with an assessment of the results. As we have stressed, the ability to make effective decisions is a distinguishing characteristic of most successful managers.[8] In the next section, we discuss two models of decision behavior.

▼ The decision-making process is not complete until the impact of the decision has been evaluated. Managers often work together to evaluate feedback and determine whether progress is being made toward goals.

MODELS OF DECISION MAKING

Many models of the decision-making process can be found in the management literature. Although these models vary in scope, assumptions, and applicability, they are similar in that each focuses on the complexity of decision-making processes. In this section, we examine two decision-making models: the rational-economic model and the behavioral model. Our goal is to demonstrate the variety in how decision making is perceived and interpreted.[9]

RATIONAL-ECONOMIC MODEL

The **rational-economic model** is prescriptive rather than descriptive; that is, it concentrates on how decisions should be made, not on how they actually are made. Such models, which focus on how a decision maker should behave, are said to be normative. The model makes several important assumptions about the manager and the decision-making process:

- The manager is assumed to have "perfect"—completely accurate—information and to have all the information that is relevant to the situation.

- The model assumes the decision maker operates to accomplish objectives that are known and agreed upon and has an extensive list of alternatives from which to choose.

- As the model's name implies, it assumes that the manager will be rational, systematic, and logical in assessing each alternative and its associated probabilities.

- The model assumes that the manager will work in the best interests of the organization.

Also implicit in the model is the assumption that ethical dilemmas do not arise in the decision-making process.

As these assumptions suggest, the rational-economic model does not address the influences that impact the decision environment or describe how managers actually make decisions; instead, it provides guidelines to help the organization or group reach an ideal outcome. As a consequence, in practice the model may not always be a realistic depiction of managerial behavior. For example, the model portrays decision making as a straightforward process. In reality, making a decision is rarely that simple. First, people hardly ever have access to complete and perfect information. Second, even if information about all possible alternatives were available, individuals are limited in their ability to comprehend and process vast amounts of information. Third, decision makers seldom have adequate knowledge about the future consequences of alternatives. Furthermore, in most decision-making situations, personal factors such as fatigue or individual personalities, emotions, attitudes, motives, or behaviors are likely to intervene to prevent a manager from always acting completely rational. In addition, an individual's culture and ethical values will influence the decision process.

From a global perspective, it is especially important to be sensitive to how culture influences decision making. Individuals from different backgrounds and cultures will have different experiences, values, and behaviors, which in turn will influence the way they process information and make decisions. For example, as Global Perspective explains, the Japanese have a very different approach to decision making.[10]

Managerial decision making is also influenced by the individual's ethics and values. As we discussed in Chapter 3, managers have power by virtue of their positions to make decisions that affect people's lives and well-being; consequently the potential for ethical dilemmas is always present.[11] In an **ethical dilemma,** managers must decide whether or not to do something that will benefit themselves or the organization but may be considered unethical and perhaps illegal.

Several recent publications have suggested that ethical dilemmas are going to occur more and more frequently in the future as a result of the dramatic changes the business environment is undergoing. For example, managers may have to answer questions such as the following: What do companies owe employees who are let go after 30 years of service? Is it right to cancel a

Rational-economic model
A prescriptive framework of how a decision should be made that assumes managers have completely accurate information.

Ethical dilemma
A situation in which a person must decide whether or not to do something that, although benefiting oneself or the organization, may be considered unethical and perhaps illegal.

GLOBAL PERSPECTIVE

DECISION MAKING IN OTHER CULTURES

Culture influences the way decisions get made in organizations. For example, do groups from different cultures do any of the following?

- Perceive problems in the same way.
- Use the same decision-making processes.
- Gather similar types and amounts of information while investigating the problem.
- Follow the same thinking patterns.
- Construct similar types of solutions.
- Use similar strategies for choosing between alternatives.

The answer in each case is *no*. Research indicates that the cultural context has a lot to do with the decision-making processes used in different parts of the world.

For example, Japanese managers follow a unique consensual decision-making process in which subordinates are involved in considering the future direction of their companies. Individuals and groups who have ideas for improvement or change discuss them extensively with a large number of peers and managers. During this lengthy information communication process, some agreements (*nemawashi*) are hammered out. At this point, a formal document is drafted and circulated for the signature or personalized stamp (the seal or chop) of every manager who is considered relevant to the decision (*ringi*). Only after all the relevant managers have put their seals on the proposal is the idea or suggestion implemented.

contract with a loyal distributor when a cheaper supplier becomes available? Is it proper to develop condominiums on land that is an unofficial wildlife refuge?

The following questions may help you when you face a situation that has ethical implications:[12]

- Have you accurately assessed the problem?
- Do you have all the necessary information?
- Where are your loyalties?
- Have you generated a list of possible alternatives and considered how each will affect the other parties involved?
- Have you tested each alternative by asking whether it is legal, fair, and just to all parties involved?
- Would your decision change if you were to disclose it to your family, your boss, or society as a whole?
- Does your decision have any symbolic potential? Could it be misunderstood?

Managers should encourage ethical decision making throughout the organization by providing subordinates with clear guidelines for making decisions and establishing rules for enforcing the guidelines. Both the guidelines and the rules should be communicated to subordinates on a regular basis.

Behavioral decision model
A descriptive framework for understanding that a person's cognitive ability to process information is limited.

BEHAVIORAL DECISION MODEL

Unlike the rational-economic model, the **behavioral decision model** acknowledges human limitations that make rational decisions difficult to achieve.

The behavioral decision model is descriptive and provides a framework for understanding the process that managers actually use when selecting from among alternatives.

The behavioral decision model suggests that a person's cognitive ability to process information is limited. In other words, a human being can handle only so much information before overload occurs. Even if complete information were available to decision makers, these cognitive limitations would impede them from making completely rational decisions.

Applying this assumption to managerial decision making, the model suggests that managers usually attempt to behave rationally within their limited perception of a situation. But most organizational situations are so complex that managers are forced to view problems within sharply restricted bounds. They frequently try to compensate for their limited ability to cope with the information demands of complex problems by developing simple models. Thus, the managers' behavior can be considered rational, but only in terms of their simplified view of the problem.

The behavioral decision model introduces several concepts that are important to understanding how we make decisions. These concepts include bounded rationality, intuition, satisficing, and escalation of commitment.

Bounded Rationality

The notion of **bounded rationality** recognizes that people cannot know everything; they are limited by such organizational constraints as time, information, resources, and their own mental capacities.[13] Bounded rationality is a useful concept because it explains why different individuals with exactly the same information may make different decisions.

Bounded rationality affects several key aspects of the decision-making process. First, decision makers do not search out all possible alternatives and then select the best. Rather, they identify and evaluate alternatives only until an acceptable solution is found. Having found a satisfactory alternative, the decision maker stops searching for additional solutions. Other, and potentially better, alternatives may exist, but will not be identified or considered because the first workable solution has been accepted. Therefore, only a fraction of the available alternatives may be considered due to the decision maker's information processing limitations.

Intuition

Intuition has been described as everything from an unconscious analysis based on past experience to a paranormal ability called a "sixth sense."[14] Several theories have attempted to explain intuition, but none has been proved. We do know that intuition is based on the individual's years of practice and experience. For example, a decision maker who detects similarities between the current situation and one encountered previously will select or modify actions that proved effective in that situation in the past.[15] Managers use intuition to obtain a quick understanding of a situation and to identify solutions without going through extensive analysis. Many critics feel that many U.S. corporations place too much emphasis on decision analysis and suggest that managers should trust their feelings and experience more often.[16]

Satisficing

Satisficing means searching for and accepting something that is satisfactory rather than insisting on the perfect or optimal. "Satisficers" do not try to find optimal solutions to problems but search until they find an acceptable or satisfactory solution and then adopt it. In short, managers tend to "satisfice" rather than optimize in considering and selecting alternatives. Some satisficing behavior is unavoidable because managers do not have access to all possible contingencies in making decisions. As we see in Entrepreneurial Approach,

Bounded rationality
Recognizes that people are limited by such organizational constraints as time, information, resources and their own mental capacities.

Intuition
An unconscious analysis based on past experience.

Satisficing
The search and acceptance of something that is satisfactory rather than perfect or optimal.

ENTREPRENEURIAL APPROACH

CHATWAL'S SATISFICING BEHAVIOR LEADS TO PROBLEMS

Sant Singh Chatwal, an entrepreneur and the founder of Bombay Palace Restaurants, Inc., discovered that satisficing behavior has some potential pitfalls. When Chatwal wanted to expand his New York–based restaurant chain, he found that leasing property in Manhattan was extremely expensive. Rather than evaluating many alternatives, he sought a quick solution to his problem and merged with another chain, Lifestyle Restaurants, Inc., a publicly owned chain that owned, operated, or franchised close to 50 Beefsteak Charlie's restaurants. Chatwal was attracted to Lifestyle because it owned a number of inexpensive leases, many of them in very expensive parts of Manhattan.

While Chatwal admits that he had heard that Lifestyle's chairman had a reputation for unsavory business practices and problems with liquor boards in New York and Maryland, he still sought a quick solution to his leasing problems. After the merger, Chatwal retained Lifestyle's chairman as president and chief executive and guaranteed him a generous salary of $400,000 per year, other benefits, and attractive financial concessions involving stock. Within a few months, however, Chatwal and his company were in court attempting to break the contract on the ground that Lifestyle had allegedly failed to disclose certain tax liabilities and other problems.

Chatwal became distracted by these problems, and the Bombay Palace chain began to experience losses. Thus, Chatwal found that satisficing behavior may lead to difficulties in the long run.

Sant Singh Chatwal, the founder of Bombay Palace Restaurants, discovered that satisficing behavior has some potential pitfalls.[17]

Escalation of Commitment

Escalation of commitment
The tendency to increase commitment to a previously selected course of action beyond the level that would be expected if the manager followed an effective decision-making process.

When managers face evidence that an initial decision is not working, they frequently react by committing more resources, even when feedback indicates the action is wrong.[18] This **escalation of commitment** phenomenon is the tendency to commit more to a previously selected course of action than would be expected if the manager followed an effective decision-making process.[19] One reason for escalation of commitment is that individuals feel responsible for negative consequences and try to justify their previous decisions. Managers may also stay with a course of action simply because they believe consistency is a desirable behavior. In addition, managers may worry that if they change course, others may regard the original decision as a mistake or a failure.

In contrast, consider how Fred Smith, the CEO of Federal Express, changed course and cut the company's losses on ZapMail. ZapMail was a satellite-based network that was to provide businesses with two-hour document delivery service. Believing Federal Express's hard-copy delivery services would be severely eroded by the burgeoning electronic mail market, Smith decided to invest heavily in ZapMail. Unfortunately, he failed to anticipate the impact of low-cost fax machines, and Federal Express lost over $300 million in the first year alone. Smith admits that making the decision to disband ZapMail after the organization had committed so many resources to the concept and the technology was difficult.

WHAT MAKES A QUALITY DECISION?

How can managers tell whether they have made the best possible decision? One way is to wait until the results are in, but that can take a long time. In the meantime, managers can focus on the decision-making process. Although nothing can guarantee a "perfect" decision, using vigilance can make a good decision more likely. **Vigilance** means being concerned for and attentive to the correct decision-making procedures. Vigilant decision makers use the following procedures:[20]

- Survey the full range of objectives to be fulfilled and identify the values and qualities implicated by the choices.
- Thoroughly canvas a wide range of alternative courses of action. This is the idea-gathering process, which should be quite separate from idea evaluation.
- Carefully weigh whatever they know about the costs and risks of both the negative and positive consequences that could flow from each alternative.
- Intensively search for new high-quality information relevant to further evaluation of the alternatives.
- Assimilate and take into account any new advice or information to which they are exposed, even when the information or advice does not support the course of action initially preferred.
- Reexamine all the possible consequences of all known alternatives before making a final choice, including those originally regarded as unacceptable.
- Make detailed provisions for implementing or executing the chosen course of action and give special attention to contingency plans that might be required if various known risks materialize.

While vigilance will not guarantee perfect decisions every time, this approach can help managers be confident they have followed procedures that will yield the best possible decision under the circumstances. Spending more time at this stage can save time later in the decision process.

▼ Although nothing can guarantee a perfect decision, using vigilance can increase the quality of the decision. John Yeh, president of Integrated Microcomputer Systems, encourages top-level managers to be attentive and concerned for the decision-making process.

Vigilance
The concern for and attention to the process of making a decision that occurs when the decision maker considers seven critical procedures.

GROUP CONSIDERATIONS IN DECISION MAKING ▬▬▬

So far in this chapter we have been examining how managers make decisions individually. In practice, managers often work with their employees and peers in the company and may need to solicit input from them. Decision making is frequently entrusted to a group—a board, standing committee, ad hoc committee, or task force. Group decision making is becoming more common as organizations focus on improving customer service through quality management and push decision making to lower levels.[21] Accordingly, this section examines some of the issues related to using groups to make decisions.

PARTICIPATIVE DECISION MAKING

Participative decision making is not a single technique that can be applied to all situations. As we will see, managers can use a variety of techniques to involve the members of the organization in decision making. The appropriate level of subordinate participation in decision making depends on the manager, the employees, the organization, and the nature of the decision itself.

Participative Models

Vroom and Yetton developed a model for participation in decision making that helps managers determine when group decision making is appropriate.[22] According to this participative model, the effectiveness of a group decision is governed by both its quality and its acceptance (the degree to which group members are committed to the decision they have made). Updated by Vroom and Jago to reflect the decision-making environment of managers more adequately, this model expands the three basic decision-making methods (individual, consultative, and group) into five styles of possible decision participation.[23] To arrive at the best decision, a manager needs to analyze the situation and then choose one of the five decision-making styles.

As Table 6.1 shows, the five styles can be arranged along a continuum. The decision methods become progressively more participative as one moves from the highly autocratic style (AI), in which the manager decides alone, to the consultative style (CI), where the manager consults with the group before deciding, to the group style (GII), where the manager allows the group to decide.[24]

According to Vroom and Jago, the nature of the decision itself determines the appropriate degree of participation, and they provide diagnostic questions to help managers select the appropriate level. Figure 6.2 shows how these questions can be used in a decision tree format to arrive at the appropriate decision style. (The structure and use of decision trees will be discussed in more detail in Chapter 7.) For the sake of simplicity, the decision tree in Figure 6.2 treats each question as having only two answers, yes or no. By starting at the left and answering the questions, managers can follow the tree to arrive at one of the decision styles described in Table 6.1.

▼ **TABLE 6.1**   Decision Styles

	DECISION STYLE	DESCRIPTION
Highly autocratic		
	AI	The manager solves the decision problem alone using information available at the time.
	AII	The manager solves the decision problem alone after obtaining necessary information from subordinates.
	CI	The manager solves the decision problem after obtaining ideas and suggestions from subordinates individually. The decision may or may not reflect their counsel.
	CII	The manager solves the decision problem after obtaining ideas and suggestions from subordinates as a group. The decision may or may not reflect their counsel.
	GII	The group analyzes the problem, identifies and evaluates alternatives, and makes a decision. The manager acts as coordinator of the group of subordinates and accepts and implements any solution that has the support of the group.
Highly democratic		

NOTE: A = autocratic; C = consultative; G = group.

QR	Quality requirement	How important is the technical quality of this decision?
CR	Commitment requirement	How important is employee commitment to the decision?
LI	Leader's information	Do you have sufficient information to make a high-quality decision?
ST	Problem structure	Is the problem well structured?
CP	Commitment probability	If you were to make the decision by yourself, is it reasonably certain that your employees would be commited to the decision?
GC	Goal congruence	Do employees share the organizational goals to be attained in solving this problem?
CO	Employee conflict	Is conflict among employees over preferred solutions likely?
SI	Employee information	Do employees have sufficient information to make a high-quality decision?

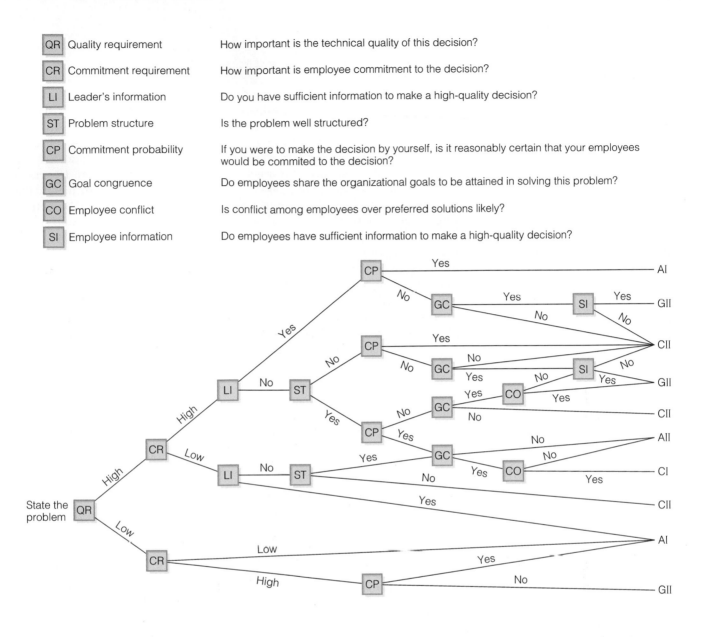

In general, a participative decision style is desirable when subordinates have useful information and share the organization's goals, when subordinates' commitment to the decision is essential, when timeliness is not crucial, and when conflict is unlikely. At the same time, group decision making is more complex than decision making by individuals, but good communication and conflict management skills can overcome this difficulty.[25] As we see in Service Challenge, New York Life Insurance Company has found that participative decision making helps it provide quality service to its customers.[26]

It is important to note that the inappropriate use of either group or individual decision making can be costly. Using groups ineffectively wastes organizational resources because the participants' time could have been spent on other tasks; it also leads to boredom and reduces motivation because participants feel that their time has been wasted. Making decisions individually that would have been better made by groups can lead to poor coordination among organization members, less commitment to quality, and little emphasis on creativity, as well as to poor decisions.[27]

▼ **FIGURE 6.2**
Vroom and Jago Decision Tree

SOURCE: Reprinted from V. H. Vroom and A. G. Jago, *The New Leadership: Managing Participation in Organizations,* (Englewood, Prentice-Hall, 1988), 184.

SERVICE CHALLENGE

NEW YORK LIFE'S GRAVEDIGGERS DELIVER QUALITY AND SERVICE

At New York Life Insurance Company, a new group decision-making approach is allowing people to pool their skills and knowledge to provide better service to their customers. Throughout the New York Life organization, teams with such unlikely names as Hot Pursuit, Watch Dogs, Just the Fax, French Connection, and Raiders of the Lost Transactions are streamlining operations.

One of the most successful team efforts to date is the work of an 18-person team formed to discover why 7000 letters a week were being returned by the U.S. Post Office as "undeliverable." Since most of the undeliverable letters were premium notices, the potential value of the project was estimated at $80 million. Dubbed the Gravediggers because of their tenacity in "digging up" addresses, the team—composed of employees from around the country—met first weekly and then biweekly via teleconferences. Using a step-by-step decision-making process, the team began identifying root problems: policyholders moved and forgot to notify the company; addresses did not fit into mailing envelope windows; addresses on applications were difficult to read; and procedures for locating more accurate addresses were inadequate.

Next, the team generated alternatives and chose several ways to solve the problems. The team then implemented a number of corrective measures; these included creating units in each New York Life service office to find more accurate addresses and update company records in a more timely manner; working out an agreement with the Post Office to forward mail and provide correct addresses; arranging with outside databases to provide addresses the Post Office couldn't supply; improving the use of software to validate addresses as they're put into the computer system; and bar-coding and sorting mail in greater detail.

The results to date are impressive, with even more to come. The volume of returned mail has been reduced by more than 20 percent. Over $600,000 has already been saved through bar-coding and sorting. According to Wynne M. Gannon, vice president for quality, "It is evident that highly empowered teams are the best vehicle for delivering enhanced quality and service to our customers. A focus on customers is just good business."

Group Size

In deciding whether a participative model of decision making is appropriate, a manager must also consider the size of the group. In general, as group size increases, the following changes in the decision-making process are likely to be observed:[28]

- The demands on the leader's time and attention are greater, and the leader is more psychologically distant from the other members. This becomes much more of a problem in self-managing teams, where several individuals can take on leadership roles.
- The group's tolerance of direction from the leader is greater, and the team's decision making becomes more centralized.
- The atmosphere is less friendly, actions are less personal, more subgroups form, and in general, members are less satisfied.
- Rules and procedures become more formalized.

As our discussion thus far suggests, both group and individual decision making offer potential advantages and disadvantages. These are examined in

▼ A manager must consider size as an important factor when using groups to make decisions. These two groups will function differently and impact the decision-making process because of differences in size.

the next sections. Then we turn our attention to structured techniques managers can use to improve group decision making.

ADVANTAGES OF GROUP DECISION MAKING

Committees, task forces, and ad hoc groups are frequently assigned to identify and recommend decision alternatives or, in some cases, to actually make important decisions. In essence, a group is a tool that can focus the experience and expertise of several people on a particular problem or situation. Thus, a group offers the advantage of greater total knowledge. Groups accumulate more information, knowledge, and facts than individuals and often consider more alternatives. Each person in the group is able to draw on his or her unique education, experience, insights, and other resources and contribute those to the group. The varied backgrounds, training levels, and expertise of group members also help overcome tunnel vision by enabling the group to view the problem in more than one way.

Participation in group decision making usually leads to higher member satisfaction. People tend to accept a decision more readily and to be better satisfied with it when they have participated in making that decision. In addition, people will better understand and be more committed to a decision in which they have had a say than to a decision made for them. As a result, such a decision is more likely to be implemented successfully. A summary of the advantages of group decision making appears in Table 6.2.

In Managing for Excellence, we see how Spurling Fire & Burglar Alarm Company uses group decision making to support organizational goals and implement new programs.[29]

DISADVANTAGES OF GROUP DECISION MAKING

While groups have many potential benefits, we all know that they can also be frustrating. In fact, the traditional interacting group is prone to a variety of difficulties. One obvious disadvantage of group decision making is the time required to make a decision (see Table 6.2). The time needed for group discussion and the associated compromising and selecting of a decision alternative can be considerable. Time costs money, so a waste of time becomes a disadvantage if a decision made by a group could have been made just as effectively by an individual working alone. Consequently, group decisions should be avoided when speed and efficiency are the primary considerations.

MANAGING FOR EXCELLENCE

SPURLING FIRE & BURGLAR ALARM: MANAGING BY COMMITTEE

Aspersions are often cast at managing by groups or committees. Supposedly, it slows you down to the point of paralysis, so that nothing gets decided. Not so at Spurling Fire & Burglar Alarm Company, a seller and servicer of fire and burglar alarms that has branched out into electronic devices for keeping tabs on paroled criminals. Spurling, based in Fort Smith, Arkansas, has outlets there, in Springdale to the north, and in Little Rock to the east.

The company's sales were flat and its collections lagging when it tried a new system. It formed "The Committee," consisting of owner W. K. McGehee, Jr., the general manager, the sales manager, the northwest Arkansas manager, and the Little Rock manager. Several ideas initiated by "The Committee" have been implemented successfully.

Meeting monthly, "The Committee" makes decisions on prices, collecting procedures, purchasing, marketing, and personnel. These meetings, notes McGehee, have given more people input into daily operations and long-range planning. "They started coming up with some great ideas which have been instituted with good results," he says. "We are operating like a team now."

Since sales were slow, service crews weren't spending much time on new installations of leased alarm systems. "The Committee" suggested that crews be sent to update older systems. The result was more available time; once updated, the systems needed less service. However, the crews soon had more installations to do. Pleased by the updating, customers referred Spurling to more businesses. Salespeople paid courtesy calls on customers and got good leads. Commercial and industrial firms were not always aware that Spurling did work for residential customers—and vice versa. Many customers didn't know the firm took jobs in other parts of the state.

As for slow collections, "The Committee" changed procedures on sales commissions. Previously, salespeople received commissions when down payments were made. Now they wait until the company gets all its money— an inspiration for them to press customers for prompt payment.

Today 42-year-old Spurling is prospering. Its annual sales top $1 million, reflecting a 15 percent growth in three years, and it expects much more growth. Who says management by committee can't work?

A second disadvantage is that the group discussion may be dominated by an individual or subgroup. Effectiveness can be reduced if one individual, such as the group leader, dominates the discussion by talking too much or being closed to other points of view. Some leaders try to control the group and provide the major input. Such dominance can stifle other group members' willingness to participate and could cause decision alternatives to be ignored or overlooked. All group members need to be encouraged and permitted to contribute.

Another disadvantage of group decision making is that members may be less concerned with the group's goals than with their own personal goals. They may become so sidetracked in trying to win an argument that they forget about group performance. On the other hand, a group may try too hard to compromise and consequently may not make optimal decisions. Sometimes this stems from the desire to maintain friendships and avoid disagreements. Often groups exert tremendous social pressure on individuals to conform to

▼ **TABLE 6.2**   Advantages and Disadvantages of Group Decision Making

ADVANTAGES	DISADVANTAGES
• Experience and expertise of several individuals available	• Greater time requirement
• More information, data, and facts accumulated	• Minority domination
• Problems viewed from several perspectives	• Compromise
• Higher member satisfaction	• Concern for individual rather than group goals
• Greater acceptance and commitment to decisions	• Social pressure to conform
	• Groupthink

established or expected patterns of behavior. Especially when they are dealing with important and controversial issues, interacting groups may be prone to a phenomenon called groupthink.[30]

Groupthink is an agreement-at-any-cost mentality that results in ineffective group decision making. It occurs when groups are highly cohesive, have highly directive leaders, are insulated so they have no clear ways to get objective information, and, because they lack outside information, have little hope that a better solution might be found than the one proposed by the leader or other influential group members.[31] These conditions foster the illusion that the group is invulnerable, right, and more moral than outsiders. They also encourage the development of self-appointed ''mind guards'' who bring pressure on dissenters. In such situations, decisions, often important decisions, are made without consideration of alternative frames or alternative options. It is difficult to imagine conditions more conducive to poor decision making and wrong decisions.

Recent research indicates that groupthink may also result when group members have preconceived ideas about how a problem should be solved.[32] Under these conditions the team may not examine a full range of decision alternatives or they may discount or avoid information that threatens the team's preconceived choice.

Irving Janis, who coined the term groupthink, focused his research on high-level governmental policy groups faced with difficult problems in complex and dynamic environments. The groupthink phenomenon has been used to explain numerous group decisions that have resulted in serious fiascoes. Examples of such decisions include the Bay of Pigs invasion, the Watergate coverup, and NASA's decision to launch the *Challenger* on January 28, 1986, as described in the Managerial Incident.[33] Of course, group decision making is quite common in all types of organizations, so it is possible that groupthink exists in private-sector organizations as well as in those in the public sector. Table 6.3 summarizes the characteristics of groupthink and the types of defective decision making that will likely result.

Groupthink is common in tightly knit groups that believe in what they are doing: citizen groups who censor book acquisitions for the local library, environmental groups who will save us from ourselves at any price, business leaders who presume that they control other people's economic destinies, or government functionaries who think that they know better than the voters what is in the national interest. None of the decisions made by these groups is necessarily wrong, but that is not the point. Rather, it is the single-mindedness of the decision process, the narrow framing, and limited deliberation that are of concern.[34]

Groupthink
An agreement-at-any-cost mentality that results in ineffective group decision making.

▼ **TABLE 6.3**   Characteristics of Groupthink and the Types of Defective Decisions that May Result

CHARACTERISTICS OF GROUPTHINK	TYPES OF DEFECTIVE DECISIONS
• Illusion of invulnerability • Collective rationalization • Belief in the morality of group decisions • Self-censorship • Illusion of unanimity in decision making • Pressure on members who express arguments	• Incomplete survey of alternatives • Incomplete survey of goals • Failure to examine risks of preferred decisions • Poor information search • Failure to reappraise alternatives • Failure to develop contingency plans

TECHNIQUES FOR QUALITY IN GROUP DECISION MAKING

Managers can use several structured techniques to foster quality in group decision making.[35] Here we will briefly explore brainstorming, the nominal group technique, the Delphi technique, devil's advocacy, and dialectical inquiry.

Brainstorming

Brainstorming

A technique used to enhance creativity that encourages group members to generate as many novel ideas as possible on a given topic without evaluating them.

Brainstorming is a technique that encourages group members to generate as many novel ideas as possible on a given topic without evaluating them. As a group process, brainstorming can enhance creativity by overcoming pressures for conformity that can retard the development of creative decision making. Brainstorming primarily focuses on generating ideas rather than on choosing an alternative. The members of the group, usually 5 to 12 people, are encouraged to generate ideas during a specific time period while withholding criticism and focusing on nonevaluative presentation.[36] In this way, individuals who may be concerned about being ridiculed or criticized feel more free to offer truly novel ideas.

The following rules should guide the brainstorming process:[37]

- Freewheeling is encouraged. Group members are free to offer any suggestions to the facilitator who lists ideas as people speak.
- Group members will not criticize ideas as they are being generated. Consider any and all ideas. No idea can be rejected initially.
- Quantity is encouraged. Write down all the ideas.
- The wilder the ideas the better.
- Piggyback on or combine previously stated ideas.
- No ideas are evaluated until after all alternatives are generated.

Brainstorming enhances creativity and reduces the tendency of groups to satisfice in considering alternatives. One advocate of brainstorming is Bill Gates, the CEO of Microsoft. He often joins programmers in the brainstorming sessions that give birth to new products. According to Gates, it is very important to him and to those who work with him at Microsoft to encourage creative group decision making.[38]

Nominal Group Technique

Nominal group technique (NGT)

A structured process designed to stimulate creative group decision making where agreement is lacking or the members have incomplete knowledge concerning the nature of the problem.

The **nominal group technique (NGT)** is a structured process designed to stimulate creative group decision making where agreement is lacking or the members have incomplete knowledge of the nature of the problem.[39] It is a means of enhancing creativity and decision making that integrates both indi-

▼ Brainstorming enhances creativity and reduces the tendency of groups to satisfice in considering alternatives. This company brainstorming session encourages group members to generate as many novel ideas as possible on a given topic without evaluating them.

vidual work and group interaction with certain basic guidelines. NGT was developed to foster individual, as well as group, creativity and further overcome the tendency of group members to criticize ideas when they are offered.

NGT is used in situations where group members must pool their judgments to solve the problem and determine a satisfactory course of action. First, individual members independently list their ideas on the specific problem. Next, each member presents his or her ideas one at a time without discussion. As with brainstorming, members are asked to generate ideas without direct comment, but the idea generation phase of NGT is more confined than it is with brainstorming because group members present ideas in a round robin manner rather than through freewheeling. Members' ideas are recorded so everyone can see them. After all the members' ideas are presented, the group discusses the ideas to clarify and evaluate them. Finally, members vote on the ideas independently, using a rank-ordering or rating procedure. The final outcome is determined by the pooled individual votes and is thus mathematically derived.

NGT may be most effective when decisions are complex or where the group is experiencing blockages or problems, such as a few dominating members. NGT is generally effective in generating large numbers of creative alternatives while maintaining group satisfaction.[40]

Delphi Technique

The **Delphi technique** was originally developed by the Rand Corporation to enable groups to consult experts and use their predictions and forecasts about future events.[41] Using survey instruments or questionnaires, a group leader solicits and collects written, expert opinions on a topic. The leader collates and summarizes the information before distributing it to the participants. This process continues until the experts' predictions are systematically refined through feedback and a consensus emerges.

Like NGT, the Delphi technique can be used to define problems and to consider and select alternatives. The Delphi technique is also best used under special circumstances. The primary difference between NGT and the Delphi technique is that with the Delphi technique participants do not meet face-to-face.

Delphi technique
Uses experts to make predictions and forecasts about future events without meeting face-to-face.

A significant advantage of the Delphi technique is that it completely avoids group interaction effects. Even NGT is not completely immune to social facilitating pressure that results from having an important person in the same room. With Delphi, participant experts can be thousands of miles apart.

Devil's Advocacy Approach

The last two techniques to enhance group decision making, devil's advocacy and dialectical inquiry, were developed to deal with complex, strategic decisions. Both techniques encourage intense, heated debate among group members. A recent study found that disagreement in structured settings like meetings can lead to better decision making.[42] Disagreement is particularly useful for organizations operating in uncertain environments.

Devil's advocacy

An individual or subgroup appointed to critique a proposed course of action and identify problems to consider before the decision is final.

The **devil's advocacy approach** appoints an individual or subgroup to critique a proposed course of action. One or more individuals are assigned the role of devil's advocate to make sure that the negative aspects of any attractive decision alternatives are considered.[43] The usefulness of the devil's advocate technique was demonstrated several years ago by Irving Janis in his discussion of famous fiascoes attributed to groupthink. Janis recommends that everyone in the group assume the role of devil's advocate and question the assumptions underlying the popular choice. An individual or subgroup can be formally designated as the devil's advocate to present critiques of the proposed decision. Using this technique avoids the tendency of groups to allow their desire to agree to interfere with decision making. Potential pitfalls are identified and considered before the decision is final.

Dialectical Inquiry

Dialectical inquiry

Approaches a decision from two opposite points and structures a debate between conflicting views.

With **dialectical inquiry,** a decision situation is approached from two opposite points, and advocates of the conflicting views conduct a debate, presenting arguments in support of their position. Each decision possibility is developed and assumptions are identified. The technique forces the group to confront the implications of their assumptions in the decision process.[44] Bausch and Lomb successfully uses this technique by establishing "tiger teams" composed of scientists from different disciplines. Team members are encouraged to bring up divergent ideas and offer different points of view. Xerox uses round table discussions composed of various functional experts to encourage divergent and innovative decision making.

MANAGERIAL IMPLICATIONS

The most important characteristic of successful decision makers is that they do not approach decisions unprepared. Responsibility for decision making only comes to those who have earned it. Responsibility is earned by decision makers who demonstrate both a record of success and an understanding of their organization. As a manager, you need to realize that successful decision making means understanding the organization's basic beliefs and culture, its goals and vision, and its activities and the plans that guide them.[45]

How will changes in the managerial role in the next decade impact the decision making of tomorrow's manager? The following guidelines, developed by Robert Denhardt in his recent book *The Pursuit of Significance,* reflect current thinking about managerial techniques that foster quality decision making:[46]

- Be committed to the decision-making process; use it, and let data, not emotions, drive decisions.
- Seek employees' input before you make key decisions.

- Believe in, foster, and support group decision making in the organization.
- Believe that the best way to improve the quality of decisions is to ask and listen to employees who are doing the work.
- Seek and use high-quality information.
- Avoid ''top-down'' power-oriented decision making wherever possible.
- Encourage decision-making creativity through risk taking, and be tolerant of honest mistakes.
- Develop an open atmosphere that encourages organization members to offer and accept feedback.

In this chapter we have set forth some fundamentals of how managers in organizations make decisions. We examined the steps in the decision-making process, issues related to ethical decision dilemmas, and two models of decision behavior. Since managers are often involved with groups, we discussed group decision-making concerns and techniques that managers can use to improve the group decision process. In Chapter 7 we will build on these fundamentals by presenting quantitative tools for making better decisions.

AN ILL-FATED DECISION WATCHED BY MILLIONS

MANAGERIAL INCIDENT RESOLUTION

In retrospect, many experts regard the *Challenger* disaster as an example of faulty decision making that resulted from top management's isolation from the technical personnel. At the time, NASA's top managers were under intense pressure to reach a decision and were influenced by many factors.

In the aftermath of the accident, NASA significantly overhauled the decision-making process used for shuttle launches. The new system incorporates a number of reviews by several committees and uses much more information than in the past. Several critical reviews take place before the terminal countdown begins; the most important is the Flight Readiness Review (FRR). To keep NASA's management in touch with all levels of the organization, the new decision-making process includes checks and verifications by more than 300 NASA employees as well as by numerous outside contractors. To date, the revised decision-making launch procedures appear to be working successfully.[47] ▼

SUMMARY

- The decision-making process includes seven steps: (1) identifying and diagnosing the problem, (2) identifying objectives, (3) generating alternatives, (4) evaluating alternatives, (5) reaching decisions, (6) choosing implementation strategies, and (7) monitoring and evaluating.
- Ethical dilemmas often occur as alternatives are being evaluated. An ethical dilemma is a situation in which the decision makers must decide whether or not to do something that will benefit themselves or the organization but may be considered unethical and perhaps illegal.
- The rational-economic model assumes that the manager has completely accurate information and an extensive list of alternatives from which to choose; it also assumes that he or she will be rational and systematic in assessing each alternative and will work in the best interests of the organization.

- The behavioral decision model acknowledges human limitations to decision making and addresses the issues of bounded rationality, intuition, satisficing, and escalation of commitment. Bounded rationality recognizes that people cannot know everything and are limited by such organizational constraints as time, information, resources, and their own mental capacities. Intuition has been described as everything from an unconscious analysis based on past experience to a paranormal ability called a sixth sense. Satisficing means searching for and accepting something that is satisfactory rather than optimal. Escalation of commitment is the tendency to commit more resources to a previously selected course of action than would be expected if the manager followed an effective decision-making process.

- The increased involvement of groups and teams in management actions requires that managers understand group considerations in decision making. The participation model of group decision making provides guidelines for the appropriate level of subordinate participation in decision making.

- A manager must consider both the advantages and disadvantages to group decision making. The advantages include greater experience and expertise, more information, higher satisfaction, and greater acceptance and commitment to the decisions. The disadvantages are that group decisions take more time, one member or subgroup may dominate, individual goals may supplant group goals, social pressure to conform may be brought to bear on members, and groupthink may develop.

- Managers can use several structured techniques to aid in group decision making. These include brainstorming, the nominal group technique, the Delphi technique, devil's advocacy, and dialectical inquiry.

KEY TERMS

Decision making (p. 180)
Objectives (p. 184)
Rational-economic model (p. 187)
Ethical dilemma (p. 187)
Behavioral decision model (p. 188)
Bounded rationality (p. 189)

Intuition (p. 189)
Satisficing (p. 189)
Escalation of commitment (p. 190)
Vigilance (p. 191)
Groupthink (p. 197)
Brainstorming (p. 198)

Nominal group technique (NGT)
  (p. 198)
Delphi technique (p. 199)
Devil's advocacy (p. 200)
Dialectical inquiry (p. 200)

REVIEW QUESTIONS

1. Define decision making.
2. Explain the steps a manager can use to handle ethical dilemmas in decision making.
3. How does bounded rationality affect the decision-making process?
4. What are the seven steps of the decision-making process? Which step is most important?
5. Under what conditions would a manager use a group to make a decision?
6. Describe the advantages and disadvantages of group decision making compared to individual de-

cision making. Provide specific examples to demonstrate your understanding.
7. What is groupthink? What are the signs a manager should look for to recognize groupthink?
8. What are the key guidelines for brainstorming?
9. How can brainstorming be used to improve group decision making?
10. What are the three basic categories of decision making in the Vroom-Jago participation model?

DISCUSSION QUESTIONS

Improving Critical Thinking

1. Is the rational-economic model of decision making so unrealistic that it is of no value to a decision maker? Why or why not?

2. Describe a situation in which you satisficed when making a decision.

Enhancing Communication Skills

3. What types of ethical dilemmas do you think future managers will face? How can you prepare yourself to handle ethical dilemmas? To develop your written communication skills, find some recent examples in current business publications and write a short paper on this subject.

4. Consider a recent decision that you have made such as choosing a major or buying a car. How vigilant were you in making your decision? To practice your oral communication skills, be prepared to present your decision process to the class or a small group as directed by your instructor.

Building Teamwork

5. Interview a manager in a local business. Ask the manager to describe a business decision that she or he recently made and to explain the process that led to that decision. Analyze the manager's decision with regard to the two models of decision making described in the chapter. Form small groups and share the results of your interview with the team. Did the team members find any issues in common among all the managers interviewed?

6. Think about a group decision that you have been involved with. Did the group experience any signs of groupthink? Why or why not? Form small groups and look for common problems that members have experienced. Summarize your findings and be prepared to report them to the class.

ETHICS: TAKE A STAND

Harry was a senior member of the outside auditing team of a public company. Among his many responsibilities was the accurate and complete reporting of all financial information and transactions that could affect potential and current investors in the company. Inadvertently, a copy of a private memo from the company's controller to members of top management was placed in Harry's mail. The memo dealt with an acquisition that was about to take place, but the controller had not mentioned the acquisition to Harry. Harry therefore asked the controller about the acquisition when he returned the memo.

The controller seemed disturbed that Harry had received the memo. She grabbed the memo from Harry's hand and said that the acquisition was only under consideration. Thus, it should not be reported in the financial statements. She also said that if Harry mentioned the situation to anyone, he would look foolish because the transaction did not have to be reported under Generally Accepted Accounting Principles.

Harry was taken aback by the controller's reaction. The memo provided significant detail about the transaction, and he was sure that the deal was final. In accordance with his firm's policy, Harry decided to bring the situation to the attention of the manager in charge of the auditing job. The manager said that he knew of the acquisition, but because the deal was not final when he completed his fieldwork, he had decided to ignore it at the request of the chief financial officer. The partner on the job agreed with the decision.

Harry was certain that the acquisition would be very important to potential and current investors in the company. He was not comfortable with the way the problem had been handled and felt that some serious ethical issues were involved. He knew his next decision would be critical.

For Discussion:

1. If you were Harry, what would you do?

2. What criteria would you use in taking action?

3. Develop a plan for Harry based on the steps of the decision-making process outlined in the chapter.

THINKING CRITICALLY
Debate the Issue

WHO SHOULD MAKE THE DECISION?

Form teams as directed by your instructor. Half of the teams should take the position that group decision making leads to high-quality decisions and high organizational performance. The other teams should take the position that group decision making impedes organizational performance and that decisions should not be made by groups. Research the topic using current business publications to provide support for your team's position. Your instructor will select two teams to present your arguments in a debate format.

VIDEO CASE

Motorola Challenges Employees with Team Competitor

 Motorola is a large manufacturing organization that supplies electronic equipment, system components, and services to markets worldwide. The company is headquartered near Chicago and has operating locations throughout the United States and the world. Motorola takes great pride in its long history of creating world-class products.

Motorola's goals include building a corporation that is continually moving forward while strengthening its foundation of uncompromising integrity. Motorola plans to grow rapidly around the world and gain global marketshare by providing customers with exciting high-quality products and services when they need them.

In 1988 Motorola's excellence was recognized when it won the first Malcolm Baldrige National Quality Award. The company did not view the award as an end in itself but rather as a symbol of its long-term drive for competitive excellence through product and service quality. Although the company learned many lessons along the way to this award, top management was above all seeking to challenge employees to be more creative and innovative, especially in achieving customer satisfaction.

To achieve this lofty goal, Motorola's management created the Customer Satisfaction Team Competition. The competition, now in its third year, has unleashed the creative spark of employee teams by empowering and encouraging them to develop high-quality prod-

ucts and provide excellent service. The event challenges employees to use their team problem-solving skills to look at concerns from the customer's point of view.

Teams from around the world are entered in the competition. They present their ideas to a panel of Motorola managers and customers who judge and rank the teams. The teams are evaluated on (1) teamwork, (2) problem selection, (3) analysis, (4) remedies, (5) results, (6) institutionalization of remedies, and (7) team presentation. The competition focuses attention on a significant cultural change at Motorola and shows employees' ability to work together to drive initiative and provide the best products and service to customers.

The Customer Satisfaction Team Competition is one way Motorola challenges and rewards employees for being creative and innovative. At Motorola, total customer satisfaction is more than a corporation vision.

For Discussion

1. Discuss ways that Motorola encourages its employees to be creative.

2. How are the criteria for evaluating the competition related to the decision-making process?

3. If you were an employee at Motorola, how would you view the Customer Satisfaction Team Competition?

CASE

Cypros Computer Design: A Case of Mixed Blessings

As manufacturing vice president for Cypros Computer Design, Jessica Okaty ponders the problem she faces. Cypros's management is always searching for ways to increase efficiency and recently installed new equipment (robots) along with a new simplified work system. To the surprise of everyone, including Jessica, the expected increase in productivity has not materialized. In fact, production has begun to drop, quality has fallen off, and employee turnover has risen.

Jessica does not believe that there is anything wrong with the new equipment. She has obtained reports from other companies that are using the robots, and they confirm this opinion. In addition, representatives from the firm that designed the equipment have inspected it and report that it is operating at peak efficiency.

Jessica suspects that some aspects of the new work system may be responsible for the declining productivity, but this view is not shared by her immediate subordinates—four unit supervisors, each in charge of a section, and her supply manager. They attribute the drop in production to insufficient training of the robot operators, lack of an adequate system of financial incentives, and poor morale. Clearly, this issue is arousing considerable feeling and is a source of potential disagreement among Jessica's subordinates.

This morning Jessica received a phone call from her division manager. He had just received her pro- duction figures for the last six months and was calling to express his concern. He said that the problem was hers to solve as she thought best, but that he would like to know within a week what steps she was planning to take.

Jessica shares her division manager's concern about the falling productivity and knows that her subordinates are also concerned. Her problem is to decide what steps to take to rectify the situation.

For Discussion:

1. Using the Vroom-Jago participation model of decision making in Figure 6.2, decide upon the appropriate decision style for Jessica to use. Support your answer.

2. Form groups of three to five persons and repeat the process from question 1. Try to achieve a consensus. Pick a spokesperson to report your group's solution to the class.

3. How much agreement was there within the group and within the class about the appropriate decision style for the case? Why?

4. Even though the Vroom-Jago model seems clear-cut, people often offer different answers to the diagnostic questions (in Figure 6.2) about the situation. What factors may account for differences in the way managers diagnose decision situations?

EXPERIENTIAL EXERCISE 6.1

Brainstorming: Creative Group Decision Making

Step 1: Form small groups as directed by your instructor. Each group will have an opportunity to develop some creative solutions to problems that typically arise on a college campus. Before beginning the exercise, review the rules for brainstorming discussed earlier in the chapter.

Step 2: From a current campus newspaper, select a problem or issue that needs to be solved on your campus. Possible issues might include student apathy about elections, the need for recycling programs, or the lack of funding for student programs.

Step 3: You have 10 minutes after the words "Begin brainstorming" to generate ideas. Have one person write down all the alternatives. Remember, do not evaluate ideas.

Step 4: You have 10–15 minutes to discuss and evaluate the ideas that were generated in step 3.

Step 5: You have 5 minutes to decide on the final solution that you will present to the class.

Step 6: Discuss as a class what happened in your group. How did your ideas emerge? Did you experience frustrations? What did you find most difficult about trying to use the brainstorming process?

EXPERIENTIAL EXERCISE 6.2

Examining Decision Making: An Organizational View

Examine current issues of business periodicals such as *Business Week*, the *Wall Street Journal*, or *Fortune*, and identify a significant decision recently made by a major company. Choose a company located in your city or state or one that you are familiar with. Possible decisions include the decision to expand into international markets, restructure, or hire a new CEO.

1. In the decision you identified, did the manager or managers appear to use good decision-making skills?

2. Did they follow the decision-making steps?

3. How successful was the company in implementing its decision?

4. Was the decision made by a group or an individual?

5. If you were advising the managers who made the decision, what criteria would you use?

SOURCE: Adapted from P. Fandt, *Management Skills: Practice and Experience* (St. Paul, Minn.: West Publishing Company, 1994).

NOTES

1. H. Mintzberg, ''The Manager's Job: Folklore and Fact,'' *Harvard Business Review* (March/April 1990): 163-76.

2. Adapted from D. E. Sanger, ''Engineers Tell of Punishment for Shuttle Testimony,'' *New York Times*, May 11, 1986, B1; ''NASA's Challenge: Ending Isolation at the Top,'' *Fortune*, May 12, 1986, 26-28; G. Whyte, ''Group-think Reconsidered,'' *Academy of Management Review* 14 (1989): 40-56; and A. W. Kruglanski, ''Freeze-think and the Challenger,'' *Psychology Today*, August 1986, 48-49.

3. P. Fandt, *Management Skills: Practice and Experience* (St. Paul, Minn.: West Publishing Company, 1994).

4. C. O'Reilly, ''Variations in Decision Makers' Use of Information Sources,'' *Academy of Management Journal* 25 (1982): 756-71; and C. O'Reilly, ''The Use of Information in Organizational Decision Making: A Model and Some Propositions,'' in B. Staw and L. Cummings, eds., *Research in Organizational Behavior*, Vol. 5 (Greenwich, Conn.: JAI Press, 1983), 103-39.

5. D. Vaughan, ''Autonomy, Interdependence, and Social Control: NASA and the Space Shuttle Challenger,'' *Administrative Science Quarterly* 35 (1990): 225-57.

6. K. Eisenhardt, ''Making Fast Strategic Decisions in High-Velocity Environments,'' *Academy of Management Journal* 32 (1989): 543-76.

7. S. W. Floyd and B. Wooldridge, ''Managing the Strategic Consensus: The Foundation of Effective Implementation,'' *Academy of Management Executive* 6 (1992): 27-39.

8. Mintzberg, ''The Manager's Job.''

9. J. G. March, ''Decision Making Perspective,'' in A. H. Van de Ven and W. S. Joyce, eds., *Perspectives on Organization Design and Behavior* (New York: John Wiley & Sons, 1981).

10. N. J. Adler, *International Dimensions of Organizational Behavior*, 2d ed. (Boston: PWS-Kent Publishing Company, 1991); and P. Sethi, N. Maniki, and C. Swanson, *The False Promise of the Japanese Miracle* (Marshfield, Mass.: Pitman, 1984).

11. F. N. Brady, *Ethical Managing: Rules and Results* (New York: Macmillan, 1990).

12. Adapted from S. W. Gellerman, ''Why 'Good' Managers Make Bad Ethical Choices,'' *Harvard Business Review* (July/August 1986): 85-90; and K. H. Blanchard and N. V. Peale, *The Power of Ethical Management* (Homewood, Ill.: Richard D. Irwin, 1987).

13. H. A. Simon, *Model of Man* (New York: John Wiley & Sons, 1957).

14. O. Behling and N. L. Eckel, ''Making Sense out of Intuition,'' *Academy of Management Executive* 5 (1991): 46-54.

15. R. Rowen, *The Intuitive Manager* (Boston: Little, Brown, 1986).

16. Behling and Eckel, ''Making Sense out of Intuition.''

17. P. Gupte, ''Merge in Haste, Repent in Leisure,'' *Forbes*, August 22, 1988, 85.

18. C. R. Schwenk, ''Information, Cognitive Biases, and Commitment to a Course of Action,'' *Academy of Management Review*, 11 (1986): 298-310.

19. M. H. Bazerman, *Judgment in Managerial Decision Making* (New York: John Wiley & Sons, 1986).

20. I. Janis and L. Mann, *Decision Making: A Psychological Analysis of Conflict, Choice, and Commitment* (New York: Free Press, 1977).

21. D. Ciampa, *Total Quality* (Reading, Mass.: Addison-Wesley, 1992).

22. V. H. Vroom and P. W. Yetton, *Leadership and Decision Making* (Pittsburgh: University of Pittsburgh, 1973).

23. V. H. Vroom and A. G. Jago, *The New Leadership: Managing Participation in Organizations* (Englewood Cliffs, N.J.: Prentice-Hall, 1988).

24. V. H. Vroom, ''A New Look at Managerial Decision Making,'' *Organizational Dynamics* (Spring 1973): 69-70.

25. Vroom and Jago, *The New Leadership*.

26. ''Gravedigging at New York Life,'' *Fortune*, September 21, 1992, 160.

27. R. A. Cooke and J. A. Kernagan, ''Estimating the Difference between Group versus Individual Performance on Problem-Solving Tasks,'' *Group and Organization Studies* 12 (1987): 319-42.

28. W. L. Ury, J. M. Brett, and S. B. Goldberg, *Getting Disputes Resolved* (San Francisco: Jossey-Bass, 1989).

29. "Spurling Fire & Burglar Alarm: Managing by Committee," in *Real-World Lessons for America's Small Businesses: Insights from the Blue Chip Enterprise Initiative* (published by Warner Books for Connecticut Mutual Life Insurance Company and the U.S. Chamber of Commerce, 1992), 143–44.

30. I. L. Janis, *Victims of Groupthink* (Boston: Houghton Mifflin, 1972).

31. L. R. Beach, *Making the Right Decision: Organizational Culture, Vision, and Planning* (Englewood Cliffs, N.J.: Prentice-Hall, 1993).

32. Whyte, "Groupthink Reconsidered," 40–55.

33. Adapted from C. R. Schwenk and R. A. Cosier, "Effect of the Expert, Devil's Advocate, and Dialectic Inquiry Methods on Prediction Performance," *Organizational Behavior and Human Performance* 1 (1980): 409–24.

34. Beach, *Making the Right Decision.*

35. D. M. Schweiger, W. R. Sandberg, and J. W. Ragan, "Group Approaches for Improving Strategic Decision Making: Analysis of Dialectical Inquiry, Devil's Advocacy, and Consensus," *Academy of Management Journal* 29 (1986): 51–71.

36. A. F. Osborn, *Applied Imagination*, rev. ed. (New York: Scribner, 1957).

37. Ibid.

38. B. Schlender, "How Bill Gates Keeps the Magic Going," *Fortune,* June 18, 1990, 82–89.

39. A. Delbecq, A. Van de Ven, and D. Gustafson, "Guidelines for Conducting NGT Meetings," in *Group Techniques for Program Planning* (Glenview, Ill.: Scott Foresman, 1975).

40. R. DeStephen and R. Hirokawa, "Small Group Consensus: Stability of Group Support of the Decision, Task Process, and Group Relationships," *Small Group Behavior* 19 (1988): 227–39.

41. D. M. Hegedus and R. V. Rasmussen, "Task Effectiveness and Interaction Process of a Modified Nominal Group Technique in Solving an Evaluation Problem," *Journal of Management* 12 (1986): 545–60.

42. R. Cosier and C. Schwenk, "Agreement and Thinking Alike: Ingredients for Poor Decisions," *Academy of Management Executive* 4 (1990): 69–74.

43. Schwenk and Cosier, "Effect of the Expert, Devil's Advocate, and Dialectic Inquiry Methods on Prediction Performance."

44. Ibid.

45. Beach, *Making the Right Decision,* 6.

46. Developed from D. C. Couper and S. H. Lobitz, *Quality Policing: The Madison Experience* (Washington, D.C.: Police Executive Research Forum, 1991); and R. B. Denhardt, *The Pursuit of Significance* (Belmont, Calif.: Wadsworth, 1992).

47. Adapted from Sanger, "Engineers Tell of Punishment for Shuttle Testimony"; "NASA's Challenge: Ending Isolation at the Top"; Whyte, "Groupthink Reconsidered"; and Kruglanski, "Freeze-think and the Challenger."

Decision-Making Tools and Techniques

CHAPTER 7

▼ CHAPTER OVERVIEW

As we saw in Chapter 6, every day managers face situations where they must make a decision. Many times a decision is needed because a problem has arisen. Other times a decision is needed because an opportunity has presented itself. Regardless of the reason, when a decision is needed, successful managers will be ready to leap into action and make the decision to avoid losing ground in the increasingly competitive marketplace. We also learned from Chapter 6 that decision making is a multistep process, and that tomorrow's managers must possess decision-making skills.

Merely understanding the steps in the decision-making process is not enough, however. Many quantitative tools and techniques can be used to evaluate alternative courses of action prior to making a decision. Tomorrow's managers must be equipped with these analytical tools, for their proper use will help managers improve the quality of their decision making.

Organizational decisions are often categorized as either long-range strategic decisions or short-range operational decisions. Analytical tools and techniques have evolved to help managers make better decisions in both of these areas. This chapter focuses on the methodologies, procedures, and applications for some of the more prominent decision-making aids.

▼ LEARNING OBJECTIVES

When you have finished studying this chapter, you should be able to:

- Discuss the different classifications for managerial decisions.
- Recognize the difference between strategic decision making and operational decision making.
- Describe the strategic decision-making matrix approach for strategy selection.
- Identify the differences between the growth-share matrix and the industry attractiveness/business strength matrix approaches for evaluating business portfolios.
- Discuss the differences between decision making under certainty, risk, and uncertainty.
- Describe the solution approaches that would be taken for risk and uncertainty situations.
- Explain the structure of and use of decision trees.
- Discuss the basics of breakeven analysis, linear programming, and PERT analysis.

THE SATURN RECALL DILEMMA

In 1981 the General Motors Corporation embarked upon a study to determine how to build a small automobile that could compete in price, quality, and performance with the products of Japanese automakers. More than 190 organizations around the world were examined in an attempt to find the best manufacturing processes available. As a result of its study, GM decided that it would have to start from the ground up, with an entire new factory and a new automobile. In 1982 the new automobile was conceived and given the name *Saturn,* which was to be the first new nameplate in GM's automobile line since Chevrolet was added in 1918. The goal of the Saturn project was to build automobiles in the United States and would be among the world leaders in cost, quality, and customer satisfaction. In 1990 Saturn automobiles began rolling off the assembly line of GM's state-of-the-art manufacturing facility in Spring Hill, Tennessee.

In its first few years of operation, Saturn became a modern-day success story for General Motors, which has been beset by heavy financial losses and image problems in its other car-making operations. A 1993 market research survey revealed that Saturn ranked behind only the Lexus and Infinity (two high-priced Japanese luxury automobiles) in customer satisfaction. But, in August 1993, Saturn's top managers faced a problem that required an immediate decision. Over 380,000 cars manufactured during 1991, 1992, and the first four months of 1993 had a wiring problem in the alternator that could potentially ignite an engine fire. As of that time, only 34 fires had been reported, indicating that the odds were less than one in 10,000 that a fire might occur. Nevertheless, Saturn's top managers faced a tough dilemma. They had to decide whether they would simply deal with the few rare fires after the fact or recall all affected automobiles and repair the wiring.[1] ▼

INTRODUCTION

In the opening Managerial Incident, we saw that Saturn's top management faced a dilemma. Since the likelihood that any given automobile might experience an engine fire was very small, they could choose to address each problem as it occurred. In all probability this was the less costly option. A total recall to replace the affected part would cost over $8 million in repairs, as well as the publicity and postage costs to notify Saturn owners. Saturn is a company that was built on the premise that through creativity, technology, and innovation, it could build quality automobiles that could compete with the Japanese imports. Furthermore, Saturn had staked its early reputation on customer satisfaction and a quality image. How would a recall affect this image?

In the previous chapter we saw that any person or organization faced with a decision has a rather straightforward task at hand. By following a systematic set of steps, the decision maker can select a course of action (the decision) from a set of many potential alternatives. After implementing the decision, follow-up monitoring will enable the decision maker to assess whether the chosen alternative has been producing desirable results. As routine as the decision-making process may seem, however, it requires considerable preparation to assemble and analyze all available information.

We begin this chapter with a discussion of the different categories of decision-making situations and then distinguish between strategic decision making and operational decision making. Several analytical tools and techniques have been developed to aid in making both strategic decisions and operational decisions, and we will examine them here. Much of the material that you will encounter in this chapter is a direct outgrowth of the quantitative perspective on management that was described in Chapter 2.

MANAGERIAL DECISION SITUATIONS

Before examining specific tools and techniques for decision making, let's review the conditions under which a decision situation might arise and the different ways of classifying those situations.

SOURCES OF ORGANIZATIONAL AND ENTREPRENEURIAL DECISIONS

Managers are faced with decisions when a problem occurs or when an opportunity arises. A **problem** occurs when some aspect of organizational performance is less than desirable. This definition is purposely broad so that it will cover any aspect of organizational performance, such as overall bottom-line profits, market share, output productivity, quality of output, and worker satisfaction and harmony, to name just a few of the countless possibilities. When such unsatisfactory results have occurred, the successful manager will both recognize the problem and find a solution for it.[2] The decision that Saturn would eventually have to make would also be in response to a problem—the wiring problem and the potential for engine fires.

Look at the decision made by the Coca-Cola Company in Global Perspective, which illustrates that decisions do not always turn out as planned.[3] Coca-Cola's decision to change the Coke formula was precipitated by what management perceived as a problem. Even though Coke held the largest domestic and global market share in the soft drink industry, the company's executives were concerned about Pepsi's gains in certain segments of the market and thought that changing the formula would help them regain some of the lost share of the global market. Unfortunately, Coca-Cola's response to the problem of declining market share led to an even bigger problem—the negative backlash from loyal Coke drinkers. To Coca-Cola's good fortune, the subsequent decision to reintroduce the old Coke formula as Classic Coke resulted in a larger market share than Coke had enjoyed before the reformulation.

Managers do not always make decisions in response to problem situations. Often decisions are made because an opportunity arises. An **opportunity** is any situation that has the potential to provide additional beneficial outcomes. When an opportunity presents itself, success will be achieved by those who recognize the potential benefits and then embark upon a course of action to achieve them. A good example of a successful response to an opportunity is the founding of Big Bob's Used Carpet Shops of America. After replacing the carpeting in his home, David Elyacher placed a classified ad in the Sunday newspaper offering his old carpet for sale. He received 50 phone calls on the day of the ad and sold the carpet that same day. When would-be buyers continued to call, Elyacher ran another ad offering to buy used carpet and told local carpet installers that he was interested in buying any carpeting they had replaced. He then leased warehouse space and opened a store. Within nine months he had opened a second store, and three more followed within the next few years, all in the greater Kansas City area. Big Bob's now has stores in seven states and has signed contracts for outlets in several others.[4]

Sometimes it can be difficult to clearly determine whether a problem or an opportunity precipitated a management decision. Consider the decision by

Problem
Situation where some aspect of organizational performance is less than desirable.

Opportunity
Situation which has the potential to provide additional beneficial outcomes.

COCA-COLA'S BOLD NEW DECISION

In 1985 the Coca-Cola Company made a bold decision that most of you will undoubtedly remember. The company decided to change the formula of Coke, its mainstay product. Although Coke's market share was the highest in the soft drink industry, Coca-Cola executives perceived an opportunity to increase Coke's market share at the expense of Pepsi-Cola, Coke's main competitor. Market research and taste tests convinced the executives that a sweeter formula would be the ticket to those market share gains. With considerable advertising fanfare and endorsement by celebrity pitchman Bill Cosby, the new Coke was introduced. To the executives' amazement, the backlash from loyal Coke drinkers was overwhelming. The company had not anticipated the degree of emotional attachment that longtime Coke drinkers held for this product. It became painfully obvious that removing the old Coke formula from the market had been a mistake, and that a new decision was needed quickly.

Even though the company had spent millions of dollars to taste-test the new Coke on almost 200,000 consumers and had obtained favorable results, the old formula Coke was back in the stores within three months of the decision to change the formula. Coca-Cola's follow-up analysis revealed that millions of people had developed a strong, emotional attachment to the original Coke formula through many years of loyalty. The original Coke formula was reintroduced as Coca-Cola Classic, which took its place beside the new Coke on supermarket shelves. Although the company hadn't originally considered this alternative, now there were two Coke formulas to battle the competition. Follow-up and control indicated that the two Coke formulas had a combined market share that exceeded Coke's share prior to reformulation, an unplanned but welcome result.

▼ In the never ending battles between the cola giants, one of Pepsi's decisions was to introduce this new product—*Crystal Pepsi.*

Pepsi to introduce a new product—Crystal Pepsi. Was this decision precipitated by Pepsi's perception of a problem (i.e., some of the smaller soft-drink companies were beginning to gain market share by touting the natural qualities of a clear, colorless beverage)? Or was the decision by Pepsi precipitated by a perceived opportunity to capture health and image-conscious consumers who favor colorless, clear beverages? For another example, consider Pepsi's recent decision to add a freshness date on its beverage containers.[5] Was this decision precipitated by a perceived problem (dissatisfaction on the part of the customers due to their inability to know whether the product's taste had deteriorated at the time of purchase or consumption)? Or was the decision precipitated by a perceived opportunity to capture additional market share by offering something that Pepsi's competitors were not offering? For each of these decisions the answer may be that it was a combination of both!

Regardless of whether a decision is precipitated by a problem, an opportunity, or both, it is important to understand the nature of the decision situation. Accordingly, let's turn our attention to methods of classifying decision situations.

CLASSIFICATION OF DECISION SITUATIONS

On a very basic level, Herbert Simon, a management scholar and prolific researcher in the area of decision making, proposed that decisions can be clas-

AGSCO, INC.

Agsco, Inc., a family-owned agricultural chemicals firm in Grand Forks, North Dakota, has been overcoming business problems for 55 years, but coping with heightened environmental concerns looked like it would be the company's biggest challenge yet. Not only are government regulations raising standards for cleanup and disposal of chemical wastes, but farmers are under pressure to increase yields while producing less chemical residue. Meanwhile U.S. landfills are rapidly filling with chemical containers. "This seemed to be a no-win situation," admits Agsco President Russ Brown.

The company committed time and money to finding ways to meet the challenge. The result was a radically new method of distributing farm chemicals. Agsco calls it the "Out-N-Back" system. Now, when a farmer needs a pesticide, Agsco delivers a sealed container to the farm. The farmer uses as much pesticide as he needs, but never actually has to touch it. A small, low-pressure air tank and quick-connect fittings are used to extract the container's contents in measured quantities, eliminating the need for pumps or batteries. When the farmer has used all he needs, Agsco picks up the container, and the farmer gets credit for the unused contents. The pressure on landfills is reduced, and farmers no longer must store partly used containers or triple rinse empties as required for landfills. Nor are farmers tempted to spill leftovers, a great source of pollution.

Farmers have embraced the system, and Agsco enjoys an image as a responsible, concerned company. Agsco's sales rose 1 percent last year to $15 million, and its workforce grew 13 percent to 65 employees. The company has been rewarded with steady growth in a depressed market because it tackled its "no-win" situation with determination and creativity.

sified as either programmed or nonprogrammed.[6] When the decision situation is one that has occurred in the past and the response is routine, the decision is referred to as a **programmed decision.** Identifying alternative courses of action in such situations is usually routine, for the alternatives are quite familiar to the decision maker. As an example of a programmed decision, consider the customer assistance operator for the Charleswood Company, a manufacturer of kits of unassembled furniture. If a customer discovers that a component or hardware item is missing from her kit, she can call an 800 number for assistance. The operator routinely obtains the missing part number from the customer, and then authorizes immediate UPS shipping of that part.

When decisions are made in response to situations that are unique, unstructured, or poorly defined, they are called **nonprogrammed decisions.** These decisions often require considerable creativity, cleverness, and innovation to elicit a list of reasonable alternative courses of action. As we saw with Saturn in the opening Managerial Incident, the response to these decision situations often requires considerable judgement, intuition, and even plain old gut-feeling reaction. Another example of innovative decision making can be found in Entrepreneurial Approach, which describes how the president of a family-owned agricultural chemicals firm found an ingenious solution to environmental problems with its unused chemical fertilizers.[7]

The changing nature of today's business environment presents an interesting dilemma for decision makers. On the one hand, the rapidly changing, global business environment creates a need for more nonprogrammed deci-

Programmed decisions
Decisions made in response to routine situations that have occurred in the past.

Nonprogrammed decisions
Decisions made in response to situations that are unique, unstructured, or poorly defined.

sions than ever before. With quality and continuous improvement as major strategic initiatives, organizations are constantly being challenged to find creative and innovative solutions to unique new problems and opportunities. At the same time, the changing composition of the workforce suggests that more programmed decisions might be beneficial. Today's workforce is constantly becoming more diverse in racial, ethnic, and gender composition. Workers with diverse backgrounds and cultural values often have different perceptions of appropriate organizational goals and objectives and therefore respond differently to the same decision situation. In such circumstances, the more programmed the decision responses can be, the more likely that workers will make consistent, quality decisions.

Whatever the type of decision situation, managers can use certain tools and techniques to achieve excellence in the decision-making process. We will first examine tools that aid in making long-range strategic decisions and then shift our attention to tools and techniques that would be useful for making shorter-range operational decisions.

STRATEGIC DECISION-MAKING TOOLS

Strategic decision making occurs at the highest levels in organizations. As we saw in Chapter 5, this type of decision making involves the selection of a strategy that will define the long-term direction of the firm. Two important areas for strategic decision making are in strategy selection and evaluation of portfolios.

STRATEGY SELECTION

Many times organizations find that there is not one clear-cut, obvious strategy that should be pursued. Instead, several potentially attractive alternatives may exist. The task for management is to select the strategy that will best facilitate the achievement of the multiple objectives of the organization. A tool that can be helpful in such cases is the **strategic decision-making matrix.**[8]

Strategic decision-making matrix
Two-dimensional grid used to select the best strategic alternative in light of multiple organizational objectives.

Strategic Decision-Making Matrix

When management faces several strategic alternatives and multiple objectives, it is helpful to organize these factors into a two-dimensional decision-making matrix.[9] To illustrate, let's consider the case of an organization that has established a goal of strong growth and has operationalized that goal by specifying three objectives: increased profit, increased market share, and increased production output. Suppose management has determined that three alternative growth strategies are reasonable options for the organization—product development, horizontal integration, and a joint venture. To form the strategic decision-making matrix, the alternative strategies are listed along the side of the matrix, while the objectives are listed along the top, as in Table 7.1.[10]

Since the objectives of the organization won't always be equally important, different weights can be assigned to them. Management usually assigns the weights based upon its subjective assessment of the importance of each objective. The weights are shown directly below the objectives in Table 7.1. In this example, increased profit is the most important objective; therefore it has received the highest weight. Note that the sum of the weights must equal 1.0.

To use the matrix, management must first rate each alternative strategy on its potential to contribute to the achievement of each objective. A 1–5 rating scale is used, with 1 indicating little or no potential for achieving an objective and 5 indicating maximum potential. Once an alternative strategy has been

▼ **TABLE 7.1**   Strategic Decision-Making Matrix

		OBJECTIVES			
		Increased Profit	Increased Market Share	Increased Production Output	
ALTERNATIVE STRATEGIES	WEIGHT	.5	.3	.2	TOTAL WEIGHTED SCORE
Product Development		2	2	3	$.5(2)+.3(2)+.2(3)=2.2$
Horizontal Integration		4	2	2	$.5(4)+.3(2)+.2(2)=3.0$
Joint Venture		5	3	3	$.5(5)+.3(3)+.2(3)=4.0$

rated for each objective, the strategy's total weighted score can be computed by multiplying its rating for each objective by the corresponding weight of the objective, and then summing across all objectives, as shown in the last column in Table 7.1. The decision maker can then select the strategy with the highest weighted score. In this example, the joint venture strategy is the most desirable alternative, because it will allow the organization to achieve the best combination of profitability, market share, and production output.

EVALUATING DIVERSIFIED PORTFOLIOS

Whenever an organization becomes involved in several businesses and industries or with several products and services, it becomes necessary to make decisions about the role each business line will play in the organization and the manner in which resources will be allocated among these business lines.* The most popular technique for assessing the balance of the mix of business lines in an organization is portfolio matrix analysis. A **business portfolio matrix** is a two-dimensional grid that compares the strategic positions of each of the organization's businesses.

A portfolio matrix can be constructed using any reasonable pair of indicators of a firm's strategic position. As we will see, usually one dimension of the matrix relates to the attractiveness of the industry environment and the other to the strength of a business within its industry.[11] The two most frequently used portfolio matrices are the growth-share matrix and the industry attractiveness/business strength matrix.

The Growth-Share Matrix
The earliest business portfolio approach to be widely used for corporate strategy formulation is the growth-share matrix. This technique was developed by the Boston Consulting Group (BCG), a leading management consulting firm.[12] Figure 7.1 illustrates a BCG matrix.[13]

The **BCG matrix** is constructed using market growth rate and relative market share as the indicators of the firm's strategic position. Each of these indicators is divided into two levels (high and low), so that the matrix contains four cells. The rows of the matrix show the market growth rate, while the columns show the relative market share. **Market growth rate** is the percentage at which the market in which the business operates is growing annually.

Business portfolio matrix
Two-dimensional grid that compares the strategic positions of each of the organization's businesses.

BCG matrix
Business portfolio matrix that uses market growth rate and relative market share as the indicators of the firm's strategic position.

Market growth rate
A measure of the annual growth percentage of the market in which the business operates.

*Although the following discussion of the portfolio approaches focuses on the evaluation of multiple business lines, these approaches can also be used at the product or service level. This is done by replacing "business lines" on the matrix with products or services.

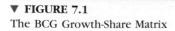

▼ **FIGURE 7.1**
The BCG Growth-Share Matrix

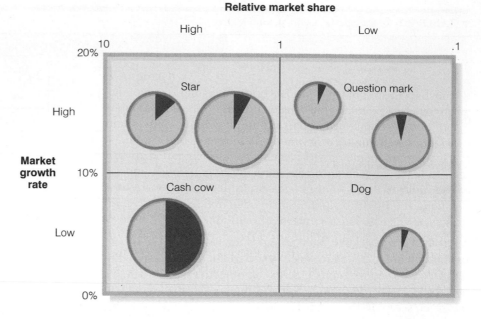

Relative market share
The firm's market share divided by the market share of its largest competitor.

Stars
Businesses that fall into the high market growth/high market share cell of a BCG matrix.

Cash cows
Businesses that fall into the low market growth/high market share cell of a BCG matrix.

Dogs
Businesses that fall into the low market growth/low market share cell of a BCG matrix.

In the BCG matrix 10 percent is generally considered the dividing line between a low rate and a high rate of market growth. **Relative market share** is computed by dividing the firm's market share by the market share of its largest competitor. For example, a relative market share of 0.4 means that the sales volume of the business is only 40 percent of the market leader's sales volume. In the BCG matrix a relative market share of 1.0 is usually set as the dividing line between high and low relative market share.

To use the BCG matrix, each of the organization's businesses is plotted in the matrix according to its market growth rate and relative market share. Figure 7.1 illustrates a BCG matrix for an organization with six businesses. Each circle represents a business unit. The size of a circle reflects the proportion of corporate revenue generated by that business, and the pie slice indicates the proportion of corporate profits generated by that business.[14] Note that each cell in the BCG matrix has a descriptive label; these labels reflect the roles that the businesses in the cells play in the overall strategy of the firm.

Stars   Businesses that fall into the high market growth/high market share cell are referred to as **stars.** These businesses offer attractive profit and growth opportunities. However, they also require a great deal of money to keep up with the market's rate of growth. Consequently, in the short term they are often cash-using rather than cash-generating units, but usually this situation reverses in time. BCG analysis advocates retaining stars in the corporate portfolio.

Cash Cows   Businesses that fall into the low market growth/high market share cell are referred to as **cash cows.** These businesses generate substantial cash surpluses over what they need for reinvestment and growth. Cash cows are generally yesterday's stars whose industries have matured. Although not attractive from a growth standpoint, they are quite valuable, for the cash surpluses they generate can be used to pay bills, cover dividends, provide funds for investment, or support struggling businesses (such as, the question marks described below). BCG analysis also views the cash cows favorably and advocates keeping them in the corporate portfolio.

Dogs   Businesses that fall into the low market growth/low market share cell are known as **dogs.** These businesses typically generate low profits, and in some cases they may even lose money. They also frequently consume more

**MEETING THE
CHALLENGE**

DEVELOPING A BCG MATRIX FOR YOUR COLLEGE

To get experience in developing a BCG matrix, examine the various academic departments of your business school. Consider that the total market consists of your university's school of business and its three geographically closest competing business schools. The academic departments in your school will be the "business units" being analyzed. Construct a BCG matrix using the following guidelines:

• Allow the market growth rate axis to reflect a unit's average annual growth.

• Allow the relative market share axis to reflect the ratio of a particular department's student enrollment to the enrollment of that department's largest competitor (from among the four schools being studied).

Use a circle to plot each department on the BCG matrix. The size of the circle can represent the proportion of the total business school enrollment generated by students majoring in that department's curriculum. The circle's pie slice can reflect the percentage of the total business school faculty assigned to that department.

Even though this is a nonprofit organization, the location of the circles on the matrix will be some indication of the stature of the different departments. Some departments may have large student enrollments with low faculty staffing levels, while others may have relatively small student enrollments but high faculty staffing levels. This analysis can then be used in allocating resources to individual departments or in making expansion and contraction decisions about individual departments.

SOURCE: Reprinted with the permission of Macmillan College Publishing Company from *Strategic Management*, 4th ed. by F. R. David. Copyright © 1993 by Macmillan College Publishing Company, Inc.

management time than they are worth. Unless there is some compelling reason to hold onto a dog (such as an expected turnaround in market growth rate), BCG analysis suggests that such businesses be removed from the portfolio.

Question Marks   Businesses that fall into the high market growth/low market share cell are referred to as **question marks.** The rapid market growth makes these businesses look attractive from an industry standpoint. Unfortunately, their low market share makes their profit potential uncertain. Question mark businesses are often called "cash hogs" because they require large infusions of resources to keep up with the rapid growth and product development of the market. BCG analysis suggests that the organization must very carefully consider whether continued funding for a question mark is worthwhile. Management must consider the question mark's potential to gain market share and move into the star category.

Question marks
Businesses that fall into the high market growth/low market share cell of a BCG matrix.

BCG portfolio analysis can be used in both for-profit and not-for-profit organizations and in manufacturing and service organizations. Turn your attention, for the moment, to Meeting the Challenge.[15] Here is an opportunity for you to gain hands-on experience in developing a BCG matrix using your own business school as the industry and the various academic departments as the business units.

The BCG business portfolio matrix makes valuable contributions in the area of strategic decision making. It enables a corporation to highlight the flow of cash resources among the units in its portfolio, and it provides a sound rationalization for resource allocation, investment, expansion, and contraction

▼ Balanced portfolio of General Mills Restaurants: Red Lobster is a cash cow, Olive Garden is a star, and China Coast is a question mark.

decisions. It also enables management to assess the balance among the units within its portfolio. A balanced portfolio should contain units in several cells. The status of individual business units can shift over time. For example, question marks can move into the star category, and stars will eventually evolve into cash cows. For these reasons, it is important to have question marks "waiting in the wings" to replace stars, and stars waiting to replace any cash cows that might slip into the dog category.

General Mills Restaurants provide a classic example of a service organization that has balanced its portfolio to ensure its long-term success. The restaurant group currently operates three restaurant chains: Red Lobster, Olive Garden, and China Coast. Each chain is in a different stage of development and occupies a different position on the BCG matrix. Red Lobster is a mature chain in a mature segment of the restaurant industry. Although Red Lobster still has opportunities for expansion, its growth rate has subsided from the early 1980s when units were popping up everywhere. Olive Garden, General Mills Restaurants' entry into the Italian dinnerhouse segment, was started in 1980. The intention was to build this chain into a leader in its segment by penetrating the domestic market. And while Olive Garden has already achieved this leadership position, it is still in the early growth stage and will continue to enjoy significant growth for several years to come. China Coast, General Mills Restaurants' newest chain, has just begun operations. With only a handful of units currently in existence, the intention is to eventually duplicate the success Red Lobster has experienced in the seafood dinnerhouse segment and Olive Garden has experienced in the Italian segment—only this time in the Chinese segment. Placing these restaurant chains on a BCG matrix reveals an interesting balance. Red Lobster is a cash cow, Olive Garden is a star, and China Coast is a question mark. As long as General Mills Restaurants continues to generate new concepts as the older concepts mature and saturate their relevant markets, the company is destined for long-term success.[16]

The BCG business portfolio matrix approach is not without its shortcomings. Some critics have argued that the four-cell classification scheme is overly simplistic. Others contend that accurately measuring market share and growth rate can be difficult. Furthermore, when the analysis is based on just these two factors, other important variables may be overlooked.[17] In an attempt to overcome some of the limitations of the BCG approach, more refined models have been proposed. One of the early refinements of the BCG approach is the General Electric model, which attempts to overcome some of the BCG shortcomings.

The Industry Attractiveness/Business Strength Matrix

GE matrix

Business portfolio matrix that uses industry attractiveness and business strength as the indicators of the firm's strategic position.

General Electric (GE) developed a nine-cell business portfolio matrix that overcomes some of the limitations of the BCG matrix. The **GE matrix** uses several factors to assess industry attractiveness and business strength. Table 7.2 lists the various factors that can contribute to industry attractiveness and business strength.[18] Furthermore, the GE approach allows for three levels of industry attractiveness and business strength, resulting in its nine-cell structure.

▼ **TABLE 7.2**   Factors Contributing to Industry Attractiveness and Business Strength

INDUSTRY ATTRACTIVENESS	BUSINESS STRENGTH
Market Forces	
Size (dollars, units, or both)	Your share (in equivalent terms)
Size of key segments	Your share of key segments
Growth rate per year:	Your annual growth rate:
Total	Total
Segments	Segments
Diversity of market	Diversity of your participation
Sensitivity to price, service, features, and external factors	Your influence on the market
Cyclicality	Lags or leads in your sales
Seasonality	
Bargaining power of upstream suppliers	Bargaining power of your suppliers
Bargaining power of downstream suppliers	Bargaining power of your customers
Competition	
Types of competitors	Where you fit, how you compare in terms of products, marketing capability, service, production strength, financial strength, and management
Degree of concentration	
Changes in type and mix	
Entries and exits	Segments you have entered or left
Changes in share	Your relative share change
Substitution by new technology	Your vulnerability to new technology
Degrees and types of integration	Your own level of integration
Financial and Economic Factors	
Contribution margins	Your margins
Leveraging factors, such as economies of scale and experience	Your scale and experience
Barriers to entry or exit (both financial and nonfinancial)	Barriers to your entry or exit (both financial and nonfinancial)
Capacity utilization	Your capacity utilization
Technological Factors	
Maturity and volatility	Your ability to cope with change
Complexity	Depths of your skills
Differentiation	Types of your technological skills
Patents and copyrights	Your patent protection
Manufacturing process technology required	Your manufacturing technology
Sociopolitical Factors in Your Environment	
Social attitudes and trends	Your company's responsiveness and flexibility
Laws and government agency regulations	Your company's ability to cope
Influence with pressure groups and government representatives	Your company's aggressiveness
Human factors, such as unionization and community acceptance	Your company's relationships

SOURCE: Derek F. Abell and John S. Hammond, *Strategic Market Planning: Problems & Analytical Approaches,* © 1979, p. 214. Adapted by permission of Prentice Hall, Englewood Cliffs, New Jersey.

To use the GE matrix, each of the organization's businesses is rated as to industry attractiveness and business strength. To measure the attractiveness of an industry, the decision maker first selects from Table 7.2 those factors that are likely to contribute to the attractiveness of the industry in question. Each factor is assigned a weight based upon its perceived importance. These weights must sum to 1.0. The industry is then assigned a rating for each of these factors using some uniform scale (for example, a 1–5 rating scale). Finally, a weighted score is obtained by multiplying weights by factor scores, and then adding to obtain a total weighted value. To arrive at a measure of business strength, each business is rated using the same procedure as for industry attractiveness. Table 7.3 illustrates these calculations for a hypothetical business in a corporation's portfolio.[19]

The total weighted scores for industry attractiveness and business strength are used to locate the business on the nine-cell matrix. Figure 7.2 illustrates a GE business portfolio matrix that contains eight businesses, with each circle reflecting one business.[20] The area of a circle is proportional to the size of the entire industry, while the pie slice within the circle represents the business's share of that market.

The GE matrix provides the decision maker with rationalization for resource allocation, investment, expansion, and contraction decisions within dif-

▼ **TABLE 7.3**   Illustration of Industry Attractiveness and Business Strength Computations

INDUSTRY ATTRACTIVENESS	WEIGHT	RATING (1–5)	VALUE
Overall market size	0.20	4.00	0.80
Annual market growth rate	0.20	5.00	1.00
Historical profit margin	0.15	4.00	0.60
Competitive intensity	0.15	2.00	0.30
Technological requirements	0.15	3.00	0.45
Inflationary vulnerability	0.05	3.00	0.15
Energy requirements	0.05	2.00	0.10
Environmental impact	0.05	1.00	0.05
Social/political/legal	Must be acceptable		
	1.00		3.45

BUSINESS STRENGTH	WEIGHT	RATING (1–5)	VALUE
Market share	0.10	4.00	0.40
Share growth	0.15	4.00	0.60
Product quality	0.10	4.00	0.40
Brand reputation	0.10	5.00	0.50
Distribution network	0.05	4.00	0.20
Promotional effectiveness	0.05	5.00	0.25
Productive capacity	0.05	3.00	0.15
Productive efficiency	0.05	2.00	0.10
Unit costs	0.15	3.00	0.45
Material supplies	0.05	5.00	0.25
R&D performance	0.10	4.00	0.80
Managerial personnel	0.05	4.00	0.20
	1.00		4.30

SOURCE: La Rue T. Hosmer, *Strategic Management: Text and Cases on Business Policy,* © 1982, p. 310. Adapted by permission of Prentice Hall, Englewood Cliffs, New Jersey.

Business strength

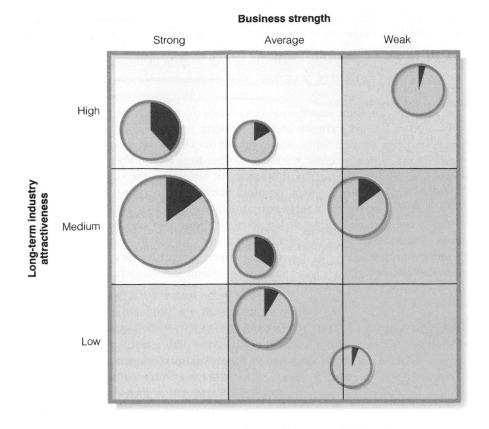

▼ FIGURE 7.2
The GE Industry Attractiveness/
Business Strength Matrix

ferent cells, in much the same way as the BCG matrix. Businesses that fall into the three yellow cells at the upper left of the GE matrix are given top investment priority. These are the combinations of industry attractiveness and business strength that are most favorable. The strategic prescription for businesses located in these three cells is to invest and grow. Businesses positioned in the three blue cells are next in priority. These businesses deserve selective reinvestment to maintain and protect their industry positions. Finally, businesses positioned in the three pink cells at the lower right of the matrix are serious candidates for divestiture due to their low overall strength.[21]

Although similar to the BCG approach, the GE matrix offers several improvements. For one thing, it allows for intermediate rankings between high and low and between weak and strong, yielding nine rather than four cells. A second improvement is that it incorporates a much wider variety of strategically relevant variables. Whereas the BCG matrix considers only two factors (industry growth rate and relative market share), the GE matrix takes many factors into consideration (see again Table 7.2) to determine industry attractiveness and business strength. Finally, and perhaps most importantly, the GE approach emphasizes allocating corporate resources to businesses with the greatest chance of achieving competitive advantage and superior performance.[22]

Despite these improvements, the GE matrix does have its critics. Like the BCG matrix, it prescribes only a general strategic posture and provides no real guidance on the specifics of the business strategy. Another criticism of the GE approach (and the BCG approach, for that matter) is that they are static. They portray businesses as they are at one point in time and do not take into account that businesses evolve over time. Consequently, these approaches do not detect businesses that are about to become winners because their industries are entering the takeoff stage or businesses that are about to become losers as their industries enter the decline stage.[23]

OPERATIONAL DECISION MAKING

The strategic decision making just examined is typically conducted at high levels within the organization and covers long time horizons. Operational decision making, on the other hand, relates to decision situations that cover much shorter spans of time. While these decisions are typically made at lower levels within the organization, this need not always be the case. Consider the decision faced by Saturn in the opening Managerial Incident. Whether or not to recall is by no means a long-term strategic decision. This decision applied to the immediate short-term future. Nevertheless, you can be sure that it received the full attention of top management.[24] In the next sections, we will introduce structure to the operational decision-making process. Once that structure is in place, a variety of computational decision-making techniques can be applied.

APPLYING STRUCTURE TO THE DECISION-MAKING PROCESS

Several basic elements of decision making can be identified in the decision-making steps described in Chapter 6. They are referred to as alternative courses of action, states of nature, and payoffs. These elements can often be conveniently arranged into a structured array to aid in the decision analysis. Such an array is called a payoff matrix.

Alternative Courses of Action

Alternative courses of action
Strategies that might be implemented in a decision-making situation.

The **alternative courses of action** in a decision-making situation are the strategies that the decision maker might implement to solve the problem or respond to the opportunity. In the opening Managerial Incident, Saturn officials had two alternative courses of action from which to choose. One alternative was to sit back and wait for trouble spots (engine fires) to occur and then make the appropriate response (repair or replace the damaged automobile). The other alternative was to recall all affected automobiles and replace the defective wiring.

To make quality decisions, the decision maker must first identify viable and potentially attractive alternative courses of action. The necessity of recognizing viable alternatives is illustrated in Managing for Excellence, which describes how management of the Computer Service Supply Corporation identified a new alternative course of action when the market for its existing products had severely eroded.[25]

States of Nature

States of nature
Conditions over which the decision maker has little or no control.

States of nature are future conditions that can occur. They will affect the outcome of the decision, yet the decision maker has little or no control over them.[26] For example, corporate financial officers must often decide how to invest surplus funds. Future interest rates are a state of nature that will affect the outcome of their decisions. States of nature can reflect any type of future event that is likely to affect the outcome of a decision, including such events as weather, competitor behavior, economic conditions, political events, new laws, and consumer behavior. The more certain the decision maker is about the likelihood of various states of nature, the easier will be the decision making. Unfortunately, as we will see later, decision makers are rarely able to foresee future events with complete certainty. The degree of certainty that the decision maker possesses will affect the decision-making process.

MANAGING FOR EXCELLENCE

COMPUTER SERVICE SUPPLY CORPORATION: WHEN THE MARKET VANISHES

Computer Service Supply Corporation (CSSC) of Londonderry, New Hampshire, was founded in 1987 as a distributor of mainframe-computer parts. Thomas Barnes started the company with a $2000 investment. CSSC quickly grew to 20 employees, but by 1990 the company was down to 6 employees and was losing money. The mainframe market had eroded with the advent of more powerful personal computers and the introduction of new software. As a result, CSSC's business all but disappeared in the span of 18 months.

Barnes realized that he needed to find an alternative to his current way of doing business. He recognized that personal computers were replacing mainframes and that his company would have to change its focus. CSSC switched from mainframes to distributing, servicing, and remanufacturing personal-computer boards and subassemblies. Since there was little working capital, employees voluntarily took pay cuts. Innovative packaging of services and a reputation for quality work helped CSSC get business. And how that business has grown! Sales were $1.4 million in 1990, $2.4 million in 1991, close to $6 million in 1992, and more than $12 million in 1993. CSSC foresees a continuation of this phenomenal growth in the future. Because Barnes was able to identify a viable and attractive new alternative for doing business, Computer Service Supply Corporation has been recognized as one of the country's fastest growing companies.

Payoffs

The interaction of each alternative course of action with each state of nature will result in a decision outcome. Each combination of alternative and state of nature will produce a separate outcome. Suppose that a company can choose to invest surplus funds in fixed-rate certificates of deposit (CDs) or in a money market account. If the company invests in CDs and interest rates rise, the yield will not be as great as it would have been if the money had been invested in

▼ Although meteorologists are constantly improving their equipment and techniques for forecasting the weather, this future state of nature can rarely be predicted with complete certainty.

▼ **TABLE 7.4**   Structure of a Payoff Table

ALTERNATIVE COURSES OF ACTION	STATES OF NATURE		
	S_1	S_2	S_3
A_1	O_{11}	O_{12}	O_{13}
A_2	O_{21}	O_{22}	O_{23}
A_3	O_{31}	O_{32}	O_{33}
A_4	O_{41}	O_{42}	O_{43}

NOTE: A_i = alternative courses of action; S_j = states of nature; O_{ij} = outcome associated with alternative i and state of nature j.

Payoffs
The outcomes of decision situations.

Payoff table
A matrix which organizes the alternative courses of action, states of nature, and payoffs for a decision situation.

a money market account. Outcomes of decision situations are often referred to as **payoffs** since the objective in many business decisions can be measured in units of monetary value.

Payoff Tables
By properly organizing these elements, a systematic decision analysis can be undertaken. In decision theory, payoffs are called conditional values because each payoff is conditional upon a particular alternative course of action having first been selected and a particular state of nature having subsequently occurred. Whenever a decision situation is to be analyzed, the basic elements of the situation can be arranged in a matrix that is called a **payoff table** or a conditional value matrix due to the conditional nature of the payoffs.[27] The alternative courses of action form the rows of the table, and the states of nature form the columns, as in Table 7.4.[28] Then each cell in the table contains the outcome, or payoff, for a particular combination of an alternative course of action and state of nature. Organizing the decision-making elements in this structured format allows for the systematic analysis of the decision problem and the eventual selection of an appropriate course of action.

If you compare the payoff table for operational decision making with the strategic decision-making matrix discussed earlier, you will see some similarity. Both use a two-dimensional matrix with decision alternatives arranged along the left side. But here the similarity ends. The strategic decision-making matrix employs multiple objectives and arranges them across the top of the matrix. The payoff table uses a single objective, whose measurements appear within the cells of the matrix. External factors (i.e., states of nature) affecting the outcomes of the decisions are arranged across the top of the payoff table.

TECHNIQUES THAT ENHANCE QUALITY IN DECISION MAKING

The manner in which the information in the payoff table is analyzed is a function of the decision-making environment. At a basic level of analysis, three different decision-making environments are generally identified depending on the amount of knowledge that exists about future conditions that might occur: (1) decision making under certainty, (2) decision making under risk, and (3) decision making under uncertainty.[29] The more information the decision maker has about future conditions, the easier will be the selection of an alternative course of action. As the future becomes more clouded, it becomes more difficult to identify one best tool for analyzing the decision. As a result, in such cases decision makers tend to have less confidence in the alternative they select for implementation.

Decision Making under Certainty

In decision making under certainty, the decision maker knows with certainty what conditions will subsequently occur and affect the decision outcomes. Hence, the decision maker knows what the outcome will be for each alternative course of action. In such a situation, a rational decision maker will logically select the alternative with the most desirable outcome. For example, suppose you have $1000 that you would like to place in your neighborhood bank for one year. Suppose further that your alternatives are limited to depositing the money in a savings account that yields 5 percent annual interest or a CD that yields 6 percent annual interest. If both investments are equally secure, you will not need access to this money during the year, and your objective is to maximize your monetary payoff, then you would choose the CD.

Decision Making under Risk

Decision makers, however, seldom encounter conditions of certainty. In most instances decision makers do not know with certainty which future state of nature will occur and subsequently influence the decision outcome. In many cases, however, the decision maker may have a reasonable idea of the chances, or probability, of each state of nature occurring. Consider the financial officer's decision on investing surplus funds. Examination of economic forecasts might provide the officer with the likelihood, or probability, that future interest rates will reach certain levels. When such probabilities are present, the process is referred to as decision making under risk. In decision making under risk, the probabilities are used to obtain expected values of outcomes for each decision alternative. The decision maker then selects the alternative that maximizes the expected outcome, assuming that the outcomes in the payoff table are attractive (for example, profits). If the outcomes in the payoff table represent an undesirable parameter (such as cost), then, of course, the decision maker should select the alternative that minimizes the expected outcome.

Table 7.5 shows the structure of a decision situation that has been scaled down for ease of illustration.[30] In this situation, an organization has a surplus of $100,000 available for short-term (one-year) investment. The financial officer is considering three simple investment alternatives: the stock market, bonds,

▼ Daily trading on the New York Stock Exchange involves decisions that are made under conditions of risk and uncertainty.

▼ **TABLE 7.5**   Payoff Table for Sample Illustration: Conditional Value Matrix

ALTERNATIVES	STATES OF NATURE		
	Rising Economy	Stationary Economy	Falling Economy
Stock Market	$20000	$5000	−$8000
Bonds	$ 5000	$5000	$5000
Money Market	$10000	$7000	$4000

or a money market account. In this example, the gain to be realized after one year will depend upon the economic conditions that prevail during that year. For simplicity, assume that the economy might rise, remain stationary, or fall. The conditional payoffs for each combination of alternative and state of nature are shown in the payoff table of Table 7.5. Notice that in one cell the return is a negative number, indicating a loss if the money is invested in the stock market and the economy subsequently falls.

Expected value
The product of a payoff and its probability of occurrence.

Expected monetary value (EMV)
The sum of each expected value for an alternative.

Expected Monetary Value   An **expected value** is the product of a conditional value and the probability of its occurrence. In a decision-making matrix, each alternative strategy has a total **expected monetary value (EMV),** which is the sum of each expected value for that alternative.[31] In Table 7.6 probabilities have been assigned to each state of nature.[32] The decision maker would have estimated these probabilities after careful analysis of various economic indicators.

The matrix of Table 7.6 illustrates the calculation of the EMVs for each alternative course of action. This is referred to as an expected value matrix. The expected values within Table 7.6 are obtained by multiplying Table 7.5 conditional values by their probabilities of occurrence. The figures indicate that the most desirable alternative is the money market option, which yields $7300, the highest expected monetary value. This highest EMV of $7300 is an interesting figure. You might mistakenly conclude that the money market will generate a return of $7300, but in fact this can never happen. If the money market account is the selected alternative, the conditional values, as shown in Table 7.5, indicate that the only possible returns are $10,000, $7000, or $4000. Then what does the $7300 figure reflect? The $7300 value is the long-run average return that would occur if the decision maker faced this situation repeatedly and selected the money market alternative each time. On some occasions the return would be $10,000 (30 percent of the time, assuming that

▼ **TABLE 7.6**   Calculation of Expected Monetary Values: Expected Value Matrix

	STATES OF NATURE			
Probability	.3	.5	.2	Expected Monetary Value
ALTERNATIVES	Rising Economy	Stationary Economy	Falling Economy	
Stock Market	$6000	$2500	−$1600	$6900
Bonds	$1500	$2500	$1000	$5000
Money Market	$3000	$3500	$ 800	$7300

Maximum expected monetary value = $7300, associated with the money market alternative.

the probabilities reflect long-run frequencies for different economic conditions). Furthermore, 50 percent of the time, the return would be $7000, and 20 percent of the time, a return of $4000 would be realized. Averaging the returns from repeated decisions over a long period of time gives the $7300 figure.

Decision making is not always as simple as selecting the alternative that maximizes expected profit or minimizes expected cost. Consider again the dilemma faced by the Saturn managers. Recalling all the affected automobiles would result in a total cost of approximately $10 million ($8 million for repairs plus the costs of publicity, postage, and phone calls to notify Saturn owners). That $10 million would be enough to totally replace approximately 1000 damaged automobiles—an unlikely necessity given that only 34 cars out of more than 380,000 have had a fire problem. If cost were the only consideration, attending to fire problems as they occurred would be the better alternative. But Saturn was concerned here with more than just cost. After all, this company has staked its reputation on quality, customer satisfaction, and responsiveness to customer needs.

Decision Trees   As we have just seen, the payoff matrix is a convenient way to analyze alternatives in decision making under risk situations. Our investment example might also have been structured in a **decision tree** format, with various tree branches and junctions (or nodes) depicting the same decision scenario.[33] Figure 7.3 displays this problem in a decision tree format.

In this tree diagram, the box represents a decision point, with alternatives emanating from it. Circles represent points in time after the potential decision has been made when states of nature (future events) are about to occur. Each circle in this diagram has the three states of nature emanating from it. Each state of nature is followed by its probability of occurrence. Finally, payoffs are shown at the termination of each state of nature branch. Each payoff is still a

Decision tree
A branching diagram that illustrates the alternatives and states of nature for a decision situation.

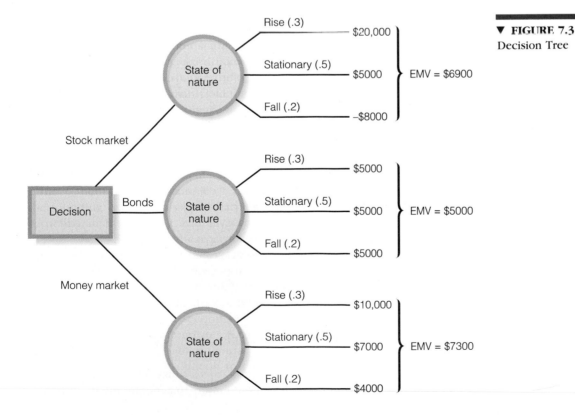

▼ **FIGURE 7.3**
Decision Tree

conditional value. The events the payoffs are conditional upon can be found by tracing from the decision point to the payoff. For example, if the money market alternative is selected and the economy remains stationary (with a .5 probability), the payoff will be $7000. The tree can be used to compute expected monetary values and will give the same results as the payoff table, as Figure 7.3 shows. Although a decision tree can be used for simple problems such as this, this approach is most useful for situations where sequential decisions must be made over time. In such cases an alternative choice branch will be followed by a state of nature branch, which may be followed by another decision point with more branches emanating from it. With such a complex series of interrelated decisions, decision trees are the only recourse for obtaining a solution.

A decision tree approach proved to be quite helpful to the United States Postal Service (USPS) in the early 1980s when it began to explore the possibility of expanding the five-digit ZIP Code. The USPS viewed the developmental study as a two-phase decision process. Phase I focused on information dissemination and the acquisition of automated equipment for pilot testing. Phase II dealt with the continuation of the postal automation strategy. Six alternatives were included in this phase (one of which was to cancel Phase II and terminate the expanded ZIP Code concept). We all know through our daily dealings with the USPS that the expanded ZIP Code concept (called ZIP + 4) was adopted. What we probably didn't know is that this decision was prompted by an extensive decision tree analysis of the alternatives based on internal rate of return and net present value of cash flows.[34]

Decision Making under Uncertainty

In some cases a decision maker cannot assess the probability of occurrence for the various states of nature. When no probabilities are available, the situation is referred to as decision making under uncertainty. In such situations the decision maker can choose among several possible approaches for making the decision. Each approach takes a different view of the likelihood of future events.[35] To illustrate two extremes, consider an optimistic approach and a pessimistic approach to decision making under uncertainty. The optimistic approach assumes that the best payoff will occur regardless of the alternative selected by the decision maker. If you were an optimistic decision maker facing the investment decision described earlier, you would choose the stock market alternative, because it has the highest of the optimistic payoffs ($20,000). On the other extreme, a pessimistic approach assumes that the worst payoff will occur regardless of the alternative selected by the decision maker. If you were a pessimistic decision maker facing the same investment decision, you would choose the bond alternative, because it has the highest of the pessimistic payoffs ($5000).

Different decision makers will have different perceptions about which future events are likely to occur and different levels of aversion to risky ventures; both will influence their decision making. To accommodate these differences, several uncertainty approaches have been developed. Although the details will not be covered here, we can note that these approaches generally fall between the optimistic and pessimistic extremes described above. None of these approaches can be described as the "best approach," for there is no one best uncertainty approach. Each has utility for different decision makers, since different people often have different ways of looking at a problem.[36]

ETHICAL AND SOCIAL IMPLICATIONS IN DECISION MAKING

The treatment of decision making presented thus far may leave the impression that all managers need to do is plug in the numbers to generate the best choice of an alternative. However, managers must also be careful to consider more than just the numbers. Often they will have to look beyond the numbers, as the Saturn managers did in the opening Managerial Incident. In addition, they will have to consider the ethical and social implications of their actions, as the city of Orlando, Florida, did when it hired workers for a new expressway project. In 1993 the Orlando/Orange County Expressway Authority made hiring the homeless a condition for contractors bidding on highway landscaping and maintenance contracts worth millions of dollars. The intent was to provide the homeless with basic on-the-job training, an opportunity to move into better jobs, and a chance to break out of their endless cycle of poverty.[37]

QUANTITATIVE DECISION-MAKING AIDS

Many quantitative models, tools, and techniques are available that can aid in various types of decision-making situations. Although a detailed presentation of these models is beyond the scope of this book, it is important to have some awareness of these tools and techniques. The next sections provide a brief overview of some of the more important models.

Breakeven Analysis

Breakeven analysis is a quantitative technique that allows managers to examine the relationships between output levels, revenues, and costs. By analyzing these factors, managers can determine the level of output at which the firm will break even (i.e., where total revenue equals total cost; at this point the firm makes no profit, but incurs no loss). Furthermore, managers can project the profit or loss associated with any level of output. For a familiar example, consider the situation faced by the promoter of a rock concert. Revenue generated by the concert will be determined largely by the price charged per ticket and the number of tickets sold. (In some cases concession and souvenir sales might add to this revenue.) Expenses, for the most part, will consist of the contracted fee negotiated with the rock act, concert hall rental charges, and other personnel services (such as ticket takers and security guards). The promoter can use breakeven analysis to help determine ticket prices and the number of tickets that must be sold to break even or, more importantly to the promoter, to generate varying levels of profit.

Breakeven analysis
A graphic display of the relationship between volume of output and revenue and costs.

Breakeven analysis depicts the output, revenue, and cost relationships in a graphical format, as illustrated in Figure 7.4.[38] In this format, output volume (in units of product) is represented on the horizontal axis of the graph, while the vertical axis indicates the levels of costs and revenues (in dollars).

Seven elements can be defined and illustrated on the breakeven graph.[39]

1. *Fixed cost.* Fixed cost includes those costs that remain constant regardless of the volume of output. Fixed cost is comprised of such items as overhead, administrative salaries, rent, and mortgage payments. It is shown by a horizontal line on the graph.

2. *Total variable cost.* This reflects the costs that increase as the volume of output rises. Variable costs include such items as raw material cost, direct labor cost, and the cost of energy consumed in the manufacture of the product. Total variable cost is obtained by multiplying the output level by the variable cost per unit (i.e., the material, labor, and energy costs consumed per unit of output). On the graph, the total variable cost is zero when there is no output, but then increases as the output level rises.

3. *Total cost.* The sum of fixed cost and total variable cost is the total cost. It is represented by a line that is parallel to the total variable cost line, but shifted upward due to the addition of the fixed cost.

▼ FIGURE 7.4
Breakeven Analysis

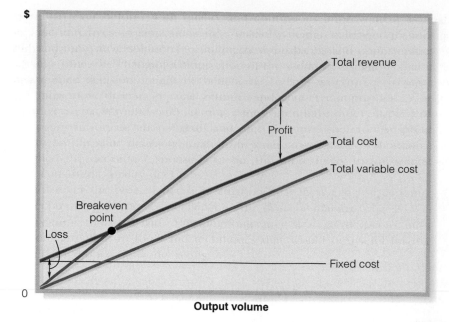

4. *Total revenue.* This is the total dollars received from the sale of the output. Total revenue is obtained by multiplying the per unit selling price by the output level. On the graph, revenue is zero when there is no output, but then increases as the output level rises.

5. *Breakeven point.* On the graph, there is one level of output where total cost equals total revenue. This is defined as the breakeven point, for it is here that the organization will realize no profit, but incur no loss.

6. *Profit.* Profit is the amount by which total revenue exceeds total cost on the graph. Profit will be realized at all output levels to the right of the breakeven point.

7. *Loss.* Loss is the amount by which total cost exceeds total revenue. On the graph, a loss will be incurred at all output levels to the left of the breakeven point.

Breakeven analysis is a useful tool for analyzing the costs, revenues, profits, and losses at various levels of output. The simple linear structure displayed here does have its limitations, though. Often fixed cost does not remain constant through all levels of output. For example, to exceed some critical volume of output, it may be necessary for the organization to expand its plant, thereby incurring a sudden increase in its overhead, administrative expenses, and other contributors to fixed cost. A situation like this would be reflected as a step increase in the fixed cost line.

Similarly, price and unit variable cost may change as output volume changes. Higher levels of output may result in quantity discounts in the purchase of raw materials. Lower raw material costs would lead to a decrease in the slope of the variable cost line. Higher levels of output may also require more overtime from workers. The higher cost of labor would lead to an increase in the slope of the variable cost line. If higher levels of output occur, management must often reduce the selling price to encourage consumption of this additional output. Lowering the selling price would lead to a decrease in the slope of the revenue line. When situations such as these occur, the breakeven graph will not display the crisp, uniform, linear relationships shown in Figure 7.4. Instead, the lines may contain bends, curves, breaks, and/or kinks. Furthermore, these lines generally represent estimates of costs and revenues that will occur in the future. Since estimates are rarely exact, the lines will not be precise and sharp. Instead, the actual values might be above or below those lines. Consequently, the breakeven point should be regarded not as a single, indisputable value, but as an indication of an approximate range of output levels where breakeven is most likely to occur. Regardless of the amount of irregularity in these graphs, however, the fundamental relationships will remain intact. Profit will occur when total revenue exceeds total cost, losses will occur when total cost exceeds total revenue, and breakeven will occur when total cost equals total revenue.

Linear Programming

Often managers are faced with the decision of how to allocate limited resources among competing users in a manner that optimizes some objective. These resources can be as diverse as materials, machines, money, energy, employees, and the like. Linear programming is a powerful tool that can help the manager solve such allocation problems.

Although the linear programming computations are quite technical, desktop computer software for solving this type of problem is available. Nevertheless, managers need to be familiar with the basic structure of a linear programming problem. After all, they will be responsible for recognizing these allocation situations and will have to structure the linear programming formulation for the decision situation before the computer can take over and perform the calculations.

To develop a linear programming formulation, the decision maker must structure two basic components: the objective function and a set of constraints.[40] **An objective function** is a symbolic, quantitative representation of the primary goal that the decision maker is seeking to optimize. **Constraints** are algebraic statements, in equation form, that reflect any restrictions on the decision maker's flexibility in making decision choices. Before developing these two components, the decision maker must have a clear understanding of the decision variables in the problem. **Decision variables** represent the factors that the decision maker can manipulate, that is, the decisions that must be made. Table 7.7 illustrates a simple production decision where two products (bookcases and compact disc racks) are to be manufactured from three raw materials (wood, plastic laminate, and glue) whose supplies are limited. The data in the table indicate the amount of each raw material used in making each product, the amount of each raw material available, and the profit contribution for each product. The decision maker must decide how much of each product to manufacture to maximize profit, while at the same time being careful not to exceed the available supplies of each raw material. Steps 1–4 at the bottom of Table 7.7 show how the decision maker would define algebraic symbols to represent the number of units of each product to make (the decision variables) and the subsequent objective function and constraints that would have been formulated. This linear programming model is now ready for desktop computer solution.

The linear programming situation illustrated in Table 7.7 was kept exceedingly simple for illustration purposes. In reality, managers often face resource allocation problems consisting of hundreds or even thousands of decision variables and similar numbers of constraint equations. Linear programming has seen some very diverse applications over the years. For example, Owens-Corning Fiberglass uses it to develop multiproduct production schedules, American Airlines uses it for scheduling flight crews and aircraft, and Major League Baseball uses it to assign umpires to baseball games.[41]

PERT

Organizations must often undertake large, unique, projects that involve many highly interrelated work activities. In such cases, managers must be prepared

Objective function
A symbolic, quantitative representation of the primary goal that the decision maker is seeking to optimize.

Constraints
Algebraic statements, in equation form, that reflect any restrictions on the decision maker's flexibility in making decision choices.

Decision variables
The factors that the decision maker can manipulate.

▼ **TABLE 7.7**   Linear Programming

PRODUCT INFORMATION			
Raw Material	BOOK CASES	COMPACT DISC RACKS	Raw Material Available
Lumber	8	5	400
Plastic Laminate	4	2	120
Glue	1	2	60
Profit per unit	$15	$10	

Step 1. Definition of decision variables:
   Let X_1 = the number of books cases manufactured.
   Let X_2 = the number of CD racks manufactured.

Step 2. Establish object function:
   Maximize profit, or MAX $15X_1 + 10X_2$.

Step 3. Establish constraints:
   Resource constraints: Amount of each raw material used must be less than or
      equal to the amount available.
   Lumber constraint: $8X_1 + 5X_2 \leq 400$.
   Plastic laminate constraint: $4X_1 + 2X_2 \leq 120$.
   Glue constraint: $1X_1 + 2X_2 \leq 60$.
   Nonnegativity constraints: You cannot make a negative number of book cases or
      CD racks.
$$X_1 \geq 0$$
$$X_2 \geq 0$$

Step 4. Summarize problem:
$$\text{MAX } 15X_1 + 10X_2$$
$$\text{subject to: } 8x_1 + 5X_2 \leq 400$$
$$4X_1 + 2X_2 \leq 120$$
$$1X_1 + 2X_2 \leq 60$$
$$X_1 \geq 0$$
$$X_2 \geq 0$$
   (Solution: $X_1 = 20$; $X_2 = 20$; profit = $500)

to schedule all of those activities and the resources they consume so that the project can be completed in a timely fashion. General Motors had to coordinate thousands of activities as the Saturn project moved from the concept stage to a working factory producing automobiles.

**PERT (Program Evaluation and
Review Technique)**
A network approach for scheduling
project activities.

PERT (Program Evaluation and Review Technique) is a technique designed to aid in scheduling project activities. The PERT approach uses a network diagram to arrange and visually display project activities. Such a diagram can help managers to plan far in advance, pinpoint potential bottlenecks and trouble spots, and determine whether resources should be reallocated among activities.

In the PERT approach, four preliminary steps must be performed before the project analysis can begin: (1) activity identification, (2) precedence identification, (3) activity time estimation, and (4) network construction.[42] Activity identification requires that managers determine all of the elements of work (activities) that must be performed for the project to be completed. To establish the activity precedence relationships, managers must determine which activities can be conducted simultaneously and which must be performed sequentially. It is also necessary to estimate the amount of time each activity will consume so that a time schedule can eventually be developed for the project activities. Finally, all of this information must be assembled into a network model to facilitate the analysis.

Figure 7.5 shows a network model for a very simple project, consisting of only five activities. In this project, a team of fraternity brothers will build a bicycle shed for the fraternity house. The arrows in the PERT diagram represent the activities, while the circles (nodes) represent events. The amount of time each activity will take is indicated on the appropriate arrow. The nodes (events) represent points in time. For example, at node 2, activity A (design the dimensions of the shed) has been completed, and activities B and C (set the forms for the concrete slab, and cut the lumber for the shed) are ready to be started. Furthermore, precedence relationships can be recognized immediately from the diagram. For example, setting the forms for the concrete slab (activity B) and cutting the lumber for the shed (activity C) cannot begin until after the shed has been designed and its dimensions are known (activity A). Also, activities B and C (setting forms and cutting lumber) can be conducted simultaneously, since no precedence relationship exists between them.

▼ Major construction endeavors like this require formal project scheduling techniques like PERT to ensure timely completion of all project activities.

Once the preliminary PERT steps have been performed, the network can be analyzed to determine reasonable start and finish times for each activity and a likely project duration. Project duration is determined from the network's critical path. A path is any sequence of activities that extends from the beginning to the end of the project. In our simple illustration two paths extend from the beginning to the end of the project (path A–B–D–E and path A–C–E). The most time-consuming path in the network is the critical path. The critical path dictates the minimum amount of time in which the project can be completed and also indicates which activities are most critical to getting the project completed on time. In this example, the critical path is path A–B–D–E (10 days). Any delays on these activities will lengthen the duration of the project. We have assumed in this example that the fraternity brothers' main concern is finishing the project in 14 days, so that it will be completed when the other brothers return for the fall semester. Figure 7.5 summarizes the results from all the calculations of start and finish times for each of the project's activities.

This overview of PERT has described the technique in its most basic form. By expanding this form, managers can deal with situations where the time required for activities is uncertain or where resources can be reallocated among activities to alter a project's completion time and cost. British Airways successfully used PERT to analyze the necessary activities in a program to create a new image for the corporation.[43]

MANAGERIAL IMPLICATIONS

Decision making has always been one of the primary activities of managers. As the global business economy continues to expand and change dramatically, the level of managerial decision making can only be expected to increase in the future. If they are to make quality decisions, managers will have to become thoroughly familiar with the structure of decision making and at the same time must equip themselves with the tools and techniques that can aid in the decision-making process. This means that tomorrow's managers should:

▼ FIGURE 7.5
PERT Analysis

Data generated in preliminary analysis of project:

Activity		Immediate Predecessors	Activity Time (Days)
A	Design dimensions of shed	—	2
B	Set forms for concrete slab	A	1
C	Cut lumber for shed to proper dimensions	A	2
D	Pour concrete slab and allow to cure	B	4
E	Assemble shed	C, D	3

Resulting project network generated:

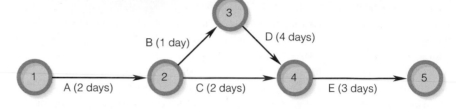

Identification of critical path:

Path	Time
ABDE	10 days (critical path)
ACE	7 days

Earliest start (ES), earliest finish (EF), latest start (LS), and latest finish (LF) time estimates:

Activity	ES	EF	LS	LF
A	0	2	4	6
B	2	3	6	7
C	2	4	9	11
D	3	7	7	11
E	7	10	11	14

ES for first activity = 0, or today's calendar date.

ES for other activities = largest EF of activity's immediate predecessors.

EF for activity = its ES + its activity time.

LF for last activity = some target completion time (14 days here).

LF for other activities = smallest LS of activity's immediate successors.

LS for activity = its LF – its activity time.

- Be able to recognize quickly problems and opportunities that call for a decision.
- Be able to recognize the different time frames and scopes of strategic decisions versus operational decisions.
- Be equipped with all the tools and techniques that can aid in making strategic decisions.
- Be familiar with the framework for operational decision making as well as the structural components for displaying operational decisions.
- Be able to recognize the different decision-making environments under which her operational decisions will be made.
- Have an awareness and understanding of the various quantitative tools that can aid in making the operational decisions.

This chapter has presented several quantitative tools and techniques that can aid in making both strategic and operational decisions. These tools and techniques are quite analytical, suggesting that we need only "plug in the numbers" to select the best alternative. As we saw several times in our discussions, however, decision making cannot always go entirely by the numbers. Many times experience, good judgment, and even intuition are valuable commodities when making decisions about future courses of action, especially since we can never be entirely certain about what the future holds in store for us.

THE SATURN RECALL DILEMMA

MANAGERIAL INCIDENT RESOLUTION

Saturn's response to the electrical wiring problem was swift and decisive. On August 11, 1993, came a media blitz announcing Saturn's intention to recall the more than 380,000 affected automobiles and make the necessary repairs. Radio and television news programs carried the story, as did all newspapers. To ensure that all affected Saturn owners were informed, notices were mailed to them with instructions to call their dealership to make an appointment for repairs. Richard Lefauve, president of Saturn Corporation, was a guest on NBC's "Today Show," where he explained that Saturn's decision was prompted by its commitment to its customers. Saturn was going to do whatever was necessary to demonstrate that commitment. In fact, Lefauve said that any Saturn owner who did not come in for repairs would receive a phone call from his or her dealer to ensure that the owner knew of the problem.

Saturn spokesman Bob Tripolsky issued a statement saying that "our number one priority is to keep our stakeholders (our customers and retailers) aware of what is going to be happening." Saturn dealers canceled vacation plans, extended service department hours, and provided customers with snacks in an attempt to turn the recall into a campaign of reassurance that Saturn's service was superior. Saturn's swift and decisive response to the problem proved to be a good decision. Surveys of affected Saturn owners and dealers revealed that customer response was positive. The recall effort simply confirmed most Saturn owners' belief that they had made the correct choice when they purchased their automobiles.[44] ▼

SUMMARY

- Programmed decisions are routine responses to decision situations that may have occurred in the past or with which the decision maker is quite familiar. Nonprogrammed decisions are responses to situations that are unique, unstructured, or poorly defined.

- Strategic decision making occurs from a very broad perspective and is performed at the highest levels within organizations. It involves the selection of a corporate-level strategy and the choice of competitive strategies to be pursued by the various business units of the organization. Strategic decision making is most often nonroutine in nature. Operational decision making pervades all levels in the organization and is usually concerned with day-to-day routine decisions.

- Selection of a business strategy can be facilitated by means of the strategic decision-making matrix approach. This tool allows the decision maker to evaluate a variety of potential strategies in conjunction with several objectives. Objectives are ranked by their importance, and strategies are rated by their likelihood of achieving those objectives. This method ultimately allows for the ranking of alternative strategies.

- Two popular matrix approaches for evaluating a business portfolio are the BCG growth-share matrix and the GE industry attractiveness/business strength matrix. Although both have two dimensions, they measure different factors and include a different number of levels for each factor. The two factors in BCG matrix are market growth rate and relative market share. With two levels for each factor, a four-cell matrix results. The GE matrix uses industry attractiveness and business strength as its factors. Three levels for each factor are defined, resulting in a nine-cell matrix. In both approaches, an organization's business units are placed in the appropriate cell; then prescriptions for strategic decision making are made relative to the cell occupied by the business unit.

- In decision making under certainty, the decision maker knows exactly which future state of nature will occur. In decision making under risk, the decision maker is not sure which state of nature will occur, but can assess the probability, or likelihood, of each occurring. In decision making under uncertainty, the decision maker not only is not sure which state of nature will occur, but has no estimate of the probability that each will occur.

- Various computational criteria exist for analyzing decision making under conditions of certainty, risk, and uncertainty. When risk conditions prevail, payoff tables can be used in conjunction with state of nature probabilities to arrive at expected payoffs for each alternative. The alternative with the best expected payoff will then be selected. When uncertainty conditions prevail, decision makers must assess their degree of optimism about the likely occurrence of future events in order to make a choice.

- Decision trees provide another format for assessing decision making under risk situations. Alternative courses of action and states of nature are laid out in a tree diagram rather than in a matrix. Decision trees are particularly useful when the decision maker faces a sequence of interrelated decisions that occur over time.

- Breakeven analysis is a quantitative technique that allows managers to graphically examine the relationships between output levels, revenue, and costs. Linear programming is a technique that allows managers to determine how to best allocate limited resources among competing users in a manner that optimizes some objective. PERT is a network technique that allows managers to schedule a complex set of interrelated activities that must be performed to complete large, unique projects.

KEY TERMS

Problem (p. 211)
Opportunity (p. 211)
Programmed decisions (p. 213)
Nonprogrammed decisions (p. 213)
Strategic decision-making matrix (p. 214)
Business portfolio matrix (p. 215)
BCG matrix (p. 215)
Market growth rate (p. 215)
Relative market share (p. 216)

Stars (p. 216)
Cash cows (p. 216)
Dogs (p. 216)
Question marks (p. 217)
GE matrix (p. 218)
Alternative courses of action (p. 222)
States of nature (p. 222)
Payoffs (p. 224)
Payoff table (p. 224)

Expected value (p. 226)
Expected monetary value (EMV) (p. 226)
Decision tree (p. 227)
Breakeven analysis (p. 229)
Objective function (p. 231)
Constraints (p. 231)
Decision variables (p. 231)
PERT (Program Evaluation and Review Technique (p. 232)

REVIEW QUESTIONS

1. Identify the two situations that are liable to result in a business decision being made.

2. Describe the strategic decision-making matrix technique for selecting from among strategy alternatives. In what way is this approach similar to the format for decision making under risk for operational decision making?

3. Describe the structure, purpose, and approach of the four-cell BCG matrix.

4. Describe the structure, purpose, and approach of the nine-cell GE matrix.

5. What is a state of nature?

6. What is the difference between a conditional value and an expected value?

7. Describe how decision making under certainty, risk, and uncertainty differ.

8. What are decision trees, and where are they most useful?

DISCUSSION QUESTIONS

Improving Critical Thinking

1. Discuss the pros and cons associated with the two business portfolio matrix techniques described in this chapter. Which, if any, do you find more appealing? Why?

2. Assume that you are about to prepare for an examination in one of your business courses and have several alternatives as to the amount of studying that you can do. The exam can have several possible degrees of difficulty (depending upon how tough your professor decides to make it!). Discuss how this situation could be cast into a decision-making matrix format. What would you use as a measure of payoffs for this situation?

3. Refer back to question 2. Think for a moment about your own personal feelings and premonitions as to how difficult the exam might be. Using these premonitions on exam difficulty and the payoffs you described in Question 2, which alternative would you select and why?

Enhancing Communication Skills

4. Assume that you are employed as a counter attendant in a fast-food restaurant. What are two requests that a customer might make that would require a routine decision? Two requests that would require a nonroutine decision? To enhance your oral communication skills, prepare a short (10–15 minute) presentation for the class in which you describe these requests and explain why you classified them in this way.

5. Think of some task, project, or endeavor that you have recently faced that required you to make a series of interrelated decisions. Thoroughly describe that situation and the decisions you made. Then convert this verbal description into a decision tree diagram that displays these interrelationships. To enhance your written communication skills, write a short (1–2 page) essay describing this endeavor, the decisions you faced, and the tree diagram displaying these interrelationships.

Building Teamwork

6. Put yourself in the position of a student member of your campus homecoming committee. One of your committee's duties is to book a successful comedian (fee $10,000) for one of your homecoming events, and develop a plan to conduct that event. To refine your teamwork skills, meet with a small group of students who have been given this same assignment. Assign each team member some aspect of this endeavor to research in order to determine the costs you are likely to incur, potential sources of revenue, available concert halls or auditoriums, and any other pertinent information. Then, use break-even analysis to develop a thorough plan for staging this entertainment event. Finally, select a spokesperson to present the details of your plan to the rest of the class.

7. List several objectives with different units of "payoff measure" that might be encountered in various business decisions. To refine your teamwork skills, meet with a small group of students who have been given the same assignment. Compare your lists for common items, then consolidate your ideas into a single list. Select a spokesperson to present to the rest of the class your list of payoff measures and where they might be encountered.

ETHICS: TAKE A STAND

Pennsylvania's largest health insurer, Pennsylvania Blue Shield, has invested almost $10 million since 1986 in Philip Morris, Inc., the world's largest cigarette manufacturer. The money represents about 0.5 percent of Blue Shield's total investment in stocks and bonds, according to financial reports filed with the Pennsylvania State Insurance Department. In 1992 alone, Blue Shield bought 1.8 million shares of Philip Morris stock. Currently, the insurer has a total of more than $4.3 million invested in Philip Morris.[45]

For Discussion:

1. Discuss the ethics of the health insurer's decision to invest in an industry that arguably has a negative impact on human health.

2. Can this investment be justified on the basis of Blue Shield's obligation to generate sufficient cash to service claims by policyholders?

3. Does the fact that the investment is less than 1 percent of Blue Shield's total portfolio have any bearing in this matter?

THINKING CRITICALLY
Debate the Issue

BCG ANALYSIS—GOOD OR BAD?

Form teams of four or five students as directed by your instructor. Research the use of the BCG growth-share matrix for business portfolio analysis. In particular, try to ascertain and understand both the positive and negative aspects of this approach. Prepare to debate either the positive or the negative aspects of the BCG approach. When it is time to debate this issue in front of the class, your instructor will tell you which position you will take.

VIDEO CASE

Allwest Fire and Sound

Allwest Fire and Sound, Inc., which is located in Denver, Colorado, installs special electronic systems, such as fire alarm, security, paging, intercom, and closed-circuit television systems. When President Peter Perry and Chief Financial Officer Steve Pickett purchased Allwest in 1990, they realized that the company had some serious problems.

One of the most glaring problems was the lack of control on installation projects, which ranged from small two-week jobs to a lengthy $5 million fire alarm installation at Denver International Airport. Allwest's managers had no comprehensive way to check on projects (i.e., how far along they were, whether materials had been delivered, and whether the performance was satisfactory). Too often Perry and Pickett learned the answers to such questions through irate phone calls from outraged customers.

In addition, Allwest needed to find more bank financing and more business, to increase profitability, to heighten employee effectiveness, and to improve the company's quality image. But first, the company had to do something about monitoring the progress of its projects.[46]

For Discussion

1. Describe the quantitative tool that would be most helpful to Allwest in tackling its problem with project monitoring.

2. Describe what you would do if you were asked to assist Allwest in straightening out this problem.

CASE

Word Processing 'R Me

Ann Houser was lying on the beach in Clearwater, Florida, enjoying the last weeks of the summer vacation before her senior year in college. As she lay there, she was trying to think of a way to earn extra money during the school year. "Why not take advantage of my excellent typing skills?" she thought. "I could type term papers and reports for my classmates. There is sure to be plenty of work." The more she thought about it, the more she liked the idea. She rolled off her beach blanket, picked up a small piece of driftwood, and began scrawling a decision plan in the sand.

Ann thought aloud: "I must lease hardware right now for one semester and will have to choose between a simple word processing machine and a more sophisticated personal computer with word processing software and a laser printer. Then I will see how much work comes in. At the end of the fall semester, I will have to decide what I will do during the spring semester, which will be my last semester in this business venture. At that time I must decide whether to change equipment or continue with what I originally leased. If I originally leased a word processor, I might be approaching my capacity, so I'll have to decide whether to continue with the word processor or trade up to a microcomputer. If I originally leased a microcomputer, I might have too much firepower, so I'll have to decide whether to continue with the microcomputer or trade down to a word processor. Of course, my decision will be influenced by the demand for my services during the fall semester. But regardless of whether demand was high or low during the fall, it could change during the spring. It seems to me that the profit I realize will depend upon the type of hardware I lease coupled with the demand level that occurs."

At the end of all this musing, Ann realized that she had developed a tree diagram that reflected the sequence of decisions she was facing over the next academic year. The diagram put everything into perspective for her, and as she folded up her blanket, she had a very good feeling about her new venture.

For Discussion

1. Try to develop a diagram like the one Ann scratched into the sand, showing the sequence of decisions, alternatives, and states of nature that she would be facing during the upcoming academic year.

2. Discuss the additional information that Ann will have to obtain or estimate if she is to use her diagram to systematically analyze the sequence of decisions that she faces.

EXPERIENTIAL EXERCISE 7.1

Decision Making under Risk

Purpose: To gain experience in the analysis of a risk decision situation through the use of payoff tables.

Procedure: Review the conditional values provided in the accompanying payoff table. Then, assuming that the probabilities for the states of nature are .2, .2, and .6 for S_1, S_2, and S_3, respectively, perform the analysis requested.

Step 1: Use the conditional values and the probabilities to derive an expected value matrix.

Step 2: Calculate the total expected value for each alternative.

ALTERNATIVES	STATES OF NATURE		
	S_1	S_2	S_3
A_1	32	25	19
A_2	21	28	29
A_3	18	20	26

Step 3: Select the best alternative and provide an interpretation for its total expected value.

EXPERIENTIAL EXERCISE 7.2

Using Decision Trees in Everyday Life

Purpose: To gain a better appreciation for the fact that many everyday decision situations are composed of a sequence of interrelated decisions that could be displayed as a decision tree.

Procedure: Think about the decisions you make each semester before registering for your college courses. Your course selections are no doubt driven to a large extent by the requirements for your program of study. Your selection of specific class sections, however, is probably influenced by such factors as the instructor, the time of day and days of the week the class meets, conflicts with other classes, conflicts with work schedules, and conflicts with sleep schedules. Your decision process probably has some sequential elements to it: for example, "if I schedule this class at this time, then these classes cannot be scheduled because . . . ." Develop a tree diagram to illustrate the sequential decision aspects of the class scheduling process that you went through in a recent semester.

NOTES

1. Based on A. Adler, "Saturn Recalls All Cars Made before April '93 for Fire Risk," *The Columbia SC State,* August 11, 1993, A1+; B. Meier, "Engine Fires Prompt G.M. to Issue Recall of 80% of Saturns, *The New York Times,* August 11, 1993, Alt; O. Suris, "Recall by Saturn Could Tarnish Its Reputation," *The Wall Street Journal,* August 11, 1993, A3+; R. Truett, "Calls Swamp Saturn Dealers Since Recall," *The Orlando Sentinel,* August 11, 1993, Alt; J. B. Treece, "Here Comes GM's Saturn," *Business Week,* April 9, 1990, 55-62; D. Williams, "Inside Saturn," *Automotive Industries,* May 3, 1989, 50-53; "Striking Back: GM Readies a New Mid-Size Line," *Wall Street Journal,* May 1, 1987; S. L. Brooks, "The GM Saturn Experience," *Production,* March 1986, 74-76; and B. H. Berry, "It's Now or Never for World-Class Automaking at GM," *Iron Age,* November 7, 1986, 34-35.

2. M. J. Hicks, *Problem Solving in Business and Management* (London: Chapman & Hall, 1991).

3. "How Coke Decided a New Taste Was It," *Fortune,* May 27, 1985, 80; and "Coke's Brand-Loyalty Lesson," *Fortune,* August 5, 1985, 44-46.

4. Adapted from "Big Bob's Used Carpet Shops of America," in *Real World Lessons for America's Small Businesses: Insights from the Blue Chip Initiative.* (*Nation's Business* on behalf of Connecticut Mutual Life Insurance Company and the U.S. Chamber of Commerce, 1992), 92-93.

5. Pepsi Puts Freshness Dates on Diet Soda Bottles, Cans. *The Orlando Sentinel,* March 31, 1994, B-5.

6. H. A. Simon, *The New Science of Management* (Englewood Cliffs, N.J.: Prentice-Hall, 1977), 47.

7. Adapted from "Agsco, Inc." in *Real World Lessons for America's Small Businesses: Insights from the Blue Chip Initiative* (*Nation's Business* on behalf of Connecticut Mutual Life Insurance Company and the U.S. Chamber of Commerce, 1992), 36-37.

8. J. M. Kopf, J. G. Krevze, and H. H. Beam, "Using a Strategic Planning Matrix to Improve a Firm's Competitive Position," *Journal of Accountancy* 175 (July 1993): 97-101.

9. F. David, "The Strategic Planning Matrix—A Quantitative Approach," *Long Range Planning* 19 (October 1986): 102.

10. F. R. David, *Strategic Management,* 4th ed. (New York: Macmillan, 1993), 234.

11. A. A. Thompson, Jr. and A. J. Strickland, III, *Strategic Management: Concepts and Cases* (Homewood, Ill.: Richard D. Irwin, 1992), 193.

12. A. C. Hax and N. S. Majluf, *Strategic Management: An Integrative Perspective* (Englewood Cliffs, N.J.: Prentice-Hall, 1984), chapter 7.

13. J. A. Pearce, III and R. B. Robinson, Jr., *Strategic Management: Formulation, Implementation, and Control,* 4th ed. (Homewood, Ill.: Richard D. Irwin, 1991), 263.

14. David, *Strategic Management,* 225-27.

15. Adapted from David, *Strategic Management,* 251-52.

16. Personal interview with Blain Sweat, Olive Garden Restaurants.

17. P. Haspeslagh, "Portfolio Planning: Uses and Limitations," *Harvard Business Review* 60 (January/February 1982): 58-73.

18. D. F. Abell and J. S. Hammond, *Strategic Market Planning: Problems & Analytical Approaches* (Englewood Cliffs, N.J.: Prentice-Hall, 1979).

19. P. Kotler, *Marketing Management: Analysis, Planning, and Control,* 6th ed. (Englewood Cliffs, N.J.: Prentice-Hall, 1988).

20. Thompson and Strickland, *Strategic Management.*

21. S. C. Certo and J. P. Peter, *Strategic Management: Concepts and Applications,* 2d ed. (New York: McGraw-Hill, 1991), 107-10.

22. Pearce and Robinson, *Strategic Management,* 267-72.

23. C. W. Hofer, and D. Schendel, *Strategy Formulation: Analytical Concepts* (St. Paul, Minn.: West Publishing Company, 1978), 33.

24. M. Bacharach and S. Hurley, eds., *Foundations of Decision Theory: Issues and Advances* (Cambridge, Mass.: B. Blackwell, 1991).

25. Adapted from "Computer Service Supply Corporation," in *Real-World Lessons for America's Small Businesses: Insights from the Blue Chip Enterprise Initiative* (*Nation's Business* on behalf of Connecticut Mutual Life Insurance Company and the U.S. Chamber of Commerce, 1993), 139–40.

26. T. M. Cook and R. A. Russell, *Introduction to Management Science,* 3d ed. (Englewood Cliffs, N.J.: Prentice-Hall, 1985), 399–402.

27. D. W. Miller and M. K. Starr, *The Structure of Human Decisions* (Englewood Cliffs, N.J.: Prentice-Hall, 1967), 106.

28. B. Render and R. M. Stair, Jr., *Introduction to Management Science* (Boston: Allyn & Bacon, 1992), 598.

29. E. F. Harrison, *The Managerial Decision-Making Process* (Boston: Houghton Mifflin, 1975), 151–58.

30. Render and Stair, *Introduction to Management Science,* 598.

31. D. Samson, *Managerial Decision Analysis* (Homewood, Ill.: Richard D. Irwin, 1988), 148–51.

32. Render and Stair, *Introduction to Management Science,* 600.

33. Samson, *Managerial Decision Analysis,* 23–32.

34. "Decision Tree Analysis in the United States Postal Service," *Interfaces* March/April 1987.

35. Cook and Russell, *Introduction to Management Science,* 402–4.

36. J. Sengupta, *Decision Models in Stochastic Programming: Operational Methods of Decision Making under Uncertainty* (New York: North Holland, 1982).

37. R. Roy, "Expressway Not a Dead End for Homeless—Program Will Give Them Jobs," *Orlando Sentinel,* April 21, 1993, p. 1+.

38. L. J. Krajewski and L. P. Ritzman, *Operations Management: Strategy and Analysis,* 3d ed. (Reading, Mass.: Addison-Wesley, 1993), 45.

39. Ibid., 44–46.

40. Render and Stair, *Introduction to Management Science,* Chap. 2.

41. Ibid., chapters 2, 4, 6.

42. Ibid., chapter 9.

43. Ibid.

44. Based on Adler, "Saturn Recalls All Cars Made before April '93 for Fire Risk"; B. Meier, "Engine Fires Prompt G.M. to Issue Recall of 80% of Saturns, *The New York Times,* August 11, 1993, A1t; O. Suris, "Recall by Saturn Could Tarnish Its Reputation, *The Wall Street Journal,* August 11, 1993, A3+; R. Truett, "Calls Swamp Saturn Dealers Since Recall," *The Orlando Sentinel,* August 11, 1993, A1t; Treece, "Here Comes GM's Saturn"; Williams, "Inside Saturn"; "Striking Back: GM Readies a New Mid-Size Line"; Brooks, "The GM Saturn Experience"; and Berry, "It's Now or Never for World-Class Automaking at GM."

45. "Health Insurer Holds Stock in Cigarette Maker," *Orlando Sentinel,* March 31, 1993, C-5.

46. Adapted from "Allwest Fire and Sound," in *Real-World Lessons for America's Small Businesses: Insights from the Blue Chip Enterprise Initiative* (*Nation's Business* on behalf of Connecticut Mutual Life Insurance Company and the U.S. Chamber of Commerce, 1993), 137–38.

IBAX: PUTTING A RETRENCHMENT STRATEGY INTO ACTION

Recall the situation at IBAX—the IBM and Baxter partnership that provides health care information systems software. The company, which had been projected to break even in the first year of the partnership (1989), lost more than $25 million over its first two years of operation. Poor product quality and customer service had led to widespread customer dissatisfaction. Coupled with internal productivity problems, these difficulties had resulted in a very unfavorable financial position for IBAX.

Jeff Goodman, who was hired as CEO of IBAX at the beginning of 1991, was faced with the challenge of turning IBAX around. Based on his assessment of the situation, Goodman knew that this would not be an easy task. He needed a strategic plan.

DEVELOPING THE PLAN

In developing the strategic plan for IBAX, Goodman worked his way through the strategic planning process. He conducted a strategic analysis, formulated a strategy, developed implementation plans, and established strategic control mechanisms (see Chapters 4 and 5 for a discussion of the process of strategic planning).

STRATEGIC ANALYSIS

Goodman began by conducting a strategic analysis of IBAX. The information provided in "The Assessment" section of the Part I cohesion case details much of the information that was evaluated during the strategic analysis. This information is summarized in Table 1, which outlines the major strengths, weaknesses, opportunities, and threats that Goodman identified. It is apparent from Table 1, that the internal analysis revealed few strengths, and many weaknesses which would have serious implications for the long-term performance of the company. Further, while the external environmental analysis revealed some very significant threats, there were also opportunities that the company could capitalize on in the long term. It was clear from strategic analysis, however, that the first priority at IBAX had to be on overcoming its many weaknesses.

STRATEGY FORMULATION

Once the strategic analysis was completed, a strategy had to be formulated. This involved assessing the mission of the company, establishing strategic goals, identifying and evaluating strategic alternatives, and choosing a strategy.

The mission of IBAX was fairly clear: to be a leading provider of high-quality information systems software to health care organizations. The mission didn't need to be changed; rather, IBAX needed to fulfill its mission more

▼ **TABLE 1** SWOT Analysis for IBAX

STRENGTHS
• Relatively large installed base • Qualified employees • Partners' (IBM and Baxter) commitment to the company
WEAKNESSES
• Poor product quality • High cost structure as a result of overstaffing • Low customer satisfaction • No senior management team • No homogeneous corporate culture/no evolved values • Low employee morale • Ineffective sales force • No performance standards • Ineffective organizational structure
OPPORTUNITIES
• Health care reform focused on improved efficiency • Growth in alternative methods of delivering health care
THREATS
• Economic recession of 1990–1991 • Strong competition in the health care information systems industry • Stagnant market in terms of hospital growth • Small hospitals merging with larger hospitals • Fast pace of technology change making products obsolete • Health care regulatory reform creating an uncertain future

effectively. The strategic goals of the organization were equally clear and had been established by the partners from the outset—improve product quality, customer satisfaction, and the financial position of the company.

IBAX appeared to have only one feasible strategic alternative—retrenchment/turnaround. The retrenchment strategy would require IBAX to reduce its assets and costs to become more efficient, as well as develop an entirely new organizational system including such things as organizational structure, culture, product quality standards, performance standards, and reward systems.

STRATEGY IMPLEMENTATION

Implementing the retrenchment strategy began early in 1991 and continued throughout the year and into the next. The company's organizational design underwent a radical transformation, and the way employees were managed with regard to communication, motivation, and leadership also changed. Since subsequent cases will discuss each of these aspects of the turnaround in greater detail, just a brief overview of the changes that were made at IBAX will be provided here.

It was clear that IBAX was operationally inefficient. To improve efficiency, geographically dispersed units would have to be merged, and employees would have to be released. Goodman started by closing and consolidating locations. By 1991, IBAX had only two main locations—one in Orlando, Florida, where approximately 75 percent of the organization is housed, and the other in New York, where a technology development center is located.

After consolidating facilities, Goodman looked for other ways to improve efficiency. Based on the benchmarks of other companies in the industry, IBAX should have been generating $125,000 in revenues per employee. The company was far below that target, which seemed to indicate that it was heavily overstaffed. Goodman cut $15 million of labor costs from the company's cost structure by reducing the workforce from 750 employees to 580.

Once facilities had been closed and the employee base had been reduced, it was time to change the internal functioning of the organization. Goodman moved the company from a functionally based organizational structure to a structure based on product lines. Self-managed teams were created as the primary unit within each product-based group, and decision making was pushed down to the lowest levels of the organization. To support this new structure, many changes were made in the human resource management function and the culture of the organization.

Goodman put a priority on developing a strong leadership team within the company. Then he enlisted that team to help him deliver the message regarding the need for change. He knew that employees had to really understand the problems facing IBAX before they would be convinced to change their behaviors. He implemented what he calls "open book management"—that is, the financial statements were open and accessible to all employees. Where necessary, Goodman taught employees how to read and understand financial statements so they would be better informed.

Once the employees were convinced that radical and dramatic changes were needed, Goodman set about getting their input on what needed to be changed and how to make those changes. He set up a motivation and reward system that encouraged broad-based participation in the turnaround. He was committed to doing everything he could to help the employees feel ownership of IBAX and to empower them to do whatever was necessary to make the company a success.

STRATEGIC CONTROL

The final phase of Goodman's strategic planning efforts related to establishing strategic controls. Developing and implementing clear performance standards were crucial to the success of the retrenchment strategy. Each business unit engaged in a benchmarking process to establish financial and product quality standards that it would be held accountable for meeting. These control measures ensured that the company was making progress toward achieving both its strategic and operational goals.

THE RESULTS

As you will learn as you work your way through the IBAX case, Goodman's plan was a success. Product quality began to improve, customer satisfaction began to rise, and the company began to recover financially—all areas of significant weakness for the company at the outset. Through the retrenchment strategy, IBAX was able to meet the strategic goals set by the IBM and Baxter partners. The cohesion cases that follow will provide additional details on how the retrenchent strategy was actually put into place.

For Discussion:

1. What were the benefits to Goodman of following a systematic model of strategic planning?
2. Do you think Goodman could have chosen any strategic alternatives other than retrenchment? If so, what were they?
3. What steps did Goodman take to ensure successful implementation of the strategy?

ORGANIZING CHALLENGES IN THE 21ST CENTURY

PART III

CHAPTER 8

Organizing for Quality, Productivity, and Job Satisfaction

▼ CHAPTER OVERVIEW

This chapter, and the three that follow, focus on the managerial function of organizing. Increasingly, organizations are finding that their long-term success is dependent upon their ability to organize activities effectively, efficiently, and with a priority on quality. Management theory clearly recognizes the importance of organizing to support the strategic and operational needs of the contemporary organization.

   This chapter describes organizing as a process and focuses on the first stage of that process. Special attention is given to contemporary approaches to organizing that support delegation and employee empowerment, and improve the organization's ability to respond to environmental change.

▼ LEARNING OBJECTIVES

   When you have finished studying this chapter,
   you should be able to:

- Explain why organizing is an important managerial function.
- Describe the process of organizing and outline the primary stages of the process.
- Discuss the concept of job design and identify the core job dimensions that define a job.
- Describe the evolution of job design theory.
- Describe reengineering as a management tool and discuss the effect of reengineering programs on job design.
- Identify the concepts related to developing effective organizational relationships including chain of command, span of control, line versus staff personnel, and delegation.
- Discuss why it is important for managers to delegate.
- Explain why managers often fail to delegate and suggest methods for improving delegation skills.

MANAGERIAL INCIDENT

A BABY BELL REORGANIZES FOR EXCELLENCE

U.S. West is one of the seven regional Bell operating companies that were spun off from AT&T in 1984. Like many of its counterparts in the telecommunications industry, U.S. West faced many strategic and operational challenges. Cost structures were high, customer service was mediocre, and the administrative processes within the organization were bureaucratic and inflexible. In an age when excellence makes the difference between success and failure, U.S. West was ill prepared to compete.

This scenario was the backdrop for the "Winning in the '90s" program initiated by U.S. West in early 1990. The program, guided by an employee task force of 17 senior and middle managers, involved a review of all aspects of U.S. West's operations. The purpose of Winning in the '90s was to develop creative approaches to improving the efficiency, effectiveness, and quality of the company's product delivery system. The intent was not to tinker with existing administrative and operational processes, but to redesign the entire organizational system to improve the operations of the organization.

Much of the redesign effort was directed toward improving the way the company's activities were organized. A task force was charged with addressing organizational issues such as subordinate/supervisor relationships, jobs design, line versus staff functions, and hierarchical levels. The rather complacent, bureaucratic U.S. West was in desperate need of an organizational system that would support its efforts to achieve quality in the next decade and beyond.[1] ▼

INTRODUCTION

U.S. West was in trouble. The company was not prepared to compete effectively in an industry that was becoming increasingly competitive. Reversing that situation would require some fairly radical organizational adjustments. U.S. West's Winning in the '90s program was the company's attempt to respond to the challenges it faced. After conducting a rigorous analysis of the existing organizational design of the company, the Winning in the '90s task force began building an entirely new organizational system. That new design would enable U.S. West to compete more effectively in the telecommunications industry of the future.

As you will recall, all organizations exist for a purpose—to fulfill a specific mission and achieve a specific set of goals. If an organization is to fulfill its mission and achieve its goals, certain activities must occur. When an organization is small and relatively simple, those activities may be defined and coordinated fairly easily. As organizations become larger and more complex, however, organizational activities may be more difficult to define and coordinate. In general, the challenges associated with organizing activities and allocating resources among those activities become greater as the size and complexity of the organization increase. Nevertheless, organizing is an important managerial function in organizations of all sizes and types.

This chapter focuses on the managerial function of organizing. It begins by defining the concept of organizing and outlining the primary stages of the organizing process. That process includes determining tasks, designing jobs, and defining working relationships. Accordingly, we will outline the core job dimensions associated with job design and review them in relation to various job design approaches. The development of working relationships involves several organizing concepts including the chain of command, span of control, line versus staff personnel, and delegation, all of which are discussed here. Special attention is given to the trend toward greater employee participation in designing jobs and coordinating the activities of the organization.

WHAT IS ORGANIZING?

Organizing refers to the process of determining the tasks to be done, who will do them, and how those tasks will be managed and coordinated. It is an interactive and ongoing process that occurs throughout the life of the organization. As an organization develops and matures, so must its organizational system. As you will read in Managing for Excellence, Chaparral Steel has achieved success in a very troubled industry by adjusting its organizational design in response to changes in both the company and the steel industry as a whole.[2]

As Figure 8.1 shows, the process of organizing can be divided into two primary stages. In the first stage, the foundation of the organizational system is developed. Work activities are determined and assigned to specific job positions, and working relationships between individuals and work groups are defined. This chapter will focus specifically on these aspects of the organizing process, beginning with a discussion of how jobs are designed. The second stage of the organizing process involves developing an organizational design that supports the strategic and operational plans of the firm. This requires grouping organizational members into work units, developing integrating mechanisms to coordinate the efforts of diverse work groups, and determining the extent to which decision making in the organization is centralized or decentralized. These aspects of organizing will be addressed in Chapter 9.

Organizing
The process of determining the tasks to be done, who will do them, and how those tasks will be managed and coordinated.

JOB DESIGN

As we noted, the first stage of the organizing process involves outlining the tasks and activities to be completed and assigning them to individuals and

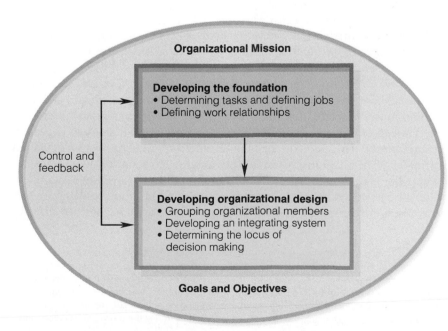

▼ **FIGURE 8.1**
The Process of Organizing

MANAGING FOR EXCELLENCE

CHAPARRAL STEEL: JOB DESIGN BASED ON PARTICIPATORY MANAGEMENT

Chaparral Steel of Midlothian, Texas, is one of the most successful steel minimills in the United States. Chaparral's executives credit their success to "... a marketing strategy sympathetic to customer needs, an insatiable thirst for technological improvement, and the application of participatory management techniques that encourage employee creativity."

During the 1970s, the average U.S. steel mill had 11 levels of management; Chaparral Steel had 4 levels. Jobs are designed very differently at Chaparral than at many of its competitors, and work relationships take on new dimensions. Some notable examples include:

• Decision making is pushed to the lowest level—the shop floor. Chaparral does not have a separate R&D department because it considers R&D to be the responsibility of each employee on the production line. This ensures that ideas are realistic and that the people who are affected by production changes are involved in their development.

• Chaparral has an annual sabbatical program for first-line supervisors. To avoid job complacency and stimulate commitment to the company's future, employees are given time off to visit competing mills, investigate the latest technology, and visit customers.

• *Every* employee is responsible for quality control. In fact, it is not uncommon to send employees from the shop floor to solve customer problems. This creates an awareness of customer service at all levels of the organization and communicates to customers that Chaparral cares about their problem.

• Job responsibilities are very broad. For example, the position of security guard is combined with that of a paramedic. Supervisors are responsible for the hiring, training, and benefit system of their employees.

Chaparral's leadership position is built on a foundation of enriched jobs and employee participation in decision making. In an industry that has struggled for two decades, Chaparral's strength is even more distinctive.

groups within the organization. Before managers can design specific jobs, they need to identify the work that must be done to achieve the organization's strategic and operational goals.

Consider, for example, an organization that manufactures and distributes small appliances.* In order to fulfill its mission and achieve its goals, the organization must complete a number of tasks and activities. Raw material must be acquired and inventoried; people must be hired, trained, and compensated; the plant must be managed and maintained; and the product must be delivered to customers. These are just a few of the activities that must occur.

Once the tasks and activities that must be completed have been identified, jobs must be designed and assigned to employees within the organization. **Job design** refers to the set of tasks and activities that are grouped together to

Job design
The set of tasks and activities that are grouped together to define a particular job.

---

*Although this example describes a very rational and sequential approach to the organizing process, it is important to note that the organizing function does not always operate in such a manner. Today, many companies reorganize relatively frequently and seek input into the decisions surrounding the reorganization from many organizational members. It is helpful, however, to consider the rational model of organizing when learning about some of the fundamental concepts and principles of organizing. Later in the chapter, we will discuss more participatory and contemporary approaches to organizing.

▼ **TABLE 8.1**   Job Description of an Office Manager

> • Serves as general office manager of the department. Duties include supervising all administrative functions necessary for the operation of the department. These duties involve interviewing applicants, selecting new assistants, and training assistants. Also supervises assistants' daily work assignments and coordinates their assignments.
>
> • Keeps accurate payroll records, payroll certifications, and personnel action forms on all department employees. Coordinates maintenance of leave records for all employees and management. Sends weekly reports to payroll departments. Distributes paychecks to departmental personnel. Prepares all recruiting and hiring records for the department.
>
> • Prepares all travel requests, travel reimbursement requests, short invoices, requisitions, work orders, and purchase orders. Orders all appropriate materials and supplies for employees and management on a quarterly basis.
>
> • Sets up as needed and maintains all office records and files, including administrative files, forms, memos, and correspondence. Coordinates scheduling and duplicating of reports and correspondence. Assigns workloads and priorities so that deadlines are met in a timely fashion. Supervises the security of all files, including personnel files of employees.
>
> • Opens and closes the four offices used. Responsible for the security of each office, the maintenance of telephone coverage, and the routing of messages and visitors. Supervises the distribution of incoming and outgoing mail including fax and priority mailings. Responsible for annual and quarterly reports, promotion papers, and employee evaluations.
>
> • Handles replies to routine inquiries from employees, customers, and the community. Refers nonroutine items to appropriate persons or manager. This includes telephone responses as well as initiating correspondence for manager's signature.

constitute a particular job position. The importance of effective job design should not be underestimated as the overall productivity of the organization will be affected by the way jobs are designed.[3] While managers commonly blame an employee's poor performance on his or her lackluster efforts, in many cases the real problem is poor job design.[4]

The design of a job can be assessed, to a degree, by reviewing the associated job description. **Job descriptions** detail the responsibilities and tasks associated with a given position. Table 8.1 provides a job description for an office manager position. This job description is intended to provide the job holder, as well as other organizational members, with an understanding of the responsibilities associated with the job of an office manager.

Although job descriptions are commonly used to describe how jobs are designed, some relevant job characteristics may not be evident from a job description. Before we go on to discuss the various job design models that have evolved over the years, it is important to examine the fundamental characteristics that can be used to describe most jobs.

Job description
An outline of the responsibilities and tasks associated with a given job.

CORE JOB DIMENSIONS

A number of core job dimensions can be used to characterize any job: (1) skill variety, (2) task identity, (3) task significance, (4) autonomy, and (5) feedback.[5] Each of these core job dimensions can significantly affect the satisfaction and performance of the individual who occupies the job. As Table 8.2 illustrates, these dimensions affect the degree to which employees find their work mean-

▼ **TABLE 8.2**   The Core Dimensions of a Job

CORE JOB DIMENSIONS	EFFECT OF DIMENSION
• Skill variety • Task identity ⎤ • Task significance ⎦ →	Meaningfulness of the work
• Autonomy →	Responsibility for outcomes of the work
• Feedback →	Knowledge of results of the work activities

SOURCE: Adapted from J. R. Hackman, G. Oldham, R. Janson, and K. Purdy, "A New Strategy for Job Enrichment." Copyright © 1975 by The Regents of the University of California. Reprinted from the *California Management Review*, Vol. 17, No. 4. By permission of The Regents.

ingful, feel responsibility for the outcomes of their job, and understand the results of their work activities. More specifically, as discussed next, skill variety, task identity, and task significance can affect the degree to which employees find their work meaningful; autonomy can affect the extent to which employees feel responsible for the outcomes of their jobs; and feedback can affect the degree to which employees understand the results of their work activities.[6] Let's explore these relationships in more detail.

Skill Variety

The first of the job dimensions, **skill variety,** refers to the degree to which a job challenges the job holder to use his or her skills and abilities. When a variety of skills is necessary to complete a task and those skills are perceived to be of value to the organization, employees find their work to be more meaningful.

Consider, for example, how a production manager and a mailroom clerk might feel about the meaningfulness of their work. The production manager's job requires the use of a relatively diverse and highly valued set of skills and abilities, and he may therefore perceive the job to be quite meaningful. The job of the mailroom clerk, in contrast, is narrower in terms of skill variety and of less perceived value to the organization than the production manager's job. As a result, the mailroom clerk is likely to feel that his job is less meaningful.

Task Identity

Task identity, the second dimension, refers to the degree to which the job requires the completion of an identifiable piece of work—a tangible outcome to which employees can attribute their efforts. For example, individuals who build entire computers will likely find their job to be more meaningful than employees who simply slide a chip into place on the circuit board of the computer.

Task Significance

The third job dimension, **task significance,** relates to the degree to which the job contributes to the overall efforts of the organization or to the world at large. Where task significance is high, the work will be more meaningful. For example, civil engineers who design an entire highway system will likely find their jobs to be more meaningful than assembly line workers who are responsible for producing a component that goes into other products. This is particularly true when the employees don't know what the end product is, what it does, or who uses it.

AMP, Inc., a leader in the connector market, found a way to improve job satisfaction by increasing task significance for the individuals who make the components the company sells. Sales engineers from companies who use AMP's products met with the workers and talked with them about their customers and their products. Some of the salespeople even brought along end

---

Skill variety
The degree to which a job challenges the job holder to use various skills and abilities.

Task identity
The degree to which a job requires the completion of an identifiable piece of work.

Task significance
The degree to which a job contributes to the overall efforts of the organization.

products, such as power tools, took them apart, and showed the AMP workers how the components they built fit in. One worker summed up the reaction by saying: "I sometimes felt that we made millions of these parts and they simply dumped them in the ocean after we shipped them out. Now I know where most of them go." The jobs of these workers had greater task significance as a result of this experience.[7]

Autonomy

The fourth job dimension, **autonomy,** reflects the degree to which job holders have freedom, independence, and decision-making authority in their jobs. When employees are highly autonomous in their work roles, their success is dependent upon their own capabilities and their desire to complete the task. Therefore, they tend to feel greater responsibility for the success or failure of their efforts. When there is low autonomy, employees are less likely to feel accountable for the outcome of their work.

Consider, for example, organizational trainers who teach a seminar that prepares participants to pass a national certification exam. These trainers may have little latitude in selecting the material to be covered in the course and often must employ a course design that is prescribed by the testing agency. They have little autonomy in conducting their jobs. In contrast, consider trainers who teach a management development seminar that is intended to help participants learn more about their own management style. These trainers are free to determine both the material to be covered and the methods by which it should be delivered. They are likely to feel more personal responsibility for their work than will the trainers who deliver a prepackaged training seminar.

Autonomy
The degree to which job holders have freedom, independence, and decision making authority.

Feedback

The final dimension of job design is **feedback,** or the extent to which job holders are provided information about the effectiveness of their efforts. When feedback is frequent and constructive, employees develop a better understanding of the relationship between their efforts and the outcomes of their work. Where feedback is insufficient, employees have little understanding of the value of their efforts.

Although feedback typically comes from the employee's supervisor, some organizations have begun to use customer feedback to motivate employees to be more customer-oriented in their work. Caterpillar, for example, provides regular customer feedback to employees to focus their attention on the need for quality in all aspects of the business.[8]

Chaparral Steel, profiled in Managing for Excellence, employed very innovative approaches to providing feedback to employees. Not only were employees advised of customer feedback, but they were also given time off annually to visit the plants of competitors. This provided employees with an opportunity to compare their efforts to those of their competitors.[9]

Feedback
The information provided to job holders regarding the effectiveness of their efforts.

Because the core dimensions of job design affect the extent to which job holders find their work meaningful, feel responsibility for their efforts, and understand the relationship between their activities and the results of those activities, they have a significant effect on the job holders' attitude.[10] Motivation, quality of work performance, job satisfaction, absenteeism, and turnover will all be a function of the core job dimensions to some degree. Consequently, managers should consider the effect of various job designs on each core dimension as they assign tasks and work activities to individuals within the organization.

The increasing diversity of the workforce has made the assessment of job design more complicated. Individuals from diverse cultural backgrounds may view certain job characteristics differently. For example, while many people

MEETING THE CHALLENGE

JOB ASSESSMENT AND REDESIGN

This exercise enables you to assess a job that you currently hold or have held in the past in terms of the five core job dimensions and to make recommendations for improving its design.

Part A: Using the following scales, rate the job you are assessing in terms of its skill variety, task identity, task significance, autonomy, and feedback.

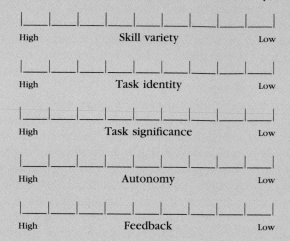

|___|___|___|___|___|___|___|___|___|
High   Skill variety   Low

|___|___|___|___|___|___|___|___|___|
High   Task identity   Low

|___|___|___|___|___|___|___|___|___|
High   Task significance   Low

|___|___|___|___|___|___|___|___|___|
High   Autonomy   Low

|___|___|___|___|___|___|___|___|___|
High   Feedback   Low

To the extent that your responses fall toward the left end of the scales, you probably find the job to be meaningful and challenging. To the extent that your responses fall toward the right end of the scales, the job could probably be redesigned to improve job satisfaction and enhance productivity.

Part B: Based on your responses to Part A, how might you redesign your job to improve each of the five core job dimensions? Would any of the participatory approaches to job redesign be appropriate? If so, which one(s)? Why do you feel it (they) would be appropriate?

from an American culture may perceive a job with low autonomy negatively, people from some Hispanic cultures may perceive low autonomy favorably. Similarly, managers who work in the international environment must also consider how perceptions of job design may differ among diverse cultures. As a general rule of thumb, managers should avoid making broad generalizations about employees' perceptions of specific job characteristics. Rather, where possible, managers should assess their employees' suitability for a particular job on an individual basis.

How does your job stack up with regard to these job characteristics? Meeting the Challenge provides an opportunity for you to assess a past or present position you've held in an organization (e.g., a business, church, social club, or student organization) in terms of skill variety, task identity, task significance, autonomy, and feedback. At this point, you are prepared to complete the assessment aspect (Part A) of the exercise. After reading the next section, you'll be prepared to suggest ways in which the job could be redesigned to improve job satisfaction (Part B).

It is interesting to examine how the principles of job design have evolved over time and, more specifically, how changes in design theory have affected the five core job dimensions. Table 8.3 outlines how job theory has evolved, the major job design approaches that have resulted from each school of

▼ **TABLE 8.3**   Job Design Theory Evolution

THEORY	CORE JOB DIMENSIONS	EFFECT*
Classical theory/scientific management (mechanistic approaches)	Skill variety	Negative
	Task identity	Negative
	Task significance	Negative
	Autonomy	Negative
	Feedback	Negative
Human relations (behavioral approaches)	Skill variety	Positive
	Task identity	None
	Task significance	None
	Autonomy	Positive
	Feedback	None
Contemporary management (participatory approaches)	Skill variety	None
	Task identity	Positive
	Task significance	None
	Autonomy	Positive
	Feedback	Positive

*None = no appreciable effect.

thought, and how each approach affects core job dimensions. The discussion that follows provides a rationale for the evolution of job design theory.

THE EVOLUTION OF JOB DESIGN THEORY

As management theory has evolved, so have many of the basic principles of job design. As we discussed in Chapter 2, classical management theory and scientific management lent support to the concept of division of labor and specialization. These early theories of management gave rise to a mechanistic approach to job design where jobs are highly structured and rigidly defined. The movement toward the human relations school of thought, however, in-

▼ At this electronics factory, jobs on the production line are routine and highly specialized. These employees are involved in an assembly process that is designed to maximize the efficiency of the line.

troduced other job design variables, most of which dealt with human behavior. As a result, more behavioral approaches to job design gained acceptance. Contemporary management thought is now affecting how jobs are designed, and participatory approaches are gaining popularity today. Let's examine how each of these approaches has affected the concept of job design, as well as the core job dimensions.

Mechanistic Approaches: Focus on Efficiency

As you should recall from Chapter 2, scientific management theorists emphasized the benefits of division of work and specialization. Productivity and efficiency were the driving forces for job design. Repetition, skill simplification, and time and motion efficiency were the primary focus of job design efforts. The result was highly specialized jobs that were routine, repetitive, and highly efficient.

One need only recall the classic example of a pinmaking operation in Adam Smith's *Wealth of Nations* to understand the potential efficiencies of division of labor and highly specialized work roles. Smith suggested that the productivity of 10 pinmakers could be greatly improved by applying these concepts. One pinmaker performing all the tasks necessary to make a pin could make only 10 pins per day. The total productivity of 10 pinmakers making pins in this fashion would be 100 pins per day. But if the 10 pinmakers organized the activities of the group so that one pinmaker drew the wire, another straightened it, a third cut it, and a fourth sharpened it to a point, while others were performing the operations necessary to complete the head of the pin and prepare the final product, the group could produce 48,000 pins per day— an average of 4800 pins per pinmaker per day. Obviously, the productivity of the group improved dramatically when jobs were redesigned to be highly specialized.

The benefits of specialization are easy to identify (see Table 8.4). Specialized tasks are considered to be more efficient because work activities are broken down into routine, repetitive actions. Further, such actions can be mastered readily by individual workers and require less training than more complex tasks. Additionally, when tasks are highly specialized, workers may be selected based on specific characteristics that make them uniquely qualified to perform the task effectively and efficiently.

Specialization also has disadvantages, however (see Table 8.4). Often, the skill variety, task identity, and task significance associated with such tasks are low. Further, job holders typically have less autonomy and may receive no feedback or feedback that is inconsequential. To the extent that these conditions exist, job holders will find little challenge in their work and may lose interest in their jobs.

In cases where excessive specialization has created jobs that are perceived to be unrewarding and uninteresting, it is difficult to motivate workers to perform well. Absenteeism and turnover are often greater, and even when

▼ **TABLE 8.4**   Potential Advantages and Disadvantages of Job Specialization

ADVANTAGES	DISADVANTAGES
• Greater efficiency due to repetition	• Low skill variety, task identity, and task significance
• Tasks easier to master and require little training	• Little autonomy and feedback, resulting in low interest and motivation
• May select workers based on specific qualifications	• Lower productivity due to high absenteeism and frequent breaks

▼ This automobile manufacturing plant utilizes robotics technology to accomplish tasks that are highly specialized. At this plant, robotics systems perform many tasks including basic welding as is illustrated here.

employees are on the job, they may take frequent and lengthy breaks or socialize with other employees excessively. In some cases, the benefits of specialization may be offset by the loss of productivity associated with job dissatisfaction and nonproductive work time.

Historically, many manufacturing firms have sought the benefits of specialization in designing jobs. The assembly line production scheme is founded on the concept of highly routinized and specialized tasks. Consider, for example, the traditional automobile manufacturing plant. As the chassis of the car flows through the assembly line, workers perform a series of highly specialized tasks that contribute in some way to the production of the final product. While any given worker may do little more than attach a specific component or insert and tighten several screws, the result of the combined efforts of all the participants in the assembly process is a complete and fully functioning vehicle.

Today, there are fewer highly specialized jobs in the U.S. than in the past. Robotics technology has replaced many specialized jobs, particularly in the manufacturing environment. In addition, many organizations that require low-skilled labor have moved their operations overseas where there is access to less expensive labor. Finally, other organizations have found alternative job design options that overcome some of the negative aspects of highly specialized jobs.

The human relations theorists were the first to suggest alternate job design methods. As we will discuss next, the emphasis moved from division of labor and specialization toward job designs with greater breadth, depth, and challenge.

Behavioral Approaches: Focus on Motivation, Satisfaction, and Productivity

Behavioral approaches to job design became popular during the movement toward the human relations school of thought. When the human relations theories of management began to emerge, the net benefits of specialized job design became the subject of some controversy. As concerns about the disadvantages of highly specialized job designs continued to mount, managers began to explore methods for enhancing the ways jobs were structured. Such efforts led to the development of more innovative approaches to job design including job enlargement, job enrichment, and job rotation programs.

Job scope
The number of different activities required in a job and the frequency with which each activity is performed.

Job Enlargement   To understand job enlargement programs, you must understand the concept of job scope. **Job scope** refers to the number of different activities that a specific job requires and the frequency with which each activity is performed. Jobs that involve many different activities have broader scope than jobs that are limited to a few activities. Jobs with broad scope typically rate more favorably in terms of skill variety, task identity, and task significance than do jobs with a narrower scope. As a consequence, jobs with broad scope are often more meaningful for job holders than jobs with narrow scope.

Consider, for example, how the job scope of an office manager and a typist in a clerical pool might differ. The office manager's job will involve a relatively broad set of tasks and thus will have relatively wide scope. In any given day, the office manager may take dictation, type a letter, complete and sign time cards, make travel arrangements, schedule appointments, and interview, hire, or fire office staff. The typist's job, in contrast, is much narrower in that it only involves typing documents.

Job enlargement
Programs designed to broaden job scope.

Job enlargement programs are designed to broaden the scope of a specific job. The intent of job enlargement is to increase the horizontal tasks and responsibilities associated with a given work position to reduce the monotony of the job and provide greater challenge for the employee. For example, to enlarge the job of the typist, the manager might require her to assume additional job responsibilities such as answering the phones, processing payroll forms, and providing copying services. The typist would be responsible for a greater variety of tasks and might be less bored and more highly satisfied with her job.

While many companies have implemented job enlargement programs in an effort to redesign highly specialized and routine jobs, many other firms have been forced to enlarge jobs in response to changes in their strategy. In recent years, we have seen industries consolidate, companies merge, and organizations downsize and streamline to remain competitive. Such strategic initiatives often require changes in the way jobs are designed.

Consider, for example, the changes that have occurred in recent years in the banking industry (recall NationsBank's merger with C&S from Chapter 4). The deregulation of that industry led to mergers, bankruptcies, downsizing, and streamlining—all of which led to the elimination of literally thousands of jobs industry-wide. While many banking employees have lost their jobs entirely, the employees who have remained have been forced to assume much broader job responsibilities. With broader job scope, these individuals have an opportunity to make a more significant contribution to their organizations in the long term.[12]

Job depth
The degree of control given to a job holder to perform their job.

Job Enrichment   Central to the concept of job enrichment is the notion of **job depth,** which refers to the degree of control that individuals have over the jobs they perform. Job depth is high when the planning, doing, and controlling aspects of the job are the responsibility of the job holder. When one or more of these aspects is the responsibility of some other organization member, job depth is low. Jobs that have high job depth typically rate more favorably on the core job dimensions of skill variety, task identity, and autonomy than jobs with low job depth.

Just as specialization has led to jobs with a narrow job scope, highly specialized jobs often lack depth. In such cases, the planning and controlling aspects of a job are often separate from the doing aspect of the job. For example, the manager of a clerical pool may assume responsibility for receiving work to be typed, clarifying instructions with the originator of the work, setting priorities for scheduling work orders, checking the final document for typographical errors and neatness, delivering the completed work to the individual who brought the document in to be typed and communicating with that individual about the acceptability of the work. When the manager assumes these responsibilities, the actual typing of the document is all that is left for the typist to do. Clearly, the job depth of the typist's position is quite low.

Job enrichment programs are designed to increase the depth of individual jobs and to close the gap between planning, doing, and controlling a particular set of activities.[13] Through "vertical loading," the job holder may be given greater discretion in setting schedules and planning work activities, determining appropriate methods for completing the task, and monitoring the quality of the output from the work process. For example, the job depth of the typist would be increased if she assumed responsibility for accepting and logging in the work, scheduling work orders, and communicating with the originator of the work about its acceptability.

Just as downsizing has led to enlarged jobs, such efforts have also led to enriched jobs. When a layer of management is eliminated, the group of employees above and below that management level must assume greater responsibility. This creates a situation of vertical loading of job responsibilities and leads to jobs with greater job depth. As we will see at the conclusion of this chapter, U.S. West increased the job depth associated with many positions when layers of management were eliminated as part of the Winning in the '90s reorganization program.

In addition, quality management programs have also created greater job depth in some organizations. Individual accountability for contributing to the goals of the organization increases in quality-oriented companies, and with that accountability often comes greater job depth. Caterpillar, for example, in an effort to ensure high-quality products, has redesigned jobs so that individual employees (rather than inspectors at the end of the line) are accountable for the quality of the product at each stage of the manufacturing process. As part of this new system, employees participate in both the planning and control aspects of the manufacturing process.[14]

Chaparral Steel also serves as an excellent example of an organization that has increased job depth to enhance the commitment of its employees to its mission and goals. Employees are responsible for planning and controlling their own work, and quality is the responsibility of every member of the organization. Chaparral even sends shop floor employees to respond to customer concerns. This not only increases the employees' awareness of customer needs, but it communicates to Chaparral's customers that the company is concerned with their problems.

Job Rotation   Job rotation is a third method of reducing the level of specialization associated with a given job. **Job rotation** involves shifting individuals from one position to another once they have mastered their original job. Employees rotate through a number of job positions that are at approximately the same level and have similar skill requirements. For example, an individual who works in a bank might rotate between being a teller, a customer service representative, a loan processor, a proof operator, and a safe deposit box attendant. At a higher organizational level, a financial manager who works for a multinational firm might rotate between positions at various foreign subsidiaries to gain international business experience.

Job rotation offers several advantages. Organizations that use job rotation typically have more flexibility in developing work schedules, making work assignments, and filling vacancies within the company quickly. In addition, employees are often more challenged and less bored with their jobs and usually have a better understanding of the organization as a whole. At the same

Job enrichment
Programs designed to increase job depth.

Job rotation
Assigning individuals to a variety of job positions.

▼ This bank employee is involved in a job rotation program. While she currently serves as a teller, she has also worked as a customer service representative and a loan processor. The breadth of experience that she has gained provides a broader perspective of the overall goals of the organization.

time, job rotation can be disruptive to the organization. More time and resources must be spent in training, and optimal performance in any given job may be difficult to achieve on a consistent basis.

Today, a new form of job rotation is emerging in response to downsizing. Since many organizations have reduced their workforce in recent years, employees have far fewer internal career opportunities available. With fewer promotions to hand out, some companies are trying to motivate employees by shifting them sideways instead of up. American Greetings has found lateral moves to be very effective in rejuvenating employees who have become bored in their present positions. Nabisco Foods, Corning, Inc., and Eastman Kodak are other companies that are looking to lateral job moves as a method of motivating employees whose career progression has been stymied by the restructuring efforts of the organization.[15] This new form of job rotation may have long-term promise for organizations that hope to retain good employees by providing greater challenge in their jobs.

Job enlargement, enrichment, and rotation programs represent methods of redesigning specialized jobs to increase the motivation, job satisfaction and, in some cases, productivity of employees. Such efforts often have a very positive effect on overcoming the disadvantages of more mechanistic approaches to job design. Many managers who are concerned with maintaining a quality orientation in their work units have embraced these programs as one way to do so. In addition, many managers have turned toward more participatory approaches to job design.

Participatory Approaches: Focus on Quality

In recent years, both management theorists and practitioners have been rethinking the traditional approaches to job design. Efforts to develop more innovative and effective approaches to job design have been inspired by increasing competitive pressures in many industries.[16] Consider the experiences of ALCOA, for example. Global Perspective describes how this company has restored its competitive position in the world marketplace though the use of innovative approaches to job design.[17]

Several participatory approaches to designing jobs have emerged in recent years and have begun to gain fairly widespread acceptance. The benefits of such approaches are similar to the benefits associated with participatory decision making discussed in Chapter 6. Jobs that are designed with the involvement of the affected individuals often provide greater satisfaction for the job holder and lead to greater productivity.

Participatory approaches to job design are not intended to replace previous methods of job design, but rather to supplement both the mechanistic and the behavioral theories of job design. The most popular participatory approaches, and the ones that will be discussed here, include employee-centered work redesign programs and self-managed teams.

Employee-centered work redesign
An approach whereby employees design their work roles to benefit the organization and satisfy their individual goals.

Employee-Centered Work Redesign   **Employee-centered work redesign** is an innovative approach to job design that presents a practical solution to the one of the most significant challenges of job design—bridging the gap between the individual and the organization. This method of job design links the mission of the organization with the needs of the individual by allowing employees to design their work roles to benefit the organization, as well as themselves. The unique aspect of this job design approach is that employees are accountable for justifying how their job will support the mission of the organization, as well as improve their productivity and job satisfaction.[18]

A number of benefits are associated with employee-centered work redesign programs. Because jobs are designed by the job holder, these programs tend to favorably affect the core job dimensions that are most relevant to the

ALCOA: WORK REDESIGN AS A MEANS OF MEETING WORLD LEADER STANDARDS

GLOBAL PERSPECTIVE

As the recovery slowed and ALCOA CEO Paul O'Neill summoned all his business unit heads from around the world to Pittsburgh, many people outside the company figured they knew what was coming—layoffs and maybe even the relocation of headquarters to a less expensive location. The mood in Pittsburgh was anxious.

But O'Neill surprised everyone with a far bolder move: a major reorganization that would make operating units much more autonomous and redesign work at every level and every location of the organization. A change like that turns life upside down throughout a company, but ALCOA has pulled out of this downturn without a loss at the operating level. In addition, O'Neill thinks the reorganization could eventually raise operating profits $1 billion to $2 billion a year.

As O'Neill noted recently: "In a slow-growth environment, redesigning the organization allows a company to pick off a big part of the market because your company is producing more value with fewer resources." ALCOA has reduced the time it takes to fill an order in its can sheet business, which supplies the beer and beverage industry, by about 60 percent. Quality dropped briefly, although the company insists it was for reasons unrelated to the reorganization, before bouncing back. But in a number of key processes ALCOA has closed the gap to 80 percent of world leader standards in less than a year and is increasing its global market position.

individual employee. Studies suggest that very tangible improvements in both productivity and job satisfaction result from employee-centered work redesign efforts. Further, such programs foster an organizational climate that supports cooperative efforts between individuals and work groups. Finally, employee-centered work redesign programs are very much in line with the quality improvement efforts of many companies. Because the employees of an organization are in the best position to know where quality improvements can be achieved, jobs can be designed so quality problems can be identified and resolved more quickly.

Table 8.5 outlines some of the factors that are critical to the success of an employee-centered work redesign program, as well as some of the anticipated benefits for both the employee and the organization.[19] Table 8.6 outlines the process that one would follow in implementing an employee-centered work redesign program.[20]

Amoco Oil Company is an excellent example of a firm that uses an employee-centered work redesign program to support its strategic goals. This company offered detailed training sessions to help employees at its Yorktown, Virginia refinery to identify their roles in pursuing the company's mission. The benefits of involving employees in this process have been tremendous, and the company plans to implement a similar program in other refineries.[21]

Self-Managed Teams   All of the approaches to job design discussed so far have focused on designing the jobs of individual organizational members. The **self-managed team** approach to job design shifts the focus from the individual to a work group (recall the discussion of self-managed teams in Chapter 1). Instead of managers dictating a set of narrowly defined tasks to each individual employee, responsibility for a substantial portion of the organization's activities

Self-managed teams
Groups of individuals who design their jobs to fulfill the overall responsibilities of the group.

▼ **TABLE 8.5**   Employee-Centered Work Redesign

CRITICAL FACTORS	EMPLOYEE BENEFITS	ORGANIZATIONAL BENEFITS
• Strong commitment from management to the program to ensure success	• Career and professional growth opportunities realized within the organization	• Greater use of employees
• Teamwork between employees and managers to redesign work roles	• Increased job satisfaction	• Taps into employee skills, knowledge, and creativity
• Organizational benefits in work productivity, work quality, and cost containment	• Gain insights into the organization	• Increased productivity and improved quality
• Demonstrate positive impact on staff and existing systems	• Opportunity to contribute to organizational goals	• Reduced employee turnover
• Hands-on problem-solving format	• Learn to communicate needs, concerns, and interests	• Employees become stakeholders, not job holders, in the organization
	• Broaden organization perspective	• Increased accountability leads to cost-effective behavior
	• Career growth opportunities enhanced	• Promotes positive work attitude to discourage employee grievances
	• Access to information	• Supports cooperative teamwork between employees and management
	• Critical skills identified	

SOURCE: Excerpts from "Employees Redesign Their Jobs" by S. L. Perlman, copyright November 1990. Reprinted with the permission of *Personnel Journal*, ACC Communications, Inc., Costa Mesa, California; all rights reserved.

is assigned to a team of individuals who must determine the best way to fulfill those responsibilities. Today, self-managed teams (also known as autonomous work groups) exist in organizations of all sizes and types and in and across departments within those organizations.[22]

The distinguishing feature of the self-managed team approach to job design is that the group is completely independent. The team must justify their choice of work methods only in terms of strong productivity and contribution to the overall effort of the firm. Like employee-centered work redesign programs, jobs that are designed by self-managed teams tend to reflect the core job dimensions that are most relevant to the individual employees of the work group.

While research has suggested that self-managed teams have higher productivity and deliver better quality products and services with lower relative costs, a number of situational factors appear to influence the effectiveness of such groups. These factors include the personalities of the group members, the ability of the group to exercise control and assume responsibility, and the nature of the tasks to be completed.[23] Therefore, the success of a self-managed team will depend upon the particular individuals involved and the nature of the job responsibilities.

Organizations that have designed very narrow, highly specialized jobs in an effort to maximize efficiency may find self-managed teams to be advantageous. The team approach has been credited with avoiding redundant efforts, increasing cooperation between organizational members, spawning new ideas, generating solutions to problems, maintaining motivation, improving product quality, and increasing profits.[24] In fact, using a team approach rather than the traditional assembly line approach to manufacturing has worked successfully for many organizations.[25] Few would dispute the success of the team concept at NUMMI (New United Motors Manufacturing, Inc.), the joint venture between General Motors and Toyota. This facility is organized around self-managed teams that establish their own work standards, work flow,

▼ **TABLE 8.6**   How to Execute an Employee-Centered Work Redesign Program

Employee-centered work redesign programs focus on treating employees as partners rather than subordinates. To execute such a system, the following steps must be taken:

- Teach employees about the mission and goals of the organization and their department.

- Have employees complete a needs assessment survey to help them identify personal job satisfaction and professional development goals. These should be consistent with the mission and goals of the department and the organization.

- Conduct an exercise to help employees learn to recognize possible obstacles to achieving their goals and identify methods for eliminating or minimizing such barriers.

- Ask employees to prepare an inventory of their existing work responsibilities. This inventory should be broken into three distinct categories: work that will be retained, work that will be modified, and work that will be eliminated. Employees should also identify new work that should be added to their current job.

- Employees should outline methods for accomplishing all modified and new tasks in the inventory. This process increases the employees' sense of accountability for their newly designed jobs.

- Finally, a careful review of the proposal by management should be followed by implementation on a trial basis. This provides for monitoring of the new job design and allows for corrections to be made quickly and easily.

SOURCE: Excerpts from "Employees Redesign Their Jobs," by S. L. Perlman, copyright November 1990. Reprinted with the permission of *Personnel Journal*, ACC Communications, Inc., Costa Mesa, California; all rights reserved.

production process, tools to be used and work schedules. The significant improvements in productivity and quality experienced by NUMMI can be attributed, in large part, to its team orientation.[26] Other organizations that have successfully implemented self-managed teams include Xerox, Chrysler, and British Telecom. As we will see later, IBAX also achieved greater productivity and better quality through the use of self-managed teams.

Perhaps the most challenging, yet rewarding teams are those that are interfunctional in nature. Many self-managed teams include engineers, financial managers, marketing managers, and production managers—all of whom must work together toward common goals and objectives. General Foods, a strong proponent of the team approach, claims that organizing the company into interfunctional work teams has been, in general, the most critical factor in creating a work environment that supports peak performance.[27] In fact, some would argue that the effective use of interfunctional work teams is the key to achieving a quality orientation within an organization.

REENGINEERING AND JOB DESIGN

As we know, quality has become the key competitive weapon of the 1990s. Few organizations will prosper in today's environment without a focus on quality and continuous improvement. Corporations across the globe have implemented quality improvement programs in an effort to reduce costs, improve customer satisfaction, increase market share, and, last but not least, improve the bottom line.

Closely related to the quality movement, though separate and distinct in some very important ways, is one of the latest management tools—business process reengineering. For organizations that compete on the basis of quality,

▼ These managers are using business process reengineering to redesign jobs and improve organizational performance. The objective of the process is to rebuild the organization to maximize both efficiency and effectiveness.

Reengineering
Radically changing the organizational processes for delivering products and services.

achieving simplicity, speed, and flexibility within the organizational system can be crucial. And, according to some experts, the way to achieve those qualities is through business process reengineering.

During **reengineering,** an organization seeks out and implements radical change in the processes that it uses to produce and deliver its products and services. Every manager and employee becomes involved in the process of assessing every aspect of the company's operations and rebuilding the organizational system with a focus on improving efficiency, identifying redundancies, and eliminating waste in every way possible.

Reengineering is neither easy nor cheap, but the results have been remarkable for some companies. Consider the following: through reengineering Union Carbide reduced its fixed costs by $400 million in three years; GTE expects to double its revenues and reduce its costs by half in its telephone division as a result of reengineering; and AlliedSignal's vice president for materials management estimates that reengineering his unit will save the company $100 million a year.[28] Even small companies, like the one profiled in Entrepreneurial Approach, can benefit from such programs. Shelby Die Casting Company avoided closing a plant in Shelby, Mississippi, by involving its workers in redesigning the way the plant functioned.

Reengineering efforts have a significant effect on the way jobs are designed.[29] Any reengineering project will raise critical questions about how work and work processes can be optimally configured. Answering such questions will require managers to look for creative approaches to job design—approaches that maintain or improve the effectiveness and efficiency of the organization. Table 8.7 outlines one method for reengineering that will help to identify appropriate job design.[30]

Now that we have concluded our discussion of job design, take a moment to go back to Part B of Meeting the Challenge. How might you redesign the position you evaluated to improve job satisfaction? Would a participatory approach to job design be appropriate? Why or why not? How could you redesign the job to support improved quality in the organization?

Thus far, we have explored how managers determine the work to be done and assign that work to individual employees or work groups. Equally important, however, is the process of defining the working relationships, both vertical and horizontal, that exist within the organization. The next section examines how working relationships can be established to ensure that the organization fulfills its mission and achieves its goals.

ORGANIZATIONAL RELATIONSHIPS

The working relationships that exist within an organization will affect how its activities are accomplished and coordinated. Consequently, it is essential to understand both the vertical and horizontal associations that exist between individuals and work groups within the organization. Relevant to this topic are (1) the chain of command, (2) span of control, (3) line and staff responsibilities, and (4) delegation.

SHELBY DIE CASTING: INVESTING IN PEOPLE

To buyers of the aluminum castings Shelby made, price was of the essence. Shelby was well prepared to compete since their plant was located in the heart of the impoverished Mississippi Delta where labor costs were very low. The plant was run autocratically, with layers of supervisors managing unskilled, and often illiterate, workers.

Then, stimulated by global competition, customer requirements began to change. Zero defects were expected; just-in-time delivery called for better and more efficient service. Management put pressure on workers as the expectations of the company as a whole began to rise. Employee morale plummeted, scrap rates and absenteeism rose, and financial losses began to mount.

G. Rives Neblett, a lawyer who had bought a majority interest in the company in 1984, left his law practice to make a last-ditch effort to save the plant. He studied the plant and concluded that the main problems were the management style and the employees' educational level. Aided by two of his executives, he set out to change both factors at Shelby.

Educators called in to test employees reported average reading skills were close to the third-grade level. Neblett figured that managers who blamed workers for incompetence, laziness, and insubordination had actually failed at their own jobs by not ensuring that workers were adequately trained. The local community college designed a curriculum, and classes built around workers' job needs were opened.

Managers went to class to learn about shifting to a management style based on teamwork and increased worker responsibility. Those who did not buy into the new model left the company. Problem-solving work teams, each with a manager assigned as a facilitator, were organized for different plant projects. Meetings held between normal work duties "turned into name-calling and shouting matches where everyone blamed everyone else for plant inefficiencies," Neblett says. But eventually, he adds, solutions to problems were found, and with workers no longer afraid of management, new management-labor relations were forged.

Next came an even more radical step: supervisors were taken off the floor. Through their project teams, "associates" were to run the plant. Supervisors were reassigned to technical training and improving production efficiency. Production teams of representatives of different disciplines in the plant—tooling, maintenance, and so forth—were formed to advise project teams. Leaders emerged among minority members; some now hold managerial jobs.

In less than a year, "nothing short of a miracle" had taken place. A plant that had been targeted for closing was showing a strong profit.

CHAIN OF COMMAND

The vertical relationships that exist within an organization are defined by its chain of command. The **chain of command** delineates the line of authority and responsibility that flows throughout the organization and defines the supervisor and subordinate relationships that govern decision making.

One of the most basic principles of organizing, unity of command, is used in defining vertical relationships. The **unity of command** principle suggests that each employee in the organization should be accountable to one, and only one, superior. When individual employees must report to more than one superior, they may be forced to prioritize their work assignments and resolve conflicting demands on their time.

Chain of command
The line of authority and responsibility that flows throughout the organization.

Unity of command
A principle that each employee in the organization is accountable to one, and only one, supervisor.

▼ **TABLE 8.7**   Steps in Process Engineering

1. *Seize control of the process.* Many processes vitally important to a firm's success "just happen." The sequence of activities that count the most usually require interventions from many organization units. Good ideas for new products dissipate in the path from one unit to another. Seizing control of a process means giving it an owner who has authority to break through the departmental walls.

2. *Map it out.* Most companies are organized in ways that make it difficult to identify key processes. Reengineering can only be accomplished if the organization is mapped out, usually graphically, so as to provide a step-by-step description of how the process works. Then, by carefully identifying and eliminating problem areas, a more streamlined operation can be reengineered.

3. *Eliminate sources of friction.* One method of eliminating organizational friction is to devise an alternative to the traditional passing of work down the established hierarchy. Many companies have set up coordinating "brand management" or "czar" positions to keep things moving along. Other methods include streamlining administrative processes (purchasing, billing, etc.), minimizing handoffs by having as few units processing transactions as possible, creating new, higher-paying positions with greater authority, and time compression through responsibility expansion.

4. *Close the loop.* Becoming a fast-cycle company involves mind-set change as well as technique adoption. In reengineered businesses, the most common phrase you hear is "Life is short." This is not so much a philosophical justification as a plea to get on with it. Reengineering studies can create volumes of paperwork and creative and colorful flowcharts. But the only studies worth doing are those that make change happen.

5. *Don't drop the ball.* The only studies whose changes will stick are those done with eyes wide open about the transitory nature of improvement programs. Few improvements last indefinitely. Technologies will change, allowing for further enhancements in speed. Also, superior approaches will be developed for common problems. Knowing that the results of this year's reengineering will need reengineering at some point is essential to making any effort successful.

SOURCE: R. M. Tomasko, "Intelligent Resizing: View from the Bottom Up (Part II)," 18–23. Reprinted by permission of publisher, from *Management Review*, June 1993, © 1993. American Management Association, New York. All rights reserved.

As you will recall from Chapter 2, the concept of a well-defined chain of command was originally advanced by the classical management theorists. In its purest form, the concept is consistent with the bureaucratic organizational system. Although contemporary managers still embrace the idea of a chain of command, the flexibility of the organization to respond quickly and proactively to change may be severely limited when decision making is rigidly tied to the official hierarchy. For that reason, organizations that operate in very dynamic environments may prefer to maintain flexibility in their chain of command so that they can respond more effectively to change. Eastman Kodak is an example of an organization that has been experimenting with a complex, but relatively flexible chain of command in an effort to improve its responsiveness to changing business conditions. While efforts to date have been largely within the information systems department, the structure holds promise for other divisions of Kodak's business.[31]

SPAN OF CONTROL

Span of control
The number of employees reporting to a particular manager.

A second important aspect of working relationships is **span of control,** which refers to the number of employees that report to a single manager. At one time it was thought that there was a universally appropriate span of control (i.e., six employees should report to every manager), but managers now recognize that span of control will vary in accordance with a number of variables. Organizational characteristics such as task complexity, the volatility of the competitive environment, and the capabilities of both the employees and the manager will influence the appropriate span of control.

As an example of how certain conditions might effect span of control, consider the job characteristic of task complexity. In theory, when tasks are very complex, span of control should be relatively narrow. This allows the manager to spend more time with each individual subordinate to help him or her deal with the complexity of the job. In contrast, where jobs are highly standardized and routine (low complexity), a manager will not need to spend as much time supporting individual subordinates, and span of control may be larger.

Which comes first—job design or span of control? That depends. Although one typically thinks of jobs being designed first and span of control being determined by the nature of the job, the reverse can happen. Jobs may be designed to support a company's preferred span of control. For example, in an effort to cut costs, Ameritech recently reduced management levels, consolidated staff functions, and increased the average span of control. To do so, the company had to create common internal operating systems that standardized and simplified job design.[32]

Span of control is a critical organizational variable for a number of reasons. It defines the layers of management that exist within the company. An organization that maintains a relatively narrow span of control will have more hierarchical levels than an organization with the same number of employees but a wider span of control. As Figure 8.2 illustrates, the span of control and the resulting layers of management determine whether the organization maintains a tall or a flat structure.[33]

In general, tall structures are associated with a long chain of command and bureaucratic controls. Consequently, they are often thought to be ineffective in rapidly changing environments. On the other hand, managers in tall structures have fewer subordinates to supervise and are less likely to be overcommitted and overburdened. Free from the burden of excessive subordinates, such managers may have more time to analyze situations, make effective decisions, and execute the actions associated with their decisions. Consequently, they may be more effective than managers in flat organizations.

Managers in flat organizations, by contrast, have greater demands in terms of direct supervision because they have wider spans of control. They may feel hassled, frustrated, and incapable of coping effectively with the nonsupervisory demands of their job. Yet flat structures are often thought to facilitate decentralized decision-making, participatory management, and responsiveness to the challenges inherent in highly competitive environments. Wide spans of control suggest a need for greater self-direction and initiative on the part of individual employees and may result in more effective employee development. As will be discussed in the Managerial Incident Resolution at the close of the chapter, U.S. West's effort to reorganize led to wider spans of control and more opportunities for employees.

Clearly, advantages and disadvantages are associated with both tall and flat structures. Therefore, organizations must choose a span of control that supports their particular strategic and operational goals. For example, many global firms may find they need a relatively small span of control at the upper levels of the organization. The challenges of managing geographically dispersed and culturally diverse operating units may require a narrower span of control.

General Electric has changed its span of control as a part of a major restructuring program. Ten years ago, managers supervised 6 people on average;

Tall structure

Flat structure

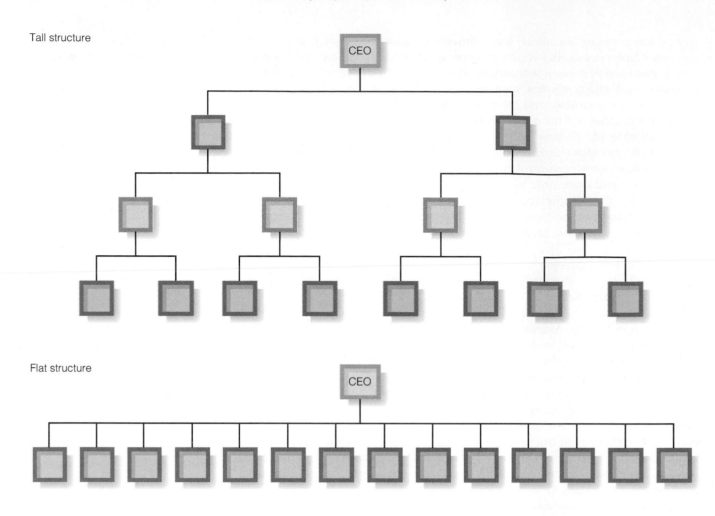

▼ **FIGURE 8.2**
Tall versus Flat Structure

SOURCE: Adapted from H. Mintzberg, *The Structuring of Organizations* (Englewood Cliffs, N.J.: Prentice-Hall, 1979), 136.

Line personnel
Those organizational members that are directly involved in delivering the products and services of the organization.

Staff personnel
Those organizational members that are not directly involved in delivering the products and services of the organization, but provide support for line personnel.

today they supervise 12. The reasons for the change are many. GE wanted to improve its products, get closer to its customers, and trim costs. Some say that GE's greatest challenge was convincing managers that they did not need to have complete control over every aspect of their operation. They had to learn to rely on the individuals in their work groups to make the decisions necessary to achieve the goals of the unit.[34]

LINE AND STAFF RESPONSIBILITIES

The third aspect of organizational relationships is that of line and staff responsibilities. Line and staff positions exist within virtually all organizations, but the individuals who occupy these positions play very different roles within the organization.

Line positions are directly involved in delivering the product or service of the organization. The individuals and work groups that have formal authority for decisions that affect the core production efforts of the firm are the line personnel. **Staff** positions, in contrast, are not part of the product or service delivery system chain of command, but rather provide support to line personnel. Line personnel or work groups may call upon staff personnel to provide expert advice or perform specific support services. Staff personnel do not have authority or responsibility for decisions that relate to the core delivery system of the organization.

As organizations experiment with less rigid hierarchical structures and team-oriented approaches, the distinction between line and staff responsibili-

▼ If one were to look at the titles of the individuals on this Chrysler vehicle development team, it would be apparent that the team is comprised of both line and staff personnel. This diverse group of employees possesses the skills and expertise needed to develop a top quality product.

ties is blurring. U.S. West, for example, has moved away from making distinctions between line and staff, preferring to call employees either supervising managers or individual contributors. This is consistent with the quality management movement, which suggests that all members of the organization must contribute to fulfilling the mission and achieving the goals of the organization. The differences in the way employees contribute is far less important than the commonality inherent in working to achieve the same organizational goals. As a consequence, the distinction between line and staff has become less important.

In addition, line and staff personnel now frequently coexist within work teams that collectively pursue a specific set of tasks. Consider, for example, Chrysler's efforts to gain a competitive advantage through the team approach to vehicle design. This company provides an example of a company that has grouped line and staff personnel together in product development teams.[35]

DELEGATION

Another important aspect of organizational relationships involves delegation. One of the most challenging skills that successful managers must master is the ability to delegate effectively. **Delegation** refers to the process of transferring the responsibility for a specific activity or task to another member of the organization and empowering that individual to accomplish the task effectively. Traditionally, supervisors delegate tasks to those in their work group. The **scalar principle** of management suggests that a clear line of authority should run through the organization (chain of command) so that all persons in the organization understand to whom they can delegate and from whom they should accept delegated tasks.

The Process of Delegation
To delegate effectively, managers must understand that delegation involves three distinct but highly related activities: (1) assignment of responsibility,

Delegation
The process of transferring the responsibility for a specific activity or task to another member of the organization and empowering that individual to accomplish the task effectively.

Scalar principle
A clear line of authority must run throughout the organization.

(2) granting of authority, and (3) establishing accountability.[36] All are essential to the success of the delegation process.[37]

Responsibility
An obligation on the part of an employee to complete assigned activities.

Assignment of Responsibility   The delegation process begins when a manager assigns a subordinate the responsibility for a specific task or set of tasks. **Responsibility** refers to the employee's obligation to complete the activities that he or she has been assigned. Clear communication of the specific activities for which the employee is responsible is essential if the task is to be delegated successfully.

Authority
The formal right of an employee to marshall resources and make decisions necessary to fulfill work responsibilities.

Granting of Authority   Secondly, managers must give their employees the authority to accomplish their work successfully.[38] **Authority** is the formal right of an employee to marshal the resources and make the decisions necessary to fulfill her or his work responsibilities. Without sufficient authority, it is unlikely that employees will complete delegated tasks successfully.

Consider, for example, a restaurant manager who has to leave early one evening and says to one of the waiters: "Make sure all the employees complete their closing duties." Assuming that the statement is made only to the waiter and not to the other employees, the manager has put the waiter in a very difficult position. She has just delegated the responsibility for ensuring that closing activities are completed properly without giving the waiter the authority he needs to succeed at that task. The other employees are unlikely to feel compelled to cooperate with the waiter so that he can fulfill his responsibility to the restaurant manager. To complete any task successfully, one must be given the authority necessary to carry out that task.

Accountability
Employees must justify their decisions and actions with regard to the task they have been assigned.

Establishing Accountability   Managers must hold their employees accountable for completing the tasks for which they assume responsibility and are given the necessary authority. When there is **accountability** for performance, employees understand that they must justify their decisions and actions with regard to the tasks for which they have assumed responsibility. Delegating decision-making responsibility without the associated accountability will compromise the overall benefits of the delegation process.

As Figure 8.3 illustrates, delegation can be thought of as a triangle, with each of these elements representing a point. Should one element be missing, the delegation process will be ineffective. To delegate successfully, managers must clearly communicate the responsibilities they are delegating, provide their employees with the formal authority necessary to fulfill those responsibilities, and develop the necessary control and feedback mechanisms to ensure that the employee is held accountable for successfully completing the delegated task.[39]

The Benefits of Delegation and Empowerment
Delegation offers a number of advantages. When used properly, delegation can lead to a more involved and empowered workforce.[40] As we discussed in Chapter 1, empowerment can lead to heightened productivity and quality, reduced costs, more innovation, improved customer service, and greater commitment from the employees of the organization.[41] Delegation involves empowering employees at all levels to make decisions, determine priorities, and improve the way work is done.[42]

Delegating decisions and activities to individuals lower in the organizational hierarchy often leads to better decision making. Those who are closest to the actual problem to be solved or the customer to be served, may be in the best position to make the most effective decisions. In addition, response time may be improved since information and decisions need not be passed up and down the hierarchy. This will be particularly critical in organizations where delays in decision making can make the difference between success and failure. At Hewlett-Packard, for example, decision making has traditionally

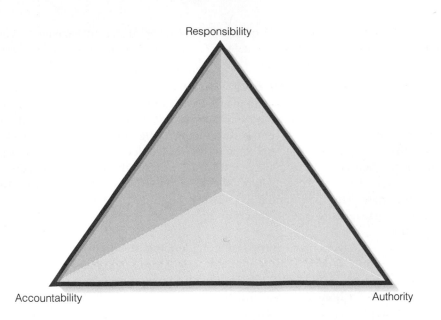

Responsibility

Accountability

Authority

▼ **FIGURE 8.3**
The Delegation Triangle

SOURCE: C. O. Longnecker, "The Delegation Di
lemma," *Supervision* 52 (February 1991): 3–5.
Reprinted by permission of © National Research
Bureau, P.O. Box 1, Burlington, Iowa
52601-0001.

taken place at the top levels of the organization. Recently, however, top management realized that the delegation of decision making to the lower ranks of the organization was the only way to function effectively in an industry that was rapidly changing and highly competitive.[43]

Additionally, delegation is beneficial from an employee development perspective. By delegating tasks and decision-making responsibility to their employees, managers provide an opportunity for the development of analytical and problem-solving skills. The employees are forced to accept responsibility, exercise judgement, and be accountable for their actions. The development of such skills will benefit the organization in the long term.

Finally, through delegation and empowerment managers magnify their accomplishments. By delegating tasks that their employees have the ability to complete, managers can use their time to accomplish more complicated, difficult, or important tasks. This can lead to a more creative and productive work group as a whole.[44]

Many organizations have benefited from empowering employees through delegation. Xerox, the American Society for Quality Control, and Federal Express are a few examples of organizations that have claimed significant success from employee empowerment. As we saw in Managing for Excellence, delegation and empowerment at Chaparral Steel had a very positive effect on the quality of its product and the efficiency of its production process. By forcing decision making to the lowest levels of the organizational hierarchy, Chaparral empowered its employees to do what was necessary to improve the operations of the company.

Managers should be cautioned about the potentially negative perceptions that ineffective delegation can create. Delegation must never be used to avoid work responsibilities that should legitimately be assumed by the manager. Delegation is not a way to "pass the buck," but rather a method for enhancing the overall productivity of the work group. If employees perceive the delegation as a way to reduce the manager's responsibilities and increase their own, their respect for the manager will undoubtedly deteriorate. This may be particularly problematic in diverse work groups where perceptions of delegation may vary. In such situations, it may be appropriate for managers to explain to their employees how delegation benefits the entire work group.

In general, effective delegation is a vital skill for successful managers. Yet it is a skill that many managers lack. Why? There are a number of reasons why managers fail to delegate.[45]

Reasons for Failing to Delegate

Delegation requires planning—and planning takes time.[46] How often have you heard someone say "by the time I explain this task to someone, I could do it myself?" This is a common excuse for maintaining responsibility for tasks rather than delegating them.[47] In some cases, such a decision may make sense. However, when tasks are recurring and would warrant the time to train someone who could assume responsibility for the work, such a decision would not be appropriate. The Experiential Exercise at the end of this chapter provides a tool for managers to use in determining whether a task is appropriate for delegation.

Second, managers may simply lack confidence in the abilities of their subordinates. Such a situation fosters the attitude "if you want it done well, do it yourself." This problem is particularly difficult to overcome when the manager feels pressure for high-level performance in a relatively short time frame. The manager simply refuses to delegate, preferring to retain responsibility for tasks to ensure that they are completed properly.

As a further complication, managers experience dual accountability. Managers are accountable for their own actions and the actions of their subordinates. If a subordinate fails to perform a certain task or does so poorly, it is the manager who is ultimately responsible for the subordinate's failure. Therefore, when the stakes are high, managers may prefer to perform certain tasks themselves.[48]

Finally, managers may refrain from delegating because they are insecure about their value to the organization.[49] Such managers may refuse to share the information necessary to complete a given task or set of tasks because they fear they will be considered expendable to the organization.

Learning to Delegate Effectively

Despite the perceived disadvantages of delegation, the reality is that managers can improve the performance of their work groups by empowering their employees through effective delegation. So how do managers learn to delegate effectively? They apply the basic principles of delegation.

Principle 1: Match the Employee to the Task   Managers should carefully consider the employees to whom they delegate.[50] The individual selected should possess the skills and capabilities needed to complete the task and, where possible, should stand to benefit from the experience. Further, managers should delegate duties that challenge employees somewhat, but which they can complete successfully.[51] There is no substitute for success when it comes to getting an employee to assume responsibility for more challenging assignments in the future.

Implicit in this principle is an acceptance of an "incremental learning" philosophy. This philosophy suggests that as employees prove their ability to perform effectively in a given job, they should be given tasks that are more complex and challenging. In addition to employee development benefits, such a strategy will be beneficial for the overall performance of the work group.[52]

Principle 2: Be Organized and Communicate Clearly   Most cases of failed delegation can be attributed to either poor organization or poor communication. When managers or employees do not clearly understand what is expected, the delegation process is sure to fail. The manager must have a clear understanding of what needs to be done, what deadlines exist, and what special skills will be required.[53] Delegation is a consultative process whereby managers and employees gain a clear understanding of the scope of their responsibilities and how their efforts relate to the overall efforts of the group or organization.[54]

Further, managers must be capable of communicating their instructions effectively if their subordinates are to perform up to the managers' expectations.[55] Effective communication about delegated tasks is particularly important in diverse work groups. As we know, people from different cultures may have different frames of reference and may interpret messages differently. Consequently, managers should be sure to clarify their instructions very carefully if they have any reason to believe that they may not be understood.

Principle 3: Transfer Authority and Accountability with the Task   The delegation process is doomed to failure if the individual to whom the task is delegated is not given the authority to succeed at accomplishing the task and is not held accountable for the results. The manager must expect the employee to carry the ball and let them do so.[56] This means providing employees with the necessary resources and power to succeed, giving them timely feedback on their progress, and holding them fully accountable for the results of their efforts.

Principle 4: Choose the Level of Delegation Carefully   Delegation does not mean that the manager can walk away from the task or the person to whom the task is delegated. The manager may maintain some control of both the process and the results of the delegated activities. Depending upon the confidence the manager has in the subordinate and the importance of the task, the manager can choose to delegate at several levels (see Figure 8.4).[57]

Many good managers find it difficult to delegate. Yet few managers have been successful in the long term without learning to delegate effectively.[58] This is particularly true in situations where growth and expansion are critical. For example, consider the experience of Debi Fields, the successful entrepreneur who created Mrs. Field's Cookies. To support the growth goals of her company, Mrs. Fields had to abandon her hands-on, control-oriented leadership style for a more participative, delegation-oriented style.[59]

Managers can delegate in degrees. Consider the following alternative levels of delegation.

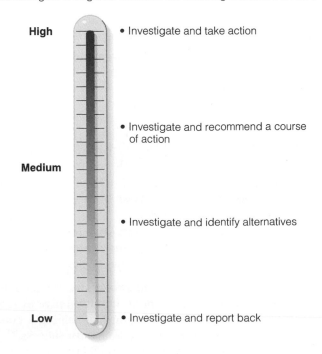

▼ **FIGURE 8.4**
Degree of Delegation

SOURCE: Adapted from M. E. Haynes, "Delegation: There's More to It Than Letting Someone Else Do It!", 9–15. Reprinted, by permission of publisher, from *Supervisory Management*, January 1980, © 1980. American Management Association, New York. All rights reserved.

MANAGERIAL IMPLICATIONS

In this chapter, we have learned how jobs are designed and organizational relationships are determined. As a future manager, you should keep the following organizing tips in mind:

● Identify the tasks and activities that must be completed in order for the goals of the organization to be achieved.

● Design jobs so that job holders will find their jobs interesting and challenging.

● Look for ways to use participatory approaches to job design as a means of improving quality.

● Consider reengineering business processes as a means of improving organizational performance.

● Don't be trapped by traditional hierarchical organizational relationships. More flexible and adaptable organizational designs are appropriate in many situations.

● Remember—all successful managers delegate. Develop a system of delegation that works for you and your work group.

This chapter has focused on some of the foundation principles of organization theory and, more specifically, on the first stage of the organizing process. The next chapter will address the second stage of the process and the concept of organizational design. The design of an organization defines the way organizational members are configured or grouped together; the types of mechanisms used to integrate and coordinate the flow of information, resources, or tasks between organizational members; and the degree of centralization or decentralization of decision making within the organization. An understanding of these organizing concepts, along with those discussed in this chapter, is essential for understanding the managerial function of organizing.

MANAGERIAL INCIDENT RESOLUTION

A BABY BELL REORGANIZES FOR EXCELLENCE

U.S. West's Winning in the '90s program was a tremendous success. The task force worked closely with employees from all levels in the organization to identify several key areas that needed attention. Some of the most notable results included:

● Management layers were reduced by half leading to faster decision making and clearer communication between and within departments.

● Span of control was nearly doubled. This both reduced costs and increased the job depth of many employees.

● Jobs were redesigned so that fragmented tasks were combined, resulting in broader, more challenging work roles.

● Role clarification for employees simplified work assignments. Line versus staff distinctions were minimized. All employees were identified as either supervising managers or individual contributors—no other distinctions were made.

The bottom line—U.S. West emerged from the process as an organization committed to excellence in both its products and its administrative processes. The foundation has been laid, but challenges remain. Maintaining a commitment to quality will be the key to this organization's long-term success.[60]

SUMMARY

- The managerial function of organizing is critical for all managers and all organizations. The activities of the organization must be organized so that it can fulfill its mission and achieve its goals.

- Organizing is a two-stage process. The first stage involves delineating the work that needs to be done, assigning that work to specific job holders, and creating the work relationships necessary to support the product and service delivery system of the organization. The second stage involves assigning organizational members to work groups, developing an integrating system to coordinate the work of those groups, and defining the locus of decision making in the organization.

- Job design issues relate to the first stage of the organizing process. Job design refers to the way tasks and activities are grouped to constitute a particular job. Core job dimensions that can be used to describe a job include: (1) skill variety, (2) task identity, (3) task significance, (4) autonomy, and (5) feedback. The first three dimensions determine the meaningfulness of jobs; the fourth dimension, autonomy, determines the degree to which individuals feel responsible for their work; and the final dimension, feedback, relates to the extent to which job holders understand the outcome of their jobs.

- Job design principles have evolved along with management theory. Classical management theory and scientific management suggested relatively mechanistic approaches to designing jobs. The human relations school of thought supported behavioral approaches to job design. Job enlargement, enrichment, and rotation programs became accepted methods of increasing the motivation, job satisfaction, and overall productivity of job holders. Contemporary management theory prescribes more participatory approaches to job design. Employee-centered work redesign programs and self-managed teams are two examples of job design programs that are participatory in nature.

- Reengineering involves a search for and implementation of radical change in the processes by which the organization produces and delivers its products and services. Through this process, organizations redesign the ways work is done with a focus on improving efficiency, identifying redundancies, and eliminating waste in everything the company does. Reengineering has a significant impact on the way jobs are designed.

- Organizational work relationships are defined by the concepts of: (1) chain of command, (2) span of control, (3) line versus staff personnel, and (4) delegation. The chain of command defines the vertical relationships that exist within the organization. Span of control refers to the number of subordinates who report to any supervisor. Line personnel are individuals or work groups that have direct responsibility for the delivery of the organization's product or service, while staff personnel provide an advisory or support function to the line personnel. Delegation refers to the process of transferring the responsibility for a specific activity or task to another member of the organization and empowering them to accomplish it effectively.

- Effective delegation requires the assignment of responsibility for a task, the granting of the authority necessary to complete the task, and the transfer of accountability to the individual to whom the task has been delegated.

- Effective delegation is essential for successful managers. Managers often fail to delegate because of a failure to plan, a lack of confidence in their subordinates, hesitancy to assume dual accountability for the actions of those to whom they delegate, or insecurity about their own value to the organization. Effective delegation requires matching the employee to the task, clearly communicating task responsibilities, giving authority to and imposing accountability on the person to whom the task is delegated, and choosing the appropriate level of delegation.

KEY TERMS

Organizing (p. 249)
Job design (p. 250)
Job description (p. 251)
Skill variety (p. 252)
Task identity (p. 252)
Task significance (p. 252)
Autonomy (p. 253)
Feedback (p. 253)
Job scope (p. 258)

Job enlargement (p. 258)
Job depth (p. 258)
Job enrichment (p. 259)
Job rotation (p. 259)
Employee-centered work redesign (p. 260)
Self-managed teams (p. 261)
Reengineering (p. 264)
Chain of command (p. 265)

Unity of command (p. 265)
Span of control (p. 266)
Line personnel (p. 268)
Staff personnel (p. 268)
Delegation (p. 269)
Scalar principle (p. 269)
Responsibility (p. 270)
Authority (p. 270)
Accountability (p. 270)

REVIEW QUESTIONS

1. Why is organizing an important managerial function?
2. Describe the process of organizing. What does each stage in the process entail?
3. Define job design. What are the core job dimensions that define a specific job?
4. How has job design theory evolved? What do the mechanistic, behavioral, and participatory approaches to job design prescribe, and how does each affect the core job dimensions?

5. What is reengineering? How will reengineering programs affect the ways jobs are designed?
6. Discuss the following concepts: (1) chain of command, (2) span of control, and (3) line versus staff personnel.
7. What is delegation and why is it important to delegate?
8. Why might managers find it difficult to delegate? How might they improve their delegation skills?

DISCUSSION QUESTIONS

Improving Critical Thinking

1. Consider an organization that you have either worked for or been affiliated with in some way. How might you redesign the jobs that must be done in that organization to achieve: (a) increased efficiency, (b) enhanced quality of the product or service, and (c) improved employee satisfaction? Are these objectives mutually exclusive? Could you design the jobs so that all of these objectives could be achieved?

2. The concept of self-managed teams has gained popularity in recent years. Consider moving toward that type of job design in a job you have held or hold currently. What would be the advantages and disadvantages to this approach?

Enhancing Communication Skills

3. Certain advantages and disadvantages are associated with having a fairly rigid chain of command. What are they? Can you identify certain business conditions and/or organizations where a rigid chain of

command would be appropriate? What conditions and/or organizations would benefit from the use of a more flexible chain of command? Present your conclusions to the class orally.

4. Consider the job design of the following grocery store positions: (a) cashier, (b) produce manager, and (c) general manager. How would these jobs differ with regard to the core job dimensions discussed in this chapter? How would these jobs rate in terms of meaningfulness, the responsibility the job holder feels for outcomes, and the job holder's understanding of the results of work activities? To practice writing, develop a written summary of your response.

Building Teamwork Skills

5. The competitive pressures of today's business climate (e.g., stronger global competition, weakened economic conditions, greater demands from consumers) have forced many firms to reconsider how they might operate more efficiently and effectively.

Form a team with four or five fellow students. As a group, identify and research at least three firms that have responded to such pressures by reassessing and adjusting their organizational system. Have their efforts been effective?

6. Your boss is a terrible delegator. She rarely delegates tasks, preferring to retain the responsibility for the efforts of your entire work unit rather than take a risk by assigning the task to a member of the group. Even when she does delegate a meaningful task, she rarely gives the authority necessary to complete the task successfully. Form a team of four to five fellow students and discuss ways to encourage your boss to delegate more.

ETHICS: TAKE A STAND

Playtime Toys recently restructured its operations in an effort to achieve a stronger competitive position within its industry. The competitiveness of the toy industry had intensified in the last two years, and more efficient, low-priced competitors had begun to chip away at Playtime's market share. If Playtime's restructuring plan was not successful at driving down costs, the company would likely not survive the next year.

Playtime's restructuring plan included the elimination of an entire layer of management, as well as the selective elimination of certain job positions. As a result, the job responsibilities of a number of individuals throughout the organization had changed dramatically over the last month.

Susan Pilcher was one of those individuals. Susan was one of two managers on the production lines for baby swings. When the other production line manager's job was eliminated in the restructuring, Susan's span of control doubled. Where she originally supervised 15 employees on one line, she now supervised 30 employees working on two production lines. Managing the two lines effectively was very difficult. Susan was determined to maintain productivity goals, however. Otherwise she felt certain that she would be the next supervisor eliminated.

Unfortunately, the pressure to maintain productivity was affecting the quality of the company's products. Playtime was a small operation, and production managers performed quality checks as part of their normal job responsibilities. Like Susan, many of the company's production managers had been forced to assume increased responsibilities, leaving little time to perform regular quality checks.

Susan was particularly aware of this issue, as the company had received two customer complaints about weak straps on baby swings that she knew had not been checked. But pressure to perform had left her in a quandary as to how to resolve this problem. Thus far, no serious incidents had occurred, but what if a child was hurt next time? On the other hand, if she complained about this problem how would upper management view her ability to supervise, and how would this affect her future in the company?

For Discussion
1. Why was Susan experiencing this dilemma?
2. What would you do if you were Susan?

THINKING CRITICALLY
Debate the Issue

Form teams of four to five students. Half of the teams should prepare to argue the benefits of job specialization. The other half of the teams should prepare to argue the benefits of job enlargement. Your instructor will select two teams to present their arguments to the class in a debate format.

VIDEO CASE

Cormier Equipment

 Cormier Equipment Corporation rents, services, and sells heavy industrial equipment. When the President of the company began to suspect that the economy was going into a recession, he began to prepare for a potential loss of revenues. Through a reengineering project that affected job design, as well as other aspects of the organization, Cormier continued to prosper even through the recession.

When describing the reengineering project, Cormier says, "we reviewed the way we did business." All aspects of organization's operation were reviewed with an eye on improving quality and efficiency. The following were among the actions eventually implemented:

• Managers were told to be more attentive to worker suggestions.

• Jobs were enlarged and workers were given more responsibilities.

• Monetary incentives were provided for doing better jobs.

• Cost-reduction goals were set and strategies for achieving them were developed.

• Annual reviews of paperwork eliminated duplication and unneeded reports.

• A new billing system produced quicker, more error-free invoicing.

• A system of processing before it was rented out again, improved service quality.

• In need of improved marketing, Cormier created a marketing director's position. The new marketing director's primary emphasis was on creating long-term client loyalty.

Through reengineering with a focus on changing the way jobs were designed and tasks were completed, Cormier weathered the recession successfully. As evidence of that success, profitability rose 2½ times from October, 1990 to October, 1992.

For Discussion

1. Discuss how Cormier adapted job design to prepare for an economic downturn.

2. How can reengineering improve productivity, quality, and job satisfaction?

CASE

Major Appliances Scales Down

Recently, customer service problems and employee morale problems surfaced at Major Appliances. The problems, precipitated by recent downsizing of the organization, put a damper on management's enthusiasm for the benefits of their new organizational design.

Six months ago, the company had downsized to cope with the increasingly competitive global environment. The growth of the company in the early 1980s had led to expansion of the workforce at all ranks within the company. However, growth had stabilized, and sales were expected to remain flat for the next several years. In addition, the company had recently installed a new computer system that performed many functions previously accomplished by employees. These two factors influenced the decision to downsize to improve the efficiency of the organization. As Dave Fick, CEO, told the key management

group, "the purpose of the restructuring plan is to remain competitive in the increasingly mature appliance industry. We need to stretch the capabilities of each employee to achieve this goal."

The impact of the downsizing efforts seemed to be particularly negative for the Accounting Support Department. Originally, three people worked in this department, with one assigned to each of the following jobs: accounts payable, accounts receivable, and payroll. Management felt that, given the new computer system, one person should be able to perform all three functions. Consequently, management terminated two workers and shifted the responsibility for all three jobs to the remaining person—Mr. Matsuda.

Initially, Mr. Matsuda was excited about his additional responsibilities and the opportunity to expand his role in the company. But he soon became disillusioned. He found it nearly impossible to fulfill his responsibilities in a timely fashion. Bills were not paid on time, errors were made in employee paychecks, and Mr. Matsuda was falling further and further behind in all of his duties. He was working every Saturday but was still unable to catch up with his work. While the company had to pay additional overtime costs, the problems continued. Customers and suppliers had begun to complain, and so had employees. Something needed to be done to correct the situation.

For Discussion

1. What was the management at Major Appliances trying to accomplish by redesigning the way work was done in the Accounting Support Department?

2. Using the terms introduced in this chapter, describe what happened to Mr. Matsuda's job. How were the five core job dimensions affected by the changes in his job design?

3. Was his reaction to his new job design what you would expect? Why or why not?

4. How could the problems in the Accounting Support Department have been avoided?

EXPERIENTIAL EXERCISE 8.1

Assure Positive Delegation

Using either your present job or a past job as an example, think about a task that you would like to delegate. Answer the following questions about the task and the existing situation. Based on your answers, decide if the task should have been delegated.

1. *Precise task.* Could I specify in writing the precise task I'm going to delegate? In other words, could I specify what it is, how much of it needs to be done, and within what time frame?

2. *Benefits.* Could I specify in writing why delegating this particular task to this particular individual is good for her, good for the organization, and good for me?

3. *Measure of results.* Could I specify in writing how I will know whether the task: (a) has been done, and (b) how well it has been done?

4. *Competence.* Is the person to whom I intend to delegate this task: (a) competent to do it (b) require step-by-step instructions or supervision?

5. *Motivation.* Is there any evidence in my past relationship with this person that he wants, needs, or is motivated to do work outside the customary job?

6. *Measure of cost.* If the person makes an error, specifically what would be the dollar costs? The human costs?

7. *Check performance.* Is it possible for me to oversee or measure the employee's performance on the task without interfering with his work?

8. *Correct mistakes.* If problems arise, can we correct mistakes quickly without great cost or difficulty?

9. *Clearance.* Do I need to check this delegation with my boss?

10. *Rewards.* What are the rewards, both formal and informal, that I can give this person if the delegated task is done well? Do I need to tell the person what these rewards are?

11. *Next tasks.* If the person masters the task that has been delegated, what are the specific subsequent tasks that should be delegated to her?

12. *Responsibility and authority.* Can I, in delegating this task, delegate both the responsibility and the authority to this person?

SOURCE: J. Lawrie, "Turning around Attitudes about Delegation," 2. Reprinted by permission of publisher from *Supervisory Management*, December 1990, © 1990. American Management Association, New York. All rights reserved.

NOTES

1. R. Lynch, "A Baby Bell Reexamines Itself," *Journal of Business Strategy* (September/October 1991): 8–11.

2. J. A. Pierce and R. B. Robinson, *Strategic Management* (Homewood, Ill.: Irwin, 1991), 526–40; and T. Peters, *Thriving on Chaos* (New York: Alfred A. Knopf, 1988), 167–69.

3. P. C. Grant, "Managing the Downside of Top Performance," *Supervisory Management* (November 1989): 25–27.

4. M. A. Campion and P. W. Thayer, "How Do You Design a Job?" *Personnel Journal* 68 (January 1989): 43–46.

5. J. R. Hackman, G. R. Oldham, R. Janson, and K. Purdy, "A New Strategy for Job Enrichment," *California Management Review* 17 (Summer 1975): 57–71.

6. Ibid., 58.

7. C. L. Fowler, "ASQC/Fortune Special Report," *Fortune*, 1992.

8. Caterpillar, Inc., *Annual Report*, 1991.

9. Peters, *Thriving on Chaos,* 167-69.

10. See, for example, J. W. Dean Jr. and S. A. Snell, "Integrated Manufacturing and Job Design: Moderating Effects of Organizational Inertia," *Academy of Management Journal* 34 (1991): 776-804; and G. Johns, J. L. Xie, and F. Yongqing, "Mediating and Moderating Effects in Job Design," *Journal of Management* 18 (1992): 657-76.

11. G. Stix, "No Tipping Please," *Scientific American,* January 1992, 141.

12. T. Carson, "Bittersweet Future in Store for Survivors of Cutbacks," *Wall Street Journal,* March 2, 1992, 1+.

13. J. B. Cunningham and T. Eberle, "A Guide to Job Enrichment and Redesign," *Personnel* 67 (February 1990): 56-61.

14. Caterpillar, Inc., *Annual Report,* 1990, 8.

15. J. E. Rigdon, "Using Lateral Moves to Spur Employees," *Wall Street Journal,* May 26, 1992, PB1(W), PB1(E), col. 3, B1.

16. M. H. Safizadeh, "The Case of Workgroups in Manufacturing Operations," *California Management Review* 33 (Summer 1991): 61-82.

17. R. Jacob, "Thriving in a Lame Economy," *Fortune,* October 5, 1992, 44-54.

18. S. L. Perlman, "Employees Redesign Their Jobs," *Personnel Journal* 67 (November 1990): 37-40.

19. Ibid.

20. Ibid.

21. Amoco Corporation, *Annual Report,* 1990, 12.

22. See, for example, P. J. Keating and S. F. Jablonsky, "Get Your Financial Organization Close to the Business," *Financial Executive,* May/June 1991, 44-50; and Safizadeh, "The Case of Workgroups in Manufacturing Operations."

23. P. Chance, "Great Experiments in Team Chemistry," *Across the Board,* May 1989, 18-25.

24. Ibid.

25. T. R. Horton, "Delegation and Team Building: No Solo Acts Please," *Management Review* (November 1989): 25-27.

26. Ibid.

27. M. Bassin, "Teamwork at General Foods: New & Improved," *Personnel Journal* (May 1988): 62-70.

28. A. K. Naj, "AlliedSignal's Chairman Outlines Strategy for Growth," *Wall Street Journal,* August 17, 1993, PB4(W), PB4(E), col. 3.

29. J. Oberle, "Quality Gurus: The Men and Their Message," *Training.* January 1990, 47-52.

30. R. M. Tomasko, "Intelligent Resizing: View from the Bottom Up (Part II)," *Management Review* (June 1993): 18-23.

31. A. Laplante, "Kodak Experiments with Local Support," *Computerworld,* December 1990, Vol. 24, No. 50, p. 90(1).

32. Ameritech, *Annual Report,* 1992.

33. H. Mintzberg, *The Structuring of Organization* (Englewood Cliffs, N.J.: Prentice-Hall, 1979), 136.

34. J. S. McClenahen, "Managing More People in the '90s," *Industry Week,* March 20, 1989, 31-38.

35. Chrysler Corporation, *Annual Report,* 1990.

36. S. C. Bushardt, D. L. Duhon, and A. R. Fowler Jr., "Management Delegation Myths and the Paradox of Task Assignment," *Business Horizons,* March/April 1991, 34, 37-43.

37. Chrysler Corporation, *Annual Report,* 1990.

38. M. E. Douglas, "How to Delegate Safely," *Training and Development Journal* (February 1987): 8.

39. C. O. Longnecker, "The Delegation Dilemma," *Supervision* 52 (February 1991): 3-5.

40. J. D'O'Brian, "Empowering Your Front-line Employees to Handle Problems," *Supervisory Management,* Vol. 38, No. 1, p. 10 (1) January 1993.

41. D. Vinton, "Delegation for Employee Development," *Training and Development Journal* (January 1987): 65-67.

42. M. C. Dennis, "Only Superman Didn't Delegate," *Business Credit,* February 1993, 41.

43. T. Peters, "Letting Go of Controls," *Across the Board,* June 1991, 14-18.

44. M. Yate, "Delegation: The Key to Empowerment," *Training and Development Journal* (April 1991): 23-24.

45. J. H. Carter, "Minimizing the Risks from Delegation," *Supervisory Management* (February 1992): 1-2.

46. J. Lawrie, "Turning Around Attitudes about Delegation," *Supervisory Management* 35 (December 1990): 1-2.

47. R. Wilkinson, "Eight Supervisory Tips," *Supervision* (July 1991): 12+.

48. Lawrie, "Turning Around Attitudes about Delegation."

49. R. Rohrer, "Does the Buck Ever Really Stop?" *Supervision* 52 (July 1991): 7-8.

50. J. T. Straub, "Do You Choose the Best Person for the Task?" *Supervisory Management* (October 1992): 7.

51. Vinton, "Delegation for Employee Development."

52. Douglas, "How to Delegate Safely."

53. Yate, "Delegation: The Key to Empowerment."

54. Vinton, "Delegation for Employee Development."

55. R. Wilkinson, "Think before You Open Your Mouth!" *Supervision* 52 (May 1991): 17-19.

56. M. Townsend, "Let the Employees Carry the Ball," *Personnel Journal* 69 (October 1990): 30-31.

57. M. E. Haynes, "Delegation: There's More to It Than Letting Someone Else Do It," *Supervisory Management* 25 (January 1980): 9-15.

58. T. R. Horton, "Delegation and Team Building: No Solo Acts Please," *Management Review* (September 1992): 58-61.

59. A. Prendergast, "Learning to Let Go," *Working Woman,* January 1992, 42-45.

60. Lynch, "A Baby Bell Reexamines Itself."

61. Adapted from "Vortex Industries," in *Real-World Lessons for America's Small Businesses: Insights from the Blue Chip Enterprise Initiative (Nation's Business* on behalf of Connecticut Mutual Life Insurance Company and the U.S. Chamber of Commerce, 1993), 13-14.

Designing the Contemporary Organization

CHAPTER 9

▼ CHAPTER OVERVIEW

Developing an organizational design that supports the strategic and operational goals of an organization can be a very challenging managerial task. This is particularly true today as many organizations struggle to find that delicate balance between organizational responsiveness and operational efficiency. Achieving success will depend, to a large degree, on the ability of managers to develop an effective and flexible organizational design.

This chapter focuses on a number of issues related to organizational design. Special attention is given to the effect of various strategic orientations on the structure of organizations, the impact of interdependence between operating units on the integration needs of organizations, and the extent to which environmental stability or volatility affects how decision making occurs within organizations.

▼ LEARNING OBJECTIVES

When you have finished studying this chapter,
you should be able to:

• Explain why organizational design is important for organizational success.
• Identify the three major components of organizational design.
• Discuss the four types of organizational structure and the strategic conditions under which each might be appropriate.
• Describe the factors that affect an organization's need for coordination and explain how integrating mechanisms can be used to coordinate organizational activities.
• Explain the concept of locus of decision making and the advantages and disadvantages of centralized and decentralized decision making.
• Describe organic and mechanistic organizational systems and discuss the relationships between these systems and environmental stability.
• Describe an adaptive organizational design.

MANAGERIAL INCIDENT

IBM

BIG BLUE: DEVELOPING AN ORGANIZATIONAL DESIGN THAT WORKS

Few companies have enjoyed such great success as International Business Machines (IBM). "Big Blue," as it is affectionately called by many, built a worldwide reputation for the delivery of high-quality, advanced information technology for use by organizations across the globe. Its aggressive growth strategies earned it a place at the top of the highly volatile and rapidly changing computer industry year after year.

Surprisingly, however, the company's competitive edge has deteriorated significantly in the last several years. In fact, due to a number of factors (a sluggish world economy, a general slowdown in the computer industry, and intensified competition), IBM experienced a substantial decline in revenues and profits in 1991 and 1992. The company's problems eventually resulted in the ousting of Jim Akers, who had been the CEO for many years. As Lou Gerstner took the helm as CEO, restoring IBM's profitability was his first priority.

One aspect of the company that received significant scrutiny was its organizational design. Many criticized IBM's excessively bureaucratic organizational system, suggesting that it hampered decision making and stifled creativity. Such a design was likely inappropriate for an organization operating in a dynamic industry where innovation is critical to long-term success.

The management at IBM was considering a number of possible changes in the organizational design. Among the options under consideration were the elimination of middle levels of management, the decentralization of decision making, and the regrouping of work activities along product lines. Complicating the situation, however, was the fact that IBM's organizational design had been in existence for a very long time. It was deeply rooted and would be difficult to change. Nevertheless, the long-term success of this firm would depend, to some degree, on its ability to make the necessary changes in its organizational design.[1] ▼

INTRODUCTION

Management at all levels of IBM were concerned about the company's declining competitive position. Was the company's organizational design simply inappropriate for the industry in which it operated? Burdened with excessive layers of management that complicated and delayed decision making, IBM found itself incapable of competing effectively with its more flexible and proactive competitors. A major restructuring of the firm's organizational design was imperative.

Organizational design is an important aspect of management. The way in which an organization is designed will determine how efficiently and effectively its activities are carried out. Organizations must be designed so that the mission of the organization can be fulfilled and its goals can be achieved. Increasingly, managers are looking to organizational design as a method for competing more effectively in global markets and achieving a quality orientation across the organization as a whole.[2]

This chapter begins with a discussion of the concept of organizational design from a contingency perspective. The primary components of organizational design are identified, and the role that each plays in the overall design of the organization is examined. The implications of various organizational and environmental variables (i.e., strategy, interdependence, and external environmental pressures) will be evaluated for each organizational design component. Finally, the chapter concludes with a discussion of adaptive organizations and offers some guidelines for managers who must design their organizations for the business environment of the future.

ORGANIZATIONAL DESIGN FROM A CONTINGENCY PERSPECTIVE

Organizational design is a plan for arranging and coordinating the activities of an organization for the purpose of fulfilling its mission and achieving its goals. More specifically, design defines: (1) the configuration of organizational members, (2) the types of mechanisms used to integrate and coordinate the flow of information, resources, and tasks between organizational members, and (3) the locus of decision making—the level of the organizational hierarchy at which most decision making occurs. The ultimate success of an organization will depend, in part, on the ability of its managers to develop an organizational design that supports its strategic and operational goals.

Design provides a mechanism for coping with the complexity that results from managing multiple tasks, functions, products, markets, or technologies. Although organizational design issues are important to all organizations, the more complex its operations, the more sophisticated its design must be.

For example, a small organization that produces a single product with a small workforce will likely find it easier to organize and coordinate its organizational members than will a multinational organization with multiple product lines, operating facilities spread across the globe, and a highly diverse workforce. Further, growth-oriented organizations will find that effective design is a key to managing the complexity that results from developing new products, entering new geographic markets, or pursuing new customer groups. In sum, all organizations (small, large, and growing) must maintain an organizational design that is appropriate for the level of complexity they face.

There is no "universal" design that is appropriate for all organizations. In fact, the contingency approach to organizing suggests that organizational design must be consistent with a fairly broad range of variables that are largely a function of the organization's strategy (e.g., size, level of development, product diversity, geographic coverage, and customer base).[3] Consequently, just as strategy varies among organizations, so will organizational design.

COMPONENTS OF ORGANIZATIONAL DESIGN

As noted earlier and illustrated in Figure 9.1, an organization's overall design is defined by three primary components: (1) organization structure, (2) integrating mechanisms, and (3) locus of decision making. As a system, these components enable the members of the organization to fulfill its mission and work toward the achievement of its goals. Each of these components will vary with the overall strategy of the organization.

ORGANIZATION STRUCTURE

Organization structure is the first component of organizational design. **Organization structure** refers to the primary reporting relationships that exist

Organizational design
The way in which the activities of an organization are arranged and coordinated so that its mission can be fulfilled and its goals achieved.

Organization structure
Defines the primary reporting relationships that exist within an organization.

▼ **FIGURE 9.1**
Dimensions of Organizational Design

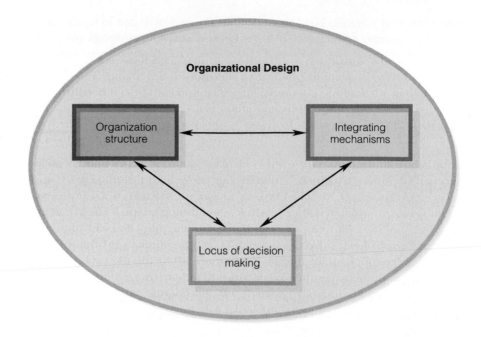

within an organization. The chain of command and hierarchy of responsibility, authority, and accountability are established through organizational structure and are often illustrated in an organizational chart.

The structuring process involves creating departments by grouping tasks on the basis of some common characteristic such as function, product, or geographic market. If, for example, work units are created by grouping all production tasks together, all marketing tasks together, and all finance tasks together, then the units are organized by function. In contrast, if work units are formed by grouping together all tasks related to serving a specific region of the U.S. market (i.e., Northeast, Southeast, Central, West), then the geographic market served is the basis for departmentalization.

An organization's strategy has significant implications for its structure.[4] Organizations group their members along that aspect of their operations that is most complex. For example, an organization with significant product diversity will likely find a structure departmentalized by product to be most suitable for managing its broad range of products. If, in contrast, a firm has a relatively narrow product line but serves a wide geographic market, it might find a geographic-based structure to be most appropriate.

In general, four types of organizational structure are predominant in organizations today. Three of these, the functional, divisional, and matrix structures, are traditional organizational forms that have been used by U.S. corporations for decades. The last structure, the network structure, has emerged more recently and represents a contemporary approach for meeting the challenges of today's business environment. In the next several sections, we will describe each structural alternative, suggest some strategic conditions for which each might be appropriate, and outline some of the major advantages and disadvantages associated with each structure.

Functional Structure: Enhancing Operational Efficiency

Functional structures are the most commonly used organizational form today.[5] The **functional structure** groups organizational members according to the particular function that they perform within the organization and the set of resources that they draw upon to perform their tasks. Figure 9.2 illustrates a functional organizational chart for Colgate-Palmolive Company. As the chart

Functional structure
Members of the organization are grouped according to the function they perform within the organization.

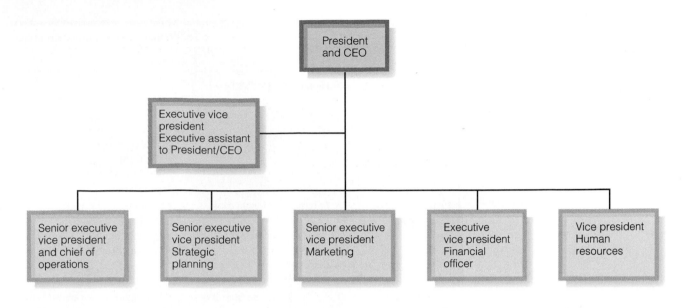

▼ **FIGURE 9.2**
Functional Structure: Colgate-Palmolive Company

SOURCE: Adapted from *The Conference Board Chart Service* (New York: The Conference Board, Inc., 1988). Reprinted with permission of *The Conference Board.*

shows, this firm structures its activities according to the functions of operations, strategic planning, marketing, finance, and human resources.[6]

When an organization's greatest source of complexity comes from the diverse tasks and responsibilities that must be performed, rather than from its products, geographic markets or customer groups, a functional structure may be appropriate. Entrepreneurial organizations or organizations that are in the early stages of the organizational life cycle often have limited product diversity and geographic scope. Task diversity may represent the organization's greatest source of complexity, and as a consequence, a functional structure may be most suitable.

Table 9.1 outlines the major advantages and disadvantages associated with the functional structure. On the positive side, functional structures support task specialization and may help employees develop better job-related skills. In addition, work groups may be more cohesive because employees work with individuals with similar skills and interests and the group's leader has a common functional orientation with the group members. Finally, this structure supports tight, centralized control and may result in greater operational efficiency.

But this structure has disadvantages as well (see Table 9.1). Most of these disadvantages stem from the problems associated with coordinating diverse work groups. Work groups organized along functional lines are often insulated from the activities of other departments and may not truly understand the priorities and initiatives of other work groups. Further, the functional structure leads to the development of specialized managers rather than generalists who may be more appropriate for top-level management positions. Finally, profit centers usually do not exist in a functionally structured organization. Therefore only top-level corporate executives can be held clearly accountable for bottom-line profitability.

Divisional Structures: Providing Focus

A second common form of organizational structure is the divisional structure. Most **divisional structures** are designed so that members of the organization are grouped on the basis of common products, geographic markets, or customers served. The primary advantage of a divisional structure is the focus it provides in supporting the strategic goals of the organization. The primary disadvantage is that resources and efforts may be duplicated across divisions (see Table 9.1).

Divisional structure
Members of the organization are grouped on the basis of common products, geographic markets, or customers served.

▼ **TABLE 9.1**   Advantages and Disadvantages of Traditional Organizational Structures

	ADVANTAGES	DISADVANTAGES
Functional	• Facilitates specialization • Cohesive work groups • Improved operational efficiency	• Focus on departmental versus organizational issues • Difficult to develop generalists needed for top management • Only top management held accountable for profitability
Product divisional	• Enhanced coordination • Better assessment of manager performance and responsibility • Development of generalist managers	• Managers may lack expertise to operate in wide geographic regions • Duplication of resources
Geographic divisional	• Allows focus on specific new markets • Good structure for growth along geographic lines • Adaptable to local needs	• Duplication of product or product/technology efforts • Coordination and integration are difficult • May be difficult to manage diverse product lines
Matrix	• Can achieve simultaneous objectives • Managers focus on two organizational dimensions, resulting in more specific job skills	• Complex, leading to difficulties in implementation • Behavioral difficulties from "two bosses" • Time-consuming from a planning/coordination perspective
Network	• Maximizes the effectiveness of the core unit • Do more with less resources • Flexibility	• Fragmentation makes it difficult to develop control systems • Success is dependent on ability to locate sources • Difficult to develop employee loyalty

Product divisional structure
A structure in which the activities of the organization are grouped according to specific products or product lines.

Product Divisions   In a **product divisional structure,** product managers assume responsibility for the manufacture and distribution of a specific product or product line to all the geographic and customer markets served by the organization. These managers coordinate all functional tasks (finance, marketing, production, and so on) related to their product line. As an example of such a structure, consider Black & Decker. This company operates with a product divisional structure organized along its primary product segments—commercial and industrial tools, power tools and home improvements, and household products.[7]

Product divisional structures are considered most appropriate for organizations with relatively diverse product lines that require specialized efforts to achieve high product quality. When products are targeted to different, distinct groups, require varied technologies for production, or are delivered through diverse distribution systems, a product-based structure may be suitable. Consider, for example, IBM's move to create autonomous operating divisions based on the firm's distinct product lines. Recognizing the importance of a product

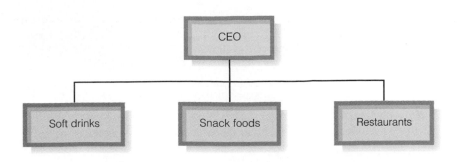

▼ **FIGURE 9.3**
SBU-Based Structure: Pepsi Cola
Company

Note: Staff departments have been eliminated to
illustrate the product dimension of PepsiCo's
structure more clearly.

orientation to IBM's overall success, top management believed that a product
divisional structure would provide the product focus necessary to regain their
competitive edge.[8]

Many large organizations not only have diverse product lines, but actually
operate several diverse and distinct businesses. In such cases, the product
divisional structure actually takes the form of an SBU (strategic business unit)
divisional structure where each business unit is maintained as a separate and
autonomous operating division. PepsiCo, Inc. provides an excellent example
of a company organized around its three primary businesses—soft drinks,
snack foods, and restaurants (see Figure 9.3). Interestingly, PepsiCo uses a
variety of structural alternatives within each business unit. The snack foods
SBU, for example, is organized primarily along product lines, whereas the soft
drinks SBU is organized by geographic region.[9]

Geographic Divisions   The **geographic divisional structure** groups the activities of the organization along geographic lines. Each geographic division is
responsible for distributing products or services within a specific geographic
region. Coopers & Lybrand is an example of a firm that uses this type of
structure quite effectively. This accounting firm maintains nine separate units
that are organized by geographic region. Operational decisions are made at
the unit level; corporate headquarters assumes responsibility for determining
the overall strategic direction of the firm and allocating resources among ge-

Geographic divisional structure
A structure in which the activities of
the organization are grouped according to the geographic markets served.

▼ These employees work in a geo-
graphically-based division of their
company. This meeting has focused
on comparing the sales and profit performance of their region with the performance of other regions in the
country.

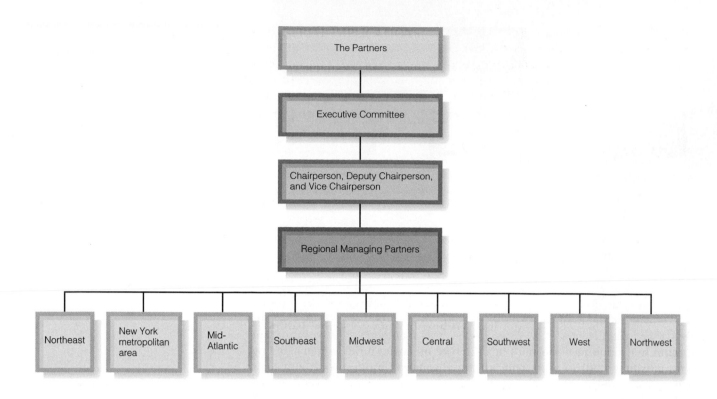

▼ **FIGURE 9.4**
Geographic Divisional Structure:
Coopers & Lybrand

SOURCE: Adapted from *The Conference Board Chart Service* (New York: The Conference Board, Inc., 1988). Reprinted with permission of *The Conference Board.*

ographic units. Figure 9.4 illustrates the organizational chart for Coopers & Lybrand.[10]

A geographic divisional structure is appropriate for organizations of varying strategic conditions. In general, this structure is most appropriate for organizations with limited product lines that either have wide geographic coverage or desire to grow through geographic expansion. This structure permits organizations to concentrate their efforts and allocate their resources toward penetrating multiple regional markets with products and services that are, when necessary, adapted to meet local needs and preferences.[11]

Organizations pursuing international strategies often choose a geographic-based structure.[12] Companies with relatively narrow, mature product lines may find their primary growth opportunities are in the international marketplace. Entering those markets effectively often requires a strong understanding of local market conditions and customer preferences. A geographic divisional structure provides a mechanism for learning more about local markets and making the necessary adaptations to the company's products and services. Multinational organizations in the food, beverage, and cosmetic industries have found that this organizational structure supports their efforts to respond to local market demands.

The Caterpillar Tractor Company, headquartered in Peoria, Illinois, is an excellent example of a company that uses a global geographic structure. Its four major divisions are segmented on the basis of geographic location: (1) United States, (2) Europe, Africa, and Middle East, (3) Asia/Pacific, and (4) Canada and Latin America. The geographic differentiation makes strategic sense for Caterpillar. Not only is the company's international involvement extensive, but it also maintains a relatively narrow product line (nearly all of its products are categorized as either earthmoving or engines). This narrow focus has always been a strength for Caterpillar and has led to the development of a worldwide reputation for outstanding product quality.[13]

Customer Divisions   **Customer divisional structures** group tasks according to different customers. Each customer-based unit focuses on meeting the needs

Customer divisional structure
A structure in which the tasks of the organization are grouped according to customer segments.

of a specific group of the organization's customers. CIGNA Property and Casualty is an example of a company that uses a customer divisional structure. CIGNA abandoned a product-based structure in 1990 in favor of a structure organized around customer business segments. The company feels that this change will provide the strong customer focus that is essential in the insurance industry.[14]

A customer-based structure is appropriate for organizations that have separate customer groups with very specific and distinct needs. With the quality movement in full swing, and the emphasis on meeting the needs of the customer first and foremost, this structure is highly appropriate for organizations that must adapt their products and services for different customer groups. It may also be suitable for organizations that wish to grow by targeting new and distinct customer groups. Resources can be allocated to support the customer groups with the greatest growth potential.

Matrix Structure: An International or Project Perspective

The organizational structures discussed so far have grouped activities along a specific, single dimension of the organization's operations (function, product, geographic region, or customer base). Rather than focusing on a single dimension of the organization's operations, a **matrix structure** defines work groups on the basis of two dimensions simultaneously (i.e., product/function, product/geographic region, etc.). Davis and Lawrence defined a matrix structure as one that "employs a multiple command system that includes not only a multiple command structure but also related support mechanisms and an associated organizational culture and behavior patterns."[15] In other words, the distinguishing characteristic of the matrix structure is its dual chain of command.[16]

For illustrative purposes, consider the organizational chart in Figure 9.5. The chart is for PGP, Inc., a fictitious multinational company that distributes

Matrix structure
A structure in which the tasks of the organization are grouped along to organizing dimensions simultaneously (e.g., product/geographic market, product/function).

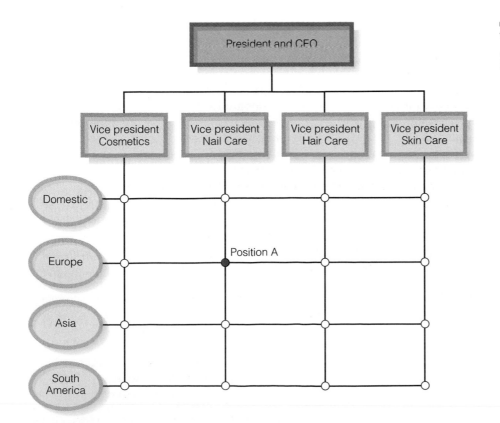

▼ **FIGURE 9.5**
A Multinational Matrix Structure. PGP, Inc.

a relatively broad range of health and beauty products. The vice presidents of the product and geographic divisions report directly to PGP's CEO and assume full responsibility for the operations of their respective divisions. For example, the vice president for South America is ultimately responsible for the distribution of all products (hair care, nail care, cosmetics, skin care) to the South American market. In contrast, the vice president of the nail care division assumes responsibility for the distribution of nail care products worldwide. Theoretically, these vice presidents have equal organizational power.

The dual chain of command is illustrated at the next level of the hierarchy. Consider the manager occupying position A. What are her job responsibilities? Who is her boss? Is it the vice president of nail care products or the vice president for Europe? The person who occupies position A on PGP's organizational chart is responsible for distributing nail care products in Europe. Therefore, this manager has both a product and area focus to her job, and as a result, she can develop more specific job skills. In addition, she has two bosses to whom she is equally accountable—the vice president of nail care products and the vice president for Europe.

The matrix structure provides PGP with a viable way to focus on both specific products and geographic markets, thereby enabling the company to achieve simultaneous objectives. If forced to organize around only one organizational dimension, PGP would forgo the benefits associated with the other dimension. The matrix structure enables many global organizations to focus both on enhancing the quality of their products through the product dimension and on achieving greater penetration of discrete national or regional markets through the geographic dimension of the structure.

Despite the obvious advantages of the matrix structure, it also has a number of disadvantages (see Table 9.1). Most notable is the complexity inherent in a dual chain of command. Managing within this structure requires extraordinary planning and coordination between work groups.[17]

Network Structures: The Key to Flexibility

For decades organizations have aspired to be large. Growth was considered to be synonymous with success, and the "bigger is better" syndrome governed the strategic decision making of most companies.[18] This is not so today. Organizations are finding that being lean and flexible is often preferable to being big.[19] This is particularly true for companies that operate within rapidly changing industries or face intense global competition.[20]

In response to these changes, a number of successful organizations have abandoned the traditional organizational structures of the past and have moved toward a more contemporary form of organizational structure—the **network structure**.[21] At the foundation of the network structure is a sophisticated product delivery system that is built around alliances with other groups. These groups perform some of the activities necessary to deliver the products and services of the organization.[22] They may be independent, market-driven internal work units, or in many cases, they may be outside the organization.

For example, the central organization may coordinate production, marketing, financing, and distribution activities necessary to market a particular product without owning a single manufacturing plant, creating a single line of advertising copy, or even taking possession of the product. The central organization simply coordinates the activities of others so that the product reaches the ultimate consumer in the most efficient method possible.[23] Figure 9.6 illustrates the network organizational structure.[24]

Three primary types of network structures are found in organizations today—internal, stable, and dynamic networks.[25] These structures vary in terms of their commitment to outsourcing. Recall from Chapter 4 that out-

Network structure
A contemporary organizational structure that is founded on a set of alliances with other organizations that serve a wide variety of functions.

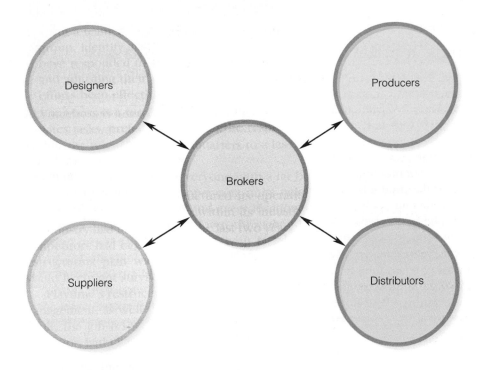

▼ **FIGURE 9.6**
Network Structure

SOURCE: R. E. Miles and C. C. Snow, "Organizations: New Concepts for New Forms," 62–73. Copyright © 1986 by The Regents of the University of California. Reprinted from the *California Management Review*, Vol. 28, No. 3. By permission of The Regents.

sourcing occurs when one organization contracts with another organization to perform some aspect of its operations.

An **internal network** exists in organizations that choose to avoid outsourcing, but wish to develop internal entrepreneurial ventures that are driven by market forces and, thus, are competitive with alternative sources of supply. These internal units operate independently and negotiate with the central unit like any outside vendor. Each unit functions as a profit center that specializes in a particular aspect of the organization's product delivery system.

The component business of General Motors serves as an excellent example of an internal network structure. GM's component business maintains eight independent divisions that specialize in the production of some aspect of the automotive system (e.g., AC Spark Plugs). These divisions are encouraged to conduct business on the open market, yet they cooperate with the central unit of GM's component business whenever appropriate. The net result is greater effectiveness for the corporation as a whole.[26]

Organizations that maintain a **stable network** rely to some degree on outsourcing to add flexibility to their product delivery system. The central organization contracts with outside vendors to provide certain products and services that are essential to its product delivery system. Although these vendors are independent of the central organization, they are typically highly committed to the core firm.

BMW is an example of a company that has adopted a stable network structure. Somewhere between 55 and 75 percent of BMW's production comes from outsourcing. Partnerships with vendors serve a critical function in the company's product delivery system. Although BMW does not own its vendor firms outright (as GM does), it does maintain stable relationships with them and may even make a financial investment in these organizations where appropriate.[27]

A **dynamic network** differs from internal and stable networks in that organizations with this structure make extensive use of outsourcing to support their operations. Partnerships with vendors are less frequent, and less emphasis is placed on finding organizations to service the central organization only.

Internal network
A network structure that relies on internally developed units to provide services to a core organizational unit.

Stable network
A network structure that utilizes external alliances selectively as a mechanism for gaining strategic flexibility.

Dynamic network
A network structure that makes extensive use of outsourcing through alliances with outside organizations.

ENTREPRENEURIAL APPROACH

LEWIS GALOOB: A DYNAMIC NETWORK

Lewis Galoob Toys is one of the few privately held toy companies left in an industry that is dominated by such kingpins as Hasbro and Mattel. Its uniqueness is not limited to its ownership structure, however. Lewis Galoob is unique in other ways as well.

The survival and success of this company are based largely on its unique organizational structure—a dynamic network. A few more than 100 employees run the entire operation. Independent inventors and entertainment companies create the products, and outside specialists design and engineer them. Manufacturing and packaging are contracted through vendors in Hong Kong who pass the labor-intensive portions on to factories in China. When the toys arrive in the United States, they are sold and distributed by commissioned manufacturing representatives. Finally, Commercial Credit Corporation acts as the collector of receivables for Galoob. Galoob is the chief broker for many specialists involved in creating its products.

In the words of Robert Galoob, "Our business is one of relationships."

Typically, the central organization focuses on some core skill and contracts for most other functions. For example, Motorola capitalizes on its manufacturing strengths, Reebok on its design strength, and Dell Computer on its design and assembly strengths; in each case, the company prefers to outsource most other aspects of its product delivery system.[28] Entrepreneurial Approach describes how Lewis Galoob Toys managed to capture a significant share of the toy market by developing a dynamic network structure in which it performs only a brokering or coordinating function and contracts out all other aspects of its business.[29]

A number of advantages and disadvantages are associated with the network structure (see Table 9.1).[30] The effectiveness and efficiency of the core unit are maximized by the use of a network structure. The organization can do more with less because it is using others' resources. Flexibility is an inherent benefit of this organizational form, because the core unit can change vendors quickly should product changes be necessary. Many international firms have found that the network structure provides them with the speed and flexibility necessary to compete effectively in highly competitive global markets.[31] In fact, some multinationals are abandoning the matrix structure in favor of the more adaptable network form.[32]

The primary disadvantage of a network structure is that because operations are fragmented, it may be difficult to develop a control system that effectively monitors all aspects of the product delivery system.[33] Consequently, comprehensive quality management programs may be more difficult to implement effectively.

It is not uncommon for an organization to use some type of network structure to get into a specific market very quickly and then adopt a more traditional structure later. IBM, for example, utilized a dynamic network structure to enter the personal computer market. Lagging the competition in this market, IBM assembled a network of suppliers, designers, and marketers to bring its product to market very quickly. Once the company had established itself in the personal computer arena, it reintegrated many of these functions into its central operating system.[34]

We have examined the four basic types of structures that are commonly used in organizations today. These structures define how the work groups of the

ASSESSING ORGANIZATIONAL STRUCTURE

MEETING
THE CHALLENGE

Select an organization for which you can develop an organizational chart (e.g., a business, university, church, social organization, student organization). Develop an organizational chart that shows how the organization is departmentalized. Then answer the following questions about its structure:

- Is the structure consistent with the strategy of the organization?
- Are the work units grouped according to the aspect of the organization that presents the greatest complexity (e.g., task/function, products, geographic market)?
- Would another organizational structure make more sense than the existing structure? If so, why?

organization are structured and specify reporting relationship within the organizational hierarchy. Meeting the Challenge gives you an opportunity to assess the organizational structure of an organization with which you are familiar. Take some time to work through that exercise before moving on to learn about the second component of organizational design—integrating mechanisms.

MANAGING COMPLEXITY THROUGH INTEGRATION

Integrating the activities of an organization involves controlling and coordinating the flow of information, resources, and tasks among organizational members and work groups. Whereas structure serves to segregate organizational members into different work units, the goal of the integration component of organizational design is to coordinate the work of these distinct groups. An organization's many and diverse work groups are linked together through integrating mechanisms. As we will soon learn, integrating mechanisms include such things as management information systems, liaison personnel, and interfunctional work teams.

The complexity of an organization's operations will affect its need for integration. For example, a purely domestic firm with a narrow product line and a single manufacturing facility will find the integration of its work groups to be more manageable than a multinational corporation with broad product lines and manufacturing facilities spread across the globe. In general, the more complex an organization's operations, the more sophisticated its coordinating mechanisms must be.

In general, an organization's integration needs will vary with the level of interdependence that exists among work groups.[35] In organizations where work groups must closely coordinate their activities to achieve organizational goals, integration needs will be high. In contrast, where work groups exist relatively independently and without significant interaction, integration needs are low. Before we discuss specific integrating mechanisms that might be used to coordinate the activities of an organization, let's examine the various levels of interdependence that may exist in an organization and how that interdependence affects its integration needs.

Interdependence and Integration Needs
Central to the discussion of integration is the concept of interdependence. **Interdependence** refers to the degree to which work groups are interrelated and the extent to which they depend upon one another to complete their work. The level of interdependence between work groups will affect the need

Interdependence
The degree to which work groups are interrelated.

▼ **FIGURE 9.7**
Levels of Work Unit interdependence

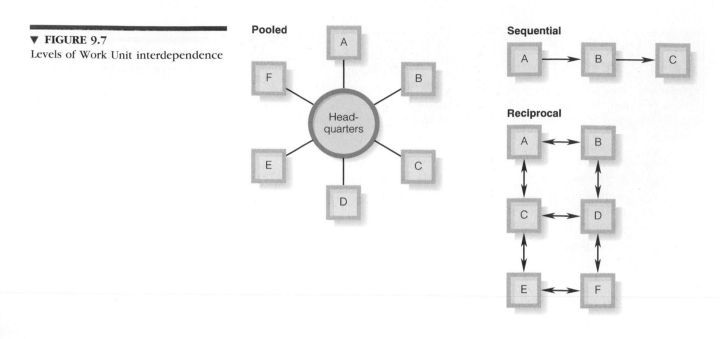

for integrating mechanisms.[36] Figure 9.7 illustrates the three primary levels of work group interdependence, and the following discussion describes each in greater detail.

Pooled interdependence
Occurs when organizational units have a common resource but no interrelationship with one another.

Pooled Interdependence   **Pooled interdependence** occurs when organizational units have a common source of resources, but have no interrelationship with one another. Consider, for example, a local bank with branch offices spread around the city. Though all branches must coordinate their efforts with the central office, they have very limited interaction with one another. They have little need to cooperate and coordinate with one another to achieve their goals. Managers work independently to achieve the goals of their own work group, which, in turn, contributes to the overall performance of the organization.

Sequential interdependence
Occurs when organizational units must coordinate the flow of information, resources, and tasks from one unit to another.

Sequential Interdependence   **Sequential interdependence** exists when work groups must coordinate the flow of information, resources, or tasks from one unit to another. Sequential interdependence is associated with a typical manu-

▼ Many manufacturing plants experience sequential interdependence in their assembly processes. At this automobile manufacturing plant, workers assume responsibility for a certain aspect of the assembly process. As the automobile travels down the assembly line, employees perform a specific task. Each employee depends on the worker ahead of him on the assembly line to complete his or her task effectively and efficiently.

▼ The student registration process at most universities provides an excellent example of reciprocal interdependence. Different units within the university system must coordinate the processing of the students' records so that they can be registered in a timely fashion.

facturing assembly line. The output of one unit becomes the input for another unit. Organizations with sequentially interdependent units have greater coordination needs than organizations with units that have pooled interdependence.

Reciprocal Interdependence   **Reciprocal interdependence** represents the greatest level of interrelatedness between work groups in that work is passed back and forth between work units. The final product requires the input of a number of different departments at varying times during the production process. Consider a university system, where students' registration materials must be shuffled from one administrative unit to another and back. These work groups are interrelated, and the effective functioning of the system requires a high level of integration between the groups.

The higher the level of interdependence of an organization's work groups, the greater its needs for coordination. The sophistication of an integrating system should be in alignment with its specific coordination needs. For example, an organization with pooled interdependence between its work groups may be able to function effectively with a few, relatively simple integrating mechanisms. In contrast, an organization with reciprocal interdependence between work groups will require more sophisticated integrating mechanisms.

Integrating mechanisms are not without costs. As we will discuss, many of the tools for coordinating the activities of the organization have human or financial costs that are tangible and measurable. Therefore, organizations must carefully evaluate their coordination needs so that they can develop integrating mechanisms that are cost-effective and in line with those needs.

Integrating Mechanisms

At the foundation of an organization's ability to coordinate the activities of its subunits is its information processing capacity. Effective coordination is dependent upon the flow of information between the individual units of the organization so that work can be scheduled, resources shared and transferred, and conflicting objectives resolved. Toward this end, organizations develop integrating mechanisms that enhance their information processing capacity and support their need for coordination. **Integrating mechanisms** are methods for managing the flow of information, resources, and tasks throughout the organization.

Many different mechanisms can be used to process information and coordinate the activities of interdependent work units. Some of these mechanisms are characteristic of general management systems. Others are developed

Reciprocal interdependence
Occurs when information, resources, and tasks must be passed back and forth between work groups.

Integrating mechanisms
Methods for managing the flow of information, resources, and tasks within the organization.

▼ **FIGURE 9.8**
Integrating Mechanisms

SOURCE: Adapted from J. R. Galbraith, "Organizational Design: An Information Processing View," *Interfaces* 4 (May 1974): 3.

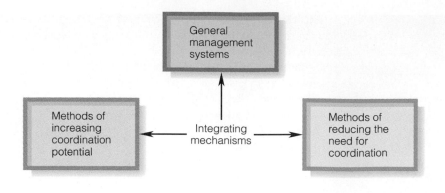

specifically to increase the coordination potential of the organization. Still others are designed to reduce the organization's need for coordination. Figure 9.8 illustrates the three major categories of integrating mechanisms, each of which is discussed below.[37]

General Management Systems   Some coordination of work units may be achieved through the development of general management systems such as the managerial hierarchy, basic rules and procedures, and plans and goals. Such mechanisms form the foundation of an organization's integration system.

As we have discussed, an organization's managerial hierarchy is established by its organizational structure. Recall that organizational structure defines work groups on the basis of the task characteristic that presents the greatest source of diversity (i.e., function, product, geographic, market, customer). By grouping organizational members in this fashion, coordination within the groups is enhanced.

Similarly, most organizations develop basic rules and procedures that govern the behavior of their members. Organizations that make extensive use of rules and procedures are often thought to be bureaucratic, highly formalized, and closely governed. In contrast, organizations that use fewer rules and procedures are considered to be more flexible, less formal, and participatory in nature.

Most universities make extensive use of rules and procedures to coordinate the activities of their colleges and departments. Student records must be processed according to specific guidelines; overrides into classes must be handled systematically; and parking tickets and overdue library books must be dealt with before the registration process can be completed. These rules and procedures are mechanisms that ensure that the activities of the various units of the university are well coordinated.

The development of plans and goals can also serve as a means of integrating the operations of an organization. Plans that require implementation by multiple work groups provide a foundation for action by those units. A well-developed business plan will detail the activities of specific departments within an organization, thereby providing guidance about how those activities are to be coordinated. Similarly, certain behaviors are implied by specific achievement-based goals.

Quality management programs serve as an excellent integrating mechanism for many companies. The plans that result from such programs provide a foundation for integrating and coordinating the activities of diverse groups toward common quality-oriented goals.

Increasing Coordination Potential   For most organizations, general management systems do not provide sufficient coordination potential. Additional integrating mechanisms are needed to coordinate the organization's activities effectively.

Information systems and lateral relationships are two of the most common mechanisms for increasing coordination potential both vertically and horizontally within the organization.

Information systems facilitate the flow of information up and down the traditional chain of command and across organizational units. Management information systems have become increasingly important mechanisms for increasing coordination potential in recent years. The computerized transfer of important information and data provides a powerful tool for coordinating diverse departments or operating units.[38]

Many multinational corporations have developed sophisticated management information systems to support their global operations. With the advent of more sophisticated and affordable computer technology, decision-making data can be transmitted almost simultaneously from division to division around the globe. Computer and telecommunication networks provide the infrastructure for coordinating operations on a worldwide scale. Electronic mail, teleconferencing, and high-speed data systems are a few of the mechanisms used by multinational companies.

For example, managers at Digital Equipment Corporation have developed a formalized system for quickly accessing "expertise" around the globe. A general query sent out on DEC's electronic mail system can solicit a timely response from the people in the organization with the greatest knowledge on the matter. DEC vice president of international engineering, David Stone, commented, "Instead of calling somebody on the telephone for information and having him call other people, who in turn call more people, which can take days or weeks, I can send out a request and have a report back in 24 hours."[39] Global Perspective illustrates how Royal/Dutch Shell has utilized information technology to coordinate its activities and enhance its worldwide performance.

The second important method for increasing coordination potential is to establish lateral relationships. Such relationships exist across horizontal work units and serve as mechanisms for exchanging decision-making information. In general, lateral relationships can be thought of as **boundary-spanning roles.** The primary purpose of the boundary-spanning function is to develop an understanding of the activities of units outside the boundaries of one's own work group. Such knowledge helps employees and work groups understand how their actions and performance affect others within the organization, as well as the organization as a whole.

The boundary-spanning function can be served through a number of different relationships that vary in formality and level of commitment to the coordinating function. Integrating relationships include liaisons, committees and task forces, and integrating positions and interfunctional work teams.

When two or more work units have a recurring need to communicate with each other, it may be beneficial to establish a *liaison* position to support their communication needs. People who occupy such positions retain their association with their primary unit, but also assume responsibility for interacting with other work groups. For example, the marketing department of an organization might identify an individual to act as a formal liaison with the company's engineering department. Although this individual remains in his marketing role, he also serves as the primary contact point for the interaction between the marketing department and the engineering department.

Boundary-spanning roles
Lateral relationships that help to integrate and coordinate the activities of the organization (i.e., liaisons, committees, task forces, integrating positions, and interfunctional work teams).

▼ This interfunctional work team provides an important method of integration for this financial services company. By meeting regularly to coordinate their activities, these managers ensure that the company's customers get the best possible service.

**GLOBAL
PERSPECTIVE**

USING INFORMATION TECHNOLOGY FOR INTERNATIONAL BUSINESS

Management information systems provide an excellent mechanism for improving coordination in many organizations. Royal Dutch/Shell Group is an example of a company that has found information technology to be the key to developing an integrated global strategy.

At one time, Dutch/Shell consisted of several hundred, virtually autonomous companies located across the globe. Its original strategy was to have all operating subsidiaries purchase their supplies from local vendors, provide their products to the local market only, and stay in concert with the local political and cultural situation.

Today, all that has changed. Faced with unpredictable oil prices and intense competition, Dutch/Shell has enhanced its effectiveness through better coordination of its units around the world. To a large extent, this has been accomplished through the development of a multibillion dollar management information system. The system supplies local managers with up-to-date information on oil prices, currency fluctuations, management expertise, and resource availability across the globe.

Some argue that the system has some negative side effects. Most notably, some managers feel that information is *too* readily available. Information that was previously available to only the top cadre of managers is now available at multiple levels of the organization. Such openness initially made Dutch/Shell's conservative upper echelon uneasy.

Regardless of any disadvantages associated with the enhanced communication structure, top management is committed to the system. Organizational performance is improving—despite some loss of formal control.

When the effective management of multiple interdependent units is critical to the success of the organization, it may be appropriate to establish a *committee* (permanent group) or a *task force* (temporary group) to facilitate communication between the groups. The committee or task force would be made up of representatives from each of the work groups involved. As was the case with the formal liaison position, the committee or task force assignment is only a part of each representative's job—their primary job responsibilities remain with the unit they represent.[40] Multinational corporations, for example, often use committees or councils comprised of corporate executives and representatives from both their domestic and foreign subsidiaries. This council assumes responsibility for both assimilating and disseminating critical information needed by the operating units of the company.

When an organization has very high integration needs, it may become necessary to establish a standing *integrating position* or *interfunctional work teams*. The primary responsibility of individuals serving in integrating positions is to facilitate communication between work groups. Such individuals do not represent a specific operating unit and thus are not formally associated with any of the work groups with which they work. Their full-time work responsibilities are associated with managing the interdependence between work units. Interfunctional work teams are a more radical approach to integration in that members from various functional groups are permanently assigned to a team that is given responsibility for completing a particular set of tasks (see the discussion of self-managed teams in Chapters 1 and 8).

▼ This control room of a dry process cement company demonstrates how information technology can be used to improve the coordination of multiple units within an organization. The technology in this room monitors activities throughout the plant.

Although integrating mechanisms designed to increase coordination potential can be quite costly, they may be warranted when strategic effectiveness requires close coordination and cooperation between organizational subunits. IBM, for example, has established interfunctional work teams that focus on issues of product and service quality throughout the organizational system.[41] These teams provide the integration and coordination necessary to support IBM's efforts to improve quality.

Philip Morris has developed formal lateral relationships in an effort to integrate the activities of its various subunits more effectively. Through an extensive network of committees, task forces, and other lateral associations, this company has developed a sophisticated information processing system that supports its strategic and operational goals.

Reducing the Need for Coordination   The third and final method of integration is to reduce or eliminate the need for coordination between work groups. In essence, the organization creates "slack resources" that reduce the interdependence of the work groups and, as a result, the need for integrating mechanisms. For example, the organization might establish longer lead times for sequentially interdependent work to be completed or maintain larger inventories of work in progress. Both measures would reduce the need for tight coordination between units. Although this is an effective way to reduce the need for coordination, it is not necessarily the most efficient. Creating slack resources in this way is inconsistent with recent trends toward quality management and improved productivity and efficiency. As a result, such a practice may lead to suboptimal organizational performance.

Another way organizations can reduce the need for coordination is to create work units that have only pooled interdependence. By doing so, the need for integration is minimized. One benefit of interfunctional work teams is that work groups are relatively independent, thereby reducing the need for integration between diverse functional units. However, forming interfunctional teams simply to reduce integration needs may not be appropriate if it results in redundant resource utilization. In general, independent units should be formed only when there are other strategic reasons to do so.

Matching Integrating Mechanisms with Coordination Needs

As mentioned previously, integrating mechanisms have costs. The hardware and software support for management information systems have very tangible costs. So do the personnel who must manage the information system. Integrating positions have clearly identifiable costs as well. While not as easily measured, the management time and energy that go into developing effective management systems (managerial hierarchy, rules and procedures, plans and goals) and acting in lateral relationship roles (liaisons, committees and task forces, integrating positions) also have costs. Therefore, it is important for an organization to develop a cost-effective integration system that satisfies its coordination needs while minimizing the financial and managerial resources required to maintain the system.

Managing for Excellence describes how one company, Mearthane Products, designed its organization and integration system to improve performance. A sophisticated computer system and a comprehensive quality management program provided the foundation for communication and coordination throughout the organization. In fact, this system enabled Mearthane Products to be certified as one of the 110 "Team Xerox" suppliers.[42]

LOCUS OF DECISION MAKING

Locus of decision making
The degree to which decision making is centralized versus decentralized.

The third component of organizational design involves the locus of decision making within the organization. Essentially, **locus of decision making** refers to whether the organization's decision making is centralized or decentralized. This may be determined by examining how decision-making authority is divided between corporate headquarters and the operating units or between top management of an operating unit and the departmental work groups.[43]

If, for example, an organization's decision-making authority rests with corporate headquarters or the top levels of management of an operating facility, its organizational design is centralized. An organization that maintains its locus of decision making at lower levels (i.e., subsidiary or departmental level) is decentralized. IBM's plan to restructure into autonomous operating units, for example, was an attempt to decentralize by pushing decision-making authority down to the lower levels of the organizational hierarchy.

It is helpful to think of centralized and decentralized decision making as two ends of a continuum. Most organizations' locus of decision making will fall somewhere between those two extremes. In addition, the locus of decision making in most organizations is mixed, with decisions in some areas (e.g., finance) being relatively centralized, while decisions in other areas (e.g., marketing) may be relatively decentralized.

Centralized versus Decentralized Decision Making

Certain advantages and disadvantages are associated with both centralized and decentralized decision making. Their respective advantages and disadvantages are nearly mirror images of each other.

In general, centralized decision making gives top management more control than does decentralized decision making. This may be appropriate when work groups are highly interdependent or when maximizing the efficient use of resources is essential to the success of the organization. The primary disadvantage of centralized decision making is that it may limit the organization's ability to respond quickly and effectively to changes in its environment.

In contrast, the primary advantage of decentralized decision making is that organizations can respond to environmental changes more rapidly and effectively when decisions are being made by the people closest to the situation.[44]

MEARTHANE PRODUCTS: TOPPING JAPANESE QUALITY

In the 1960s the challenge for Mearthane Products Corporation was to expand its line, originally polyurethane shoe soles and heels. Mearthane, which is based in Cranston, Rhode Island, developed such products as the first polyurethane feed roller for office copiers and self-lubricating valve seals for nuclear submarines. The 1970s brought a new challenge—how to manage the company's technology for continued growth. Proper planning and hands-on management by objective helped Mearthane become a $4 million a year operation. Today, Mearthane's sales top $10 million. They have reached that level because the firm, through the 1980s and into this decade, struggled to meet a third challenge: equaling or topping the quality of its Asian competitors' products.

Mearthane had a 10-year goal of remaking itself so that a major customer, Xerox Corporation, would certify it as one of 110 "Team Xerox" suppliers, chosen from a field of 5000 worldwide. Mearthane's improvements also helped it with other customers such as IBM, Eastman Kodak, and Pitney Bowes. The changes included the following:

- English-as-a-second-language training was started. Mearthane, the epitome of the American melting pot, has many employees whose native language is Portuguese, Spanish, French, Russian, or an Asian tongue, Communication is better now.

- Just-in-time manufacturing became a watchword. Purchasing was changed drastically so the company could order and get deliveries when needed, avoiding the cost of holding inventory for long periods.

- Computerizing, the company adopted a manufacturing resource planning philosophy and linked every facet of the business, from order entry to financial planning, in one system.

- Mearthane launched a $100,000 total quality management training program. All personnel, from the CEO's office to the shop floor, were retrained in communicating and facilitating so the company could achieve world-class quality. All of the company's 150 employees learned how the details of their work could affect customer satisfaction.

- The company paid for outside education for numerous employees. Lab technicians pursued chemistry degrees; people in the company's manufacturing group studied for business administration degrees or certification by the American Production and Inventory Control Society.

Such efforts have helped Mearthane stay technologically competitive. And last December Mearthane was certified as one of those 110 Team Xerox suppliers worldwide.

In addition, many proponents of quality management would argue that the individuals who are closest to the customers and suppliers are best prepared to make many decisions. Coordination between units may be hindered by decentralized decision making, however, and achieving efficiency through standardization may be more difficult to accomplish. Further, the growing diversity of the workforce has increased the variance in decision-making styles.

Organizations must determine their locus of decision making in light of the advantages they seek, as well as the specific strategic and operational conditions they face. There are many examples of firms that have used each form of decision making very successfully. Consider, for example, Apple Computer.

A shift to a more centralized organizational design rescued Apple when it was floundering in the mid-1980s. John Sculley, who replaced Steven Jobs as the CEO of Apple, concluded that the decentralized system of the past had resulted in organizational inefficiencies that were unacceptable in an industry that had become highly competitive and, to a significant degree, efficiency driven. As a result, Sculley decided to centralize decision making, consolidate manufacturing facilities, reduce overhead by eliminating redundant activities among work units, and adopt a more consistent marketing focus across product lines. These efforts to centralize and standardize the company's activities enabled Apple to increase its efficiency and regain its position as an industry leader. By the late 1980s, Apple was enjoying a sales growth rate twice that of the industry, and profit margins that tripled since Sculley had taken the helm.[45] Of course, today, Michael Spindler has taken over as CEO of Apple, and his decision-making style is clearly different from both Jobs's and Sculley's.

In contrast to Apple, consider Nestlé. This Swiss company employs a highly decentralized decision-making system in support of its efforts to penetrate the international marketplace. The company's on-the-spot geographic managers are allowed to make all decisions with respect to production, administration, marketing, and pricing of the company's food products within their geographic market. As a consequence, Nestlé has been able to respond proactively and effectively to changes in its local markets.[46]

Mechanistic versus Organic Systems

An organization's locus of decision making will determine the extent to which it is mechanistic or organic.[47] This typology, originally advanced by Tom Burns and Gene Stalker, describes organizations according to the level of centralization or decentralization in their decision-making process.

Mechanistic systems

Highly centralized organizations in which decision-making authority rests with top management.

Mechanistic systems are associated with highly centralized organizations where decision-making authority rests with the top levels of management. Tasks are highly specialized, and work procedures are governed by detailed rules and guidelines. Interorganizational communication flows primarily from superior to subordinate, and hierarchical relationships serve as the foundation for authority, responsibility, and control. Mechanistic systems are usually designed to maximize specialization and improve efficiency. However, organizations with this design many find it difficult to respond quickly and effectively to changes that affect their operations.

Organic systems

Decentralized organizations that push decision making to the lowest levels of the organization in an effort to respond more effectively to environmental change.

Organic systems, in contrast, are designed to enhance an organization's ability to respond to environmental change by decentralizing decision making to those in the organization who are closer to customers, suppliers, and other external constituents. Organizational members are not only permitted to participate in decision making, but are encouraged to do so. Tasks are often broader and are more interdependent than in mechanistic systems. Rules and guidelines are far less prevalent and may exist only to provide the parameters within which organizational members can make decisions. The patterns of communication are far more intricate, and horizontal communication is common. While a vertical hierarchy typically exists, extensive use of teams and other lateral relationships facilitates communication and decision making across vertical lines. An organic system may be less efficient than a mechanistic system, however.

Experiential Exercise 9.2 provides an assessment instrument that can be used to evaluate the degree which an organization demonstrates mechanistic versus organic characteristics. Think of an organization with which you have been associated. How does it rate according to this assessment instrument?

The Impact of Environmental Stability

Which system is better—the mechanistic system that enhances efficiency or the organic system that enhances responsiveness? There is no simple answer to that question. The most effective system for any organization will vary as a function of the specific circumstances that the organization faces. More specifically, the stability of the environment in which the organization operates will have a significant impact on the effectiveness of either system.

The external environment for any given organization can be characterized along a continuum ranging from stable to turbulent. In general, **stable environments** experience relatively little change, or the change is of low impact to the organization. Product life cycles are long and enduring; marketing strategies remain relatively constant; and economic and political factors have little influence on the strategic or operational aspects of the firm. Competitive pressures are manageable and changes in buyers' needs are minimal. Although few industries would fit this description, some organizations do face relatively stable environments. For example, manufacturers of staple items such as detergent, cleaning supplies, and paper products enjoy relatively stable environmental conditions.

Turbulent environments, in contrast, are characterized by rapid and significant change. An organization that faces turbulent environmental conditions must cope with shorter decision windows, changing buyer patterns, fragmented markets, greater risk of resource and product obsolescence, and a general lack of long-term control.[48] Such conditions intensify the pressure for organizations to respond effectively to change. IBM, for example, faces a relatively turbulent environment where technological change creates competitive pressures for all industry players. The key to success in such an environment lies in developing an organizational design that allows managers to identify and respond to the opportunities and threats facing the organization.

In general, organizations that operate in stable external environments find the mechanistic system to be advantageous. This system provides a level of efficiency that enhances the long-term performance of organizations that enjoy relatively stable operating environments. In contrast, organizations that operate in volatile and frequently changing environments are more likely to find that an organic system provides the greatest benefits. This system allows the organization to respond to environmental change more proactively.

ORGANIZATIONAL DESIGN FOR A CHANGING ENVIRONMENT

While many organizations have been coping with changing environmental conditions and intense competition for decades, others are just beginning to feel the effects of escalating rates of technological change and an increasingly competitive global marketplace. Such business conditions will continue to affect a wide variety of organizations and industries in the future. As this occurs, organizations will continue to seek innovative organizational designs to cope with the challenges of the business environment.

Although most organizations will maintain traditional hierarchical structures to some degree, many will increasingly make use of alliances among people and organizations. Surrounding the conventional chain of command will be a complex network of committees, task forces, interfunctional teams, partnerships, and other informal relationships that will provide a forum for creativity and innovation. As Raymond Gilmartin, CEO of the high-tech medical equipment manufacturer Becton Dickinson, says, "Forget structures invented by the guys at the top. You've got to let the task form the organization."[49]

This new model of organizational design goes by a number of names— Two of the most common are the **adaptive organization** or the **horizontal corporation**.[50] The purpose of this design is to reduce the bureaucracy that stifles employee creativity and puts an unacceptable distance between the customer and the decision makers in the organization. Such organizations will pull

Stable environments
Environments which experience little change.

Turbulent environments
Environments which are characterized by rapid and significant change.

Adaptive organizations (horizontal corporation)
Organizations that eliminate bureaucracy that limits employee creativity and brings the decision makers of the organization closer to the customer.

▼ **Table 9.2**   McKinsey's 10-Point Plan for Developing an Adaptive Organization

- Organize primarily around process, not task.
- Flatten the hierarchy by minimizing subdivision of processes.
- Give senior leaders responsibility for processes and process performance.
- Link performance objectives and evaluation of all activities to customer satisfaction.
- Make teams, not individuals, the focus of organization performance and design.
- Combine managerial and non-managerial activities as often as possible.
- Emphasize that each employee should develop several competencies.
- Inform and train people on a just-in-time, need-to-perform basis.
- Maximize supplier and customer contact with everyone in the organization.
- Reward individual skill development and team performance instead of individual performance alone.

out all the stops to capitalize on their human resources, develop partnerships with other organizations with common objectives, and let the needs of the customer drive the actions of the organization. Doing this effectively may be the key to success for the organization of the future. Table 9.2 describes McKinsey & Co.'s 10-point blueprint for developing an organizational design that is appropriate for the organization of the future.

MANAGERIAL IMPLICATIONS

The manager of tomorrow must be aware of the importance of organizational design to the long-term performance of his or her company. The increasing availability and sophistication of technology will change the way organizations are designed and coordinated. Further, the ever increasing demands for quality will create additional pressures for achieving maximum efficiency and effectiveness in every aspect of an organization's operations. And as more and more industries globalize, organizations will be faced with the challenge of coordinating their efforts across different nations and among diverse people. In preparing to meet these challenges, managers must:

- Remember that organizational design provides an important mechanism for achieving the strategic and operational goals of the organization.
- Structure their organizations to cope with the source of greatest complexity.
- Consider ways partnerships between members of the organization, as well as alliances with other organizations, can create synergy and improve organizational performance.
- Look for ways to increase the integration potential of the organization or to reduce the need for integration.
- Evaluate the advantages and disadvantages associated with centralized versus decentralized decision making given the specific circumstances of the organization.
- Strive to develop an adaptive organization that is prepared to meet the challenges of the twenty-first century.

Managers must create an organizational design that is adaptable, flexible, and supportive of the strategy of their organizations. Doing so will be one of the major challenges of the twenty-first century.

BIG BLUE: DEVELOPING AN ORGANIZATIONAL DESIGN THAT WORKS

Top management at IBM faced significant challenges as they prepared to re-design their organizational system. Yet, given the changes in the competitive structure of the computer industry, it seemed imperative for the company to realign the components of its organizational design.

IBM began by reducing its workforce by more than 20,000 people. While layoffs were avoided, the company offered buyout packages and early retire-ment to middle managers throughout the organization. In addition, IBM de-veloped six independent and highly autonomous business units that were based on its primary product lines. This new structure provided the strong product focus that management felt was essential for success. Further, in an attempt to decentralize decision making, top management gave these product divisions significant latitude with respect to their strategic and operational ac-tivities. Along with this increased decision-making authority came the associ-ated accountability. Each division is responsible for producing its own financial statements at year-end and is evaluated on the basis of its individual performance.

IBM, according to Sam Albert, a computer industry consultant and former IBM executive, "is very creatively and judiciously looking for anything and everything to eliminate bureaucracy to speed up the process and to do things on economy of scale." The jury is still out on whether these organizational changes will make a long-term difference in IBM's performance, but 1993's financial picture was somewhat improved. Although sales were still down slightly, total profits remained stable, suggesting that the difficult decline ex-perienced in 1991 and 1992 may have come to an end. Further, top manage-ment appears committed to doing whatever it takes to ensure the company's success for many years into the future.[51] ▼

SUMMARY

- Organizing is an important managerial function that leads to the develop-ment of organizational design. An organization's design serves as a mecha-nism for managing its tasks, functions, products, markets, and technologies effectively.

- Organizational design determines the configuration of organizational mem-bers (structure); the flow of information, resources, and/or tasks throughout the organizational system (integration); and the centralization or decentrali-zation of decision-making authority (locus of decision making).

- Organizations structure their activities by grouping certain tasks and respon-sibilities into work units. The four primary forms found in organizations today are functional, divisional, matrix, and network structures. Certain stra-tegic conditions imply certain organizational structures. In general, organi-zations should employ a structure that enables them to cope with their greatest source of complexity (e.g., function, product diversity, geographic market diversity).

- Integrating mechanisms help to coordinate the flow of information, re-sources, and tasks between work groups. The level of interdependence be-tween the subunits of an organization will determine, to a large degree, the organization's need for integrating mechanisms. Integrating mechanisms in-clude general management systems (managerial hierarchy, rules and proce-dures, plans and goals), methods for increasing coordination potential (information systems and lateral relationships), and methods for reducing the need for coordination (creation of slack resources and independent work units).

- The extent to which an organization centralizes or decentralizes decision-making authority will determine its locus of decision making. While centralized decision making facilitates control and enhances organizational efficiency, decentralized decision making provides for faster and more effective responses to change.

- An organization can be described as mechanistic or organic depending on its locus of decision making. Mechanistic systems maintain a centralized locus of decision making and are most suitable for organizations that operate in mature, stable environments. Organic systems maintain a decentralized locus of decision making and are most appropriate for firms operating in dynamic, rapidly changing environments.

- Many organizations will implement an adaptive organizational design in the future. Adaptive organizations rely on teams, lateral relationships, and alliances to supplement the traditional hierarchy. This network of relationships is designed to foster creativity and support proactive responses to environmental changes that affect the organization.

KEY TERMS

Organizational design (p. 285)
Organization structure (p. 285)
Functional structure (p. 286)
Divisional structure (p. 287)
Product divisional structure (p. 288)
Geographic divisional structure
   (p. 289)
Customer divisional structure
   (p. 290)

Matrix structure (p. 291)
Network structure (p. 292)
Internal network (p. 293)
Stable network (p. 293)
Dynamic network (p. 293)
Interdependence (p. 295)
Pooled interdependence (p. 296)
Sequential interdependence (p. 296)
Reciprocal interdependence (p. 297)

Integrating mechanisms (p. 297)
Boundary-spanning roles (p. 299)
Locus of decision making (p. 302)
Mechanistic systems (p. 304)
Organic systems (p. 304)
Stable environments (p. 305)
Turbulent environments (p. 305)
Adaptive organizations (horizontal
   corporation) (p. 305)

REVIEW QUESTIONS

1. What is organizational design? Why is it important for an organization to develop an effective design?

2. What are the three primary components of organizational design?

3. Identify and describe each of the four types of organizational structure discussed in the chapter.

4. How does interdependence affect the need for coordination and integration?

5. Outline the three major categories of integrating mechanisms.

6. Explain the concept of locus of decision making. Under what strategic conditions would a centralized locus of decision making be appropriate? A decentralized locus of decision making?

7. What are the differences between mechanistic and organic organizational systems? What effect would the environment have on an organization's choice of a mechanistic versus an organic system?

8. How is organizational design likely to change in the future?

DISCUSSION QUESTIONS

Improving Critical Thinking

1. How might the organizational design of research and development firm in the pharmaceutical industry differ from the organizational design of a consumer food products manufacturer?

2. Consider the organization you currently work for or one that you worked for in the past. Would you characterize that organization as centralized or de-

centralized? What are the advantages and disadvantages associated with the locus of decision making in that organization? If you had the power to change the locus of decision making in that organization, what would you do?

Enhancing Communication Skills

3. Suppose the dean of the College of Business Administration hired you to coordinate the efforts of five different student organizations, each of which was affiliated with a different functional department within the college. What integrating mechanisms might you use? To practice your oral communication skills, make a brief presentation of your ideas to the class.

4. Develop a plan to redesign an organization with which you are familiar using McKinsey & Co.'s blue-

print for developing an adaptive organizational design (see Table 9.2). Develop a written draft of the plan for your instructor to review.

Building Teamwork Skills

5. Think of several different businesses that might be started on your campus to serve the needs of students. Select one of those business concepts and, with a team of students, discuss how that business might be developed using a dynamic network system.

6. With a group of fellow students, identify a set of organizations that maintains relatively mechanistic organizational systems. Also develop a list of organizations that are more organic. Share your lists with the class, as well as your rationale for classifying these organizations as you did.

ETHICS: TAKE A STAND

At Dobbs Electronics Manufacturing Company there is an important need for open communication between the Production Department and the Sales Department. The success of the sales people often depend on whether they can promise timely shipment to their customers, and the Production Department has to be able to fulfill those promises. To be competitive in the industry, Dobbs's sales representatives frequently promise customers earlier shipping dates than the Production Department can comfortably meet. In the past, the Production Department has attempted to meet these earlier dates, even though it meant rushing jobs, working overtime, and reducing machine down time for scheduled maintenance. Production has tired of the situation, however. The relationship between the two departments has deteriorated dramatically in recent months and, at this point, communication between the groups has literally come to a halt.

The top management at Dobbs has recognized the problem and knows that they need to take steps to reestablish the communication channels between the two groups. They decided to appoint a formal liaison for both departments. These liaisons will meet and set reasonable production/sales schedules that will work for both departments and will be in the best interest of the organization as a whole.

Tom Short, who has been appointed the liaison for the Production Department, is faced with a tough situation. The manager of production, with the support of most of the employees within the department, has insisted that Tom add three weeks to the production schedule he negotiates with the Sales Department. While everyone in production knows they could deliver the product in a much shorter time frame, they are determined to allow more than enough time to complete their tasks. In addition, some members of the group feel strongly that the department should "show those guys in sales that we won't be pushed around."

Tim is very uncomfortable about this situation. He feels as though his department is pressuring him to lie to his counterpart in the Sales Department. To complicate things further, Tom believes that to delay the production schedule would not be in the best interest of the company as a whole. Yet, if he doesn't comply with the wishes of his department, he stands to be heavily criticized by both his boss and his peers.

For Discussion

1. How would you feel if you were in Tom's situation?

2. What actions would you recommend for Tom?

3. Can you think of other organizational relationships or situations that might lead to similar problems?

THINKING CRITICALLY
Debate the Issue

Form teams of four to five students. Half of the teams should prepare to argue the benefits of a dynamic network structure. The other half of the teams should prepare to argue the disadvantages of such a structure. Where possible, identify companies that have adopted a dynamic network structure and assess their performance as related to this structural form. Choose two teams to present their arguments in a debate format.

VIDEO CASE

AT&T's Microelectronics

 Communications giant AT&T reorganized the top job at its Microelectronics Division. The division, headquartered in Berkeley Heights, New Jersey, had had a conventional product divisional structure, with six divisional vice presidents reporting to the president.

The top level at AT&T's Microelectronics was changed to the Office of the President. Two individuals—Bill Warwick and Curtis Crawford—share power and responsibility, acting as co-presidents. Warwick is directly responsible for three Integrated Circuit businesses, and Crawford is responsible for the three Systems and Technology businesses.

The goal of this shared work load is to provide greater customer service by making Warwick and

Crawford more accessible. AT&T believes that this power-sharing arrangement will make the top people more responsive to their customers, employees, and business units and will speed up decision making.

For Discussion

1. How would you describe the structure at AT&T Microelectronics?

2. What kinds of coordinating mechanisms might Warwick and Crawford use?

3. How much does the success of this arrangement depend on the personal working relationship between Warwick and Crawford?

CASE

Chocolate and Much More

David Troy addressed the executive board at their planning meeting. "As you know, our company has developed a relatively diverse product line over the past 30 years. We began as a small chocolate manufacturer operating in San Francisco. Opportunities arose, and we moved into assorted other candies and became a major player in the U.S. market. Our next endeavor was to move into specialty cookies and candy in the German market and, as you know, we achieved great success in that market as well."

"Our strategic plan is now focused on expanding into Europe, Southeast Asia, and Japan. We recognize that these markets are very different culturally and, consequently, have different preferences for candy and cookies. In addition, the impending unification of Europe has resulted in increased competition and regulation for firms that wish to compete in that market. As we formulate our plan, let's consider the importance of competing on an international level and its impact on our product development and marketing strategies. Our success depends on our ability to remain flexible and react quickly to customer desires!"

For Discussion

1. As Chocolate and Much More attempts to formulate its strategic plan, what issues must it consider with respect to its organizational design?

2. Evaluate the repercussions of moving into new international markets without the appropriate organizational design.

3. What recommendations might you make to this company?

EXPERIENTIAL EXERCISE 9.1

Organizational Characteristics Questionnaire

This brief instrument measures the degree to which five characteristics are present in a particular organization's structure. It can be used to examine any real organization.

Instructions: The 10 questions that follow ask about certain organizational conditions. You must refer to a specific organization in order to respond to these questions. Give your best overall judgment about how well each statement actually describes conditions in the organization that you have in mind. There are no "right" or "wrong" answers, since the purpose is to describe an existing organization's conditions and characteristics.

	Completely	Mostly	Partly	Slightly	Not at All
1. Work roles in this organization are highly specialized; each person has clear-cut authority and responsibility.	____	____	____	____	____
2. The formal hierarchy in this organization is formal to the point of being rigid and inflexible.	____	____	____	____	____
3. In this organization people are selected and promoted on the basis of their demonstrated technical competence.	____	____	____	____	____
4. People in this organization often seem so concerned with conforming to rules and procedures that it interferes with their mental health.	____	____	____	____	____
5. Everyone in this organization expects to be subject to the same set of rules and controls; there are no favorites.	____	____	____	____	____
6. People in this organization are often so wrapped up in their own narrow specialties that they can't see that we all have common interests; this causes unnecessary conflicts.	____	____	____	____	____
7. The offices and positions in this organization are arranged in a clear and logical hierarchy.	____	____	____	____	____
8. Overall, this organization is a political bureaucracy, with a "managerial elite" who got where they are through political savvy.	____	____	____	____	____
9. Managers in this organization see themselves as being on a clear "career ladder" and expect to make regular progress in their career paths.	____	____	____	____	____
10. Many of the rules in this organization have either become ends in themselves, with no logical function, or have come to specify the minimum tolerable performance levels.	____	____	____	____	____

Scoring

To score your answers, use the key below. Add up the points for all 10 questions to get your score. A high score indicates a "good" bureaucracy, while the lower the score, the less the organization is a good bureaucracy. It either lacks the right bureaucratic characteristics or goes far overboard on some. A score between 25 and 35 is about average; scores above 35 are suggestive of a "good" bureaucratic structure. Scores from 18 to 24 are a cause for concern, and scores below 18 indicate serious problems, either overbureaucratic rigidity or under-bureaucratic chaos.

	RESPONSE				
Question Numbers	Completely	Mostly	Partly	Slightly	Not at All
1, 3, 5, 7, 9	5 points	4 points	3 points	2 points	1 point
2, 4, 6, 8, 10	1 point	2 points	3 points	4 points	5 points

EXPERIENTIAL EXERCISE 9.2

ORGMECH Survey

This instrument places an organization along the organic-mechanistic dimension first defined by Tom Burns and G. Stalker. The mechanistic end of the dimension approximates the classic highly formalized bureaucracy, while the organic end can be used to describe a more participatory type of organization.

Instructions: Consider an organization with which you are familiar. Indicate the extent to which each of the following 10 statements is true of or accurately characterizes the organization in question.

	To a Very Great Extent	To a Considerable Extent	To a Moderate Extent	To a Slight Extent	To Almost No Extent
1. This organization has clear rules and regulations that everyone is expected to follow closely.	___	___	___	___	___
2. Policies in this organization are reviewed by the pople they affect before being implemented.	___	___	___	___	___
3. In this organization a major concern is that all employees be allowed to develop their talents and abilities.	___	___	___	___	___
4. Everyone in this organization knows who his or her immediate supervisor is; reporting relationships are clearly defined.	___	___	___	___	___
5. Jobs in this organization are clearly defined; everyone knows exactly what is expected in any specific job position.	___	___	___	___	___
6. Work groups are typically temporary and change often in this organization.	___	___	___	___	___
7. All decisions in this organization must be reviewed and approved by upper-level management.	___	___	___	___	___

	To a Very Great Extent	To a Considerable Extent	To a Moderate Extent	To a Slight Extent	To Almost No Extent
8. In this organization the emphasis is on adapting effectively to constant environmental change.	‾‾‾	‾‾‾	‾‾‾	‾‾‾	‾‾‾
9. Jobs in this organization are usually broken down into highly specialized, smaller tasks.	‾‾‾	‾‾‾	‾‾‾	‾‾‾	‾‾‾
10. Standard activities in this organization are always covered by clearly outlined procedures that everyone is expected to follow.	‾‾‾	‾‾‾	‾‾‾	‾‾‾	‾‾‾

Scoring

On the scoring grid, note the numbers that correspond to your response to each of the 10 questions. Enter the numbers in the boxes, then add up all the numbers in the boxes. This is your ORGMECH Score.

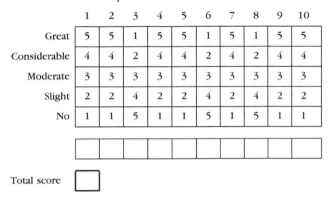

	1	2	3	4	5	6	7	8	9	10
Great	5	5	1	5	5	1	5	1	5	5
Considerable	4	4	2	4	4	2	4	2	4	4
Moderate	3	3	3	3	3	3	3	3	3	3
Slight	2	2	4	2	2	4	2	4	2	2
No	1	1	5	1	1	5	1	5	1	1

Total score [ ]

Interpretation

High scores indicate high degrees of mechanistic/bureaucratic organizational characteristics. Low scores are associated with adaptive/organic organizational characteristics.

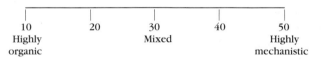

10	20	30	40	50
Highly organic		Mixed		Highly mechanistic

For Discussion

- How would you feel (or do you feel) about working in a "mechanistic" organization?
- How would you feel (or do you feel) about working in a "organic" organization?
- Is it desirable to have as low a score as possible? Why or why not?
- Are certain characteristics of the organization you describe inconsistent with one another? What effects does this have?

SOURCE: M. Sashkin and W. C. Morris, *Organizational Behavior,* © 1984. Reprinted by permission of Prentice-Hall, Englewood Cliffs, New Jersey.

NOTES

1. S. Fatsis, "Restructuring Revives IBM PC's," *Orlando Sentinel,* May 23, 1993, F-1.

2. See, for example, A. P. Carnevale, *America and the New Economy* (American Society for Training and Development and the U.S. Department of Labor Employment and Training Administration, 1993); and W. Kiechel, "How We Will Work in the Year 2000: Six Trends Reshaping the Workplace," *Fortune,* May 17, 1993, 38–41.

3. See, for example, R. K. Kazanjian and R. Drazine, "Implementing Internal Diversification: Contingency Factors for Organization Design Choices," *Academy of Management Review*[12] (1987): 342–54; and D. Miller, "The Genesis of Configuration," *Academy of Management Review*[12] (1987): 686–701.

4. D. Miller, "Relating Porter's Business Strategies to Environment and Structure: Analysis and Performance Implications," *Academy of Management Journal* 31 (1988): 280–308; and D. Miller, C. Droge and J. M. Toulouse, "Strategic Process and Content as Mediators between Organizational Context and Structure," *Academy of Management Journal* 31 (1988): 544–69.

5. R. B. Duncan, "What Is the Right Organization Structure," *Organizational Dynamics* (Winter 1989): 59–80.

6. *The Conference Board Chart Service* (New York: The

Conference Board, Inc., 1988).

7. Black & Decker Annual Report, 1993.

8. M. W. Miller and L. Hays, "Gerstner's Nonvision for IBM Raises a Management Issue," *Wall Street Journal,* July 29, 1993, B1.

9. Pepsico, *Annual Report, 1992.*

10. *The Conference Board Chart Service.*

11. R. Sookdeo, "The New Global Consumer," *Fortune,* Autumn/Winter 1993, 68-77.

12. P. S. Lewis and P. M. Fandt, "The Strategy-Structure Fit in Multinational Corporations: A Revised Model," *International Journal of Management* (June 1990): 137-46.

13. Croce, Ginty, Okpamen, and Unger, *Cases in Strategic Management for Business.*

14. C. L. Fowler, "Focusing Expertise at CIGNA. ASQC/Fortune Special Report," *Fortune,* 1992.

15. M. Davis and P. R. Lawrence, *Matrix* (Reading, Mass: Addison-Wesley, 1977), 3.

16. J. R. Galbraith, "Matrix Organization Designs: How to Combine Functional and Project Forms," *Business Horizons,* February 1971, 29-40.

17. E. W. Larson, and D. H. Gobeli, Matrix Management: Contradictions and Insights. *California Management Review,* Summer 1987, 126-38.

18. J. A. Byrne, "Is Your Company Too Big?" *Business Week,* March 27, 1989, 84-94.

19. Kiechel, "How We Will Work in the Year 2000."

20. Carnevale, *America and the New Economy.*

21. R. E. Miles and C. C. Snow, "Organizations: New Concepts for New Forms," *California Management Review.* 28 (Spring 1986): 62-71.

22. S. Tully, "The Modular Corporation," *Fortune,* February 8, 1993, 106-14.

23. J. A. Byrne, "The Virtual Corporation," *Business Week,* February 8, 1993, 98-103.

24. Miles and Snow, "Organizations: New Concepts for New Forms."

25. C. C. Snow, R. E. Miles, and H. J. Coleman, Jr., "Managing 21st Century Network Organizations," *Organizational Dynamics* 10 (February 1992): 5-20.

26. Ibid.

27. Ibid.

28. Ibid.

29. J. W. Wilson and J. H. Dobrzynski, "And Now, the Post-Industrial Corporation," *Business Week,* March 3, 1986, 64-71.

30. R. E. Miles, "Adapting to Technology and Competition: A New Industrial Relations System for the 21st Century," *California Management Review* 31 (Winter 1989): 9-28.

31. R. Charan, "How Networks Reshape Organizations—For Results," *Harvard Business Review* (September/October 1991): 104-15.

32. F. V. Guterl, "Goodbye, Old Matrix," *Business Month,* February 1989, 32-38.

33. J. B. Bush, A. L. Frohman, "Communication in a 'Network' Organization," *Organizational Dynamics* (1991): 23-36.

34. Miles and Snow, "Managing 21st Century Network Organizations."

35. See, for example, J. L. Chency, "Interdependence and Coordination in Organizations: A Role-System Analysis," *Academy of Management Journal* 26 (1983): 156-62; J. K. Ito and R. B. Peterson, "Effects of Task Difficulty and Interunit Interdependence on Information Processing Systems," *Academy of Management Journal* (1986): 139-49; and J. E. McCann and D. L. Ferry, "An Approach for Assessing and Managing Inter-unit Interdependence," *Academy of Management Review* 4 (1979): 113-20.

36. J. D. Thompson, *Organizations in Action* (New York: McGraw-Hill, 1967).

37. J. R. Galbraith, "Organizational Design: An Information Processing View," *Interfaces* 4 (May 1974): 3.

38. P. G. Keen, "Redesigning the Organization through Information Technology," *Planning Review,* May/June 1991, 4-9.

39. Guterl, "Goodbye, Old Matrix."

40. W. J. Altier, "Task Forces: An Effective Management Tool," *Management Review* (February 1987): 52-57.

41. M. Hardaker and B. K. Ward, "How to Make a Team Work," *Harvard Business Review* (November/December 1987): 112-20.

42. Adapted from "Mearthane Products," in *Real-World Lessons for America's Small Businesses: Insights from the Blue Chip Enterprise Initiative (Nation's Business* on behalf of Connecticut Mutual Life Insurance Company and the U.S. Chamber of Commerce, 1993), 52-53.

43. G. Garnier, "Context and Decision Making Autonomy in Foreign Affiliates of U.S. Multinational Corporations," *Academy of Management Journal* 25 (1982): 893-908.

44. T. Peters, "Letting Go of Controls," *Across the Board,* June 1991, 15-18.

45. See, for example, B. R. Schlender, "Yet Another Strategy for Apple," *Fortune,* October 22, 1990; and J. Sculley, *Odyssey: Pepsi to Apple—A Journey of Adventure Ideas for the Future* (New York: Harper & Row, 1987).

46. R. L. Drake and L. M. Caudill, "Management of the Large Multinational: Trends and Future Challenges," *Business Horizons* (May/June 1981): 83-91.

47. T. Burns and G. Stalker, *The Management of Innovation* (London: Tavistock, 1961), 119-22.

48. See, for example, R. Hayes and W. Abernathy, "Managing Our Way to Economic Decline," *Harvard Business Review,* 58 (July/August 1980): 67-77; H. Stevenson and D. Gumpert, "The Heart of Entrepreneurship," *Harvard Business Review* 63 (March/April 1985): 85-94; and H. H. Stevenson, M. J. Roberts, and D. E. Grousbeck, *New Business Ventures and the Entrepreneur* (Homewood, Ill.: Irwin, 1989).

49. B. Dumain, "The Bureaucracy Busters," *Fortune,* June 17, 1991, 36+.

50. J. Byrne, "The Horizontal Corporation," *Business Week,* December 20, 1993, 76-81.

51. Fatsis, "Restructuring Revives IBM PC's."

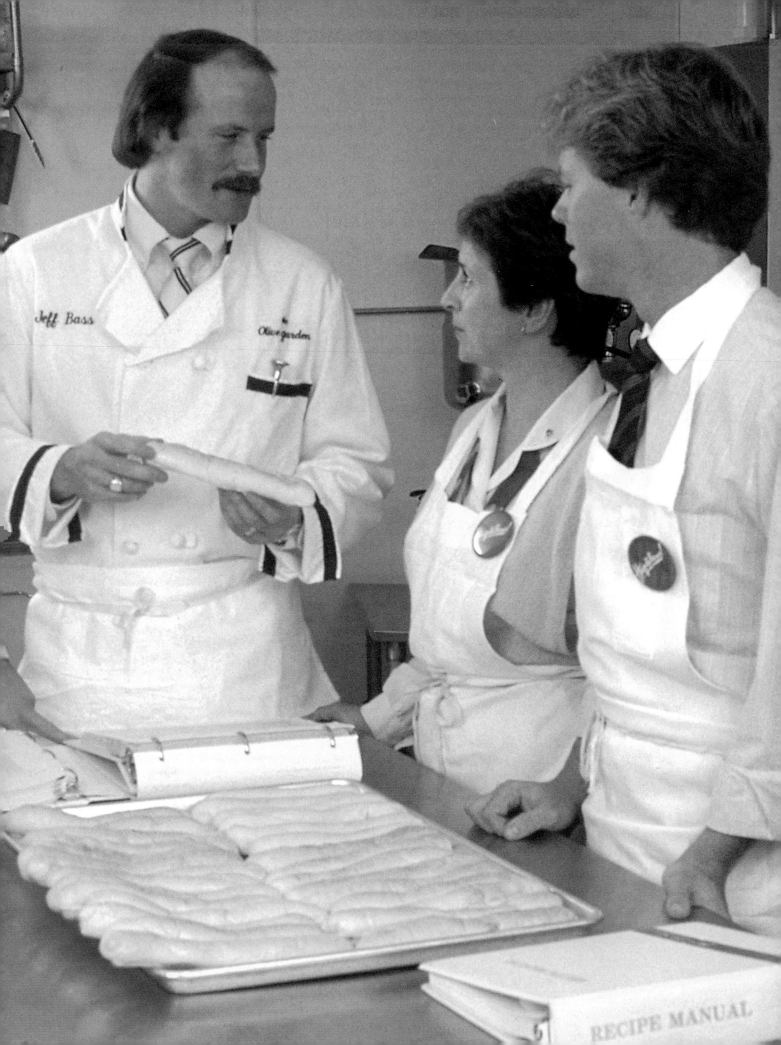

Managing Human Resources

CHAPTER 10

▼ CHAPTER OVERVIEW

At McDonald's Corporation, there is a Vice President for Individuality. At Carson Pirie Scott & Company, there is a Vice President of Customer Satisfaction through People Involvement. Although the titles are very different, both positions involve the same managerial function—the management of people in organizations. Increasingly, managers have recognized that people are "human resources" and that human resources are often the organization's most critical resource. The effective management of human resources leads to greater productivity, quality, and organizational performance.

In the two previous chapters, we considered the organizing function as it related to designing the organization to achieve its goals and objectives. In this chapter, we continue our discussion of the organizing function by examining how organizations acquire and develop human resources. We focus on the human resource planning process as it occurs within organizations. Legal human resource issues, including discrimination concerns and affirmative action programs, are also considered. Finally, we explore some emerging issues that are affecting human resource management today.

▼ LEARNING OBJECTIVES

When you have finished studying this chapter,
you should be able to:

- Describe the legal environment of human resource management.
- Discuss the human resource planning process.
- Describe different recruiting techniques used by organizations.
- Explain the four major selection methods.
- Describe the problems inherent in performance appraisals.
- Demonstrate how managers use performance appraisal information.
- Explain how compensation and benefits are used in organizations.
- Define and discuss labor-management relations.
- Discuss current issues in human resource management.

MANAGERIAL INCIDENT

CORNING: IT SIMPLY MAKES GOOD BUSINESS SENSE

Corning, Inc., is best known for popular consumer products, such as Corning-ware, Corelle, and Pyrex brands of housewares. More recently, Corning has earned a reputation as one the most quality-oriented companies in the world by creating a work environment that supports and rewards a quality orientation in everything the company does.

Much of the credit for the changes at Corning is attributed to James R. Houghton, the founder's great-great-grandson, who took over as chair and chief executive officer in 1983. Houghton had three major goals for Corning: total quality, high return on equity, and improved human resource management systems. For the challenges to be met, new partnerships had to be formed with employees, and human resources had to be better utilized.

Revising the human resource management system required extensive planning. Workforce diversity programs, teamwork and group-based tasks, performance-based incentives and reward systems, intense training and development programs, and strategies for continuous improvement were all intensively studied, designed, and implemented. The company wanted to create an environment in which all employees could realize their potential and contribute effectively to the goals of the organization. Individual differences were to be valued and celebrated, not simply tolerated.

The issue of workforce diversity became a top priority for Houghton. He believed that Corning's workforce should more closely mirror the company's customer base. This meant changing many of the traditional human resource management practices. The company had higher attrition rates for minorities and women than for white males, which suggested that recruiting, selecting, training, and development programs were ineffective. Talented women and blacks joined the company only to plateau or resign. Few reached upper management levels, and no one could say exactly why. Reversing this trend represented a significant management challenge for Corning.[1] ▼

INTRODUCTION

As managers at Corning realized, achieving the goals of the organization requires effective human resource management. Corning's reputation for quality was a function, to a large degree, of its highly effective human resource management system. Nevertheless, continued success will be dependent upon the company's ability to maintain a work environment that encourages and rewards a quality orientation among employees and meets the needs of a more diverse workforce.

Human resource management (HRM) involves the management of the organization's employees. HRM consists of all the activities required to enhance the effectiveness of an organization's workforce and to achieve organizational goals and objectives. In today's highly competitive marketplace, human resource management has become critical to improving the competitiveness of many firms. It is particularly important in industries where success is dependent upon achieving the highest possible product and service quality. At the same time, changing legal requirements, along with changes in the workforce, have forced human resource managers to recognize and respond to a multitude of external environmental forces.

The focus of this chapter is on the role of human resource managers and the activities that are involved in the HRM function. Because of the increasing importance of legal issues, we begin by examining those aspects of the legal

Human Resource Management (HRM)
The management of the employees of the organization consisting of all the activities required to enhance the effectiveness of an organization's work force and to achieve organizational goals and objectives.

environment that affect HRM practices, focusing on the major legislation regulating employment practices and affirmative-action programs. Next, we explore the major HRM activities that help the organization attract, retain, and develop the quality and quantity of employees needed to meet organizational goals. More specifically, we examine HRM planning and job analysis, staffing, training, performance appraisal, compensation, and labor relations. In the last part of the chapter, we turn our attention to some current issues affecting HRM including international HRM, workforce diversity, sexual harassment, and health concerns in the work environment.

LEGAL ENVIRONMENT OF HUMAN RESOURCE MANAGEMENT

One factor that has contributed to the increased importance of human resource managers is the number and complexity of legal issues faced by organizations. Federal and state laws that specify required, acceptable, and prohibited employment practices place many constraints on recruitment, selection, placement, training, and other human resource activities. For example, Xerox sets recruitment and representation goals in accordance with federal guidelines and reviews them continually to make sure that they reflect workforce demographics. While all companies with federal contracts are required to make this effort, Xerox extends the guidelines by setting diversity goals for its upper-level jobs and holding division and group managers accountable for reaching those goals.[2]

EQUAL EMPLOYMENT OPPORTUNITY LEGISLATION

In an effort to reduce employment discrimination based on racial bigotry and sexual stereotypes, Congress passed several laws that directly address the problem of employee discrimination.[3] The Civil Rights Act of 1964, the Civil Rights Restoration Act of 1988, and the Civil Rights Act of 1991 are equal employment opportunity (EEO) laws that prohibit the use of race, color, religion, national origin, or sex in employment decision making. Other legislation such as the Americans with Disabilities Act of 1990 and the Age Discrimination in Employment Act of 1967 prohibits employment decisions based on biases toward the handicapped and elderly. In general, the purpose of EEO legislation is to ensure that unemployment decisions are based on job-related criteria only. Toward that end, a substantial amount of legislation deals with various forms of employee protection. Table 10.1 summarizes the major federal laws and regulations that affect the management of human resources.

The Civil Rights Act of 1964 established the Equal Employment Opportunity Commission (EEOC). This organization is responsible for enforcing federal laws related to job discrimination. Although the EEOC can prosecute an organization that violates the law, the commission usually tries to persuade offending organizations to change their policies and pay damages to anyone who has encountered discrimination. To help organizations comply with federal employment regulations, the EEOC also publishes written guidelines that clarify the law and instruct organizations on their legal obligations and responsibilities. Current federal law prohibits discrimination on the basis of gender, age, physical or mental disabilities, military experience, religion, race, ethnic origin, color, or national origin.

AFFIRMATIVE-ACTION PROGRAMS

Affirmative action refers to the legal requirement that employers must actively recruit, hire, and promote members of minority groups and other protected

▼ **Table 10.1**   Major Federal Laws Protecting Employees

LAW OR REGULATION	YEAR	DESCRIPTION
Fair Labor Standards Act	1938	Established minimum wages paid to employees and the 40-hour workweek; regulates child labor.
Social Security Act	1935	Established the Social Security System.
Equal Pay Act	1963	Requires that men and women receive equal pay for equal work.
Title VII of Civil Rights Act	1964 (amended in 1972)	Makes it illegal to discriminate on the basis of race, color, religion, national origin, or sex.
Age Discrimination in Employment Act	1967 (amended in 1986)	Prevents age discrimination in employment against persons between 40 and 70 years of age.
Occupational Safety and Health Act	1970	Requires organizations to provide safe, nonhazardous working conditions for employees.
Pregnancy Discrimination Act	1978	Broadens discrimination to include pregnancy, childbirth, and related conditions.
Americans with Disabilities Act	1990	Prohibits discrimination in employment against persons with physical or mental disabilities or those who are chronically ill.
Civil Rights Act	1991	Amends and clarifies Title VII, Americans with Disabilities Act, and other EEO laws.

Protected class
Composed of individuals who fall within a group identified for protection under equal employment laws and regulations.

classes, if such individuals are underrepresented in the organization. Individuals who fall within a group identified for protection under equal employment laws and regulations are a **protected class.** That is, if the qualified labor pool in a community is 20 percent African American and 5 percent Hispanic American, then 20 percent and 5 percent of the labor force of an organization operating in that community should be African American and Hispanic American, respectively.

Organizations often have patterns of employment in which protected groups are underrepresented relative to the number of group members who have appropriate credentials in the marketplace. To correct imbalance in their workforce, organizations may adopt affirmative action programs. An affirmative-action program is a written, systematic plan that specifies goals and a timetable for hiring, training, promoting, and retaining groups protected by federal EEO laws and regulations. While affirmative action is not synonymous with quotas, under federal regulations all companies with federal contracts greater than $50,000 and with 50 employees or more are required to establish annual plans in the form of numerical goals or timetables for increasing employment of women and minorities.[3]

Many organizations have found that simply dictating affirmative action in hiring cannot change an organization's culture. It takes more than simply hiring members of protected classes. Education and management development are often necessary to encourage the general workforce to appreciate individuals of different genders, race, or ethnic background.

Monsanto, the St. Louis–based maker of chemicals and drugs, serves as an excellent example of an organization that tries to encourage workplace diver-

AVON CALLING: AFFIRMATIVE ACTION FROM THE BOTTOM UP

Avon wanted its workforce, especially at the decision-making level, to reflect its customer base. But top-down affirmative-action programs, inspired by legal mandates or the CEO's interest, failed to fulfill this goal. Avon found a bottom-up approach was more successful. All minority employees belong to in-house race-based networks—advocacy groups that have become a crucial part of minority relations at the company. The networks provide Avon with a barometer of how well the company is doing in terms of affirmative action and workforce diversity.

Developed first as social groups in the mid-1980s, the Black Professional Association (BPA), Avon Hispanic Network (AHN), and Avon Asian Network (AAN) were originally independent of one another. Soon the networks evolved into self-help organizations devoted to encouraging minority recruiting and career development. Currently, Avon's 1525-person workforce is 13 percent black, 6 percent Hispanic, and 4 percent Asian.

The three networks, whose officers are elected annually by employee members, meet separately each quarter. Although they provide a source of support for staffers, they deliberately stay away from matters of discrimination or harassment. They focus on workplace issues such as flextime, maternity leave, and work stress rather than on complaints. Often, they sponsor events that get people together in a nonconfrontational way.

The network heads take their agendas directly to top managers including the CEO, the president, and Avon's Diversity Task Force chair, who handles minority-related issues. Recently, the networks sponsored an effort to get Avon to fund three-day seminars, outside the office, where minority employees could discuss how to acclimate to Avon's predominately white organizational culture.

While the networks play an advocacy role and continually challenge management, the strong sense of cooperation at Avon has allowed its networks to thrive, whereas similar programs at other companies have failed.

sity. The company began by conducting exit interviews with minorities and women who left the organization. Based on information obtained from the interviews, the company developed a series of managing diversity programs to help it retain such employees. One program, called "Consulting Pairs," trains employees throughout the company to serve as in-house consultants (working in race- or sex-matched pairs) on race and gender issues.[4] As another example of a proactive affirmative-action plan, Managing for Excellence describes the efforts of Avon Products to maintain a more diverse workforce.[5] This company wanted its workforce to reflect its customer base and developed a program that took a bottom-up approach to achieving diversity in the workplace.

Organizations meet their human resource requirements through staffing. **Staffing** entails bringing in or placing people in the organization and making sure they serve as productive members of the workforce. The staffing process consists of recruiting and selecting the employees an organization needs to accomplish its goals and objectives. As a manager, you must be prepared to cope with a changing workforce. How aware are you of these changes? Test your knowledge on this important issue in Meeting the Challenge.[6]

Perhaps more than any other area of management, the HRM process is affected by the legal environment.[7] Moreover, due to societal and political

Staffing
Bringing in or placing people into the organization and making sure they serve as productive members of the workforce.

HOW AWARE ARE YOU OF THE CHANGING WORKFORCE?

As a manager, how prepared are you to handle the requirements of a changing workforce? Respond true or false to the following statements. Within the next few years:

1. Almost half of the workforce will be women.
2. Less than 25 percent of the workforce will be white men.
3. Hispanic Americans will make up more than 20 percent of the workforce.
4. African Americans will comprise more than 25 percent of the workforce.
5. Almost 5 percent of the workforce will be Asian Americans.
6. More than 75 percent of the companies in some industries will have diversity training programs.
7. More than 75 percent of the companies in some industries will implement specific minority recruiting programs.
8. Fifteen percent of the net addition to the workforce will be white men.
9. More than 60 percent of women over the age of 16 will be working.
10. The greatest percentage of population growth will occur in the Western hemisphere.

Answers: Items 2 (40 percent), 3 (10 percent), and 4 (11 percent) are false. Items 1, 5, 6, 7, 8, 9, and 10 are predicted to be true.

forces, the legal landscape of HRM is constantly changing. Therefore, it is important for managers to keep abreast of which employment practices are permissible and which are prohibited. For example, many organizations have appearance and grooming rules and guidelines for employees, especially those who deal with the public. Although there have been cases of "appearance" discrimination, businesses generally retain the right to require their employees to meet appearance standards. In contrast, there is growing pressure to prohibit employment decisions based on sexual preferences. Because of such trends, human resource managers are becoming increasingly important members of the organization.

HUMAN RESOURCE PLANNING

Have you ever wondered why some organizations, such as Corning, have been successful so consistently? Or why some college and professional sports teams consistently win championships? As we know from Chapters 4 and 5, planning is one ingredient for achieving the goals and objectives of the organization. It would be unthinkable for a company not to plan for its future material needs, plant capacity, or financing. Similarly, organizations must plan for their human resource needs.

Human resource planning is the process of determining future human resource needs relative to an organization's strategic plan and taking actions necessary to meet those needs in a timely manner. The planning process is shown in Figure 10.1. In planning to meet human resource requirements, managers must be familiar with both the organization's job requirements and labor

Human resource planning
The process of determining future human resource needs relative to an organization's strategic plan and taking the actions necessary to meet those needs in a timely manner.

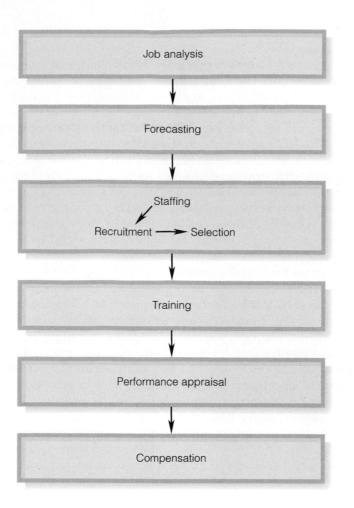

▼ FIGURE 10.1
Human Resource Planning Process

demand and supply issues; they must also know how to reconcile supply and demand through recruitment, selection, training, performance appraisal, and compensation programs. We will discuss each of these aspects of human resource planning in the following sections.

JOB ANALYSIS

Job analysis involves assimilating all of the information about a particular job. Job analysis information, in turn, is used to develop two important documents: job descriptions and job specifications. As we know from Chapter 8, **job descriptions** detailed the responsibilities and tasks associated with a given position. **Job specifications** identify the knowledge, skills, abilities, and other employee characteristics needed to perform the job. Taken together, the job descriptions and job specifications provide the human resource manager with a foundation for forecasting the supply of and demand for labor within the organization and developing programs to meet the company's human resource requirements. Job descriptions and job specifications also help the organization comply with EEO laws by assuring the HRM decisions are based on job-related information.

FORECASTING

An important aspect of human resource planning is forecasting the supply of and demand for human resources for both short-term planning (one to two

Job analysis
Assimilating all of the information about a particular job including job descriptions and job specifications.

Job descriptions
Detail the responsibilities and tasks associated with a given position.

Job specifications
The identification of the knowledge, skills, abilities, and other employee characteristics needed to perform the job.

years) and long-term planning (three to five years). Both types of forecasts require looking into the future.

Demand forecasting involves determining the number of employees that the organization will need at some point in the future as well as the knowledge, skills, and abilities that these employees must possess. The organization's external and internal environments are the major determinants of the demand for human resources. For example, changes in the economy may affect the demand for a product or service and, thus, affect the need for certain types of employees. In addition, demand is based on the organization's strategic goals and plans and internal workforce changes, such as retirements, resignations, terminations, and leaves of absence. If Wal-Mart, for example, planned to open three new stores two years from today, its human resource managers must begin planning now to staff those facilities. Likewise, if the company intended to close or relocate a branch or regional facility, there would be less demand for certain employees.

Supply forecasting involves determining what human resources will be available, both inside and outside the organization. Internal programs such as promotions, transfers, training, and pay incentives are designed to meet demand through existing employees. Internal supply forecasts simply estimate the effect of internal programs will have on turnover, termination, retirement, promotion, and transfer rates.[8] For example, monetary incentives are often used to induce employees to accept transfers or obtain the training needed for promotion. To meet human resource demand, most organizations must rely on some extent on bringing in employees from the outside. Labor market analysis and human resource professionals are used to forecast external labor supply. Together, internal and external supply forecasts allow the organization to estimate the number of people who will enter and leave various organizational jobs, as well as the effects of HRM programs on employee skills and productivity.[9]

After estimating the demand for and potential supplies of human resources, the human resource manager develops programs that reconcile the two forecasts. If a shortage is forecast, HRM programs to increase employee hiring, promotions, transfers, and training are devised. If an excess is predicted, workforce reduction programs must be implemented.

STAFFING

The staffing function has two primary components: recruitment and selection. We will examine each of these aspects in more detail.

Recruitment

Recruitment is the process of finding and attracting job candidates who are qualified to fill job vacancies. Job descriptions and job specifications, both discussed earlier, are important in the recruiting process because they specify the nature of the job and the qualifications required of candidates.

Recruitment, or the search process, can occur in a variety of settings, both inside and outside the organization. Both internal and external recruitment have certain advantages and disadvantages.[10] These are summarized in Table 10.2 and discussed in more detail in the next paragraphs.

Most vacant positions in organizations are filled through internal recruitment. Internal recruitment involves identifying potential internal candidates and encouraging them to apply for and be willing to accept organizational jobs that are vacant. Methods of internal recruitment include job banks, employee referral systems, job postings, and advertisements in company newsletters.

Recruitment
The process of finding and attracting job candidates who are qualified to fill job vacancies.

▼ **Table 10.2**   Internal versus External Recruitment

	ADVANTAGES	DISADVANTAGES
Internal Recruitment	• Helps morale of promotee • Better assessment of abilities • Lower cost for some jobs • Motivator for good performance • Causes a succession of promotions • Have to hire only at entry level	• Inbreeding • Possible morale problems of those not promoted • Political infighting for promotions • Strong management development program needed
External Recruitment	• New blood and new perspectives • Cheaper than training a professional • No group of political supporters in the organization already • May bring new ideas, creativity, and insights	• May not select someone who will fit • May cause morale problems for internal candidates not promoted • Longer adjustment or orientation time needed

Every organization represents an internal labor market to some degree. Many employees, both entry level and upper level, aspire to move up the ranks through promotion. Promotion-from-within becomes more feasible when companies invest in training and development activities. At higher levels, transfers can be an important development tool for acquiring additional job knowledge, as well as a means of creating new job ladders for upward mobility. Both promotion and transfer policies can create a favorable climate for attracting qualified employees and retaining valued ones.

External recruitment involves advertising for and soliciting applicants from outside the company. If internal sources do not produce an acceptable candidate, a wide variety of external sources are available. These sources differ in terms of ease of use, costs, and the quality of applicants obtained.

External sources include walk-ins, public employment agencies, temporary help agencies, labor unions, educational institutions, referrals from current and past employees, competitive sources, and newspaper/trade publications. The source used will depend upon the job skills required and the current availability of those skills in the labor market. For example, organizations frequently use external placement firms and private employment agencies to find applicants for upper-level managerial positions, but look to educational institutions for candidates for entry-level managerial positions. As technology develops, human resource managers are increasingly using computerized databases in the recruitment task.

Finding and hiring the best people is a top priority for many organizations. For example, to hire 2000 people each year, Microsoft Corporation visits nearly 150 college campuses, reviews more than 120,000 résumés, and conducts 7,500 face-to-face candidate interviews.[11] Through this process, Microsoft helps to ensure that it identifies and recruits the very best candidates.

Selection

Once applicants have been recruited, the organization must select the right person for the job. **Selection** is the process of evaluating and choosing the best-qualified candidate from the pool of applicants recruited for the position. It entails the exchange of accurate information between employers and job

Selection
The process of evaluating and choosing the best qualified candidate from the pool of applicants recruited for the position.

candidates to optimize the person-job match. Although organizations usually make these decisions, applicants also select organizations to meet their economic and occupational needs.

The procedure of selecting and matching applicants to jobs begins after an adequate number of applicants has been recruited. At the heart of the selection process is the prediction of whether or not a particular applicant is capable of performing the job tasks associated with the position for which he or she is being considered.

Careful selection procedures can be time-consuming and costly. However, a wrong decision can also be costly when it results in litigation, lost time, or wrongful discharge complaints. Some organizations are now using expensive selection procedures, even for positions that historically would have been filled without much screening. For example, when Toyota Motor Corporation wanted to fill positions at its new automobile assembly plant in Kentucky, it received 90,000 applications from 120 countries for its 2700 production positions and thousands more for the 300 office jobs. To select workers who would conform to the Japanese emphasis on teamwork, loyalty, and versatility, Toyota required applicants to spend approximately 25 hours completing written tests, workplace simulations, and interviews. The tests examined not only literacy and technical knowledge, but also interpersonal skills and attitudes toward work. In addition, each person took a physical examination and a drug test.[12] This process enabled Toyota to select those candidates that had the greatest likelihood of succeeding in their jobs.

During the selection process, managers must determine the extent to which job candidates have the skills, abilities, and knowledge required to perform effectively in the positions for which they are being considered. To make such judgments, managers and human resource professionals rely on various tools and techniques for selection including application forms, tests, interviews, and assessment centers.

Application Forms   The application form is the first source of information about a potential employee. It records the applicant's desired position, serves as a prescreening device to help determine whether an applicant meets the minimum requirements of a position, and allows preliminary comparisons with the credentials of other candidates.

The application form contains a series of inquiries about job-related qualifications and experience, such as an applicant's educational background, previous job experience, physical health, and other information that may be useful in assessing an individual's ability to perform a job. If you currently hold a job or have ever looked for one, chances are that you have completed an application form for employment.

In collecting information on a candidate's background and current status, the application form should ask only questions pertaining to the applicant's ability to perform the job. If the information helps the employer select more qualified candidates, then it is job related. In nearly all instances, questions regarding sex, age, or race, or national origin are not predictive of future employment success and should be avoided.

Employment tests
Any instrument, device, or information used to make an employment decision is considered a test by the EEOC's Uniform Guidelines of Employee Selection.

Employment Tests   Any instrument, device, or information used to make an employment decision is considered a **test** by the EEOC's Uniform Guidelines on Employee Selection. An employment test is a means of assessing a job applicant's knowledge, skills, and abilities through paper-and-pencil responses (such as a math test) or simulated exercises (such as a motor skills test). The major types of tests used in the selection process are intelligence tests, job aptitude and knowledge tests, personality inventories, and job performance tests.

▼ These job candidates are participating in a work place simulation as part of the selection process.

Interviews   Interviews are relatively formal, in-depth conversations conducted for the purpose of assessing a candidate's knowledge, skills, and abilities, as well as providing information to the candidate about the organization and potential jobs. They are used with more than 90 percent of all people hired for industrial positions.

Interviews permit a two-way exchange of information. Most interview questions are straightforward inquiries about the candidate's experience or education. At Microsoft, however, prospective employees are asked seemingly off-the-wall, brain-teaser questions, such as those in Table 10.3.[13] Recruiters at Microsoft aren't looking for a definitive answer. Instead, they are testing how an applicant thinks. How well would you respond to Microsoft's questions?

If interviews are used, steps should be taken to maximize their effectiveness. Typically, a structured interview format works best. A specific list of

▼ Interviews are relatively formal, in-depth conversations conducted for the purpose of assessing a candidate's knowledge, skills, and abilities. Both the employer and the candidate need strong communication skills to exchange accurate information and to optimize the person-job match.

▼ **Table 10.3**   Can You Pass Microsoft's Test?

1. Why are manhole covers round?
2. How many gas stations are there in the United States?
3. If you were to put artificial turf on all the Major League ball fields, how many square yards would you need?
4. Why do many vending machines and jukeboxes have both letters and numbers?
5. If you were a product, how would you position yourself?

Answers:

1. They can be moved by rolling, and if they were square, they could fall down the hole.
2. If you figure there are 250 million people and one car per every four people and may be 500 cars for each gas station, the answer is 125,000.
3. Same type of process as question 2.
4. There would be too many buttons otherwise.
5. As high-energy, high-bandwidth, and hardcore.

SOURCE: K. Rebello and E. I. Schwartz, "Can You Pass the Test?", 65. Reprinted from February 24, 1992 issue of *Business Week* by special permission, copyright © 1992 by McGraw-Hill, Inc.

topics and the order in which they will be covered should be determined in advance. When managers are responsible for interviewing potential candidates, they need to keep the following points in mind:

- Ask precise, specific questions that are job related.
- Probe for details and be a careful listener.
- Avoid biases such as making snap judgments, stereotyping, or looking only for negative information.
- Be careful to avoid prohibited discriminatory questions.
- Keep written records of the interview.
- Use multiple interviewers.
- Keep in mind that candidates from diverse backgrounds and cultures may interpret questions differently. Be sure that the candidate understands your questions.

Interviews should never be the sole basis for selecting a candidate. Instead, they should be used along with other selection devices to provide additional information on candidates' strengths and weaknesses. Chase Manhattan Bank, for example, developed an analytical interview because of its interest in the thought processes of its future employees. According to Vice President Stanley Burns, Chase's recruiting efforts generally include several types of interviews. An initial interview, either on campus or in New York, determines whether the candidate's overall abilities, motivation, and interpersonal skills seem to fit the bank's requirements. Candidates are subsequently interviewed by a human resource specialist who informs the candidate about Chase's organizational structure and career opportunities and determines if the candidate meets the general criteria for a specific business unit. Finally, the candidate is interviewed by managers who assess very specific analytical skills. In describing the analytical interview, Burns notes that Chase is looking at the specific mental abilities that are required for successful performance in both its training program and its management jobs. The company recognized that while many job requirements varied depending on the specific business unit, certain mental abilities were needed for strong analytical skills to develop.

Consequently, Chase studied the content and structure of its training program and its entry-level management jobs to identify critical mental abilities. Six abilities were determined to be necessary: memory, learning speed, logical reasoning, divergent thinking, convergent thinking, and an affinity for numbers. The bank then developed a series of cases that could be used in a structured interview to focus on these six mental abilities. The cases, along with probing interviewer questions, are used to see if the candidate has the basic problem-solving capabilities necessary for success at Chase Manhattan.[14]

Although it is illegal to ask job applicants questions that violate EEO law, a recent study by New York's Hanigan Consulting Group found that managers ask for information that could be considered prohibitive in nearly 70 percent of all interviews.[15] Most managers do this because they are uninformed. Some managers, however, knowingly ask questions that put the interviewee in a position of revealing information prohibited by EEO law. What would you do if you were asked such a question? Table 10.4 provides some examples of "loaded" questions and possible responses.[16]

Assessment Centers   Many organizations approach the employee selection process very systematically through an assessment center that combines a variety of procedures. An **assessment center** is a controlled environment used to predict the probable success of job applicants based on their behaviors in simulated situations. Assessment centers are most often used for selecting can-

Assessment center
A controlled environment used to predict the probable success of job applicants based on their behaviors in simulated situations.

▼ **Table 10.4**   How to Handle Loaded Interview Questions

Here's a sampling of what interviewers *shouldn't*, but might ask:
- *What they ask:*   "Our division is spread out over several floors. Is that OK?"
- *What they mean:*   We spend a lot of our day running up and down the stairs, but in that wheelchair you might have difficulties.
- *How to answer:*   "Getting from place to place is not a problem for me."

Note: Under the Americans with Disabilities Act, the employer must make stairways more accessible.

- *What they ask:*   "Will it be a problem for you to work long hours?"
- *What they mean:*   Do you have to get home every night to young children?
- *How to answer:*   "I value my personal life, but I can make myself available when necessary."

- *What they ask:*   "Does your family mind you traveling?"
- *What they mean:*   Are you a single parent with child-care concerns?
- *How to answer:*   "Will travel be part of my job responsibilities?"

- *What they ask:*   "What were the dates of employment for your past jobs?"
- *What they mean:*   How old are you?
- *How to answer:*   Give them the dates and say, "As you see from the longevity of my employment, I'm very dependable."

Note: Anyone over 40 is protected from age discrimination.

- *What they ask:*   "As a consulting firm, we must be responsive to our clients. Will you be readily available?"
- *What they mean:*   Are you going to be taking off a lot of religious holidays?
- *How to answer:*   "My attendance record is exemplary."

- *What they ask:*   "We are looking for people who have a long-term commitment to the company. Is that what you have in mind?"
- *What they mean:*   You're a young woman with a wedding ring. Will you get pregnant and leave?
- *How to answer:*   "I like this company. Maybe you can tell me what it takes to move up here."

didates for managerial positions and sales personnel. Some organizations, however, use them to evaluate current nonmanagerial employees for supervisory training and advancement and to select college graduates for entry-level supervisory positions.

The situations or exercises in the assessment center are essentially performance tests that reflect the type of work done in managerial positions, such as decision making, writing, speaking, managing time, giving feedback, and completing leadership tasks. Presumably, simulations provide a good indication of how well the individual will do on the job. Assessment ratings of candidates are provided by trained observers who are usually human resource managers.

Although assessment centers are costly, virtually every study has found they are better predictors of employee performance than other selection approaches. Further, employees typically report that assessment centers have given them a fair chance to show their abilities. AT&T, the pioneer of this technique, is perhaps the best-known user, but more than 2000 organizations have assessment center programs in operation.[17]

Regardless of the selection method used, the organization must be able to demonstrate that its selection methods are valid and do not illegally discriminate against employee classes protected by EEO legislation. **Validity** means that a test actually measures what it says it measures and refers to inferences about tests. It may be valid to infer that college admission test scores predict college academic performance, but it is probably invalid to infer that those same test scores predict athletic performance. To validate their tests, organizations must show that test performance is related to subsequent job performance. If not, then use of the tests may adversely affect protected employees and could result in legal problems for the organization. Employment selection tests that were unrelated to job performance and excluded women and minorities were the catalyst for much of the legislation that affects the HRM function today. The EEOC publishes comprehensive guidelines on test validation and employee selection. Currently, most organizations make great efforts to use valid selection methods and to make selection decisions based upon anticipated job performance.

TRAINING

Training is a planned effort to assist employees in learning job-related behaviors that will improve their performance. The primary reason that organizations train new employees is to prepare them to work toward achieving the goals and objectives of the organization. At the same time, effective training should help trainees bring their skills, knowledge, and abilities up to the level required for satisfactory performance. As employees continue on the job, additional training provides them with the opportunity to acquire new knowledge and skills and improve their effectiveness on the job.

Training is vital to the success of modern organizations, both large and small. This is evidenced by the fact that organizations spend $100 billion every year on training.[18] Rapidly changing technology requires that employees possess the knowledge, skills, and abilities needed to cope with new processes and production techniques. Further, changes in management philosophy create a need for management development as well. For example, when faced with a tough global challenge, Xerox and Motorola increased their investment in employee training.[19] Training has helped Xerox regain market share from Japan. At Motorola, training gave the company the edge to grow in the face of strong Japanese competition in cellular phones and semiconductors.

Validity
A relationship between what a test proposes to measure and what is actually measured.

Training
A planned effort to assist employees in learning job-related behaviors in order to improve performance.

The organization's training needs can be identified through three types of analysis: (1) organizational, (2) task, and (3) individual.[20] Organizational analysis uses the company's strategic plan to identify the knowledge, skills, and abilities that will be needed in the future as jobs and the organization change. Task analysis uses job descriptions and job specifications to compare present job requirements with employee knowledge, skills, and abilities. Finally, individual training needs can be determined by focusing on how individuals perform their job. Performance appraisal information is often used to identify performance weaknesses that may be overcome with training.

Types of Training Programs

Once the training needs of the organization have been assessed, training programs must be designed and developed. Here we examine a few of the various kinds of training programs that typically exist in organizations.

The first step in the training process is to get new employees off to a good start. This is generally accomplished through an orientation program. **Orientation** is the formal process of familiarizing new employees with the organization, their job, and their work unit. Orientation procedures vary widely from company to company. Generally, their purpose is to enable new employees to fit in so that they become productive members of the organization. The newcomer may need several hours, several weeks, or several months of work with other employees to become completely familiar with the organization.

Technical training programs are designed to provide nonmanagerial employees with specialized skills and knowledge in the methods, processes, and techniques associated with their job or trade. In union settings, apprenticeship training programs are common for skilled occupations. With advances in training technology, many organizations are using computer-assisted instruction and interactive video training for their nonmanagerial employees. However, approximately 90 percent of technical training programs still use on-the-job training methods.[21]

On-the-job training is conducted while employees perform job-related tasks. This type of training is the most direct approach and offers employers the quickest return in terms of improved performance. At Solectron Corporation, a California electronic parts manufacturing company, on-the-job training has been essential for maintaining the high performance levels of a diverse workforce. This emphasis on training is driven by the enterpreneurial spirit of the company's CEOs, as described in Entrepreneurial Approach.

Management development programs are designed to improve the technical, interpersonal, and conceptual skills of supervisors, managers, and executives. On-the-job training for managers might include rotating through a variety of positions, regular coaching and mentoring by a supervisor, committee assignments to involve individuals in decision-making activities, and staff meetings to help managers become acquainted with the thinking of other managers and with activities outside their immediate area. Most of these on-the-job training methods are used to help managers broaden their organizational knowledge and experience. Some popular off-the-job training techniques include classroom training, simulations, role-playing, and case discussion groups.

Training and Quality Management

Organizations that implement aggressive quality improvement programs often find that additional training and employee development are essential to the success of the program. Through quality-oriented training programs, organizations ensure that employees know the quality goals of the organization, understand how their jobs relate to achieving those goals, and possess the skills and abilities necessary to contribute effectively.

Orientation
The process of familiarizing new employees with the organization, their job, and their work unit, that enables them to become productive members of the organization.

ENTREPRENEURIAL APPROACH

AN ENTREPRENEURIAL SPIRIT INSPIRES A DIVERSE WORKFORCE

Winston Chen spent 8 years at IBM, and Ko Nishimura put in 24 years. Chen and Nishimura are co-CEOs of Solectron Corporation, a manufacturer of internal components of electronic products, based in San Jose, California. An immigrant from Taiwan and a Harvard Ph.D., Chen bought into the floundering company for $100,000. Fifteen years later, growth at Solectron is spectacular with sales of $300 million and profits at $9 million. In 1991, Solectron won a Malcolm Baldrige National Quality Award.

What makes Chen and Nishimura so successful? Their entrepreneurial spirit is fueled by a diverse workforce of 3300. More than half of their employees are immigrants from the Middle East, Asia, and Latin America. The company devotes an average of 85 hours training each new employee, and that number is rising by 10 percent each year.

According to Nishimura and Chen, being average is not acceptable at Solectron. They continually challenge employees to work hard and managers to use sound management principles. At 7:30 A.M. every Wednesday, Nishimura and Chen meet with 80 or more of their managers to review quality improvements right down to solder joints. Defects have fallen from several hundred parts per million five years ago to five or six per million today. At 7:30 A.M. each Thursday, the team zeros in on how customers, including IBM, Sun Electronics, and Apple Computer, rated their performance the week before. Grading is tough: 100 points if the customer gives you an A: minus 100 for a D.

In the search for quality over quantity, many companies are finding that they must modify their training techniques. Companies in the service industry, such as Federal Express, Bell Canada, USAA, and Northwest Airlines, have found that some types of training actually hindered customer service and increased employee stress and job dissatisfaction as well.[22]

In developing training programs to support a quality orientation in the organization, HRM professionals must be aware of the economic, social, and political forces that have implications for training.[23] For example:

- Increased global and domestic competition has led to greater need for competitive strategies that often require extensive training.
- Rapid advances in technology have created an acute need for people with specialized technical skills.
- Widespread mergers, acquisitions, and divestitures have created a need to redesign many jobs. As a result, new training programs and reward systems may be necessary.
- A better-educated workforce that values self-development and personal growth has an enormous desire for learning and a growing need for new forms of participation at work.
- As some occupations become obsolete and new occupations emerge due to the changing nature of the business environment, flexible training policies are needed to prevent increased turnover and lower productivity.

PERFORMANCE APPRAISAL

Performance appraisal
A systematic process of evaluating employee job-related achievements, strengths, weaknesses, as well as determining ways to improve performance.

After employees have been trained and have settled into their jobs, managers usually begin to evaluate their performance. **Performance appraisal** is a systematic process of evaluating each employee's job-related achievements, strengths, and weaknesses, as well as determining ways to improve performance.

Performance is almost never one dimensional—there are always several dimensions to job performance. For example, the leading home run hitter on a baseball team may not be the best fielder or have the highest batting average. Consider that students evaluate university professors on one dimension of their performance—teaching. But, for most professors, their job has at least two other important dimensions—research and professional service.

Performance appraisals are invaluable aids in making many HRM decisions and are essential for distinguishing between good and poor performers. Managers can use performance appraisal information in four ways:

▼ Performance appraisals are invaluable aids in making any human resource management decision. A division manager is providing feedback to one of her staff members as part of his annual performance review.

1. *Motivation.* Organizations try to motivate employees by basing pay, bonuses, and other financial rewards on performance. Since performance is frequently a basis for rewards, it is important to evaluate performance so that those rewards can be provided fairly and serve as a motivator for future performance. Merit pay plans, for example, are designed to compensate people according to their job performance.

2. *Personnel movement.* Performance appraisal information helps managers develop an inventory of people appropriate for personnel movement. In other words, performance appraisals can be used to determine who should receive a promotion, transfer, demotion, or be dismissed.

3. *Training.* By identifying areas of poor performance, performance appraisals help the manager suggest training or other programs to improve certain skills or behaviors.

4. *Feedback.* Performance appraisals provide a mechanism for giving employees feedback about their work performance. If employees are to do their jobs better in the future, they need to know how well they have done them in the past so that they can adjust their work patterns as necessary.

Rating Performance

Effective performance appraisals usually consider various dimensions of a job. A variety of methods are available, but the most widely used approaches evaluate either behaviors or performance results.[24]

Behavior-Oriented Approaches   Behavior-oriented approaches to performance appraisal focus on assessing employee behavior. Two commonly used methods are graphic rating scales and behavioral-anchored rating scales.

When graphic ratings scales are used to assess performance, employees are evaluated on a series of performance dimensions, such as initiative, tardiness, and accuracy of work, using a five- or seven-point scale. For example, a typical rating scale ranges from 1 to 5, with 1 representing poor performance and 5 representing outstanding performance. The rater evaluates the employee on each performance dimension by checking the appropriate place on the scale.

Performance dimensions on a graphic rating scale tend to be fairly general, and as a result, the scales are relatively flexible and can be used to evaluate individuals in a number of different jobs. But, because the graphic rating scale is general, considerable interpretation is needed to apply it to specific jobs. As a result, the scale sometimes produces inconsistent and inaccurate ratings of employees. In general, the more clearly and specifically the scales and performance dimensions are defined, the more effective the evaluation system.

To define various aspects of an employee's job more clearly, some organizations use behavioral-anchored rating scales (BARS). BARS are similar to graphic rating scales, but use more detailed examples of job behaviors to represent different levels of performance. The BARS approach relies on job analysis information to describe a range of desirable and undesirable behaviors for each performance dimension. Each of these behavioral descriptors is used as an anchor to distinguish between high, moderate, and low performance. Using BARS reduces subjective interpretation of performance because they are based on clearly stated job-related activities. They are costly to construct, however, and both subordinates and supervisors require training in their use.[25]

Results-Oriented Approach   An alternative to the behavior-oriented approaches to performance appraisal is a results-oriented method. One of the most common results-oriented performance appraisal systems is management by objectives (MBO). As you will recall from Chapter 4, MBO is a system of guided self-appraisal that is useful in evaluating an employee's performance. Through the MBO process, specific goals are set for individual members of the organization. Employees are evaluated on the basis of how well they have achieved the results specified by their goals.

Because results-oriented approaches to performance appraisal use objective performance criteria, there is less bias in the evaluation process. Such approaches are not very useful for training purposes, however, because they provide little information that can be used to improve performance. Results can also be contaminated by factors beyond the employee's control. Equipment breakdowns, economic changes, and the availability and quality of supplies are just a few of the factors that can affect performance. When using this approach, organizations must also guard against encouraging a "results at any cost" mentality among their employees.

Problems with Performance Appraisal

While we would like to believe that every manager carefully assesses each employee's performance, most people who have given or received a performance appraisal are aware of the subjective nature of the process. This subjectivity can lead to the following common problems.

Halo Effect   The halo effect occurs when a manager rates an employee high or low on all items because of one characteristic. For example, a worker who has few absences might receive high ratings in all other areas of work, including quantity and quality of output. The manager may not really think about the employee's other characteristics separately. While an employee may perform at the same level across all dimensions, most people do some things better than others. Thus, the ratings should differ from one dimension to another.

Rater Patterns   Students are well aware that some professors tend to grade easier or harder than others. Likewise, a manager may develop a rating pattern. For example, some managers have a problem with central tendency. Central tendency occurs when the rater judges all employees as average, even though their performance varies. Managers with wide spans of control and, thus, many subordinates may have less opportunity to observe the behavior of individual employees. Such managers are more likely to play it safe and rate most of them in the middle of the scale rather than high or low.

Another common rater pattern is the leniency-severity error. Leniency error occurs when the rater evaluates some in a group higher than they should be or when the rater is unjustifiably easy in evaluating performance. In contrast, a severity error occurs when a rater tends to be unjustifiably harsh in evaluating employee performance.

Contrast Error   A contrast error is the tendency to rate employees relative to each other rather than to performance standards. If almost everyone in a group is doing a mediocre job, then a person performing somewhat better may be rated as excellent because of the contrast effect. But, in a higher performing group, the same person might have received only an average rating. Although it may be appropriate to compare people at times, performance appraisal ratings should evaluate performance against job requirements rather than against other employees.

There is no simple way to eliminate the problems associated with performance appraisal. However, making raters aware of the potential problems through training programs is beneficial in overcoming the errors and the problems that result.

COMPENSATION

Compensation consists of wages paid directly for time worked, incentives for better performance, and indirect benefits that employees receive as part of their employment relationship with the organization. Together, these elements make up the compensation that employees receive for the work they do for the organization.

Base pay refers to wage and salaries employees receive in exchange for performing their jobs. Base pay rates are determined by economic forces in the labor market by competitor wages, and, in unionized firms, by negotiation. In most noncommission jobs, base pay represents the majority of the compensation an employee receives.

To attract, retain, and motivate employees, however, many organizations offer compensation beyond base pay in the form of bonuses, commissions, and profit-sharing plans. These incentives are designed to encourage employees to produce results beyond expected performance norms. Today, in an effort to improve the quality of products and services, many organizations are experimenting with various incentive plans to reward employees who contribute toward meeting the quality goals of the organization.

An example of a particularly creative approach to improving service quality can be found at E.T.C. Carpet Mills in Santa Ana, California. This company has successfully used incentives to encourage its employees to provide better customer service. Since customers often had to wait more than an hour for an order at competing firms, E.T.C. tried to establish a 10-minute or less waiting period for customers. When an order is finished within 10 minutes, the company puts $1 into a bonus fund. Every three months the balance of the fund is divided evenly among the company's 10 employees. As a result, employees often receive bonuses of $600 each, and the company has developed a reputation for superior customer service.[26]

Benefits, a more indirect type of compensation, are payments beyond wages or salaries that are given to employees as a reward for organizational membership. Benefits can be categorized into several types: required and voluntary security, retirement, time-off, insurance and financial, and social and recreational. Examples of the benefits an organization can provide are listed in Table 10.5.[27]

Compensation
Wages paid directly for time worked (base pay), incentives for better performance, and indirect benefits that employees receive as part of their employment relationship with the organization.

▼ **Table 10.5**   Examples of Different Benefits by Category

REQUIRED SECURITY	VOLUNTARY SECURITY	RETIREMENT	TIME-OFF	INSURANCE	FINANCIAL	SOCIAL AND RECREATIONAL
• Worker's compensation • Unemployment compensation • Old age, survivors' and disability insurance • State disability insurance • Medicare hospital benefits	• Severance pay • Supplemental unemployment benefits • Leave of absence	• Social Security • Pension fund • Early retirement • Preretirement counseling • Retirement gratuity • Retirement annuity • Disability retirement benefits	• Vacation time • Company subsidized travel • Holidays • Sick pay • Military reserve pay • Social-service sabbatical	• Medical • Dental • Travel accident insurance • Group insurance rates • Disability insurance • Life insurance • Auto insurance	• Credit union • Profit sharing • Company-provided housing or car • Legal services • Purchase discounts • Stock plans • Financial counseling • Moving expenses • Tuition assistance/reimbursement • Relocation planning and assistance	• Recreational facilities • Company publications • Professional memberships • Counseling • Company-sponsored events • Child-care services • Food services • Wellness and health services/facilities • Service awards

Organizations commonly provide health, dental, disability, and life insurance coverage for employees and sometimes for their families. The costs of these plans may be paid entirely by the company or shared with the employee. Also, employees usually receive some pay for time that they don't work, such as vacations, sick days, and holidays. Retirement programs are also a common benefit.

Some companies even provide benefits such as counseling, wellness programs, credit unions, legal advice, and tuition reimbursement for educational expenses. For example, RJR Nabisco pays for the educational expenses of its employees. It has committed $5 million annually to help employees and their children attend college or job-training programs. The company offers a wide range of financial assistance for high school graduates, including scholarships to college, trade, or vocational schools. While RJR Nabisco can't pay the full college bill, the company's goal is to ensure that nobody is denied a post-secondary education for financial reasons. This focus on education is part of a benefits package that includes giving workers time off for parent-teacher conferences and even for a child's first day of school.[28]

A benefit package can represent a significant cost to an organization. In a recent survey of major U.S. manufacturing firms, benefits represented an average of 37.7 percent of the organizational payroll.[29] Although benefits represent a major cost to an organization, they are also a key factor in attracting and retaining employees.

Compensation programs reflect the overall culture, life-cycle stages, and strategic plans of the organization.[30] As shown in Table 10.6, for example, the compensation practices appropriate for a newly formed organization may be different than for a more mature organization.[31] For example, to encourage innovation, flexibility, and an entrepreneurial culture, a new organization might offer stock equity programs to encourage employees to participate in

▼ Employees at U-Haul International Inc. take part in an exercise program that is just one of many employee health related benefit campaigns sponsored by the company.

the growth and success of the company. In contrast, highly structured pay and benefit programs may be more appropriate for a large, stable organization.[32]

Designing Equitable Reward Systems

Most organizations attempt to develop a compensation system that carefully considers issues of equity or fairness. Compensation is often the prime reason an individual works. However, compensation usually has several meanings to employees. Compensation has economic meaning because it allows people to obtain the necessities and luxuries they need and want; compensation is symbolic because it is a means of keeping "score" and a measure of achievement; an increase in compensation indicates growth because it reflects how well employees' performance and capabilities have grown.

In practice, developing an equitable or fair compensation system is quite challenging, primarily because most organizations have very complex compen-

▼ **Table 10.6**   Matching Compensation and Organizational Life Cycles

| Compensation | ORGANIZATIONAL LIFE-CYCLE STAGE | | | |
	Introductory	Growth	Maturity	Decline
Pay	Competitive, but conservative wages/salaries	Moderate wages/salaries	Above-market wages/salaries	High wages/salaries with pressure for reductions
Incentives	Stock/equity possibilities	Bonuses tied to objective; stock options	Bonuses, incentive plans, stock options	Reduced bonuses cost-saving incentive plans
Benefits	Core benefits	Complete benefits at moderate level; limited executive perks	Comprehensive benefits; expanded executive perks	Cost-consciousness limit benefit costs; frozen executive perks

sation systems. Equity theory, discussed in Chapter 15, is the basis for designing fair pay plans. Compensation designers are concerned with three sources of fairness expectations: (1) external fairness, (2) internal fairness, and (3) employee fairness.[33] External fairness refers to expectations that the pay for a job in one organization is fair relative to the pay for the same job in other organizations. Wage surveys are used to compare the organization's pay rates with other organizations in the industry to ensure that the pay remains competitive. Internal fairness refers to expectations that the pay for the job the individual is performing within the organization is fair relative to the pay of higher- and lower-level jobs in the same organization. Job evaluation procedures use job specifications to determine the relative worth of jobs in the organization. Employee fairness refers to expectations that individuals on a given job are paid fairly relative to co-workers on the same job. Differences in pay among co-workers are acceptable if the variations are based on differences in performance or seniority. Because compensation can be so complex, many organizations have compensation specialists in the human resource department who develop, administer, and oversee the compensation system. They ensure that the organization provides compensation that is both competitive and equitable.

In many organizations, the human resource planning process that we have been examining is affected by labor-management relations. In the next part of the chapter, we examine the role of unions and the strategies organizations use in dealing with them.

LABOR-MANAGEMENT RELATIONS

Labor-management relations
The formal process through which employees and unions negotiate terms and conditions of employment including pay, hours of work, benefits, and other important aspects of the working environment.

The term **labor-management relations** refers to the formal process through which employees and unions negotiate terms and conditions of employment including pay, hours of work, benefits, and other important aspects of the working environment. Unions are employee groups formed for the purpose of negotiating with management regarding the terms and conditions related to their work. Unions represent workers and seek to protect and promote their members' political, social, and economic interests through collective bargaining.

Given the turbulent history of labor-management relations, it should come as no surprise that the process of forming a union is closely regulated by the government. The National Labor Relations Board (NLRB) is the government agency that oversees this process in the private sector. It enforces the provisions of the Wagner Act of 1935 and the Taft-Hartley Act of 1947 (an amendment to the Wagner Act), two major laws governing labor-management relations. When recognized by the NLRB, unions have the legal right to negotiate with private employers over terms and conditions of employment and to help administer the resulting contract.

Unions have political power and use their lobbying efforts to support legislation that is in their own interests and the interests of all employees. They also can provide workers with an opportunity to participate in determining the conditions under which they work.

Management can pursue several different strategies in dealing with organized labor. With a conflict orientation, management refuses to "give in" to labor and only recognizes the union because it is required to do so by law.[34] This approach is exemplified by Frank Lorenzo's use of hardball tactics to cut labor costs at two airlines, Continental and Eastern. Others use a more cooperative approach commonly associated with Japanese-style management practices. Each party recognizes that the other party is necessary for attaining their respective goals. Recognition of shared interests has led to labor-management relationships characterized by mutual trust and friendly attitudes.[35] Ford Motor Company, Cummins Engine Company, Bridgestone/Firestone, Inc., and others have established cooperative relations with unions in the hope that teamwork will boost productivity and quality and hold down costs.[36] In general, management prefers that employees do not belong to unions. Why then do employees join unions? Unionization is attractive to employees who believe that employment conditions are deteriorating and that, as individuals, they have little power to change those conditions.[37] Studies have shown that workers who are dissatisfied with various aspects of the workforce, such as wages, job security, benefits, unfair treatment, and workplace governance, are more likely to join a union if they believe that the union will be effective in remedying the situation.[38]

What is the future outlook for unions? Union membership has declined in the last decade for several reasons. One reason for this trend is that effective HRM in organizations has reduced the need for union protection. Other reasons include a decrease in union-organizing attempts, a decline in the traditional union industries, a decline in the economic well-being of companies (making it more difficult for unions to pressure for better wages and benefits), and effective management opposition to unions.

CURRENT ISSUES IN HUMAN RESOURCE MANAGEMENT

We conclude our examination of HRM by discussing several current issues facing today's managers. These include HRM in the multinational corporation, workforce diversity, sexual harassment, and health concerns in the work environment.

HRM IN THE MULTINATIONAL CORPORATION

The effective management of human resources is of critical importance to multinational corporations that compete in the global marketplace. Multinational organizations face greater diversity in both their labor and managerial workforce and, as a result, must develop an HRM system that is flexible and adaptable to a wide variety of cultural situations. As a result, the job of the HRM manager in a multinational is far more complex than that of his or her domestic counterpart.

Perhaps one of the most significant challenges associated with the HRM process in multinational organizations lies in managing expatriate personnel. An expatriate is an organizational member who is a citizen of the country in which the multinational is headquartered, but is assigned to a position in one of the company's foreign operating facilities. If, for example, a French firm sends a French manager to oversee its plant in Australia, it has chosen to use an expatriate in that position.

Managing expatriates presents some unique challenges for human resource professionals in terms of selection, training, and compensation.[39] For example, expatriates must be selected based on a broader set of characteristics than domestic personnel. Situational factors such as stage of career development and family commitments[40] become more important, as do personnel characteristics such as flexibility, cultural empathy, and maturity. Further, the training process is more complex for expatriate managers.[41] Language and cross-cultural training for both the expatriate and his or her family is essential. An expatriate's compensation package is also more complex than a domestic manager's compensation package. In addition to the traditional base salary, incentives, and benefits, expatriates may receive a cost-of-living adjustment, an overseas premium to compensate for the hardship of living in a foreign environment, and other perquisites such as membership in social clubs, transportation allowances, and home leave expenses to make the overseas assignment more attractive.

Historically, many multinationals have experienced disappointing results from managers sent on overseas assignments. This has been particularly true for U.S.-based firms.[42] In general, U.S. multinationals have achieved much less success with expatriates than have most Japanese and many European firms.[43] While this has been attributed, in large part, to ineffective HRM practices in many U.S. firms, all indications are that American organizations are improving their international HRM systems tremendously. It is clear that multinationals that employ careful selection procedures, require and administer effective training programs, and offer compensation packages that reward and motivate the expatriate will achieve greater success in the global environment of today and tomorrow.

WORKFORCE DIVERSITY

The changing nature of the workforce represents a challenge for many organizations. For example, the influx of women and ethnic minorities is having a tremendous impact on the workplace. Women accounted for 60 percent of the total growth of the U.S. workforce between 1970 and 1985, and they are expected to make up a similar percentage of new entry-level employees between 1991 and 2000. Many of these women have children. In fact, one of the fastest growing segments of the labor market is mothers with infants.[44] In addition, it is projected that a third of the newcomers into the workforce between now and the year 2000 will be minority group members.[45]

Demographic changes in the workforce have forced organizations to introduce new HRM programs and adapt existing programs and policies. For example, today's managers must be prepared to interact with people of different cultures as superiors, peers, and subordinates. Consequently, many organizations are developing training programs to enhance their managers knowledge and awareness of cultural differences. Other organizations have found it necessary to offer language training to employees for whom English is a second language. Flexible work schedules and telecommuting are often used to accommodate the needs of mothers with infants, and maternity leave and child-care assistance programs are offered in more organizations.

Increases in the number of highly capable women and minorities in the workforce have created a need for many organizations to review their promotion and compensation policies. Corporate America has been accused of maintaining attitudes and prejudices that have created a "glass ceiling" denying women access to managerial and executive positions.[46] As a result, women continue to occupy jobs that pay less than male-dominated jobs.

The historical earnings gap between men and women has led to calls for comparable worth legislation. Comparable worth is the concept that jobs requiring comparable levels of knowledge, skills, and abilities should be paid similarly even if the job tasks and market rates are significantly different. To date, only a few states and local municipalities have passed laws mandating equal pay for comparable worth in public sector jobs.[47] Although comparable worth legislation affecting private employers is unlikely, organizations must continue to monitor the status of women and minorities and proactively work to remove the vestiges of non-job-related biases.

Throughout this chapter we have presented examples of organizations that are adapting to these changes successfully. Avon, Corning, Monsanto, Solectron, IBM, and Du Pont are just a few of the organizations that have recognized the trends toward a more diverse workforce and have developed plans for managing that diversity effectively.

SEXUAL HARASSMENT

Sexual harassment refers to actions that are sexually directed, unwanted, and subject the worker to adverse employment conditions.[48] The Supreme Court and the EEOC recognize two major forms of sexual harassment.[49]

The first is "quid pro quo" harassment in which sexual compliance is required for job-related benefits and opportunities such as pay and promotions. Harassment by supervisors and managers who expect sexual favors as a condition for a raise or promotion is inappropriate and unacceptable behavior in the work environment. The second form of sexual harassment has been termed "hostile" environment harassment. In this case, the victim does not suffer any tangible economic injury, but workplace conduct is sufficiently severe to create an abusive working environment. A pattern of lewd jokes and comments in one instance and sexually oriented graffiti and posters in another have been viewed by the courts as sexual harassment.[50]

Sexual harassment can occur between a boss and subordinate, among co-workers, and among people outside the organization who have business contacts with employees. The vast majority of situations involve harassment of women by men. As a result of losing suits and appeals, companies are becoming more conscious of sexual harassment and are doing more to protect the rights of women. Training sessions, booklets, guidelines, and company policies regarding acceptable workplace behavior are some of the proactive methods for discouraging sexual harassment.[51] Some actions suggested by the EEOC guidelines are listed in Table 10.7.

Sexual harassment
Actions that are sexually directed, unwanted, and subject a worker to adverse employment conditions.

▼ **Table 10.7**   EEOC Guideline Suggestions for Preventing Sexual Harassment

- Establish a policy on sexual harassment and distribute a copy of the policy to all employees. Such policies make a major contribution to the prevention and control of sexual harassment.
- Develop mechanisms for investigating complaints. The organization needs a system for complaints that ensures that they are satisfactorily investigated and acted upon. This will also deter fear of retaliation.
- Develop mechanisms for handling the accused so that they are assured of a fair and thorough investigation that protects their individual rights.
- Communicate to all employees, especially to supervisors and managers, concerns and regulations regarding sexual harassment and the importance of creating and maintaining a work environment free of sexual harassment.
- Discipline offenders by using organizational sanctions up to and including firing the offenders.
- Train all employees, especially supervisors and managers, about what constitutes sexual harassment, and alert employees to the issues and behaviors involved.

HEALTH CONCERNS IN THE WORK ENVIRONMENT

Employee health problems are inevitable in any organization. These problems can range from simple illness, such as colds, to far more serious health problems. Some employees have emotional problems; others have drinking or drug problems; still others may have chronic illnesses that cause excessive absenteeism. All these difficulties may significantly affect the ability of employees to fulfill their job responsibilities. Many organizations are taking a proactive role to assist employees in dealing with these issues. Some of the more popular approaches are employee assistance programs and wellness programs.

Employee assistance programs
Designed to help employees cope with physical, personal, and emotional problems including substance abuse, alcoholism, stress, emotional illness, and family disturbances.

Employee assistance programs (EAPs) are designed to help employees cope with physical, personal, and emotional problems. These problems may include substance abuse, alcoholism, stress, emotional illness, and family disturbances. In such programs, employers establish a liaison with a social service counseling agency. Employees who have problems may contact the agency voluntarily or by employer referral. The employer pays the counseling costs up to a predetermined limit.

The growing interest in EAPs is due, in part, to an increase in the incidence of physical and emotional problems in the working population. In the long run, EAPs can save a company money. For example, alcoholism costs corporate America an estimated $86 billion a year due to employee health problems and poor performance. The expense of helping an alcoholic recover through an EAP is a fraction of the long-term potential cost.[52]

Unlike EAPs, which deal with problems after they have occurred, wellness programs are designed to maintain or improve employee health before problems arise. Wellness programs are activities that organizations engage in to promote good health habits, identify and correct health problems, direct lifestyle changes, and/or encourage a healthy work environment.

According to the Centers for Disease Control in Atlanta, Georgia, more than half of all deaths in the United States are directly related to lifestyle. Companies overwhelmed with medical costs are spending millions on wellness

▼ "Exercise for the health of it" is the central theme for the U-Haul International Inc. Employee Health Fair. During this four-day event, employees are encouraged to try new exercise programs and adopt healthy lifestyles.

programs, an extremely popular addition to an organization's benefit program. These programs are a viable option when an employer desires to improve productivity, decrease absenteeism, and lower health-care costs. Estimates are that more than 50,000 U.S. firms provide some type of company-sponsored health promotion program.

U-Haul, Control Data, Southern California Edison, Adolf Coors, and Baker Hughes are companies that emphasize wellness by providing their employees with financial incentives to meet certain "wellness" criteria, such as not smoking and maintaining a normal weight. These incentives can be in the form of lower employee health insurance premiums or higher benefits. For example, Baker Hughes saves $2 million annually because nonsmoking employees are charged less for health insurance. Adolf Coors saves $3.2 million by offering its employees incentives to meet weight, smoking, blood pressure, cholesterol, and other health criteria.[53]

MANAGERIAL IMPLICATIONS

In this chapter you were introduced to the role of human resource management in today's organizations. As a manager, you will be called upon to make human resource decisions; therefore, it is important to remember the following points:

- Recognize that human resource planning is a critical element of the strategic planning process and is essential for long-term organizational success.
- Base all HRM decisions on job-related criteria and not on racial, sexual, or other unjustified biases.
- Remember that job analysis is essential to effective human resource planning and the development of programs that satisfy the organization's human resource requirements.
- Carefully evaluate both internal and external sources of recruitment.
- Be innovative in scheduling work, designing jobs, and rewarding employees so that you can respond effectively to the changing composition and needs of the workforce.
- To keep pace with rapid changes in technology, be sure to upgrade the knowledge and skill base of their employees through training programs.
- Remember that equitable pay systems, unbiased performance appraisals, and equal access to training opportunities are just a few of the steps organizations can take to avoid unionization.

Many corporate public relations documents refer to people as "the most valuable resource" of the organization.[54] These organizations realize that human resources must be well managed to succeed in the business environment of today and tomorrow. A well-developed human resource management system results in a more productive workforce, higher morale and job satisfaction, and a reputation for being a great place to work.

CORNING: IT SIMPLY MAKES GOOD BUSINESS SENSE

MANAGERIAL INCIDENT RESOLUTION

To break the cycle of high attrition rates for minorities and women, Corning established a human resource plan and goals that involved more than producing excellent products. First, the plan organized two quality improvement teams headed by senior executives; one targeted black employees and the other targeted female employees. New selection and recruitment programs were developed, and Corning established a nationwide scholarship program that provided renewable grants in exchange for a summer of paid work at some Corning installation. The majority of program participants have come to work for Corning full-time after graduation, and very few have left the company so far. The company also expanded its summer intern program, with an emphasis on minorities and women, and established formal recruiting contacts with campus groups like the Society of Women Engineers and the National Black MBA Association.

Corning also wanted to create a high-quality work environment for employees. Part of its plan included mandatory awareness training for some 76,000 salaried employees. One goal of the training was to identify unconscious company values that work against minorities and females. Corning made an effort to improve communications by printing regular stories and articles about the diverse workforce in its in-house newspaper and by publicizing employee success stories that emphasized diversity. It worked hard to identify and publicize promotion criteria. Career planning systems were introduced for all employees.

At Corning, corporate staff is being cut; layers of management are being eliminated; and the number of employees is decreasing. What is left is a leaner and trimmer organization staffed by a more diverse group of employees who share power as they go about their daily tasks. All of these changes focused on the proper utilization of human resources. In the words of CEO Houghton, "it simply makes good business sense."[55] ▼

SUMMARY

- A substantial amount of legislation deals with various forms of employee rights including protection against discrimination, equal employment opportunity, and affirmative-action programs. These laws prohibit discrimination on the basis of sex, race color, religion, or national origin in all areas of employment.

- Human resource planning is the process of determining future human resource needs relative to an organization's strategic plan and devising the steps necessary to meet those needs. It includes job analysis, forecasting, staffing, training, performance appraisal, and rewarding.

- During the process of selection, managers must determine the extent to which job candidates have the skills, abilities, and knowledge required to perform effectively in the positions for which they are being considered. The major selection methods—application forms, tests, interviews, and assessment centers—must be job related and have no discriminatory effects.

- Training is a planned effort to facilitate employee learning of job-related behaviors in order to improve performance. Organizations train new employees to help achieve the organization's objectives and help employees develop their skills, knowledge, and abilities.

- Performance appraisal is a systematic process of evaluating each employee's job-related achievements, strengths, and weaknesses, as well as determining ways to improve performance.

- Employees are rewarded with compensation, such as pay and incentives, and benefits. Most organizations attempt to develop a compensation system that carefully considers issues of equity or fairness.

- The term labor-management relations refers to the formal process through which employees and unions negotiate conditions of employment. Numerous government regulations define and regulate labor-management relations.

● Some of the current issues facing today's managers include HRM in the multinational corporation, workforce diversity, sexual harassment, and health concerns in the work environment.

KEY TERMS

Human Resource Management (HRM) (p. 318)	Job specifications (p. 323)	Orientation (p. 331)
Protected class (p. 320)	Recruitment (p. 324)	Performance appraisal (p. 345)
Staffing (p. 321)	Selection (p. 325)	Compensation (p. 335)
Human resource planning (p. 322)	Employment tests (p. 326)	Labor-management relations (p. 338)
Job analysis (p. 323)	Assessment center (p. 329)	Sexual harassment (p. 341)
Job descriptions (p. 323)	Validity (p. 330)	Employee assistance programs (p. 342)
	Training (p. 330)	

REVIEW QUESTIONS

1. Describe the steps in the human resource planning process.
2. Distinguish between supply and demand forecasting.
3. Describe the different recruiting techniques used by organizations.
4. What are the different methods organizations use to select employees?
5. Distinguish between behavior- and results-oriented performance appraisal methods.
6. Explain ways in which interviewing can be improved.
7. What are some of the common problems inherent in performance appraisals?
8. When is it appropriate to use MBO?
9. Discuss the three key laws that address discrimination in employment.
10. Explain the various ways that managers can use performance appraisal information.
11. What are some of the current HRM issues facing managers in organizations today?

DISCUSSION QUESTIONS

Improving Critical Thinking

1. Evaluate the reward system of an organization with which you are familiar in terms of how equitable it is.
2. Look for a current article in a newspaper or magazine that describes sexual harassment. Why is this a problem for managers?
3. Describe an orientation program that you have attended. What suggestions would you make to improve the program?
4. Discuss why union membership is declining. Would you be interested in joining a union? Why or why not?

Enhancing Communication Skills

5. Write a report that describes an interview that you have had. Was it structured or unstructured? What was your impression of the interviewer? Of the organization? What could have been done to improve the interview? Present your experiences and suggestions for improvement to the class.

6. Obtain an application form from a local organization. Analyze the form and discuss the impact of any questions that could be discriminatory. Present the form and your analysis to the class.

Building Teamwork Skills

7. Form small groups as directed by your instructor. Discuss the following issue: Organizations need to increase their focus on training to improve competitiveness.
8. Have you ever been the victim of illegal discrimination? Form a team of six to eight students. Exchange your experiences with members of your team. How do your experiences and reactions to discrimination compare with those of your team members? Do gender, race or other characteristics affect the amount and type of experiences?

ETHICS: TAKE A STAND

Seth had just been recognized by his law firm for his outstanding performance on the Donner case. He had masterfully convinced the jury of the innocence of his client. He had been thorough, well prepared, and persuasive. Linda, a partner in the firm, asked Seth to join her in a celebratory lunch to discuss his "future with the firm."

During the course of the meal, the conversation took an unexpected turn. Linda began commenting on how attractive and sexy she thought Seth was and expressed a desire to spend more time with him. When Seth refused the advances, she reminded him of how much a partner could do to further his career at the firm and said the firm needed an "attractive" asset like Seth.

The working relationship between Linda and Seth quickly deteriorated after this encounter. Unwelcome innuendos became commonplace, and Linda would often rub her shoulder against his or put her hand on his arm when they were alone. Discussions about work often resulted in comments about "how new associates really got ahead in the firm." Because of these confrontations, Seth tried being rude to Linda or simply avoiding her whenever possible. He began to dread going to the office each day.

Although Seth was certain he was being subjected to sexual harassment, he was hesitant to pursue it any further. After all, shouldn't a man be immune to such behavior? He felt that making a formal complaint would irreparably damage his future in this firm or in any other law firm. After all, Linda was a prominent law partner and a well-known author. Seth was concerned that no one would believe him because her advances were made in private. Since he was the newest associate lawyer at the firm, he feared any complaints might hurt the chances of other new associates succeeding at the firm. Furthermore, he was afraid people would think he was "weak." After all, shouldn't he have been able to handle these verbal assaults on his own? How would he ever be able to deal with "tough" clients? If he did come forward, would people wonder why he had allowed things to escalate to this point? Because of his embarrassment, he had not revealed the situation to anyone. Although these questions weighed heavy on his mind, he also felt he had a responsibility to himself and other young associates in the workplace. Seth hoped he would make the right decision.

For Discussion

1. Discuss what action you think Seth should take.
2. What are the possible problems that Seth may face with his peers? With his supervisor?
3. Would the situation be any different if the advances had been made by a man to a woman?

THINKING CRITICALLY
Debate the Issue

COMPENSATION—PUBLIC OR PRIVATE

Form teams of four to five students as directed by your instructor. As assigned by your instructor, prepare to argue one side of the following issue: Compensation practices in the organization, including all employees/management salaries and benefits, should (should not) be made public. Research your team's position, and be prepared with specific company examples, rules, and policies. Your instructor will select two teams to present their findings to the class in a debate format.

VIDEO CASE

Studio 904

Although Studio 904 had a strong customer base of about 1,800 regular customers, the company faced some serious issues concerning its future growth. The Seattle-based hairdressing company utilized commissioned sales, leased chairs, and tipping systems in its operating procedures. While these practices were standard for the industry, Studio 904's management believed the company's long-term growth goals could not be achieved unless drastic changes were made.

The most significant change at Studio 904 shifted the company's emphasis from profits to customer service. Instead of focusing on the acquisition of new customers, the company began to focus on increasing the satisfaction of its current customers by establishing long-term relationships. Although attracting new customers remained an essential component of the company's future growth, Studio 904 planned to generate greater loyalty among its current customers in order to increase repeat business. To support its new emphasis on customer service, Studio 904 developed a quality assurance program that included weekly training sessions for all employees. An environmental awareness program was also established to emphasize the company's use of environmentally safe products and its sensitivity to environmental issues. To further support Studio 904's emphasis on customer service, the method of employee compensation was changed

from a tip-based system to hourly or, in most cases, salary-based compensation. Studio 904 also provided its employees with medical and dental benefits, sick pay, and vacation pay.

Studio 904 has received many benefits from its new emphasis on customer service and satisfaction. In particular, its customer base has risen from 1,800 to more than 5,000 customers. As a result of its rapid growth, Studio 904 has opened a second location in Seattle. The greater number of satisfied, repeat customers and improved compensation benefits have led directly to increased employee satisfaction, which in turn has resulted in a reduction in the level of employee turnover. Finally, because of its environmental awareness program, Studio 904 has been recognized by the city of Seattle for its leadership and responsibility within the community. With these factors in place, Studio 904 has positioned itself to attain greater profitability and to achieve its future growth goals.

For Discussion

1. How did the management at Studio 904 alter its human resource management practices to improve the overall performance of the company?

2. What other human resource management changes might Studio 904 make to further improve employee relations, quality, and financial performance?

CASE

The Campus Interview

After four years of college, Courtney was excited and looking forward to pursuing a career as a CPA in one of the top accounting firms in New Orleans. During her four years in college, she had maintained a 3.7 grade point average in her accounting classes, had been president of the Student Accounting Association, was an active member of a business fraternity, and worked part-time for an accounting professor. She used the Campus Placement Services to develop her résumé and prepare for interviews and felt prepared to present herself to potential employers.

Her first interview was going quite well until the interviewer, Jon Hall, asked her, "Courtney, I see from your application materials that you have a five-year-old son, but I don't see a wedding ring. If you are a single parent, what are you going to do about him if you get

the job and have to travel?" Courtney was caught off guard by the question but responded, "Gee, Mr. Hall, do you mean I have to get rid of him if I get the job?" Jon's face turned red. He quickly thanked Courtney for her time and ended the interview.

As Courtney left the placement office, she wondered if she had handled the situation correctly. She also wondered if she should take any further action.

For Discussion

1. Discuss Courtney's handling of the interviewer's question. Are there any other ways she could have handled the situation?

2. Are there any general rules applicants can follow in dealing with potentially illegal questions asked either on an application form or in an interview?

EXPERIENTIAL EXERCISE 10.1

Career Stages Profile

Purpose: The Career Stages Profile (CSP) measures primary central activities and relationships and provides an understanding of your career stage.

Procedure: For each of the following statements, indicate how much you agree or disagree that the statement applies to you now in your current job. Use the following scale and place the appropriate number in the blank next to the statement.

Strongly Agree	Agree	Neither Agree Nor Disagree	Disagree	Strongly Disagree
5	4	3	2	1

_____ 1. My work involves assisting others and learning from the experience.

_____ 2. My work includes supportive work relationships with my peers.

_____ 3. My supervisor's responsibility is to provide me with challenging assignments that allow me opportunities to grow and learn.

_____ 4. I am involved in training possible successors who can perform my job.

_____ 5. I expect my supervisor to give me guidance, help me develop skills, and provide opportunities that will increase my level of understanding.

_____ 6. I depend on my supervisor to provide challenging assignments that will give me exposure to higher levels in the organization and increase my visibility.

_____ 7. One of my important roles is developing younger employees.

_____ 8. I am sometimes concerned that my career is over, worry about my identity outside work, and resent the idea of losing my influence over the organization's future.

_____ 9. I need feedback, coaching, and personal acceptance from my supervisor.

_____ 10. My supervisor respects my competence and knows he or she has my full personal commitment.

_____ 11. I am very concerned about not being able to achieve all the things I had hoped in both my work and my personal life.

_____ 12. My current work activities consist primarily of completing major long-term projects and assignments.

_____ 13. My major work responsibilities are to provide technical assistance and support to my supervisor.

_____ 14. I am concerned about the number of important decisions I make on my own and about the conflicts between my work and my personal life.

_____ 15. A lot of my time at work is spent training new people and handling special assignments.

_____ 16. My most important work-related relationships center on professional involvements outside the organization.

_____ 17. I often feel concerned about coping with organizational politics and the conflicting demands placed on me.

_____ 18. Most of my current work is done independently and requires specialized technical contributions.

_____ 19. My most important work relationships are with the younger employees I am mentoring.

_____ 20. I expect my supervisor to provide me with a lot of freedom and autonomy.

Scoring: Transfer the values from the statements above to the following columns. Next, add up the points for each column. These are your scores on the Career Stages Profile.

Stage 1	Stage 2	Stage 3	Stage 4
1. _____	2. _____	3. _____	4. _____
5. _____	6. _____	7. _____	8. _____
9. _____	10. _____	11. _____	12. _____
13. _____	14. _____	15. _____	16. _____
17. _____	18. _____	19. _____	20. _____
Total _____	_____	_____	_____
Exploration and testing	Establishment and advancement	Maintenance	Withdrawal

Interpretation: Scores in each stage can range from a low of 5 to a high of 25. Scores of 20 or higher shoud indicate the stage of your career at the present time. Scores of 10 or less would normally indicate that you have already passed or not yet started that stage.

NOTES

1. J. Hoerr, "Sharpening Minds for a Competitive Edge," *Business Week,* December 17, 1990, 72–78; R. R. Thomas, "From Affirmative Action to Affirming Diversity," *Harvard Business Review* (March/April 1991): 107–17; T. A. Steward, "New Ways to Exercise Power," *Fortune,* November 6, 1989, 52–64; and S. Sherman, "A Brave New Darwinian Workplace," *Fortune,* January 25, 1993, 50–56.

2. T. L. Leap and M. D. Crino, *Personnel/Human Resource Management* (New York: Macmillan, 1993).

3. J. Ledvinka and V. G. Scarpello, *Federal Regulation of Personnel and Human Resource Management,* 2d ed. (Boston: PWS-Kent, 1991).

4. J. E. Ellis, "Monsanto's New Challenge: Keeping Minority Workers," *Business Week,* July 8, 1991, 60–61.

5. H. Keets, "Avon Calling—On Its Troops," *Business Week,* July 8, 1991, 53; S. B. Garland, "How to Keep Women Managers on the Corporate Ladder," *Business Week,* September 2, 1991, 64; and N. J. Perry, "If You Can't Join 'Em, Beat 'Em," *Fortune,* September 21, 1992, 58–59.

6. G. Graham, "Companies Forced to Become More Sensitive as Work Force Diversifies," *Orlando Sentinel,* July 2, 1992, B-1; *Monthly Labor Review* (June 1992); and T. Cox, Jr., "Managing Cultural Diversity: Implications for Organizational Competitiveness," *Academy of Management Executive* 3 (1991): 45–56.

7. Ledvinka and Scarpello, *Federal Regulation of Personnel and Human Resource Management.*

8. V. G. Scarpello and J. Ledvinka, *Personnel/Human Resource Management: Environments and Functions* (Boston: PWS-Kent, 1994).

9. L. Dyer, "Human Resource Planning," in K. M. Rowland and G. R. Ferris, eds., *Personnel Management* (Boston: Allyn & Bacon, 1992), 52–78.

10. Based in part on a discussion in R. L. Mathis and J. H. Jackson, *Personnel/Human Resource Management,* 7th ed. (St. Paul, Minn.: West Publishing, 1994), 210.

11. K. Rebello and E. I. Schwartz, "How Microsoft Makes Offers People Can't Refuse," *Business Week,* February 24, 1992, 65.

12. R. Koenig, "Toyota Takes Pains and Time Filling Jobs at its Kentucky Plant," *Wall Street Journal,* December 1, 1987, 1.

13. K. Rebello and E. I. Schwartz, "Can You Pass the Test," *Business Week,* February, 24, 1992, 65. Reprinted with permission.

14. S. Burns, "From Student to Banker: Observations from the Chase Bank." Paper presented at the Association of American Colleges and the National Endowment for the Humanities Conference, Princeton, New Jersey, April 1993.

15. M. Davids, "How to Handle Loaded Questions," *Working Woman,* July 1992, 12.

16. Based in part on a discussion in M. Davids, "How to Handle Loaded Questions," *Working Women,* July 1992, 12.

17. G. M. McEvoy and R. W. Beatty, "Assessment Centers and Subordinates Appraisals of Managers: A Seven-Year Examination of Predictive Validity," *Personnel Psychology,* 42 (1989): 37–52.

18. M. E. Grossman and M. Magnus, "The $5.3 Billion Tab for Training," *Personnel Journal* 68 (1989): 54–56.

19. E. Lawler, S. Mohrman, and G. Ledford, *Employee Involvement and Total Quality Management* (San Francisco: Jossey-Bass, 1992).

20. Mathis and Jackson, *Personnel/Human Resource Management.*

21. Bureau of National Affairs, Planning the Training Program, *Personnel Management,* (Washington, D.C.: BNA Books, 1975).

22. A. Berstein, "How to Motivate Workers: Don't Watch 'Em," *Business Week,* April 29, 1991, 56.

23. Adapted from Cassner-Lotto and Associates, *Successful Training Strategies* (San Francisco: Jossey-Bass, 1988).

24. W. F. Cascio, *Managing Human Resources,* 2d ed. (New York: McGraw-Hill, 1989).

25. For a review of BARS literatures, see G. P. Latham and K. N. Wesley, *Increasing Productivity through Performance Appraisal* (Reading, Mass.: Addison-Wesley, 1981), 61–64.

26. "Motivation," *INC.,* December 1986, 120.

27. For a more detailed discussion of benefits see Mathis and Jackson, *Personnel/Human Resource Management,* 413–39.

28. M. A. Littell, "Family Friendly Employee Benefits," *Good Housekeeping,* July 1992, 100.

29. J. R. Morris, *Employee Benefits* (Washington, D.C.: Chamber of Commerce of the United States, 1986).

30. L. L. Cummings, "Compensation, Culture, and Motivation: A System Perspective," *Organizational Dynamics* (Winter 1984): 33–44.

31. Mathis and Jackson, *Personnel/Human Resource Management,* 359.

32. A. C. Hax, "A New Competitive Lesson: The Human Resource Strategy," *Training and Development Journal* (May 1985): 76–82.

33. V. Scarpello and J. Ledvinka, *Personnel/Human Resource Management: Environments and Functions* (Boston, Mass.: PWS-Kent, 1994); and G. T. Milkovich and

J. Newman, *Compensation* (Homewood, Ill.: BPI/Irwin, 1990).

34. R. E. Walton and R. B. McKersie, *A Behavioral Theory of Labor Negotiations: An Analysis of a Social Interaction System* (New York: McGraw-Hill, 1965).

35. Ibid.

36. A. Bernstein, "Busting Unions Can Backfire on the Bottom Line," *Business Week,* March 18, 1991, 108.

37. J. M. Brett, "Why Employees Want Unions," *Organizational Dynamics,* 8 (1980): 47–59.

38. W. C. Hammer and F. J. Smith, "Work Attitudes as Predictors of Unionization Activity," *Journal of Applied Psychology,* 63 (1978): 415–21; and C. A. Schriesheim, "Job Satisfaction, Attitudes towards Unions and Voting in a Union Representation Election," *Journal of Applied Psychology,* 63 (1978): 548–52.

39. M. E. Mendenhall, E. Dunbar, and G. R. Oddou, "Expatriate Selection, Training and Career-Pathing: A Review and Critique," *Human Resource Management* 26 (Fall 1987): 340.

40. M. G. Henry, "The Executive Family: An Overlooked Variable in International Assignments," *Columbia Journal of World Business* (Spring 1985): 84–92.

41. C. Lee, "Cross-Cultural Training: Don't Leave Home without It," *Training,* 1983, 20–25.

42. A. L. Hixon, "Why Corporations Make Haphazard Overseas Staffing Decisions," *Personnel Administrator,* March 1986, 91–95.

43. M. A. Conway, "Reducing Expatriate Failure Rates," *Personnel Administrator,* July 1984, 31–38.

44. A. M. Morrison and M. A. Von Glinow, "Women and Minorities in Management," *American Psychologist* 45 (1990): 200–208.

45. W. B. Johnson, "Global Workforce 2000: The New Labor Market," *Harvard Business Review* (March/April 1991): 115–19.

46. S. B. Garland, "Throwing Stones at the Glass Ceiling," *Business Week,* August 19, 1991.

47. Ledvinka and Scarpello, *Federal Regulation of Personnel and Human Resource Management.*

48. G. N. Powell, "Sexual Harassment: Confronting the Issue of Definition," *Business Horizons,* July/August 1983, 24–28.

49. *Meritor Savings Bank v. Vinson,* 477 U.S. 57 (1986); EEOC: Policy Guidance on Sexual Harassment, March 1990.

50. *Robinson v. Jacksonville Shipyards,* USDC MFLA, No. 86-927-J-12 (1991); *Ellison v. Brady,* 54 FEP Cases 1346 (1991).

51. For a more thorough discussion, see M. Galen, Z. Schiller, J. Hamilton, and K. Hammonds, "Ending Sexual Harassment: Business Is Getting the Message," *Business Week,* March 18, 1992, 98–100.

52. W. C. Symonds, "How to Confront and Help an Alcoholic Employee," *Business Week,* March 25, 1991, 78.

53. G. Koretz, "An Incentive a Day Can Keep Doctor Bills at Bay," *Business Week,* April 29, 1991, 22.

54. Perpetual Financial Corporation, *Profiles in Quality: Blueprints for Action from 50 Leading Companies* (Needham Heights, Mass.: Allyn & Bacon, 1991), 85–86.

55. Hoerr, "Sharpening Minds for a Competitive Edge"; Thomas, "From Affirmative Action to Affirming Diversity"; Steward, "New Ways to Exercise Power"; and Sherman, "A Brave New Darwinian Workplace."

Organizational Culture, Change, and Development

CHAPTER 11

▼ CHAPTER OVERVIEW

As we approach the beginning of a new century, a transformation is occurring in many organizations—from the giants in the auto industry to the small software design firms. At all levels of operations, people are striving for quality, innovation, value, and excellence in management practices. Managers recognize that to build viable organizations, change must be viewed as an integral rather than a peripheral responsibility. This means changing the old methods of control and command that emphasized bureaucracy, rigidity, and impersonal human relationships to new methods involving participation, involvement, flexibility, and entrepreneurial behavior. These issues reflect a fundamental challenge faced by organizations as they strive to produce quality products and services and learn to manage changing cultures, strategies, and practices.

   This chapter explores the issues associated with understanding and managing change. It is based upon the viewpoint that the important responsibility of managing change can best be undertaken and accomplished by first understanding an organization's culture and then by analyzing the forces that drive and resist change. Only when managers have this foundation will their change processes and interventions be successful.

▼ LEARNING OBJECTIVES

   When you have finished studying this chapter,
   you should be able to:

- Discuss the foundations of organizational culture.
- Describe two basic components of organizational culture.
- List and explain the three forms of organizational artifacts.
- Explain the impact of culture on an organization.
- Demonstrate an understanding of organizational change.
- Identify and describe the four targets of planned change.
- Describe the three-step process of planned change.
- Identify the six strategies for overcoming resistance to change.
- List and describe four people-focused approaches to organizational change.
- Discuss ethical issues in organizational change.

MANAGERIAL INCIDENT

PEPSICO: CHANGES FROM THE BOTTOM UP

"Act like an owner, not a hired hand." So goes the message from Wayne Calloway, CEO of PepsiCo. Calloway sounds like many other CEOs in that he's preaching the philosophy of empowerment. The difference is that PepsiCo's CEO is doing much more than preaching. He's betting the future of PepsiCo on employee empowerment, or what he calls "ownership," and is depending on it to generate the changes that will be needed if PepsiCo is to succeed in today's hotly competitive business environment.

For five years, PepsiCo experienced steady growth and impressive revenue increases. But the recession in 1991 dampened PepsiCo's soft drink (Pepsi, Diet Pepsi, Mountain Dew, 7-Up, Slice, Mug Root beer), restaurant (Pizza Hut, Kentucky Fried Chicken, Taco Bell) and snack food (Doritos, Ruffles, Lay's, Sun Chips, Smart Foods) businesses.

For PepsiCo to get back on track, CEO Calloway feels it needs more than new products, packaging, and distribution channels. With 300,000 employees worldwide, PepsiCo has become burdensome to manage. To prevent the company from staggering under its own weight, Calloway is trying to change and reshape the organizational culture, working from the bottom up. He feels that PepsiCo's growth depends ultimately on its employees, and no conversation with Calloway goes far without returning to the idea of empowerment. Although more freedom for employees can mean bigger mistakes, Calloway thinks that this is the only way PepsiCo can change.

Will empowerment at PepsiCo work? Can Calloway make the necessary changes in the organization's culture?[1] ▼

INTRODUCTION

The contemporary manager faces extraordinary challenges. As we have mentioned in previous chapters, today's dynamic, complex, and sometimes unpredictable environment demands that managers and organizations take a proactive role in keeping up with and responding to change. Change is a pervasive, persistent, and permanent condition for all organizations. When organizations fail to change in necessary ways, the costs can be high. According to MIT professor David Birch, "For every corporation in the U.S., the best predictor of death is stability."[2] Innovation, flexibility, and the ability to change have become necessary business survival skills.

This chapter examines the issues associated with managing change beginning with the organization's culture. We will explore the components of organizational culture by examining organizational artifacts and then will look at how culture impacts the organization. Next, we turn our attention to the responsibility of managing change; as we will see, this can best be accomplished by analyzing the forces that drive and resist change. Finally, we examine the processes and interventions that can be used to manage change successfully.

FOUNDATIONS OF ORGANIZATIONAL CULTURE

Before we can understand the issues involved in organizational change, we need to examine the foundations of the organization, or its culture. Because culture guides the behavior of and gives meaning to organizational members, it has a direct and powerful influence on the change process.[3] We define

organization culture as the system of shared beliefs and values that develops within an organization. In simple terms, organizational culture is the personality of the organization.

Culture influences how people act in organizations; the ways people perform, view their jobs, work with colleagues, and look at the future are largely determined by cultural norms, values, and beliefs.[4] Just as no two individual personalities are the same, no two organizational cultures are identical.[5] For example, the organizational culture at MCI focuses on putting the customer first. Since no two customers or businesses have the same needs, MCI develops flexible systems that are tailored to meet specific customer demands.[6] As we read in the opening Managerial Incident, the culture at PepsiCo focuses on the delegation of authority and empowerment. Employees in this organization are encouraged to take risks and be innovative.

Cultures develop from a variety of factors. When a new organization is formed, the culture reflects the drive and imagination of the founding individual or group. Ray Kroc, the founder of McDonald's, espoused quality, service, cleanliness, and value, and these are still the corporate creed. Reward systems, policies, and procedures instituted within an organization also impact culture by further specifying notions of appropriate behavior. The culture at Walt Disney Corporation has been influenced by its creative founder, Walt Disney. Disney created entertainment that was focused on family values and traditional beliefs.

Cultures evolve and change over time in even the most stable periods.[7] In times of trouble, they may change rapidly because, whatever else the culture may value, it prizes survival most of all. Economic crises, changes in laws or regulations, social developments, global competition, demographic trends, and other events influence what the organization must do to survive, and the culture tends to evolve accordingly.[8]

Cultures also change when an organization discovers, invents, or develops solutions to problems that it faces. Successful approaches to solving problems tend to become part of the culture and are used whenever the organization faces similar conditions. For example, the culture at Chrysler has been influenced by changed market conditions, competition, and union demands, as well as by Lee Iacocca's personality when he first took the helm of the organization.

COMPONENTS OF AN ORGANIZATION'S CULTURE

As Figure 11.1 shows, organizational culture has two basic components. These components can be visualized as an iceberg because what you see on the surface is based on a much deeper reality.[9] The visible elements are the routines (practices) that constitute the organization's culture. These are sustained by hidden ideologies, shared values, expectations, and norms that are at the deepest level or core of the organization. Managers must recognize that it may not be possible to change the surface without changing what lies below.[10]

Examining Culture through Organizational Artifacts
The visible elements in Figure 11.1 consist of a number of artifacts. **Artifacts** are cultural routines that form the substance of public functions and events staged by the organization. Artifacts support and reinforce the organization's hidden ideologies, shared value systems, and norms.

Symbolism of Rites, Rituals, and Ceremonies   Some of the most obvious displays of organizational culture are rites, rituals, and ceremonies.[11] **Rites** are a relatively dramatic, planned set of recurring activities used at special times to influence the behavior and understanding of organizational members.

Organizational culture
The system of shared beliefs and values that develops with an organization. In simple terms, organizational culture is the personality of the organization.

Artifacts
Cultural routines that form the substance of public functions and events staged by the organization.

Rites
A relatively dramatic, planned set of recurring activities used at special times to influence the behavior and understanding of organizational members.

▼ **Figure 11.1**
Components of Organizational Culture
Visualized as an Iceberg

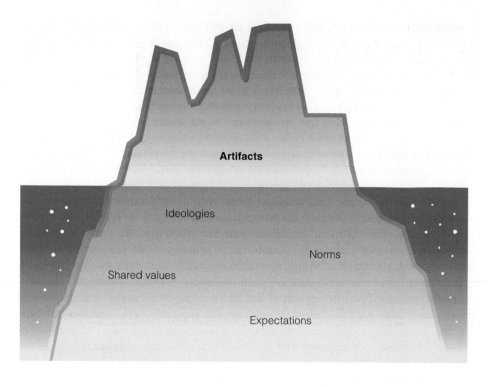

Rituals and ceremonies are usually more elaborate systems of rites. Evaluation and reward procedures, farewell parties, award banquets, and product promotions are examples. They are carried out through social interaction and usually occur for the benefit of an audience.

Microsoft Corporation celebrated the successful introduction of its software package Windows with a gala party for 5000 employees at the Seattle Kingdome. A red Corvette with the word "Windows" written on its door was placed on stage next to an Edsel emblazoned with "OS/2" (IBM's competing software). The employees chanted: "Windows, Windows, Windows." The climax of the evening came when 10 leather-clad bikers led by President Bill Gates roared on stage riding Harley-Davidsons, while the song "Leader of the Pack" blared from the loudspeakers.[12] This celebration reflects Microsoft's unorthodox and creative management culture.

Through rituals and ceremonies, participants gain an understanding of and cement beliefs that are important to the organization's culture. Mary Kay Cosmetics schedules regular ceremonies to spotlight positive work achievements and reinforce high performance expectations. At the company's annual meeting, an affair marked by lavish pomp and intense drama, top employees are recognized and rewarded for high sales. The celebration goes beyond the fancy setting and presentation of pink Cadillacs to star salespeople. Members praise the opportunities provided to them by Mary Kay, the heroine of the company. The process gives all Mary Kay employees a sense of purpose—not merely to sell cosmetics but to reach their full potential.

Language systems and metaphors
The way that organizational members typically express themselves and communicate with each other.

Language Systems and Metaphors   **Language systems** and **metaphors** are the way that organizational members typically express themselves and communicate with each other. Metaphors use familiar elements or objects to make behavior or other unfamiliar processes or actions comprehensible.[13] They include special terminology, abbreviations, jargon, slang, and gestures that are almost unintelligible to outsiders, but are used inside the organization to convey a sense of belonging or community. For example, the eleventh commandment at 3M is "never kill a new product idea." Disney employees label

▼ At Mary Kay Cosmetics, ceremonies regularly spotlight positive work achievements and reinforce high performance expectations. Through this celebration, employees are recognized, praised, and rewarded.

anything positive a ''good Mickey'' and anything negative a ''bad Mickey.'' And, at Levi Strauss, management calls its open door policy the ''fifth freedom.''[14]

Stories, Sagas, Myths   Organizations are rich with stories of winners, losers, successes, and failures. **Stories** are accounts based on true events; they often contain both truth and fiction. For a new employee, the organization is like a foreign culture—the person has to learn how to fit in and avoid major blunders. Organizational stories tell new members the real mission of the organization, how it operates, what behavior is acceptable, and how individuals can fit into the organization.

For example, most employees at a West Coast electronics firm know the story of how the company avoided a mass layoff when other companies in the industry laid off many employees. Instead of dismissing 10 percent of its employees, the company had everyone take a 10 percent cut in salary and work only 9 out of every 10 working days. This experience became known as the ''nine-day fortnight.'' Several years later, when the company again faced a drop in orders, it reinstituted the ''nine-day fortnight'' scheme for a short period. Today, old-timers use this story to quiet the anxiety of concerned newcomers and to predict the behavior of the company. Managers use this story to guide decision making when layoff pressures mount.[15]

Stories also serve as symbols of the organization's entrepreneurial orientation and promote values that unify employees from diverse organizational units. For example, Entrepreneurial Approach tells the story of the discovery of Scotch tape—a favorite story at 3M.[16]

In many organizations, the members have a collection of stories that they tell repeatedly. Often one of the most important stories concerns the founding of the organization. Such stories may convey the lessons to be learned from the heroic efforts of an entrepreneur whose vision may still guide the organization. The founding story may become so embellished that it becomes a saga.

Sagas are historical accounts describing the unique accomplishments of a group and its leaders or heroes. According to Peters and Waterman, members of ''strong culture'' companies are likely to have an enormous fund of sagas that tell about the exploits of the founder or other strong leaders.[17] At Hewlett-Packard (HP), sagas feature the legendary accomplishments of the founders,

Stories
Accounts based on true events; they often contain both truth and fiction.

ENTREPRENEURIAL APPROACH

NEVER KILL A NEW PRODUCT IDEA AT 3M

Employees at 3M are encouraged to be entrepreneurs and to try out new ideas in the marketplace rather than putting their trust in market forecasts. The culture of 3M encourages all employees to pursue innovation. This is reflected in the eleventh commandment, "thou shalt not kill a new product idea." Any idea that leads to product diversity such as the worker safety mask, which was developed from a failed plastic cup project for brassieres, is acceptable. 3M researchers are encouraged to spend 15 percent of their time pursuing pet projects that might have a payoff down the line. In 1990 more than one-fourth of 3M's worldwide sales came from new products—products that did not exist 10 years ago.

This emphasis on innovation is supported by a story about the discovery of transparent cellophane tape. According to the story, an employee accidentally discovered the tape, but was unable to get his superiors to buy the idea. Marketing studies predicted a relatively small demand for the new material. Undaunted, the employee found a way to sneak into the boardroom and tape down the minutes of the upcoming executive meeting with his transparent tape. The board members were impressed enough with the novelty to give it a try, and the cellophane tape—Scotch tape—became an incredible success.

In essence, 3M's culture promotes an entrepreneurial environment based on the belief that failure can lead to success. Not only do such stories serve as symbols of the company's entrepreneurial orientation, but they help unify diverse organizational units as employees come to share the same values.

Myths
Unproven beliefs that are accepted uncritically and used to justify current actions by communicating the practical benefits of certain techniques and behaviors.

Bill (Hewlett) and Dave (Packard), and are used to communicate the unique way of doing things at HP to outsiders or newcomers.

Myths differ from stories and sagas in that they lack a factual basis. Even though myths are unproven beliefs, they are accepted uncritically and are used to justify current actions by communicating the practical benefits of certain techniques and behaviors. Old-timers' stories about how things were "in the good old days" are frequently examples of myths.

THE IMPACT OF CULTURE ON THE ORGANIZATION

In organizations with strong cultures, shared values and beliefs create a setting in which people are committed to one another and share an overriding sense of mission. This culture can be a source of competitive advantage. Unique, shared values can provide a strong corporate identity, enhance collective commitment, create a stable social system, and reduce the need for formal and bureaucratic controls.

A strong culture can be a double-edged sword, however. A strong culture and value system can reinforce a singular view of the organization and its environment. If dramatic changes are needed, it may be very difficult to change the organization. General Motors (GM), which has a strong culture, experienced enormous problems in adapting to a dynamic and highly competitive environment. GM found it necessary to establish a new division (and thus a new culture) to produce the Saturn automobile. At Harley-Davidson, a new senior management team had to replace virtually all of the company's middle managers to establish a new competitive culture. At what was once U.S. Steel, now USX, the problems with the old steel division were so ingrained in the

culture that executives sold the division and purchased a series of divisions
with strong, resilient cultures.

Many companies are striving to achieve high levels of quality, customer
service, and satisfaction. For example, the U.S. automobile industry feels that
quality is the key to competing effectively with the Japanese automobile industry. These companies are learning that to achieve this goal, they must provide
new employee reward systems, organizational designs, and customer-service
training that focuses on interpersonal skills for salespeople as well as dealers.
Changes such as these can have dramatic effects on the organization's culture.[18]

CHANGING AN ORGANIZATION'S CULTURE

Changing an organization's culture can be very complicated. Well-known management expert Peter Drucker suggests that managers can modify the visible
aspects of culture such as the language, stories, rites, rituals, and sagas. They
can change the lessons to be drawn from common stories and even encourage
employees to see a different reality. Because of their positions, senior managers
can interpret situations in new ways and adjust the meanings attached to important organizational events. They can also create new rites and rituals. Mod-
fiying the culture in these ways takes time and enormous energy, but the
long-run benefits can be positive.[19] At American Express, President Harvey
Golub is attempting to change the organizational culture from a highly political
bureaucracy to a collaborative team approach.[20] Golub's vision is to have employees focus on service rather than growth, as we see in Managing for
Excellence.

Top managers can set the tone for a culture and for cultural change.
Throughout this book, we illustrate how managerial excellence is shaping the
corporate landscape of the 1990s. In most of these incidents, we see that
managers are building on the shared values in the culture of their organizations. Wayne Calloway at PepsiCo has focused on delegation of authority to
empower employees to be risk takers and innovators. Managers at Aetna Life
& Casualty Company built on the company's humanistic traditions to provide

▼ The CEO meets with top-level managers to emphasize the value of individuals becoming involved in
changing the organization's culture.

MANAGING FOR EXCELLENCE

CHANGES AT AMERICAN EXPRESS: FOCUSING ON SERVICE RATHER THAN GROWTH

With a combination of bluntness and humor, Harvey Golub, president of American Express (AmEx) and CEO of the Travel Related Services Company (TRS) is trying to jolt employees out of their complacency and rally them to the tasks of solving the problems (both internal and external) faced by the organization. His tasks include trying to rebuild fading customer loyalty, bolstering the company's image, and demonstrating to merchants the uniqueness of the AmEx card. Under siege from lower-priced bankcards, restless merchants, and defecting customers, AmEx has had to face up to the end of TRS's phenomenal growth.

Golub's vision for AmEx is a renewed focus on service instead of growth at any cost; he is stressing profitability. He has implemented new "health of the franchise" measures to determine the precise rate at which long-time members are dropping the card. The AmEx sales force is making more sales calls on existing merchants and is retreating from the 1980s push to sign up as many establishments as possible. AmEx is also trying to bolster its ties with cardholders, who are being polled on their likes and dislikes and bombarded with promotional offers by other credit card companies.

Golub is also betting on "reengineering," a management process that cuts costs while improving service by running the business more efficiently. For example, AmEx has consolidated seven worldwide data processing centers into two, with 1560 fewer employees and a savings of $25 million. The company is currently implementing 57 reengineering programs that are expected to save from $500,000 to $50 million each. For reengineering to work, AmEx needs more cooperation among its managers. To get managers to work together, Golub has modified the bonus system so that bonuses are no longer determined by each individual business unit's results but by TRS's profitability as a whole. To reduce feuding between TRS and AmEx corporate staff, Golub for the first time invited AmEx corporate managers to a TRS management meeting. He made the four-day event a family affair by inviting spouses to strategy meetings and even welcoming children at the event.

Golub is widely acknowledged to have introduced a welcome dose of reality at AmEx. He is seeking to change AmEx corporate culture from a highly political bureaucracy to a collaborative team approach where employees focus on customer service. He has brought a down-to-earth style that stresses employee loyalty. Golub frequently holds meetings with employees to explain strategy and extends a "Lunch with Harvey" invitation to the first 15 employees who sign up. He has even taped a video for a new program he initiated for AmEx's 50,000 employees and their spouses to help them convince neighbors and friends to use the AmEx card. His goal—convert 50,000 employees into 50,000 salespeople.

basic skills to highly motivated but underqualified individuals. Frances Hesselbein of the Girl Scouts stressed a clear mission of helping girls to reach their highest potential in today's world, not yesterday's. Even in the highly cost-competitive steel industry, F. Kenneth Iverson of Nucor built on basic entrepreneurial values in U.S. society to decrease the number of management levels by half. At Procter & Gamble, Richard Nicolosi fostered greater participation in decision making to dramatically improve creativity and innovation.

Managers who strive for quality products and services understand they must involve the keepers and holders of the culture, build on what all organizational members share, and teach new members how to behave. Sometimes managers attempt to revitalize an organization by dictating minor changes rather than building on shared beliefs and values. While things may change a bit on the surface, a deeper look often finds whole departments and key people resisting change. To be successful, change must be consistent with important values in the culture and emerge from participants within the organization.

THE CHALLENGE TO UNDERSTAND ORGANIZATIONAL CHANGE

Change is essential to an organization's survival. Change leads to new ideas, technology, innovation, and improvement. Therefore, it is important that organizations recognize the need for change and learn to manage the process effectively. For example, Bally Manufacturing Corporation was the largest and most respected builder of slot machines. In the late 1980s, it lost its number one position to International Game Technology. Industry executives say that Bally's management failed to change with the times. They were reluctant to adopt the computer technology that addressed quality-control problems and revolutionized machines.[21]

Organizational change is any alteration of activities in an organization. Alterations can involve the structure of the organization, the transfer of work tasks, the introduction of a new product, or attitudes among members. According to Michael Stephen, president of Aetna Life & Casualty Company's international operations, the change process is even more difficult in organizations with multiple facilities in several nations. He contends that change can be (and has been for Aetna) a painful process for any organization that wants to be a high-performing competitor in the global marketplace.[22] Managers must learn to recognize not only when change is occurring in an organization, but also when it is needed and the appropriate targets for change. A pertinent example is how Xerox's organizational changes in the 1980s, which focused

Organizational change
Any alteration of activities in an organization that can be in the structure of the organization, the transfer of work tasks, introduction of a new product, or in attitudes among members.

▼ Managers at Aetna Life & Casualty meet regularly to focus on key changes with the organization.

on quality improvements, resulted in phenomenal performance increases that were rewarded in 1989 when the company received a Malcolm Baldrige National Quality Award—an award bestowed by the U.S. Commerce Department for "preeminent quality leadership."[23]

TARGETS FOR CHANGE

A variety of elements in an organization can be changed. Which elements are chosen is partly determined by the manager's ability to diagnose the organization's problems or opportunities accurately. The following sections briefly describe each of the possible target areas for change.

Individual Targets

At an individual level, organizations can target several areas. These changes fall under the general category of human resource changes and include changing the number and skills of the human resource component as well as improving levels of employee motivation and performance. Changes in these areas usually occur either as a result of new staffing strategies or because the company has embraced the strategic goal of recognizing and valuing diversity in the workforce. Individual targets are accomplished through employee training or development programs.[24]

Interpersonal and Group Targets

In this area, managers may consider changing the nature of the relationships between managers and subordinates or the relationships within work groups. This might include changes or redirection of management leadership styles, group composition, or decision-making procedures. For example, at Fort Knox Security Products, a manufacturer of home safes located in Orem, Utah, rapid growth had led to groups that did not feel responsible for problem solving. It completely reorganized the group production structure. Instead of some workers making large batches of small parts and others assembling them, "work cells" were established. Teams within each cell soon were cooperating to develop efficiencies that enabled the cell to deliver its scheduled quantity each day. The new system functioned so well that the company was able to reduce its workforce while increasing bonuses and salaries paid to employees. By targeting change at the interpersonal or group level, the organization was able to make manufacturing more efficient, improve working relationships, and increase product quality.[25]

Organizational Targets

At the organizational level, managers can change the (1) basic goals and strategies of the organization; (2) products, quality, or services offered; (3) organizational structure; (4) composition of work units; (5) organizational processes such as reward, communication, or information processing systems; or (6) culture. For example, to survive in the global environment and avoid bankruptcy, Navistar International redesigned its organizational structure. By transforming its sluggish bureaucracy and becoming a streamlined, world-class manufacturer and innovator, Navistar was able to revitalize its competitive advantage.[26] Another example, shown in Table 11.1, is National Westminister Bank, which encouraged quality improvements through a quality achievement program.[27]

Environmental Targets

An organization can also work to change sectors of its environment. As we discussed in earlier chapters, sectors in the external environment can be influenced and changed in a number of ways. It is virtually impossible to change

▼ **Table 11.1**   Rewards That Encourage Quality Improvements at National
                   Westminster Bank USA

National Westminster Bank USA was experiencing a number of problems,
including a seeming lack of direction. The bank chose to concentrate its efforts on
quality improvement, one of the strategic elements for outdistancing its
competitors. It formally launced a "Quality Achievement Program." To encourage
employee involvement in the changes, Quality Action Teams and Quality
Improvement Teams were developed.

   According to Neil Metviner, vice president and manager of the Quality
Achievement Program, the following situations must exist if an organization is
going to get employees to take the time to improve their jobs and improve
quality. The first two are internal, or personal rewards, while the third is an
external or system reward. Does your organization offer these?

1. Employees must realize that they will have the opportunity to take
   responsibility for the way they perform their jobs.
2. Employees must realize that by getting rid of the problems that plague their
   daily work life, they will enjoy their work more and be rewarded with a sense
   of accomplishment.
3. Employees must be rewarded for their efforts with incentive and recognition
   programs.

   National Westminster Bank's Quality Achievement Program developed several
types of rewards and incentives for employees. For example, managers who see
employees doing something outstanding can write the incidents up and send them
to Metviner's department. Metviner will then give the employees $100 and make
them eligible for year-end lotteries with prizes that include a one-week, all-
expenses-paid vacation for two—including the vacation time from work.

SOURCE: National Westminster Bank USA, *Profiles in Quality: Blueprints for Action from 50 Leading
Companies* (Boston: Allyn & Bacon, 1991), 175–78. Copyright © 1991 by Allyn and Bacon. Adapted by
permission.

one aspect of an organization and not affect other aspects. Changes in products
or services offered may require new technology or a new distribution system.
Adopting new technology may necessitate hiring different types of employees
or revamping the corporate training system. Once again, the interconnection
of systems and subsystems makes the job of management extremely complex
and challenging.

MANAGING ORGANIZATIONAL CHANGE

In recent years, a great deal of research and practical attention has focused on
the necessity for change and the change process. If managers could design
perfect organizations and if the scientific, market, and technical environments
were stable and predictable, there would be no pressure for change. But such
is not the case. The statement that we live in the midst of constant change is
a cliché, but is relevant nevertheless. As you recall, Chapters 4 and 5 discussed
change at the strategic level. This chapter addresses change at the behavioral
level.

   Not only is change a constant of the modern business environment, but
it is becoming more complex. According to Jack Welch, CEO of General Electric, globalization compounds the problem of effectively managing change.[28]
One well-known business writer states that contemporary business organizations are facing change that is more extensive, more far-reaching in its implications, and more fundamental in its transforming quality than anything since
the modern industrial system took shape.[29] Popular literature, including best-

sellers, warns that organizations' futures depend on their managers' ability to master change.

Managers must recognize that the forces of change are significant and pervasive. Learning to recognize and manage change is one of the most important skills a manager can develop. Change is natural, and managers must help their organizations work with change, not against it. It seems reasonable to assert that organizations must manage change in order to be responsive to changing environments.[30]

A FRAMEWORK FOR CHANGE

One useful tool for taking a systematic look at the forces in play around a proposed change is called force-field analysis.[31] While this may sound like something from a Steven Spielberg movie, a **force-field analysis** is really just a systematic process for examining the pressures that are likely to support or resist a proposed change. This framework was proposed by the organizational researcher Kurt Lewin, who visualized change as the three-step process shown in Figure 11.2. Lewin's approach recognizes that merely introducing a change does not guarantee that the change will be successful. Let's take a closer look at the three steps in the change process.

Unfreezing

The first step, **unfreezing,** involves developing an initial awareness of the need for change and the forces supporting and resisting change. Most people and organizations prefer stability and the perpetuation of the status quo. In such a state, forces for change are equally offset by forces that want to maintain the status quo. Lewin called these driving forces and restraining forces, respectively. They are shown in Figure 11.3.

Driving forces for change can be conveniently classified into two groups—external forces and internal forces. **External forces,** which are in the environment, are fundamentally beyond the control of management. **Internal**

Force-field analysis
A systematic process for examining the pressures that are likely to support or resist a proposed change.

Unfreezing
Developing an initial awareness of the need for change and the forces supporting and resisting change.

External forces
Environmental factors that are fundamentally beyond the control of management.

Internal forces
Inside factors that are generally within the control of management.

▼ **Figure 11.2**
Lewin's Three Phases of the Planned Change Process

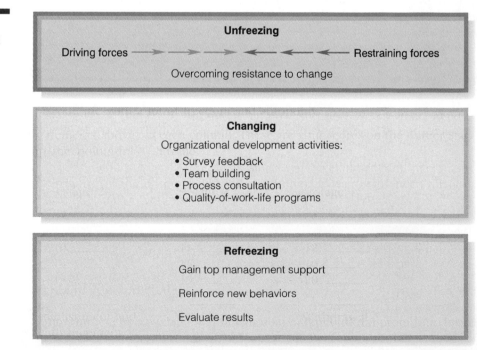

forces operate inside the firm and are generally within the control of management. Recall from Managing for Excellence 11.1 how Harvey Golub, president of American Express, acts as an internal driving force trying to jolt employees out of their complacency and rally them to the task of solving the organization's problems.[32]

Changes in one or more of the key environmental sectors discussed in Chapter 5 might be the external forces that provide the impetus for change in an organization. The environment includes many economic, technological, political, and social forces that can trigger the change process. For example, in the economic domain, changes in the inflation rate, interest rates, and money supply can affect the ability of an organization's managers to get needed resources. New laws and regulations, trade tariffs, and court decisions emanating from the political domain can affect the way an organization conducts its business.

Managers must also react to changes in the marketplace or changes in customer tastes and incomes. Efforts to change production processes or install new technologies may be the result of competitive pressures or exposure to advances in other industries. A strike at a major supplier or an embargo on new materials may force a change in management techniques such as the introduction of work groups. The introduction of new products or services, increases in advertising, price reductions or changes in customer service by competitors all require a response if an organization is to maintain market share and visibility. For example, Wayne Rosing, vice president for advanced development at Sun Microsystem, Inc., concedes that a driving force at Sun is the fear of what a competitor might do especially given the global marketplace.[33]

Change may also be initiated in response to internal forces at an organization.[34] Changes can result from (1) organizational growth, decline, or a shift in goals; (2) products, as in the case where the introduction of new products necessitates higher levels of quality in production, marketing, and accounting methods; (3) tasks, as when the transfer of existing technology requires retraining personnel; and (4) people, as when organizational members' values or levels of motivation change.

Managers must recognize that external and internal driving forces can be highly interrelated. Because organizations operate as open systems, external and internal driving forces will always be connected. For example, employees' attitudes toward work may change because of a new organizational policy or as a result of new legislation. Additionally, employees must cope with changes in their personal lives as well as changes in the organization. How much change are you currently experiencing? How much change can you handle? To better understand the issue of personal change, take a few minutes to complete the exercise in Meeting the Challenge.[35] It will help you better understand how change affects you as an employee and as a potential manager.

Managers must be able to identify not only the cause of change, but also the external and internal situations in which the change is taking place. Only then will management be able to respond correctly to the forces driving change and take the actions necessary to ensure that the organization and its employees are effective.

Regardless of the pressure these driving forces exert, the most important driving force (after survival) is the presence of a felt need for change among those most affected. Individuals must be able to see why the change is necessary or understand the benefits to be derived. Therefore, anything that can be done to strengthen this driving force will serve the unfreezing process.

If the presence of a felt need for change is a key driving force for change, then the absence of a felt need for change is a critical restraining force. **Restraining forces** promote organizational stability or the status quo and resist

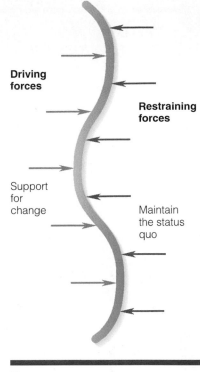

Driving forces

Restraining forces

Support for change

Maintain the status quo

▼ **Figure 11.3**
Driving and Restraining Forces

Restraining forces
Promote organizational stability or the status quo and resist change.

**MEETING
THE CHALLENGE**

HOW MUCH CHANGE ARE YOU EXPERIENCING?

Circle any of the following life events you have experienced in the past year. The findings could indicate how much stress you are experiencing due to changes in your life.

		Value
1.	Death of a spouse	100
2.	Divorce	73
3.	Marital separation	65
4.	Detention in jail/institution	63
5.	Death of close family member	63
6.	Major personal injury/illness	63
7.	Marriage	50
8.	Being fired at work	47
9.	Marital reconciliation	45
10.	Retirement from work	45
11.	Major change in the health or behavior of family member	44
12.	Pregnancy	40
13.	Sexual difficulties	39
14.	Gaining a new family member (birth, adoption, etc.)	39
15.	Major business readjustment (merger, reorganization, etc.)	39
16.	Major change in financial state	38
17.	Death of a close friend	37
18.	Changing to a different line of work	36
19.	Major change in the number of arguments with spouse	35
20.	Taking out a mortgage or loan for major purchase	31
21.	Foreclosure on a mortgage or loan	30
22.	Major change in responsibilities at work	29

change. Examples include external groups who fight against change and internal groups who have vested interests in maintaining the status quo.

People resist change for several reasons. First, they may genuinely believe, and could be right, that the change is not in their own best interests. Change can be threatening, and individuals may assess the consequences of the change in a totally different way from those who are initiating the change. During Xerox's recent reorganization, employees changed to a new form of corporate structure that evolved around self-managed work teams. While the purpose of this change was to encourage new thinking inside the company and promote high-performance work systems, it also meant that top managers had to facilitate the process and provide employees with the skills needed to be successful.[36] When employees are unsure what a new situation means in terms of the skills required to succeed, the impact of new reporting relationships, or possible disruptions, they will likely resist change. Information about a change can decrease anxiety, uncertainty, feelings of insecurity, and fear of the unknown.

Second, change may represent a loss and threaten vested interests. Managers and employees may feel threatened by a loss of power, responsibility, authority, control, and/or prestige. For example, a major obstacle to the successful introduction of personal computers in many organizations was middle

23.	Son or daughter leaving home	29
24.	Trouble with in-laws	29
25.	Outstanding personal achievement	28
26.	Spouse beginning or ceasing work outside the home	26
27.	Beginning/ceasing formal school	26
28.	Major change in living conditions	25
29.	Revision of personal habits	24
30.	Troubles with the boss	23
31.	Major change in working hours or conditions	20
32.	Change in residence	20
33.	Changing to a new school	20
34.	Major change in usual type and/or amount of recreation	19
35.	Major change in church activities	19
36.	Major change in social activities	18
37.	Taking on a mortgage or loan for lesser purchase	17
38.	Major change in sleeping habits	16
39.	Major change in number of family get-togethers	15
40.	Major change in eating habits	15
41.	Vacation	13
42.	Christmas	12
43.	Minor violations of the law	11

Scoring: Using the values on the right, total up your score. A score of 300 or above indicates that you are experiencing a high level of change in your life. Research shows that you have an 80 percent probability of encountering a major illness in the next two years; scores between 150 and 300 indicate a 50 percent chance; scores below 150 indicate a 33 percent chance.

managers' fear that they would become expendable, because upper-level managers could now monitor and control lower-level operations and direction.

Third, people may resist change because they lack the abilities or skills to cope with it. Diversity in the workforce may exacerbate this resistance. If proposed changes are going to require new skills, the organization has to include skill training as part of the planned change effort.

Finally, organizations have built-in resistance to change. Policies, rules, standard operating procedures, work methods, organizational charts, and job descriptions are examples of organizational infrastructure that serve to maintain the status quo. An organization's traditions, culture, and top management philosophy also resist change because they are developed over a long period of time and are not easily cast aside by organizational leaders. As we saw in the Managerial Incident with PepsiCo, organizational culture can have a major impact on the way an organization operates. Changes that seem to violate the accepted culture will be more difficult to implement successfully than changes that seem to emerge naturally out of the culture.

Just as some organizations are innovative and develop entrepreneurs and encourage the work of idea champions (individuals who sponsor or advance new products or services throughout the organization), other organizations are traditionally conservative and avoid change of any sort at all costs. When these

▼ As part of the unfreezing process, employees here are engaged in a self-managed work team.

organizations attempt change, the changes are usually incremental rather than major innovations. PepsiCo and American Express are examples of how organizations with a conservative tradition have undertaken major changes.

Strategies for Unfreezing   To be successful, any change process must overcome the status quo—by unfreezing old behaviors, processes, or structures. To call on a physics metaphor, unfreezing occurs only if the strength of the driving forces exceeds the strength of the restraining forces. If the restraining forces cannot be sufficiently reduced or the driving forces sufficiently increased, the change should not be attempted. If these forces can be managed, however, the next step is to design a strategy that will reduce resistance and stimulate support.

Six general strategies for dealing with resistance to change have been identified.[37]

1. ***Communication and education.*** This approach includes the use of one-on-one discussions, presentations to groups, memos, reports, company newsletters, training programs, and demonstrations to educate people about an imminent change and help them see the logic of the change. This approach requires the greatest commitment.

2. ***Participation and involvement.*** This approach allows others to help design and implement the changes. Individuals are asked to contribute ideas and advice or to form task forces or committees to work on the change. This process is time-consuming because it requires individuals and groups to make decisions.

3. ***Faciliation and support.*** This approach provides socioemotional support for the hardships of change. Training, open door policies, and active listening to problems and complaints are used to overcome performance pressures.

4. ***Negotiation and agreement.*** This method offers incentives to actual or potential resisters. Tradeoffs and compromises that provide special benefits in exchange for assurance that the change will not be blocked can be negotiated.

5. ***Manipulation and co-optation.*** This strategy uses covert or secret attempts to influence others. Selected pieces of information and consciously structured events are provided to ensure that the desired change receives maximum support.

6. ***Explicit and implicit coercion.*** This approach uses force to get people to accept change. Resisters are threatened with a variety of undesirable consequences if they do not go along with the plan. This is a risky process. But when speed is essential, it requires the least amount of time.

The advantages and disadvantages of these six strategies are explained further in Table 11.2.[38] Effective managers understand that resistance to change is something to be recognized and constructively addressed rather than feared. The presence of resistance typically suggests that something can be done to achieve a better fit among the change, the situation, and the people the change will affect. A manager needs to listen to such feedback and act accordingly.

▼ **Table 11.2**   Methods for Dealing with Resistance to Change

APPROACH	COMMONLY USED	ADVANTAGES	DRAWBACKS
Education and communication	Where there is a lack of information or inaccurate information and analysis	Once persuaded, people will often help with the implementation of the change	Can be very time-consuming if lots of people are involved
Participation and involvement	Where the initiators do not have all the information they need to design the change, and where others have considerable power to resist	People who participate will be committed to implementing change, and any relevant information they have will be integrated into the change plan	Can be very time-consuming if participants design an inappropriate change
Facilitation and support	Where people are resisting because of adjustment problems	No other approach works as well with adjustment problems	Can be time-consuming and expensive and can still fail
Negotiation and agreement	Where someone or some group will clearly lose out in a change, and where that group has considerable power to resist	Sometimes it is a relatively easy way to avoid major resistance	Can be too expensive in many cases if it alerts others to negotiate for compliance
Manipulation and co-optation	Where other tactics will not work or are too expensive	It can be a relatively quick and inexpensive solution to resistance problems	Can lead to future problems if people feel manipulated
Explicit and implicit coercion	Where speed is essential, and the change initiators possess considerable power	It is speedy and can overcome any kind of resistance	Can be risky if it leaves people mad at the initiators

SOURCE: Reprinted by permission of the *Harvard Business Review.* Excerpt from *Choosing Strategies for Change* by John P. Kotter and Leonard A. Schlesinger, Vol. 57 (March/April 1979): 111. Copyright © 1979 by the President and Fellows of Harvard College; all rights reserved.

Changing

The second step of the change process, **changing,** focuses on learning new required behaviors. Many changes that occur in an organization—new equipment, policies, or products—are relatively easy to implement in isolation. However, major difficulties can arise when dealing with human reactions to such organizational changes or attempting to change human actions and relationships directly. For example, organizational change that involves individuals directly or indirectly can require changes in roles, technical skills, interpersonal skills, or values and attitudes. Global Perspective, profiling Chanut Piyaoui, one of Thailand's most successful businesswomen, provides a clear example of how an individual changed a situation that restricted her ability to be successful.[39]

Closely tied to strategies for dealing with resistance to change are the tactics available for actually implementing the change. According to Lewin's model, if the status quo can be unfrozen, then it is possible to introduce a change or set of changes. While these changes can be implemented through a planned program, how to effectively introduce this change has been hotly debated. In the next section, we will examine a set of planned change strat-

Changing
The second step in the change process focusing on learning new required behaviors.

GLOBAL PERSPECTIVE

REJECTION LEADS TO CHANGE AND SUCCESS

A self-made entrepreneur, Chanut Piyaoui, struggled upward without the male financial support enjoyed by many Thai women who enter business. Wealthy Thai men often have minor wives, as mistresses are respectfully described, whom they set up in small businesses. This system of near polygamy inspires prudent Thai wives to persuade their husbands to back their business ventures as insurance against being abandoned. Chanut admits that trying to change the Thai business environment was not her original goal.

Chanut, who calls herself the chairperson, says, "I didn't have a good education, but I like for work to be done properly." After World War II, she went to the United States hoping to attend Columbia University. When she failed to get in, she traveled around the country, becoming fascinated with hotels. When she got into the business back home, hotels in Thailand had a somewhat unsavory reputation as "places of entertainment," in her delicate phrase. Chanut decided this image would have to change because she wanted to own a hotel like the ones she had encountered in the United States.

With little initial capital and endless determination, Khunying Chanut Piyaoui has created Thailand's leading hotel chain, which is now expanding abroad. In addition to eight hotels in Thailand, Khunying (an honorary title given to outstanding women by the Thai king) Chanut manages hotels in Indonesia, is setting up a Thai restaurant in Tokyo, and is shopping for an American hotel. *Asiamoney*, a regional magazine, ranks her Dusit Thani Group among the 100 best-managed companies in Asia, accurately describing it as "run from the top by steel-edged Mrs. Chanut, Bangkok's most famous business woman." She even owns a 40 percent share of the business.

Now that Chanut has been successful, she often serves as a role model for other women who have entrepreneurial desires. She believes strongly in the equality of women but understands that changing the status quo involves a fundamental change in attitudes and values. According to Chanut, "Thai women are trained to walk behind men, but in the rice fields you see them working side by side. I have no patience with the old attitude that women are the hind legs of the elephant."

---

egies and then discuss change tactics that are available to organizations and managers.

Tactics for Planned Change

The primary tool for planned change is called organizational development. **Organizational development (OD)** is a process of planned change that uses behavioral science knowledge, theory, and technology to help an organization improve its capacity for effective change.[40]

In recent years, a number of OD intervention activities have emerged that can be useful in facilitating planned change. The most widely used approaches concentrate primarily on people-focused change. These approaches tend to rely a great deal on active involvement and participation by many members of the organization. If successful, people-focused approaches improve individual and group processes in such areas as decision making, problem identification and solving, communication, and interpersonal relationships. We will examine

Organizational Development (OD)
A process of planning change in organizations that use behavioral science knowledge, theory, and technology to help an organization improve its capacity for effective change.

four of the most popular and effective techniques of people-focused organizational change: survey feedback, team building, process consultation, and quality-of-work-life programs.

Survey Feedback   The primary objective of **survey feedback** is to improve relationships among the members of groups or between departments through the discussion of common problems.[41] As an organizationwide intervention, survey feedback requires the administration of standardized or customized survey questionnaires to appropriate managers and their employees. The intent is to gather accurate information, perceptions, and attitudes anonymously about various aspects of an organization, work unit, and individual managers. The information is then presented or "fed back" to participants as they engage in a collaborative process to discuss the meaning and explore possible interpretations of the findings.

Survey feedback requires that managers (1) encourage open and free discussion of the findings, probable causes of problems, and possible implications for performance; (2) propose and encourage suggestions for resolving problems; and (3) carry out agreed-upon changes as quickly as possible.[42] A major strength of survey feedback is that it deals with managers and employees in the context of their own jobs, problems, and work relationships. It helps to bring problems to the surface and clarifies issues.

Team Building   One possible result of the survey feedback process is an awareness that a manager and his or her work group are not functioning as a team. Through the **team-building** process, members of a work group can diagnose how they work together and plan changes to improve their effectiveness.[43]

Like survey feedback at the organizational level, team building involves some form of data collection and feedback. Teams may consist of members who work alongside one another daily or are together on a project for a short time. The key elements, however, are the collaborative assessment of the information by all members of the group and the achievement of a consensus about what might be done to improve group effectiveness. A series of activities and exercises is designed to solve problems, enhance communication among team members, and develop a sense of teamwork.[44]

Survey feedback
A method of improving relationships among members of groups or departments that gather information, perceptions, and attitudes through a customized survey questionnaire and present the information to participants to discuss.

Team building
A process by which members of a work group diagnose how they work together and plan changes to improve their effectiveness.

▼ A number of OD intervention activities have emerged in recent years that can be useful in facilitating planned change. Here department managers are working with a consultant to better understand survey feedback results.

The advantage of team building is that it can often provide a useful way to involve employees in an organizational change program and increase collaborative behavior. In order for team building to be an appropriate OD approach, however, several conditions must be present. First, a lack of effective teamwork must be seriously hindering organizational effectiveness. Second, the culture of the organization must support a team approach to getting work done. Third, the teams must be receptive to undertaking the team-building process. For example, the team must be willing to devote time and energy to team building. Also, the active support of the team leader and his or her superior is critical to success. Fourth, adequate resources must exist internally to support team building.[45]

Process consultation

Involves structured activities directed toward key "processes" through which members of a group work with one another on specific issues and activities.

Process Consultation   Process consultation is related to team building in that it involves structured activities designed to improve group functioning. **Process consultation** directs attention toward the key "processes" through which members of a group work with one another. Thus, this tactic has a more specific focus than team building. Process consultation helps a group function better on such things as group norms and roles, decision making, conflict resolution, communication, and task activities.

Process consultation is characterized by the use of a skilled third party or facilitator, such as an external consultant, a human resource professional, or a manager skilled in process activities. It is often effective in changing attitudes and group norms, improving interpersonal and decision-making skills, increasing group cohesiveness, and enlarging interactions and appreciation for team members.

Quality-of-work-life (QWL) Programs

Programs undertaken by an organization for the purpose of (1) improving the quality of employee's work life, or (2) improving group or organizational productivity.

Quality-of-Work-Life Programs   **Quality-of-work-life (QWL) programs** are activities undertaken by an organization for the purpose of (1) improving the quality of employees' work life or (2) improving group or organizational productivity. QWL programs may focus on security, safety and health, participation in decision making, meaningful work, protection from unfair treatment, and/or opportunities to satisfy social needs. The programs can include a wide variety of specific techniques to improve conditions affecting employees' work experiences, such as team building, job redesign, participative management, quality circles, work environment improvements, and alternative work schedules. General Electric, Ford Motor, Proctor & Gamble, Westinghouse, Digital Equipment, Hewlett-Packard, Polaroid, and AT&T are just a few of many American companies that have active QWL programs.[46]

Refreezing the Change

The third and final step in the changing process, **refreezing,** centers on reinforcing new behaviors, usually by positive results, feelings of accomplishment, or rewards from others. Once management has implemented changes in organizational goals, products, processes, structures, or people, they cannot sit back and simply expect the change to be maintained over time. Laws of physics dictate that an object moved from equilibrium will tend to return to the original equilibrium point unless new forces are present to prevent this. Lewin reminds managers that new goals, structures, behaviors, and attitudes must be solidified or refrozen if that change is to become the new status quo.

Refreezing

The third step in the change process, centers on reinforcing new behaviors, usually by positive results, feelings of accomplishment, or rewards from others.

To make sure that change sticks, the manager or organization must undertake some additional activities. Let's look at three commonly employed approaches that are useful in accomplishing the refreezing step of the change process.

Gain Top Management Support   Formal or informal sponsorship of a change by top management gives legitimacy to new behaviors. If employees elsewhere in the organization see that top managers support and accept the change, they will more readily do so themselves. Thus, if a change involves the redesign of a communication or information processing system, top management must encourage the use of the new system by using it themselves.

Reinforce New Behaviors   Behaviors that are positively reinforced tend to be repeated. In designing a change, attention must be paid to how the new behaviors will be reinforced and rewarded. The reward systems should be carefully considered when planning change, and redesigned, if necessary. If the rewards or reinforcements inherent in the change fall short of employee expectations, the change will likely fail. Table 11.1 demonstrates how National Westminster Bank USA used rewards to reinforce new behaviors and make its Quality Achievement Program successful.[47]

Evaluate the Change   Finally, an important and often overlooked step in the refreezing process is evaluation. Management needs to know if the change has had the intended effects. Too many managers install changes, undertake training programs, and redesign structures with the mistaken belief that simply because the change was made, it will be successful. In many cases, this assumption proves incorrect., This is particularly true when the change was unilateral or was made without those affected perceiving the need for change. Sabotage of changes imposed by management has been known to occur in such situations.

Evaluation is also beneficial because it forces the manager making the change to establish the criteria for judging its success before the change is instituted. Doing so provides additional guidance when planning the tactics for making the change. It also forces managers to give careful thought to how the results of the change will be measured at some point in the future.

ETHICAL ISSUES IN ORGANIZATIONAL CHANGE

Regardless of how carefully managed a change might be, it will usually raise ethical issues. Managers and employees need to be aware of potential ethical concerns during organizational change. Asking some of the following questions can serve as a guide for managing the change ethically.[48]

- Does the manager or OD consultant have any vested interests in using a particular technique? Do all the alternative techniques receive a fair hearing?
- Who will determine the target(s) of change? Which members of the organization will participate in diagnosing, planning, and implementing the change and to what degree?
- To what extent should the organization disclose all aspects of the change in advance?
- Whose values influence the adoption of goals and the methods chosen to accomplish them?
- Do employees feel manipulated? To what extent do employees have the right to participate in changes that affect them?

These are difficult questions that managers and employees can use as a basis for recognizing the potential ethical concerns involved in organizational change.[49] With these questions, informed choices can be made. A starting point is the need to be sensitive to the potential for ethical problems during planned change programs.

MANAGERIAL IMPLICATIONS

Current research suggests a number of activities that will help managers achieve effective organizational culture, change, and development:[50]

- Solicit input from those who will be affected by organizational change. Involvement is essential to accepting the need for change.
- Carefully formulate your message regarding the need for and nature of organizational change. The success of the change process will depend on effective communication.
- Assess your organizational environment and be sure that the tone and the tempo of the change fit the organization. Timing is everything.
- Serve as a role model for the behaviors sought by the organizational change. Actions speak louder than words.

This chapter has focused on the need for managers to understand the culture of their organization and the role that culture plays in managing change. Cultures themselves change through evolution in light of changes in activities, in response to changing internal and external events, or through revolution as the organization deals with major challenges. Yet change is especially difficult in today's business environment of global competitiveness and diverse workforces. It is part of the manager's job to help the organization and its members overcome resistance to needed changes in its culture. Doing this requires an understanding of both the organization as it currently exists and its vision of what it wants to become.

MANAGERIAL INCIDENT RESOLUTION

PEPSICO: CHANGES FROM THE BOTTOM UP

The notion of empowerment is hardly new at PepsiCo, for it has long stressed decentralization. CEO Calloway often pushes power and decision making down the organizational hierarchy. Employees from route salespeople to restaurant workers are encouraged to come up with ideas to improve the business. They are rewarded through a plan called SharePower, introduced in 1989. The plan grants all 300,000 employees (from Pepsi-Cola truck drivers to KFC counter workers) yearly stock options on shares equivalent to 10 percent of their compensation. PepsiCo was the first major corporation to extend that traditional executive privilege on such a scale.

To ensure that PepsiCo is staffed with managers prepared to handle empowerment, Calloway spends far more time on the hiring process than most CEOs. No one at vice president level or above gets a job without seeing him. He interviews about 75 executives a year and is personally involved in roughly 600 twice-yearly evaluations of management-level employees.

Risk taking is encouraged and rewarded, win or lose. Calloway supports risk if it makes sense. PepsiCo can never get better if it doesn't learn from its mistakes. According to Calloway, the idea of employee empowerment has spurred changes in many areas. For example, a 17-year-old worker at a KFC in Oklahoma City helped his store increase catering revenues almost sevenfold after he created signs advertising the service and put them in store windows. A Moscow Pizza Hut manager sent 150 free pizzas and 20 cases of Pepsi to Boris Yeltsin in the midst of the government's 1991 failed coup. The manager didn't ask the permission of a district office or follow the rules—he just did it. These are the kind of changes that Calloway is trying to stimulate at all levels of the organizations.

Calloway's most recent agenda has focused on dreaming up new ways to make employees think like owners. He put together the company's first ever "SharePower Rally" in Atlanta, at which employees from every division gathered to hear him explain how individual initiative drives the company's growth. At PepsiCo headquarters in Purchase, New York, Calloway initiated the "Great PepsiCo Brainstorm," in which employees won prizes for contributing ideas on everything from thrift to improving menus.

Although PepsiCo manufactures what it sells, it ultimately is a service business. Calloway tells PepsiCo employees, "Frito-Lay salespeople supply 200,000 accounts every day. Unlike General Electric or IBM, we don't just win a couple of big contracts each year and make $50 billion. We have to win them (customers) one pizza at a time, one bag of chips, every day." Many credit PepsiCo's transformation to Calloway's revolutionary approach.[51] ▼

SUMMARY

- Organizational culture is the system of shared beliefs and values that develops within an organization and influences the way people act, perform their jobs, work with collegues, and view the future.

- Culture can be viewed as an iceberg. The visible elements of an organization's culture consist of the practices or routines referred to as artifacts. These are sustained by hidden ideologies, shared values, expectations, and norms that are at the deepest level or core of the organization. By studying the artifacts, or visible elements, one can better understand an organization's culture. These artifacts are (1) rites, rituals, and ceremonies, (2) language systems and metaphors, and (3) stories, sagas, and myths.

- A strong culture can be a source of competitive advantage for an organization. It can provide a stable social system and reduce the need for formal and bureaucratic controls. Conversely, it can reinforce a singular view of the organization and its environment and make it difficult to change the organization.

- Organizational change is any alteration of the activities in an organization such as (1) changes in the organizational structure, (2) transfer of work tasks, (3) introduction of new products, or (4) changes in member attitudes. Targets of change can be at the individual, group, organizational, or environmental level.

- A force-field analysis is a systematic process for examining the pressures that are likely to support or resist a proposed change. It involves three steps: unfreezing, changing, and refreezing.

- Six strategies for overcoming resistance to change were identified: (1) communication and education, (2) participation and involvement, (3) facilitation and support, (4) negotiation and agreement, (5) manipulation and co-optation, and (6) explicit and implicit coercion. Each offers advantages and disadvantages and is appropriate under certain conditions.

- People-focused approaches to change tend to rely a great deal on active involvement and participation by many members of the organization. These methods include survey feedback, team building, process consultation, and quality-of-work-life programs.

- Regardless of how carefully a change is managed, it usually raises ethical issues. Managers and employees need to be aware of potential ethical concerns during the organizational change process.

KEY TERMS

Organizational culture (p. 355)
Artifacts (p. 355)
Rites (p. 355)
Language systems and metaphors
   (p. 356)
Stories (p. 357)
Myths (p. 358)
Organizational change (p. 361)

Force-field analysis (p. 364)
Unfreezing (p. 364)
External forces (p. 364)
Internal forces (p. 364)
Restraining forces (p. 365)
Changing (p. 369)
Organizational development (OD)
   (p. 370)

Survey feedback (p. 371)
Team building (p. 371)
Process consultation (p. 372)
Quality-of-work-life (QWL) programs
   (p. 372)
Refreezing (p. 372)

REVIEW QUESTIONS

1. Define organizational culture.
2. How does an organization's culture evolve?
3. Describe the two basic components of organizational culture.
4. List and explain three types of organizational artifacts. Give an example of each.
5. How can culture influence an organization's competitive advantage?

6. Define organizational change.
7. Identify and describe four targets of planned change.
8. Describe the three-step process of planned change.
9. Explain six strategies for overcoming resistance to change.
10. Describe the use of team building as an approach to organizational change.

DISCUSSION QUESTIONS

Improving Critical Thinking

1. Since managers cannot actually see an organizational culture, what aspects of the organization might allow them to make some guesses about the nature of the culture?
2. As a manager, which of the six strategies for overcoming resistance to change would you most like to be involved with?
3. What does the statement "You can't make just one decision" mean in the context of organizational change?
4. What ethical issues are of concern with organizational change?

Enhancing Communication Skills

5. Suggest ways in which a manager can maintain a culture. To practice your oral communication skills, prepare a presentation using some examples from current successful organizations.

6. Why do people resist change? Write a brief paper that gives some examples of this concept.

Building Teamwork Skills

7. Describe the major differences between cultures in:
   a. a high school and a college or university.
   b. different college or university classes.
   c. different campus organizations.
   d. a public and a private college.
   e. a government (public) and a private organization.
   As a small group, discuss each of these settings and report your findings to the class.
8. Working in a small group, think of a recent change that has taken place at your college or university. Analyze the driving and restraining forces. Write down the key issues that should be considered and report your findings to the class or instructor.

ETHICS: TAKE A STAND

As an administrative manager for Visystem, Inc., for over eight years, Jeri is very satisfied with the company and her work. The culture of the organization is one of the reasons she has been so happy. As she describes it, the company isn't really a company, it's a big family where members support and care about each other. Often, Jeri has seen ideas that looked good for the company be voted down because they were bad for individual employees. Visystem is very decentralized, so Jeri makes decisions in her department without having to follow a lot of rigid rules or be closely supervised by top managers. Employee satisfaction is high, turnover is low, and a recent attitude survey found that 95 percent of the people said that they would recommend Visystem to a friend as a good place to work.

In Jeri's department employees work in small project groups and are supportive and friendly. They celebrate weddings and birthdays together, support the local college football team, spend holidays together, and often help out when an employee has a personal problem. Although most of Jeri's subordinates are hourly workers, they strive to complete assignments, even if it means coming in on weekends or staying late.

James, a member of Jeri's department, is a very dedicated employee who has worked hard and been loyal to the company for 25 years. In addition to working at Visystem, he takes care of his family and attends a community college to earn some credits. In the last two years, virtually every possible disaster has happened to James: death of both parents, divorce, major physical problems, and personal problems with relatives. As a result, James got very sick. After his sick leave was used up, Jeri let him use vacation time until that was gone. Visystem has a system for this type of problem: its short-term disability program pays 80 percent of an employee's salary for a month and then two-thirds of the salary for a year. Jeri knew that James couldn't live on this limited income, however, so she gave him time off without docking his pay. James assured her that he would make up the time when things were straightened out at home.

Jeri felt she could adjust the disability policy because (1) the company believed in treating people differently, as long as the different treatment was not discriminatory, (2) the role of policy in the company was not clear, and (3) she reported her actions to the company president who backed her decision.

For Discussion

1. Did Jeri's actions set a precedent that could erode respect for policies, rules, and procedures in the organization?
2. What kind of message did Jeri's actions send to people in the department? Was she a humane manager? Does her message say that this company really cares about its people?

MEASURING AND STUDYING CULTURE

THINKING CRITICALLY
Debate the Issue

Form small teams as directed by your instructor. Half of the teams should prepare to argue that culture cannot be measured or studied. The other half of the teams should take the perspective that culture can be measured and studied to understand how organizations function. Use current periodicals and organizational examples to strengthen your team's arguments. Your instructor will select two teams to present their findings to the class in a debate format.

VIDEO CASE

Southwest Airlines: Twentieth Anniversary

 In 1991, Southwest Airlines celebrated its twentieth anniversary with a Texas-sized celebration. Herb Kelleher, the 63-year-old chairman of Southwest, was a San Antonio attorney looking for start-up opportunities when he met banker Rollin King in 1966. King believed Texas could benefit from a short-haul commuter airline, and he and Kelleher mapped out the basic plan for Southwest. Although Braniff and Texas International Airlines were able to delay the new airline with litigation, Southwest's first flight took off in June 1971 from Dallas's Love Field.

Southwest became profitable in its second year of operation and has been profitable ever since—a record unmatched in the airline industry. Industry analysts attribute much of Southwest's success to its unique culture, which blends an identification with the Lone Star State with a zany sense of humor and a real concern for people.

Kelleher, for example, has been known to dress up like the Easter Bunny and Elvis. In an effort to get Southwest designated the official airline of Sea World, Southwest employees painted one of their planes like Shamu the whale. And it is not unusual for passengers to open overhead luggage compartments and find a flight attendant hiding there. Notes Kelleher on his employees: "What we are looking for, first and foremost, is a sense of humor. Then we are looking for people who have to excel to satisfy themselves and who work well in a collegial environment. We don't care that much about education and experience, because we can train people to do whatever they have to do. We hire attitudes."

For Discussion:

1. What are some of the rites, rituals, and ceremonies in the video that exemplify Southwest's culture?

2. The uniform for female flight attendants at Southwest originally included hot pants, and Kelleher is known to hug and kiss his female employees; the company also has contributed money for programs on professional women. How can two apparently opposing views of women in the workplace coexist at Southwest?

3. Would you want to work at Southwest? Why or why not?

CASE

Changing the System at SCLD

The Seminole County Library District (SCLD) has six branches and employs 42 full-time staff members, including 12 librarians. SCLD has an excellent reputation for community service, thanks to Charles Klee, the director who ran SCLD for 25 years until his recent retirement. Charles knew every staff member personally, having hired and indoctrinated (with his community service ideals) all 42. None of the 12 librarians has a college degree, but Charles trained all of them and promoted them into librarian positions. His approach to management was traditional, and he rarely delegated or involved the staff in policy making.

Upon Charles's retirement, Shannon Miller was hired as director. After two weeks on the job, Shannon discovered two major problems. First, the state library accreditation commission had put SCLD on probation, limiting the availability of state grants and funding sources if immediate action was not taken to raise standards. The level of computer use in catalog-ing, maintenance of reference sources, linkage with other resource centers, and tracking of borrowed materials was totally inadequate. Second, she was notified that the State University had dropped SCLD from the approved list of library systems for its graduate interns. Interns were an important source of inexpensive labor and a force for improvement and revitalization.

Shannon had experience with computerized library systems and was promised the resources and trained personnel to implement a new computer system. She called a staff meeting to discuss her concerns and objectives and explain the changes that needed to take place to put SCLD back on the approved internship program and have the computer system up and operational in one year. The staff members voiced suspicions about computers and suggested the new system was an excuse to weed out unneeded personnel. Some argued that it would require people to learn extensive programming skills that they didn't have or weren't interested in learning. Still others felt it would dilute their efforts at delivering personal service. They made negative comments about the university internship program. In the last two days, Shannon has received phone calls from 15 community patrons who have heard that the new computer system would reduce personal service.

For Discussion

1. What are the possible targets of change? Use a force-field analysis to examine the pressures that are likely to support or resist a proposed change.

2. What approach should Shannon use for dealing with the resistance to change?

EXPERIENTIAL EXERCISE 11.1

Understanding the Culture of Your Organization

Purpose: To better understand and describe the culture of an organization. This can be done either individually or in a small group if several members of the class work in the same organization.

Procedure: Think about an organization with which you are familiar. It could be one in which you are employed or a campus organization such as a fraternity/sorority or service club. How would you describe the organization's culture to a friend or new employee? Try to be objective in your analysis and identify examples of the artifacts in use. Answer each of the following questions. After you have completed the questions, share the information about the culture of your organization with a small group or the class.

1. What are the main norms (i.e., the do's and don'ts)?

2. What are the main ceremonies and rituals and what purpose do they serve?

3. What metaphors and language dominate everyday conversations?

4. What kinds of beliefs and values dominate the organization (officially and unofficially)?

5. What are the images that people use to describe the organization?

6. What are the favorite topics of informal conversation?

7. What reward systems are in place? What messages do they send in terms of which activities or accomplishments are valued and which are not?

8. What are the dominant stories or sagas that people tell? What measures are they trying to convey?

9. Think of two influential people in the organization. In what ways do they symbolize the character of the organization?

EXPERIENTIAL EXERCISE 11.2

Planning for Change

Purpose: To better understand how to develop and implement change as a manager. This exercise can be done either individually or in small work groups as directed by your instructor.

As a manager, one of the problems you face involves mistakes made by employees who perform a particular task. The same mistakes seem to occur in more than one department. You believe a training program for the people concerned will help reduce errors.

You are aware, however, that your supervisors may defend existing procedures simply because the introduction of training may imply criticism of the way they have been operating. You realize, too, that the supervisors may fear making changes because some employees may be concerned that they will not do well in the training program.

Procedure: Using the material from this chapter, develop a plan for change, along with a recommendation for your subordinates and supervisor on how training will be implemented to reduce errors and handle possible employee resistance to change.

1. Share the results of your plan with your group or the class as directed by your instructor.

2. What are the major problems you had to consider?

3. Where did you start?

4. Where would you anticipate the greatest resistance to your plan to occur?

NOTES

1. "Can Wayne Calloway Handle the Pepsi Challenge?" *Business Week,* January 27, 1992, 90–94; T. J. Murray, "PepsiCo's Fast Track," *Business Month,* June 1987, 50–52; "Go There and Get the Business," *Directors and Boards,* Winter 1991, 15–19; J. E. Rigdon, "PepsiCo's KFC Scouts for Blacks and Women for Its Top Echelons,"

Wall Street Journal, November 13, 1991, A1, A6; see also a discussion in M. Hammer and J. Champy, *Reengineering the Corporation: A Manifesto for Business Revolution* (New York: Harper Business, 1993).

2. K. C. Green and D. T. Seymour, *Who's Going to Run General Motors?* (Princeton, N.J.: Peterson's Guides, 1991), 134.

3. R. H. Kilmann, M. J. Saxon, and R. Serpa, "Issues in Understanding and Changing Culture," *California Management Review* 28 (1986): 87-94; and E. H. Schein, *Organizational Culture and Leadership* (San Francisco: Jossey-Bass, 1985), 223-43.

4. J. S. Ott, *The Organizational Culture Perspective* (Monterey, Calif.: Brooks Cole Publishing, 1989).

5. L. R. Beach, *Making the Right Decision: Organizational Culture, Vision, and Planning* (Englewood Cliffs, N.J.: Prentice-Hall: 1993); and G. Morgan, *Imaginization: The Art of Creative Management* (Newbury Park, Calif.: Sage Publications, 1993).

6. B. H. Peters and J. Peters, "The New Corporate Order," *Business Week,* January 27, 1992, 52-55.

7. Beach, *Making the Right Decision.*

8. G. G. Gordon, "Industry Determinants of Organizational Culture," *Academy of Management Review* 2 (1991): 396-415.

9. H. M. Trice and J. M. Beyer, "Using Six Organizational Rites to Change Culture," in R. H. Kilmann, M. J. Saxton, and R. Serpa, eds., *Gaining Control of the Corporate Culture* (San Francisco: Jossey-Bass, 1985).

10. Ibid.

11. Adapted from ibid., 372.

12. K. Rebello and E. Schwartz, "The Magic of Microsoft," *Business Week,* February 24, 1992, 60-64.

13. For a very detailed discussion of metaphors and metaphorical thinking, see Morgan, *Imaginization: The Art of Creative Management.*

14. T. J. Peters and R. H. Waterman, *In Search of Excellence* (New York: Harper & Row, 1983).

15. A. Wilkins, "Corporate Culture: The Role of Stories," in G. Morgan, ed., *Creative Organization Theory* (Newbury Park, Calif.: Sage Press, 1989), 159-62.

16. Adapted from Peters and Waterman, *In Search of Excellence,* 224-34; J. Galbraith, "The Innovating Organization," *Organizational Dynamics* (Winter 1982): 5-25; B. Dumaine, "Ability to Innovate," *Fortune,* January 29, 1990, 43, 46; and C. Knowlton, "What America Makes Best," *Fortune,* March 28, 1988, 40-54.

17. Peters and Waterman, *In Search of Excellence.*

18. D. Woodruff, "May We Help You Kick the Tires?" *Business Week,* August 3, 1992, 49-50.

19. P. F. Drucker, "Don't Change Corporate Culture—Use It!" *Wall Street Journal,* March 28, 1991, A14.

20. L. N. Spiro, "What's in the Cards for Harvey Golub?" *Business Week,* June 15, 1992, 112-24; and R. Wells, "American Express CEO Charges into Problems," *Orlando Sentinel,* September 20, 1993, F-1, F-7.

21. R. Stevenson, "Slot Machine Maker Hits Jackpot," *New York Times,* September 12, 1989, C1.

22. J. A. Bryne, "Management's New Gurus," *Business Week,* August 31, 1992, 44-52.

23. D. Keams, "Leadership through Quality," *Academy of Management Executive* 4 (1990): 86-89; R. Howard, "The CEO as Organizational Architect: An Interview with Xerox's Paul Allaire," *Harvard Business Week,* September/October, 1992, 107-21; and S. Herman, "A Brave New Darwinian Workplace," *Fortune,* January 25, 1993, 50-56.

24. J. Kennedy and A. Everest, "Put Diversity in Context," *Personnel Journal,* September 1991, 50-54.

25. Real-World Lessons for America's Small Businesses: Insights from the Blue Chip Enterprise Initiative, 1992. Fort Knox Security Products: A New Production Concept.

26. C. Borucki and C. Barnett, "Restructuring for Self-Renewal: Navistar International Corporation," *Academy of Management Executive* 4 (1990): 37-49.

27. National Westminster Bank USA, *Profiles in Quality: Blueprints for Action from 50 Leading Companies* (Boston: Allyn & Bacon, 1991), 175-78.

28. N. M. Tichy and S. Sherman, *Control Your Destiny or Someone Else Will* (New York: Doubleday, 1993).

29. R. M. Kanter, *The Change Masters* (New York: Simon & Schuster, 1983).

30. Bryne, "Management's New Gurus."

31. K. Lewis, *Field Theory in Social Science* (New York: Harper & Row, 1951).

32. Keams, "Leadership through Quality"; and Wells, "American Express CEO Charges into Problems."

33. "Sun Microsystems Turns on the Afterburners," *Business Week,* July 18, 1988, 115.

34. Gordon, "Industry Determinants of Organizational Culture."

35. Adapted from T. H. Holmes and R. H. Rahe, "Social Readjustment Rating Scale," *Journal of Psychosomatic Research* 11 (1967): 213-18.

36. Bryne, "Management's New Gurus."

37. J. P. Kotter and L. A. Schlesinger, "Choosing Strategies for Change," *Harvard Business Review,* March/April 1979, 109-12.

38. Reprinted by permission of the *Harvard Business Review,* Excerpt from *Choosing Strategies for Change* by John P. Kotter and Leonard A. Schlesinger, 57 (March/April 1979), 111. Copyright 1979 by the President and Fellows of Harvard College.

39. L. Kraar, "Iron Butterflies," *Fortune,* October 7, 1991, 143-54.

40. W. W. Burke, *Organizational Development* (Reading, Mass.: Addison-Wesley, 1987).

41. Adapted from W. L. French and C. H. Bell, *Organization Development: Behavioral Science Interventions for Organization Improvement,* 4th ed. (Englewood Cliffs, N.J.: Prentice-Hall, 1990), 169-72.

42. E. F. Huse and T. G. Cummings, *Organization Development and Change*, 4th ed. (St. Paul, Minn.: West Publishing, 1989).

43. W. G. Dyer, *Team Building: Issues and Alternatives*, 2d ed. (Reading, Mass.: Addison-Wesley, 1987).

44. D. G. Ancona, "Outward Bound: Strategies for Team Survival in an Organization," *Academy of Management Journal* 33 (1990): 334–65.

45. C. Larson and F. LaFasto, *Teamwork: What Must Go Right: What Can Go Wrong* (Newbury Park, Calif.: Sage Publications, 1989).

46. "Management Discovers the Human Side of Automation," *Business Week*, September 29, 1986, 70–75.

47. National Westminster Bank USA, *Profiles in Quality: Blueprints for Action from 50 Leading Companies.*

48. Based on G. Boccialetti, "Organization Development Ethics and Effectiveness," in W. Sikes, A. B. Drexler, and J. Gants, eds., *The Emerging Practice of Organization Development* (Alexandria, Va.: NTL Institute for Applied Behavioral Sciences, 1989), 83–92.

49. A set of ethical guidelines for OD practitioners was published in *Consultation*, Fall 1986, 21–218.

50. R. Denhardt, *The Pursuit of Significance* (Belmont, Calif.: Wadsworth Publishing Co., 1992).

51. "Can Wayne Calloway Handle the Pepsi Challenge?"; Murray, "PepsiCo's Fast Track"; "Go There and Get the Business"; Rigdon, "PepsiCo's KFC Scouts for Blacks and Women for Its Top Echelons"; see also a discussion in Hammer and Champy, *Reengineering the Corporation: A Manifesto for Business Revolution.*

IBAX: Reorganizing to Achieve Performance Improvements

Recall the IBAX situation, profiled in the cohesion cases at the close of Parts I and II. IBAX, a vendor of health care information systems software, is a partnership between IBM and Baxter. The company had experienced significant strategic, operational, and financial problems since its inception in 1989. As we began the case, Jeff Goodman had just been hired as the CEO of IBAX. His challenge was to turn the company around.

In the cohesion case that closed Part II, we learned about Goodman's strategic plan for IBAX. The plan was based on a retrenchment strategy. Goodman had closed several facilities and had reduced the workforce from 750 to 580. Once the downsizing efforts were complete, Goodman started changing the internal functioning of IBAX. In this cohesion case, we will examine the changes that Goodman made in the organizational design of the company, its human resource management practices, and its organizational culture.

CHANGING THE ORGANIZATIONAL DESIGN OF IBAX

Historically, IBAX had been organized in a traditional functional structure. A senior vice president was in charge of each functional department such as human resources, finance, product development, sales and marketing, and so on. As with most functional structures, profit centers did not exist, and there was little direct accountability for the bottom-line performance measures that were most critical for the company (i.e., net profit margins, product quality measures, customer satisfaction levels, and the like).

Goodman believed that a product-based structure would bring employees closer to the products and the customers that drove IBAX's performance. So he reorganized the company into six independent operating units based on the three core product lines of the company (Series 3000, 4000, 5000), and three other categories of products offered by IBAX (Value-added Products, Physician Series, and Point-of-Care Clinical Series). He called these units "businesses" and intended for them to operate as such. He identified teams of people to run each business, worked with them to establish performance objectives for their business with regard to such things as revenues, expenses, and customer satisfaction, and gave them the authority to do whatever necessary to make sure those objectives were achieved. Along with delegating the responsibility and authority associated with running the business, Goodman also made it very clear that these self-managed teams were accountable for the performance of their businesses. The locus of decision making in the organization shifted from being highly centralized to being very decentralized.

Once the teams understood their responsibilities, they began to reengineer their units, looking for redundancies in tasks and inefficient processes. Tasks were regrouped and jobs were redesigned. In many cases, both job scope and depth increased as employees took on additional tasks and responsibilities to improve the efficiency of their units. Where necessary, employees were provided with the training and development to do their jobs better or, in some cases, to do an entirely new job.

The product-based structure created relatively independent units and therefore the need for integration between work groups was reduced to some degree. Nevertheless, there was still a need for some communication between work groups and with the functional managers that had remained part of the structure (e.g., the vice presidents of human resources and finance). Team leaders served as liaisons with other groups where necessary, but it was generally understood that any employee could go directly to any other employee in the organization to get the information necessary to do his or her job. There was not a rigid hierarchy to be respected; doors were open, and everyone in the company was available to help as necessary.

A NEW APPROACH TO HUMAN RESOURCE MANAGEMENT

The human resource management (HRM) function changed dramatically as part of the retrenchment strategy. While the human resource management function had been fulfilled in very traditional ways in the past, Goodman and the vice president of Human Resources, Meigann Putnam, designed more creative and innovative methods to better serve the HRM function.

Rather than providing the traditional services of recruitment, selection, compensation, training and development, and employee relations centrally, the HRM function was decentralized. An HRM adviser was assigned to each business unit at IBAX. This adviser worked within the business so he or she could better understand the products and markets of the business and, therefore, better assess its human resource needs. The adviser would involve the team members in the business in all elements of the HRM process. For example, the teams assumed responsibility for hiring their own people based on the assessed needs of their business. What had once been a top-down approach to human resource management was transformed into an integrated, team-based process.

INSTILLING A NEW ORGANIZATIONAL CULTURE

Changing the culture of IBAX was critical to the implementation of the organizational and human resource management changes. As you will recall from the cohesion case at the close of Part I, there was no homogeneous culture at IBAX and no evolved, shared values among employees. Goodman knew from the outset that developing a strong and healthy corporate culture at IBAX would be a prerequisite to all the other changes that needed to take place.

Communication was the key to changing the culture at IBAX. From the beginning, Goodman was open with the employees about his concerns, goals, and plans. He involved them in both the assessment of the business and the development of the plan to turn it around. Employees started to believe that Goodman was committed to involving the employees in decision making. Further, he promised to reward organizational commitment, creativity, and hard work, and he followed through. Trust began to build within the ranks. As one person put it, "for the first time, the words and the music started to match." As trust continued to grow, the culture began to change. Morale began to improve, and employees started to feel empowered to make a difference at IBAX.

THE RESULTS

Much of the success of the retrenchment strategy can be attributed to the organizational changes described above. The move to a product-based structure put the focus of the company on the products it marketed and the customers it served. Responsibility and authority were delegated to those who could make a difference in product quality and customer service. Decision making was in the hands of self-managed teams who understood their performance objectives clearly and knew they were accountable for achieving those objectives. The overall effect of these changes was improved product quality, greater productivity, better customer satisfaction and stronger bottom-line profitability for all of IBAX's product lines.

For Discussion:

1. Discuss the ways Goodman changed the organizational design of IBAX.
2. What were the benefits of decentralizing the HRM function?
3. How will the new organizational culture at IBAX help with the implementation of its retrenchment strategy?

LEADERSHIP CHALLENGES IN THE 21ST CENTURY

PART IV

Communicating Effectively Within Diverse Organizations

CHAPTER 12

▼ CHAPTER OVERVIEW

An effective manager spends more time communicating—informing, persuading, listening, and inspiring—than doing anything esle. Communication skills are the manager's most important asset or biggest liability. Recent studies show that managers spend from 66 to 80 percent of their time communicating with superiors, subordinates, peers, and outside constituents.[1] If managers do not understand the processes involved in good communications, their best-laid plans can fail. The challenge for effective communication is even greater for managers in diverse organizations.

We therefore devote a chapter to providing an understanding of communication and to the task of achieving excellence in managerial communication. We start by defining communication and examining the different types of communication including oral, written, nonverbal, and information technologies. Then we turn our attention to the basic elements in the communication process such as the social context, sender and message encoding and decoding, the medium, feedback, and noise. Next, we examine some of the sources of communication breakdowns. These include cultural factors, trust and credibility issues, information overload, perception, and language characteristics. We move on to explore ways in which managers handle organizational communication including both formal and informal communication channels as well as communication networks. Finally, we conclude by focusing on ways managers can achieve communication competency by improving their feedback and listening skills.

▼ LEARNING OBJECTIVES

When you have finished studying this chapter, you should be able to:

- Describe the elements of the communication process and explain their relationship to one another.
- Give examples of the types of communication managers use.
- Discuss the changing role of information technologies in the communication process.
- Explain the importance of feedback.
- Describe the sources of communication breakdowns.
- Discuss the differences between formal and informal communication channels.

- Evaluate the effects and implications of different types of communication networks.
- Improve your feedback and listening competencies.

MANAGERIAL INCIDENT

EASTMAN KODAK: ALIGNING PEOPLE WITH COMMUNICATION

Most people at Eastman Kodak knew there were problems in the copy products group when they were forced to write off $40 million in inventory. But, when Chuck Trowbridge became the group's new general manager, he tackled those problems with his strongest tool—effective communication. His first task was to develop crucial communication links with nearly every key person inside and outside the group, including Bob Crandall, head of the engineering and manufacturing organization.

The situation for Crandall at Kodak was more a communication challenge than a performance problem. He had to talk not only with his subordinates but also with his bosses, peers, and staff in other parts of the organization as well as suppliers, government officials, and even customers. That meant he had to tap all of the communication channels at Kodak.

Trowbridge and Crandall had an immense problem that had to be resolved. How could they create and communicate a vision that would inspire Kodak's employees? Would it be possible for Trowbridge and Crandall to create a less bureaucratic and more decentralized organization while also striving to become a world-class manufacturing operation? This message was difficult to convey because it was such a radical departure from previous Kodak communications, not only for the copy products group but for most of the organization as well. This was the challenge that Kodak faced.[2] ▼

INTRODUCTION

Chuck Trowbridge and Bob Crandall know that every manager must demonstrate effective communication skills to stay successful in a highly competitive global environment. Communication is the process through which managers coordinate, lead, and influence their subordinates. The ability to communicate effectively is the characteristic managers consider most critical in determining managerial success. This ability involves a broad array of activities, from writing to speech making and the use of symbolic gestures.

Communication skills can make or break a career—and an organization. Communication is essential to management because it encompasses all aspects of an organization and pervades organizational activity; it is the process by which things get done in organizations. Yet communication is a complicated and dynamic process with many factors influencing effectiveness.[3] First, communication is a process in which sender, messages, channels, and receivers do not remain constant or static. Second, communication is complex. A number of communication theorists suggest that even a simple two-person interaction involves many variables, such as the individuals, the setting, the experiences each person has had, and the nature of the task, that effect the efficiency and effectiveness of the process. Third, communication is symbolic. We use a variety of arbitrary words and signs to convey meaning to those with whom we are communicating. While there is some agreement about the meaning of most of our words and signs, these change over time.

Consider Jan Carlzon, president of Scandinavian Airlines (SAS). From his first day at SAS, he made communicating, particularly with his employees, a top priority. During his first year as president, he spent exactly half of his working hours out in the field talking to SAS people. It was Carlzon's way of accepting responsibility and showing employees that his enthusiasm and involvement were genuine.[4]

Clearly, then, communication skills are essential for managerial success. This chapter explores the ways managers communicate, both formally and informally. Like the other aspects of the business environment we have examined, communication is being affected by change. In particular, information technology is changing the way managers communicate, and we will look at its effects in some details. Throughout the chapter, emphasis will be placed on ways managers can develop communication competency.

WHAT IS QUALITY COMMUNICATION?

An accountant prepares a memo on the tax implications of a proposed business merger. A department chair praises the accomplishments of a faculty member. A supervisor gives directions to a welder. A professor compliments a student's term paper. You will probably agree that all these incidents involve some form of communication. But what exactly is meant by communication? Communication is a complex and dynamic process, and like other management terms, it has no universally accepted definition.

For our purposes we will define **communication** as a process in which one person or group transmits some type of information to another person or group.[5] In some cases, this is all that occurs—communication is a one-way process. One-way communication is common when top executives in a large company send directions to subordinates. Often they do not expect any information in return, at least not immediately. But in most situations, the process of communication involves another aspect, for the receiver responds in some manner. For example, the person or group that receives the initial message returns a message to the person or group that initiated the communication. The receiver provides feedback to the sender. When this occurs, communication is a two-way, reciprocal event, involving the mutual exchange of information between two or more sides.

Communication
A process in which one person or group transmits some type of information to another person or group.

Defining communication is relatively simple, but achieving quality communication expertise is both complicated and difficult. Successful and high-quality communication results when the message is received and conveys the exact meaning the sender intended. In the next section, we will examine the types of communication managers most commonly use.

CATEGORIES OF COMMUNICATION

Managers use several different types of communication in their work. Each type, or category, plays an important role in managerial effectiveness. We organize managers' communication into four categories: (1) oral, (2) written, (3) nonverbal, and (4) information technology.

Oral

Oral communication consists of all forms of spoken information and is by far the most preferred type of communication used by managers. Research indicates that mangers prefer face-to-face and telephone communication to written communication because it permits immediate feedback. For example,

Oral communication
All forms of spoken information.

▼ Most professionals will eventually be called upon to use oral communication skills such as making a formal oral presentation either to a large audience, small committee or team, client, customer, or national conference.

individuals can comment or ask questions, and points can be clarified. Managers spend most of their time sharing information by communicating orally.[6] Experiential Exercise 12.2 at the end of the chapter provides an opportunity for you to develop your oral communication skills and effectiveness within a group setting.[7] It takes practice and time to develop these valued managerial skills.

Every professional will eventually be called upon to use oral communication such as making a formal oral presentation to a large audience, small committee or team, client, customer, or national conference. As we discussed in Chapter 11, professionals are change agents. Changes have to be presented effectively and sold to achieve acceptance and implementation.[8] As a manager, your oral communication skills are vital to your work and your career success.[9] Table 12.1 provides a checklist of key items to keep in mind when you are asked to make an oral presentation, whether to a small group or a large audience.[10]

Written

Written communication
Letters, memos, policy manuals, reports, forms, and other documentation used to share information in the organization.

Written communication includes letters, memos, policy manuals, reports, forms, and other documents used to share information in an organization. Managers use written communication less often than oral, but there are many occasions when written documentation is important. Writing down a message and sending it as a letter or memo enables a precise statement to be made, provides a reference for later use, aids in systematic thinking, and provides an official document for the organization. Written messages can also be disseminated to many members of the organization at the same time in the form of newsletters or memos. Meeting the Challenge enables you to examine your

▼ **Table 12.1**   Checklist for Planning More Effective Oral Presentations

1. *Establish your goals.* Have a clear image of your goals or purpose. Ask yourself, what is it that I want to accomplish?

2. *Analyze the audience.* Know your audience so you can effectively select the appropriate content, vocabulary, and visual aids. When the members of your audience are from diverse backgrounds or occupations, it is especially important to find a common bond. Pinpoint some shared concerns members of the audience may have, whether they are economic, political, or cultural.

3. *Diagnose the environmental conditions.* Be aware of how much time you will have and use your time effectively. Determine in advance, if possible, the audience size, physical layout of the room and speaking area, and technical equipment.

4. *Organize your material.* Remember that your message can be followed easily if your material is organized. A logical flow of thoughts will help your listeners follow the message. Start with a brief introduction that provides a preview, follow with a body that develops, and finish with a conclusion that reviews.

5. *Design and use visual aids.* Keep in mind that visual aids not only help to clarify material and heighten its impact but also keep an audience alert. Keep the visual aids simple and use them to emphasize, clarify, or pull together important information.

SOURCE: Adapted from P. Fandt, *Management Skills: Practice and Experience* (St. Paul, Minn.: West Publishing Co., 1994), 156–60.

written communication skills and also offers you an opportunity for improvement through peer evaluation and feedback.[11]

Nonverbal

Nonverbal communication involves all messages that are nonlanguage responses. It can be anything that sends a message. Although managers recognize that communication has a nonverbal side, they often underestimate its importance. Nonverbal communication may contain hidden messages and can influence the process and outcomes of face-to-face communication.[12] Even a person who is silent or inactive in the presence of others may be sending a message that may or may not be what is intended.

Consider how nonverbal communication affects the impressions we make on others. For example, interviewers respond more favorably to job candidates whose nonverbal cues (such as eye contact and erect posture) are positive than to those displaying negative nonverbal cues (such as looking down and slouching).[13]

Nonverbal communication can also take place through the physical arrangement of space, such as that found in various office layouts. For example, visitors tend to be uncomfortable in offices where a desk is placed between them and the person to whom they are speaking. Other things that communicate nonverbal messages about an individual are the artwork and decorations found in an office, as well as its orderliness and neatness.[14]

The following are six basic types of nonverbal communication:

1. *Kinesic behavior* or body motion such as gestures, facial expressions, eye behavior, touching, and any other movement of the body.

2. *Physical characteristics* such as body shape, physique, posture, height, weight, hair, and skin color.

3. *Paralanguage* such as voice quality, volume, speech rate, pitch, and laughing.

Nonverbal communication
All messages that are nonlanguage responses.

▼ Nonverbal communication involves all messages that are nonlanguage responses. What messages are these individuals communicating?

MEETING THE CHALLENGE

A COMMUNICATION SELF-ASSESSMENT

In response to each item, circle the answer that reflects how well the statement applies to you: (SA) strongly agree, (A) agree, (D) disagree, and (SD) strongly disagree.

1. When people talk, I listen attentively and do not think of other things, read or talk on the telephone.   SA A D SD
2. I provide the information the group needs, even if another member of the group was its source.   SA A D SD
3. I get impatient when people disagree with me.   SA A D SD
4. I ask for and carefully consider advice from other people.   SA A D SD
5. I cut off other people when they are talking.   SA A D SD
6. I tell people what I want, speaking rapidly, in short, clipped sentences.   SA A D SD
7. When people disagree with me, I listen to what they have to say and do not respond immediately.   SA A D SD
8. I speak candidly and openly, identifying when I am expressing opinions or feelings rather than reporting facts.   SA A D SD
9. I finish other people's sentences for them.   SA A D SD
10. I find it difficult to express my feelings, except when pressure builds up and I become angry.   SA A D SD
11. I am conscious of how I express myself nonverbally, including facial expressions, body language, voice tone, and gestures.   SA A D SD
12. When people disagree with me, I avoid arguments by not responding.   SA A D SD
13. During meetings, I prefer to listen rather than talk.   SA A D SD
14. When I talk, I am concise and to the point.   SA A D SD
15. I prevent arguments during team meetings.   SA A D SD

Agreeing (SA or A) with items 1, 4, 7, 8, 11, and 14 and disagreeing (D or SD) with all the rest suggests you encourage openness and candor. You create a climate of trust and teamwork by involving team members in important decisions that affect their lives. You communicate clearly and concisely and balance task and interpersonal aspects of the group.

Agreeing (SA or A) with items 2, 3, 5, 6, and 9 means you are probably task oriented and dominate the team. Such team leaders are frequently intolerant of disagreement and may squelch involvement and discussion. You would thus need to develop a more collaborative style to build and enhance teamwork. To become better at teamwork, modify your approach so your behavior would be accurately characterized by items 1, 4, 7, 8, 11, and 14.

4. *Proxemics* such as the way people use and perceive space, seating arrangements, and conversational distance.
5. *Environment* such as building and room design, furniture and interior decorating, light, noise, and cleanliness.
6. *Time* such as being late or early, keeping others waiting, and other relationships between time and status.

▼ **Table 12.2**   Watch Those Nonverbal Messages

NONVERBAL BEHAVIOR		COMMON INTERPRETATION
Facial Expressions	Frown	Displeasure, unhappiness
	Smile	Friendliness, happiness
	Raised eyebrows	Disbelief, amazement
	Narrow eyes, pursed lips	Anger
	Biting lip	Nervousness
Gestures	Pointing finger	Authority, displeasure, lecturing
	Folded arms	Not open to change or communication
	Arms at side	Open to suggestions, relaxed
	Hands on hips	Anger or defensiveness
	Hands uplifted outward	Disbelief, uncertainty
Voice	Shaky	Nervous
	Broken speech	Unprepared
	Strong/clear	Confident
Body Postures	Fidgeting, doodling	Boredom or nervousness
	Hands on hips	Anger, defensiveness
	Shrugging shoulders	Indifference
	Sitting on edge of chair	Listening, great interest
	Slouching	Boredom, lack of interest
	Shifting	Nervousness
Eye Contact	Sideways glance	Suspicion
	Steady	Active listener, interest
	No eye contact	Disinterest

Table 12.2 provides a guide to some nonverbal behaviors and common interpretations. These examples illustrate the numerous ways people can and do communicate without speaking or writing a word.

Information Technology

Information technology is a broad category of communication techniques that are rapidly influencing how managers communicate. For example, videotape recorders, telephone-anwsering devices and services, closed-circuit television systems, and facsimile machines all provide new communication flexibility. Computers networked together create an easy means to store and communicate vast amounts of information. Networking ties computers together, permitting individuals to share information, communicate, and access tremendous amounts of information. As we see in Managing for Excellence, this new information technology has led to more productive meetings.[15] Marriott Corporation, IBM, and Boeing are three companies that have successfully experimented with this type of information technology.

Telecommuting refers to the practice of working at home or at a remote site by using a computer linked to a central office or other employment location. It may also include those who work out of a customer's office or communicate with the office or plant via a laptop computer or mobile phone. More than two million corporate employees are now telecommuting full-time, and three times that number are involved in this form of communication one or two days a week. When the small, yet profitable Lepsch and Stratton Travel Agency faced the challenge of needing more office space and an unacceptably

Information technology
A broad category of communication techniques that includes videotape recorders, telephone-answering devices and services, closed-circuit television systems, and facsimile machines.

Telecommuting
The practice of working at a remote site by using a computer linked to a central office or other employment location.

MANAGING FOR EXCELLENCE

COMPUTER NETWORKING: THE KEY TO PRODUCTIVE MEETINGS

The typical business meeting is often less than productive. Although participants may arrive with an agenda in hand, the gathering may provide an excellent opportunity for individuals to settle other business matters and socialize with infrequently seen co-workers. Once the meeting begins, some participants may decide to make speeches in an attempt to make favorable impressions on superiors. As a result, they often digress from the subject at hand. Furthermore, others at the meeting may be less inclined to speak because they feel intimidated or think their ideas have no merit. Finally, some people with insight on an important topic may not be able to attend the meeting because they are out of town. Thus, another meeting must be held on the same topic. Under these circumstances, a skilled leader and a lot of cooperation from the participants are necessary to accomplish the meeting's objectives in an efficient manner.

An increasingly popular way of alleviating these problems and increasing efficiency is to conduct meetings with participants connected via computer networks. Marriott Corporation, IBM, and Boeing are three companies that have successfully experimented with this type of information technology. Studies support their claims that they accomplish more in less time. For example, Boeing analyzed 64 groups using a meeting room equipped with personal computers and IBM's TeamFocus software. Its findings indicated that total meeting time was cut 71 percent and calendar time required for team projects was cut 91 percent.

This method of electronic communication helps participants to be more efficient by encouraging succinct communication. Further, the ability to make statements anonymously increases the likelihood that people will express their true feelings and reduces participants' desire to talk purely for the sake of talking.

While electronic communication will never entirely replace verbal communication, it does offer managers a way to overcome some of the problems associated with the traditional business meeting. In the increasingly global business world, this type of information technology is sure to play an important role.

---

high turnover of support staff, it successfully implemented a program of telecommuting and had several employees conduct their work from home and communicate with the office by computer, telephone, and mail.[16] Many freelance creative workers, contract and temporary workers, and small companies are using this form of information technology, as are many better-known organizations, including IBM, Xerox, American Express, Du Pont, Apple Computer, and the Environmental Protection Agency.[17]

Electronic mail (E-mail)
A computer-based system that allows individuals to exchange and store messages through computerized text-processing and communication networks.

The emerging technology of **electronic mail (E-mail),** a computer-based system that allows individuals to exchange and store messages through computerized text-processing and communication networks, provides a very fast, inexpensive, and efficient means of organization. Text-based messages can be sent and received by anyone who has access to a computer terminal and is in a computer mailbox on the network. Messages can be transmitted in seconds between employees in the same building or overseas. The use of E-mail enhances vertical and horizontal communication because it can lead to greater information exchanges.[18] At Microsoft Corporation, CEO Bill Gates keeps up with his 10,000-employee empire via E-mail. Available to all employees, the system is considered the lifeblood of the company. All employees are encouraged to use E-mail to share suggestions and information—even send ideas to Gates without going through a supervisor.[19]

Videoconferencing is an umbrella term referring to the technologies that use live video to unite widely dispersed company operations. This technology offers tremendous savings of time, energy, and money. Business television networks enable companies to communicate to thousands of employees simultaneously. For example, televised instructions can provide training as well as technical assistance for employees. Videoconferencing enables organizations to hold interactive meetings where groups communicate live with each other via camera and cable transmission of the picture and sound, even though they are hundreds or even thousands of miles apart.[20]

Although information technology makes it easier for managers to communicate with their subordinates, it has also created managers who are "communicaholics."[21] Communicaholic managers are individuals who become extremely uncomfortable when they don't have ready access to subordinates, peers, and superiors. They lose track of the line separating work and nonwork time by seeking to be in constant touch with the office. They stay in touch with a portable or a car phone and rely excessively on fax machines, computer networks, and voice mail systems.

While good communication is valuable and an essential part of the manager's job, more information is not necessarily better information or even relevant information. Communicaholic managers can cause more problems than they solve. First, they may become prone to make decisions too quickly. The rapid access to data can preclude thoughtful deliberation. Communicaholic managers also tend to become obsessed with control and closely monitor employees' actions and decisions. In addition, they often fail to build face-to-face relationships, so the personal touch in managing is lost. More, faster, and easier

Videoconferencing
The technologies that use live video to unite widely dispersed company operations.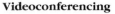

▼ Teleconferences are becoming increasingly necessary communication links as organizations expand internationally.

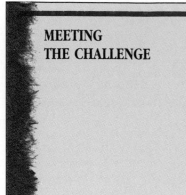

MEETING
THE CHALLENGE

USING FEEDBACK TO IMPROVE YOUR WRITING SKILLS

Bring two samples of your own writing to class. These can be samples from course work or from writing tasks you have completed on your job or in various organizations. Exchange samples with a classmate. Informally assess the strong points as well as the areas that need improvement in each other's writing samples. Keep in mind that as editors or evaluators you are just operating as readers reacting to one another's writing. Provide feedback to your classmate. Suggest improvements in his or her writing sample.

After each of you has provided feedback, make any changes in your own writing sample that you think are appropriate.

communication opens up the possibility for managers to waste a lot of time on junk communication.[22]

UNDERSTANDING MANAGERIAL COMMUNICATION

Managers communicate for many reasons—to motivate, inform, control, and satisfy social needs. Motivational communication serves the function of influencing the behavior of organization members. Communication that is intended to motivate must be designed to influence employees to work toward the accomplishment of organizational goals. Communication has an informational purpose when it provides facts and data to be used for decision making. In addition, managers give employees information they need to perform tasks, and employees inform managers of their progress toward meeting their objectives.

Communication also serves a control function. As you recall from the discussion on control in an earlier chapter, through communication work is coordinated and integrated, tasks and responsibilities are clarified, and records are kept to create order. Communication that controls serves the purpose of creating order in an organization, so that multiple goals and tasks can be pursued.

Finally, managers communicate to satisfy social needs. Communication fulfills social needs relating to the emotional and nontask-oriented interactions that occur in every organization. For example, employees need to talk about football games, the weather, politics, the boss's personality, and so forth. While this communication may not directly affect the performance of organizational tasks, it serves important needs and can influence how employees feel about their work conditions and how connected they are with others at work.

Assess your personal level of communication in Meeting the Challenge. Does your communication style enhance teamwork? Do you develop trust and teamwork through your communication?

THE COMMUNICATION PROCESS

To better understand why communication is problematic in organizations, managers must understand how the process of communication works. The communication process begins when an individual or group has an idea or concept and wishes to make that information known to someone else. Let's explore the elements of the process in more detail.

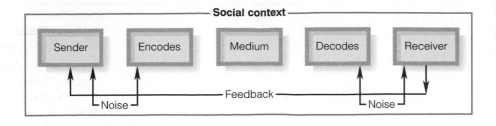

BASIC ELEMENTS IN THE COMMUNICATION PROCESS

The elements of the communication process are shown in Figure 12.1.[23] These elements include the social context, the sender who encodes the message, the receiver who decodes the message, the medium, feedback, and noise.

Social Context: Considerations of Global Impact and Diversity

The **social context** is the setting in which the communication takes place. The setting has an impact on the other components of the communication process. For example, communication between a manager and a subordinate in the manager's office will likely be more formal and reserved than if it occurred at a football game. Fewer distractions may occur under these circumstances. However, the subordinate may be less inclined to give the manager candid feedback. The social context is an important consideration in light of the global nature of business and the diversity of employees' or customers' cultural backgrounds. Conducting business in this arena presents many challenges to managers.

Social context
The setting in which a communication takes place.

Sender and Message Encoding

The sender initiates the communication process by encoding his or her meaning and sending the message through a channel. The **encoding** process translates the sender's ideas into a systematic set of symbols or a language expressing the communicator's purpose. The function of encoding, then, is to provide a form in which ideas and purposes can be expressed as a message.

Vocabulary and knowledge play an important role in the sender's ability to encode. But our ability to encode ideas, thoughts, and feelings is far from perfect. Some professionals have difficulty communicating with the general public because they tend to encode meanings in a form that can be understood only by other professionals in the same field. For example, legal contracts that directly affect consumers often have been written with the assumption that only lawyers will decode them. Consumer groups have pressed to have such contracts written in language that everyone can understand.

Encoding
Translating the sender's ideas into a systematic set of symbols or a language expressing the communicator's purpose.

Message and Medium

The result of encoding is the message. **Messages** are the tangible forms of coded symbols that are intended to give a particular meaning to the data. Words and symbols have no meaning in and of themselves. Their meaning is created by the sender and the receiver and, to a certain extent, by the situation or context. As we see in Table 12.3, sometimes messages are conveyed in ways that can be interpreted very differently.[24]

Once the encoding is accomplished, another issue arises. How can this information be transmitted to the receiver? The answer depends in part on how the message has been encoded. If the message is in the form of a written report, it can be transmitted by mail or, if urgent, by messenger or fax machine. If it has been entered into computer storage, it can be sent directly to another computer over phone lines or even by satellite. If it is expressed vocally, it can be presented directly in a face-to-face meeting or over the

Messages
The tangible forms of coded symbols that are intended to give a particular meaning to the data.

▼ **Table 12.3**   Sign of the Times: Thumbs Up

The day after falling ill at a state dinner, then President George Bush chose to communicate that he was alive and well by flashing a "thumbs-up" sign. President Bill Clinton used the same signal when he stepped off Air Force One upon returning from a recent policy meeting, only he communicated the gesture with both hands.

For years, the thumbs-up sign has been the national symbol for "don't worry, be happy." The gesture has become a sign for the times, preferred by heroic generals, buoyant athletes, returning astronauts, and just about anybody who wants to communicate the "all's well" message in a photo-opportunity way. For example, when former relief pitcher Rollie Fingers was told he had been voted into the Baseball Hall of Fame, he flashed a thumbs up. When General H. Norman Schwarzkopf returned home triumphantly from victory in the Gulf War, the no-nonsense general raised his thumb in the air, and the nation applauded. After suffering an injury in a football game that left him paralyzed, Detroit Lions lineman Mike Utley courageously raised his thumb as he was carried off the field. The gesture became the Lion's team symbol throughout the playoffs.

According to legend, the thumbs-up sign was first used by Roman emperors and audiences at coliseums where gladiators battled. A thumbs up meant that the victor should spare his rival's life; a thumbs down meant the loser would be killed. Today, the same symbol communicates ratings for arts and entertainment, thanks largely to film critics Gene Siskel and Roger Ebert.

But be careful using the thumbs-up sign in a different culture. Order a beer in Germany with a raised thumb and the bartender will bring you one brew. Use the same symbol in Japan and you'll get five beers. In Nigeria it is extremely insulting to use the thumbs-up gesture, as one innocent traveler found out when he raised his thumb to hitchhike and was beaten up by locals. The sign has similar obscene connotations in Iran and Australia.

SOURCES: J. Brownell, "Communicating with Credibility: The Gender Gap," *The Cornell Hotel and Restaurant Administration Quarterly*, April 1993, 52–61; B. Pauly, "Thumbs Up," *Los Angeles Daily News*, January 14, 1992, A12; and L. Harrisberger, *Succeeding: How to Become an Outstanding Professional* (New York: Macmillian, 1994).

Medium
The carrier of the message or the means by which the message is sent.

phone. The overriding consideration in choosing a method of transmission is to ensure that the receiver can comprehend the message.

The **medium** is the carrier of the message or the means by which the message is sent. Organizations provide information to members through a variety of mediums, including face-to-face communication, telephone conversations, group meetings, fax messages, memos, policy statements, reward systems, production schedules, and/or videoconferences. Fax machines have made it possible to send and receive written messages thousands of times faster than was possible a few years ago.

Sometimes managers fail to understand or consider how the choice of a medium affects a communication's effectiveness. The results of a three-year study of managerial communication indicate that the selection of the appropriate medium can have a major impact on communication effectiveness and even managerial performance.[25]

Receiver and Message Decoding: Challenges of Diversity

The receiving person or group must make sense of the information received. **Decoding** involves the translation of received messages into interpreted meanings. Once again, our abilities to accomplish this task are limited. As the workforce becomes more diverse, managers are challenged to decode messages accurately. Since receivers interpret the message based upon previous experience, frames of reference, vocabulary, and culture, this process is not always successful.

Decoding
The translation of received messages into interpreted meanings.

▼ Organizations provide information to members in a variety of mediums. Here we see a group receiving information via a videoconference.

Feedback

In our communication model, **feedback** refers to the process of verifying messages and the receiver's attempts to ensure that the message he or she decoded is what the sender really meant to convey. Feedback is a way to avoid communication failure because it provides preliminary information to the sender. Through feedback, communication becomes a dynamic, two-way process rather than just an event.

Many companies are beginning to realize the value of feedback from their customers. For example, at Xerox Corporation, executives spend one day a month taking complaints from customers about machines, bills, and services. At Hyatt Corporation Hotels, senior executives put in time as bellhops.[26] These types of activities provide managers with valuable feedback that they can use to improve the working relationships within the organization as well as strengthen the quality of customer service.

Feedback
The process of verifying messages and the receiver's attempts to ensure that the message decoded is what the sender meant to convey.

Noise

Noise is any internal or external interference or distraction with the intended message that can cause distortion in the sending and receiving of messages. In addition to physical conditions that make communication more difficult, emotional states can also create noise. For example, a radio playing loud music while someone is trying to talk, static on a line during a telephone conversation, or stressful working conditions are examples of noise. Noise can occur during any stage of communication process, and it reduces the probability of achieving common meaning between sender and receiver. Messages that are poorly encoded (e.g., written in an unclear way), improperly decoded (e.g., not comprehended), or transmitted through inappropriate mediums may result in reduced communication effectiveness.

Noise
Any internal or external interference or distraction with the intended message that can cause distortion in the sending and receiving of messages.

SOURCES OF COMMUNICATION BREAKDOWNS

Despite its apparent simplicity, the communication process rarely operates flawlessly. As we point out in the next section, communication breakdowns often interfere with communication excellence. Consequently, the information

▼ **Table 12.4**   Sources of Communication Breakdowns

• *Cross-cultural diversity*	When senders and receivers come from different cultural backgrounds, breakdowns in the communication process are more likely. Cultural differences may arise between persons from different geographical or ethnic groups within one country as well as between persons from different national cultures.
• *Trust and credibility*	Trust and credibility between the sender and receiver must be established. Without trust, the communicating parties concentrate their energies on defensive tactics, rather than on conveying and understanding meaning.
• *Information overload*	Individuals can experience information overload when they are asked to handle too much information at one time.
• *Perception*	A variety of factors such as experiences, needs, personality, and education can affect individuals' perceptions. As a result, two people may perceive the same thing in different ways.
• *Language characteristics*	The nature of our language means that many words or phrases are imprecise. Individuals often use different meanings or interpretations of the same word and do not realize it.
• *Gender differences*	Gender differences can result in breakdowns and lead to distorted communication and misunderstandings between men and women. Since males and females are often treated differently from childhood, they tend to develop different perspectives, attitudes about life, and communication styles.
• *Other factors*	Time pressures may cause us to focus on information that helps us make a choice quickly. Feedback may be impaired or absent.

transmitted from one party to another may be distorted, and communication problems may result. We turn now to some common sources of communication breakdowns; these are summarized in Table 12.4.

Cross-Cultural Diversity

Communication, as an exchange of meaning, is bounded by culture. As we have seen, during encoding an idea is translated into a message represented in symbols and language; then, during decoding the message is translated into interpreted meanings. This means that the message must be encoded in a form that the receiver will recognize, but the symbols and language used for encoding depend on cultural background, which varies from person to person.

Managers need to understand that senders and receivers from different cultures may encode and decode their messages differently, leading to breakdowns in the communication process. These difficulties may arise between persons from different geographical or ethnic groups in the same country, as well as between persons from different national cultures.[27] Read Global Perspective to better understand how cross-cultural communication has the potential for miscommunication.[28]

LEARNING THE LANGUAGE OF CROSS-CULTURAL COMMUNICATION

In organizations all over the world, people use time to communicate with each other. But the language of time varies from culture to culture. There are different languages of time just as there are different spoken languages. Deadlines may indicate a degree of urgency or relative importance in the United States, but in the Middle East, the time required to get something accomplished depends on the relationship between individuals.

The language of space refers to perceptions about interactions and status. The American businessperson, familiar with the pattern of American corporate life, has no difficulty appraising an individual's relative importance simply by noting the size of his or her office in relation to other offices nearby. In the American pattern, the president or board chair has the biggest office, and the more important offices are usually located at the corners of the building and on the top floor. The French, on the other hand, are much more likely to lay out space as a network of connecting points of influence, activity, or interest. The French Manager will ordinarily be found in the middle of his or her subordinates to make it easier to supervise them.

The language of things refers to the status associated with material possessions. Lacking a fixed class system and having an extremely mobile population, Americans have become highly sensitive to how others make use of material goods. The French, English, and Germans, however, have different ways of using material possessions. Things that represent the height of dependability and respectability to the English would be considered old-fashioned and backward by most Americans. Middle East businesspersons attach status to family, connections, and friendship rather than to material things. The Japanese take pride in tasteful though often inexpensive possessions that are used to create the proper emotional setting.

The language of friendship refers to the depths, length, and type of relationship that develops between individuals. Americans perceive friendships in terms of a series of favors that must be repaid, at least by gratitude. In India, however, friendship involves sensing a person's needs and filling them without any expectation of gratitude.

Finally, the language of agreements refers to the importance of knowing the rules for negotiating in different organizations and various countries. It's not essential to know the details of the legal practice, but one should be aware that differences exist. Sensitivity to these differences is critical.

A common problem in cross-cultural communications is ethnocentrism, the tendency to consider one's culture and its values as being superior to others. Very often such tendencies are accompanied by an unwillingness to try to understand alternative points of view and take seriously the values they represent. This attitude can be highly disadvantageous when trying to conduct business and maintain effective working relationships with persons from different cultures.[29]

Studies show that the greater the differences between the sender's and receiver's cultures, the greater the chance for miscommunication.[30] Miscommunication in this context is the result of misperception, misinterpretation, and misevaluation. For example, the Coca-Cola Company lost sales in many

Asian markets when consumers misinterpreted the advertisement "Coke Adds Life" to mean "Coke Brings You Back from the Dead."

Trust and Credibility

One potential barrier to effective communication is a lack of trust between the sender and the receiver. This lack of trust can cause the receiver to look for hidden meanings in the sender's message. A trusting relationship is almost a prerequisite for communication excellence. In the absence of trust, the communicating parties divert their energies to defensive tactics, rather than trying to convey and understand meaning.[31]

A work environment characterized by trust does not just happen. It takes time and effort to develop. It must be nurtured and reinforced by honesty and accuracy in communication and mutual respect between communication parties. General Electric Government Services, for example, has a special program that tries to break down the adversarial relationships between management and the workforce. Based on a highly developed set of corporate ethical principles devised through employee participation, the program looks for ways the company can earn the trust and commitment of its employees.[32]

Managers must develop trust in their working relationships with subordinates and take advantage of all opportunities for face-to-face communications. Management by wandering around (MBWA) is now popularly acclaimed as one way to do this.[33] MBWA simply means that managers get out of their offices and communicate regularly with employees as they do their jobs. Managers who spend time walking around can greatly reduce the perceived distance between themselves and their subordinates. They can also create an atmosphere of open and free-flowing communication, which makes more and better information available for decision making and makes decisions more relevant to the needs of lower-level personnel. Of course, the wandering around must be a genuine attempt to communicate.[34] It should not be perceived as just another way to "check up" on employees.

Information Overload

Although information is the lifeblood of the organization, it is possible for managers and organizations to have too much information. We all have a limit to the amount of information we can decode and understand at any given time. **Information overload** exists whenever the capacity of a communication medium to process information is exceeded. Individuals can experience information overload when they are asked to handle too much information at one time. For example, the new employee who is presented with too much information to comprehend on her first few days on the job may experience information overload. Similarly, it is difficult for a student to read and comprehend several chapters of material the night before an exam if he is reading them for the first time.

As we discussed earlier, with the widespread use of communication technology, the information age is upon us. With so much information available, managers are often dazzled and do not know what to do with it all. Individuals may respond to information overload in a variety of ways, including the following:[35]

- Failing to process or ignoring some of the information.
- Processing the information incorrectly.
- Delaying the processing of information until the information overload abates.
- Searching for people to help process some of the information.

Information overload
Occurs whenever the capacity of a communication medium to process information is exceeded.

- Lowering the quality of information processing.
- Withdrawing from the information flow.

Managers are not the only ones who experience overload. It can also trouble consumers. Organizations are looking for creative ways to help consumers handle the abundance of information and are trying to make products more "consumer-friendly." This emphasis has led to the emergence of a new discipline called information graphics, or "infographics." The idea behind infographics is to make every mark on the page carry meaning. This allows people to learn more with less effort. Anything that doesn't serve a purpose is referred to as "chartjunk" and is eliminated.[36] The infographics approach to reducing information overload is getting attention. For example, Pacific Bell hired an infographer to revitalize its yellow pages, and the IRS used one to make its forms less confusing to taxpayers.

Perception

As we discuss in Chapter 14, perception is the process of selecting, organizing, and interpreting environmental stimuli to provide meaningful experiences. It deals with both the sensory and mental processes used by an individual in interpreting information. A variety of factors such as experiences, needs, personality, and education can affect individuals' perceptions. As a result, two people may perceive the same thing in different ways. For example, sales and production managers of the same company are likely to perceive the weekly sales data differently.

Language Characteristics

The very nature of our language constitutes a source of communication breakdown. Many words are imprecise. For example, a manager tells a subordinate to do this task "right away." Does the manager mean for the subordinate to drop what she is doing and work on the new task immediately or to finish what she is currently working on and then do the new task?

When two individuals are using different meanings or interpretations of the same word and do not realize it, a communication barrier exists. For example, some words sound the same but have multiple meanings. "Write" (communicate), "rite" (ceremony), "right" (not left), and "right" (privilege) all sound alike, right (correct)? Don't assume the meaning you give a word will be the one the receiver uses in decoding the message. Language characteristics can lead to encoding and decoding errors and mixed messages that create semantic barriers to communication. For example, a word may be interpreted differently depending on the facial expressions, hand gestures, and voice inflection that accompany it.

The imprecision and multiple meanings of words are one reason why jargon develops. **Jargon** is pretentious terminology or language specific to a particular profession or group. For example, at Disney, customers are called "guests" and employees are called "cast members." If cast members do a job correctly, it is called a "good Mickey"; if they do a bad job, it is a "bad Mickey."[37] At Microsoft Corporation, learning the company jargon is an important part of acceptance as an organizational member.[38] Although jargon is designed to avoid communication breakdowns, in some cases it may lead to inefficiency because not everyone will understand what is being communicated, especially new members of the organization or group.

Language characteristics, including imprecision and multiple meanings, are posing an even greater threat to communication as society becomes more interconnected and mobile. The possibility of contact with someone from a different background or culture who uses words differently is increasing.

Jargon
Pretentious terminology or language specific to a particular profession or group.

Gender Differences

Gender differences can result in breakdowns and lead to distorted communication and misunderstandings between men and women. Because males and females are often treated differently from childhood, they tend to develop different perspectives, attitudes about life, and communication styles. Historically, stereotypical assumptions about the differing communication styles of males and females have stimulated discrimination against female managers. In recent years, however, more realistic images of how professional men and women behave and communicate have replaced the old stereotypes.

Research shows that women and men listen differently.[39] Women tend to speak and hear a language of connection and intimacy while men tend to speak and hear a language of status and independence. Women are more likely to hear emotions and to communicate empathy. For example, when co-workers socialize at work, women are more likely to share their problems and respond with sensitivity to others' concerns.[40]

Women's oral communication differs from men's in significant ways. Women are more like to use qualifiers, phrases like "I think" or "It seems to me."[41] Generally, women tend to end statements with an upward inflection that makes the statements sound like questions. Female voices are generally higher and softer than male voices. This makes it easy for men to overpower women's voices, and men commonly interrupt women or overlap their speech.

Another obvious difference is that men spend much more of their oral communication time telling stories.[42] When you listen closely to men's conversations, you will find that they retell tales of past incidents, often adding enhancements to improve the story's entertainment value. In contrast, women personalize their messages, often emphasizing the emotional aspects.

Although a wide range of gender differences can exist in verbal communication, nonverbal differences are even more striking. Men lean back and sit in an open leg position that takes up considerable space, thereby communicating higher status and a greater sense of control over their environment.[43] Women use much more eye contact than men yet avert their gaze more often, especially when communicating with a man or someone of higher status. Women smile more frequently and are generally better at conveying and interpreting emotions.

Both men and women can work to change the perception that women are less capable of being competent managers. Women need to monitor their verbal and nonverbal communication and choose behavior that projects professionalism and competence. Men should become more aware of their communication behavior and its impact on female colleagues and choose responses that will facilitate an open exchange of ideas.[44]

Other Factors

Several other factors can lead to communication breakdowns. Time pressures may cause us to focus on information that helps us make decisions quickly, although the information may not be of high quality. Feedback may be impaired or absent. In one-way communications, like the written memo, the sender does not receive any direct and immediate feedback from the receiver. Studies show that two-way communication is more accurate and effective than one-way, but it is also more costly and time-consuming.

MANAGING ORGANIZATIONAL COMMUNICATION WITHIN DIVERSE ORGANIZATIONS

Communication permeates every organization. Some messages are clear and effective; others cause confusion and errors. In addition, some messages sent throughout the organization contain misinformation or secret information that may impede organizational processes. As organizations become more diverse, managers must strive to provide clear guidelines for effective communication. In this section, we describe formal and informal communication channels.

FORMAL COMMUNICATION CHANNELS

Formal communication follows the chain of command and is recognized as official. One way to view formal communication in organizations, shown in Figure 12.2, is to examine how it flows—downward, upward, or horizontally. Specific types of communication are often associated with directional flow. Briefly examining each type of directional flow will help us appreciate the problems inherent in organizational communication and identify ways to overcome these problems.

Vertical Communication
Vertical communication is the flow of information both up and down the chain of command. It involves an exchange of messages between two or more levels in the organization.

Downward Communication   When top-level management makes decisions, standing plans, and so forth, they are often communicating downward. **Downward communication** flows from individuals in higher levels of the organization to those in lower levels. The most common forms of downward communication are meetings, official memos, policy statements, procedures, manuals, and company publications. At the Walt Disney Company, a newsletter called *Eyes and Ears* informs employees of any new attractions and improvements and provides information on "Donald Deals," which offer discounts on meals and local amusements. This type of downward communication helps involve employees and makes them feel that they are an integral part of the organization.

Information sent downward may include new company goals, job instructions, procedures, and feedback on performance. Studies show that only 20 percent of the intended message sent by top management is intact by the time it reaches the entry-level employee. The information loss in downward communication is shown in Figure 12.3.[45] This information loss occurs for several reasons. First, managers tend to rely too heavily on written channels; an avalanche of written material may cause the overloaded subordinate to ignore some messages. Second, the oral face-to-face message that commands more attention and provides immediate feedback is often underutilized. Finally, subordinates may perceive many downward messages as irrelevant or obsolete.

Downward communication
Flows from individuals in higher levels of the organization to those in lower levels.

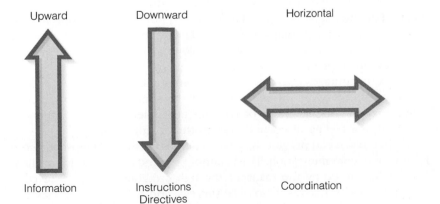

Upward   Downward   Horizontal

Information   Instructions   Coordination
                 Directives

▼ **Figure 12.2**
Organizational Communication Flows

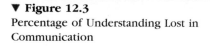

▼ **Figure 12.3**
Percentage of Understanding Lost in
Communication

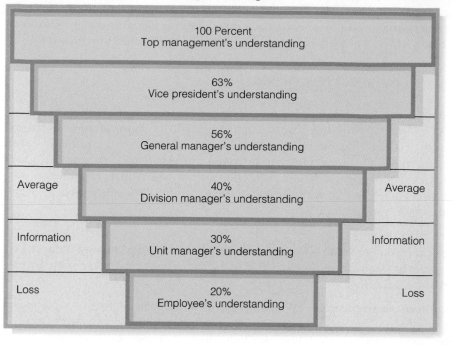

Table 12.5 provides a humorous account of information loss and distortion that can occur in downward communication.[46]

Upward communication
Information to managers from their
subordinates.

Upward Communication   **Upward communication** typically provides information to managers from their subordinates. Effective organizations need upward communication as much as downward communication.

Upward communication, from subordinates to managers, usually falls into one of the following types:

1. Personal reports of performance, problems, or concerns.
2. Reports about others and their performance, problems, or concerns.
3. Reactions to organizational policies and practices.
4. Suggestions about what tasks need to be done and how they can be accomplished.

This type of communication is frequently sent up only one level in the organization to the immediate supervisor. The supervisor may send some of the information to the next higher level, but usually in a modified form. Both written and oral channels may be used in those instances.

Upward communication is beneficial to both the manager and the subordinate. For the manager, it is often necessary for sound decision making. Upward communication helps managers know employees' accomplishments, problems, and attitudes and allows employees to make suggestions and feel that they are part of the decision making process. Additionally, it provides feedback, encourages ongoing two-way communication, and indicates the subordinates' receptiveness to messages. For the subordinate, upward communication may provide a release of tensions and a sense of personal worth that may lead to a feeling of commitment to the organization.

As we discussed previously, a trusting relationship is almost a prerequisite for effective communication. Trust cannot be mandated by policy or directives; it must be earned by the manager through credible behavior and communication. Suggestion boxes, employee surveys, and open door policies are often

▼ **Table 12.5** Is That What I Said?

- A COLONEL issued the following directive to his EXECUTIVE OFFICER: "Tomorrow evening at approximately 2000 hours Halley's comet will be visible in this area, an event that occurs only once every 75 years. Have the men fall out in the battalion area in fatigues, and I will explain this rare phenomenon to them. In case of rain, we will not be able to see anything, so assemble the men in the theater, and I will show them films of it."

- EXECUTIVE OFFICER to COMPANY COMMANDER: "By order of the colonel, tomorrow at 2000 hours, Halley's comet will appear above the battalion area. If it rains, fall the men out in fatigues. Then march to the theater, where the rare phenomenon will take place, something that occurs only once every 75 years."

- COMPANY COMMANDER to LIEUTENANT: "By order of the colonel in fatigues at 2000 hours tomorrow evening, the phenomenal Halley's comet will appear in the theater. In case of rain in the battalion area, the colonel will give another order, something that occurs once every 75 years."

- LIEUTENANT to SERGEANT: "Tomorrow at 2000 hours, the colonel will appear in the theater with Halley's comet, something that happens every 75 years. If it rains, the colonel will order the comet into the batallion area in fatigues."

- SERGEANT to SQUAD: "When it rains tomorrow at 2000 hours, the phenomenal 75-year-old General Halley, accompanied by the colonel, will drive his comet through the batallion area theater in fatigues.

SOURCE: Adapted from J. W. Gould, "Quotations That Liven a Business Communication Course," *The Bulletin,* December 1985, 32.

used to encourage upward communication. General Electric Government Services has encouraged the use of upward communication through some unique programs as Service Challenge describes.[47]

Achieving effective upward communication—getting open and honest messages from employees to management—is an especially difficult task. Some research has shown that upward communication is the most ineffective type of communication. Upper-level managers often do not respond to messages from lower-level employees, and lower-level employees often are reluctant to communicate upward, especially if the message contains bad news.

Since most organizations are characterized by top-down information flows, managers must make a concerted effort to seek information from employees. It is not always enough for senior managers to talk with the layer of people immediately beneath them because this group may have a vested interest in presenting only positive information. This is why the concept of managing by wandering around is so important.[48]

Perhaps more importantly, we should note that upward communication often tends to suffer from serious inaccuracies.[49] A recent study revealed that less than 15 percent of managers' total communication was directed toward their superiors.[50] When managers communicate upward, their conversations tend to be shorter than discussions with peers, and they often highlight their accomplishments and downplay their mistakes if the mistakes will be looked upon unfavorably.[51]

Horizontal Communication

Horizontal communication is the lateral information flow that occurs both within and between departments. The purpose of horizontal communication is coordination. As you will recall from the discussion of the coordination function in an earlier chapter, communication provides a means for members on the same level of an organization to share information without directly involving their superiors. Examples include the communication that may occur

Horizontal communication
The lateral information flows that occur both within and between departments for the purpose of coordination.

SERVICE CHALLENGE

GEGS: LISTENS TO EMPLOYEES

Top executives at General Electric Government Services (GEGS) don't just send messages down the organizational chain of command. By estimating several new programs to encourage upward communication, GEGS management has shown a commitment to getting quality information from employees.

To increase two-way communication and a business/customer focus, GEGS devised a program called Work-Out. The program initiated a set of values that encouraged employee participation in management decisions.

To enhance open communication channels, a program called Skip Level Luncheons was launched. The purpose of the luncheons is to provide employees an opportunity to make suggestions about improving quality and discuss issues that pertain to their work.

Finally a program called ACTION (Accessibility, Communication, Trust, Integrity, Openness, and Nonretaliating) was inaugurated. The purpose of ACTION is to assure that employee questions are dealt with in a timely, fair, and nonretaliatory fashion.

between members of different departments of an organization and between co-workers in the same department. Both written and oral channels may be used for horizontal communication. In addition, more formal liaison roles may be created to support horizontal information flows. These are important to coordinate activities that support the organizational objectives.

INFORMAL COMMUNICATION CHANNELS

The upward, downward, and horizontal communications described so far are part of the formal communication channels used to accomplish the work of the organization. In addition to these formal channels, organizations have informal channels of communication. Informal communication channels arise from the social relationships that evolve in the organization. These are neither required nor controlled by management.

The **grapevine** is the informal flow of messages throughout the organization. The grapevine is a useful and important source of information for managers and employees at all levels. It typically involves small clusters of people who exchange information in all directions through unsanctioned organizational channels and networks. The grapevine should be considered as much a communication vehicle as the company newsletter or employee meetings.

The grapevine can be quite beneficial. For example, research shows that the more involved people are in their organizations' communication channels, the more powerful and influential they become on the job.[52]

Information carried by the grapevine is often quite accurate. In fact, one well-known study found that approximately 80 percent of the information transmitted through the grapevine was correct.[53] The remaining 20 percent, though, can often lead to serious trouble. As you probably know from your own experience, a story can be mainly true but still be quite misleading because essential facts are omitted or distorted. The information in the informal network is usually unverified and often includes rumors that are exaggerated and frequently wrong. To help prevent incorrect rumors, the manager must keep the information flowing through the grapevine as accurate and rumor-free as possible. To do so, managers should share as much information as

Grapevine
The informal flow of messages throughout the organization.

possible with employees, tell them of changes as far in advance as possible, and encourage employees to ask questions about rumors they hear.

To some extent, the grapevine is always present in any organization and is more than just a means of conveying corporate gossip. Its information may be less official but is no less important for understanding the organization. The grapevine is an influence to be considered in all management actions. Indeed, the grapevine's influence suggests that mangers must listen to it, study it, learn who its leaders are, how it operates, and what information it carries.

COMMUNICATION NETWORKS

Our model of the communication process in Figure 12.1 includes only two individuals. However, communication frequently takes place among many individuals and groups. For example, when tasks require inputs from several individuals, managers must link up with a variety of people inside and outside the organization.

A managers' **communication network** represents a pattern of information flow among task group members. The importance of communication networks lies in their potential influences on effectiveness, task efficiency, group leadership, member satisfaction, decision quality, and other variables.[54] Five major group communication network structures, categorized as either centralized or decentralized, are shown in Figure 12.4.

Centralized Networks

In a **centralized communication network,** group members must communicate through another group member. Since information more often flows through central members, they are likely to be perceived as leaders and to have high status. They are also likely to be more satisfied than their less central counterparts. Centralized networks tend to permit rapid decision making, but member satisfaction is usually low. Centralized networks may be efficient for

Communication network
A pattern of information flow among task group members.

Centralized communication network
Communication that flows through a centralized group member.

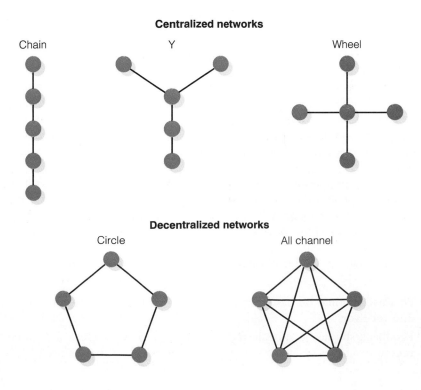

Centralized networks

Chain   Y   Wheel

Decentralized networks

Circle   All channel

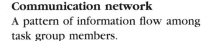

▼ **Figure 12.4**
Communication Networks

simple problems, but as complexity increases, more decentralization (and thus more participation in decision making) is needed.

The chain pattern of communication links members sequentially and results when group members communicate only with certain people in the group. In this pattern, the leader is not defined, although the person in the center of the chain tends to emerge as the controller of the information. The biggest drawback of chain patterns is the lack of coordinated effort. The group does not function like a team, and leadership is also weak.

The Y network is a modified chain. One member, usually at the fork of the Y, becomes the information coordinator to all others in the network. While most tasks are centralized, members of Y networks do not experience high

With the wheel network, all communication must flow through a central individual. The wheel network might be appropriate for routine, well-structured tasks, especially if there are time constraints. This pattern can be very effective for simple tasks if group members accept the leader's authority.

Decentralized Networks

Decentralized communication network
Communication that flows to all group members equally.

In **decentralized communication networks**, such as the circle and all-channel networks, all members are equally central, and anyone in the group can emerge as leader. Since members can communicate with any other member, decentralized networks are more effective for solving complex problems and encouraging creativity.

ACHIEVING COMMUNICATION COMPETENCY

Defining good communication is much easier than achieving competent communication skills because communication is both complicated and difficult. Managers agree that the ability to communicate effectively is crucial to success.[55] Even a fairly simple and straightforward exchange of factual information is subject to distortion and miscommunication. In this section, we will focus on ways to prevent distortion and improve two critical aspects of communication—feedback skills and listening skills.

DEVELOPING QUALITY FEEDBACK SKILLS

As we discussed earlier, feedback refers to the process of verifying messages from the sender. Through feedback, communication becomes a dynamic, two-way process, rather than just an event. Feedback can include very personal feelings or more abstract thoughts, such as reactions to others' ideas or proposals. The emotional impact of feedback varies according to how personally it is focused.

The first requirement of quality feedback is to recognize when it is truly intended to benefit the receiver and when it is purely an attempt to satisfy a personal need. A manager who berates an employee for accounting errors may actually be angry about personally failing to give clear instructions in the first place.

If feedback is to be effective, managers need to observe the following principles:

• Feedback should be based on a foundation of trust between the sender and receiver.

• Feedback should be specific rather than general, with clear and preferably recent examples. Saying "You are a poor listener" is not as useful as saying "I watched you interact with that customer and you did not listen to what she was saying."

- Feedback should be given at a time when the receiver appears ready to accept it. Therefore, when a person is angry, upset, or defensive, it is probably not the time to bring up other new issues.

- Feedback should be limited to things the receiver may be capable of doing something about.

- Feedback should provide descriptive information about what the person said or did and should avoid evaluative inferences about motives, intent, or feelings.

- Feedback should not include more than the receiver can handle at any particular time. For example, the receiver may become threatened and defensive if the feedback includes everything the receiver does that annoys the sender.

In addition to giving feedback, being able to receive feedback is also important for effective communication. According to Robert Kaplan, senior fellow at the Center for Creative Leadership in Greensboro, North Carolina, managers can develop feedback competency not only through giving feedback but by actively soliciting feedback about their own performance. This means managers need to ask subordinates and peers for feedback and take a realistic stock of their strengths and weaknesses. Kaplan tells managers not to ask questions unless they are willing to hear the answers. Accept the comments about what you don't do well, and work hard to make improvements.[56]

▼ Feedback can include very personal feelings or more abstract thoughts, such as reactions to others' ideas or proposals. This manager is providing feedback that will help to improve a client's proposal.

IMPROVING LISTENING SKILLS

Since a large proportion of a manager's time is spent communicating with other people, the ability to listen well is a distinct asset. How good a listener are you? Experiential Exercise 12.1 helps you assess your listening skills. Take the time now to measure your listening ability. Listening involves careful attention and response to messages. Instead of evaluating the message or preparing a response, an effective listener tries to understand both direct and subtle meanings contained in messages. Be attentive to the feelings of the sender as well as the verbal content of the message. Observe people while they are speaking. Watch facial expressions, gestures, body movements, and eye contact. This will help you to understand the real content of the message. The following guidelines will help you be an effective listener:[57]

- Listen for message content. Try to hear exactly what is being said in the message.

- Listen for feelings. Try to identify how the sender feels about the message content. Is it pleasing or displeasing to the sender?

- Respond to feelings. Let the sender know that you recognize his or her feelings, as well as the message content.

- Be sensitive to both the nonverbal and the verbal content of messages; identify mixed messages that need to be clarified.

- Reflect back to the sender, in your own words, what you think you are hearing. Paraphrase and restate the verbal and nonverbal messages as feedback to which the sender can respond with further information.
- Be attentive. Don't pretend to listen when you really are thinking about what you are going to say next or what is going on in the next office. Don't squirm or fidget while someone else is talking. Find a comfortable position, and give 100 percent of your attention to the speaker.
- Be patient. Don't interrupt the speaker. Take time to digest what has been said before responding. Don't be afraid to ask questions to clarify and understand every word of what has been said. There is no shame in not knowing, only in not knowing and pretending to know.

Listening is an active process. Effective listening behaviors include maintaining eye contact, rephrasing what has been said, listening for the message beyond the obvious and overt meaning of the words that have been spoken, and observing nonverbal messages. The key to more effective listening competency is the willingness to listen and respond appropriately to the feelings being expressed, as well as to the content.

MANAGERIAL IMPLICATIONS

Organizational leaders are first and foremost in the communications business. According to Roger Smith, former chair of General Motors, effective communication has more impact on an organization's prospects than any other single factor.[58] Whether you are a financial planner, small business owner, accountant, sales representative, minister, teacher, or any other type of professional, the following issues are key points to consider for managerial effectiveness:[59]

- You spend most of your time at work communicating.
- Your success is based on strong communication skills.
- Communication is becoming increasingly important in view of recent trends, such as increased globalization, diversity, and workplace specialization.
- Communication technology offers new opportunities to communicate more often and more efficiently than ever before.

Whatever you do in the future, communication will probably take up a large portion of your time, and the more effective you are at communicating, the more successful you are likely to be.

MANAGERIAL INCIDENT RESOLUTION

EASTMAN KODAK: ALIGNING PEOPLE WITH COMMUNICATION

Chuck Trowbridge and Bob Crandall faced a major communication challenge at Kodak. Within six months after they initiated their intensive communication alignment process, Crandall and Trowbridge began to see results. Communication flows changed as Crandall set up dozens of vehicles to emphasize the new direction and align people to his vision. These vehicles included weekly meetings with his immediate subordinates; monthly "copy products forums," where Crandall met with a group including an employee from each of his departments; quarterly meetings, where he met with all 100 of his supervisors to discuss recent improvements and new projects to achieve better results;

and quarterly "State of the Department" meetings, where his managers met with everyone in their own departments.

Once a month, Crandall and all those who reported to him would also meet with 80 to 100 people from some area of the communication to discuss anything they wanted. To align his biggest supplier, Crandall and his managers met with its top management over lunch every Thursday. Based on his success, he created a format called "business meetings," where his managers meet with 12 to 20 people on a specific topic such as inventory or master scheduling. The goal was to include all of his 1500 employees in at least one of these focused business meetings each year.

Trowbridge and Crandall also used written communication in their alignment process including the "Copy Products Journal" sent to employees once a month, "Dialog Letters" that gave employees an opportunity to question Crandall and his top managers anonymously and be guaranteed a reply, and charts posted in a main hallway near the cafeteria that graphically reported the quality, cost, and delivery results of each product. A hundred smaller versions of these charts were scattered throughout the manufacturing area, reporting quality levels and costs for specific work groups.

These successes made the message Crandall and Trowbridge sent more credible and helped influence more employees to work toward accomplishing organizational goals. For example, in four years, quality on one of the main product lines increased nearly 100-fold. Defects per unit declined from 30 to 0.3. Over a three-year period, costs on another product line dropped nearly 24 percent. On-time deliveries increased by 82 percent in the first two years. Inventory levels dropped by over 50 percent, even though the product volume was increasing. And productivity, measured in units per manufacturing employee, more than doubled. Communication affects the bottom line and it pays! Clearly, the communication alignment process at Kodak was a success.[60] ▼

SUMMARY

- Communication is essential to management because it encompasses all aspects of an organization and pervades organizational activity. Managers communicate to motivate, inform, control, and satisfy social needs.

- We defined communication as a process in which one person or group transmits some type of information to another person or group. Managers use oral, written, nonverbal, and information technologies to communicate.

- The elements of the communication process include the social context, or the setting in which the communication takes place; the sender who initiates and encodes the message; the medium, or the carrier of the message; the receiver who decodes, or translates, the message; feedback, which refers to the process of verifying messages and the receiver's attempts to ensure that the message is what the sender really meant to convey; and noise, which is interference or distraction with the intended message that can cause distortion or miscommunication.

- There are six types of nonverbal communication: (1) kinesic behavior or movement of the body; (2) physical characteristics; (3) paralanguage; (4) proxemics; (5) environment; and (6) time.

- Information technology is rapidly changing the way we communicate. Technologies such as computer networks, E-mail, videoconferencing, facsimile machines, and telecommuting all offer managers easier and more flexible means of communicating with subordinates.

- Despite the apparent simplicity of the communication process, communication breakdowns may often interfere with communication excellence. Sources of breakdowns include cultural differences, trust and credibility, information overload, perception, characteristics of the language, time pressures, lack of feedback, and gender differences.
- Organizational communication functions under two systems, one formal and one informal. Formal communication flows downward, upward, and horizontally. Informal communication, referred to as the grapevine, flows in all directions.

KEY TERMS

Communication (p. 389)
Oral communication (p. 389)
Written communication (p. 390)
Nonverbal communication (p. 391)
Information technology (p. 393)
Telecommuting (p. 393)
Electronic mail (E-mail) (p. 394)
Videoconferencing (p. 395)
Social context (p. 397)

Encoding (p. 397)
Messages (p. 397)
Medium (p. 398)
Decoding (p. 398)
Feedback (p. 399)
Noise (p. 399)
Information overload (p. 402)
Jargon (p. 403)
Downward communication (p. 405)

Upward communication (p. 406)
Horizontal communication (p. 407)
Grapevine (p. 408)
Communication network (p. 409)
Centralized communication network (p. 409)
Decentralized communication network (p. 410)

REVIEW QUESTIONS

1. Describe the elements of the communication process and their relationship to one another.
2. Give examples of the six types of nonverbal communication.
3. Discuss how advances in information technology are changing the communication process.
4. Explain the importance of feedback.
5. Describe the sources of communication breakdowns.

6. Discuss the differences between formal and informal communication channels.
7. Evaluate the effects and implications of different types of communication networks.
8. What are the rules for giving effective feedback?
9. Why is it important that a manager ask for feedback from subordinates?
10. Explain how a manager can be an effective listener.

DISCUSSION QUESTIONS

Improving Critical Thinking

1. What sources of communication breakdown may result from the use of electronic transmission channels, such as E-mail, facsimile machines, and videotaping?
2. What impact do electronic communications have on the feedback component of the communication process?

Enhancing Communication Skills

3. How is nonverbal communication impacted by gender differences? Cultural differences? Write a brief paper that demonstrates your understanding of these issues and prepare to present your findings to the class.

4. How can an organization respond to rumors or messages from the grapevine that are inaccurate and destructive? Prepare a brief written report on this subject.

Building Teamwork Skills

5. Trust was identified as a prerequisite for good communication between a sender and a receiver, especially in upward communication channels. How can trust be established between two parties? Form a small group as directed by your instructor, and prepare a brief oral presentation on the subject.
6. How does managing by walking around affect the communication process in an organization? Form a

small group, and develop some specific ideas on how this technique can help a manager be more effective. Be prepared to present your ideas to the class as directed by your instructor.

Mike was the latest addition to the staff of R & S Advertising. He was bright, personable, and ambitious. He was also an experienced advertising account representative. For the past three years, he had been employed by a rival advertising agency.

As the months passed, Mike proved to be a valuable member of the agency. He worked well with clients and seemed to know just the right approach to take with their advertising campaigns. He was also instrumental in acquiring the latest client—Cantor Software, Inc. Mike had focused on Cantor's needs and come up with a cost proposal that was just below the competitive bids.

Inadvertently, Joan learned that Mike had worked on the Cantor account while at his previous job. Furthermore, in developing the bid, he had used confidential information that he gathered using various types of information technology. For example, he used several of Cantor's code words and account references to tap into, and read, confidential E-mail files. By using sophisticated computer devices provided by R & S, Mike was able to find out what Cantor was doing on a daily basis and know in advance their needs and cost figures. He also found out in advance what other companies were bidding for the account.

The next day Joan mentioned the situation to Tom, a partner in the firm. Tom said that hiring Mike was part of the agency's regular competitive surveillance procedures. Tom continued, "Everyone in the business does it. So we have to do it to stay competitive." Further, Tom said that if Joan continued to pursue the topic, it would work to her detriment because all the partners endorsed such practices.

Joan realized that competitive intelligence was important in devising effective strategies, but she did not think this was an ethical way to obtain information. The agency had guidelines on this matter, and Joan knew that she would have to make a decision soon.

For Discussion
1. Is information technology being used wisely or inappropriately by the agency?
2. Suggest how Joan can handle this situation ethically.

USING OR ABUSING THE GRAPEVINE?

Form teams of four or five students to assess whether or not managers should use the grapevine to find out what is going on in their organizations. Half of the teams should take the stand that effective managers tap into the grapevine to find out what rumors are circulating and may even "plant" some ideas of their own. The other half of the teams should take the perspective that this type of behavior is inappropriate. Use articles from current magazines and even interviews with practicing managers to strengthen your team's arguments. Your instructor will select two teams to present their arguments to the class in a debate format.

VIDEO CASE

Price/Costco

 Price/Costco was formed on October 21, 1993 as a result of a merger of The Price Company and Costco Wholesale Corporation—two of the top three membership discount retailers in the United States. Price/Costco operates a chain of cash and carry membership warehouses that sell high quality, nationally branded and selected private label merchandise at low prices. Their target markets include both businesses that purchase merchandise for commercial use or resale and individuals who are employees of select organizations. The company's business is based upon achieving high sales volumes and rapid inventory turnover by offering a limited assortment of merchandise in a wide variety of product categories at very competitive prices.

In order to coordinate the merger and manage the transition as smoothly as possible, effective communication was critical. Communication at Price/Costco occurs in many forms and at many levels. For example, formal communication, which follows the normal chain of command, was the primary channel of information about merger activities. Top management had the responsibility for communicating accurate, up-to-date, and necessary information about the merger to the company's stakeholders. In turn, this information was carried through the informal channels of communication, namely the grapevine. Surprisingly, perhaps, information passed through the grapevine was quite accurate.

The management of Price/Costco had worked diligently to ensure the effectiveness and the accuracy of the information being circulated within Price/Costco. As they found out, communication was key to the success of the merger.

For Discussion

1. Although communication is important in all organizations at all times, discuss why communication is even more important during a merger.

2. Describe some negative consequences that could have resulted if the management of Price/Costco did not pay careful attention to communication.

3. Identify ways in which the management of Price/Costco could have improved their communication regarding the merger.

CASE

The Performance Review

Dave Jenkins was scheduled to receive his first performance review at 10:00 A.M. In his office, he prepared the packet of information required for the review session and left for the conference room with 10 minutes to spare. He was nervous.

Dave enjoyed working in the branch office of the law firm Dieter, Smart, and Cohen. He expected his first review to be "above average" or possibly "excellent," since "outstanding" seemed beyond reach at the time. Although he was still learning his job, Dave felt positive about his work, the number of hours he put in weekly, client comments, and the fact that he was generating more revenue than most of his peers. If all went well, he thought he could make partner in a few years.

Five minutes before the meeting was to begin, Dave entered the conference room for his meeting with his immediate supervisor, Melissa Harris. He made himself comfortable, selected the chair at the head of the table, and began to prepare. Being nervous did not make this process any easier. At 10:15, Dave began to think he had the wrong time. He called the secretary to confirm his appointment with Melissa, or Ms. Harris as she preferred to be called. Ms. Harris was running a little late—again—and Dave had no choice but to wait for her. By 10:45, he was becoming aggravated. He had work to do and didn't like to be kept waiting.

Meanwhile Melissa Harris had had a very hectic morning. She was behind schedule and had an important client coming in at 11:15 A.M., so she only had 15 minutes to spend on Dave's review. Walking down the hall to the conference room, she recalled that she had rated Dave's job performance as "average." Dave had the least seniority of any employee in the department, and she wanted to leave room for improvement. He was consistently bringing in more revenue than his peers, but telling Dave he was average would get him to work even harder.

As Melissa entered the conference room, she saw that Dave had taken her chair at the head of the table. She decided to stand since this wouldn't take long.

"Dave, in our firm 'performance reviews' mean the systematic and regular evaluation of an individual's job performance and potential for development." Dave nodded in agreement. From a stack of papers that seemed a little disorganized, Melissa handed Dave his performance review form and asked him to sign. Dave replied, "If you don't mind, I would rather sign after I have read the review and we have discussed it."

"I really don't have a lot of time for this right now," said Melissa. "You'll notice that your overall rating is 'average.' That is good for a new employee and that is how the numbers worked out." Dave was astonished. "Average," he said in a quivering voice, "How can you rate me that low? My work has been very good. I have worked long hours to make sure I do a quality job, and you rate that average?" Raising her voice, Melissa said defensively, "Are you questioning my evaluation of your work? You are not getting paid to be the judge here!"

Realizing that things were getting a little too heated, Dave tried to explain. "I'm saying I don't understand your low rating of my job performance." Melissa shuffled through more files and pulled out a piece of paper. "Well, for one thing, you don't know anything about our automated client billing procedure." Surprised and a bit defensive, Dave protested, "I did everything you asked me to do, Ms. Harris, and I did it well. I even asked you about the computerized billing system, and you told me that you didn't have time to show me until next year. Please give me a valid reason for my low performance rating."

Melissa decided to be more firm and said sternly, "I am your supervisor. You work for me and I evaluate your progress. I complete the performance reviews for all of the new lawyers. Nobody else has complained. What is your problem, Dave?"

Dave was angry and dismayed. "This is just not fair. I know my work is better than half the others." Melissa looked at her watch and asserted emphatically, "It isn't your job to rate the performance of your peers. That's my job. We don't seem to be getting anywhere. If you'll sign and date this to indicate that we have had the required performance review interview, we'll be through here. I have an important appointment at 11:15."

Dave leaned forward and clenched his fist. "I'm not signing anything." Melissa gathered her papers and looked again at her watch. "Well, it's plain to me that you resent being rated as average. You don't respect my judgment and you won't follow my instructions. Time to get back to work." She left Dave sitting in the conference room astonished.

For Discussion

1. Describe the types of nonverbal communication that are present in this case.

2. Explain the nonverbal cues and their probable interpretation from both Dave's viewpoint and Melissa' perspective.

3. Offer feedback to Melissa and Dave about their behavior in this incident.

EXPERIENTIAL EXERCISE 12.1

Listening Skills

Purpose: To assess your listening skills.

Procedure: Complete the following listening skills inventory, and then ask several people (peers and/or a supervisor) who know you well to rate your listening skills by completing the inventory. Compare your scores.

Using the following scale, circle the number that best matches your response to the following items. There are no right or wrong answers. Complete every item.

Seldom	Occasionally	Frequently	Usually	Almost Never
1	2	3	4	5

1. I like to listen to people talk. I encourage them to talk by showing interest, smiling, and nodding. 1 2 3 4 5
2. I pay closer attention to speakers who are similar to me. 1 2 3 4 5
3. I evaluate people's words and nonverbal communication ability as they talk. 1 2 3 4 5
4. I avoid distractions; if it's noisy, I suggest moving to a quiet spot. 1 2 3 4 5
5. When people interrupt me to talk, I put what I was doing out of sight and mind and give them my complete attention. 1 2 3 4 5
6. When people are talking, I allow them time to finish. I do not interrupt, anticipate what they are going to say, or jump to conclusions. 1 2 3 4 5
7. I tune out people who do not agree with my views. 1 2 3 4 5

Seldom	Occasionally	Frequently	Usually	Almost Never
1	2	3	4	5

8. When someone else is talking or the professor is lecturing, my mind wanders to personal topics.   1   2   3   4   5

9. While the other person is talking, I pay close attention to the nonverbal communications to help me understand what the sender is trying to communicate.   1   2   3   4   5

10. I tune out or pretend I understand when the topic is difficult.   1   2   3   4   5

11. When the other person is talking, I think about what I am going to say in reply.   1   2   3   4   5

12. When I feel something is missing or contradictory, I ask direct questions to get the person to explain more fully.   1   2   3   4   5

13. When I don't understand something, I let the sender know.   1   2   3   4   5

14. When listening to other people, I try to put myself in their position and see things from their perspective.   1   2   3   4   5

15. During conversations, I paraphrase to be sure I understand correctly what has been said.   1   2   3   4   5

Record your scores below:

1. _____   4. _____   5. _____   6. _____   9. _____   12. _____   13. _____   14. _____   15. _____
Subtotal _____

For the following items, reverse the scores so that 5 = seldom; 4 = occasionally; 2 = usually; 1 = almost always.

2. _____   3. _____   7. _____   8. _____   10. _____   11. _____
Subtotal _____

Now add both subtotals for a total number of points. Your score will be between 15 and 75. Place your score here _____ and on the continuum below. Generally, the higher your score, the better your listening skills. How did your own score compare with the scores you received from others who know you well? If time permits, form small groups and discuss how each of you can improve your listening skills.

15	25	35	45	55	65	75
Poor listener						Good listener

EXPERIENTIAL EXERCISE 12.2

Thinking on your Feet: Improving Oral Communication Skills

Purpose: To improve your oral communication skills.

Procedure: Form small groups of four to six people. Each group member should write a lighthearted topic (for example, holiday excursions, your favorite hobby, postgraduation plans), on a slip of paper. Next, collect all the slips, and have the group members in turn draw a slip from the collection and give a one-minute impromptu talk on the topic. After each presentation, the group should provide feedback to the speaker on his or her oral and nonverbal communication.

Repeat this procedure until each member of the group has given a presentation and received feedback.

SOURCE: Adapted from P. Fandt, *Management Skills: Practice and Experience* (St. Paul, Minn.: West Publishing Co., 1994), 193.

NOTES

1. For a classic discussion of this, see H. Mintzberg, *The Nature of Managerial Work* (New York: Harper & Row, 1973); see also *Workplace Basics* (U.S. Department of Labor, 1992).

2. "Aligning People: Chuck Trowbridge and Bob Crandall at Eastman Kodak," *Harvard Business Review* (May/June 1990): 108; H. R. Jessup, "The Road to Results for Teams," *Training and Development*, September 1992, 67; R. Henkoff, "Cost Cutting: How to Do It Right," *Fortune*, April 9, 1990, 40-49 and; M. Hammer and J. Champy, *Reengineering the Corporation: A Manifesto for Business Revolution* (New York: HarperBusiness, 1993), 44-47, 68-71.

3. For more specific details and a thorough discussion, see M. Munter, *Guide to Managerial Communication*, 3d ed. (Englewood Cliffs, N.J.: Prentice-Hall, 1992).

4. K. Green and D. Seymour, *Who's Going to Run General Motors?* (Princetone, N.J.: Peterson's Guides, 1991).

5. K. H. Roberts, *Communication in Organizations* (Chicago: Science Research Associates, 1984).

6. Mintzberg, *The Nature of Managerial Work.*

7. Adapted from P. Fandt, *Management Skills: Practice and Experience* (St. Paul, Minn.: West Publishing Co., 1994), 193.

8. L. Harrisberger, *Succeeding: How to Become an Outstanding Professional* (New York: Macmillan, 1994).

9. For more specific details on making effective presentations, see P. Fandt, *Management Skills*; M. Martel, *The Persuasive Edge: The Executive Guide to Speaking and Presenting* (New York: Fawcett Columbine, 1989); Harrisberger, *Succeeding*; and A. Fischer and M. Northey, *Impact: A Guide to Business Communication* (Englewood Cliffs, N.J.: Prentice-Hall, 1993).

10. Adapted from Fandt, *Management Skills*, 156–60.

11. Adapted from Ibid., 135.

12. K. Blanchard, "Translating Body Talk," *Success!* April 1986, 10; and J. Baird and G. Wieting, "Nonverbal Communication Can Be a Motivational Tool," *Personnel Journal* (September 1979): 609.

13. Baird and Wieting, "Nonverbal Communication Can Be a Motivational Tool."

14. P. C. Morrow and J. C. McElroy, "Interior Office Design and Visitor Response: A Constructive Replication," *Journal of Applied Psychology* 66 (1981): 646–50.

15. W. Bulkeley, "Computerizing Dull Meetings Is Touted as an Antidote to the Mouth That Bored," *Wall Street Journal*, January 28, 1992, B1.

16. As discussed in A. DuBrin, *Contemporary Applied Management: Behavioral Science Techniques for Managers and Professionals*, 3d ed. (Homewood, Ill.: Irwin, 1989), 328–40.

17. R. O. Metzger, and M. A. Von Glinow, "Off-Site Workers: At Home and Abroad," *California Management Review* (Spring 1988): 101–11; and J. N. Goodrich, "Telecommuting in America," *Business Horizons*, July/August 1990, 31–37.

18. C. Churback, "Prepare for E-Mail Attach," *Forbes*, January 23, 1989, 82–87.

19. K. Rebello and E. Schwartz, "The Magic of Microsoft," *Business Week*, February 24, 1992, 60–64.

20. J. Zygmont, "Face to Face," *Sky Magazine*, February 1988, 10.

21. W. Kiechel, "Hold for the Communicaholic Manager," *Fortune*, January 2, 1989, 107–8.

22. Ibid.

23. C. Cantoni, "Quality Control From Mars," *Wall Street Journal*, January 27, 1992, A12.

24. J. Brownell, "Communicating with Credibility: The Gender Gap," *The Cornell Hotel and Restaurant Administration Quarterly*, April 1993, 52–61; B. Pauly, "Thumbs Up," *Los Angeles Daily News*, January 14, 1992, A12; and Harrisberger, *Succeeding.*

25. R. Lengel, and R. Daft, "The Selection of Communication Media as an Executive Skill," *Academy of Management Executive* 2 (1988): 225–32.

26. "King Customer," *Business Week*, March 12, 1990, 88.

27. N. J. Adler, *International Dimensions of Organizational Behavior* (Boston: PWS-Kent, 1991).

28. Adapted from E. T. Hall, "The Silent Language in Overseas Business," *Harvard Business Review* (May/June 1960).

29. S. Cady, P. Fandt and D. Fernadez, "Investigating Cultural Differences in Personal Success: Implications for Designing Effective Reward Systems," *Journal of Value-Based Management* 6 (1993): 65–80.

30. B. J. Reilly and J. A. DiAngelo, "Communication: A Cultural System of Meaning and Values," *Human Relations* 43 (1990): 129–40.

31. A. Farnham, "Trust Gap," *Fortune*, December 4, 1989, 70.

32. *Quality and Teamwork: Keys to Success* (Cherry Hill, N.J.: General Electric Government Services, 1988).

33. T. J. Peters and R. H. Waterman, *In Search of Excellence: Lessons from America's Best-Run Companies* (New York: Harper & Row, 1980).

34. M. Sinetar, "Building Trust into Corporate Relationships," *Organizational Dynamics* (Winter 1988): 88–93.

35. D. Katz and R. Kahn, *The Social Psychology of Organizations*, 2d ed. (New York: John Wiley & Sons, 1978).

36. J. Verity and J. Nathans, "The War on Information Clutter," *Business Week*, April 29, 1991, 66.

37. M. Cooper, D. Friedman and J. Koenig, "Empire of the Sun," *U.S. News & World Report*, May 28, 1990, 44–51.

38. Rebello and Schwartz, "The Magic of Microsoft."

39. D. Borisoff, "Gender Issues and Listening," in D. Borisoff and M. Purdy, eds., *Listening in Everyday Life: A Personal and Professional Approach* (Lanham, Md.: University Press of America, 1992).

40. E. Aries, "Verbal and Nonverbal Behavior in Single-Sex and Mixed-Sex Groups," *Psychological Reports* 51 (1982): 127–34.

41. L. Hirschman, "Female-Male Differences in Conversational Interaction," in B. Thorne and N. Henley, eds., *Language and Sex: Difference and Dominance* (Rowley, Mass.: Newbury House, 1975).

42. J. C. Pearson and D. Tannen, *Gender and Communication* (Dubuque, Iowa: William C. Brown, 1985).

43. J. C. Pearson and E. Aries, *Gender and Communication* (Dubuque, Iowa: William C. Brown, 1991).

44. Brownell, "Communicating with Credibility: The Gender Gap."

45. As discussed in P. V. Lewis, *Organizational Communication: The Essence of Effective Management*, 2d ed. (Englewood Cliffs, N.J.: Prentice-Hall, 1991); and E. Scannell, *Communication for Leadership* (New York: McGraw-Hill, 1970).

46. Adapted from J. W. Gould, "Quotations That Liven a Business Communication Course," *The Bulletin*, December 1985, 32.

47. *Quality and Teamwork: Keys to Success*; R. D. Prichard, P. L. Roth, S. D. Jones, P. J. Galgay, and M. D. Watson, "Designing a Goal-Setting System to Enhance Performance: A Practical Guide," *Organizational Dynamics* 17

(1988): 69–78; and M. Whitmire, and P. R. Nienstedt, "Lead Leaders into the 90's," *Personnel Journal* (May 1991): 80–85.

48. Peters and Waterman, *In Search of Excellence*.

49. S. L. Kirmeyer and T. Lin, "Social Support: Its Relationship to Observed Communication with Peers and Superiors," *Academy of Management Journal* 30 (1987): 138–51.

50. F. Luthans and J. K. Larsen, "How Managers Really Communicate," *Human Relations* 39 (1986): 161–78.

51. M. J. Glauser, "Upward Information Flows in Organizations: Review and Conceptual Analysis," *Human Relations* 37 (1984): 113–43.

52. D. J. Brass, "Men's and Women's Networks: A Study of Interaction Patterns and Influence in an Organization," *Academy of Management Journal* 28 (1985): 327–43.

53. E. Walton, "How Efficient Is the Grapevine?" *Personnel* 28 (1961): 45–48.

54. Y. Toshio, M. R. Gilmore, and K. S. Cook, "Network Connections and the Distribution of Power in Exchange Networks," *American Journal of Sociology* 93 (1988): 833–51.

55. F. Luthans, R. Hodgetts, and S. Rosenkrantz, *Real Managers* (New York: Ballinger Publishing Co., 1988); and *Workplace Basics*.

56. R. Kaplan, B. Drath, and J. Kofodimas, *Beyond Ambition: How Managers Can Lead Better and Live Better* (San Francisco: Jossey-Bass, 1991).

57. W. Kiechel, "Learn How to Listen," *Fortune*, August 17, 1987, 107–108.

58. See Green and Seymour, *Who's Going to Run General Motors?* 45.

59. Adapted from Munter, *Guide to Managerial Communication*, xii.

60. Adapted from "Aligning People: Chuck Trowbridge and Bob Crandall at Eastman Kodak"; Jessup, "The Road to Results for Teams"; Henkoff, "Cost Cutting: How to Do It Right"; and Hammer and Champy, *Reengineering the Corporation*.

Understanding Leadership in a Dynamic Environment

CHAPTER 13

▼ CHAPTER OVERVIEW

The study of leadership and the demand for good leaders have fascinated people throughout the ages. In fact, nearly ten thousand articles and books have been published on the subject using three major approaches—the study of traits, the study of leadership behaviors, and the study of contingencies, or the situations in which leaders act. Obviously, leadership is an important topic. What makes a good leader? What makes followers follow? Can anyone be a leader? Are leaders always necessary? What are the limits to leadership? These are some of the issues we examine in this chapter.

Our purpose in this chapter is to examine leadership as it relates to the manager's job and to provide a knowledge foundation for developing leadership effectiveness in a global and diverse organizational environment. Our emphasis is on "managerial leadership" in formal organizations such as business corporations, government agencies, hospitals, universities, and so forth. We examine the traditional approaches to leadership, explore several emerging leadership perspectives, and conclude with some guiding principles to get you started toward leadership effectiveness. Throughout the chapter, we offer many opportunities for you to apply leadership theories to practice and enhance your leadership skills.

▼ LEARNING OBJECTIVES

When you have finished studying this chapter,
you should be able to:

- Describe what is meant by the term leadership.
- Explain the sources of a leader's power.
- Describe the traits approach to leadership.
- Define the behavioral dimensions of the Ohio State and Michigan studies of leadership.
- Discuss Fiedler's LPC leadership model.
- Explain the leadership and contingency variables in the situational leadership theory (SLT) and path-goal models.
- Identify leadership substitutes.
- Describe transformational leadership.
- Explain how self-managed teams (SMTs) function.
- Suggest ways leaders influence quality management programs.

MANAGERIAL INCIDENT

⊕ Bell Atlantic

THE BELL ATLANTIC WAY: SMITH'S WAKE-UP CALL

Since becoming CEO of Bell Atlantic, Raymond W. Smith has been challenged with providing the leadership needed to guide the company out of its old bureaucratic system. To do so, he has developed a program called the "Bell Atlantic Way"—a broad initiative to cut costs, spur sales, ensure a quality orientation, and promote independent thinking among employees at the $3 billion, Philadelphia-based regional Bell phone company. While all seven "Baby Bells" are striving to break out of their bureaucratic thinking, the Bell Atlantic Way program stands out for its sheer pervasiveness.

Smith, a Carnegie Mellon University engineering graduate, keeps a plaque on his desk reading "Be Here Now," a reminder to remain focused on the business at hand. He encourages employees to carry a blue poker chip, as he does, to keep them working on "blue-chip" priorities first, leaving less important tasks for later.

Smith began the Bell Atlantic Way process by becoming thoroughly immersed in a new leadership focus that stresses motivational techniques and employee partnerships. In the past four years, Smith has sent nearly 20,000 managers through a 2-day training program to learn the Bell Atlantic Way. Similar training for nearly 60,000 other employees started in 1993. True believers wear "Coach Me" buttons, an invitation to co-workers and even subordinates to offer advice.

Smith's unrelenting message is expressed in company newsletters, training sessions, and ubiquitous Bell Atlantic Way posters. As he strives to lead Bell Atlantic in new directions, his biggest challenge will be to keep employees from slipping back into comfortable Bell habits. "We've largely overcome the old monopoly mindset, and I'd say we're in Act III, scene IV of a five-act play," the CEO says. Can Smith provide the leadership necessary for Bell Atlantic to meet this challenge?[1] ▼

INTRODUCTION

Raymond Smith obviously understands how important leadership can be to an organization. As we examine how he steered the changes at Bell Atlantic, two important behaviors emerge. First, he developed an agenda for himself and the company that included a new vision of what the organization could and should be. Second, he worked to gain cooperation from employees by motivating them to buy into this vision. Smith asked employees to work on changing corporate objectives instead of just fulfilling the narrow, bureaucratically defined objectives that marked the old Bell system. This is not an easy task for a leader.

Being an effective leader has never been more important or more challenging. As the global marketplace becomes more competitive and the workplace grows more diverse, leaders face many challenges. Meeting these challenges requires an unprecedented level of flexibility and responsiveness.

Accordingly, this chapter is devoted to exploring what leadership is and how managers can develop leadership skills. Our examination of leadership begins by discussing the nature of leadership and the sources of a leader's power. Next, we explore the three traditional approaches to the study of leadership—the traits approach, behavioral approach, and contingency approach. Finally, the chapter concludes by examining several of the emerging perspectives to understanding leadership.

MEETING
THE CHALLENGE

WHAT IS LEADERSHIP?

What is leadership? Jot down a few notes on what you think leadership is. How would you describe it to someone else? In defining leadership, consider examples from as wide a range of experiences as possible; think globally and abstractly. See how creative you can be in recalling images of leaders you have gathered over the years from your family, social, school, and work life. You may also want to consider leaders you have encountered in fiction, history, and current events through books, television, and movies.

Form groups of six to eight members to share your impressions and thoughts. What common elements seem to emerge? Have a spokesperson make a list of these elements. Spokespersons should report the findings to the class as a whole.

THE NATURE OF LEADERSHIP

We broadly define **leadership** as a social influence process. Leadership involves determining the group's or organization's objectives, motivating behavior in pursuit of these objectives, and influencing group maintenance and culture.[2] But leadership also produces change.[3] Typically, leadership involves creating a vision of the future, devising a strategy for achieving that vision, and communicating the vision so that everyone understands and believes in it. Leadership also entails providing an environment that will inspire and motivate people to overcome obstacles. In this way leadership brings about change.

A debate in the popular management literature concerns whether leading and managing are different behaviors. One view is that managers carry out responsibilities, exercise authority, and worry about how to get things done, whereas leaders are concerned with understanding people's beliefs and gaining their commitment.[4] In other words, managers and leaders differ in what they attend to and in how they think, work, and interact. A related argument contends that leadership is about coping with change, whereas management is about coping with complexity.[5]

Although the leader-manager debate has generated tremendous controversy in the literature, there is little research to support the notion that certain people can be classified as leaders rather than managers, or that managers cannot adopt visionary behaviors when they are required for success. We maintain that it is important for all managers to think of themselves as leaders, and consequently, we use the term leadership to encompass both leadership and management functions.

Meeting the Challenge asks you to consider leadership and what it means to you.[6] Complete the exercise before continuing the rest of the chapter. It will enhance your understanding of what it means to become a leader.

We tend to associate leaders with power. In fact, power, is central to successful leadership. Where does that power come from? In the next section, we examine the sources of a leader's power.

SOURCES OF A LEADER'S POWER

Anyone in an organization, regardless of rank, can have power. **Power** is defined as the ability to marshal human, informational, or material resources to get something done. The concept of ability distinguishes power from authority.

Leadership
A social influence process that involves determining the group's objectives, motivating behavior in pursuit of these objectives, and influencing group maintenance and culture.

Power
The ability to marshal human, informational, or material resources to get something done.

Authority is the right to get something done and is officially sanctioned; power is the ability to get results.

Power is important not only for influencing subordinates, but also for influencing peers, superiors, and people outside the organization, such as clients and suppliers. To understand this process better, we need to look at the various types of power. In addition, we must consider whether the power is prescribed by the person's position or is a result of personal attributes.

Position Power

Power is derived, in part, from the opportunities inherent in a person's position in an organization. Position power includes legitimate power, coercive power, reward power, and information power.

Legitimate power
Power stemming from formal authority based on the particular positions in an organization or social system.

Legitimate Power Power stemming from formal authority is sometimes called **legitimate power.**[7] This authority is based on perceptions about the obligations and responsibilities associated with particular positions in an organization or social system. Legitimate power exists when people go along with someone's wishes because they believe that person has the legitimate right to influence them and that they have a duty to accept that influence. For example, presidents, supervisors, and academic department chairs have a certain degree of legitimate power simply because of the formal position they hold. Other people accept this power, as long as it is not abused, because they attribute legitimacy to the formal position and to the person who holds that position.

Coercive power
The power to discipline, punish, and withhold rewards.

Coercive Power **Coercive power** is the power to discipline, punish, and withhold rewards. As a source of leader power, coercive power is important largely as a potential, rather than an actual, type of influence. For example, the threat of being disciplined for not arriving at work on time is effective in influencing many employees to be punctual. Similarly, the possibility that we might get a speeding ticket is enough to cause many of us to drive within acceptable speed limits.

Reward power
Derived from control over tangible benefits, such as promotion, a better job, a better work schedule, a larger operating budget, an increased expense account, and formal recognition of accomplishments.

Reward Power Another source of power that stems from the manager's position in the organization is influence over resources and rewards. **Reward power** is derived from control over tangible benefits, such as a promotion, a

▼ Legitimate power is derived from the formal position or authority an individual is given by the organization. We see this demonstrated as a Pitney-Bowes manager directs her employee in the assembly of postage meters.

▼ This professor is relying on one type of personal power, known as referent power, to influence his student.

better job, a better work schedule, a larger operating budget, an increased expense account, and formal recognition of accomplishments. Reward power is also derived from status symbols such as a larger office or a reserved parking space. For reward power to be influential, the employee must value the rewards.

Information Power   **Information power** is control over information. It involves the leader's power to access and distribute information that is either desired by or vital to others. Managerial positions often provide opportunities to obtain information that is not directly available to subordinates or peers. However, some people acquire information power through their unique skill of being able to know all the latest news and gossip that others want to hear.

Information power
Control over information that involves the leader's power to access and distribute information that is either desired or vital to others.

Personal Power

Effective leaders cannot rely solely on power that is derived from their position in the organization. Other sources of power must be cultivated. Personal power is derived from the interpersonal relationship between a leader and his or her followers. It includes both expert and referent power.

Expert Power   A major source of personal power in organizations stems from expertise in solving problems and performing important tasks. **Expert power** is the power to influence another person because of expert knowledge and competence. Computer specialists often have substantial expert power in organizations because they have technical knowledge that others need. The expertise of tax accountants and investment managers gives them considerable power over the financial affairs of business firms. A secretary who knows how to run the office may have expert power, but lack position power.

Expert power
The power to influence because of expert knowledge and competence.

Referent Power   **Referent power** is the ability to influence others based on personal liking, charisma, and reputation. It is manifested through imitation or emulation. There are numerous reasons why we might attribute referent power to others. We may like their personalities, admire their accomplishments, believe in their causes, or see them as role models. Much of the power wielded by strong political leaders, professional athletes, musicians, and artists is referent power. People who feel a deep friendship or loyalty toward someone are usually willing to do special favors for that person. Moreover, people

Referent power
The ability to influence based on personal liking, charisma, and reputation.

tend to imitate the behavior of someone whom they greatly admire, and they tend to develop attitudes similar to those expressed by a person with whom they identify. Bill Cosby (actor/comedian), Cindy Crawford (model), and Shaquille O'Neal (Magic basketball superstar) are just a few of the many individuals who have been hired to promote products because they influence potential buyers with their referent power.

Is power good or bad? Positive or negative? Keep in mind that power can be both negative and positive, good and bad. It can be used to influence behavior either constructively or destructively. Experiential Exercise 13.1 at the end of the chapter asks you to identify various power and influence techniques used in managerial settings.[8]

TRAIT APPROACHES TO UNDERSTANDING LEADERSHIP

Now that we have considered some of the ways leaders gain power to influence others, we examine the different approaches used to determine what makes a leader effective. For purposes of our discussion, we have grouped leadership approaches into the four categories shown in Figure 13.1: trait approaches, behavioral studies, contingency models, and several emerging perspectives.

    One of the earliest approaches to studying leadership was the trait approach. Underlying the **trait approach** is the assumption that some people are "natural leaders" and are endowed with certain traits not possessed by other individuals. This research compared successful and unsuccessful leaders to see how they differed in physical characteristics, personality, and ability. Evidence suggests that leaders and nonleaders differ in a number of traits.[9] In general, leaders possess greater (1) drive (i.e., achievement, ambition, energy, tenacity, initiative), (2) motivation, (3) honesty and integrity, (4) self-confidence, (5) cognitive ability, and (6) knowledge of the business.

    Despite the evidence that leaders tend to differ from nonleaders with respect to the five traits listed above, traits alone cannot predict leadership ability. To succeed, leaders do not have to be intellectual geniuses or all-wise prophets, but they do have to have certain capabilities.[10] Therefore, the particular requirements for effective leadership in each situation may well outweigh drive motivation, honesty and integrity, self-confidence, cognitive ability, and knowledge of the business, or make only certain ones important. Possession of the listed qualities does not guarantee that you will become a leader, nor does the absence of any one of them rule out the possibility of becoming an excellent leader.

    Trait research failed to predict leadership success consistently. As a result, some researchers began to examine what effective leaders *do* rather than what effective leaders *are*. We term these the behavioral approaches to leadership.

Trait approach
The assumption that some people are "natural leaders," and are endowed with certain traits not possessed by other individuals.

▼ **Figure 13.1**
Approaches to Understanding Leadership

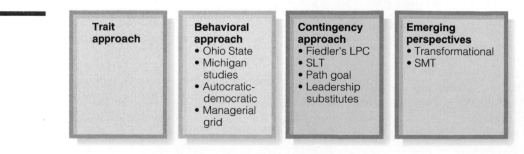

Trait approach	Behavioral approach	Contingency approach	Emerging perspectives
	• Ohio State	• Fiedler's LPC	• Transformational
	• Michigan studies	• SLT	• SMT
	• Autocratic-democratic	• Path goal	
	• Managerial grid	• Leadership substitutes	

BEHAVIORAL APPROACHES TO UNDERSTANDING LEADERSHIP

Instead of examining the personal traits of successful leaders, the behavioral approach studies patterns of behaviors or styles that are used by effective leaders. The **behavioral approach** assumes that what the leader does is the primary variable that determines effectiveness. Much of the research on leadership behavior during the past three decades has followed the pattern set by pioneering research programs at Ohio State University and the University of Michigan.

OHIO STATE LEADERSHIP STUDIES

Although there have been numerous attempts to identify the basic dimensions of leadership behavior, the Ohio State studies have had the greatest impact on this line of research. The Ohio State studies focused on two independent dimensions of leader behavior labeled initiating structure and consideration.[11]

Initiating structure is the degree to which a leader defines and structures his or her own role and the roles of subordinates toward the attainment of the group's formal goals. It is related to specific, task-oriented behaviors such as planning, directing subordinates, providing job information, and maintaining definite standards of performance.

Consideration is a second leader behavior related to the degree of trust, friendship, and respect extended to subordinates. Consideration includes specific people- or relationship-oriented behaviors, such as showing concern and support for subordinates, looking out for the personal welfare of the group, putting suggestions made by the group into action, being willing to make changes, explaining actions, and doing things that make it pleasant to be a member of the group.

The findings from the Ohio State studies have been particularly important to our understanding of leadership. First, some effective leaders were found to be high in consideration; others were high in initiating structure. Second, initiating structure and consideration were found to represent two completely separate and distinct dimensions. These four different leadership styles are shown in Figure 13.2.

Behavioral approach
What the leader does is the primary variable that determines effectiveness.

Initiating structure
The degree to which a leader defines and structures his or her own role and the roles of subordinates toward the attainment of the group's formal goals.

Consideration
The degree of trust, friendship, and respect extended to subordinates.

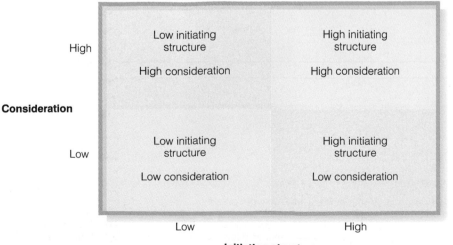

▼ **Figure 13.2**
Ohio State Leadership Dimensions

UNIVERSITY OF MICHIGAN STUDIES

A second major program of research on leadership behavior was carried out by a group at the University of Michigan. The Michigan research focused on identifying relationships among leader behavior, group processes, and measures of group performance. The researchers found that three types of leadership behavior differentiated effective leaders from ineffective leaders. Task-oriented behaviors and relationship-oriented behaviors were similar to the Ohio State research findings of initiating structure and consideration. The third behavior, participative leadership, involves the use of decision procedures that give subordinates some influence over the leaders' decisions. Other terms used to refer to the participative type of behavior include consultation, joint decision making, power sharing, and democratic management.

AUTOCRATIC-DEMOCRATIC LEADERSHIP CONTINUUM

The autocratic-democratic continuum was an early model of behavioral leadership developed in the 1950s. The model focused on the extent to which decision making is centralized in a group and describes the various factors thought to influence a manager's choice of leadership style.[12] As shown in Figure 13.3, at one end of the scale is the autocratic leader who dominates decision-making activities (boss-centered leadership). This type of manager believes that the needs of the individual must come second to the needs of the organization and is likely to take a very directive role in managing the activities of subordinates. At the other end of the continuum is the democratic leader who permits a group to make decisions within prescribed limits (subordinate-centered leadership). The manager may specify a range in which subordinates have final decision-making authority and may or may not require them to obtain approval before implementing the decisions.[13]

One of the main problems with the autocratic-democratic leadership continuum is that it views leadership as a one-dimensional concept. The model is descriptive and provides no guidance on choosing an appropriate leadership style.

Take, for example, the Procter & Gamble CEO Edwin L. Artzt, who is determined to make P&G tougher, faster, and more global. To do so, he is promoting individual accountability and turning back the clock from the team approach of recent years. He favors a "squash-the-competition" approach and focuses on building volume and profit rather than getting aligned, partnering, and team decision making. Many of his critics—who have either been silenced

▼ **Figure 13.3**
Leadership Continuum

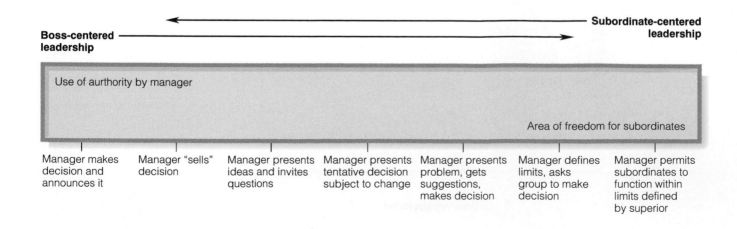

or have left the company—say he pushes hard and operates without regard for his people. Under Artzt's leadership, even training programs, officially named P&G College, have become less humanistic and more "win, win, win."[14] Where would you place Artzt's leadership behavior on the autocratic-democratic continuum shown in Figure 13.3?

MANAGERIAL GRID

The Managerial Grid® is a two-dimensional leadership model.[15] The Managerial Grid is based on two fundamental attitudes: concern for production and concern for people. Other terms used for concern for production include initiating structure and task-orientation. Concern for people is also referred to as consideration or relationship-orientation. Figure 13.4 identifies five basic leader behaviors or leader styles that can be derived from the grid styles shown on the two axes.

The Managerial Grid model, developed by Robert Blake and Jane Mouton, suggests that competent leaders should use a style that reflects the highest concern for both people and production, or the 9,9 "team-oriented" leaders. Blake and Mouton refer to the 9,9 leadership style as Team Management and consider it the most effective leader style. Supporters of the grid have asserted that team managers are sounder leaders regardless of the type of problem faced or the nature of the individuals or group being led.[16]

While this "one best style" position differs from the more widely held view that the most effective leader behavior varies with the situation, strong research results show that the grid has been, and is, a popular and successful approach to leadership training. It is intended to serve as a framework to help managers learn about their own leadership behavior and develop a plan to move toward a 9,9 team management style of leadership.

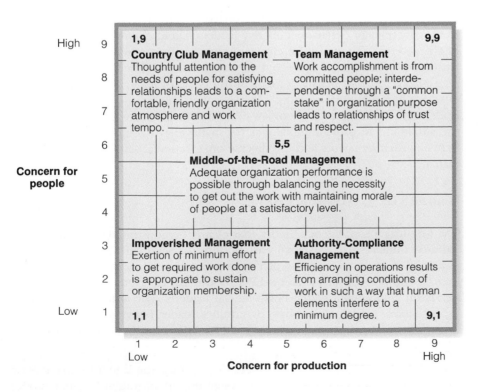

▼ **Figure 13.4**
Managerial Grid

SOURCE: The Leadership Grid Figure for *Leadership Dilemmas—Grid Solutions*, by Robert R. Blake and Anne Adams McCanse (Houston: Gulf Publishing Company) 29. Copyright 1991 by Scientific Methods, Inc. Reproduced by permission of the owners.

▼ **Table 13.1**   Effective Leadership: A Great Boss Isn't Bossy

To be an effective leader, learn to do the following:

1. *Motivate*. The most important duty is motivating people. Be supportive and positive but also offer corrective feedback.
2. *Simplify*. Make complicated situations simple.
3. *Inform*. Information has three functions: to inform, instruct, and motivate. Motivating is the most difficult part.
4. *Stay in the trenches*. People make mistakes when they become the boss. They make sweeping changes rather than slow, measured ones. They criticize their predecessor. They knock down previous policies. They establish goals and expectations that are impossible to keep.
5. *Don't be the star*. The toughest part of being a boss is recognizing strengths and letting others cover for weaknesses.

SOURCE: Adapted from M. H. McCormack, *The 110% Solution* (New York: Villard Books, 1991).

In his book *The 110% Solution*, Mark McCormack suggests that many leaders have trouble developing an effective style.[17] They confuse being boss-like with being bossy. One of the biggest mistakes managers make, according to McCormack, is "acting like the boss." An effective style is one that inspires and helps everyone to feel successful. You can see McCormack's perspective on the most effective leadership style in Table 13.1. Keep in mind that what one culture perceives as effective leadership may not be considered effective in another. This issue is especially important to remember as the workforce becomes more diverse and organizations expand their boundaries to compete in a global environment.

CONTINGENCY APPROACHES: UNDERSTANDING LEADERSHIP QUALITY

The theme in earlier approaches to understanding leadership was the desire to identify traits or behaviors effective leaders had in common. A common set of characteristics proved to be elusive, however. Researchers were continually frustrated by the lack of consistent support for their findings and conclusions. As a result, research began to focus on the style of leadership that was most effective in a particular situation. This is called the contingency approach to leadership. **Contingency theories** examine the fit between the leader and the situation and provide guidelines for managers to achieve an effective fit between their behaviors and the diverse organizational settings in which they manage.

FIEDLER'S LPC CONTINGENCY MODEL

The first major contingency theory that clearly demonstrated discipline of situational thinking was Fiedler's least preferred co-worker (LPC) model. The objective of the model is to predict work-group task performance or effectiveness.[18] The premise of **Fiedler's LPC model** is that group performance depends on a successful match between the leader's style and the demands of the situation. Let's look at what determines leader behavior and situational favorability and at how each can be used to determine an effective match.

Leadership Behavior Assessment
The first step in applying the LPC model is to assess the leader's behaviors or characteristics. A characteristic that plays an important role in Fiedler's model

Contingency theories
Examine the fit between the leader's behavior and the situations in which they manage.

Fiedler's LPC model
A contingency model that predicts workgroup effectiveness based on a match between the leader's style and the demands of the situation.

is the behavioral tendency to be motivated primarily toward either task accomplishments or people relationships. Fiedler used an instrument called the **least preferred co-worker scale (LPC)** to measure a person's basic leadership style. The people completing the LPC scale are asked to describe the co-worker with whom they have been able to work least well (least preferred co-worker or LPC). A person who describes the co-worker in positive terms (i.e., pleasant, helpful, supportive, open) earns a high LPC score. A high LPC score suggests that the person has a behavioral tendency toward people relationships and thus has a relationship-oriented style. A person who describes a co-worker in negative terms (i.e., unpleasant, frustrating, hostile, and guarded) gets a low LPC score. A low LPC score suggests that the person has a behavioral tendency toward task accomplishment and thus has a task-motivated style.

Least Preferred coworker scale (LPC)
Designed to measure relationship-oriented versus task-oriented behaviors according to a leader's choice of descriptive terms.

Situational Favorability

The next step in applying the LPC model is to understand the situation. The relationship between a leader's LPC score and group effectiveness depends on a complex situational variable called **situational favorability.** Fiedler defines *favorability* as the extent to which the situation gives a leader control over subordinates. Favorability is measured in terms of three aspects of the situation:

1. *Leader-member relations.* The extent to which the leader has the support and loyalty of subordinates.
2. *Task structure.* The extent to which there are standard operating procedures for accomplishing the task.
3. *Position power.* The extent to which the leader has authority to evaluate subordinate performance and administer rewards and punishments.

Situational favorability
A combination of leader-member relations, task structure, and position power that determines the control needed by a leader in a specific situation.

These three components—leader-member relations, position power, and task structure—combine in a number of ways to create specific organizational situations. Figure 13.5 shows the eight possible combinations and indicates the relative degree of control required in each situation.

According to the LPC model, the situation is *highly favorable* for the leader (situation 1) when leader-member relations are good, the task is highly structured, and the leader has substantial position power. When leader-member relations are good, subordinates are more likely to comply with the leader's requests and direction, rather than ignoring or subverting them. When a leader has high position power, it is easy to influence subordinates. When the task is structured, it is easy for the leader to direct subordinates and monitor their performance. An example of this situation is the well-liked supervisor of a parts assembly line crew.

	1	2	3	4	5	6	7	8
Favorability	Highly favorable						Highly unfavorable	
Leader-member relations	Good				Poor			
Task structure	High		Low		High		Low	
Leader position power	Strong	Weak	Strong	Weak	Strong	Weak	Strong	Weak

▼ **Figure 13.5**
Fiedler's LPC Leadership Model

SOURCE: F. E. Fiedler, "The Effects of Leadership Training and Experience: A Contingency Model Interpretation," *Administrative Science Quarterly* 17 (1972): 455. Reprinted by permission of *Administrative Science Quarterly.*

The situation is *highly unfavorable* for the leader (situation 8) when relations with subordinates are poor, the task is unstructured, and position power is low. An example is the unpopular chair of a volunteer committee with a vague problem to solve.

Behavior-Situation Match

The final step in applying Fiedler's LPC model is to determine the appropriate leadership style for the situation. Based on the results of the LPC, a manager whose LPC score is low, or a task-oriented leader, will be more effective in a situation that is either highly unfavorable (situations 6, 7, and 8) or highly favorable (situations 1, 2, and 3) than a relationship-oriented leader. In contrast, relationship-oriented leaders, whose scores on the LPC are high, excel when conditions are moderately favorable. Moderately favorable situations lie somewhere between the extremes of high and low control.

What if the leader's style and the situational control requirement do not match? Fiedler contends that it is easier to alter a situation than to change a leader's LPC score since LPC is a relatively stable and resistant measure. In fact, Fiedler developed a self-paced study program called LEADER MATCH to train managers to apply his theory. The program shows trainees how to compute scores for LPC and situational factors and then suggests ways to alter the situation to match the trainee's LPC.

SITUATIONAL LEADERSHIP THEORY

A second contingency approach is the situational leadership theory. Hersey and Blanchard developed a contingency leadership model, which was originally called the life cycle theory of leadership, but the name was later changed to situational leadership theory (SLT). According to the **SLT model,** quality leader behavior depends on the situational contingency of readiness and the appropriate behavior-readiness match.[19]

SLT model
States that effective leader behavior depends on the situational contingency of readiness and the appropriate behavior-readiness match.

Readiness is the extent to which a subordinate possesses the ability and willingness to complete a specific task. Subordinates have various degrees of readiness, as shown in Figure 13.6. In a specific situation, the leader provides some degree of task behavior and relationship behavior. *Task behavior* is the extent to which a leader organizes and defines the role of followers by explaining what each person must do and when, where, and how tasks are to be accomplished. *Relationship behavior* is the extent to which a leader maintains personal relationships with followers by opening up channels of communication and providing support.

Figure 13.6 shows the model linking task and relationship behaviors and subordinate readiness.[20] The appropriate style of leadership is shown by the curve running through the four leadership quadrants. As the subordinate's readiness increases from the minimum to a moderate level, the leader should use more relationship behavior and less task behavior. As the subordinate's readiness increases beyond a moderate level, the leader should decrease the amount of relationship behavior while continuing to decrease the amount of task behavior.

A leader using the *telling style* provides specific instructions and closely supervises performance. This style works best when follower readiness is low. The direction provided by this leadership style defines roles for people who are unable or unwilling to take responsibility because it eliminates any insecurity about the task that must be done.

Using the *selling style*, the leader explains decisions and provides opportunities for clarification. This style offers both task direction and support for

▼ **Table 13.2**   Enhance Your Leadership Skills: Issues for Successful Management

U.S. business desperately needs better leadership. Companies that will be successful in a new, more competitive global economy will be more flexible, responsive, and leaner than those in the past. Small groups must tackle problems and seize opportunities as they arise. Individuals at all levels need the responsibility and authority to make decisions.

The following principles, developed by Robert Denhardt in his recent book *The Pursuit of Significance*, reflect current thinking about the behaviors needed to be a quality leader:

- Believe in, foster, and support teamwork.
- Be committed to the problem-solving process, use it, and let data, not emotions, drive decisions.
- Seek employees' input before you make key decisions.
- Believe that the best way to improve the quality of work or service is to ask and listen to employees who are doing the work.
- Strive to develop mutual respect and trust among employees.
- Have a customer orientation and focus toward employees and citizens.
- Manage on the behavior of 95 percent of employees, and not on the 5 percent who cause problems. Deal with the 5 percent promptly and fairly.
- Improve systems and examine processes before placing the blame on people.
- Avoid "top-down," power-oriented decision making wherever possible.
- Encourage creativity through risk taking, and be tolerant of honest mistakes.
- Be a facilitator and coach. Develop an open atmosphere that encourages providing and accepting feedback.
- With teamwork, develop with employees agreed-upon goals and a plan to achieve them.

SOURCE: R. Denhardt, *The Pursuit of Significance* (Belmont, Mass.: Wadsworth, 1992). Copyright © 1992, Wadsworth Publishing Company.

biguous nonrepetitive jobs, achievement-oriented leadership should increase their expectations that effort will lead to desired performance.

Experiential Exercise 13.2 allows you to test your leadership style and will help enhance your understanding of the type of leader you are now. After completing this exercise, you may also want to work on Experiential Exercise 13.3 and consider the traits and behaviors of a leader whom you have known personally and reflect on his or her success.[22] This exercise, along with the information shown in Table 13.2, will provide guidelines to help you enhance your leadership skills.

Situational Contingencies

The situational contingencies defined by the path-goal model are subordinate characteristics and task structure. These characteristics influence how subordinates perceive the leader's behavior.

Subordinate Characteristics   The model uses three characteristics that help define the situation and relate to the most effective leadership behaviors: (1) ability, (2) locus of control, and (3) need structure. *Ability* relates to the subordinates' knowledge, skills, and expertise in completing a task. The greater employees' ability to perform the task, the less they will want directive leadership. High-ability employees will prefer achievement-oriented leadership.

Locus of control focuses on the employees' sense of internal and external control, or how much control over events or outcomes they believe can be gained. Research has shown that the more employees have an internal locus of control and desire control in a situation, the less they will be satisfied with directive leadership. Instead, such individuals will desire participative or achievement-oriented leadership.

Need structure refers to a hierarchy of needs. Do the employees have high- or low-level needs? The more high-level needs the employees have, the less they will want directive leadership. More specifically, people who desire safety and security will respond positively to directive leadership. Those who desire belongingness will respond positively to supportive leadership. And those desiring self-esteem and self-actualization will respond positively to participative and achievement-oriented leadership.

Task Structure   If the task is structured, supportive and participative leadership behaviors will be more effective. When the task is stressful, boring, tedious, or dangerous, supportive leadership leads to increased subordinate effort and satisfaction by increasing self-confidence, lowering anxiety, and minimizing unpleasant aspects of the work.

Subordinates working on an unstructured task will want directive leadership. In these unstructured task situations, the manager's job is to initiate structure, clarify goals, and define expectancies for the subordinates. In doing this, managers reduce uncertainty, and this leads to increased motivation and performance. When the task is unstructured and complex, subordinates are inexperienced, and there are few formal rules and procedures to guide the work, directive leadership will result in higher subordinate satisfaction and effort. When the task is unstructured, participative and achievement-oriented leadership can increase subordinate effort and satisfaction.

Path-goal is a complex leadership model. The principal contribution of this approach has been an expanded search for relevant contingency factors and clarification of ways that managers can influence employee behavior. The path-goal model of leadership can be used in guiding subordinates toward improved effort, performance, and satisfaction. This is a dramatic shift away from Fiedler's LPC model, where leadership style is considered to be relatively fixed and the solution may be to change leaders or aspects of the work situation rather than alter leadership behavior.

In sum, the contingency approach to leadership quality in diverse organizations generally concludes that effective leaders don't use a single style; they use many different styles and make adjustments based on the situation. An important but often overlooked contingency variable that may affect a leader's style is national culture. As we see in Global Perspective, national culture can affect leadership style, not because of the leader, but because of the subordinates. The cultural frame of reference and a subordinate's expectations can greatly influence what leadership style will be most effective.

LEADERSHIP SUBSTITUTES

Some argue that the importance of leadership is overrated and that in many situations leaders make little or no difference.[23] In contrast to traditional theories that assume hierarchical leadership is always important, the premise of the leadership substitutes model is that leader behaviors are irrelevant. The leadership substitutes model is fairly new, and only a few studies have been conducted to verify its propositions about specific substitutes and neutralizers.[24]

Leadership substitutes
Situational variables that tend to outweigh the leader's ability to affect subordinate satisfaction and performance.

Leadership substitutes are situational variables such as individual, task, and organizational characteristics that tend to outweigh the leader's ability to affect subordinate satisfaction and performance.[25] They make leadership behavior unnecessary or redundant. A neutralizer is a condition that counteracts

NATIONAL CULTURE: AN IMPORTANT LEADERSHIP CONTINGENCY VARIABLE

National culture can affect leadership style, not because of the leader, but because of the subordinates. Leaders cannot choose their styles at will because they are constrained by the cultural conditions that their subordinates have come to expect. For example, a manipulative or autocratic leadership style is compatible with the high power distance that is found in Arab, Far Eastern, and Latin countries. Power distance rankings are also good indicators of employee willingness to accept participative leadership. Participation is likely to be most effective in such low power distance cultures as Norway, Finland, Denmark, and Sweden. This may explain why a number of leadership theories, such as the Ohio State behavioral studies, implicitly favor the use of a participative or people-oriented style. These theories were developed by North American researchers, using North American subjects in countries like the United States and Canada, which rate below average on power distance.

GLOBAL PERSPECTIVE

leader behavior and/or prevents the leader from having an effect on a specific situation.

Individual characteristics that can serve as leadership substitutes include a high level of experience, training, ability, professional orientation, or indifference toward organizational rewards. If, for example, employees have the skills and abilities to perform the job and a high need for independence, leadership is less important, and the employees may resent a leader who provides structure and direction. A professor in a graduate-level seminar may need to provide students with just a set of readings and materials to be studied rather than a structured course outline.

Various task attributes can serve as leadership substitutes. For example, if the task is simple and repetitive, subordinates can learn the appropriate skills without extensive training. Tasks that are characterized by structure or frequent feedback can also neutralize leader behavior, as can tasks that are intrinsically satisfying.

Characteristics of the organization can also substitute for leadership. When the organization possesses high levels of formality, inflexibility, cohesive work groups, staff support, managerially independent reward structures, and spatial distance between workers and managers, the need for formal leadership decreases.[26]

EMERGING PERSPECTIVES TO UNDERSTANDING LEADERSHIP

The 1980s brought revolutionary change to many American businesses, and the pace of change is accelerating with political and economic developments in Europe, the Middle East, and other locations around the world. As we have been discussing throughout the book, the changing global environment is likely to continue to stimulate the transformation and revitalization of public and private institutions. Small as well as large U.S. companies such as IBM, AT&T, and General Motors recognize that they will have to change in order to survive. They have embarked on "transformation" programs of extensive change that must be accomplished in short periods of time. Such transformations require a new set of leadership guidelines. In this section we look at several emerging perspectives in understanding leadership—followership, transformational leadership, the changing role of women in leadership positions, self-managed teams, and leadership influences on quality management programs.

FOLLOWERSHIP

While organizations spend millions annually to train potential leaders, they are also beginning to realize the value of followership. Teaching employees how to be effective followers may be a wise decision. In many respects, an effective follower resembles an effective leader. And subordinate leadership is a skill that every leader should master. After all, every leader, regardless of position, plays the role of follower at some point. Consider Raymond Smith at Bell Atlantic, profiled in the Managerial Incident. He plays the role of follower when he reports to Bell Atlantic's board of directors and stockholders.

Large organizations, discovering that an abundance of baby-boom managers in their 30s and 40s are concerned about career plateauing, have begun to adopt followership training programs to convince employees that they are contributing even when they are not moving up the corporate ladder. Lincoln Electric, a Cleveland-based manufacturer of welding machines and electrical motors, provides an example of the value of fostering organizational followership. The structure of the organization requires each employee to be accountable for his or her own behavior. Even in recessionary times, employees are loyal to the company and show their cooperation by performing duties not required by their contracts. Employees are asked to serve on an advisory board that meets weekly to assess how the company is doing in a variety of areas. The employees understand the organization and their contributions to it. They are adaptable and take responsibility for their own actions. In essence, the employees of Lincoln Electric are good followers.[27] Lincoln, along with many other companies, is aware of the importance of effective followership to organizational success.[28]

Studies show that effective followers have most of the following characteristics:

- Capacity to motivate themselves and stay focused on tasks.
- Integrity that demands both loyalty to the organization and the willingness to act according to beliefs.
- Understanding of the organization and their contributions to it.
- Versatility, skillfulness, and flexibility to adapt to a changing environment.
- Responsibility for their own careers, actions, and development.

TRANSFORMATIONAL LEADERSHIP

Transformational leadership
The process of influencing the attitudes and assumptions of organizational members and building commitment to the organization's mission and objectives.

Transformational leadership refers to the process of influencing the attitudes and assumptions of organizational members and building commitment to the organization's mission and objectives.[29] Transformational leaders do not accept the status quo; they recognize the need to revitalize their organizations and challenge standard operating procedures; they institutionalize change by replacing old technical and political networks with new ones. In other words, transformational leaders "transform" things from what could be to what is by generating excitement.[30] Transformational leaders such as Steven Jobs, president and CEO of Next Corporation, also create new corporate visions and mobilize employee commitment to that vision as described in Entrepreneurial Approach.[31]

STEVEN JOBS: INSPIRING OTHERS THROUGH THE LANGUAGE OF LEADERSHIP

When Steven Jobs described the mission of his new computer company, Next, to his staff, he could have mechanically dictated a sales objective. Instead, he presented a vision of "revolutionizing the educational system of a nation." He intrinsically motivated the staff by appealing to their benefits and values. In addition, his speech employed stories, revealed emotion, and utilized a communication style that made the vision memorable. The potential benefits of communicating the mission in this manner are immeasurable.

The strategic objectives of Next were rhetorically crafted to have the maximum impact on the staff. Rhetoric heightens the motivational appeal of a message and increases the likelihood that it will be remembered. The message was also appropriately framed. In other words, the purpose of the organization was defined in a meaningful way. Such communication skills are essential to leadership excellence.

ENTREPRENEURIAL APPROACH

Though the literature on transformational leadership naturally focuses on CEOs and top managers, transformational leadership commonly involves the actions of leaders at all levels, not just those at the top. Transformational leadership increases follower motivation by activating the higher needs of followers, appealing to their moral ideas, and empowering them.

Most leadership research has concentrated on the leader's influence on followers. Followers are motivated to do more than originally expected because of their feelings of trust, admiration, loyalty, and respect for the leader. This motivation occurs when the leader makes subordinates more aware of the importance and values of task outcomes, helps them think beyond their own self-interest to the needs of the work teams and organization, and activates higher-order needs such as creative expression and self-actualization.[32]

The term *charismatic* is often used to describe transformational leaders. Whether they are called charismatic or transformational, such leaders inspire their followers to transcend their own interests and work exceptionally hard for the goal, cause or mission. To achieve such high levels of compliance and commitment, these leaders must pay special attention to meeting the developmental needs of their followers.[33] In the end, charismatic or transformational leaders have a profound impact on their followers by providing a vision and encouraging and inspiring their followers to look at old problems in new ways, put forth extra effort, and develop new ideas and procedures.

When a charismatic leader has a successful track record, his or her vision is often a key factor in the organization's success. Stepping down after 14 years as a programming executive at NBC Television, Brandon Tartikoff expressed concern that nobody at NBC had a vision of what they wanted the network to become. He contrasted this with the clear vision that Grant Tinker had brought to NBC when he took over as network chair 10 years earlier and lifted NBC to the top of the ratings.[34]

Bill Gates, CEO of Microsoft Corporation (the world's largest software developer), is an example of a transformational leader. Gates involves employees by recognizing the need for revitalizing the organization and by working with them as a team to share responsibility for managing. Gates is often described as full of horsepower and energy. A billionaire seven times over, Gates works 15-hour days, crosses the country in coach class, and obsesses about details that other chief executives would ignore. He scoffs at the challenges from competitors. He is not interested in mundane details such as haircuts and

▼ Transformational leaders such as Bill Gates, CEO of Microsoft, recognize the need to revitalize their organizations and challenge standard operating procedures.

fashion. The Harvard University dropout would prefer to dive headlong into intellectual pursuits. And he relies on personal sources of power to arouse intense feelings in his employees. In the 18 years since he launched Microsoft, Gates has followed a simple rule: hire smart people, challenge them to think, and ask them to be committed and to work hard. Many of Gates's employees describe him as charismatic. He gives individualized attention to his employees as well as stimulating them intellectually. He has a vision of Microsoft's future, which he communicates to his employees. He accomplishes all this in meetings that are regarded as part adolescent mischief, part marketing genius; to this, he adds lots of energy, vision, and above all, drive.[35]

How does your own management style compare with that of Bill Gates? How does it compare with a supervisor or authority figure whom you have known personally? Experiential Exercises 13.2 and 13.3 ask you to consider these questions and to compare your own management style with that of an immediate supervisor.

THE CHANGING ROLE OF WOMEN AS LEADERS

The number of women in leadership positions has increased steadily since 1970. In fact, over 25 percent of the supervisory positions in the U.S. industry were occupied by women in 1990. The number of women enrolled in business schools is yet another sign of the increasing presence of women in management. In 1990, the number of men and women enrolled in U.S. business programs was nearly equal.[36] Women's entrepreneurial spirit is also becoming apparent; more and more businesses, particularly in the service, retailing, and trade industries, are being started and managed by women.

Consider, for example, Gae Veit, the chief executive of Shingobee Builders, a commercial and industrial contracting construction firm in Loretto, Minnesota. Veit liked the work she performed in a construction firm office and went into business for herself in the 1980s. According to Veit, a female general contractor had virtually no credibility with the corporate officers and potential commercial-building owners with whom she sought contracts. In spite of the obstacles, she met the challenge head-on. Veit's response to the gender problem was to "just be myself—to be confident and knowledgeable, but when I need help with an issue not be afraid or embarrassed."[37] She was recently named woman entrepreneur of the year by the Small Business Administration.

How well do men accept women as leaders? Research indicates that men's attitudes toward women in the workplace are gradually changing as more women enter the workforce and assume leadership positions. Studies show, however, that both men and women executives believe that women have to be exceptional to succeed in the business world. Women leaders still face disadvantages in business and feel they must struggle harder than men to succeed.[38]

Do men and women differ in terms of leadership ability? In the past, successful leaders have been associated with stereotypical masculine attributes such as competitiveness, task-orientation, and willingness to take risks. Recent studies, however, show that female middle- and top-level executives no longer equate successful leadership with these masculine attributes. Experienced female managers show no differences in leadership ability from their experienced male counterparts. Both groups possess a high need for achievement and power, and both demonstrate assertiveness, self-reliance, risk taking, and other traits and behaviors associated with leadership. Actually, once men and women have established themselves as leaders in their organizations, women do not behave differently than men.[39] The first female executives, because they were entering new territory, adhered to many of the "rules of conduct" that spelled success for men.[40] Today, a second wave of women are making their way to the top and are not only adopting styles and habits that have proved successful for men, but are also drawing on the skills and attitudes they have developed from their experiences as women.

SELF-MANAGED TEAMS: FOCUSING ON QUALITY AND DIVERSITY

You will recall from our discussion in Chapter 8 that the use of self-managed teams (SMTs) has become increasingly popular for diverse organizations such as Digital Equipment, Frito-Lay, General Electric, General Foods, Hewlett-Packard, Microsoft, and Pepsi-Cola, as well as numerous smaller firms.[41] SMTs appear in many forms, such as quality circles, task forces, communication teams, and new venture teams. They are used to solve complex problems, increase productivity, foster creativity, and reduce middle management costs.

Most existing leadership theories assume a person-centered approach in which leadership is a quality that exists in one person—the leader. In contrast, the SMT is based on the premise of the distributed leadership model, which emphasizes the active cultivation and development of leadership abilities within all members of a team. SMTs assume that leadership is a collection of roles and behaviors that can be shared and rotated. At any one time, multiple leaders can exist in a team, with each member assuming complementary leadership behaviors. At Microsoft, CEO Bill Gates believes that the only way to keep the company feeling small is by sticking to SMTs, a lesson he admits he borrowed from Hewlett-Packard. He contends that all employees at Microsoft must feel that they can make a difference and that they are accountable for their performance.[42]

How can an SMT be effectively managed? The leadership behaviors required for effective SMT functioning fall into four categories: (1) envisioning, (2) organizing, (3) spanning, and (4) social.[43]

Envisioning leadership behavior revolves around creating new and compelling visions. This requires facilitating idea generation and innovative thinking and helping others in the group to develop new ideas. *Organizing*

▼ The self-managed work team shown here is based on the premise of the distributed leadership model that emphasizes the active cultivation and development of leadership abilities with a diverse team membership.

MANAGING FOR EXCELLENCE

NICOLOSI'S VISION: EVERYONE IS A LEADER

When Richard Nicolosi came to Procter & Gamble's paper products division, he found a heavily bureaucratic and centralized organization that was overly preoccupied with internal functional goals and projects. His first task as division head was to stress the need for employee creativity. He made it clear that the rules of the game had changed.

The new direction included a much greater stress on teamwork and multiple leadership roles. Nicolosi pushed a strategy of using groups to manage the division and its specific products. He and his team designated themselves as the paper division "board" and began meeting first monthly and then weekly. Nicolosi's theme was "each of us is a leader."

All these changes helped create an entrepreneurial environment where large numbers of people were motivated to realize the new vision. Most innovation came from people dealing with new products. Other employee initiatives were oriented more toward functional areas, and some even came from the bottom of the hierarchy. For example, a few of the division's secretaries, feeling empowered by the new culture, developed a Secretaries Network. This association established subcommittees on training, rewards and recognition, and the "secretary of the future." Nicolosi's leadership style inspired employees at all levels to contribute to the division's new direction.

leadership behavior focuses on quality issues such as details, deadlines, efficiency, and structure. Team members who fulfill this role help provide the group with direction and goal setting. Behaviors associated with *spanning leadership* include networking, developing and maintaining a strong team image with outsiders, bargaining, and being sensitive to power distributions. Spanning leadership links the SMT's effort to outside groups and individuals. *Social leadership behavior* focuses on developing and maintaining the team's diverse social environment. The effective social leader is concerned with members' needs, being sensitive to group processes, fostering an environment where individuals are respected, and mediating conflicts. These are issues most important as organizations become more diverse.

With the right leadership mix and enough time and support from outside, an SMT can achieve remarkable results. Although SMTs are becoming more common in the workplace, their usefulness depends on how well people in various leadership roles can communicate and unify the SMT to work toward a common goal. As we see in Managing for Excellence, Richard Nicolosi brought a new perspective on teamwork to his position at Procter & Gamble.[44] This new direction included a much greater stress on teamwork and multiple leadership roles. Nicolosi pushed a strategy of using teams to manage the division and focused on developing his subordinates, motivating innovative behavior, and encouraging them to take a leadership role, even when that role was not formalized.

LEADERSHIP INFLUENCE AND QUALITY MANAGEMENT

Achieving quality and implementing quality management sound relatively simple: just put the customer first, empower employees to meet the needs of the customer, develop a measurement system to evaluate quality, and engage in continuous improvement practices to ensure that quality improvements remain a high priority. Although it may be reduced to "four easy steps," in practice, implementing a quality management program is more difficult than it sounds. Many argue that successful quality management programs require an entire change in the organizational culture and leadership of the firm. But, as you read in Chapter 11, culture doesn't change easily or quickly. How then can an organization improve its chances of implementing a quality management program successfully?[45]

Perhaps the single most important prerequisite to effective quality management is a commitment on the part of the top management of the organization to play a leadership role in developing and implementing the program. In fact, the prestigious and coveted Malcolm Baldrige National Quality Award recognizes the importance of leadership from two important perspectives—symbolic acts and active involvement.[46]

Symbolic acts are purposeful actions that convince employees that quality will be the priority of the organization—even above financial and efficiency goals. Unless the members of the organization truly believe that quality comes first, a quality management program stands little chance of success. Consequently, it is essential that the organization's leaders do whatever is necessary to get the attention of their employees and convince them that quality is priority one.

▼ An organization can improve its chances of successfully implementing a quality management program. At Southern Bell's corporate Communications Network Center, leaders work closely with employees to focus on quality issues.

Excellent examples of such symbolic acts of leadership come from the ranks of former Baldridge Award winners. Bob Galvin, former CEO of Motorola, changed the structure of his policy committee meetings so that quality appeared at the top of the agenda. To emphasize his point, Galvin would leave the meeting immediately after the quality issues had been discussed and before financial matters had been addressed. Roger Milliken, CEO of Milliken and Company, demanded that his executive management team attend statistical methods courses prior to having the lower-level managers attend. Despite strong protests on the part of the Xerox sales team, David Kearns, former CEO of Xerox, delayed the introduction of a major new product because of a "minor" quality problem. In each case, a highly visible action got the attention of the organization's employees and reinforced the quality message.[47]

Of equal importance is the active involvement of top managers in the daily management of the quality improvement program. "Slogans and lip service" alone will never be enough to ensure the success of a quality management program. Leadership at the top must be actively involved in ensuring that quality improvement is an organizational reality. Such involvement can take many forms. Top managers may actually teach quality management training courses, meet with customer focus groups regularly, and visit employees on the shop floor to hear their ideas for improving the quality of the firm's output.

To determine top management's involvement in a quality management program, the judges for the Baldridge Award review the calendars or logbooks of a firm's top managers for a given period prior to visiting the organization. The judges look to see how much time managers spend talking to employees and to customers.

While we have used examples of CEO involvement exclusively thus far, it is essential to note that leadership must come from all ranks of management. If quality management in on the agenda of top management only, the program is sure to fail. Bright and capable individuals in the line and staff functions throughout the organization must also be willing to play a leadership role in ensuring that quality becomes the priority for all employees.

MANAGERIAL IMPLICATIONS

We conclude this chapter on leadership with a list of guiding principles to start you toward leadership effectiveness. These 10 items get to the core of what leadership is all about.[48] Following these principles will help you develop effective leadership skills.

- Know yourself. You cannot be an effective leader without knowing your own strengths and weaknesses. Knowing your capabilities will allow you to improve on your weaknesses and trade on your strengths.
- Be a role model. Expect no more than what you yourself are willing to give.
- Learn to communicate with your ears open and your mouth shut. Most problems that leaders are asked to solve are people problems created because of a failure in communication. Communication failures are the result of people hearing but not listening to one another.
- Know your team and be a team player. As a leader, make the effort to know what other members of the team are doing, not necessarily to monitor their progress but to seek ways and means of providing your own assistance.
- Be honest to yourself as well as to others. All good leaders make mistakes. Rarely do they make the same mistake more than once. Openly admit a mistake, learn from it, and forget it. Generally, others will forget it too.
- Do not avoid risks. If you are to become an effective leader, you will need to become an effective risk taker. See problems as challenges, challenges as catalysts for change, and changes as opportunities.
- Believe in yourself. All effective leaders share the characteristic of confidence in their own ability to get the job done. This personal confidence is often contagious and quick to permeate an entire organization, boosting confidence levels of all team members.
- Take the offense rather than the defense. The most effective leaders are quicker to act than react. Their best solution to any problem is to solve it before it becomes a problem. If they see something that needs fixing, they will do what they can to repair it before being told to do so by someone else.
- Know the ways of disagreement and the means of compromise. While people may disagree with one another, remember that who wins or loses is not important. The real winner is the leader who can facilitate the opposing side's goals while achieving his or her own.
- Be a good follower. Effective leaders lead as they would like to be led.

This chapter has explored many different facets of leadership effectiveness for the dynamic environment in which you are, or soon will be, working. As we noted earlier, a considerable amount of research has been done on leadership, and there are many books and articles on the topic. Although leadership means different things to different people, the focus of much of the leadership research has been on common qualities shared by all leaders. Many long lists of admirable qualities (aggressiveness, charisma, courage, wisdom) have been generated but have not been found to apply to all leaders in all situations. To be effective, a leader's qualities must be related in some way to the situation he or she is in and to the nature of his or her followers.

U.S. businesses desperately need better leadership. Companies that will be successful in the more competitive global economy will be more flexible, responsive, and leaner than those in the past. Small groups must tackle problems and seize opportunities as they arise. Individuals at all levels must be given the responsibility and authority to make decisions to be effective followers and leaders in the dynamic environment of the twenty-first century.

THE BELL ATLANTIC WAY: SMITH'S WAKE-UP CALL

The thrust of Smith's leadership style is to foster worker participation at all levels. At a reinforcement session for Bell Atlantic supervisors, a blindfolded employee is told to hit a target with a velcro-tipped dart. At first, no one lends any guidance. Then, people shout directions that help the employee hit the target. Such drills are more motivational than instructional. Indeed, employees whose esprit de corps appears to be slackening sometimes are advised to attend a ''reinforcement'' session.

The new leadership culture is already apparent in the executive suite. To set an example, Smith turned the executive dining room into an employee cafeteria. He also dispersed top brass from the executive floor and stationed them with the groups they oversee. ''What kind of message do we send employees if we're all on the same floor and lunch in a private dining room?'' Smith asks.

To some employees, Smith's leadership style seems a bit ''hokey,'' but he says it is helping transform his executives into the kind of managers who can compete in all sorts of businesses. Smith is asking employees to work on changing corporate goals, instead of just fulfilling the narrow, bureaucratically defined objectives that marked the old Bell system. While Smith concedes that some people don't want to change under any circumstances, he vows that the new leadership focus, employee partnership, and independent thinking at the heart of the Bell Atlantic Way are here to stay.[49] ▼

SUMMARY

- Leadership is broadly defined as a social influence process that involves determining group or organization objectives, motivating behavior, and influencing group maintenance and culture. We also said that leadership is a process whose function is to produce change.

- Power was defined as the ability to marshal human, informational, or material resources to get something done. There are various types of power including power that is prescribed by the person's position in the organization and power that is a result of personal attributes.

- The trait approach to leadership emphasized the personal attributes of leaders. But this research failed to find any traits that would guarantee leadership success.

- The behavioral approach to understanding leadership turned from personal traits of successful leaders to patterns of behaviors or styles that are used by excellent leaders. The Ohio State studies identified two independent dimensions of leader behavior that were labeled initiating structure and consideration.

- Fiedler's LPC model was the first contingency approach to understanding leadership. The LPC model states that effectiveness depends on two factors, which were identified as the personal style of the leader and the degree of situational favorability.

- According to the SLT contingency model, effective leader behavior depends on the match between leader behavior and the situational contingency of subordinate readiness. The four leader behaviors are telling, selling, participating, and delegating.

- The path-goal model of leadership examines how four aspects of leader behavior influence subordinate satisfaction and motivation. The four leader behaviors are supportive, directive, participative, and achievement-oriented leadership.

- Leadership substitutes are individual, task, and organizational characteristics that tend to outweigh the leader's ability to affect subordinate satisfaction and performance. They make leadership behavior unnecessary or redundant.

- Several emerging approaches to understanding leadership were discussed. Transformational leadership is the process of influencing the attitudes and assumptions of organizational members and building commitment for the organization's mission or objectives. Followership is being encouraged at many organizations as a way to influence individual accountability and independence. The emergence of women as leaders is influencing how leadership success is determined. SMTs are becoming more commonplace in high-performing diverse organizations. This concept is based on the distributed leadership model that emphasizes the active cultivation and development of leadership abilities within all members of a team. Finally, we discussed how leadership influences the successful implementation of quality management programs.

KEY TERMS

Leadership (p. 425)
Power (p. 425)
Legitimate power (p. 426)
Coercive power (p. 426)
Reward power (p. 426)
Information power (p. 427)
Expert power (p. 427)
Referent power (p. 427)
Trait approach (p. 428)

Behavioral approach (p. 429)
Initiating structure (p. 429)
Consideration (p. 429)
Contingency theories (p. 432)
Fiedler's LPC model (p. 432)
Least preferred co-worker scale (LPC) (p. 433)
Situational favorability (p. 433)
SLT model (p. 434)

Path-goal model (p. 435)
Supportive leadership (p. 436)
Directive leadership (p. 436)
Participative leadership (p. 436)
Achievement-oriented leadership (p. 436)
Leadership substitutes (p. 438)
Transformational leadership (p. 440)

REVIEW QUESTIONS

1. Define the term leadership. Identify examples of effective leadership.

2. What are a leader's sources of power?

3. Distinguish between position power and person power and provide examples of each.

4. Define the behavioral dimensions of initiating structure and consideration.

5. How does the behavioral approach to leadership differ from contingency approach?

6. How does Fiedler's LPC model describe situational favorability?

7. Examine the differences between Fiedler's LPC model and path-goal leadership.

8. Describe the term readiness from the SLT contingency model.

9. How is a transformational leader different from other leaders?

10. Under what conditions would an SMT be effective?

DISCUSSION QUESTIONS

Improving Critical Thinking

1. Suppose that a leader's behavior does not seem to match the situation. Can the leader's behavior be changed to produce a better match? What would Fiedler's LPC model predict? The SLT model? The path-goal model?

2. Under what conditions would an organization want to promote followership? How would you feel about being trained to be a follower?

3. Watch a popular television show (or cable reruns) such as "Seinfeld," "Roseanne," "The Simpsons," or "MASH," and examine how the main characters use power to influence. What types of power do they use most often? Least often?

Enhancing Communication Skills

4. Is a formal leader always necessary? If not, under what conditions does the leader not make a differ-ence? After you have developed some understanding of this topic, share your ideas either in an oral pres-entation or in a short paper.

5. Give an example of a situation in which you used your power to influence your peers, your family members, and your professor. Provide specific ex-amples either as an oral presentation or in writing as directed by your instructor.

Building Teamwork Skills

6. What are some of the major differences among the contingency leadership models? Form small teams to identify and discuss these differences.

7. Select any theory of leadership discussed in the chapter and analyze your own leadership behavior. When is your behavior effective? Ineffective? In a small group, exchange your ideas with others with whom you have worked.

ETHICS: TAKE A STAND

As the manager of a paper products division, Ken has shown remarkable lead-ership skills in achieving a 35 percent market share for his division's primary product. He has used his influence in many ways—to get the proper allocation of resources from top management and to motivate his staff to work hard to achieve the company's goals. Recently, Ken has had to deal with an employee problem, and he isn't sure how to proceed.

The problem is with Jeff, an employee who until recently had worked extremely hard and contributed significantly to the division's success. Unfor-tunately, the stress associated with meeting this objective seems to have taken its toll on Jeff. In the last few months, he has frequently come to work late or called in sick. Furthermore, he has made several critical errors, and the quality of his work has begun to decline. Ken has approached Jeff several times about the problems, and Jeff has promised improvement. Ken has not seen any change, however. In fact, several clients have called to complain about Jeff's behavior on sales calls. Apparently, Jeff got into an unnecessary conflict with a member of one of the client's purchasing department. The client also said that Jeff seemed to have had several drinks at lunch. More than one client has mentioned that Jeff had alcohol on his breath before lunch.

Ken is not sure what action he should take. He feels obligated to repri-mand Jeff because of these latest incidents. At the same time, Ken feels he should cover for Jeff until he has resolved his apparent alcohol dependency problem because of his valued contributions to the company in the past. The time has come for Ken to take some action.

For Discussion

1. What sources of power would be appropriate for Ken to use in his ac-tion toward Jeff?

2. Suggest the type of leader behavior that Ken can use to help Jeff.

THINKING CRITICALLY
Debate the Issue

LEADERSHIP—A NECESSARY EVIL?

Form teams as directed by your instructor. The teams will be responsible for debating the following question: Is leadership necessary? Half of the teams should take the position that every organization and group needs a leader to be effective. The other half of the teams should take the position that leadership is not always necessary for effective performance. Each team should research and prepare its position using organizational and group examples from current magazines, newspapers, and periodicals. Your instructor will select two teams to present their findings to the class in a debate format.

VIDEO CASE

Mary Kay Cosmetics: Spotlight on Success

This video provides highlights from an annual sales meeting for Mary Kay Cosmetics consultants. Though some people find the sight of 25,000 women getting excited about glitzy awards and mock beauty pageants amusing, no one can argue with the success of Mary Kay Ash. Ash started Mary Kay Cosmetics in 1963 with $5,000 and nine consultants. Today, the company has more than 300,000 consultants and 21,000 full-time employees in 19 countries; it also has annual revenues of over $1 billion.

The reward system at Mary Kay is noncompetitive; there are no first, second, or third place winners. Rewards are pegged to plateaus of excellence. Any consultant who reaches a stipulated plateau wins the appropriate reward for that level. Material rewards include mink coats, diamond rings, luxury vacations, and the widely recognized pink Cadillacs. There are over 5,000 pink Cadillacs on the road.

In addition to material rewards, the 76-year-old Ash also makes sure her top salespeople receive large doses of recognition and appreciation. The annual sales meeting in Dallas, the company magazine, and frequent phone calls and letters are all aimed at letting top people know that they are appreciated by the company and by Mary Kay personally.

For Discussion

1. How would you describe Mary Kay's leadership style? Is it a style that could be easily copied?

2. What aspects of followership are evident in the video?

3. What are the implications for Mary Kay Cosmetics when Ash dies?

SOURCES: Jon Anderson, "In the Pink," *Chicago Tribune*, February 14, 1991, 1, 6; and Mary Kay Ash, *Mary Kay* (New York: Harper & Row, 1981).

CASE

Weintrop's Search for Good Leadership

While I was trying to earn enough money to finish graduate school, I worked full-time as a gas station attendant for Weintrop Oil, a large petroleum refiner with gas stations located primarily in the Southwestern United States. The station operated 24 hours a day and had a staff of 20 attendants and mechanics.

During my 18 months of employment, there were two different managers. Alice Komasare, the first manager, had worked there for several months prior to my arrival and stayed for 12 months until requesting a transfer to be closer to her family. The next man-

ager, Tony Fitz, took over when Alice transferred and continued after I left.

Both Alice and Tony were in their late 20s, held bachelor's degrees in management, and had previous managerial experience. But that is where the similarities stopped. Alice and Tony had very different styles of managing the station. Alice operated in ways that circumvented the regulations laid down in the Weintrop operations manual and sought to develop a sense of camaraderie and friendship with the crew. Her willingness to bend or disregard the rules was appreciated by both myself and the others on the crew. As a result, the crew frequently helped each other out, even when they were not on the clock. Alice would often show up early in the morning with coffee and donuts for the morning crew or late in the evening with pizza for the evening crew. Her efforts on the crew's behalf were reciprocated whenever she needed an extra crew member or a task done that wasn't part of the official Weintrop job description. We felt a lot of loyalty to Alice and frequently would volunteer to work another eight-hour shift if the business needed us.

Alice also had good rapport with the customers. We often went against Weintrop's rules to help a stranded motorist, and Alice would always praise our efforts. Alice's station consistently set all-time sales records even though it didn't operate by the book. But, after a year, Alice accepted a transfer, and the crew, much aggravated, greeted our new boss, Tony Fitz.

Tony operated the station by the book in a no-nonsense attempt to establish discipline and order. Where Alice fostered camaraderie, Tony deliberately attempted to foster individual accountability. Two crew members were fired for being $2.00 short for four days' work because the operations manual set out strict rules about this situation. When the crew protested by saying that Alice had never done it that way, Tony responded by saying he was not Alice.

Tony altered the way the crew operated. Previously, the work crew had consisted of four attendants, one responsible for each island of gas pumps (three in all) and one floating assistant who was free to help

wherever needed. In fact, any attendant who was free also helped out by wiping windows, checking oil, collecting money, or talking to the customers. Under Tony's system, the crew stopped helping each other and didn't leave their assigned area. As a result of the new system, the crew's long-standing concern for customers diminished. We began to enforce the rules rigorously for fear of losing our jobs. Customers reacted at first by complaining to Tony and then by never returning.

The sales volume of the station sharply declined despite Tony's rigorous application of Weintrop's rules. The district manager told Tony that service to customers was well below Weintrop's standards. Confronted with these problems and obvious crew hostility, Tony and the district manager found a solution: fire all of the crew members who had worked for Alice. So one by one, the crew was fired.

For Discussion

1. How would you characterize the leader behaviors of Alice and Tony?

2. Compare and contrast the sources of power used by Alice and Tony.

3. Discuss the extent to which you think the leader behaviors of Alice and Tony are appropriate for the situation they faced. How would you go about deciding such appropriateness?

4. Who's to blame for the station's poor performance?

EXPERIENTIAL EXERCISE 13.1

Identifying Power Techniques

Working alone or in a small group, read each of the following situations and identify the power technique being used. Provide a brief explanation of your reasoning.

- *Situation 1*: You work as the production manager for Don Industries, a major pharmaceutical manufacturer. You have a major contract that must be finished today. You have been told by your boss that you are to keep everyone at work until the task is finished. You meet with your employees and tell them, "I am responsible for seeing that this work is finished on time. No one will be allowed to leave until the work is finished."

- *Situation 2*: As the sports editor of a major newspaper, you have one employee who has missed the last four deadlines. You have spoken with her after each missed deadline, and she always promises that she will meet the next one. You want her to change, so you tell her that the next time she is late, you will put her on probation.

- *Situation 3*: You have an employee who is beginning to take classes at the local university in business administration. You have an undergraduate business degree as well as an MBA, and you recommend a list of courses to your employee.

EXPERIENTIAL EXERCISE 13.2

Test Your Leadership Style

Read both statements in each entry in the following list, and circle either *a* or *b* to indicate whichever best describes you—or is the least incorrect about you. You must answer every question to arrive at a proper score.

1. a. You are the person people most often turn to for help.
   b. You are aggressive and look after your best interests first.
2. a. You are more competent and better able to motivate others than most people.
   b. You strive to reach a position where you can exercise authority over large numbers of people and sums of money.
3. a. You try hard to influence the outcome of events.
   b. You quickly eliminate all obstacles that stand in the way of your goals.
4. a. There are few people you have as much confidence in as yourself.
   b. You have no qualms about taking what you want in this world.
5. a. You have the ability to inspire others to follow your lead.
   b. You enjoy having people act on your commands and are not opposed to making threats if you must.
6. a. You do your best to influence the outcome of events.
   b. You make all the important decisions, expecting others to carry them out.
7. a. You have a special magnetism that attracts people to you.
   b. You enjoy dealing with situations requiring confrontation.
8. a. You would enjoy consulting on the complex issues and problems that face managers of companies.
   b. You would enjoy planning, directing, and controlling the staff of a department to ensure the highest profit margins.
9. a. You want to consult with business groups and companies to improve effectiveness.
   b. You want to make decisions about other people's lives and money.
10. a. You could deal with level upon level of bureaucratic red tape and pressure to improve performance.
    b. You could work where money and profits are more important than other people's emotional well-being.
11. a. You typically must start your day before sunrise and continue into the night six or seven days a week.

b. You must fire unproductive employees regularly and expediently to achieve set targets.
12. a. You must be responsible for how well others do their work (and you will be judged on their achievements, not yours).
    b. You have a workaholic temperament that thrives on pressure to succeed.
13. a. You are a real self-starter and full of enthusiasm about everything you do.
    b. Whatever you do, you have to do it better than anyone else.
14. a. You are always striving to be the best, the tops, the first at whatever you do.
    b. You have a driving, aggressive personality and fight hard and tough to gain anything worth having.
15. a. You have always been involved in competitive activities, including sports, and have won several awards for outstanding performance.
    b. Winning and succeeding are more important to you than playing just for enjoyment.
16. a. You will stick to a problem when you are getting nowhere.
    b. You quickly become bored with most things you undertake.
17. a. You are naturally carried along by some inner drive or mission to accomplish something that has never been done.
    b. Self-demanding and a perfectionist, you are always pressing yourself to perform to the limit.
18. a. You maintain a sense of purpose or direction that is larger than yourself.
    b. Being successful at work is the most important thing to you.
19. a. You would enjoy a job requiring hard and fast decisions.
    b. You are loyal to the concepts of profit, growth, and expansion.
20. a. You prefer independence and freedom at work to a high salary or job security.
    b. You prefer structure, clear guidelines for high performance, and job security.
21. a. You firmly believe that those who take the most risks with their own savings should receive the greatest financial rewards.
    b. There are few people's judgment that you would have as much confidence in as your own.
22. a. You are seen as courageous, energetic, and optimistic.
    b. Being ambitious, you are quick to take advantage of new opportunities.
23. a. You are good at praising others and you give credit readily when it's due.

    b. You like people, but have little confidence in their ability to do things the right way.

24. a. You usually give people the benefit of the doubt rather than argue openly with them.

    b. Your style with people is direct, "tell it like it is" confrontation.

25. a. Although honest, you are capable of being ruthless if others are playing by devious rules.

    b. You grew up in an environment that stressed survival and required you to create your own rules.

Find Your Score

Count all the *a* responses you circled and multiply by 4 to get your percentage for leadership behaviors. Do the same with *b* answers to arrive at manager behaviors.

- Leader (number of *a*'s) _____ × 4 = _____ %
- Manager (number of *b*'s) _____ × 4 = _____ %

Interpret Your Score

Consider yourself a leader if you score more than 65 percent in the leader tally, consider yourself a manager if you score more than 65 percent in the manager tally. If your scores cluster closer to a 50-50 split, you're a leader/manager.

The Leader

Your idea of fulfilling work is to motivate and guide co-workers to achieve their best and to reach common goals in their work by functioning in harmony. You are the sort of person who simply enjoys watching people grow and develop. You are commonly described as patient and encouraging in your dealings with people and are a determined self-starter in your own motivation. Since you have a natural ability for inspiring top performances, there's usually little turnover among your employees, and staff relations are harmonious. At times, however, you may be too soft on people or overly patient when their

performance lags. Where people are concerned, you may be too quick to let emotions get in the way of business judgments. Overall, you're the visionary type, not the day-to-day grinder.

The Manager

You are capable of getting good work out of people, but your style can be abrasive and provocative. You are especially competent at quickly taking charge, bulldozing through corporate red tape, or forcing others to meet tough work demands. Driven partly by a low threshold for boredom, you strive for more complexity in your work. But you love the "game" of power and the sense of having control over others. Also, your confidence in your own ideas is so strong that you may be frustrated by working as part of a team. Your tendency to see your progress as the battle of a great mind against mediocre ones is not the best premise for bringing out the best in others. Therefore, the further up the corporate ladder you go, the more heavily human relations problems will weigh against you.

The Leader/Manager Mix

As a 50–50 type, you probably do not believe in the need to motivate others. Instead, you maintain that the staff should have a natural desire to work as hard as you do, without needing somebody to egg them on. You do your job well, and you expect the same from your subordinates. This means that while your own level of productivity is high, you are not always sure about how to motivate others to reach their full potential. Generally, however, you do have the ability to get others to do as you wish without being abrasive or ruffling feathers. You may pride yourself on being surrounded by a very competent, professional staff that is self-motivated, requiring little of your own attention. But don't be too sure: almost everyone performs better under the right sort of encouraging leadership.

EXPERIENTIAL EXERCISE 13.3

Compare Your Leadership Style

Complete the leadership style scale in Exercise 13.2 to determine your personal leadership style. Then, conduct an interview with your immediate supervisor and ask him or her to take the leadership style scale in the

exercise. Compare your results with those of your supervisor and discuss the similarities or differences in the styles you each choose to employ. If you are not satisfied with the style you are using, how could you alter your behavior to change your leadership style?

NOTES

1. J. A. Lopex, "A Wake-Up Call for Bell Atlantic," *Business Week*, December 2, 1991, 133–35; R. M. Kanter, "Championing Change: An Interview with Bell Atlantic's CEO Raymond Smith," *Harvard Business Review* (January/February 1991): 119–30; P. Drucker, *The New Realities* (New York: Harper & Row, 1990); and M. Hammer and J. Champy, *Reengineering the Corporation: A Manifesto for Business Revolution* (New York: HarperBusiness, 1993), 193–99.

2. G. A. Yukl, *Leadership in Organizations*, 3d ed. (Englewood Cliffs, N.J.: Prentice-Hall, 1993).

3. J. Kotter, "What Leaders Really Do," *Harvard Business Review* (May/June 1990): 103-11.

4. W. Bennis and B. Nanus, *Leaders: The Strategies for Taking Charge* (New York: Harper & Row, 1985).

5. J. P. Kotter, *The Leadership Factor* (New York: Free Press, 1987).

6. Adapted from J. B. Lau and A. B. Shani, *Behavior in Organizations: An Experiential Approach*, 5th ed. (Boston, Irwin, 1992), 39.

7. J. French and B. Raven, "The Bases of Social Power," in D. Cartwright, ed., *Studies of Social Power* (Ann Arbor, Mich.: Institute for Social Research, 1959).

8. Adapted from P. Fandt, *Management Skills: Practice and Experience* St. Paul, Minn.: West Publishing Co., 1994), 81.

9. S. A. Kirkpatrick and E. A. Locke, "Leadership: Do Traits Matter?" *Academy of Management Executive* 5 (1991): 48-59; and R. M. Stogdill, *Handbook of Leadership* (New York: Free Press, 1974).

10. Kirkpatrick and Locke, "Leadership: Do Traits Matter?" 49-59.

11. R. M. Stogdill and A. E. Coons, *Leader Behavior: It's Description and Measurement* (Columbus, Ohio: Ohio State University Bureau of Business Research, 1957).

12. R. Tannenbaum and W. Schmidt, "How to Choose a Leadership Pattern," *Harvard Business Review* (March/April 1958): 95-101.

13. Ibid.

14. Z. Schiller, "No More Mr. Nice Guy at P&G—Not by a Long Shot," *Business Week*, February 3, 1992, 54-56.

15. R. Blake and J. Mouton, *The Managerial Grid* (Houston: Gulf Publishing, 1964).

16. R. Blake and J. Mouton, "How to Choose a Leadership Style," *Training and Development Journal* (February 1986): 39-46.

17. M. H. McCormack, *The 110% Solution* (New York: Villard Books, 1991).

18. F. E. Fiedler, "The Contingency Model and the Dynamics of the Leadership Process," in L. Berkowitz, ed., *Advances in Experimental Social Psychology* (New York: Academic Press, 1967); and F. E. Fiedler, "The Effects of Leadership Training and Experience: A Contingency Model Interpretation," *Administrative Science Quarterly* 17 (1972): 455.

19. P. Hersey and K. H. Blanchard, *Management of Organizational Behavior: Utilizing Human Resources*, 5th ed. (Englewood Cliffs, N.J.: Prentice-Hall, 1988).

20. Ibid.

21. R. J. House and T. R. Mitchell, "Path-Goal Theory of Leadership," *Journal of Contemporary Business* (Autumn 1974): 81-98.

22. J. R. Schermerhorn, Jr., J. G. Hunt, and R. N. Osborn, *Managing Organizational Behavior* (New York: John Wiley & Sons, 1985).

23. S. Kerr and J. Jermier, "Substitutes for Leadership: Their Meaning and Measurement," *Organizational Behavior and Human Performance* 22 (1978): 375-403.

24. Ibid.

25. A. Zaleznik, "The Leadership Gap," *Academy of Management Executive* 4 (1990): 7-22.

26. C. C. Manz and H. P. Sims, "Leading Workers to Lead Themselves: The External Leadership of Self-Managing Work Teams," *Administrative Science Quarterly* (March 1987): 106-29.

27. Adapted from C. Lee, "Followership: The Essence of Leadership," *Training*, January 1991, 27-35; and M. A. Abramson and J. W. Scanlon, "The Five Dimensions of Leadership," *Government Executive*, July 1991, 20-25.

28. Lee, "Followership"; Abramson and Scanlon "The Five Dimensions of Leadership"; and Zalenzik, "The Leadership Gap."

29. Yukl, *Leadership in Organizations;* J. M. Kouzes and B. Z. Posner, *The Leadership Challenge: How to Get Extraordinary Things Done in Organizations* (San Francisco: Jossey-Bass, 1990).

30. Kouzes and Posner, *The Leadership Challenge.*

31. J. A. Conger and R. N. Kanungo, "Behavioral Dimensions of Charismatic Leadership," in J. A. Conger and R. N. Kanungo, eds., *Charismatic Leadership* (San Francisco: Jossey-Bass, 1988).

32. W. Bennis, "The Four Competencies of Leadership," *Training and Development Journal* (August 1984): 119-25.

33. Conger and Kanungo, "Behavioral Dimensions of Charismatic Leadership."

34. T. Shales, "Lack of Leadership and Vision May Hurt NBC Future, Tartikoff says," *Tucson Citizen*, May 8, 1991, C19.

35. K. Rebello and E. Schwartz, "The Magic of Microsoft," *Business Week*, February 24, 1992, 60-64.

36. B. M. Bass, *Bass and Stogdill's Handbook of Leadership: Theory, Research, and Managerial Implications* (New York: Free Press, 1990).

37. Adapted from "Shingobee Builders," *Real-World Lessons for America's Small Businesses: Insights from the Blue Chip Enterprise Initiative* (Nation's Business on behalf of Connecticut Mutual Life Insurance Company and the U.S. Chamber of Commerce, 1992), 10-11.

38. Lau and Shani, *Behavior in Organizations.*

39. Bass, *Bass and Stogdill's Handbook of Leadership.*

40. J. B. Rosener, "Ways Women Lead," *Harvard Business Review* (November/December 1990): 119-25.

41. B. Dumaine, "Who Needs a Boss?" *Fortune*, October 1990, 52-60.

42. Rebello and Schwartz, "The Magic of Microsoft."

43. Adapted from D. Barry, "Managing the Bossless Team: Lessons in Distributed Leadership," *Organizational Dynamics* (Winter 1992): 31-47.

44. Kotter, "What Leaders Really Do."

45. For a more thorough discussion of this, see E. Holmes, "Leadership in the Quest for Quality," *Issues & Observations* 12 (1992): 5-7.

46. A more detailed discussion is found in D. A. Gavin,

"How the Baldrige Award Really Works," *Harvard Business Review* (November/December 1991): 80–93.

47. Ibid.

48. Adapted from L. Ludewig, "The Ten Commandments of Leadership," *NASPA Journal* (Spring 1988): 297.

49. Lopex, "A Wake-Up Call for Bell Atlantic"; Kanter, "Championing Change: An Interview with Bell Atlantic's CEO Raymond Smith"; Drucker, *The New Realities*; and Hammer and Champy, *Reengineering the Corporation*.

Effectively Managing Individual and Group Behavior

CHAPTER 14

▼ CHAPTER OVERVIEW

Management distinction in the 1990s will be achieved by those organizations with an organizational culture that allows them to move faster, communicate more clearly, react better to diverse customers and employees, produce higher-quality products and services, be globally oriented, and involve everyone in a focused effort to serve ever more demanding customers. To eliminate the barriers that separate functions within the organization, organizations must move toward a culture that helps people understand how to work together at both an individual and a group level.

In this chapter we lay the foundations of individual and group behavior. We first discuss some of the ways individuals differ—including attitudes, personalities, perceptions, and abilities. Merely placing people together does not guarantee success in organizations that are comprised of individuals with diverse backgrounds and perceptions. The real challenge comes in encouraging individuals to pull together in a group and focus on common goals. Therefore, we turn our attention to understanding groups. We explore the dimensions that affect how groups operate in an organization and the ways managers can create more effective groups that make real contributions to the continuing success of the organization as a whole.

▼ LEARNING OBJECTIVES

When you have finished studying this chapter,
you should be able to:

- Define attitudes and describe three relevant work-related attitudes that managers should understand.
- Discuss the relationship between job satisfaction and performance.
- Explain personality and describe five personality traits that are considered important in the workplace.
- Identify and explain three perceptual biases.
- Discuss how to reduce perceptual errors.
- State the differences between formal and informal groups.
- Discuss the five-stage group developmental process.
- Identify six group dimensions that influence group effectiveness.
- Explain what makes a group effective.

457

BOEING DISCOVERS A NEW STRATEGY TO ENHANCE PERFORMANCE

Boeing discovered an important "new" strategy to enhance organizational performance and increase quality products. "We recognized that if we were going to remain competitive in the marketplace in the years ahead, we were going to have to change the way we did business," says Jack Wires, former (retired) vice president of quality assurance. "We had to make a breakthrough in the way we produced our products in order to get our costs down, and at the same time increase our quality." So Boeing developed a strategy to encourage teamwork, boost employee morale, and solve quality-control problems.

To implement its strategy, Boeing had to introduce a quality improvement process that would change the way it managed its business. These changes were vigorous and to some employees, threatening. But to make any type of major improvement, Boeing had to change the system. It implemented this process by forming employees into quality improvement teams. These teams were distinctly different from quality circles, a participative management practice that Boeing had had in place since 1980. In quality circles, people worked together to identify and solve problems that involved their particular units. The problems they addressed were, by definition, relatively narrow in scope. The quality improvement teams, on the other hand, were formed to look at chronic problems that might span a number of organizational units; sometimes they looked at an entire system.

Could an organization that employs over 50,000 individuals make such drastic changes? Would Boeing be able to modify the prevailing employee attitudes from individual orientation to team orientation? Was management willing to become part of the team, rather than just acting as a leader? What were the results of Boeing's emphasis on quality improvement through teamwork?[1] ▼

INTRODUCTION

In the workplace, a new recognition and appreciation of individuals and groups are emerging. Effective organizations such as Boeing must pull together all their human resources to forge a strong, viable organizational culture that emphasizes teamwork. In recent years, U.S. industry has begun to see just how important teamwork is to quality and organization effectiveness. Indeed, the examples are all around us. More than a decade ago, the Swedish car manufacturer Volvo abandoned the traditional automobile manufacturing line, replacing it with mobile platforms for the car chassis; employee teams work on one car section or system at a time. Members of the team can exchange jobs or change teams and even vary the work pace.[2] A recent reorganization at Xerox replaced the previous system with a corporate structure that revolves around self-managed work teams.[3] As we will see in Chapter 17, teams are an important part of successful quality management programs. These approaches foster top-quality products, individual employee concern for enhancing production, increased efficiency, and high employee morale.

This chapter provides the foundations of individual and group behavior. We begin by examining some of the ways individuals differ in attitudes, personalities, perceptions, and abilities. We will look at three important work attitudes that affect behavior and performance including job satisfaction, organizational commitment, and job involvement. Since management effectiveness depends upon the ability of different individuals to pull together and focus on a common goal, we turn our attention to understanding group issues. We explore the different types of groups, how groups form and develop, and several dimensions that influence group effectiveness. Finally, we take a look at how managers can work to make groups more effective.

UNDERSTANDING INDIVIDUAL BEHAVIOR: KEY TO MANAGING DIVERSITY

An individual's behavior will be determined to a great extent by several internal elements, such as attitudes, personalities, perceptions, and abilities. People respond differently to the same situation because of their unique combination of these elements. Managers are challenged to understand and recognize the importance of individual differences in their employees. We examine some of these elements that determine individual behavior in the next few sections.

ATTITUDES

Attitudes are relatively lasting beliefs, feelings, and behavioral tendencies held by a person about specific objects, events, groups, issues, or persons. For example, when Boeing employees said they liked the new quality improvement teams, they were expressing an attitude about the process and the organization. Attitudes result from a person's background and life experiences. They may not necessarily be factual or completely consistent with objective reality.

Attitudes
Relatively lasting beliefs, feelings, and behavioral tendencies held by a person about specific objects, events, groups, issues, or persons.

Work Attitudes Affecting Behavior and Performance
While the study of attitudes is an important aspect of understanding and predicting behavior in the workplace, our focus in this chapter is on understanding some common work-related attitudes that managers encounter. These include job satisfaction, organizational commitment, and job involvement.

Job Satisfaction   The most commonly studied work attitude is job satisfaction. **Job satisfaction** is the degree to which individuals feel positively or negatively

Job satisfaction
The degree to which individuals feel positively or negatively about their jobs.

▼ The construction supervisor shown here focuses on employee input as part of the organization's emphasis on employee involvement and job satisfaction.

about their jobs. It is an emotional response to tasks, as well as to the physical and social conditions of the workplace.[4] Job satisfaction can lead to a variety of positive and negative outcomes, from both an individual and an organizational perspective. It influences how employees feel about themselves, their work, and their organizations and can affect their contribution to achieving the organization's goals.[5]

The best-known scale that measures job satisfaction—the Job Descriptive Index (JDI)—evaluates five specific characteristics of a person's job:[6]

1. The work itself—responsibility, interest, and growth.
2. Pay—adequacy of pay and perceived equity.
3. Relations with co-workers—social harmony and respect.
4. Quality of supervision—technical help and social support.
5. Promotional opportunities—chances for further advancement.

Obviously, an employee can be satisfied with some aspects of a job and, at the same time, be dissatisfied with others. A scale, such as the JDI, helps managers to pinpoint sources of dissatisfaction so they can take appropriate actions.

Of particular interest to managers is the possible relationship between job satisfaction and performance at work. Over the years, some research has shown that job satisfaction *causes* job performance, while other studies have indicated that job performance *causes* job satisfaction. The current view is that managers should not assume a simple cause-and-effect relationship between job satisfaction and job performance because the relationship between the two in any particular situation will depend on a complex set of personal and situational variables. An employee's job performance depends on a large number of factors such as his or her ability, the quality of equipment and materials used, the competence of supervision, the working environment, peer relationships, and so on.

Organizational commitment
The degree to which the employee is committed to the organization's values and goals, has a desire to remain a part of the organization, and is willing to expend considerable efforts for the organization.

Organizational Commitment   **Organizational commitment** reflects the degree to which the employee is committed to the organization's values and goals, has a desire to remain a part of the organization, and is willing to expend considerable effort for the organization.[7] In short, commitment is something like loyalty. When people are loyal to something, they want it to succeed and will work toward that end.

Given this definition, most companies would like to see high levels of organizational commitment in their workforces. While this is especially true, there may be exceptions. For example, if poor-performing employees are very committed to the organization, they may be reluctant to leave. If management is restricted from terminating poor-performing employees, such commitment could be costly to the firm. Also, consider the case in which employees are so committed to an organization or to a cause that they are afraid to criticize others in the organization. In extreme cases, commitment has led to the commission of illegal or unethical acts. Too much commitment, like most things in life, is not necessarily better.[8]

Job involvement
The job's importance in the employee's life or to the employee's self-concept.

Job Involvement   **Job involvement** is another work-related attitude that concerns managers. It may be reflected in the job's importance in the employee's life or to the employee's self-concept. When job involvement is high, the employee actively participates and considers performance important to his or her self-worth. Recent research indicates that managers must be aware of numerous issues both within the organization and in the employee's nonwork environment that can affect job involvement.[9]

PERSONALITY

Personality is the enduring, organized, and distinctive pattern of behavior that characterizes an individual's adaptation to a situation.[10] It is used here to represent the overall profile or combination of traits that characterize the unique nature of a person. In short, personality allows us to tell people apart and to anticipate their behaviors.

Personality characteristics suggest tendencies to behave in certain ways and account for consistency in various situations. In an effort to increase job satisfaction, some organizations try to match personality characteristics of employees with job requirements. According to some researchers, an individual's satisfaction and propensity to leave a job depend on the degree to which the employee's personality matches her or his occupation. Should organizations try to match personality characteristics of employees with job requirements? According to the personality–job fit theory, the answer is yes. Meeting the Challenge provides insight into this notion and may provide you with some help as you select a major or a profession.[11] After examining Meeting the Challenge, try to determine how well your personality matches your major or profession.

A number of personality traits have been convincingly linked to work behavior and performance. The next section describes several personality traits (or styles) that are particularly important for managers to understand.

Personality Characteristics Affecting Performance

Organizational researchers have tended to focus on specific personality traits (or styles) that are considered important in the workplace. We will examine five traits of special relevance to managers: self-esteem, locus of control, authoritarianism/dogmatism, Machiavellianism, and Type A/Type B orientation.

Self-Esteem   **Self-esteem** indicates the extent to which people believe they are capable, significant, successful, and worthwhile.[12] In short, a person's self-esteem is a judgment of worthiness that is expressed by the attitudes that person holds toward him- or herself. People have opinions about their own behavior, abilities, appearance, and worth. Research has shown that these assessments of worthiness are affected somewhat by situations, successes or failures, and the opinions of others.[13] Nevertheless, the assessments are stable enough to be widely regarded as a basic characteristic or dimension of personality that is credited with enhancing performance, increasing the likelihood of success, and fueling motivation.[14] Self-esteem affects behavior in organizations and other social settings in several important ways. For example, self-esteem is related to initial vocational choice. Individuals with high self-esteem take more risks in job selection, may be more attracted to high-status occupations, and are more likely to choose nontraditional jobs than individuals with low self-esteem.[15] Individuals with low self-esteem set lower goals for themselves than individuals with high self-esteem and tend to be more easily influenced by the opinions of others in organizational settings.

Locus of Control   **Locus of control** is a personality characteristic that describes the extent to which individuals believe that they can control events affecting them.[16] Do you have an internal or external locus of control? Before reading further, take a few minutes to complete Experiential Exercise 14.1 at the end of the chapter. This will give you some insight into this aspect of your personality and help you determine whether you have an internal or external locus of control.

Individuals who have an *internal locus of control* believe that the events in their lives are primarily (but not necessarily totally) the result of their own

Personality
The enduring, organized, and distinctive pattern of behavior that characterizes an individual's adaptation to a situation.

Self-esteem
The extent to which people believe they are capable, significant, successful, and worthwhile.

Locus of control
The extent to which individuals believe that they can control events affecting them. Those with an internal locus of control believe that events are primarily the result of one's own behavior and actions. Those with an external locus of control believe that much of what happens is uncontrolled and determined by outside forces.

**MEETING
THE CHALLENGE**

MATCHING PERSONALITY AND OCCUPATION TO INCREASE SATISFACTION

Should organizations try to match personality characteristics of employees with job requirements? According to John Holland's personality-job fit theory, the answer is *Yes*. Holland's model is based on the concept of the fit between a person's interests—interpreted to represent personality characteristics—and his or her occupation.

According to the theory, there are six basic personality types, which correspond to occupational preferences. An individual's satisfaction and propensity to leave a job depend on the degree to which his or her personality matches the occupation. Satisfaction is highest, and turnover lowest, when personality and occupation are in agreement. When there is a match between job and personality type, employees should be more satisfied and less likely to resign than when job and personality are at odds.

The following table lists the six personality types and gives examples of typical personality characteristics and the matching occupations.

PERSONALITY TYPE	PERSONALITY CHARACTERISTICS	MATCHING OCCUPATIONS
Artistic	Self-expression, creativity	Art, music, writing, design, architecture, emotional activities
Enterprising	Attaining power and status, verbal activities to influence/persuade	Law, small-business management, public relations
Social	Interpersonal, communication activities	Social work, teaching, counseling, foreign service
Investigative	Thinking, organizing, understanding concepts	Mathematics, reporting, biology, physical sciences
Realistic	Physical activities, strength training, coordination	Farming, forestry, assertive behaviors
Conventional	Rule-regulated activities, sublimation of personal needs to organizations or persons of power and status	Accounting, finance, corporate management

behavior and actions. In contrast, individuals with an *external locus of control* believe that much of what happens to them is uncontrolled and determined by outside forces.

The many differences between internal and external locus of control can help explain some aspects of individual behavior in organizational settings. For example, since internals believe they control their own behavior, they are more active politically and socially and are more active in seeking information about their situations than are externals. Internals are more likely to try to influence or persuade others, are less likely to be influenced by others, and may be more achievement oriented than externals. For all these reasons, internals may be more highly motivated than externals. More differences between internals and externals are shown in Table 14.1.

▼ **Table 14.1** Differences between Internals and Externals in Organizational Settings

INDIVIDUAL BEHAVIOR	INTERNALS VERSUS EXTERNALS
Use of information	Externals make fewer attempts to acquire information and are more satisfied than internals with the amount of information they have. Internals are better at utilizing information than externals.
Independence	Externals are less independent than internals and more susceptible to the influence of others.
Performance	Internals perform better than externals on learning and problem-solving tasks when performance leads to valued rewards.
Satisfaction	Externals are less satisfied than internals and more alienated. Internals have a stronger job satisfaction/performance relationship than externals.
Motivation	Internals exhibit greater work motivation, expect that working hard leads to good performance, and feel more control over their performance and time commitment than externals.
Risk	Externals show less self-control and caution but engage in less risky behavior than internals.

An internal locus of control is an important personality characteristic of an entrepreneur, since these individuals are convinced that they play a role in determining their success or failure. Entrepreneurs tend to feel that they have control of their fate through their own efforts. Read about several such individuals and their unique ideas in Entrepreneurial Approach.[17] These individuals were motivated to take the steps needed to set up and run a new business, even in the face of adversity.[18]

Authoritarianism/Dogmatism Both **authoritarianism** and **dogmatism** deal with the rigidity of a person's beliefs.[19] A person high in authoritarianism tends to adhere rigidly to conventional values, readily obeys recognized authority, is concerned with toughness and power, and opposes the use of subjective feelings. As leaders, authoritarians expect unquestioning obedience to commands; as subordinates, they willingly give it. If a leader is authoritarian and his or her subordinate is not, frustration or conflict in the workplace may result.

A person high in dogmatism is closed-minded, sees the world as a threatening place, often regards legitimate authority as absolute, and accepts or rejects others according to how much they agree with the accepted authority. She or he performs acceptably in well-defined, routine situations, especially if there are time constraints. In other situations, especially those demanding creativity, the dogmatic individual will do poorly. Superiors possessing this trait tend to be rigid and closed. Dogmatic subordinates tend to want certainty imposed upon them.

Machiavellianism An individual with **Machiavellian personality** traits is someone who vies for and manipulates others for purely personal gain. Machiavellians feel that any behavior is acceptable if it achieves their goals. They are unemotional and detached, can be expected to take control, and try to exploit loosely structured situations. They perform well when there are substantial rewards for success and in jobs that require strong negotiation skills.[20]

Authoritarianism
The tendency to adhere rigidly to conventional values, readily obey recognized authority, be concerned with toughness and power, and oppose the use of feelings.

Dogmatism
The tendency to be closed-minded, see the world as a threatening place, regard legitimate authority as absolute, and accept or reject others according to agreement with the accepted authority.

Machiavellian personality
Someone who vies for and manipulates others purely for personal gain and feels that any behavior is acceptable if it achieves one's goals.

ENTREPRENEURIAL APPROACH

ACCIDENTAL ENTREPRENEURS: CONTROLLING THEIR EFFORTS AND FATE

What do Brian O'Donnell, David Swanson, and Ray Kroc (of McDonald's hamburger fame) have in common? All three are considered to be "accidental entrepreneurs"; that is, they started out to do one thing and somehow got sidetracked into creating a successful business.

Although many accidental entrepreneurs struggle to make their companies work, few attain fame. Probably the best-known accidental entrepreneur is the late Ray Kroc, who built the McDonald's hamburger empire. He was a 52-year-old malted milk machine salesman in 1955 when he spotted the original McDonald's restaurant in San Bernardino, California. Kroc's original idea was to make a fortune selling the malted milk mixers to a national chain of franchises. That was before he discovered how profitable hamburgers could be and bought out the two McDonald brothers.

Brian C. O'Donnell is probably a more typical accidental entrepreneur. He practices law in Barrington, Illinois, and uses some of his income from that profession to finance the company he formed to sell a snow shovel he invented for people with bad backs. As a child with back problems, he invented the "Snow Bully" while shoveling his father's 144-foot-long driveway. He put $15,000 into refining and manufacturing his invention, which has been successfully marketed in many parts of the United States.

David Swanson is another entrepreneur who manages to pursue two careers. By day he runs a team of computer troubleshooters for IBM. On the weekends, he runs GATS, Ltd., which operates model train shows across the country. Swanson got into train shows as a 14-year-old freshman in high school when he joined a train club and helped it stage a few local shows in veterans' halls and church basements. The shows became so successful that by 1984, when he formed his own company to run them, they were producing over $100,000 a year in revenues, and he was packing the local fairgrounds 10 times a year.

While accidental entrepreneurship comes from inspiration as well as desperation, most entrepreneurs are convinced that they play a role in determining their success or failure. Entrepreneurs tend to feel that they have control of their fate through their own efforts.

Type A and Type B Orientation   Your orientation toward Type A or Type B behavior has implications for your work and nonwork behaviors and your personal reactions to stress.[21] This personality dimension has attracted a lot of interest from medical and organizational researchers alike. Table 14.2 lists some of the common characteristics of the Type A personality.

Individuals with a **Type A orientation** are characterized by impatience, a desire for achievement, aggressiveness, irritability, and perfectionism. Type A orientation tendencies indicate obsessive behavior. This is a fairly widespread, but not always helpful, trait of managers. Many Type A individuals are hard-driving, detail-oriented people who have high performance standards and thrive on routine. But, when work obsessions are carried to an extreme, they may lead to a greater concern for details than for results, a resistance to change, excessive control of subordinates, and interpersonal difficulties.[22]

In contrast to Type A individuals, those with a **Type B orientation** are characteristically easygoing and less competitive in daily events. Type B indi-

Type A Orientation
Characterized by impatience, a desire for achievement, aggressiveness, irritability, and perfectionism.

Type B Orientation
Characterized as easy-going, relaxed, patient, able to listen carefully, and communicate more precisely than Type A individuals.

▼ **Table 14.2**   Common Characteristics of Type A Personality

- Signs of personal tension, such as clenched jaw and tight muscles.
- Chronic sense of being in a hurry.
- Frequent knee jiggling or finger tapping.
- Doing everything rapidly.
- Impatience with the normal pace of events. Tendency to finish others' sentences.
- Feelings of guilt when relaxing or taking a vacation.
- Polyphasic thoughts and actions, that is, a tendency to do several things simultaneously.
- Speech characterized by explosive accentuation, acceleration of the last few words of a sentence, and impatience when interrupted.
- Strong need to be an expert on a subject.
- Personal commitment to having rather than being.
- Belief that Type A attributes are what lead to success.

viduals appear to be more relaxed and patient than Type A individuals and listen more carefully and communicate more precisely.

Do you have a Type A or Type B personality? Before reading further, take a few minutes to respond to the seven descriptive characteristics found in Meeting the Challenge.[23] Then, calculate your score and determine whether you fit the Type A or Type B personality.

PERCEPTION

Perception can be defined as the way people experience, process, define, and interpret the world around them. It can be considered an information screen or filter that influences the way in which individuals communicate and become aware of sensations and stimuli that exist around them. Acting as a filter, perception helps individuals take in or see only certain elements in a particular situation.

Perceptions are influenced by a variety of factors including an individual's experiences, needs, personality, and education. As a result, a person's perceptions are not necessarily accurate. But they are unique and help to explain why two individuals may look at the same situation or message and perceive it differently. For example, marketing, accounting, and production managers of the same company will perceive the weekly sales data differently. Would you expect the presidents of Delta Airlines and the Airline Pilots Association (ALPA) to agree on the distribution of corporate profits? In addition, an individual's cultural background may influence his or her perception and interpretation of certain company messages or symbols.

The Perceptual Process
The perceptual process is quite complex. It involves selection, organization, and interpretation of environmental stimuli. First, we select or pay attention to some information and ignore other information, often without consciously realizing that we are doing so. For example, a hungry person is likely to focus on the food pictured in an advertisement for china, whereas a person who is not hungry may focus on the color and design of the china.

Next, we organize the information into a pattern and interpret it. How we interpret what we perceive also varies considerably. Depending on the circum-

MEETING THE CHALLENGE

TYPE A AND TYPE B PERSONALITY ORIENTATION

Rate the extent to which each of the following statements describes your behavior most of the time. Place a 1 (not typical of me), 2 (somewhat typical of me), or 3 (very typical of me) before each statement.

_____ 1. My greatest satisfaction comes from doing things better than others.

_____ 2. I tend to bring the theme of a conversation around to things I am interested in.

_____ 3. I get impatient waiting in line or when someone pulls in front of me on the highway.

_____ 4. I move, walk, and eat rapidly.

_____ 5. I feel guilty when I relax or do nothing for several hours or days.

_____ 6. Having more than others is important to me.

_____ 7. I am extremely impatient, especially with people who are slow talkers; I often hurry their speech or finish sentences for them.

_____ 8. One aspect of my life (work, family, school) dominates all other aspects.

_____ 9. I am preoccupied with having rather than doing.

_____ 10. I frequently try to do two or more things simultaneously.

_____ 11. I simply don't have enough time to lead a well-balanced life.

_____ 12. I have nervous habits, such as finger tapping, clenching my fists, and/or rapidly blinking my eyes.

_____ 13. I always play to win, even with children.

_____ 14. I evaluate life strictly in terms of numbers—salary, grades, number of clients, number of pages read, and so on.

_____ 15. I get things done faster and faster and crowd more and more into my day.

_____ 16. I take out my frustration with my own imperfections on others.

_____ Total points

Scores from 16 to 25 indicate a Type B orientation. Scores from 35 to 48 indicate a Type A orientation. Scores that fall between 26 and 34 indicate neither Type A nor Type B. In general, the higher the score, the more Type A behaviors you exhibit.

stances and our state of mind, we may interpret a wave of the hand as a friendly gesture or as a threat.

Errors in Perception: Learning to Manage and Handle Differences

The perceptual process we just described is filled with possibilities for errors in judgment or misunderstandings. While these perceptual errors or biases allow us to make quick judgments and provide data for making predictions, they can also result in significant mistakes that can be costly to individuals and organizations. We will explore several common errors, or distortions, in perception that have particular application in managerial situations including (1) stereotyping, (2) the halo and horn effect, and (3) selective perception.

Stereotyping   **Stereotyping** is the tendency to assign attributes to someone, not on individual characteristics, but solely on the basis of a category or group to which that person belongs. We readily expect someone identified as a professor, surgeon, police officer, or janitor to have certain attributes, even if we have not met the individual. Even identifying an employee by such broad categories as older worker, female, or Asian American, can lead to errors and misperceptions. Stereotyping may lead the perceiver to dwell on certain characteristics expected of all persons in the assigned category and to fail to recognize the characteristics that distinguish the person as an individual.

When we face new situations, stereotypes provide guidelines to help classify people. Unfortunately, stereotyping based on false premises may lead to a distorted view of reality because it assumes that all people of any one gender, race, or age have similar characteristics, and this simply isn't true. Stereotypes based on such factors as gender, age, and race can, and unfortunately still do, bias perceptions of employees in some organizations.[24] A recent study even found gender bias in the college classroom and demonstrated that male professors were perceived to be more effective than females even though their performance ratings were identical.[25]

Many organizations, such as Corning and Digital Equipment, have instituted classes to demonstrate how stereotyping can lead to inefficiency and turnover and to teach employees to manage a diverse workforce.[26] Digital, for example, helps people get in touch with their stereotypes and false assumptions through what it calls "Core Groups." These voluntary groups work with company-trained facilitators who encourage discussion and self-development. In the company's words, these groups operate "to keep people safe" as they struggle with their prejudices. Digital also runs a voluntary two-day training program called "Understanding the Dynamics of Diversity," which thousands of its employees have now taken.[27]

Halo and Horn Effect   The **halo and horn effect** refers to a process in which we evaluate and form and overall impression of an individual based solely on a specific trait or dimension, such as enthusiasm, gender, appearance, or intelligence. If we view the observed trait as positive, we tend to apply a halo (positive) effect to other traits. If we think of the observed trait as negative, we apply a horn (negative) effect. For example, a student who makes a good grade on the first test in a course may create a favorable impression with the instructor. The professor may then assume that the student is tops in all of her or his classes, a leader in many situations, efficient, honest, and loyal.

Keep in mind that when evaluations are made on the basis of traits that really aren't linked, halo and horn effects result. Of course, many traits are, in fact, related. So, not all judgments based on the halo and horn effect are really perceptual errors.

Selective Perception   **Selective perception** is the tendency to screen out information with which we aren't comfortable or don't want to be bothered. We have all been accused of listening only to what we want to hear or "tuning out" what we don't wish to hear. Both are examples of selective perception.

A classic research study of how selective perception influences managers involved executives in a manufacturing company.[28] When asked to identify the key problem in a comprehensive business policy case, all executives in the study selected a problem consistent with their own functional area work assignments. For example, most marketing executives viewed the key problem area as sales; production people tended to see it as a production problem; human resources people perceived it as a personnel issue. These differing viewpoints demonstrate how errors can occur and affect the way the executives would approach the problem.

Stereotyping
The tendency to assign attributes to someone, not on individual characteristics, but solely on the basis of a category or group to which that person belongs.

Halo and horn effect
The process in which we evaluate and form an overall impression of an individual based solely on a specific trait or dimension.

Selective perception
The tendency to screen out information with which we aren't comfortable or do not consider relevant.

▼ **Table 14.3**   Enhance Your Perception Skills: Learning to Identify Problems That Can Go Wrong

1. *Information isn't available.* This may be either because the necessary information doesn't reach you or because there are no sources of information. Try to seek out knowledgeable individuals in the organization as well as searching for quality information.

2. *Information isn't analyzed correctly or thoroughly.* Be sure to check to see whether the data are contradictory and you don't realize it, or whether the data contains errors you haven't previously caught.

3. *Characteristics of the data are overlooked.* Look for trends in the data that you may have missed, learn to distinguish facts from opinions, and devise systems that make the data easy to assimilate.

4. *Interrelationships among information, people, and things are overlooked.* Relationships between a problem occurring now and a solution to a related problem in the past may be overlooked. For example, an employee's skills may fit with the requirements of a new assignment. Also, seemingly unrelated projects may require the same personnel or resources. Learn to recognize how the deadline for one project affects the assignment of people to another project.

SOURCE: Adapted from P. Fandt, *Management Skills: Practice and Experience* (St. Paul, Minn.: West Publishing Co., 1994), 216.

In organizations, employees often make this perceptual error. Marketing employees pay close attention to marketing problems and issues, research and development (R&D) engineers pay close attention to product technology or R&D funding, and accountants focus on issues specifically related to their areas. These employees selectively perceive information that deals with other areas of the organization and focus only on information that is directly relevant to their own needs.

Reducing Perceptual Errors

Since perception is such an important process and plays a major role in determining our behavior, managers must be cognizant of the common perceptual errors. Managers who fall prey to perceptual errors, such as stereotyping, lose sight of individual differences among people. The quality of their decisions can suffer, and the performance of capable people will also suffer. Simple knowledge of perceptual errors, such as halo-horn errors, stereotype bias, and selective perception, is the first step in avoiding such mistakes.

The errors discussed in this section are only a few of the many factors that can affect the perceptual process. We have identified those most critical to organizations; these are also the errors most likely to influence managers. One step in becoming more perceptive is to recognize potential problems in the perception process. Table 14.3 lists some other common perception problems along with recommendations to enhance your perception skills.[29]

ABILITY

Ability is defined as an existing capacity to perform various tasks needed in a given situation. Abilities may be classified as mental, mechanical, and psychomotor.

In the organizational setting, ability along with effort are key determinants of employee behavior and performance. For example, *mental* or *intellectual ability* is important for problem solving because it involves the capacity to transform information, generate alternatives, memorize, and consider implica-

CORNING—TEACHING WORKERS A NEW WAY TO WORK

Corning believes that U.S. workers must learn new ways to work, and it is prepared to invest in those who are willing to learn. The emphasis at Corning's Blacksburg, Virginia plant is on teamwork, job rotation, flexible scheduling, and self-management. The job requirements for production workers include problem-solving abilities and a willingness to work in a team setting.

Corning has invested heavily in both technical and interpersonal skills training for its employees. Employees spend one-fifth of their time in training and earn pay increases for mastering new skills. In the first year of production at the Blacksburg plant, 25 percent of all hours worked were devoted to training. The cost was about $750,000.

Everyone at the Blacksburg plant works shifts of 12.5 hours in alternating three-day and four-day weeks. Employees belong to 14-member teams. The teams set their own goals, make schedules, assign work, discipline co-workers for shoddy production, and make managerial decisions. All this is a stark contrast to the plant's former assembly line organization where each employee worked alone at one and only one job. There are no timeclocks in the plant and no supervisors—just eight managers. The plant has only two levels of management—the plant manager and two "line leaders" who advise teams but do not supervise them.

tions. *Mechanical ability* refers to the capacity to comprehend relationships between objects and to perceive how parts fit together. *Psychomotor ability* includes such things as manual dexterity, eye-hand coordination, and manipulative ability. The key point is that not only do employee' abilities vary substantially but different tasks will require different abilities. Such recognition is crucial to understanding and predicting work behaviors.

Up to this point, we have focused on individual behavior. However, individuals act differently in groups than when they are alone. In the next part of the chapter, we explore groups since, in most organizations, group work is required for organizational effectiveness. For example, Managing for Excellence profiles Corning's emphasis on groups.[30] Corning believes that U.S. workers must learn new ways to work, and it is willing to make an investment in those who are committed to learn. The emphasis at its Blacksburg, Virginia plant is on teamwork, job rotation, flexible scheduling, and self-management.

UNDERSTANDING GROUP BEHAVIOR: ESSENCE OF QUALITY PRODUCTS AND SERVICES

Although groups have always been a central part of the organization, they are gaining increasing attention as potentially important organizational assets. Professionals rarely work alone—they work with their colleagues and with their manager. Accordingly, managers are concerned with creating effective groups that make real contributions to quality products and services and thus the continuing success of the total organization.[31]

We define a **group** as two or more interdependent individuals who interact with and influence one another in order to accomplish a common purpose.[32] Our definition recognizes that a group can involve as few as two people, that group success depends on the interdependent and collective ef-

Group
Two or more interdependent individuals who interact with and influence one another to accomplish a common purpose.

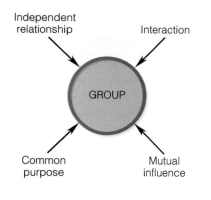

Independent relationship

Interaction

GROUP

Common purpose

Mutual influence

▼ **Figure 14.1**
Requirements of a Group

forts of various group members, and that group members are likely to have significant impacts on one another as they work together. This definition also helps us differentiate a group from a mere aggregate of individuals. In recent years, *team* has become a popular word in the business community, often replacing the word *group*. The terms group and team are similar, however, and for our purposes, they will be used interchangeably.

Four specific requirements of a group are shown in Figure 14.1.[33] First, the group members have an interdependent relationship with one another; they are dependent on one another to accomplish the group work. Second, this interdependence dictates that group members must interact through conversation or work activities. Third, a group is characterized by a condition of mutual influence between group members, rather than a situation in which all the power is held by a minority in the group. Fourth, groups have a common purpose, such as accomplishing work goals, completing a project, or preparing a report.

In the performance of organizational work, there are two basic types of groups—formal and informal. Both groups influence, either positively or negatively, the work performed. We examine the two types of groups and their influence on behavior in the next section.

TYPES OF GROUPS

Groups come in many forms, shapes, and sizes. Most managers belong to several different groups at the same time, some at work, some in the community, some formally organized, and some informal and social in nature.

Formal Groups

Formal groups
Deliberately created to accomplish goals and serve the needs of the organization.

Formal groups are deliberately created by the organization's managers to accomplish goals and serve the needs of the organization. The major purpose of formal groups is to perform specific tasks and achieve specific objectives defined by the organization. The most common type of formal work group consists of individuals cooperating under the direction of a leader. Examples of formal groups are departments, divisions, task forces, project groups, quality circles, committees, and boards of directors. Boeing's quality improvement teams, which were described in the Managerial Incident, are considered formal groups.

Informal Groups

Informal groups
Self-created groups that evolve out of the formal organization based on proximity, common interests, or needs of individuals.

Informal groups in organizations are not formed or planned by the organization's managers. Rather, they are self-created and evolve out of the formal organization for a variety of reasons, such as proximity, common interests, or needs of individuals. It would be difficult to design an organization that prohibits informal working relationships from developing.

Because human beings receive reassurance from interacting with others and being part of a group, informal groups can meet a range of individual needs. Perhaps the major reason informal groups evolve is to fulfill individuals' needs for affiliation and friendship, social interaction, communication, power, safety, and status. For example, individuals who regularly eat lunch or go to a football game together are members of an informal group that fulfills some of these needs. While some informal groups may complement the organization's formal groups, at times they can also work against the organization's goals.

A number of factors affect the way that groups operate and their ultimate effectiveness. First, we will examine the group developmental sequence, and then we will turn our attention to the five dimensions that influence group effectiveness.

▼ In an effort to assure the highest standards of quality and reliability, Boeing formed design teams like the one shown here. Team members work concurrently, share their knowledge with one another, and evaluate designs from a multidisciplinary perspective.

GROUP FORMATION AND DEVELOPMENT

The group development process is dynamic. While most groups are in a continual state of change and rarely ever reach complete stability, the group development process does follow a general pattern. Groups appear to go through a five-stage developmental sequence: forming, storming, norming, performing, and adjourning.[34]

Stages of Group Development

The types of behaviors observed in groups differ from stage to stage. The length of time spent in each stage can also vary greatly, with each stage lasting until its paramount issues are essentially resolved. The group then moves on. The stages are not clearly delineated, and there is some overlap between them. In other words, the process of group development is ongoing and complex. New groups may progress through these stages, but if the group's membership changes, the development of the group may regress to an earlier stage, at least temporarily.

Forming   In the forming stage, members focus their efforts on seeking basic information, defining goals, developing procedures for performing the task, and making a preliminary evaluation of how the group might interact to accomplish goals. There is often a great deal of uncertainty at this point as group members begin to test the extent to which their input will be valued.

Groups in the forming stage often require some time for members to get acquainted with each other before attempting to proceed with the task responsibilities. It is a time for members to become acquainted, understand leadership and member roles, and learn what is expected of them.[35] The following behaviors are common for individuals in the forming stage of group development:

- Keeping feelings to themselves until they know the situation.
- Acting more secure than they actually feel.
- Experiencing confusion and uncertainty about what is expected.
- Being polite.

▼ In the forming stage, members focus their efforts on seeking basic information, defining goals, developing procedures for performing the task, and making a preliminary evaluation of how the group might interact to accomplish goals. The group pictured here is taking time for members to get acquainted with each other before attempting to proceed with the task responsibilities.

- Trying to size up the personal benefits and personal costs of being involved in the group.
- Accepting dependence on a powerful person.

Storming   In the storming stage, group members frequently experience conflict with one another as they locate and attempt to resolve differences of opinion about key issues, relative priorities of goals, who is to be responsible for what, and the task-related direction of the leader. Competition for the leadership role and conflict over goals are dominant themes at this stage. Some members may withdraw or try to isolate themselves from the emotional tension that is generated. Groups with members from diverse backgrounds or cultures may experience greater conflict than more homogenous groups.

It is important at this stage not to suppress or withdraw from the conflict. Suppressing conflict will likely create bitterness and resentment, which will last long after members attempt to express their differences and emotions. Withdrawal can cause the group to fail more quickly.

Norming   During the norming stage, a real sense of cohesion and teamwork begins to emerge. Group members feel good about each other and identify with the group. They share feelings, give and receive feedback, and begin to share a sense of success. The norming stage is a junction point.[36] If the issues have not been resolved, then the group will erupt into serious conflict and runs the risk of falling into groupthink. Groupthink occurs when the feeling of cohesion overrides the realistic appraisal of alternative courses of action.[37] But groupthink does not have to occur. The other option for the norming stage is to develop the potential for exchanging all kinds of information relevant to a task. An organized group is primed for the exchange of information that will help the members accomplish their task effectively.[38]

Performing   The performing stage, when the group is fully functional, is the most difficult to achieve. The interpersonal relations in this stage are marked by high levels of interdependence. The group is oriented to maintaining good relations and to getting its task accomplished. Group members can now work well with everyone in the group, communication is constant, decisions are made with full agreement, and members understand the roles they need to perform for the group to be highly effective.[39]

At the performing stage, the group has learned to solve complex problems and implement the solutions. Members are committed to the task and willing to experiment to solve problems. Cohesion has progressed to the point of collaboration. Confidence reaches a high level for the few groups who achieve this stage. Unfortunately, even if a group reaches this stage, it still faces the difficult job of staying there.

Adjourning   The adjourning stage involves the termination of task behaviors and disengagement from relations-oriented behaviors. Some groups, such as a project team created to investigate and report on a specific program within a limited time frame, have a well-defined point of adjournment. Other groups, such as an executive committee, may go on indefinitely. Adjourning for this type of group is more subtle and takes place when one or more key members leave the organization.

INFLUENCES ON GROUP BEHAVIOR AND EFFECTIVENESS

Managers must understand the developmental sequence of groups because each stage can ultimately influence the group's effectiveness. In addition to the developmental process, research has identified several group dimensions that can have an effect on group behavior and effectiveness. For example, a recent study investigated the relationship between the organization's executive team and organizational performance. The results indicated a strong relationship between performance, team structure, and the team's context.[40] The next section discusses several of the key dimensions and attributes that make a group effective.

Effective Work Groups: Achieving Quality

An effective work group is one that achieves high levels of both task performance and human resource maintenance over time.[41] For example, Vans, a California-based shoe manufacturer, sells its shoes at 68 company-owned stores in California and throughout a nationwide network of retailers including Nordstroms, Athlete's Foot, and Foot Locker. Whereas most of Vans's competitors need six months to fill customer orders, Vans takes 19 days. By providing this short cycle, Vans allows its customers to sell more of a product or style when it is a hot item. Vans also keeps inventories lean and virtually eliminates end-of-season discounts that cost retailers important profits. To accomplish this type of service excellence, Vans developed two new systems and incorporated these practices throughout the organization. First, unlike most footwear companies that produce their goods in China, South Korea, or Malaysia, Vans makes its shoes in the United States. Second, an innovative team-based manufacturing system boosts productivity. Vans organizes its nonunion factory workers into teams and gives each team a daily quota; when the quota is filled, the team members go home, paid for eight hours even though the work usually takes less time. The teams minimize the need for expensive managers. In fact, the production facility has only three managers. Three managers supervise 1,700 factory workers, and Vans has never missed a deadline or lost a customer.[42]

With respect to task performance, an effective group achieves its performance goals. With respect to human resource maintenance, an effective group is one whose members are sufficiently satisfied with their task, accomplishments, and interpersonal relationships to work well together on an ongoing

▼ **Table 14.4**   Developing Your Team Member Skills About Being a Good Team Member

- ALWAYS deliver on time and alert your team ASAP when unexpected delays occur.
- ALWAYS attend all team meetings—on time, unless in the hospital or in jail.
- ALWAYS speak up, speak out, and interact at all team meetings.
- ALWAYS take personal interest in planning and problem solving.
- ALWAYS look for ways to go-the-second-mile on your own.
- NEVER tell your teammates or leader how much time and effort you are putting into your assignments.
- NEVER assume the roll of resident critic and complainer.
- NEVER tattle and conduct witch-hunts. Teams don't need bounty hunters.
- NEVER wait for someone to tell/ask you what to do next.
- NEVER procrastinate and make excuses.

SOURCE: L. Harrisberger, *Succeeding: How to Become an Outstanding Professional* (New York: Macmillan, 1994), 100. Used with permission.

basis.[43] The following is a classic listing of the characteristics of an effective group:[44]

- Members are loyal to one another and the leader.
- Members and leaders have a high degree of confidence and trust in each other.
- The group is eager to help members develop to their full potential.
- The members communicate fully and frankly all information relevant to the group's activities.
- Members feel secure in making decisions that seem appropriate to them.
- Activities of the group occur in a supportive atmosphere.
- Group values and goals express relevant values and needs of members.

In his recent career development handbook, *Succeeding: How To Become an Outstanding Professional*, Lee Harrisberger provides tips for being a good team member; following them will increase the chances that the group will be effective.[45] Review the list in Table 14.4 as you become part of a work group either in the classroom or in an organization. The tips will help to enhance your team member skills.

Achieving group effectiveness is no simple task, but managers can aid the process by being aware of the dimensions that influence groups. In the next section, we consider some of the most important dimensions influencing group effectiveness.

Dimensions Influencing Group Effectiveness

Numerous dimensions can affect how effectively the group functions. Here we will examine five important factors that managers need to consider, including size, membership composition, roles, norms, and cohesiveness. These are particularly important in the global environment where team members are often very diverse.

Size   Effective task groups can range from 2 members to a normal upper limit of 16. It is difficult to pinpoint an ideal group size because the appropriate size depends on the group's purpose.[46]

Size affects how individuals interact with each other as well as the overall performance of the group. In groups of less than five members, there will be more personal discussion and more complete participation. As a group grows beyond several members, it becomes more difficult for all members to parti-

▼ Group size affects how individuals interact with each other as well as the overall performance of the group. As a group grows it becomes more difficult for all members to participate, communicate, and coordinate effectively. As pictured here, there is a tendency to split into subgroups.

cipate effectively. Communication and coordination among members become more difficult, and there is a tendency to split into subgroups. As a result, the interactions become more centralized, with a few individuals taking more active roles relative to the rest; disagreements may occur more easily; and group satisfaction may decline unless group members put a good deal of effort into relationship-oriented roles.

As group size increases, more potential human resources are available to perform the work and accomplish needed tasks. While this can boost performance, the expanded size tends to increase turnover and absenteeism, as well as provide opportunities for social loafing. Social loafing describes a tendency of people not to work as hard in groups as they would individually. This phenomenon occurs because their contribution is less noticeable and they are willing to let others carry the workload.[47]

Social loafing directly challenges the logic that the productivity of the group as a whole should at least equal the sum of the productivity of each individual in the group. In other words, group size and individual performance may be inversely related. Most students are acquainted with the concept of social loafing, largely as a result of negative experiences they have encountered in working on group projects.[48]

Membership Composition   Two composition factors are particularly important influences on a group's effectiveness. The first factor is the members' characteristics, which include physical traits, abilities, job-related knowledge and skills, personality, age, race, and gender. The second factor encompasses the reasons why members are attracted to a particular group, such as their needs, motivations, and power.

Membership composition can be homogeneous or heterogeneous. A group is considered homogeneous when it is composed of individuals having similar, group-related characteristics, backgrounds, interests, values, attitudes, and the like. When the individuals are dissimilar with respect to these characteristics, the group is heterogeneous. Most heterogeneous groups are a function of increases in organizational diversity.

Does homogeneous or heterogeneous composition lead to more effective groups? Managers face this difficult question every time they assemble a group. A manager needs to understand the purpose of the group and the nature of the task to determine whether the group is better served by a homogeneous or a heterogeneous composition.

▼ The diverse membership of the work group pictured here makes this a heterogeneous group.

Roles
Shared expectations of how group members will fulfill the requirements of their positions.

Task-oriented roles
Behaviors directly related to establishing and achieving the goals of the group or getting the task done.

Relationship-oriented roles
Behaviors that cultivate the well-being, continuity, and development of the group.

Self-oriented roles
Behaviors that meet some personal need or goal of an individual without regard to the group's problems.

Norms
Unwritten and often informal rules and shared beliefs about what behavior is appropriate and expected of group members.

For tasks that are standard and routine, a homogeneous group functions more quickly. Membership homogeneity contributes to member satisfaction, creates less conflict, and increases the chances for harmonious working relationships among group members. If a group is too homogeneous, however, it may exert excessive pressure on group members to conform to the group's rules.[49]

For tasks that are nonroutine and require diverse skills, opinions, and behaviors, a heterogeneous group yields better results. We saw in our earlier example that Boeing's management created heterogeneous groups for their quality performance teams. A heterogeneous membership can bring a variety of skills and viewpoints to bear on problems and thus facilitate task accomplishment. The more heterogeneous the membership, however, the more skilled the manager or group leader will have to be in facilitating a successful group experience.

Roles   **Roles** are shared expectations of how group members will fulfill the requirements of their positions. People develop their roles based on their own expectations, the group's expectations, and the organization's expectations. As employees internalize the expectations of these three sources, they develop their roles.

People often have multiple roles within the same group.[50] For example, a professor may have the roles of teacher, researcher, writer, consultant, adviser, and committee member. Our roles also extend outside the workplace. The professor may also be a family member, belong to professional and civic organizations, and have social friends, all of whom may have very different expectations.

When operating in a work group, individuals typically fulfill several roles. Member roles fit into three categories: (1) task-oriented, (2) relationship-oriented, and (3) self-oriented roles. As Figure 14.2 shows, each of these categories includes a variety of different role behaviors.

Task-oriented roles focus on behaviors directly related to establishing and achieving the goals of the group or getting the task done. They include seeking and providing information, initiating actions and procedures, clarifying issues, summarizing progress, energizing the quantity and quality of output, and helping the group reach a consensus.

Relationship-oriented goals include behaviors that cultivate the well-being, continuity, and development of the group. They focus on the operation of the group and the maintenance of good relationships among members. They help foster group unity, positive interpersonal relations among group members, and the development of the members' ability to work effectively together.

Self-oriented roles occur to meet some personal need or goal of an individual without regard for the group's problems. They often have a negative influence on a group's effectiveness.[51] Examples of such behaviors include dominating the group discussion, emphasizing personal issues, interrupting others, distracting the group from its work, and wasting the group's time.

Norms   **Norms** are unwritten and often informal rules and shared beliefs about what behavior is appropriate and expected of group members. Norms differ from organizational rules in that they are unwritten and group members must accept them and behave in ways consistent with them before they can be said to exist.[52] This difference is important when dealing with heterogeneous and diverse groups.

A typical work group may have norms that define how people dress, the upper and lower limits on acceptable productivity, the information that can be told to the boss, and the matters that need to remain secret. If a group member does not follow the norms, the other members will try to enforce compliance through acceptance and friendship or through such means as ridicule, ostracism, sabotage, and verbal abuse.

As the Hawthorne Studies demonstrated many years ago, work groups establish a variety of norms, which are not always aligned with the formal standards set by the organization. Group norms can be positive, helping the group meet its objective(s), or they can be negative, hindering the group's effectiveness. Managers need to understand the norms of the groups they manage and then work toward maintaining and developing positive norms, while eliminating negative norms.

Status Relationships   **Status** refers to the perceived social ranking of one member relative to other members of the group. As group members interact, they develop respect for one another on numerous dimensions. The more respect, prestige, influence, and power a group member has, the higher his or her status within the group.

Staus is based on several factors, including a member's job title, wage or salary, seniority, knowledge or expertise, interpersonal skills, appearance, education, race, age, role, and gender. Group status depends upon the group's goals and objectives, norms, and degree of cohesiveness. Members who conform to the group's norms tend to have higher status than members who do not, although a group is more willing to overlook a high-status member breaking a norm. High-status members also have more influence on the development of the group's norms and can have a major impact on the group's performance. Lower-status members tend to copy high-status members' behaviors and standards.

Status
The perceived social ranking of one member relative to other members of the group.

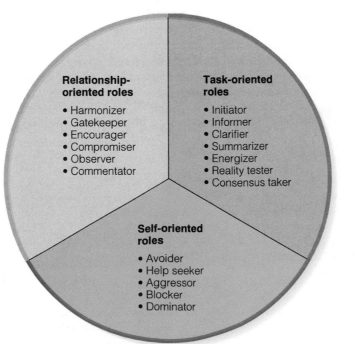

▼ **Figure 14.2**
Group Roles and Associated Behaviors

Another aspect of status that influences group effectiveness is status congruence. Status congruence is the acceptance and satisfaction members receive from their group status. Members who are not satisfied with their status may not be active participants of the group. They may physically or mentally escape from the group and not perform to their full potential. Or they may cause group conflict as they fight for a higher status level. Leadership struggles often go on for long periods or may never be resolved resulting in lowered performance levels.[53]

Cohesiveness

The strength of the members' desires to remain in the group.

Cohesiveness   Have you ever been a member of a group whose members seemed to get along and work well with one another, were highly motivated, and worked in a coordinated way? When a group behaves in this way, it is considered to be cohesive. **Cohesiveness** is defined as the strength of the members' desires to remain in the group, their commitment to it, and their ability to function together as a unit. It is influenced by the degree of compatibility between group goals and individual members' goals. A group whose members have a strong desire to remain in the group and personally accept its goals would be considered highly cohesive.

The degree of group cohesion is an important dimension influencing group effectiveness. Cohesiveness can impact communication and the job satisfaction of group members. For example, members of cohesive groups tend to communicate more frequently, are likely to feel more satisfied with their jobs, are more committed to working through issues, think more favorably of group members, and experience less conflict than members of groups that are not cohesive.[54]

Nevertheless, though we often assume that the more cohesive a group is, the better the group functions, it is important to recognize that cohesion may also have negative effects. High cohesiveness may actually be associated with low effectiveness if group goals are contrary to organizational goals or if members are more concerned with the group itself than with the goals of the organization.[55] Therefore, the relationship between cohesion and effectiveness cannot be anticipated or understood unless the group's goals and norms are also known. The relationship between group cohesiveness, group effectiveness, and group norms is shown in Table 14.5.

Overall, managers should strive to promote cohesiveness among work group members because group cohesiveness can be an extremely positive organizational force when it helps unite a group behind organizational goals. For example, the Boston Celtics have been the world basketball champions numerous times. Sportswriters and sports fans have frequently commented that Boston didn't necessarily have the most talent in the years they won the league championship. True, the Celtics had good players and a few stars, but they weren't unbeatable. What made the difference? Celtic pride and their ability to blend together as a cohesive unit are often cited as the reasons for their

▼ **Table 14.5**   The Relationship between Group Cohesiveness, Group Effectiveness, and Group Norms

Norms	COHESIVENESS OF THE WORK GROUP	
	High	Low
Aligned with organization	Highest performance	Moderate performance
Not aligned with organization	Low performance	Moderate to low performance

success. Team members were committed; they knew each others' strengths and weaknesses; they brought problems to the surface; they worked hard at being a team.[56] These abilities and people skills are basically the same regardless of whether you play for the Celtics, work for a large corporation like General Motors or IBM, or are employed by a small company with only a handful of employees.

On the other hand, cohesiveness can be a negative factor when it impedes productivity and causes opposition to needed changes. For example, recall our discussion of groupthink, an agreement-at-any-cost mentality that results in ineffective group decision making. Highly cohesive groups may be prone to groupthink.[57]

As organizations become increasingly diverse in terms of gender, race, ethnicity, and nationality, this diversity brings potential benefits such as better decision making, greater creativity and innovation, and more successful marketing to different types of customers. But increased cultural differences within a workforce can also make it harder to develop cohesive work groups and may result in higher turnover, interpersonal conflict, and communication breakdowns.[58]

Managers must be aware of these issues as they work to create high-performance groups. They need to be trained to capitalize on the benefits of diversity while minimizing the potential costs. Additionally, managers will need to work to integrate minority-culture members both formally and informally and strive to eliminate prejudice and discrimination to reduce alienation and build organizational identity among minority group members. The organization that achieves these conditions will create an environment in which all members can contribute to their maximum potential and in which the value of diversity can be fully realized.[59]

MANAGING GROUPS FOR EFFECTIVENESS

Most managers have mixed feelings about working with committees, task forces, and other groups. Sometimes they are a total waste of time and have difficulty accomplishing even the simplest tasks. Some of the most common problems encountered in work groups are described in Table 14.6.[60]

Groups can also be incredibly effective. Stephen Wolf, CEO of United Airlines (UAL), strongly believes that groups can be very effective. While running Republic Airlines in 1984, and later as CEO at Flying Tigers, Inc., he assembled close-knit management groups that helped revive the carriers and lure buyers. In his five years at UAL, Wolf has relied on a group of five vice presidents to advise him on how to run the airline. Each vice president plays a vital role in the day-to-day operations of the airline. If Wolf has to make big decisions, he depends on this inner circle, which has become an effective team at UAL.[61]

To increase the likelihood that the group will be effective, a manager can diagnose the group dimensions we discussed earlier—size, member composition, roles, status relationships, norms, and cohesiveness. Consider how each of the following tips for managing groups can enhance managerial and organizational effectiveness and how you can use them to develop a productive work group:

- Match the group size with the demands of the task that needs to be accomplished.
- For routine, standard tasks, consider a homogeneous group to increase the chances for harmonious working relationships among group members. For

▼ **Table 14.6**   Common Problems Encountered in Working with Groups

- *Personality and work style differences.* Team members bring a range of individual differences, motivations, and work styles to the group. Some people see a project, job, or class assignment as just one more of "life's little requirements." Their primary goal is to get it done and move on. For others, the project or task is an important personal statement. They take pride in their contribution. Work styles also differ. Some members will take a highly structured, meticulous approach. Such rigidity can stifle more freewheeling members.

- *Poor task/problem definition.* Groups often see their role in terms of problem solving and getting the job done. Unless the real issues are carefully identified, the group may find a quick solution to the wrong problem, and ineffective performance can result.

- *Poor preparation.* Groups often use meetings ineffectively. A lack of focus, unstructured discussions, and unprepared members can lead to wasted time and little real decision making or action.

- *Difficulties in compromising.* Inflexibility and the desire by some members to "win the argument" are common problems in groups. Some members come into a discussion with their minds made up and are not interested in new information; they fail to be good listeners.

- *Lack of empathy.* Group members may view the project only in terms of their own efforts and fail to see the contributions of other members. It becomes easy to dismiss problems that don't affect them personally.

- *Poor conflict management skills.* Conflict can be either productive or destructive. It can be helpful if it expands the pool of ideas, helps to clarify issues, and prevents a group from reaching a premature consensus. In contrast, conflict is detrimental if it becomes personal and leads to infighting and drains the energy of group members.

- *Lack of cohesiveness.* Groups that lack cohesiveness fail to function effectively as a unit. Cohesive groups share common goals, and members are committed to understanding and helping each other. Cohesion is an important variable in predicting the ability of groups of people to identify and solve problems.

SOURCE: Adapted from K. C. Green and D. T. Seymour, *Who's Going to Run General Motors?* (Princeton, N.J.: Peterson's Guides, 1991), 66–68.

nonroutine tasks that require diverse skills and opinions, consider a heterogeneous group.

- Examine the task-, relationship-, and self-oriented roles that group members have acquired.
- Investigate the various status relationships among group members.
- Consider what the group's norms are. Do the group's norms match the organization's norms?
- Determine the group's level of cohesiveness.

MANAGERIAL IMPLICATIONS

Developing effective work groups is an even greater challenge when a group or team consists of members from different cultures and with different ethnic backgrounds. Effective groups require that members shed some of their notions of individualism and accept a different set of philosophies in the workplace. We conclude this chapter by providing some guidelines for creating more effective groups. For a group to be successful, the following elements must be developed:[62]

- *Trust.* Employees and management have to learn not be wary of each other. Lack of trust is an obstacle to flexibility and information flow.
- *Involvement.* Every group member's participation counts, and people are dependent on each other, regardless of where they fit into the hierarchy.
- *Emphasis on others' strengths, not weaknesses.* Employees must look for ways to complement, rather than compete with, each other.
- *Persuasive and nonpaternalistic leadership.* Managers must become good listeners and be willing to involve others in decision making. Everyone must take personal responsibility for completing the task.
- *Precise objectives.* Members need to have clearly defined problems with precise goals and specific deadlines.

This chapter has examined the foundations of individual and group behavior. We discussed some of the ways in which individuals differ, including attitudes, personality, perceptions, and ability. When organizations are made up of individuals with diverse characteristics such as physical traits, abilities, job-related knowledge and skills, personality, age, race, and gender, merely placing employees in groups does not mean they will be effective. Clearly, the establishment of productive groups challenges managers. This is no easy task, although it can be important for managerial success.

BOEING DISCOVERS A NEW STRATEGY TO ENHANCE PERFORMANCE

MANAGERIAL INCIDENT RESOLUTION

To implement the team concept, Boeing started by increasing awareness. People had to understand what was going to change, and they had to be kept informed about what was happening. Next, managment demonstrated their commitment to the concept. Third, they developed special training courses to provide skills for implementing this new way of working together.

Now quality improvement teams are specifically charted to focus attention on a particular problem. To make sure that the right people—those with the knowledge, work skills, interest, and responsibility—are on a team, top management selects the members of each team. This means that any combination of employees may be on a team, ranging from line workers to supervisors, from engineers to managers. The team works together until it comes up with a solution, and then it is dissolved.

Teams work on developing strong relationships between management and nonmanagement people, and workers are expressing positive attitudes toward the change in the work environment. To facilitate communication, Boeing is fostering an environment in which workers will communicate with the right people when they see something wrong, or when they see something that can be done more efficiently.

Although Boeing is still in the process of implementing these team systems throughout the organization, the company has already seen a number of benefits—increased employee morale, lower turnover, reduced scrap and rework, and improvements in the bottom line.

The feedback from workers who have been involved in the new process has been overwhelmingly positive. Workers feel that management has finally recognized that they have some good ideas for improving the company. They express a more positive attitude and greater sense of belonging than before the system was put in place. Also, increased interaction between people from different departments and levels of management is giving workers a better picture of the overall product, the quality goals of the organization, and their roles in meeting those goals. One workers says, "You know, it's really great to come to work now. I really feel a part of the team. Before, I just put in my time, but now I feel like I'm really contributing and that my efforts have a greater impact on how well the company can perform."

Boeing is a believer in the team approach to running an organization. Expectations are running high that the team-designed strategy will do for Boeing what similar changes have done for Procter & Gamble, General Motors, and Champion International.[63] ▼

SUMMARY

- Attitudes are relatively lasting beliefs, feelings, and behavioral tendencies held by a person about specific objects, events, groups, issues, or persons.

- There is no direct relationship between job satisfaction and job performance. In some situations, job satisfaction may cause high job performance; in other situations, job performance may cause higher job satisfaction, or the two may be unrelated. Thus, the relationship between the two concepts will depend on a complex set of personal and situational variables.

- Personality is the organized and distinctive pattern of behavior that characterizes an individual's adaptation to a situation; it endures over time and suggests tendencies to behave in certain ways. Several personality traits that have been linked to work behavior and performance include self-esteem, locus of control, authoritarianism/dogmatism, Machiavellianism, and Type A/Type B orientation.

- Perception is the way people experience, process, define, and interpret the world around them. Perceptual biases, such as stereotyping, halo and horn effects, and selective perception, cause managers to make errors that can be costly to the organization and to individuals.

- To reduce perceptual errors, managers must make a conscious effort to attend to relevant information, actively seek evidence of whether or not their perceptions are accurate, compare their perceptions with those of others, and look for objective measures in relation to their own perceptions.

- A group is defined as two or more interdependent individuals who interact with and influence one another in order to accomplish a common purpose. Groups can be classified as formal or informal.

- While most groups are in a continual state of change, the group development process generally follows a five-stage developmental sequence: forming, storming, norming, performing, and adjourning.

- Achieving group effectiveness is no simple task, but awareness of the six dimensions that influence groups should help in this endeavor. These dimensions include group size, composition, roles, norm, status relationships, and cohesiveness.

KEY TERMS

Attitudes (p. 459)	Locus of control (p. 461)	Stereotyping (p. 467)
Job satisfaction (p. 459)	Authoritarianism (p. 463)	Halo and horn effect (p. 467)
Organizational commitment (p. 460)	Dogmatism (p. 463)	Selective perception (p. 467)
Job involvement (p. 460)	Machiavellian personality (p. 463)	Group (p. 469)
Personality (p. 461)	Type A orientation (p. 464)	Formal groups (p. 470)
Self-esteem (p. 461)	Type B orientation (p. 464)	Informal groups (p. 470)

Roles (p. 476)   Self-oriented roles (p. 476)   Status (p. 477)
Task-oriented roles (p. 476)   Norms (p. 476)   Cohesiveness (p. 478)
Relationship-oriented roles (p. 476)

REVIEW QUESTIONS

1. Define attitudes and describe three relevant work-related attitudes that are important for managers to understand.

2. Discuss the relationship between job satisfaction and performance.

3. Identify and explain the difference between stereotyping and the halo effect.

4. Name a common stereotype. What attributes do you give that person?

5. Why would a manager need to understand an employee's locus of control?

6. Explain three types of ability.

7. Distinguish between a formal group and an informal group.

8. Define and discuss the five stages of group development.

9. Identify and discuss the six key dimensions that affect group effectiveness.

10. Describe the attributes of an effective group. Provide examples from your own experience or from an organization that you have read about in a recent publication.

DISCUSSION QUESTIONS

Improving Critical Thinking

1. Why are organizations concerned with job satisfaction?

2. Have you ever violated group norm? Discuss your behavior and the group's reaction.

3. Describe an effective and an ineffective group in which you have been a member. What role(s) did you play? What status did you have in the group? How cohesive was the group? What could you have done to make the group more effective?

4. Describe a stereotypical group to which you belong. What people or things belong to the group? Give an example of a member of the group who does not fit the stereotype.

Enhancing Communication Skills

5. Explain the ways managers can learn to reduce the perceptual errors that occur in the workplace. Prepare a presentation for a small group or the class that includes specific examples.

6. Identify and describe (either in writing or in a presentation) a formal group that you are a part of, and then describe any informal groups that exist within the formal group.

Building Teamwork Skills

7. Describe a group of which you have been a member and discuss its development over time. Did the group seem to proceed through all of the stages of group development? Why or why not? If you are not already part of a group for this class, form small groups as directed by your instructor and reach some consensus on your responses.

8. Find an article in a current business magazine that describes how an organization is using groups to increase quality or organizational performance. Form a small group as directed by your instructor and share your findings with the group. Have the group select the best article and share it with the class.

ETHICS: TAKE A STAND

Steve is a member of a group of four assigned to write a report on ethics in the workplace for a management class. The irony of the situation is that he is faced with an ethical dilemma. It is the day the report is due, and he has discovered that Jane, another member of the group, has plagiarized her portion of the report.

Steve immediately told the other members of the group about the situation. The other members were good friends with Jane and were sympathetic to her personal situation. She was under a lot of pressure to perform well in this class. She had two children and was working her way through school.

Because of some personal demands last semester, she was put on academic probation. Anything less than a B in this course, and she would be forced to leave school. Besides, the group members did not want to be responsible for having her expelled. They felt justified in ignoring this new knowledge and taking their chances with the report as it was written. After all, "they hadn't plagiarized." Everyone in the group felt that the report would earn an A. Why start trouble with the professor? they asked. There was little time remaining. Steve felt his options were severely limited.

For Discussion

1. How would you suggest Steve handle the situation? What are his options?
2. Discuss the group's norms.
3. In which stage of development is the group? Will this affect the action taken?
4. If you were the professor, how would you handle the situation if Steve told you what had happened?

THINKING CRITICALLY
Debate the Issue

DO GROUPS ENHANCE PERFORMANCE?

Form small teams as directed by your instructor. Half of the teams should take the position that using groups in the organization can enhance performance. The other teams should take the position that groups do not enhance performance. Use current periodicals and references other than the material presented in the chapter to develop your team's position. Your instructor will select two teams to present their ideas in a debate format.

VIDEO CASE

Valley School Supply: Where Employees Get High Marks

For a while Valley School Supply seemed about to fail, but this school-products distributor, based in Appleton, Wisconsin, passed the crucial test of surviving technical insolvency. It now concentrates on doing what it knows best. And it does it better.

The company's near disaster was rooted in an acquisition-and-merger strategy that saw it expand into telephone and office supply and retailing. Sales jumped $11 million, to $31 million, in one year. However, losses reached $3.4 million. The company had a negative tangible net worth. New management began closing or selling all non-school-related businesses, products were eliminated, and a duplicative distribution center was closed.

Meanwhile, the company's owners anted up an extra $500,000 in capital and converted $600,000 the company owed them into equity. Another $1 million was raised through subordinated debt. The recapitalization enabled Valley School Supply to switch from a commercial finance company to a bank for short-term borrowings at a far better interest rate.

All that was important. But, says Valley School Supply President Daniel Spalding, the basic reason for the company's success since then has been its employees. There currently are 210, plus part-timers. All are involved in company programs. The company offers rewards for ideas for cutting costs and improving service. Seven hundred ideas were submitted and judged by managers in a two-year period.

One idea was the creation of the company's CARE ("customers are really everything") program. On the basis of points bestowed by their peers, customers, and managers, employees win recognition and awards for going beyond the call of duty in meeting customer needs. Another employee suggested that the firm give its suppliers annual reports on their performance. Some suppliers have been weeded out as a result.

"Result teams" of employees tackle problems by means of an eight-point solving process. A company trainer, who runs a continuing education program on Valley School Supply's operations, is chief "facilitator" for the teams. All employees are involved in developing an annual business plan and budget. Quarterly financial reports are reviewed at employee meetings. What they hear affects an important employee benefit. The company puts 20 percent of profits in a pool to be distributed to them.

Today, this company that downsized so drastically

in the late 1980s is larger and stronger than ever. Valley School Supply has learned some lessons.

For Discussion

1. Discuss the way Valley School Supply uses employee teams. Why was this idea so helpful to the organization?

2. Would the employee team concept work in all organizations? Why or why not?

3. Imagine you are an employee of Valley School Supply and develop a list of suggestions involving employee teams that the company could use to be a high-performing organization.

CASE

Are You Sure We're in the Same Class?

Teri was studying for her Management Principles exam when she spotted Clark, another student in her class. "Hey Clark, would you like to study together for this exam? I could use some help reviewing these concepts from the chapter on individual behavior." "Why bother studying?" Clark responded. "It doesn't matter how hard I try in that class, I just can't do well. Professor Danos's tests are impossible to study for—I do just as well guessing at the answers as I do studying. You know those multiple-choice questions are randomly selected, and it's just a matter of luck anyway. I guess I wasn't meant to be a management major."

"Clark, it sounds like you aren't doing well in the class. Maybe I can help. I really am enjoying the class and especially Professor Danos. I met Professor Danos at orientation my first summer on campus, and when I found out he was a scuba diver, I just knew he would be a great teacher! I like the way he explains things in language you can understand, and the examples he gives are always relevant to the topic. I think he makes the material in the text so interesting. I know I can do even better on this test if I spend

enough time looking up all the sources of information that Professor Danos gave us to read."

Clark couldn't believe Teri and he were in the same class! To Clark, the class was so disorganized. Professor Danos never followed the material in the book and was always going off on some unrelated topic that made the material even more confusing. "Professors are all alike, they just love to confuse students. If he would just tell you what you had to study and follow the textbook, the class might make sense. After all, isn't that what a textbook is for? Oh well, I guess there isn't anything I can do now anyway."

For Discussion

1. From the information given in the case, do you think Teri has an external or internal locus of control? What about Clark? Give some examples to justify your decision.

2. Why do Clark and Teri have different impressions of the same class.

3. Have Clark and Teri made any errors in perception? Has this ever happened to you?

EXPERIENTIAL EXERCISE 14.1

Locus of Control

For each of the following 10 questions, indicate the extent to which you agree or disagree using the following scale:

Strongly Disagree	Slightly Disagree	Disagree	Neither Agree nor Disagree	Slightly Agree	Agree	Strongly Agree
1	2	3	4	5	6	7

_____ 1. When I get what I want, it's usually because I worked hard for it.

_____ 2. When I make plans, I am almost certain to make them work.

_____ 3. On an exam or in competition, I like to know how well I do relative to everyone else.

_____ 4. I can learn almost anything if I set my mind to it.

_____ 5. My major accomplishments are entirely due to my hard work and ability.

_____ 6. I prefer games involving some luck over games requiring pure skill.

_____ 7. I usually don't set goals, because I have a hard time following through on them.

_____ 8. Competition discourages excellence.

_____ 9. Often people get ahead just by being lucky.

_____ 10. It's pointless to keep working on something that's too difficult for me.

Scoring: For questions 1 through 5, sum the values, and enter the results on the line: _____ . For questions 6 through 10, reverse the scale so that 1 equals strongly agree, 2 equals agree, and so on. Now add the point values for questions 6 through 10, and enter the result on the line: _____ . Sum both subtotals, and enter the total: _____ .

Scores can range from a low of 7 to a high of 70. The higher you score on this questionnaire, the more you tend to believe that you are generally responsible for what happens to you. Higher scores are associated with

an internal locus of control. In general, scores above 50 indicate an internal locus of control. In contrast, low scores (below 40) are associated with an external locus of control. Scoring low indicates that you tend to believe that forces beyond your control, such as other powerful people, fate, or chance, are responsible for what happens to you.

SOURCE: D. Hellriegel, J. W. Slocum, R. W. Woodman, "Measuring Locus of Control," in *Organizational Behavior*, 6th ed. (St. Paul, Minn.: West Publishing Co., 1991), 97–98. Used with permission.

EXPERIENTIAL EXERCISE 14.2

How Well-Suited Are You for Working in Groups?

Purpose: To gain a better understanding of your orientation to working alone or with others in a group.

Procedure: Respond either Y (yes) or N (no) to each of the following statements:

_____ 1. I usually feel uncomfortable with a group of people that I don't know.

_____ 2. I enjoy parties.

_____ 3. I do not have much confidence in social situations.

_____ 4. I am basically a shy person.

_____ 5. I like going on job interviews.

_____ 6. I usually feel anxious when I speak in front of a group.

_____ 7. Large groups make me nervous.

_____ 8. I would rather work on a group project than an individual project.

_____ 9. I am basically a loner.

_____ 10. I find that groups bring out the best in me.

Scoring: Give yourself one point for each of your responses that matches the following answer pattern: 1 = Y, 2 = N, 3 = Y, 4 = Y, 5 = N, 6 = Y, 7 = Y, 8 = N, 9 = Y, 10 = N. Total your score.

Interpretation of score: If your score is 8 or higher, you probably prefer to avoid most group situations. This means you are a group avoider. If you have a score of 2 or lower, you probably seek out group situations and activities and are thus a group seeker. Unfortunately, it is not always possible to choose your preferred situation. When people do get into situations that conflict with their orientation, they may not function as well as they would otherwise. Try to match your activities with your group preference style.

Now answer the following questions:

1. After completing this questionnaire, form a small group as directed by your instructor and discuss how the scores of the group members differ.

2. How can you best match your work activities with your group preference style? Generate a list of ideas and share them with either a small group or the class as directed by your instructor.

SOURCE: Adapted from R. A. Baron and P. B. Paulus, "Group Seekers and Avoiders: How Well-Suited Are You for Working in Groups?" in *Understanding Human Relations*, 2d ed. (Boston: Allyn & Bacon, 1991), 286–87.

NOTES

1. D. Jones-Yang, "How Boeing Does It," *Business Week*, July 9, 1990, 46–50; "Boeing Commercial Airplanes," in *Profiles in Quality: Blueprints for Action from 50 Leading Companies* (Boston: Allyn & Bacon, 1991); and B. Acohido, "Boeing Workforce Tries New Direction," *Dallas Morning News*, May 5, 1991, 8H.

2. "Management Discovers the Human side of Automation," *Business Week*, September 29, 1986, 71; and P. Bernstein, "Efficiency Is Up and Absenteeism is Down at New Volvo Plant," *World Wide Report*, December 1983, 94.

3. J. A. Bryne, "Management's New Gurus," *Business Week*, August 31, 1992, 44–52.

4. P. C. Smith, L. M. Kendall, and C. L. Hulin, *The Measurement of Satisfaction in Work and Retirement* (Chicago: Rand McNally, 1969).

5. L. Roberson, "Prediction of Job Satisfaction from Characteristics of Personal Work Goals," *Journal of Organizational Behavior* 11 (1990): 29–41.

6. Smith, Kendall, and Hulin, *The Measurement of Satisfaction*.

7. L. W. Porter, R. M. Steers, R. T. Mowday, and P. V. Boulian, "Organizational Commitment, Job Satisfaction, and Turnover among Psychiatric Technicians," *Journal of Applied Psychology* 5 (1974): 603–9.

8. K. L. Miller, "Now, Japan Is Admitting It: Work Kills Executives," *Business Week*, August 3, 1992, 35.

9. S. J. Lambert, "The Combined Effects of Job and Family Characteristics on the Job Satisfaction, Job Involvement, and Intrinisic Motivation of Men and Women Workers," *Journal of Organizational Behavior* 12 (1991): 341–63.

10. E. Robinson, *Why Aren't You More Like Me?* (Dubuque, Iowa: Kendall/Hunt, 1991).

11. J. Holland, *Making Vocational Choices: A Theory of Vocational Personalities and Work Environments*, 2d ed. (Englewood Cliffs, N.J.: Prentice-Hall, 1985).

12. S. Coopersmith, *The Antecedents of Self-Esteem* (San Francisco: Freeman, 1967).

13. G. Mitchell, and P. Fandt, "Confident Role Models for Tomorrow's Classrooms: The Self-Esteem of Education Majors," *Education* 113 (1993): 556–62.

14. R. Lovelace, *Stress Masters* (New York: John Wiley & Sons, 1990).

15. A. Korman, "Self-Esteem Variable in Vocational Choice," *Journal of Applied Psychology* 50 (1966): 479–86; and A. Korman, "Relevance of Personal Need Satisfaction for Overall Satisfaction as a Function of Self-Esteem," *Journal of Applied Psychology* 51 (1967): 533–38.

16. J. B. Rotter, "Generalized Expectancies for Internal versus External Control of Reinforcement," *Psychological Monographs* 80 (1966): 1–28.

17. D. Young, "Accidental Entrepreneurs Break All Business School Rules," *Orlando Sentinel*, February 9, 1992, D1, D2.

18. R. H. Brockhaus, Sr., "The Pscyhology of the Entrepreneur," in C. A. Kent, E. L. Sexton, and K. H. Vesper, eds., *Encyclopedia of Entrepreneurship* (Englewood Cliffs, N.J.: Prentice-Hall, 1982).

19. T. W. Adorno, E. Frenkel-Brunswick, D. J. Levinson, and B. J. Sanford, *The Authoritarian Personality* (New York: Harper, 1950).

20. R. G. Vleeming, "Machiavellianism: A Preliminary Review," *Psychological Reports*, February 1979, 295–310.

21. Based on M. Jamal, "Type A Behavior and Job Performance: Some Suggestive Findings," *Journal of Human Stress* (Summer 1985): 60–68.

22. J. Bishop, "Prognosis for the 'Type A' Personality," *Wall Street Journal*, January 14, 1992, 9H; and M. Freidman and R. Roseman, *Type A Behavior and Your Heart* (New York: Knopf, 1974).

23. Ibid.

24. "Throwing Stones at the Glass Ceiling," *Business Week*, August 19, 1991, 19.

25. P. Fandt, and G. Stevens, "Evaluation Bias in the Business Classroom: Evidence Related to the Effects of Previous Experiences," *Journal of Psychology* 125 (1991): 469–77.

26. S. Overman, "Managing the Diverse Workforce," *HR Magazine*, April 1991, 32–36.

27. R. R. Thomas, "From Affirmative Action to Affirming Diversity," *Harvard Business Review* (March/April 1992): 107–17.

28. D. C. Dearborn, and H. A. Simon, "Selection Perception: A Note on the Departmental Identification of Executives," *Sociometry* 21 (1958): 140–44.

29. Adapted from P. Fandt, *Management Skills: Practice and Experience* (St. Paul, Minn.: West Publishing Co., 1994), 216.

30. J. Hoerr, "Sharpening Minds for a Competitive Edge," *Business Week*, December 17, 1990, 72–78; T. A. Steward, "New Ways to Exercise Power," *Fortune*, November 6, 1989, 52–64; and K. H. Hammonds, "Corning's Class Act," *Business Week*, May 13, 1991, 68–76.

31. For a more detailed discussion, see L. Harrisberger, *Succeeding: How to Become an Outstanding Professional* (New York: Macmillan, 1994); and J. B. Miller, *The Corporate Coach* (New York: St. Martin's Press, 1993).

32. This definition is adapted from M. E. Shaw, *Group Dynamics: The Psychology of Small Group Behavior* (New York: McGraw-Hill, 1981), 8.

33. For a thorough discussion, see C. Larson and F. LaFasto, *Teamwork: What Must Go Right/What Can Go Wrong* (Newbury Park, Calif.: Sage, 1989); and Shaw, *Group Dynamics*.

34. B. W. Tuckman, "Development Sequence in Small Groups," *Psychological Bulletin* 63 (1965): 384–99; and

B. W. Tuckman and M. Jensen, "Stages of Small Group Development Revisited," *Group and Organization Studies* 2 (1977): 419-27.

35. J. O'Brian, "Making New Hires Members of the Team," *Supervisory Management* (May 1992): 4; and D. W. Johnson and F. P. Johnson, *Joining Together: Group Theory and Group Skills* (Boston: Allyn & Bacon, 1994), 18-21.

36. Johnson and Johnson, *Joining Together*, 20-22.

37. I. L. Janis, *Victims of Groupthink*, 2d ed. (Boston: Houghton Mifflin, 1982).

38. G. Whyte, "Groupthink Reconsidered," *Academy of Management Review* 14 (1989): 40-55.

39. R. Poe, "The Secret of Teamwork," *Success*, June 1991, 72.

40. S. L. Keck, and M. Tushman, "Environmental and Organizational Context and Executive Team Structure," *Academy of Management Journal* 36, (1993): 1314-44.

41. Harrisberger, *Succeeding*.

42. S. Neumeirer, "Vans," *Fortune*, March 9, 1992, 63.

43. W. Kiechell, III, "The Art of the Corporate Task Force," *Fortune*, January 28, 1991, 104-6; and Harrisberger, *Succeeding*.

44. Adapted from Shaw, *Group Dynamnics*.

45. Harrisberger, *Succeeding*.

46. B. Berelson, and G. Steiner, *Human Behaviors: An Inventory of Scientific Findings* (New York: Harcourt, Brace & World, 1964), 356-60.

47. For a more thorough discussion, see Johnson and Johnson, *Joining Together*, 248-52.

48. For more information on social loafing, see B. Latane, K. Williams, and S. Harkins, "Many Hands Make Light the Work: The Causes and Consequences of Social Loafing," *Journal of Personality and Social Psychology* 37 (1978): 822-32; and E. Weldon and G. Gargano, "Cognitive Effort in Additive Task Groups: The Effects of Shared Responsibility on the Quality of Multiattribute Judgments," *Organizational Behavior and Human Decision Processes* 36 (1985): 348-61.

49. See reviews on group composition, diversity, and performance in Shaw, *Group Dynamics*, 232-33; and Johnson and Johnson, *Joining Together*, 435-53.

50. Johnson and Johnson, *Joining Together*, 18-21.

51. Based on K. J. Benne, and P. Sheats, "Functional Roles of Group Members," *Journal of Social Issues* 4 (1948): 42-47.

52. K. L. Bettenhausen, and J. K. Murnighan, "The Development of an Intragroup Norm and the Effects of Interpersonal and Structural Changes," *Administrative Science Quarterly* 36 (1990): 20-35.

53. C. Larson and F. LaFasto, *Teamwork: What Must Go Right/What Can Go Wrong* (Newbury Park, Calif.: Sage, 1989).

54. N. Evans, and P. Jarvis, "Group Cohesion: A Review and Reevaluation," *Small Group Behavior* 11 (1980): 359-70.

55. A more thorough discussion of this relationship appears in P. Fandt, S. Cady, and M. Sparks, "The Impact of Reward Interdependency on the Synergogy Model of Cooperative Performance: Designing an Effective Team Environment," *Small Group Research*, 24 (1993): 101-15.

56. S. Cohen, "A Monkey on the Back, a Lump in the Throat," *Inside Sports* 4 (1992): 20.

57. I. L. Janis, *Victims of Groupthink*, 2d ed. (Boston: Houghton Mifflin, 1982).

58. H. Park, P. Lewis, and P. Fandt, "Ethnocentrism and Group Cohesiveness in International Joint Ventures," in R. Culpan, ed., *Multinational Strategic Alliances* (Binghamton, N.Y.: International Business Press, 1993).

59. Taylor Cox, Jr., "The Multicultural Organization," *Academy of Management Executive* 5 (1991): 34-47.

60. K. C. Green, and D. T. Seymour, *Who's Going to Run General Motors?* (Princeton, N.J.: Peterson's Guides, 1991), 66-68.

61. K. Kelly, "He Gets by with a Lot of Help from His Friends," *Business Week*, April 27, 1992, 68.

62. Green and Seymour, *Who's Going to Run General Motors?*

63. D. Jones-Yang, "How Boeing Does It"; "Boeing Commercial Airplanes," in *Profiles in Quality: Blueprints for Action from 50 Leading Companies*; Acohido, "Boeing Workforce Tries New Direction."

Motivating Organizational Members

CHAPTER 15

▼ CHAPTER OVERVIEW

An organization's energy comes from the motivation of its employees. Although their abilities play a crucial role in determining their work performance, so does their motivation. Managers must ensure that employees are motivated to perform their tasks to the best of their abilities. Through motivation, managers are better able to create a working environment that is conducive to good effort and where employees are inspired to work to accomplish the organization's goals.

In this chapter we discuss motivation as the force that energizes and gives direction to behavior. Many models of motivation and definitions have been developed and examined over the last 40 years. We examine need-based theories, process theories, theories that focus on how employees learn desired work behaviors, and several contemporary approaches to motivation. Finally, we will consider motivation from an international perspective and see how it differs from motivation in a purely domestic organization.

▼ LEARNING OBJECTIVES

When you have finished studying this chapter, you should be able to:

- Explain the basic motivation process.
- Describe the different approaches to motivation.
- Define need-based theories of employee motivation.
- Explain the basic elements of Herzberg's theory of motivation.
- Describe how content and process theories differ.
- Explain how expectancy theory can be applied in the workplace.
- Describe the use of equity theory to motivate employees.
- Describe how reinforcement theory applies the principles of reinforcement to employee performance.
- Identify how goal setting is used to motivate performance.
- Understand the importance of motivation from an international perspective.

MANAGERIAL INCIDENT

USAA STRIVES FOR EXCEPTIONAL SERVICE

The United Services Automobile Association (USAA), located in San Antonio, Texas, is one of the nation's largest insurers of privately owned automobiles and homes. Recently, USAA faced a myriad of difficult challenges.

According to Robert F. McDermott, the CEO of USAA for over 24 years, the underlying causes of the company's problems were the employees' lack of motivation and the resulting lack of service to customers. McDermott uncovered an unhealthy environment of competition within the organization characterized by many smaller departments that were run by what McDermott refers to as "warlords," who didn't communicate with each other and fought "perpetual turf battles." He also found little or no communication between departments. According to McDermott, employees didn't know how the whole organization fit together, they only knew and cared about their own section of the company. Another problem was the overwhelming amount of paperwork cluttering up offices. McDermott claimed that on any given day, the chances of finding a particular file were only 50–50. These problems, coupled with the lack of communication between departments, resulted in the even more serious problem of poor customer service, a problem that could eventually lead to the demise of the organization.

McDermott regarded the competitive, unfriendly, cluttered, and negative environment in the organization as demoralizing to the employees. Their dissatisfaction was reflected in a turnover rate of 44 percent and a double-digit absentee rate. How could employees be expected to remain motivated to help the company achieve its goals under these circumstances?

McDermott developed an aggressive motivational program to attack these problems. Could he successfully motivate employees and move USAA toward the goal of providing exceptional service to its customers?[1] ▼

INTRODUCTION

Robert F. McDermott, the CEO of USAA is clearly facing motivational challenges. Like most effective managers, he is concerned about motivation because the work motives of employees affect their productivity and the quality of their work. Also like most managers, one of McDermott's responsibilities is to channel employee motivation toward achieving organizational goals.[2]

As the concerns for productivity and quality are increasing at the global level, so is the search for the "right" theory or the "right" approach to work motivation. Many models have been developed and examined over the last four decades, and a variety of definitions have emerged in the process. In this chapter we explore several approaches to motivation including a broad classification of need-based theories and process theories. We begin by looking at need-based theories that examine motivation based on specific human needs or the factors within a person. Next, we focus on expectancy and equity theories—two process theories of motivation. Reinforcement theory and its application in the workplace are discussed next. We then look at several contemporary approaches to motivation including goal setting, participative management, and money as a motivator. Finally, we take an international perspective to better appreciate how diversity and the global environment can affect the motivation of employees in the international arena.

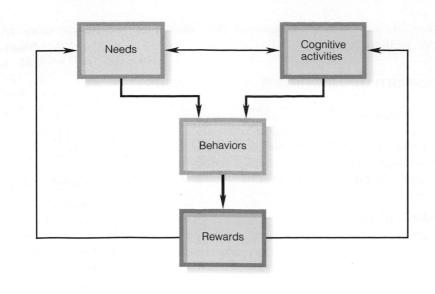

▼ **Figure 15.1**
A General Framework for the
Motivation Process

BASIC MOTIVATION PROCESS

How does motivation occur? Since the early work of the scientific management and human relations theorists, management scholars have developed a number of different theories that help us understand what motivates people at work.[3] **Motivation** is generally defined as the forces acting on or within a person that cause that person to behave in a specific, goal-directed manner.[4] It is a psychological process that gives behavior purpose and direction. Although the process of motivation is quite complex, a general framework appears in Figure 15.1. As the model indicates, needs are drives or forces that initiate behavior. For example, people often need recognition, feelings of accomplishment, food, companionship, and growth. Needs are coupled with knowledge and thoughts about various efforts we might make and the potential rewards we might receive. When needs or cognitive activities become strong enough, we do something to satisfy them. If the activity leads to satisfaction, we usually feel rewarded. This reward also informs us that our behavior was appropriate and can be used again in the future.

The motivation theories that we present in this chapter are general approaches to the "what" and "how" of behavior. But we should remember that motivation is only one of many explanations of human behavior. Though some people view motivation as a personal trait—that is, some have it and others don't—this is not true. Certainly, individuals differ in their motivational drive, but motivation is the result of the interaction between the individual and the situation. Consequently, the level of motivation varies both between individuals and within individuals at different times.[5]

APPROACHES TO MOTIVATION

Motivation can be studied through several broad approaches. Content or need-based theories emphasize specific human needs or the factors within a person that energize, direct, and stop behavior. Process theories take a more dynamic view of motivation. These theories focus on understanding the thought or cognitive processes that take place within the individual's mind and act to affect behavior. More contemporary approaches to motivation include goal

Motivation
The forces acting on or within a person that causes the person to behave in a specific, goal-directed manner.

setting and participative management. We examine each of these approaches, in the next sections.

NEED-BASED THEORIES OF EMPLOYEE MOTIVATION

Many factors are believed to influence a person's desire to perform work or behave in a certain way. Need-based theories explain motivation primarily as a phenomenon that occurs intrinsically, or within an individual. Here we look at three widely recognized need-based motivation theories: Maslow's hierarchy of needs, Herzberg's two-factor theory, and McClelland's acquired needs theory.

Maslow's Hierarchy of Needs

Maslow's hierarchy of needs is the most widely recognized theory of motivation.[6] According to this theory, a person has five fundamental needs: physiological, security, affiliation, esteem, and self-actualization.[7] Figure 15.2 shows these five needs arranged in a hierarchy.

Maslow separated the five needs into higher and lower levels. He described physiological and security needs as lower-order needs, which are generally satisfied externally, and affiliation, esteem, and self-actualization as higher-order needs, which are satisfied internally.

Physiological needs
Food, water, air, and shelter are physiological needs.

Physiological Needs   At the bottom of the hierarchy are **physiological needs.** Food, water, air, and shelter are all physiological needs and from the lowest level in Maslow's hierarchy. People concentrate on satisfying these needs before turning to higher-order needs. Managers must understand that to the extent employees are motivated by physiological needs, their concerns do not center on the work they are doing. They will accept any job that serves to meet their needs. Managers who focus on physiological needs in trying to

▼ **Figure 15.2**
Maslow's Hierarchy of Needs Requiring Fulfillment in the Work Environment

▼ Esteem needs are met from personal feelings of achievement, self-worth, recognition, respect, and prestige from others.

motivate subordinates assume that people work mainly for money and are primarily concerned with comfort, avoidance of fatigue, and their rate of pay.

Security Needs   Next in the hierarchy are **security needs,** which reflect the desire to have a safe physical and emotional environment. Job security, grievance procedures, and health insurance and retirement plans are used to satisfy employees' security needs. Like physiological needs, unsatisfied security needs cause people to be preoccupied with satisfying them. People who are motivated primarily by security needs value their jobs mainly as a defense against the loss of basic need satisfaction. Managers who feel that security needs are most important will often emphasize rules, job security, and fringe benefits.

Affiliation Needs   **Affiliation needs** include the desire for friendship, love, and a feeling of belonging. An individual with high affiliation needs focuses on obtaining love, affection, and a sense of belonging in his or her relationships with others. When physiological and security needs have been satisfied, affiliation needs become a more important source of motivation. When affiliation needs are primary sources of motivation, individuals value their work as an opportunity for finding and establishing friendly interpersonal relationships.

Esteem Needs   Fourth in the hierarchy are **esteem needs.** These needs are met by personal feelings of achievement and self-worth and by recognition, respect, and prestige from others. People with esteem needs want others to accept them for what they are and to perceive them as competent and able. Managers who focus on esteem needs try to foster employees' pride in their work and use public rewards and recognition for services to motivate them. As Managing for Excellence describes, managers with Mary Kay Cosmetics motivate the company's beauty consultants through recognition and rewards that operate on their need for higher self-esteem.[8]

Self-Actualization Needs   Finally, at the top of the hierarchy are the **self-actualization needs.** Self-fulfillment and the opportunity to achieve one's potential are considered self-actualization needs. People who strive for self-actualization accept themselves and use their abilities to the fullest and most creative extent. Managers who emphasize self-actualization may involve employees in designing jobs or make special assignments that capitalize on em-

Security need
The desire to have a safe physical and emotional environment.

Affiliation need
The desire for friendship, love, and a feeling of belonging.

Esteem needs
Personal feelings of achievement, self-worth, recognition, respect, and prestige from others.

Self-actualization needs
Self-fulfillment and the opportunity to achieve one's potential.

MANAGING FOR EXCELLENCE

RECOGNITION AT MARY KAY COSMETICS

Every year, Mary Kay Cosmetics, Inc., gives more than 300 of its top salespeople a small token of appreciation—the use of a pink Cadillac for two years. That symbol has always summed up the flamboyant spirit of the cosmetics company founded by Mary Kay Ash. The "Mary Kay Pink" Cadillacs, driven by the superstar beauty consultants, are almost legendary in some parts of the United States. Equally famous is founder Ash's skill at motivating employees through recognition and rewards.

But not long ago, a Pinto might have been a more apt symbol. By the mid-1980s, Mary Kay found it hard to recruit women as sales representatives because better-paying jobs were open to them. With more women working, the remaining reps had trouble reaching new buyers. Sales and earnings tumbled. But look at Mary Kay now. Even as rival Avon Products, Inc., is stumbling, the company seems to have regained its footing. The two competitors have an unusual relationship. Mary Kay owns a 3 percent stake in Avon and was part of a failed takeover bid launched by Chartwell Associates two years ago. But these days, Mary Kay is more concerned with making its own business grow and motivating employees than with snatching away someone else's.

Founded in 1963 on a $5,000 investment as a way to provide women with unlimited opportunity for success, the company now operates in 12 countries and is considered one of the world's largest cosmetic empires. Numerous contests and rewards in addition to regular sales commissions are used to motivate the sales force. Top beauty consultants can earn more than $250,000 a year. Beauty consultants are governed by six rules:

1. Follow the golden rule in dealing with employees and customers.
2. People are more important than the plan. Make them feel important, praise them, listen to them, and let them contribute.
3. Managers must lead by getting their hands dirty.
4. Managers have a responsibility to their employees. They must instill in their employees a sense of pride and pleasure in their work.
5. There are no "little people" in the organization. Everyone is important to the organization's success.
6. Beauty consultants are the lifeblood of this organization. They should be rewarded and respected for their efforts.

Following these rules enables beauty consultants to earn recognition and rewards. Ceremonial activities culminate with extravagant events staged at the Dallas Convention Center that Ash describes as a combination of the Academy Awards, the Miss America pageant, and Broadway opening. During this five-hour extravaganza, Ash herself crowns the top salespersons in various categories. Surrounded by a court of other outstanding salespeople, the winners receive expensive gifts. People are recognized with trophies "just for being wonderful." Other rewards for outstanding performance range from photos in monthly magazines to incentive gifts such as cars, vacation trips, and diamond jewelry.

ployees' unique skills. Many entrepreneurs who break away from jobs in large corporations to start their own business may be looking for a way to satisfy their self-actualization needs.

Maslow's hierarchy provides a convenient framework for managers. It suggests that individuals have various needs and that they try to satisfy those needs using a priority system or hierarchy. Some research indicates that higher-order needs increase in importance over lower-order needs as individuals move up the organizational hierarchy. Other studies have reported that needs vary according to a person's career stage, organization size, and even geographical location. One of the major criticisms of Maslow's theory, however, is that there is no consistent evidence that the satisfaction of a need at one level will decrease its importance and increase the importance of the next higher needs.

Herzberg's Two-Factor Theory

Herzberg's two-factor theory, provides another way to examine employee needs. Herzberg examined the relationship between job satisfaction and productivity within a group of professional accountants and engineers.[9] He found that the factors leading to job satisfaction were separate and distinct from those that lead to job dissatisfaction—hence, the term *two-factor theory*.

The two-factor model is shown in Figure 15.3. At the top are the sources of work satisfaction, otherwise termed satisfiers or motivator factors. The sources of dissatisfaction, or hygiene factors, are shown at the bottom.

Motivator Factors   **Motivator factors** are related to job content, or what people actually do in their work, and are associated with an individual's positive feelings about the job. Based on Herzberg's theory, motivator factors include the work itself, recognition, advancement, a sense of achievement, and responsibilities.

Hygiene Factors   **Hygiene factors** are associated with the job context or environment in which the job is performed. Company policy and administration, technical supervision, salary, working conditions, and interpersonal relations are examples of hygiene factors. These factors are associated with an individual's negative feelings about the job but do not contribute to motivation.

Studies on what managers value in their work support Herzberg's conclusion that factors such as achievement, recognition, and challenging work are

Motivator factors
Related to job content or what people actually do in their work.

Hygiene factors
Associated with the job context or environment in which the job is performed.

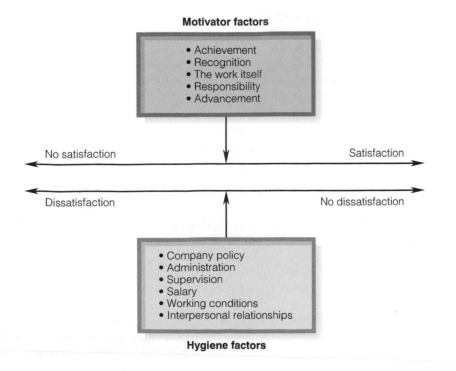

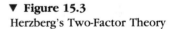
▼ **Figure 15.3**
Herzberg's Two-Factor Theory

valued more than things like pay or security. For example, a recent survey of middle- and top-level managers by the American Productivity and Quality Center found that more than half of the sample respondents, (all of whom were white males) believed that the most important characteristic of a job is that it involves work that is meaningful and provides a sense of accomplishment. They rated meaningful work most important three times more frequently than high income. Additionally, 90 percent or more of the respondents rated challenging work, participation in decision making, and recognition for their accomplishments as important or very important.[10]

But just because many people rate motivators above hygiene factors is no guarantee that the motivators will actually increase work motivation for all employees. These findings may not be applicable to the entire population. Moreover, these factors may only result in increasing employee motivation and satisfaction and have no affect on productivity.

Nevertheless, Herzberg's two-factor theory carries some very clear messages for managers. The first step in motivation is to eliminate dissatisfaction, so managers are advised to make sure that pay, working conditions, company policies, and so forth are appropriate and reasonable. Then, they can address motivation itself. But additional pay and improvements in working conditions will not accomplish this. Instead, managers should strive to provide opportunities for growth, achievement, and responsibility, all things that the theory predicts will enhance employee motivation.

McClelland's Acquired Needs Theory: Focus on Diversity

McClelland has proposed a theory of motivation, which he believes is rooted in culture; that is, needs are acquired or learned on the basis of our life experiences. His theory focuses on three particularly important or relevant needs in the work environment: achievement, affiliation, and power.[11] McClelland argues that when a need is strong, it will motivate the person to engage in behaviors to satisfy that need. How strong are your needs for achievement, affiliation, and power? Before you read further, take a few minutes to complete the questionnaire in Meeting the Challenge.[12] How do you score in the three relevant needs that McClelland proposed?

Need for achievement
The drive to excel, to accomplish challenging tasks, and achieve a standard of excellence.

Need for Achievement   Initially, McClelland's work centered on the **need for achievement,** represented by the drive to excel, accomplish challenging tasks, and achieve a standard of excellence. He primarily studied achievement motivation in relation to entrepreneurship.[13] McClelland's research shows that although almost all people feel they have an "achievement motive," probably only 10 percent of the U.S. population is strongly motivated to achieve.

The amount of achievement motivation that people have depends on their childhood, their personal and occupational experiences, and the type of organization for which they work.[14] Managers who want to motivate high achievers need to ensure that such individuals have challenging, but obtainable goals that allow relatively immediate feedback about their progress. High achievers often pursue a professional career in sales and are successful in entrepreneurial activities.

Lisa Renshaw, president of Penn Parking, Inc., is a typical self-motivated high achiever who likes to set her own goals and favors tasks that provide immediate feedback. She prefers to accept the personal responsibility for success or failure, rather than leave the outcome to chance or the actions of others. Read Lisa's profile in Entrepreneurial Approach to learn more about the need for achievement.[15]

Research consistently demonstrates that high achievers are successful in entrepreneurial activities like running their own business, managing a self-contained unit within a large organization, or holding positions where success

ACQUIRED NEEDS MOTIVATION SURVEY

Using this 1–7 scale, indicate how often each of the following statements describes you:

Almost Never	Never	Seldom	Sometimes	Usually	Almost Always	Always
1	2	3	4	5	6	7

_____ 1. I do my best work when my job assignments are fairly difficult.

_____ 2. When I have a choice, I try to work in a group instead of by myself.

_____ 3. I seek an active role in the leadership of a group.

_____ 4. I try to influence those around me to see things my way.

_____ 5. I try very hard to improve on my past performance at work.

_____ 6. I pay a good bit of attention to the feelings of others at work.

_____ 7. I find myself organizing and directing the activities of others.

_____ 8. I strive to gain more control over the events around me at work.

_____ 9. I take moderate risks and stick my neck out to get ahead at work.

_____ 10. I prefer to do my work with others.

_____ 11. I strive to be "in command" when I am working in a group.

_____ 12. I try to seek out added responsibilities on my job.

_____ 13. I do not openly express my disagreements with others.

_____ 14. I try to perform better than my co-workers.

_____ 15. I find myself talking to those around me about nonbusiness matters.

Record your responses from the 15-item survey and total the three columns. Next, divide each total by 5 to obtain your scores for need for achievement, need for affiliation, and need for power.

CATEGORY 1	CATEGORY 2	CATEGORY 3
1 _____	2 _____	3 _____
5 _____	6 _____	4 _____
9 _____	10 _____	7 _____
12 _____	13 _____	8 _____
14 _____	15 _____	11 _____
Total _____	Total _____	Total _____
÷ 5	÷ 5	÷ 5
Score = _____	Score = _____	Score = _____
Need for achievement	Need for affiliation	Need for power

Averages for a sample of 712 scientists, engineers, hospital employees, white-collar employees, and management students were as follows: need for achievement, 4.3; need for affiliation, 4.1; and need for power, 4.1.

ENTREPRENEURIAL APPROACH

LISA RENSHAW

In 1983, when Lisa Renshaw was just 21, she met the owner of a troubled downtown Baltimore parking lot and offered him a loan of $3,000 and free labor in exchange for equity in the property. Soon after, the owner left town, taking her $3,000. But Renshaw stayed, renegotiated the lease, and persuaded the garage owner to lower the monthly payments so she would have a chance at breaking even.

Lisa Renshaw is now the president of Penn Parking, Inc., and she got there by doing most of the work herself. She built the business by greeting customers daily, handing out fliers, promoting heavily to Amtrak riders who used a nearby station, offering carpooling assistance, and giving free car washes to anyone who parked in her lot for five days. The lot's occupancy rate increased from less than 10 percent to more than 70 percent in three years. Today, Lisa has four lots, garnering a 20 percent margin on annual revenues of almost $1 million.

---

depends largely on individual achievement.[16] A high need to achieve does not necessarily lead to being a good manager, however, especially in large organizations. In contrast, the needs for affiliation and institutional power are closely related to management success.

Need for Power   McClelland's research also focused on the desire to influence and control one's environment as a particularly important motivator in organizations. This **need for power** may involve either personal power or institutional power. Individuals with a high need for personal power want to dominate others for the sake of demonstrating their ability to influence and control. In contrast, individuals with a high need for institutional power want to solve problems and further organizational goals.[17]

Need for power
The desire to influence and control one's environment.

Need for Affiliation   Finally, the **need for affiliation** is the desire for friendly and close interpersonal relationships. Individuals high in the need for affiliation are likely to gravitate toward professions that involve high levels of interaction with others, such as teaching, counseling, and sales.

Need for affiliation
The desire for friendly and close interpersonal relationships.

Though not all individuals have the appropriate needs profile to be a manager, McClelland argues that employees can be trained to stimulate their achievement needs. If an organizational position requires a high achiever, management can select a person with a high need for achievement or develop its own candidate through training.

In summary, need-based approaches to motivation provide managers with an understanding of the underlying needs that motivate people to behave in certain ways. However, these theories do not explain why people choose a particular behavior to accomplish task-related goals. As useful as they are, need theories still emphasize the "what" aspect of motivation by describing what motivates individuals, but do not provide information on thought processes or the "how" aspect of motivation. We examine a more complex view of motivation in the next section.

PROCESS THEORIES OF EMPLOYEE MOTIVATION

Managers need to have a more complete perspective on the complexities of employees motivation. They must understand why different people have different needs and goals, why individuals' needs change, and how employees change to try to satisfy needs in different ways. Not all employees want the same things from their jobs. Understanding these aspects of motivation has become especially relevant as organizations deal with the diverse managerial issues associated with an increasingly global environment. Two useful theories for understanding these complex processes are expectancy theory and equity theory.

Expectancy Theory

Expectancy theory is the most comprehensive motivational model. In general, expectancy theory seeks to predict or explain task-related effort. The theory suggests that work motivation is determined by two individual beliefs: (1) the relationship between effort and performance and (2) the desirability of various work outcomes that are associated with different performance levels.[18] Simply put, the theory suggests that motivation is a function of the perceived relationship between the individual's effort, her or his performance, and the desirability of consequences associated with performance outcomes.

To help you understand expectancy theory, the next paragraphs briefly define the key terms of the model and discuss how they operate. Figure 15.4 shows how these terms are related.

Expectancy   **Expectancy** is the belief that a particular level of effort will be followed by a particular level of performance. This is best understood in terms of the effort-performance linkage or the individual's perception of the probability that a given level of effort will lead to a certain level of performance.

Instrumentality   **Instrumentality** is the individual's perception that a specific level of achieved task performance will lead to various work outcomes. This is the performance-reward linkage or the degree to which the individual believes that performing at a particular level will lead to the attainment of a desired outcome.

Valence   **Valence** is the value or importance that the individual attaches to various work outcomes. For motivation to be high, employees must value the outcomes that are available from high effort and good performance. Conversely, if employees do not place a high value on the outcome, motivation will be low.

Motivation is the force that causes individuals to spend effort. However, effort alone is not enough. Individuals must believe that their efforts will lead to some desired performance level, otherwise they will not make much of an effort. Managers can influence expectancies by selecting individuals with proper abilities, training people to use these abilities, supporting people by providing the needed resources, and identifying desired task goals.[19] In addition, managers must try to determine the outcomes that each employee values.

One of the problems with the expectancy theory is that it is quite complex. Still, the logic of the model is clear, and the steps are useful for clarifying how managers can motivate people. For example, managers should first find out which rewards under their control have the highest valences for their employees. Managers should then link these rewards to the performance they

▼ The need for affiliation is the desire for friendly and close interpersonal relationships in the work place environment.

Expectancy
The belief that a particular level of effort will be followed by a particular level of performance.

Instrumentality
The probability assigned by the individual that a specific level of achieved task performance will lead to various work outcomes.

Valence
The value or importance that the individual attaches to various outcomes.

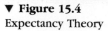

▼ **Figure 15.4**
Expectancy Theory

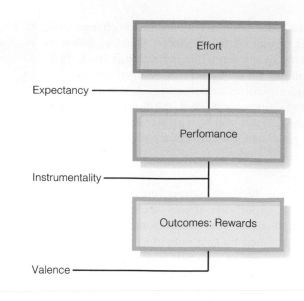

desire. If any expectancies are low, managers might provide coaching, leadership, and training to raise them.[20] For example, in Service Challenge, we see how Hilton successfully used this approach to motivate employees in its Performance for Excellence program.[21]

Equity Theory

Equity, or fairness in the workplace, has been found to be a major factor in determining employee motivation.[22] For example, when Wilber Marshall left the Chicago Bears to sign a five-year $6 million contract with the Washington Redskins, he became the highest paid defensive linebacker in the league as well as the highest paid player on the Redskins team. Marshall's contract triggered perceptions of inequity among his new teammates, many of whom called for renegotiation of their own contracts. Several years later, Marshall demanded an even higher salary and left the Redskins.

Although equity in the workplace is less visible than on the playing field, feelings of unfairness were among the most frequently reported sources of job dissatisfaction found by Herzberg and his associates. Some researchers have made the desire for fairness, justice, or equity a central focus of their theories. For example, assume that you just received a 10 percent raise. Will this raise lead to higher performance, lower performance, or no change in your performance? Are you satisfied with this increase? What if you discovered that other colleagues in your work group received 15 percent raises?

Equity theory focuses on an individual's feelings about how fairly he or she is treated in comparison with others.[23] Figure 15.5 illustrates the basic components of equity theory. The theory makes two assumptions: First, individuals evaluate their interpersonal relationships just as they evaluate any exchange process such as the buying or selling of a home, shares of stock, or a car. Second, individuals compare their situations with those of others to determine the equity of their own situation. Given the social nature of human beings, it should come as no surprise that we compare our contributions and rewards to those of others.

In the workplace, employees contribute things such as their education, experience, expertise, and time and effort, and in return they get pay, security, and recognition. According to equity theory, we prefer a situation of balance, or equity, that exists when we perceive that the ratio of our inputs and outcomes is equal to the ratio of inputs and outcomes of one or more comparison

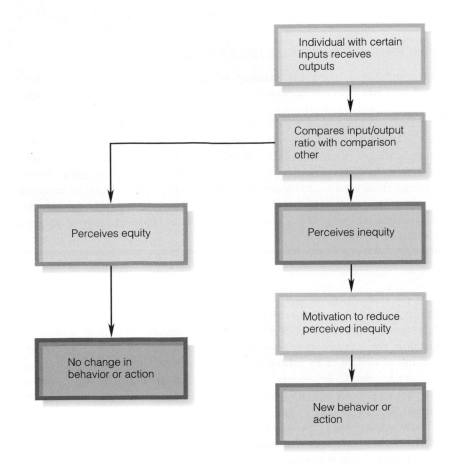

persons. If people experience inequity, they are generally motivated to change something.

This viewpoint also conveys several clear messages to managers. First, people should be rewarded according to their contributions. Second, managers should try to ensure that employees feel equity. Finally, managers should be aware that feelings of inequity are almost bound to arise, and when they do, managers must be patient and either correct the problem, if it is real, or help people recognize that things are not as inequitable as they seem.[24]

Maintaining Equity   Equity theory suggests that maintaining one's self-esteem is an important priority. To reduce a perceived inequity, a person may take one of the following actions:

- Change work inputs either upward or downward to what might be an equitable level. For example, underpaid people can reduce the quality of their production, work shorter hours, or be absent more frequently.

- Change outcomes to restore equity. For example, many union organizers try to attract nonmembers by pledging to improve working conditions, hours, and pay without an increase in employee effort (input).

- Psychologically distort comparisons. For example, a person might rationalize or distort how hard she or he works or attempt to increase the importance of the job to the organization.

- Change the comparison person he or she is using to another person.

- Leave the situation. For example, quit the job, request a transfer to another department, or shift to a new reference group to reduce the source of the inequity. This type of action will probably be taken only in cases of high inequity when other alternatives are not feasible.

SERVICE CHALLENGE

HILTON: PERFORMANCE FOR EXCELLENCE PROGRAM

In the competitive hospitality industry, where service is synonymous with success, Hilton has become famous worldwide. At Hilton, service is not left to chance. Through its Performance for Excellence program, the company carefully examined all aspects of its hotel operations. It established rigorous behavior standards and instituted a multimillion dollar training program to communicate the standards, build the skills necessary to attain them, and involve the employees in each phase of the program. The program involves everything from viewing videotapes of positive customer contact to more standard classroom instruction and discussion. Hilton expects this performance-based training will pay off in the future with better customer service and more motivated employees.

People often respond differently to the same situations, and therefore their reactions to inequity will vary. Some people are more willing to accept being underrewarded than others. If the perceived inequity results in a change in motivation, the inequity may also alter effort and performance. You can probably think of instances in school where you worked harder than others on a paper, yet received a lower grade. Although working hard doesn't necessarily imply that you wrote a high-quality paper, your sense of equity was probably violated.

These points also reinforce the fact that perception is an important aspect of equity theory. Feelings of inequity are determined solely by the individual's interpretation of the situation. Thus, it would be inaccurate to assume that all employees in a work unit will view their annual pay raise as fair. Rewards that are received with feelings of equity can foster job satisfaction and performance; rewards received with feelings of inequity can damage key work results. The burden lies with the manager to take control of the situation and make sure that any negative consequences of the equity comparisons are avoided, or at least minimized, when rewards are allocated.[25]

REINFORCEMENT THEORY

The reinforcement theory of motivation shifts the emphasis from the employee's underlying needs and thinking processes to the rewards and punishments in the work environment. Based on the work of B. F. Skinner, this theory of motivation suggests that internal states of mind (such as needs) are misleading, scientifically unmeasurable, and in any case hypothetical. Reinforcement theory rests on two underlying assumptions: First, human behavior is determined by the environment. Second, human behavior is subject to observable laws and can be predicted and changed. The foundation of reinforcement theory is the **law of effect,** which states that behavior will be repeated or not, depending on whether the consequence is positive or negative.

Behavior Modification: Applying Concepts of Reinforcement Theory
Behavior modification is the application of reinforcement theory that managers can use to motivate employees. Managers and behavioral scientists need to pay attention to behavior—the observable outcomes of situations and choices, or what people actually do. Since people repeat behaviors that are positively rewarded and avoid behaviors that are punished, managers can in-

Law of effect
Determines if a behavior will be repeated or not, depending on whether the consequence is positive or negative.

Behavior modification
The application of reinforcement theory that managers can use to motivate employees.

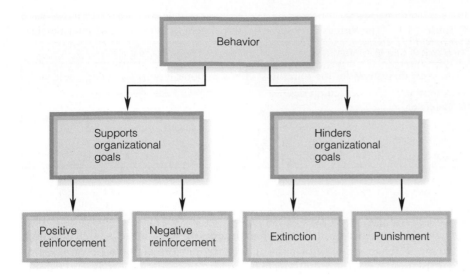

fluence employee performance by reinforcing behavior they see as supporting organizational goals.

The tools of behavior modification are four basic reinforcement strategies, in which either a pleasant or an unpleasant event is applied or withdrawn following a person's behavior. These four reinforcers are illustrated in Figure 15.6.

Positive Reinforcement   A **positive reinforcement** is the administration of positive and rewarding consequences following a desired behavior. This tends to increase the likelihood the person will repeat the behavior in similar settings. For example, a manager praises the marketing representative's high monthly sales performance; a student gets a good grade; a professor receives high teaching evaluations.

Negative Reinforcement   **Negative reinforcement** or avoidance is the removal of negative consequences following a desired behavior. This also tends to increase the likelihood the behavior will be repeated in similar settings. For example, a partner in an accounting firm scolds an employee about tardiness and then stops when the employee begins to be punctual.

Extinction   **Extinction** is the withdrawal of the positive reward or reinforcing consequences for an undesirable behavior. The behavior is no longer reinforced and therefore is less likely to occur in the future. For example, if an employee who is not meeting sales quotas fails to receive bonus checks, she will begin to realize that the behavior is not producing desired outcomes. The undesirable behavior will gradually disappear.

Punishment   **Punishment** is the administration of negative consequences following undesirable behavior. This tends to reduce the likelihood the behavior will be repeated in similar settings. For example, a manager docks an employee's pay for being rude to a customer. However, problems such as resentment and sabotage may accompany a manager's use of punishment.

Which type of reinforcer is most appropriate to use? As a result of considerable research and some popular management books such as the *One Minute Manager*, most managers prefer positive reinforcement to the use of punishment.[26] As Table 15.1 shows, there are several reasons for not using punishment. The manager who positively reinforces desirable behaviors among employees achieves performance improvements without generating the fear, suspicion, and revenge that are often the result of using punishment in the workplace.

Positive reinforcement
The administration of positive and rewarding consequences following a desired behavior.

Negative reinforcement
The removal of negative consequences following a desired behavior.

Exctinction
The withdrawal of the positive reward or reinforcing consequences for an undesirable behavior.

Punishment
The administration of negative consequences following undesirable behavior.

▼ **Table 15.1**   The Virtues of Positive Reinforcement or Why Not Use Punishment?

WHY NOT USE PUNISHMENT?	WHY USE PUNISHMENT?
• May create distress for the punisher • Attention is not focused on desired behavior • May lead to negative side effects (fear, suspicion, and revenge) • May damage employee emotionally	• Temporarily stops or lessens behavior • Quick and easy to use

When an employee's behavior is supportive of the organizational goals, a manager would use either positive or negative reinforcers to increase this desirable behavior. Managers must not allow excellent performance to be ignored or taken for granted. When employee behaviors do not support organizational objectives, a manager should use extinction or punishment (only as a last resort), since this behavior is considered to be undesirable.

Studies have shown that consistent rewards for organizationally desirable behavior result in positive performance in the long term. In contrast, punishment as a primary motivational tool contributes little to high motivation because employees learn to avoid the punisher rather than learning appropriate behaviors. Managers need to observe and manage the consequences of work-related behaviors carefully because individuals have different perceptions of what is rewarding and punishing depending on their values and needs. As the workforce becomes increasingly diverse, this issue will present greater challenges to managers. For example, one employee may consider a day off a motivating reward, but another may prefer money to a day off. Consider how USAA rewards employees for contributing suggestions and ideas to improve the workplace. It offers employees a choice of gifts such as power tools, bicycles, cameras, spa memberships, or certificates for meals at local restaurants.

Schedules of Reinforcement

To use behavior modification effectively, managers need to apply reinforcers properly. **Schedules of reinforcement** specify the basis for and timing of reinforcement. There are two basic types of schedules of reinforcement: continuous and partial.

Continuous Schedule of Reinforcement   With a **continuous schedule of reinforcement,** a desired behavior is rewarded each time it occurs. For example, a manager might praise an employee every time the worker performs a task correctly. This type of reinforcement is very effective during the initial learning process, but it becomes tedious and impractical on an ongoing basis. Further, the desired behavior tends to stop almost immediately unless the reinforcement is continued.

Partial Schedule of Reinforcement   As an alternative, a **partial schedule of reinforcement** can be used. In this case, the desired behavior is rewarded intermittently rather than each time it occurs. With a partial schedule, a desired behavior can be rewarded more often as encouragement during the initial learning process and less often when the behavior has been learned. The four major types of partial reinforcement schedules are compared in Table 15.2.

With a **fixed-interval schedule,** the manager rewards employees at specified time intervals, assuming that the desired behavior has continued at an appropriate level. An example is the Friday paycheck many employees receive.

With a **fixed-ratio schedule,** a reinforcer is provided after a fixed number of occurrences of the desired behavior. For example, a department store wants

Schedules of reinforcement
Specify the basis for and timing of reinforcement.

Continuous schedule of reinforcement
Rewarding a desired behavior each time it occurs.

Partial schedule of reinforcement
Rewarding the desired behavior intermittently.

Fixed interval schedule
Rewards at specific time intervals, assuming that the desired behavior has continued at an appropriate level.

Fixed ratio schedule
Provides a reinforcement after a fixed number of occurrences of the desired behavior.

▼ **Table 15.2**   Comparing Partial Schedules of Reinforcement

SCHEDULE	FORM OF REINFORCEMENT	INFLUENCES ON BEHAVIOR WHEN APPLIED	EFFECTS ON BEHAVIOR WHEN WITHDRAWN	EXAMPLE
Fixed Interval	Reward given on fixed time basis	Leads to average and irregular performance	Rapid extinction of behavior	Weekly or monthly paycheck
Fixed Ratio	Reward tied to specific number of responses	Quickly leads to high and stable performance	Moderately fast extinction of behavior	Piece-rate system
Variable Interval	Reward given at varying times	Leads to moderately high and stable performance	Slow extinction of behavior	Performance appraisals and rewards given at random times each month
Variable Ratio	Reward given at variable amounts of output	Leads to very high performance	Very slow extinction of behavior	Sales bonus tied to the number of new accounts opened, with random changes in the number needed

to increase charge card applications and offers to reward salesclerks each time they open four new accounts. Most piece-rate pay systems are considered fixed-ratio schedules.

With **variable-interval schedules,** reinforcement is administered at random or varying times that cannot be predicted by the employee. For example, a division manager might visit a territory five times a month to comment on employee performance, varying the days and times each month.

Variable-ratio schedules provide a reinforcer after a varying, or random, number of occurrences of the desired behavior rather than after variable time periods. For example, slot machine payoff patterns, which provide rewards after a varying number of pulls on the lever, use a variable-ratio schedule. While people anticipate that the machine will pay a jackpot after a certain number of plays, the exact number of plays is variable.

Variable interval schedule
When reinforcement is administered at random or varying times that cannot be predicted by the employee.

Variable ratio schedules
Reinforcement administered randomly.

When to Use Behavior Modification

To date, most behavior modification programs have been applied to employees at operating levels—clerical employees, production workers, or mechanics. Behavior modification is more easily applied to relatively simple jobs, where critical behaviors can be easily identified and specific performance goals readily set. For managerial jobs, these key factors may be more difficult to apply. Further, it is not clear that supervisor praise, recognition, and feedback are enough. Many times new reinforcers have to be introduced because the old ones become routine.

How successful has behavior modification been in the workplace? Its use has had some notable successes. For example, at Emery Air Freight, to use a classic case, managers wanted workers to use freight containers for shipments because of the cost savings. They established a program of positive reinforcement for employees that resulted in significant improvements in container use, cost savings of over $600,000 annually, and improved employee behavior. Dayton-Hudson used behavior modification in the men's department of one of its stores. The goal was to increase the average sale from $19 to $25. Employees were taught how to make extra sales and were congratulated by a supervisor each time a sale went above $19. Within two months, department sales averaged $23. Other companies, such as General Electric, B. F. Goodrich, Michigan Bell, and Weyerhaeuser, are also using varied forms of behavior modification.

Criticisms of Behavior Modification

Critics of behavior modification charge that it is essentially bribery and that workers are already paid for performance. Because it disregards people's attitudes and beliefs, behavior modification has been called misleading and manipulative. One critic has noted that there is little difference between behavior modification and some key elements of scientific management presented more than 60 years ago by Taylor, particularly where money is involved. Is it a motivational technique for manipulating people? Does it decrease an employee's freedom? If so, is such action on the part of managers unethical? There are no easy answers to these questions.

Consider, for example, an organization that uses behavior modification as a solution to control health care costs and keep employees healthy. While this may sound like an impractical solution to health care costs, organizations with this strategy provide employees with financial incentives if they meet certain "wellness" criteria, such as not smoking, maintaining normal weight, and following a healthy lifestyle. The rewards or incentives used are typically either a lower premium contribution required from employees or higher benefits. For example, Baker Hughes, Inc., a Texas drilling and tool company, estimates it has saved $2 million annually by charging nonsmoking employees $100 less a year for health insurance than smokers. Adolf Coors Company claims it has saved $3 million a year by offering its employees incentives to meet weight, smoking, blood pressure, cholesterol, and other health criteria. Other companies adopting the strategy of rewarding healthy lifestyles include U-Haul, Control Data, and Southern California Edison. To avoid charges of unfairness and discrimination, some companies provide cost savings to employees actively involved in improving their health.[27]

CONTEMPORARY MOTIVATIONAL ISSUES

Several contemporary issues involving motivation offer challenges to today's managers. We will look at three of these issues: goal-setting theory, participative management, and money as a means of motivating employees.

GOAL-SETTING TO SUPPORT QUALITY INITIATIVES

Goal setting
A process intended to increase efficiency and effectiveness by specifying the desired outcomes toward which individuals, groups, departments, and organizations work.

Goal setting from a planning perspective was discussed in Chapter 4. But, as we pointed out earlier with regard to MBO, goal setting can also be applied on an individual level to increase employee motivation.[28] From a motivational perspective, **goal setting** can be used to support quality initiatives. It is a process of increasing efficiency and effectiveness by specifying the desired outcomes toward which individuals, groups, departments, and organizations should work.[29] Goals are the future outcomes (results) to achieve. You may have a set goal such as "I am planning to graduate with a 2.7 grade point average by the end of the summer semester."

As a motivational tool, goal setting can help employees because goals serve three purposes:

- Guide and direct behavior toward supportive organizational goals.
- Provide challenges and standards against which the individual can be assessed.
- Define what is important and provide a framework for planning.

For goal setting to be successful and lead to higher performance levels, goals must be specific and challenging rather than vague and easy. Though it

▼ The manager of this computer software planning group works with his employees in a goal-setting session as a motivational technique.

is not always necessary to have employees participate in the goal-setting process, participation is probably preferable to managers assigning goals when they anticipate that the employee will resist accepting more difficult challenges. Managers must also provide feedback to employees about their performance. A current study found that performance review feedback followed by goal setting favorably influenced employee work satisfaction and organizational commitment to a greater extent than performance review feedback alone.[30]

To use goal setting effectively to motivate employees, managers need to (1) meet regularly with subordinates, (2) work with subordinates to set goals jointly, (3) set goals that are specific and moderately challenging, and (4) provide feedback about performance. When subordinates accept the goal-setting process, they are more likely to be committed and work hard to accomplish goals. The evidence thus far suggests that goal setting will become an increasingly important part of the motivational process in the future. Though limited, some research has suggested that employees achieve high levels of job satisfaction when they perceive that the probability of attaining goals at work is high. Also, they are more satisfied when they perceive more positive than negative goals in their environment.[31] Meeting the Challenge is an exercise that can help you develop your competency at goal setting.

PARTICIPATIVE MANAGEMENT: IMPROVING QUALITY AND PRODUCTIVITY

At a General Electric lighting plant in Ohio, work teams perform many tasks and assume many of the responsibilities once handled by their supervisors. When the plant recently experienced a decline in quality as well as in the demand for the product it manufactured, the workers decided how and when to change the production schedule and eventually which workers should be laid off. This example illustrates the use of **participative management,** an umbrella term that encompasses various activities in which subordinates share a significant degree of decision-making power with their immediate superiors. According to a recent *Business Week* article, participative management in-

Participative management
Encompasses varied activities of high involvement where subordinates share a significant degree of decision-making power with their immediate superiors.

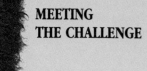

MEETING THE CHALLENGE

LEARNING TO USE GOAL SETTING AS A MOTIVATIONAL TECHNIQUE

Choose a goal for a course you are now taking, a job, or your personal life. Write a goal that is clear, specific, and challenging. Next, decide how you will implement your goal by establishing priorities, developing a work strategy, and a schedule of activities to accomplish this goal. Share the results of your plan in a small group, with a partner, or as a written paper for your instructor. How realistic is your goal and implementation plan? How easy or difficult was this exercise?

Empowering employees
To increase the amount of control and discretion employees have over their job as a means of motivating behavior.

volves any process where power, knowledge, information, and rewards are moved downward in the organization.[32]

Involvement of individuals throughout the organization is now considered essential to organizational survival. As a result of social and political developments over the past couple of decades, people today expect greater participation in choosing directions for their lives in general and their lives at work more specifically.[33] Participative management draws on and is linked to a number of motivation theories. For example, employee involvement can motivate workers by providing more opportunities for growth, responsibility, and commitment in the work itself. Similarly, the process of making and implementing a decision and then seeing the results can help satisfy an employee's need for responsibility, recognition, growth, self-esteem, and achievement.

Participative management programs represent a shift away from traditional management styles and ways of doing business.[34] For participative management to work, however, a company must change. As we discussed in Chapter 11, it is often extremely difficult for managers to give up authority and for employees to translate that surrender of power by higher-ups into lasting improvements in quality and productivity.[35] When companies increase the amount of control and discretion workers have over their jobs, they are **empowering employees** and may improve the motivation of both employees and management.[36]

Do employee participation and involvement really work to motivate individuals? In a recent survey of top U.S. executives, responses were overwhelmingly optimistic toward employee involvement and participative management.[37] Respondents viewed participative management programs as having positive influences on corporate quality, productivity, and customer service. For example, Levi Strauss managers in Fayetteville, Arkansas, responded to employees on the factory floor when they proposed ways to curb boredom and boost productivity. Machine operators designed a system to team up to learn each other's jobs. Operators did top stitching one day and creasing the next, and soon management allowed employees to develop their own work schedules and quality-control checks. The team idea was such a positive motivation for employees that the company is adopting it in other Levi plants around the globe.[38] General Mills has successfully developed an employee participative system with self-managed teams to run several plants. At some beverage plants, four shifts of 20-person teams are informed of marketing plans and production costs. These teams are involved in everything from scheduling production to rejecting products not up to quality standards. They receive bonuses based on plant performances. Some 60 percent of General Mills plants have been converted to this type of participative management work system. The approach has produced significant gains in quality, productivity, and em-

▼ **Table 15.3**   Motivating Employees Through Involvement

Strategic business objectives for involving employees include the following, listed in *decreasing* order of importance:

- To improve quality
- To improve productivity
- To improve customer service
- To reduce costs
- To increase employee commitment
- To encourage innovation
- To push accountability downward
- To change employee values
- To change the culture
- To improve employee retention
- To reduce management layers

ployee motivation.[39] Other strategic business objectives for using a participative management approach are listed in Table 15.3.

MONEY AS A MOTIVATOR

The issue of whether money motivates is particularly relevant to many managers. However, the answer to a common management question, "Does money motivate my subordinates?" depends on which theory the manager accepts. Expectancy theory asserts that money motivates people if it is contingent on performance and satisfies their personal goals. Herzberg's two-factor theory would argue that money is a hygiene factor, so it does not act as a motivator.

As a medium of exchange, money should motivate to the degree that people perceive it as a means to acquire other things they want. Money also has symbolic meaning that managers must consider. In general, to motivate, money must be important to the employees and must be perceived as a direct reward for performance.

INTERNATIONAL PERSPECTIVES ON MOTIVATION: ━━━━━ APPRECIATING DIVERSITY

Studying theories of motivation can lead us to assume that we are dealing with "human nature"—the way people really are. We must be aware, however, that most of the research for these theories has been by Americans with Americans, although some of Herzberg's work did include cross-cultural comparisons. Americans' motivation patterns and social character arise out of our unique history; they are not universal and to some degree differ from those of other cultures. These differences should be remembered when we hear that we should apply management practices from another culture to the American work scene; the past and present preoccupation with Japanese methods is a good example.[40] Further, American corporations with multinational divisions cannot assume that management practices that work well in the United States will apply to individuals in their overseas operations.

The United States is an achievement-oriented society that has historically encouraged and honored individual accomplishment and the attainment of material prosperity. Individualism, independence, self-confidence, and speak-

▼ Employees on the work team pictured here perform tasks and assume responsibilities once handled by their manager.

ing out against injustice and threats are important elements of the American character. Japanese motivations and values are quite different, with obvious implications for management practices.[41] The Japanese place greater emphasis on socially oriented qualities. Their collective society is arranged in a rigid hierarchy, and all members are expected to maintain absolute loyalty and obedience to authority. Dependency and security are part of the Japanese upbringing, whereas autonomy and early independence are typically American. In their corporate life, Japanese show great dependency and are highly conforming and obedient. Japanese managers recognize that these characteristics can inhibit creativity and innovation and are consequently encouraging programs in their schools that will develop the creativity and ingenuity they envy in Americans.[42]

The cross-cultural research on achievement has been relatively consistent across cultures,[43] stimulated by the realization that managers in multinational corporations must be sensitive to the underlying values and needs of their diverse employees.[44] For example, managers in New Zealand appear to follow an achievement pattern developed in the United States. In general, managers in Anglo-American countries such as the United States, Canada, and Great Britain tend to have a high need for achievement as well as a high need to produce and a strong willingness to accept risk. In contrast, managers in countries such as Chile and Portugal tend to have a lower need for achievement.[45] Keep in mind, however, that the word *achievement* itself is difficult to translate into other languages and this influences any cross-cultural research findings.

The implications for managerial style, practices, and motivational planning for an American firm operating branches in foreign countries are apparent. Managers must take the social character, the values, and cultural practices of each country into consideration.[46] Our large corporations operating abroad have long known this but have often failed to put it into practice. American managers seem to forget that people of other cultures perceive work differently. Individual values and attitudes, including attitudes toward work, have strong cultural ties. Managers, therefore, must be careful in designing reward systems to ensure that the rewards are truly motivational in the local cultural framework.

A well-managed diverse workforce is instrumental for a firm's competitive advantage. In order to develop or maintain such an advantage, policy makers must consider a broad definition of motivation when determining compensation packages, responsibilities, rules and procedures, organizational structure, control systems, job design, and management techniques.[47]

MANAGERIAL IMPLICATIONS

According to a recent book *Control Your Destiny or Someone Else Will* by Noel Tichy and Stratford Sherman, Jack Welch, CEO of General Electric since 1981, is known for his breakthrough management ideas and his will to apply them.[48] We conclude with some points about the lessons Welch has learned at GE and his ideas on motivation and success:[49]

- Only the most productive companies will survive the globalization of the marketplace. To be productive, companies must improve quality and productivity and increase the value they place on employees.
- The only way to be more productive is by getting people involved and excited about their jobs.
- Human values must take priority over cost cutting and restructuring.
- People must learn the value of their jobs and understand the principle that job security comes from winning.
- Invest totally in your people. Companies can't promise lifetime employment, but by constant training and education, they may be able to guarantee lifetime employability.
- Managers must create trustful environments. Trust is enormously motivational and powerful in a corporation. People won't do their best unless they believe they will be treated fairly.
- Find a way to engage the mind of every single employee. It is imperative to make every person more valuable.

In this chapter we have examined motivation as a key management tool that organizations can use to energize employees. An organization can help create a motivating atmosphere by making the work environment pleasant and conducive to productive output. The organization that achieves these conditions will create an environment in which all members can contribute to their maximum potential and in which the value of diversity can be fully realized.[50] Many companies are attempting to improve working conditions for employees based on the premise that a motivated workforce can reduce absenteeism, increase productivity, encourage labor-management harmony, and lead to a better product or service. As we see from the Managerial Resolution, USAA is finding that its motivational plan is paying off.

USAA STRIVES FOR EXCEPTIONAL SERVICE

MANAGERIAL INCIDENT RESOLUTION

To make USAA an industry leader, Robert McDermott has focused on providing quality service to customers. As a company objective, he places service before everything else and believes that the emphasis on service motivates employees. McDermott set out to empower employees by (1) updating technology, (2) offering training and education programs, (3) treating employees positively, and (4) decentralizing operations.

By updating technology, employees were able to offer faster and more reliable customer service than USAA's competitors. For example, automating the policy-writing system reduced the paper flow and employees' frustrations. This motivated employees to achieve higher levels of performance.

McDermott's plan empowered employees through job enrichment. He created more interesting jobs and established a $20 million a year training and education program (double the industry average). The company pays tuition for employees doing graduate work, including fees for CPA exams, and brings in teachers from surrounding universities to teach classes at the San Antonio office complex.

Employees also benefit in other ways under McDermott's plan. The three-million-square-foot office complex includes tennis courts, lighted softball fields, jogging trails, picnic groves, a physical fitness center, and a subsidized "dump your plump" cafeteria. Cultural events are held in the courtyards at lunchtime. The complex also includes a company store, a well-stocked library, and a clinic staffed by nine registered nurses. A subsidized van pool transports 1,700 riders a day from distances of up to 60 miles. The company also instituted a four-day, 39-hour work week. Employee's ideas and suggestions are rewarded through recognition breakfasts and gifts.

Decentralization was also part of the plan. USAA restructured into five groups, providing employees with greater authority to make decisions and take action with customers. For example, service representatives can make policy changes without having to check with the main office. Claim representatives can issue certain payments without an inspection.

The changes at USAA have been quite effective. The turnover has been reduced from 44 percent to an industry low of less than 7 percent, and absenteeism went from double digits to below 2 percent. This is evidence that the motivational techniques are affecting the bottom line. Thus, by viewing his employees as important assets to the company and using motivational tools, McDermott has improved the company in many ways.[51] ▼

SUMMARY

- Motivation is defined as the forces acting on or within a person that cause that person to behave in a specific, goal-directed manner. It is a psychological process that gives behavior purpose and direction.
- Managers can draw upon several different approaches to motivation. Content or need-based theories emphasize specific human needs or the factors within a person that energize, direct, and stop behavior. These theories explain motivation as a phenomenon primarily occurring intrinsically, or within an individual.
- Herzberg's two-factor theory examines the relationship between job satisfaction and productivity. The sources of work satisfaction are termed satisfiers or motivator factors. The sources of dissatisfaction are called dissatisfiers or hygiene factors.
- Need theories of motivation provide managers with an understanding of the underlying needs that motivate people to behave in certain ways, but they do not promote an understanding of why people choose a particular behavior to accomplish task-related goals.
- Process theories take a more dynamic view of motivation than need theories. Equity theory and expectancy theory focus on understanding the thought or cognitive processes in the individual's mind that influence behavior.

- Managers use expectancy theory in the workplace by first finding out which rewards under their control have the highest valences for their employees. Then they link these rewards to the performance they desire.

- Reinforcement theory focuses on how employees learn desired work behaviors and rests on two underlying assumptions: First, human behavior is determined by the environment. Second, human behavior is subject to observable laws and can be predicted and changed. The foundation of reinforcement theory is the law of effect, which states that behavior will be repeated or not, depending on whether the consequence is positive or negative.

- Goal setting is a process for increasing efficiency and effectiveness by specifying the desired outcomes toward which individuals, groups, departments, and organizations should work. To be successful and lead to higher performance levels, goals must be specific and challenging rather than vague and easy. Employees should participate in goal setting, especially when the manager anticipates that the employee will resist accepting more difficult challenges.

KEY TERMS

Motivation (p. 493)
Physiological needs (p. 494)
Security needs (p. 495)
Affiliation needs (p. 495)
Esteem needs (p. 495)
Self-actualization needs (p. 495)
Motivator factors (p. 497)
Hygiene factors (p. 497)
Need for achievement (p. 498)
Need for power (p. 500)
Need for affiliation (p. 500)
Expectancy (p. 501)
Instrumentality (p. 501)

Valence (p. 501)
Law of effect (p. 504)
Behavior modification (p. 504)
Positive reinforcement (p. 505)
Negative reinforcement (p. 505)
Extinction (p. 505)
Punishment (p. 505)
Schedules of reinforcement (p. 506)
Continuous schedule of reinforcement (p. 506)
Partial schedule of reinforcement (p. 506)
Fixed interval schedule (p. 506)

Fixed ratio schedule (p. 506)
Variable interval schedule (p. 507)
Variable ratio schedule (p. 507)
Goal setting (p. 508)
Participative management (p. 509)
Empowering employees (p. 510)

REVIEW QUESTIONS

1. Explain what is meant by motivation.
2. What are the basic approaches to motivation?
3. Describe the main components of Maslow's hierarchy of needs.
4. Distinguish between motivator and hygiene factors.
5. What are the characteristics of an individual who has a high need for achievement?
6. What is the basic premise of expectancy theory?
7. What possible actions would an individual take to reduce inequity?
8. Describe the four types of reinforcers. Develop specific examples of the four types of reinforcers.

9. When should a manager use punishment? Under what conditions should a manager not use punishment?
10. How can a manager apply goal-setting theory to motivate employees?
11. What makes participative management or employee involvement programs motivational?
12. Explain why managers need to be aware of cultural differences in motivation.

DISCUSSION QUESTIONS

Improving Critical Thinking

1. What is the value of Herzberg's two-factor theory?
2. Think about the best job you have ever had. What motivation approach was used in that organization?
3. How can managers apply behavior modification to improve an employee's performance?
4. What ethical considerations should be considered before using a behavior modification program at work?

Enhancing Communication Skills

5. How could a manager apply Maslow's hierarchy of needs theory to motivate employees on the job? To practice your written communication skills, write a brief paper and provide specific examples.
6. Think about the worst job you have ever had. What motivation approach was used in that organization?

Prepare a short presentation that describes this job citing specific examples of motivation approaches that you feel were (are) used incorrectly. Make suggestions for possible changes.

Building Teamwork Skills

7. What motivational lessons can be learned from Mary Kay Cosmetics' motivational programs? Form a small group as directed by your instructor and discuss. Be prepared to present your group's answers to the class.
8. In a small group, visit either a local health club or diet center and ask for an interview with the manager. What kinds of rewards does the organization give members who achieve targeted goals? Does it use punishment? Be prepared to present your findings.

ETHICS: TAKE A STAND

Arlene transferred from the corporate headquarters of Juno Company to assume the position of supervisor at a division less than a year ago. Now she must prepare for the annual performance evaluations, but she is not looking forward to this task.

Arlene had been given the objective of increasing the productivity of the department. She knew it would be a tough job. The previous supervisor had been in the department for many years and was very close to the staff. As a result, staff morale was at an all-time low when Arlene arrived. Nevertheless, she realized she would have to change many informal, unproductive procedures.

Because of the situation, Arlene had used the utmost care in implementing new procedures and making changes in the department. Initially, her changes were met with considerable resistance, but Arlene remained consistent and pleasant. In the last few weeks, the staff has begun to accept her and the new policies.

Arlene feels that the performance of the staff is improving, over the year as a whole, it was substandard. The corporate office is aware of this and expects appropriate ratings. Top management views performance appraisals as a critical human resource management tool. At the same time, Arlene is afraid that poor ratings will harm staff performance and motivation. Any gains she has made in the last few months may be lost. Further, Arlene is uncertain about the legal complications that might result if an employee with a negative permanent record seeks a new job opportunity.

For Discussion

1. Should Arlene use punishment to motivate her employees toward higher performance?
2. Should Arlene put negative performance evaluations on her employees' records? If she does give the employees poor ratings, what should be her major concerns?

BEHAVIOR MODIFICATION: USEFUL MANAGEMENT TECHNIQUE OR EMPLOYEE MANIPULATION?

Form teams as directed by your instructor to debate the issue of how managers can apply behavior modification in the workplace. Half of the teams should research and prepare to argue that behavior modification can be a useful management technique for increasing performance and productivity in the organization. The other teams should research and prepare to argue that behavior modification is essentially a technique for manipulating employee behavior.

VIDEO CASE

Financial Service Corporation: The Challenge and Rewards of Motivating Employees

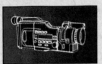
The challenges to Financial Service Corporation (FSC), of Marietta, Georgia, were basic: survival and a return to profitability. Declining sales and high costs had yielded monthly operating losses. Independent representatives on whom FSC depended for sales were deserting it. Employees felt little loyalty and no motivation to perform well.

But after finding some unique ways to motivate representatives and employees, in less than three years, FSC was in the black, and income was rising. Sales were up, and costs were under control. The number of representatives had risen, too, and revenue per representative had doubled. Net worth went from zero to more than $2 million in less than two years.

The company credits this remarkable turnaroud to the motivation of its people. The company heightened motivation primarily by getting employees involved in the organization, giving them a piece of the action, and developing a unique computer/automation system.

FSC's customers and sales representatives are scattered around the country. The company supplies information on insurance and investment opportunities—mutual funds, securities, limited partnerships—to hundreds of financial professionals who help consumers and small businesses with their insurance and investment needs. It also executes transactions, keeps records, and processes data.

Mutual Life Insurance Company of New York had bought the company from its management in 1986. Mutual Life sold it back, loss-ridden, in 1989. FSC Chairman E. James Wisner immediately met with employees and then with field representatives. Ownership of the company, he promised, would be shared with the field representative and the employees. In fact, that promise was kept in 1991 when stock was distributed—some shares were given, others sold—to

field representatives, employees, and managers in varying rations. Wisner himself owns 26 percent of the company.

Employees were then given a choice of four compensation packages with fixed and variable components that, to different degrees, gave them the choice of guaranteed income or profit sharing if the company did well. The higher the fixed component, the lower the variable; the lower the fixed component, the higher the variable. Surprisingly, many employees at modest salary levels opted for riskier—but potentially more rewarding—packages.

In addition to improving employee motivation, linking pay to profits strengthened FSC by making it easier to weather any future downturn without losing employees it wanted to keep. Normally, the fixed nature of salaries makes it difficult to cut payroll costs during business slowdowns except by firings.

Today's FSC is minus some people it didn't want to keep. The company has dropped representatives who were poor sales producers, replacing them with representatives who are more productive. It has also been able to cut the number of home-office employees, while improving quality of services, by investing $2 million in state-of-the-art computer software and taking other steps to improve efficiency.

FSC's progress is apparent not only in its better balance sheet, but in the number of the customer complaints it receives. They used to average 1,100 a month, the company says. Now they average 10.[52]

For Discussion
1. Using Herzberg's model of motivation, discuss the motivator and hygiene factors at FSC.
2. If you were an adviser to Wisner, what other techniques to motivate employees would you suggest? Why?

CASE

Can They Do It Again?

The spectators are on their feet. The clock is ticking down from 30 seconds. The score is tied and the Eagles have the ball. As the guard brings the ball down the court, the crowd chants, "Defense, defense, defense." The wave goes around the arena. A crisp pass crosses the floor to the forward. He shoots. It's off the rim. No basket is made. The Eagles get the rebound. Now there are 10 seconds, 5, 4, 3, 2, 1. The shot is off just as the buzzer sounds. It's good! The crowd goes wild. The Eagles win their first CBA Championship.

Later, at the press conference, Coach Long was asked about next year. Could the Eagles repeat their victory? He answered with a resounding "yes." Privately, Coach Long wondered if he could continue to motivate the players and control some of the behaviors that caused problems this past year. He also wondered about the off-season. Would the players be motivated to stay in physical shape and develop their skills without the staff's constant supervision? The players certainly made a lot of money playing ball, but they didn't seem to take any responsibility for their behavior off the court.

Coach Long pondered several problems that he and his staff confronted this past year. First, certain players were consistently in some kind of trouble. Recently, one player was arrested for possession of cocaine, another got in a fight at a local bar, and a third was arrested for DUI. Although the player involved in the fight claimed self-defense, and the other team members said the drug charges were false, the team had received negative publicity. The players were role models to hundreds of youngsters, and the Eagle organization just couldn't tolerate such behavior.

Other problems involved punctuality, absenteeism, and general courtesy. Three or four of the players were consistently late for practice. A few players invariably missed flights for away games. Some of the players were rude to the fans or refused to give autographs to fans who waited after the games. Several players took shortcuts across the running field to cut down on the required running distances. Heavy fines were imposed for these behaviors, but that didn't seem to work. The staff had to call players to remind them of practice times, pick them up for practice, watch them at practice, make special travel arrangements, and apologize to the fans for the players' surly attitudes.

Considering all this, Coach Long wondered how the team won the championship in the first place. He reminded himself that despite all the problems, the players did get along well together.

After a two-week vacation, the staff had their first meeting. Coach Long mentioned the concerns he had about the previous year and his doubts that the team could win another championship under the same circumstances. The staff members agreed and voiced their concerns as well. They concluded with the commitment to making the changes necessary to produce another successful year.

For Discussion

1. What seems to be the central motivational problem that plagues the Eagles?

2. Using reinforcement theory of motivation, describe the types of reinforcers the staff is using. What works? What is not working? Why?

3. What changes should the staff make? How should the changes be implemented?

EXPERIENTIAL EXERCISE 15.1

Motivation Feedback Opinionnaire

Objective: To develop an understanding of how to apply motivational tools and techniques in the workplace. Once you have completed this chart, you can see your relative strength in each area of needs motivation.

Using the scale below, circle the number that best matches your response to the following statements. There are no right or wrong answers. Complete every item.

Strongly Agree	Agree	Slightly Agree	Neutral	Slightly Disagree	Disagree	Strongly Disagree
+3	+2	+1	0	−1	−2	−3

1. Employees who do their jobs very well should receive special wage increases. +3 +2 +1 0 −1 −2 −3

2. Better job descriptions would be helpful so that employees will know exactly what is expected of them. +3 +2 +1 0 −1 −2 −3

3. Employees need to be reminded that their jobs are dependent on the company's ability to compete effectively. +3 +2 +1 0 −1 −2 −3

4. A supervisor should give a good deal of attention to the physical working conditions of his or her employees. +3 +2 +1 0 −1 −2 −3

5. A supervisor should work hard to develop a friendly working atmosphere among her or his people. +3 +2 +1 0 −1 −2 −3

6. Individual recognition for above-standard performance means a lot to employees. +3 +2 +1 0 −1 −2 −3

7. Indifferent supervision can often bruise feelings. +3 +2 +1 0 −1 −2 −3

8. Employees want to feel that their real skills and capacities are put to use in their jobs. +3 +2 +1 0 −1 −2 −3

9. The company retirement benefits and stock programs are important factors in keeping employees on their jobs. +3 +2 +1 0 −1 −2 −3

10. Almost every job can be made more stimulating and challenging. +3 +2 +1 0 −1 −2 −3

11. Many employees want to give their best in everything they do. +3 +2 +1 0 −1 −2 −3

12. Management could show more interest in employees by sponsoring social events after hours. +3 +2 +1 0 −1 −2 −3

13. Pride in one's work is actually an important reward. +3 +2 +1 0 −1 −2 −3

14. Employees want to be able to think of themselves as "the best" at their own jobs. +3 +2 +1 0 −1 −2 −3

15. The quality of the relationships in an informal work group is quite important. +3 +2 +1 0 −1 −2 −3

16. Individual incentive bonuses would improve the performance of employees. +3 +2 +1 0 −1 −2 −3

17. Visibility with upper management is important to employees. +3 +2 +1 0 −1 −2 −3

18. Employees generally like to schedule their own work and to make job-related decisions with a minimum of supervision. +3 +2 +1 0 −1 −2 −3

19. Job security is important to employees. +3 +2 +1 0 −1 −2 −3

20. Having good equipment to work with is important to employees. +3 +2 +1 0 −1 −2 −3

Scoring

1. Transfer the numbers you circled to the appropriate places in the following table:

ITEM NUMBER	SCORE		ITEM NUMBER	SCORE		ITEM NUMBER	SCORE
10	_____		2	_____		5	_____
11	_____		3	_____		7	_____
13	_____		9	_____		12	_____
18	_____		19	_____		15	_____
Total	_____		Total	_____		Total	_____
(self-actualization needs)			(safety needs)			(belonging needs)	

ITEM NUMBER	SCORE		ITEM NUMBER	SCORE
6	_____		1	_____
8	_____		4	_____
14	_____		16	_____
17	_____		20	_____
Total	_____		Total	_____
(esteem needs)			(physiological needs)	

2. Record your total scores in the following chart by marking an "X" in each row next to the number of your score for that area of needs motivation:

	−12	−10	−8	−6	−4	−2	0	+2	+4	+6	+8	+10	+12
Self-actualization													
Esteem													
Belonging													
Safety													
Physiological													

Once you have completed this chart, you can see. your relative strength in each of these areas of needs motivation. There is, of course, no "right" answer. What is right for you is what matches the actual needs of your employees and that, of course, is specific to each situation and each individual. In general, however, the "experts" tell us that today's employees are best motivated by efforts in the areas of belonging and esteem.

SOURCE: Adapted from W. J. Pfeiffer and E. E. Jones, eds., *The 1973 Annual Handbook for Group Facilitators* (San Diego, Calif.: University Associates, 1973).

NOTES

1. Adapted from T. Teal, "Service Comes First: An Interview with USAA's Robert F. McDermott," *Harvard Business Review* (September/October 1992): 117-27.

2. *Creating and Motivating a Superior, Loyal Staff* (New York: National Institute of Business Management, 1992).

3. For an integrated motivational model, see H. J. Klein, "An Integrated Control Theory Model of Work Motivation," *Academy of Management Review* 14 (1989): 150-72.

4. R. M. Steers and P. W. Porter, eds., *Motivation and Work Behavior*, 3d ed. (New York: McGraw-Hill, 1983).

5. This discussion is based on *Creating and Motivating a Superior, Loyal Staff.*

6. For a research perspective, see M. A. Wahba, and L. G. Bridwell, "Maslow Reconsidered: A Review of Research on the Need Hierarchy," *Organizational Behavior and Human Performance* 16 (1976): 212-40.

7. A. H. Maslow, "A Theory of Human Motivation," *Psychological Review* 50 (1943): 370-96.

8. M. K. Ash, *Mary Kay* (New York: Harper & Row, 1981); T. J. Peter and R. H. Waterman, *In Search of Excellence* (New York: Harper & Row, 1982); and W. Zellner, "Mary Kay Is Singing I Feel Pretty," *Business Week*, December 2, 1991, 102.

9. F. Herzberg, "One More Time: How Do You Motivate Employees?" *Harvard Business Review* (January/February 1968): 53-62.

10. "What Motivates Managers," *Inc.*, June 1989, 115.

11. D. C. McClelland, *The Achieving Society* (New York: Van Nostrand Reinhold, 1961).

12. R. M. Steers and D. N. Braunstein, "A Behaviorally-Based Measure of Manifest Needs in Work Settings," *Journal of Vocational Behavior* 9 (1976): 251-61.

13. D. Miron and D. McClelland, "The Impact of Achievement Motivation Training on Small Businesses," *California Management Review* (Summer 1979): 13-28.

14. D. C. McClelland, *Human Motivation* (Glenview, Ill.: Scott, Foresman, 1985).

15. J. Hyatt, "The Entrepreneur of the Year," *Inc.*, January 1991, 35-51.

16. Miron and McClelland, "The Impact of Achievement Motivation Training on Small Businesses."

17. For a classic discussion of power, see D. McClelland and H. Burnham, "Power Is the Great Motivator," *Harvard Business Review* 54 (March/April 1976): 100-10.

18. V. H. Vroom, *Work and Motivation* (New York: John Wiley & Sons, 1964).

19. *Creating and Motivating a Superior, Loyal Staff.*

20. R. W. Griffin, "Effects of Work Redesign on Employee Perceptions, Attitudes, and Behaviors: A Long-Term Investigation," *Academy of Management Journal* 34 (1991): 425-35.

21. As discussed in J. M. Kouzes and B. Z. Posner, *The Leadership Challenge: How to Get Extraordinary Things Done in Organizations* (San Francisco: Jossey-Bass, 1987).

22. J. S. Adams, "Toward an Understanding of Inequity," *Journal of Abnormal and Social Psychology* 67 (1963): 422-36.

23. See S. J. Adams, "Toward an Understanding of Inequity," *Journal of Abnormal and Social Psychology* 67 (1963): 422-36; and S. J. Adams, "Inequity in Social Exchange," in L. Berkowitz, ed., *Advances in Experimental Social Psychology*, vol. 2 (New York: Academic Press, 1965), 267-300.

24. J. D. Hatfield and E. W. Miles, "A New Perspective on Equity Theory: The Equity Sensitivity Construct," *Academy of Management Review* 12 (1987): 222-34.

25. E. W. Miles, J. D. Hatfield, and R. C. Huseman, "The Equity Sensitivity Construct: Potential Implications for Work Performance," *Journal of Management* 15 (1989): 581-88.

26. K. Blanchard and J. Johnson, *The One Minute Manager* (New York: Morrow, 1982).

27. G. Koretz, "Economic Trends," *Business Week*, April 29, 1991, 22.

28. For a detailed review, see E. Locke, K. Shaw, L. Saari, and G. P. Latham, "Goal Setting and Task Performance, 1969-1980," *Psychological Bulletin* 90 (1981): 125-52.

29. The work on goal-setting theory is well summarized in E. Locke and G. P. Latham, *Goal Setting: A Motivational Technique That Works!* (Englewood Cliffs, N.J.: Prentince-Hall, 1984).

30. A. Tziner and G. P. Latham, "The Effects of Appraisal Instrument, Feedback and Goal-setting on Worker Satisfaction and Commitment," *Journal of Organizational Behavior* 10 (1989): 145-53.

31. L. Roberson, "Prediction of Job Satisfaction from Characteristics of Personal Work Goals," *Journal of Organizational Behavior* 11 (1990): 29-41.

32. J. Byrne, "Management's New Gurus," *Business Week*, August 31, 1992, 44-52.

33. J. B. Miller, *The Corporate Coach* (New York: St. Martin's Press, 1994).

34. B. S. Moskal, "Is Industry Ready for Adult Relationships?" *Industry Week*, January 21, 1991, 112-99.

35. Byrne, "Management's New Gurus."

36. J. Hirsch, "Now Hotel Clerks Provide More Than Keys," *Wall Street Journal*, March 5, 1993, B1.

37. M. Hammer and J. Champy, *Reengineering the Corporation: A Manifesto for Business Revolution* (New York: HarperBusiness, 1994).

38. Moskal, "Is Industry Ready for Adult Relationships?"

39. Byrne, "Management's New Gurus"; D. W. Johnson and F. P. Johnson, *Joining Together: Group Theory and Group Skills* (Boston: Allyn & Bacon, 1994), 502-10; and Miller, *The Corporate Coach*, 3-10.

40. N. Adler, "A Typology of Management Studies Involving Culture," *Journal of International Business Studies* (Fall 1983): 29-47.

41. A. Howard, K. Shudo, and M. Umeshima, "Motivation and Values among Japanese and American Managers," *Personnel Psychology* 36 (1983): 883-98.

42. J. T. Spence, "Achievement American Style: The Rewards and Costs of Individualism," *American Psychologist* 40 (1985): 1285-94.

43. N. J. Adler, *International Dimensions of Organizational Behavior* (Boston: Kent, 1986); and M. Dolecheck, "Cross-cultural Analysis of Business Ethics: Hong Kong and American Business Personnel," *Journal of Managerial Issues* 4 (1992): 288-303.

44. S. Cady, P. Fandt, and D. Fernandez, "Investigating Cultural Differences in Personal Success: Implications for Designing Effective Reward Systems," *Journal of Value Based Management* 6 (1993): 65-80.

45. J. Lau and A. B. Shani, *Behavior in Organizations: An Experiential Approach*, 5th ed. (Homewood, Ill.: Irwin, 1992).

46. This discussion is from G. Hofstede, "The Interaction between National and Organizational Value Systems," *Journal of Management Studies* 22 (1985): 347-57; and G. Hofstede, *Culture's Consequences: International Differences in Work-Related Values* (Beverly Hills, Calif.: Sage, 1980).

47. This discussion is based on the research results found in Cady, Fandt, and Fernandez, "Investigating Cultural Differences in Personal Success: Implications For Designing Effective Reward Systems."

48. N. Tichy and S. Sherman, *Control Your Own Destiny or Someone Else Will* (New York: Doubleday, 1993).

49. This section is taken from "Managing: Jack Welch's Lessons for Success," *Fortune*, January 25, 1993, 86-93.

50. T. Cox, Jr., "The Multicultural Organization," *Academy of Management Executive* 5 (1991): 34-47.

51. Adapted from Teal, "Service Comes First: An Interview with USAA's Robert F. McDermott."

52. Adapted from "Financial Services Corporation: Up from a Downtrend," *Real-World Lessons for America's Small Businesses: Insights from the Blue Chip Enterprise Initiative* (*Nation's Business* on behalf of Connecticut Mutual Life Insurance Company and the U.S. Chamber of Commerce, 1992) 16-17.

IBAX: FACILITATING CHANGE THROUGH LEADERSHIP, COMMUNICATION, AND MOTIVATION

By now you should be very familiar with IBAX, the company profiled in the cohesion cases at the close of the major sections of the book. IBAX, a partnership between IBM and Baxter, had experienced significant strategic, operational, and financial problems since its inception in 1989. As of the beginning of 1991, Jeff Goodman, the newly hired CEO of IBAX, was in the process of implementing a retrenchment strategy designed to restore the company's product quality, customer satisfaction levels, productivity, and financial performance.

As we saw in the last cohesion case, Goodman implemented major changes in the organizational structure of IBAX, its human resource management practices, and its organizational culture. In this case, we will examine how leadership, communication, and motivation changed at IBAX.

LEADERSHIP

Goodman knew that the successful implementation of a retrenchment strategy would require strong leadership throughout the organization. He felt strongly that "leading by example" would be critical in getting employees to deal more effectively with each other, the customers, the partners, and other stakeholders of the organization.

Upon his arrival, Goodman assessed the individuals who occupied managerial positions in the company, as well as those who appeared capable of assuming such roles. Based on that assessment, he was able to identify a core group of individuals who could fulfill senior management leadership roles within IBAX, as well as other leadership roles throughout the organization. The next challenge was to turn this group of individuals into a team that would be committed to the company, as well as to each other.

He began by taking the senior management group through an intensive off-site team-building program that involved everything from classroom lectures to scaling walls and swinging on ropes. The intent of the program was to build the trust and commitment of the team. Once Goodman was convinced that his senior management group had become a team, he turned his efforts to infusing the team philosophy throughout the organization. The other managers who had been identified as leaders within the company went through the same training with their work groups. Eventually, everyone in the organization had participated in the team-building program.

Goodman's challenge was to ensure that the team-building training was transferred back into the workplace. He continued to stress the importance of the concepts within the work environment, and eventually, the team philosophy became part of the organizational culture at IBAX. The ongoing behavior of the employees began to reflect their dedication to the company and their teams. This was evidenced by a growing commitment to deliver better quality products and services to the customers.

COMMUNICATION ━━━━━━━━━━━━━━━

As was mentioned previously, communication at IBAX prior to Goodman's arrival had been limited and primarily one-way—from the bottom up. Top management rarely communicated with the employees at the lower levels of the organization. As a result, the employees were literally unaware of the severity of the problems facing the company in early 1991. Therefore, one of Goodman's primary challenges was to inform the employees of the reality of the situation at IBAX and then develop the communication infrastructure to ensure that they had the information they needed to do their jobs effectively.

Goodman began by holding company-wide meetings in which "he threw open the financial statements of the company and let the numbers tell the story." Where necessary, he explained what the financial statements said and what they meant. He also provided measures of customer satisfaction and perceived product quality to the employees. These were objective measurements that were visible to everyone and led to obvious conclusions regarding the performance of the company in the short term, as well as its long-term viability. These sessions provided employees with new insights about the situation at IBAX. They began to understand that survival depended on their ability to make radical and dramatic changes in the way the company operated.

Once Goodman knew that he had successfully communicated the need for change, he began to build a communication infrastructure that kept everyone apprised of the condition of the company and provided open access to the information they needed to do their jobs well. Everyone in each business unit had open access to revenues, expenses, statistics, and other decisional information that was relevant for their business. This information was posted on bulletin boards and distributed in reports; it was updated monthly and discussed among peers regularly. For the first time, employees had access to the information they needed to do their jobs effectively and efficiently and with a focus on achieving high-level performance as measured by critical financial and performance variables.

MOTIVATION ━━━━━━━━━━━━━━━

Goodman had a broad-based leadership team in place, had communicated the need for change to the employees, and had set up a well-defined communication infrastructure within the company. Yet he also needed to establish methods for motivating employees to do what was necessary to improve product quality, customer service, and customer satisfaction. This required an understanding of what motivates people and the development of a reward system that was based on realistic, but aggressive performance goals.

Goodman's philosophy of motivation was simple. He believed that people are motivated by the ability to be involved, make decisions, and make a difference. They want to "buy in" to their company and its products, and they want to reap the rewards associated with doing a good job. With this philosophy in mind, Goodman knew that he had to encourage the employees of IBAX to take ownership in the turnaround—to feel responsible for the company's success.

From Goodman's perspective, this translated into empowerment. He felt strongly that the employees had to be empowered to make a difference in the performance of the company. But he also knew that you can't just empower people and expect positive results. Many employees need support and development to be effectively empowered—in other words, they need to be "enabled." Some employees simply weren't capable of assuming responsibility for important tasks within the organization. Others were capable, but did not have access to the information or resources they needed to do their jobs well. Others lacked the organizational authority to get their jobs done. In all of these cases, Goodman and his leadership team stepped in and provided what was needed. For some employees, that meant additional education and training; in other cases it simply required providing information, resources, or authority. But in virtually all cases, the employees at IBAX were enabled and empowered to do their jobs well.

Even empowered employees need performance standards to work toward. And the employees at IBAX had them. Employees engaged in what Goodman calls "covenant defining." As he explains it, "when one has a job to do, they should build a covenant with the person to whom they report. This covenant should define their responsibilities and how they will be measured and evaluated in light of those responsibilities. This covenant becomes a binding agreement between the parties involved as to their commitment to one another." The performance standards that resulted from this process of covenant defining provided the measures by which employees were evaluated and rewarded.

The formal reward system was based on these performance standards, as well as on attributes and behaviors related to team leadership and team behavior. Employees were measured over time, and those who met their standards and contributed to the team were rewarded. Beyond the formal reward system, IBAX implemented an awards program that was based on both individual and team performance. For example, one award, the Best Demonstrated Practices Award, recognized work teams that showed substantial creativity or significant performance improvements.

THE RESULTS

Through effective leadership, enhanced communication, and a well-defined system of motivating and rewarding employees, IBAX began to realize gains in quality, productivity, and financial performance. When the employees who are closest to the products and customers are enabled and empowered to make decisions and are rewarded for their efforts, dramatic improvements in organizational performance can be achieved.

For Discussion
1. How did Goodman develop his leadership team and what role did the team play in facilitating organizational change?
2. Why was improved communication so important to the retrenchment efforts at IBAX?
3. Describe how Goodman used motivation and reward systems to effect change within the company.

CONTROL CHALLENGES IN THE 21ST CENTURY

PART V

Organizational Control in a Complex Business Environment

CHAPTER 16

▼ CHAPTER OVERVIEW

Control is the last of the four major management functions to be covered in this text. It is an extremely important managerial function because it helps to ensure that all of our planning, organizing, and leading have gone as we had hoped they would. In today's rapidly changing and highly competitive global business environment, organizations can experience a very rapid reversal of their fortunes if they fail to control all aspects of their operations adequately. Individual and group behaviors and all organizational performance must be in line with the strategic focus of the organization. When economic, technological, political, or competitive forces change, control systems must be capable of adjusting behaviors and performance to make them compatible with these strategic shifts. The essence of the control process requires that managers determine performance standards, measure actual performance, compare actual performance with standards, and take corrective action when necessary.

In this chapter we begin by examining the steps in the control process. After this, we discuss several control system design considerations, criteria for effective control, and keys to selecting the proper amount of control. Since the control process can be implemented at almost any stage in an organization's operations, we examine the three basic organizational control focal points. In addition, we explore two opposing philosophies toward control and raise some thought-provoking ethical issues in the control of employee behavior.

▼ LEARNING OBJECTIVES

*When you have finished studying this chapter,
you should be able to:*

- Define and discuss the importance of organizational control.
- Identify the sequence of steps to be undertaken in a thorough control system.
- Identify the factors that are important considerations in the design of a control system.
- Describe the various characteristics of effective control.
- Identify the factors that help determine the proper amount of control.
- Define feedforward control, concurrent control, and feedback control.

- Describe the difference between the philosophies of bureaucratic control and organic control.
- Describe some of the more important techniques and methods for establishing financial control.
- Discuss some of the ethical issues related to the control of employee behavior.

MANAGERIAL INCIDENT

MOTOROLA, INC.—SURVIVAL THROUGH CONTROLS

Motorola, Inc. headquartered in Schaumburg, Illinois, is a leading manufacturer of electronic equipment, systems, and components in the United States and worldwide. The company was founded in 1928, and by the 1960s, it had expanded from consumer electronics into high-tech products for industrial, commercial, and government applications. During the mid-1970s, Motorola's sales declined dramatically as a result of several Japanese competitors' efforts to gain market share. Motorola's decline was directly related to its failure to institute control mechanisms to ensure that worker performance and product quality were on the same level as its Japanese competitors. As the Japanese poured higher-quality products into the U.S. market, Motorola discontinued the production of televisions, stereo equipment, and car radios. Eventually, it even abandoned some semiconductor markets.

The MicroTac cellular telephone, a product that is composed of approximately 400 parts, illustrates some of Motorola's problems. To avoid repairs after final assembly, all 400 parts must be free of defects. But consider this sobering law of basic statistics. Because this product contains so many parts, unless each of the component parts is of very high quality, the probability that the finished product will be defect-free is low. Problems like this were contributing to Motorola's declining market share. In this increasingly competitive, global industry, relatively high component quality was not good enough. Motorola needed control mechanisms that would ensure that worker performance and production output were close to perfect. This was the challenge facing Motorola—it needed to design and implement effective systems for control so that it could compete on an even basis with its Japanese competitors.[1] ▼

INTRODUCTION

As we can see in the Managerial Incident, Motorola was facing a difficult situation. Poor control of product quality had driven Motorola out of many of its long-time businesses and was now threatening its very existence. To survive in the highly competitive electronics market, Motorola would have to develop control mechanisms that would ensure that its products could compete in quality with those of its Japanese competitors. This would require the institution of control mechanisms that could ensure that worker behavior and performance were consistent with newly defined, high standards.

Control is the last of the four major management functions that we have been discussing. By its very nature, control is concerned with making sure that all of our planning, organizing, and leading have gone as we anticipated. Control is a very critical managerial function because the consequences of not meeting the standards of performance can be very negative for the organization. For example, poor inventory control can result in lost business because of a product shortage. Poor quality control may result in angry customers, lost business, and the necessity to provide customers with replacement products. Poor cost control can lead to negative profitability and perhaps even bankruptcy. The list of potential control problems is almost limitless. These problems all point to the fact that improving operational effectiveness and quality is virtually impossible without stringent control mechanisms.

Furthermore, in a world where quality often means the difference between success and failure, organizations simply cannot tolerate substandard product or service outputs. Organizations must develop and maintain control mechanisms capable of identifying and responding to deviations in organizational performance. And while the need for control is evident in all organizations, multinational organizations have particularly challenging and unique control needs. Maintaining internal control of units located in markets and regions around the globe can be far more problematic than maintaining control over a set of domestic operating units. Thus, control mechanisms must often be specifically designed to meet the challenges of global management.

In this chapter we examine several aspects of the control process. We begin by describing the basic steps in the control process and then build upon these basics.

A PROCESS OF CONTROL FOR DIVERSE AND MULTINATIONAL ORGANIZATIONS

Organizational control is defined as the systematic process through which managers regulate organizational activities to make them consistent with the expectations established in plans and to help them achieve all predetermined standards of performance.[2] This definition implies that managers must determine performance standards and develop mechanisms for gathering performance information in order to assess the degree to which standards are being met. Control, then, is a systematic set of steps that must be undertaken. Figure 16.1 illustrates this sequence of steps. As you can see, the process of control involves four steps: (1) setting standards of performance, (2) measuring actual

Organizational control
Process through which managers regulate organizational activities to make them consistent with expectations and help them achieve predetermined standards of performance.

▼ By instituting a coordinated system for control, Federal Express has been able to achieve one of the highest customer approval ratings in the package delivery industry.

▼ **FIGURE 16.1**
Steps in the Control Process

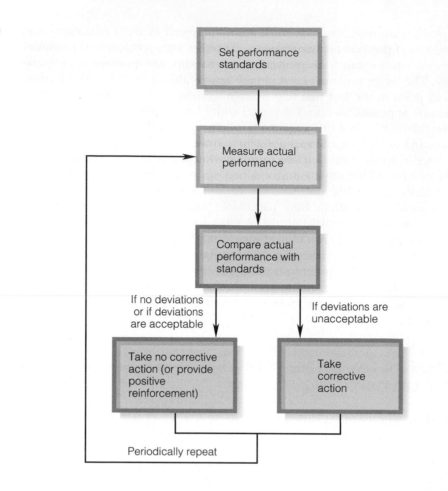

performance, (3) comparing actual performance with standards, and (4) responding to deviations.[3]

Managing for Excellence describes a control system that was developed and implemented by Federal Express.[4] This system (which was quite successful, incidentally) parallels the four steps in the control process. Let's now examine each of these steps in greater detail.

SETTING STANDARDS OF PERFORMANCE

The control process should begin with the establishment of standards of performance against which organizational activities can be compared. Standards of performance begin to evolve only after the organization has developed its overall strategic plan and managers have defined goals for organizational departments. In some instances the performance standards are generated from within the organization. Sometimes, however, the impetus for specific performance standards may originate with some outside source. For example, government laws on safety standards for electrical appliances will have a huge impact on what a manufacturer sets as the allowable current leakage from its handheld hair dryers. In other cases the desires and needs of the customer may dictate the standards set by both manufacturers and the providers of services. In fact, in today's environment, the emphasis on quality and customer satisfaction is increasing the influence that customers have on organizational standards of performance. Photronics, showcased in the video case in Chapter 5, provides a good example of a company that looks to its customers to set standards of performance.[5]

FEDERAL EXPRESS CORPORATION

Federal Express Corporation began operations in 1973 with a fleet of eight airplanes. By 1990 its approximately 89,000 employees were processing 1.3 million shipments daily. Annual revenues reached $1 billion within 10 years of the company's founding.

Federal Express's number one task, according to CEO Frederick Smith, is to improve the quality of its service. To this end Smith laid down a five-step system for control to improve quality. The plan called for (1) establishment of clear quality goals, (2) accurate measurement of what is done, (3) identification of critical links in the value chain, (4) demonstration of discipline in operations, and (5) provision of immediate and accurate feedback to employees. Smith then established a goal of 100 percent customer satisfaction. This meant that each shipment should be delivered on schedule 100 percent of the time, and that 100 percent accuracy should be maintained in all information about each item. To achieve this goal, Federal Express replaced its former measure of quality performance (percentage of on-time deliveries) with a 12-component index that comprehensively describes how its performance is viewed by customers. Measures such as the number of invoice adjustments, damaged packages, lost packages, and missed pickups are included.

The system of quality control has worked quite well. Since it was implemented, overall customer satisfaction with domestic service has averaged better than 95 percent, and international service satisfaction has averaged 94 percent. Furthermore, in a survey of air-express customers, 53 percent gave Federal Express a perfect score, as compared to 39 percent for the next-best competitor. The crowning glory came in 1990 when Federal Express was named as a recipient of the coveted Malcolm Baldrige award for quality.

The organizational activities to be controlled may involve individual behavior, group behavior, production output, service delivery, and so forth. Whenever possible, the standards should be set in a manner that allows them to be compared with actual performance. For example, it would not be very useful for Intel Corporation to state that "output quality in the integrated circuit manufacturing operation should be high." Such a standard lacks the detail needed to make comparisons with performance. A more appropriate statement of performance standard might be "the integrated circuit manufacturing operation should have no more than five defective units manufactured per day." Such a standard contains the degree of clarity needed for comparative purposes.

Or consider the professor who wishes to communicate to students the standards of classroom performance for his management class. Simply stating that "students should be prepared for class" is vague and provides little guidance to the students. But, if the syllabus says that "students should have read the assigned material prior to each class and should be prepared to discuss the issues when called upon in class," much more clarity is provided.

These two examples hardly illustrate the wide diversity of performance standards that might be established. Standards of performance can be set for virtually any activity or behavior within an organization. For example, it is not unusual to find organizations that set standards for employee dress or grooming. For several years IBM required the men in its male-dominated supervisory positions to wear white dress shirts. The Walt Disney Company maintains strict standards for employee dress, grooming, jewelry, cosmetics, and even artificial hair coloring. As today's workforce becomes more diverse, setting and enforcing standards of individual behavior and performance can sometimes be more difficult. We have seen repeatedly throughout this book that the workplace is no longer composed of homogeneous individuals. Ethnic, racial, and gender differences often lead to different sets of individual values and expectations.

Furthermore, multinational corporations with operations in several countries often find it difficult, if not impossible, to maintain the same standards in all countries. It is difficult to establish corporate-wide standards for subsidiaries that function within diverse sociocultural, technological, political-legal, and economic environments. For example, a multinational organization's facilities may have very different productivity targets in light of the different work attitudes in the various countries. Similarly, plants in different nations may employ technologies with various levels of sophistication suitable to the education/skill levels of the local workforce; consequently, the plants may experience significant variation in productivity rates. Clearly, such circumstances can impede the development of corporate-wide performance standards.

MEASURING ACTUAL PERFORMANCE

In some cases measuring actual performance can be relatively simple, but in others it can be quite complex. We have to decide such things as (1) what to measure (i.e., a single item or multiple things such as sales, costs, profits, rejects, or orders), (2) when to measure, and (3) how frequently to measure. As we noted earlier, standards should be stated as clearly as possible so they can be compared with performance. Doing this is quite simple when the performance criteria are quantitative in nature and can be objectively measured. The standard in our earlier Intel example—"the integrated circuit manufacturing operation should have no more than five defective units manufactured per day"—is a quantitative performance criterion. Sometimes, however, performance criteria are more qualitative in nature and do not easily lend themselves to absolute units of measure. Instead, they require a subjective assessment to determine whether the standard is being met. For example, even though a management student has read the assigned material and discussed the issues when called upon in class, the professor's assessment of the student's performance can be quite subjective when the issues do not have a single correct interpretation.

Suppose that the Chicago Cutlery Company states that its knives "must be honed to a high degree of sharpness, and the wooden handles must be polished to a bright luster." This is also a qualitative performance measure, for determining whether a particular knife was sharp enough or bright enough would not be easy. But regardless of whether the stated performance measure is quantitative or qualitative in nature, actual performance must be recorded for subsequent comparison with the performance standard.

COMPARING ACTUAL PERFORMANCE WITH STANDARDS

The first two steps of the control process provide managers with the information that allows them to make comparisons between actual performance and standards. If the actual performance is identical to the standard, then no deviation has occurred. Rarely, however, is there absolutely no deviation between actual and planned performance. Fortunately, in most real-world situations, actual performance does not always have to be identical to the standard. Typically, the performance standard has a stated acceptable deviation. For example, suppose Motorola management set an average productivity standard of 50 cellular telephones per worker per hour, with an acceptable deviation of plus or minus 5 telephones per worker per hour. The acceptable deviations would define the control limits for this process. If productivity is between 45 and 55 cellular telephones per worker per hour, then the process is said to be "in control," meaning that no corrective action is necessary. Measurements outside this range indicate an "out of control" situation that requires corrective action.

Continuing with the Motorola example, if actual productivity is 47 telephones per worker per hour, then the deviation from the standard is acceptable, and no corrective action is required. Suppose, on the other hand, that productivity is 58 telephones per worker per hour. Now the deviation from the standard is unacceptable, and the subsequent steps in the control process should attempt to correct it. One might initially think that this deviation (with its extra output) would be considered desirable and that no attempts would be made to correct it. But this deviation could lead to problems if the company has no market for the excess output or no room to store it; possibly, too, the extra production is using resources that were to be used elsewhere.

For a more personal example, suppose that you have established a performance standard of at least 85 for your scores on the mid-term and final exams to help you achieve your goal of receiving a grade of B in your principles of management course. If your mid-term exam score is only 75, you would have an undesirable deviation. But if your score is greater than 85, you would have an acceptable deviation from your established standard.

PROVIDING CORRECTIVE ACTION AND FEEDBACK

After comparing actual performance with standards, we can choose to either (1) take no corrective action or (2) take corrective action. If the deviation was acceptable or if there was no deviation, then the response should be to take no corrective action, since the performance or behavior is acceptable in light of the standards. If, however, the deviation was unacceptable, then the response should be to take corrective action. Corrective action usually requires making a change in some behavior, activity, or aspect of the organization to bring performance into line with the standards. Even when no corrective action is necessary, it is often useful to provide positive feedback (and in some cases even rewards) to the responsible individuals so that they are motivated to continue performing to the standards.

Return to the earlier example in which you set a standard of 85 for your mid-term and final exam scores. If your mid-term exam score is only 75, the undesirable deviation would require a response on your part. You might attempt to compensate by preparing more thoroughly for the final exam. (Or you might decide to drop the course and try again in another semester!) If your score on the mid-term exam is 90, you would not need to take corrective action in preparing for the final exam (unless, of course, you decide to raise your goal to a course grade of A and reestablish your performance standard for the final exam to achieve this goal).

When exercising control in business organizations, a variety of types of changes are possible depending upon the particular situation. Changes in materials, equipment, process, or staffing might be made. In some cases the corrective action might even involve changing the original performance standards. For example, the company might determine that the standards were set un-

SERVICE CHALLENGE

FULLWOOD FOODS

Harlow Fullwood, Jr., launched a Kentucky Fried Chicken (KFC) restaurant in a Baltimore suburb in the early 1980s without two key requirements that KFC normally imposes on franchisees. He had neither experience nor a big bankroll. But, how could KFC not take a chance on him? The company had pledged to encourage minority entries in business. Here was an African-American man with a track record of community service during nearly 24 years as a police officer, a man whose application to KFC was bolstered with letters from congressman and Maryland's governor, plus press clippings about fund-raising he had undertaken for good causes.

The company gambled and put Fullwood in charge of converting a fish-and-chips restaurant in Parkville, Maryland, into a KFC outlet. KFC expected first-year sales of about $600,000. They were nearly $1 million. Fullwood won the franchise, and more franchises followed. In the early 1990s, his Fullwood Foods, Inc., with four KFC restaurants in the Baltimore area, had $3.3 million in sales.

From the beginning Fullwood met the challenge of intense competition for fast-food customers by focusing on his strength—relationships with people. As a police officer he had been known for recruiting potential officers for Baltimore's department. He used his persuasiveness now to get good help for his KFC outlet and retained that help by providing employee benefits that were beyond what many large companies provide.

---

realistically high, making them too difficult to achieve consistently. Regardless of whether or not corrective action is taken, the control process does not end here. Even if performance standards are currently being achieved, there is no guarantee that this will be true in the future. Consequently, the measurement and comparison steps must be periodically repeated.

In some instances the response to a deviation from standards can be quite different than the formal control system might have suggested. As an illustration, Service Challenge describes a situation in which Kentucky Fried Chicken (KFC) granted a franchise to an entrepreneur who failed to meet two key standards that KFC normally imposes on franchisees.[6] KFC's response in this case was precipitated by its commitment to diversity within the managerial ranks of its restaurants.

Developing and implementing creative and constructive responses to undesirable deviations can be exceptionally difficult for multinational organizations. Because the company's understanding of each individual unit is less when units are scattered around the globe, developing solutions requires a substantial amount of information gathering. Further, the development of solutions that are acceptable to both subsidiary and headquarters management may require active participation by key personnel at each level. Consequently, it may take longer to determine and implement the necessary corrective action, and that action may come at the expense of significant managerial time and energy.

Up to this point, we have seen that the basic process of control involves a few very fundamental steps: (1) establish standards of performance, (2) measure actual performance, (3) compare actual with standards, and (4) take corrective action when necessary. But knowing the four steps in the control process is not enough to ensure that an effective control system will be developed. As we will see in the next sections, several other issues must be considered.

DESIGNING QUALITY AND EFFECTIVENESS INTO THE CONTROL SYSTEM

Designing an effective control system can be far more complex than simply performing the four steps in the control process. Several other important factors must be considered as well. Once the control system has been designed and implemented, several criteria are available to help determine how effective it will be. Finally, it is necessary to select the amount of control to be used and the point in the organization where the control effort will be focused. These issues must be considered as each step in the control process unfolds, as Figure 16.2 illustrates. We begin our treatment of control system design issues by examining several important design factors.

DESIGN FACTORS AFFECTING CONTROL SYSTEM QUALITY

When designing a control system, four important factors must be considered: (1) the amount of variety in the control system, (2) the ability to anticipate problems, (3) the sensitivity of the measuring device, and (4) the composition of the feedback reports. Let's examine each of these factors more thoroughly.

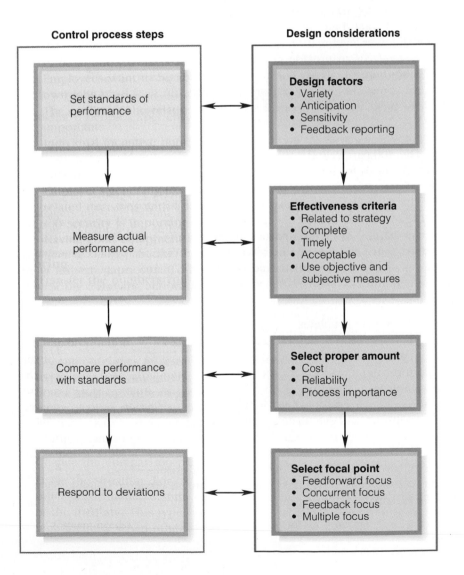

Control process steps

- Set standards of performance
- Measure actual performance
- Compare performance with standards
- Respond to deviations

Design considerations

Design factors
- Variety
- Anticipation
- Sensitivity
- Feedback reporting

Effectiveness criteria
- Related to strategy
- Complete
- Timely
- Acceptable
- Use objective and subjective measures

Select proper amount
- Cost
- Reliability
- Process importance

Select focal point
- Feedforward focus
- Concurrent focus
- Feedback focus
- Multiple focus

▼ **FIGURE 16.2**
Control System Design Issues

Law of requisite variety
Control systems must have enough variety to cope with the variety in the systems they are trying to control.

Amount of Variety in the Control System

One important design consideration is the amount of variety in the control system. Variety refers to the number of activities, processes, or items that are measured and controlled. Systems become more complex as the number of system elements and number of possible interactions among them increase. There is more uncertainty in complex systems because more things can go wrong with them. In other words, more variety leads to less predictability. To maintain adequate control in any system, the control system must contain as much variety as the system being controlled. This is known as the **law of requisite variety.**[7] Although a simple control system might seem attractive, the law of requisite variety suggests that simple control systems may not have sufficient variety to cope with the complex system they are trying to control.[8]

Consider the plight of General Motors or any other automobile manufacturer. Because so many materials and parts go into the complex finished product and those components have so many sources, the system's elements and their interactions contain considerable variety. Consequently, extensive control systems are needed at all stages in the manufacturing process to ensure that the finished automobiles meet the performance standards.

Requisite variety can be achieved by either (1) increasing the amount of variety in the control system or (2) reducing the amount of variety in the system being controlled. Increased variety in the control system can be achieved by increasing the number of performance standards and the number of items controlled. In the case of General Motors, top management will set a performance standard for finished product quality. To ensure that this standard is achieved, lower-level managers and supervisors will employ additional performance standards to provide raw material input control, production scrap control, labor control, quality control, and similar other control systems. If the lower-level managers and supervisors are successful in achieving these standards, it is likely that the top-level standard for product quality will also be achieved.

Let's now look at an example of how Motorola might achieve requisite variety. The 400-part cellular telephone described in the Managerial Incident illustrates the need for increased variety in the control system. To increase the chances of defect-free telephones, the company would have to establish controls for the manufacturing of all 400 parts. As an alternative, Motorola might consider reducing the amount of variety in the telephone by designing a phone with fewer parts. This would reduce the variety in the elements and their interactions. Since there would be fewer places where failures could occur, a simpler set of control systems could be put into place. Such actions were central to Motorola's survival, as we will see in the Managerial Incident Resolution.

Ability to Anticipate Problems

A second consideration in designing a control system is its ability to anticipate problems. When the control process is instituted, several distinct events occur when performance fails to meet the established standards. First, the undesirable deviation from standards is observed. Then, the situation is reported to the person or persons responsible for taking corrective action. Next, corrective action is instituted, and eventually, performance should return to an acceptable value. Inevitably, time lags occur between observation, reporting, instituting, and return. During these time lags, the performance continues to be unacceptable. Figure 16.3 illustrates this sequence of events.

The damage caused by these time lags can be reduced by building the ability to anticipate problems into the control system. If a deviation can be

▼ Fire towers such as this enable timber companies to anticipate and detect problems quickly, thereby reducing the time lag between when the problem (fire) occurs and when it is corrected.

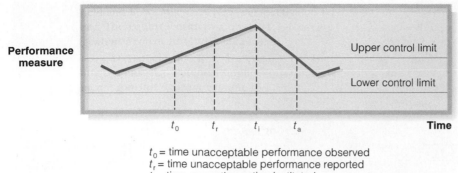

▼ FIGURE 16.3
Time Lags in Control

t_0 = time unacceptable performance observed
t_r = time unacceptable performance reported
t_i = time corrective action instituted
t_a = time acceptable performance returns

anticipated before it occurs, corrective action can be instituted more quickly and the negative consequences of the deviation reduced. To illustrate, consider how Weyerhauser Company manages its timber reserves. It is a fact of nature that forest fires sometimes occur. If standard performance is defined as a fire-free forest, then a forest fire represents an undesirable deviation that needs corrective action. Weyerhauser can anticipate that fires are more likely to occur during prolonged dry periods. By staffing watch towers, using spotter aircraft, and keeping fire-fighting equipment in a state of readiness during these periods, the company increases its anticipatory capability, enabling it to respond more quickly to the undesirable situation.

Sensitivity of the Measuring Device
A third consideration in control system design is the sensitivity of the measuring device. Sensitivity refers to the precision with which the measurement can be made. Care must be taken to use the appropriate device for the system under consideration. For example, the Teac Company, which manufactures computer components and other electronic equipment, might need a high-precision micrometer to measure the diameter of the spindles used in its computer disk drive. But, for Georgia-Pacific, a lumber company, to use such a measuring device to check the thickness of two-by-four wall studs would be highly unnecessary. A simple tape measure will suffice in this situation, for tolerances only need to be expressed in fractions of inches, not microns. The old maxim applies here: you don't need a sledgehammer to insert a thumbtack!

Composition of Feedback Reports
A final consideration in control system design involves the composition of feedback reports. As the control process measures performance and compares it with standards, much information and data are generated. Reports to management will be based upon these data. But what data should be included in the reports? A simple answer, and one that users of such reports will view favorably, is "don't tell me what is right with the system, tell me what is wrong." **Variance reporting** fulfills this desire by highlighting only those things that fail to meet the established standards. Focusing on the elements that are not meeting the standards provides the capability for **management by exception.** In this approach, management targets the trouble areas. If the system is operating acceptably, no information needs to come to the manager's attention.

Now that we have examined the factors that are important in the design of a control system, let's look at several criteria that measure the system's effectiveness.

Variance reporting
Highlighting only those things that fail to meet the established standards.

Management by exception
Focusing on the elements that are not meeting the standards.

▼ While the sensitivity of these measuring devices is appropriate for construction projects, they would not be appropriate to measure tolerances in the manufacture of computer hard disk drives.

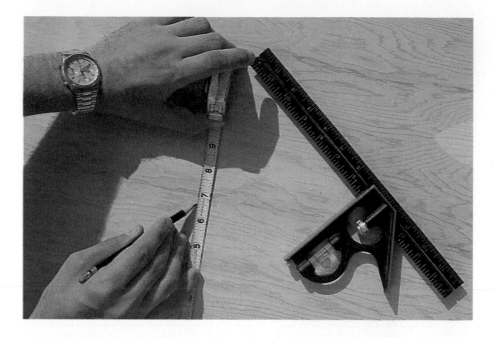

CRITERIA FOR EFFECTIVE CONTROL

To be effective in detecting and correcting unacceptable performance, a control system must satisfy several criteria. The system must be (1) related to organizational strategy, (2) complete, (3) composed of objective and subjective measures, (4) timely, and (5) acceptable.[9] The next sections examine these criteria more closely.

Related to Organizational Strategy

In designing a control system, one must make sure that it measures what is important now and what will be important in the future, not what was important in the past. As an organization's strategic focus shifts over time, the measures and standards of performance that are important to the organization must also shift. When the control system is linked to organizational strategy, it recognizes strategic shifts and is flexible enough to measure what is important as indicated by the firm's strategy.

This issue also has implications for the standards of behavior and performance that are set for individuals and groups within the organization. As the workforce becomes more racially, ethnically, and gender diverse, organizations will often have to adjust their expectations of workers and performance standards in response to the differing attitudes, abilities, and cultural biases of their employees.

Multinational corporations often find it useful to maintain a centralized, integrated system of controls consistent with the strategic orientation of the organization. If the network of organizational units is to benefit from the company's global orientation, there must be sufficient coordination and control of the units to ensure that such benefits are achieved. For example, General Motors maintains a number of units that are interdependent through each of the sequential steps in the manufacturing process (for example, GM's Brazilian subsidiary supplies its U.S. subsidiary with engines); therefore, GM must have control systems that ensure that production processes are not disrupted.[10]

Utilizes All Steps in Control Process

To be effective, a control system must employ all of the steps in the control process. Standards of performance must be set, measurements of actual performance taken, comparisons of standards with actual performance made, and, when necessary, corrective action taken. Omitting any of these steps will detract from the system's effectiveness. For example, we will see in the Managerial Resolution that Motorola set some very lofty quality performance standards. What if Motorola managers measured actual performance and made comparisons with standards, but then failed to take corrective action when they observed undesirable deviations (the final step in the control process)? By omitting this step, performance would never be brought into line with the standards, and the survival of the company would be doubtful.

To return to our more personal example of your quest for a grade of B in your principles of management course, suppose you never bothered to check your posted grade on the mid-term exam. In that case, your control system would be incomplete. Without knowing your mid-term exam score, you could not compare your actual performance with your standard. Consequently, you would not know whether there was an undesirable deviation and whether you should study harder for the final exam.

Composed of Objective and Subjective Measures

It is very unlikely that a control system will lend itself to the use of a single performance measure. More often than not, a number of performance measures are needed. As we discussed earlier, some of these performance measures may be objective and very easily quantified, while others may be qualitative and more subjective. For example, management may have set specific targets for productivity. This performance objective has a precise formula for measurement, as we will see in the next chapter. Suppose that in that same situation, management has also expressed a desire to achieve high levels of worker satisfaction. Such a qualitative criterion is more difficult, if not impossible, to measure accurately. Situations like this often require managers to blend quantitative (objective) and qualitative (subjective) performance measures in their control systems.

Incorporates Timeliness in Feedback Reporting

Timeliness is the degree to which the control system provides information when it is needed. The key issue here is not how fast the feedback information is provided, but whether it is provided quickly enough to permit a response to an unacceptable deviation. For example, consider the air traffic controller at Chicago's O'Hare Airport who observes on the radar screen that the positions of two aircraft are becoming alarmingly close. Feedback information on the changing positions of the two aircraft is needed very quickly if a tragedy is to be avoided. Here timeliness would be measured in seconds. Now consider the manager of a Christmas tree farm who monitors the annual growth rate of the trees. If the amount of growth falls below standards in a particular year, an application of fertilizer is called for as a corrective action. In this case timeliness might be measured in weeks or even months.

Return again to the personal example of your grade. Suppose that the mid-term exam was administered in the eighth week of the semester and the results were not posted until the tenth week. This feedback would not be timely if the deadline for dropping the course was in the ninth week of the semester.

Acceptable to a Diverse Work Force

To be effective, organizational controls must be accepted by employees. The control system should motivate workers to recognize standards and act to achieve them. If the control system discourages employees, they are likely to ignore the standards, and undesirable deviations are likely to follow. The more committed employees are to the control system, the more successful the system will be.[11] In the increasingly diverse workplaces of today's organizations,

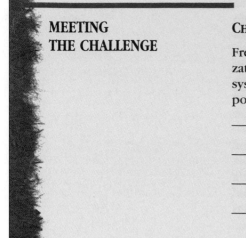

CHECKLIST FOR DESIGNING EFFECTIVE CONTROL SYSTEMS

Frequently, systems for management control of some process in an organization are inadequately designed or ill thought out. After designing your system for control, answer the following questions to ensure that all important aspects of the control system have been included.

_____ Have performance standards been explicitly stated with a degree of clarity that allows them to be compared with actual performance?

_____ Have standards been defined in a manner that permits measurement of actual performance?

_____ Are guidelines in place for responding with corrective actions to undesirable deviations?

_____ Is there sufficient variety in the control system to deal with the variety in the process being controlled?

_____ Does the control system have the capability to anticipate problems before they get out of hand?

_____ Is the precision of the measuring devices appropriate for the performance being measured?

_____ Is the feedback system designed to report what is wrong with the process rather than what is right with the process?

_____ Is the control system measuring what is important as indicated by the firm's strategy?

_____ Is feedback information provided in a timely fashion?

_____ Is the control system acceptable to your employees?

one of the challenges to management is to develop control systems and establish standards that are acceptable and understandable to all workers.

To illustrate acceptability, consider your situation as a student in a management course. Suppose that your professor has no problem assigning course grades of B or lower, but says that a grade of A can only be achieved by students who read a new chapter and five related journal articles every day and submit a 20-page, typewritten synopsis of these readings each day. Would you be discouraged from attempting to earn a grade of A? Most, if not all, students probably would be discouraged and would resign themselves to a grade of no higher than a B for the course.

Up to this point, we have seen several factors that are essential to the design of an effective control system. To assist managers in developing effective control systems, Meeting the Challenge presents a checklist that can be used to make sure that all important factors and characteristics have been included in any control system that has been designed.

Now that the control system has been established, it is necessary to determine how much control should be used. The amount of control needed depends upon several factors, as we see in the next section.

SELECTING THE PROPER AMOUNT OF CONTROL

In almost any task, there are reasonable limits on the amount of energy that should be expended. This is also true in the area of control. In theory the amount of control that a manager exercises over some aspect of the organization can vary from a minimum of zero control to a maximum of infinite control. It is possible for management to go too far and overcontrol some aspect of the organization, or not go far enough and thereby undercontrol. The end result in either case is a suboptimal control system and suboptimal performance, which will decrease the overall effectiveness and efficiency of the organization.

Choosing the proper amount of control is critical to organizations that strive for quality in everything they do. Deciding how much control is enough is not a simple matter, however. Several factors can be used to help determine the proper amount of control. These factors, which vary in their degree of objectivity, include the costs and benefits of a control system, the reliability of the thing or process being controlled, and the importance of the thing or process being controlled.[12]

Costs in Control Systems

Two basic categories of costs need to be considered in control systems: (1) the costs associated with the information needed to perform the control process, and (2) the costs associated with undesirable deviations from standards. These costs behave differently as the amount of control effort varies.[13]

Control systems rely on information. As the amount of control effort increases, information feedback is needed in greater amounts and with greater frequency. This information does not come without a cost. Time, effort, resources, and money must be expended to gather and assimilate information. Consequently, as the level of control effort increases, the information costs of the control system also increase.

As the level of control effort increases, undesirable deviations from performance standards will decrease. As a consequence, the costs associated with undesirable performance will also decrease. Reductions in the costs due to undesirable performance represent the benefits of control systems. Examples of these costs include costs to correct the problem that is causing the undesirable deviations; material scrap costs and rework costs when defective parts are detected in the manufacturing process; product warranty, repair, and replacement costs when defective output reaches the consumer; and worker compensation costs when workers are injured due to behaviors or actions that do not conform to standards. When these relationships are displayed in a graphical format as in Figure 16.4, they reveal that, from an economic stand-

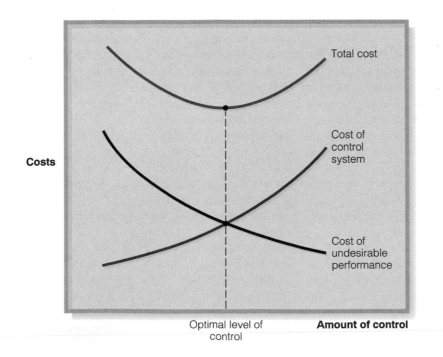

▼ FIGURE 16.4
Cost Tradeoffs in a Control System

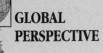

GLOBAL PERSPECTIVE

YOKOGAWA-HEWLETT-PACKARD: PROBLEMS WITH QUALITY

When the American electronics manufacturer Hewlett-Packard entered into a joint venture with the Yokogawa Electric Corporation of Japan, the anticipated synergy benefits of this partnership were slow to follow. Several years after the alliance was formed, Yokogawa-Hewlett-Packard (YHP) was still experiencing low product quality and poor productivity. Defect rates were deemed to be too high, manufacturing lead times were too long, excessive product warranty costs were being incurred, product research and development cycles were too long, and the time needed to get products to the market was lengthy. These problems were beginning to impact negatively on YHP's ability to compete effectively.

Performance took a dramatic turn for the better when YHP began to institute a control program that focused on product quality. The control program was instituted on a pilot basis on one production line. This program made liberal use of statistical quality-control procedures. The success of the pilot program prompted its introduction on a company-wide basis. Some of the approximate improvements that resulted from the program included:

- 80% overall reduction in defects
- 75% reduction in manufacturing lead time
- 85% reduction in product warranty costs
- 33% reduction in time needed to get products to market
- 42% reduction in manufacturing cost
- 64% reduction in inventory levels
- 91% increase in productivity
- 177% increase in profit
- 200% increase in market share

The control program was so successful that YHP won the Deming Prize, Japan's most coveted industrial award.

point, there is an ideal amount of control to be exercised. This optimal amount of control corresponds to the minimum total cost.

To help clarify the relationships in Figure 16.4, let's go back to the Managerial Incident and consider the situation that Motorola faced in manufacturing its cellular telephone. Management can increase the level of control by increasing the number of parts, components, and finished products that are inspected and tested. Additionally, more sophisticated testing and measuring devices might be obtained. These actions will increase the costs of obtaining the information needed in the control process, but will also reduce the likelihood that defective units will be produced. When fewer defective units are produced, scrap, rework, product repair, product warranty, and product replacement costs all decline. When the opposing costs are combined, the total cost is U-shaped, and its lowest point indicates the optimal level of control.

From a practical standpoint, this optimal value is not always easy to identify. When performance improvements are many and varied, it may be difficult to quantify the precise cost benefit of the control system. In such cases, the value of the control system might be assessed by simply examining the number of areas of improvement and the level of improvement in each area. This is certainly the case for the Yokagawa-Hewlett-Packard organization described in Global Perspective.[14] This company experienced improvements in several areas. Many of these areas have different measures of performance, and some would be quite difficult to translate into a cost tradeoff graph such as Figure 16.4.

Reliability of the System

Reliability refers to the probability that the object or process being controlled will consistently behave in an acceptable manner. The basic premise is that the more reliable the process, the less control that is needed. Process reliability is difficult to assess because it will be affected by the operating characteristics of the physical equipment and by the experience and attitudes of the workers. Equipment reliability can often be objectively measured. Human operators present a bit more uncertainty. Although reliability can be expected to increase with worker experience, there is no way to accurately predict when a worker will have a "bad day." Management must often make subjective judgments on the human aspect of reliability to aid in determining the proper amount of control.

Importance of the Process Being Controlled

Common sense would suggest that the more important the object or process being controlled, the greater the amount of control that should be exercised. The difficulty here lies in selecting a measure for importance. Frequently, cost or value is used as a substitute for importance. The more valuable the item, the more important it is; therefore, the more control it deserves. In the area of inventory control, a relatively small percentage of a company's inventory items (perhaps 20 percent) often account for a large percentage of the total inventory value (perhaps 80 percent). Although the percentages may vary, this "20/80 rule," as it has become known, would suggest that an "important few" items deserve close inventory control. The others (the "trivial many") require considerably less control.[15]

You should not automatically assume that importance can always be measured by cost or value. At first glance it might seem that extensive control systems are not needed to monitor quality in the manufacture of an inexpensive bolt. However, if that bolt is used to secure a window washer to the outside of a high-rise building, it has assumed a high level of importance despite its low cost. In a similar vein, refer to the opening Managerial Incident in Chapter 6, which described the space shuttle *Challenger* disaster. Although the O-rings in the shuttle booster rockets were relatively inexpensive items, we are all painfully aware of the importance they played in this highly complex spacecraft.

Now that the question of how much control has been addressed, let's examine where in the transformation process control should be used. The place where control is applied is called the focal point for control.

SELECTING THE FOCAL POINT FOR CONTROL

Before managers design and implement a control system, they must decide where the control effort will be focused. Virtually all organizations maintain a structure in which inputs are subjected to a transformation process that converts them into usable and marketable outputs. Despite this similarity, inputs, transformations, and outputs can vary considerably among organizations.

Although Chapter 17 provides a much more extensive examination of the operations aspects of the input transformation process, we do need to note here that inputs can include such items as raw materials, supplies, people, capital, land, buildings, equipment, utilities, and information. Outputs of the transformation process will be either physical products or services. The list of transformation processes is lengthy and quite varied. Table 16.1 provides descriptions and examples of these processes.

▼ **Table 16.1**   Descriptions and Examples of Operations Transformation Processes

TRANSFORMATION	DESCRIPTION	EXAMPLES
Physical or chemical	Cutting, bending, joining, or chemically alternating raw materials to make a product	Manufacturing company, chemical processor, oil refinery
Locational	Provide transportation function	Airlines, trucking companies, package delivery services, U.S. Postal System
Storage	Hold and then release a commodity or item	Warehouses
Exchange	Transfer possession and ownership of a commodity or item	Wholesale and retail organizations
Physiological	Improve the physical or mental well-being of sick and injured people	Hospitals, health-care clinics
Informational	Transmit information to customers	Radio and television news departments, and computer information services
Entertainment	Impart an attitudinal change to their customers	Motion picture industry and programming departments of television networks
Educational	Impart knowledge to customers	Schools, universities

Control can focus on the inputs, the transformation process, or the outputs of the operating system. The three different focal points yield three different types of control: (1) feedforward control, (2) concurrent control, and (3) feedback control.[16] These control focal points are illustrated in Figure 16.5. The next sections examine them in greater detail.

Feedforward Control

When control focuses on the material, financial, or human resources that serve as inputs to the transformation process, it is referred to as **feedforward control.** This type of control is sometimes called **preventive control** because it is designed to ensure that the quality of inputs is high enough to prevent problems in the transformation process. For example, think about the preventive controls that might take place prior to the manufacture of blue jeans. A primary input for manufacturers such as Levi Strauss is denim fabric. Long bolts of this material will have patterns overlaid and cut prior to the sewing operations. Before the patterns are laid out on the fabric, a system of feedforward control could be used to inspect the denim fabric for knots, runs, tears, color variations, and other similar imperfections. If the fabric contains many imperfections, there could well be excessive levels of imperfections in the finished blue jeans. In such a case, the corrective action suggested by the feedforward control system might be to reject the entire bolt of fabric rather than trying to cut around the imperfections.

Concurrent Control

When control focuses on the transformation phase, it is referred to as **concurrent control.** This form of control is designed to monitor ongoing activities to ensure that the transformation process is functioning properly and

Feedforward (preventive) control Focuses on detecting undesirable material, financial, or human resources that serve as inputs to the transformation process.

Concurrent control Focuses on the transformation process to ensure that it is functioning properly.

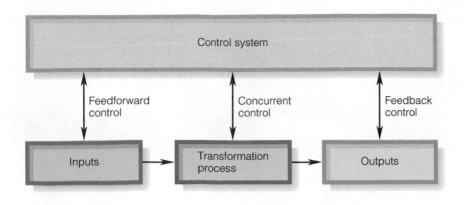

achieving the desired results. To illustrate, consider again the manufacture of blue jeans by Levi Strauss. Sewing machine operators must continually monitor their process to ensure that seams are being sewn straight and threads are interlocking appropriately. If these standards are not being met, it may be necessary to take such corrective actions as changing needles, adjusting thread tension, lubricating machines, and so forth.

Feedback Control

When control focuses on the output phase of Figure 16.5, it is referred to as **feedback control.** This type of control is sometimes referred to as **corrective control** because it is intended to discover undesirable output and implement corrective action. We can illustrate this focal point by again considering the manufacture of blue jeans. After the jeans have been assembled, a final inspection is normally performed. Individuals responsible for assessing the quality of the jeans compare the finished product with established standards of performance. If there is an undesirable amount of deviation from the standards, then corrective action must be prescribed. For example, if the design stitching on the back pockets is misaligned, corrective action would be needed at the pocket-stitching operation to correct this problem.

Feedback (corrective) control
Focuses on discovering undesirable output and implementing corrective action.

Multiple Focal Points

Very few organizations rely on a single point of focus for their control process. Instead, most organizations use several control systems focused on various phases of the transformation process.[17] This way managers are better able to control resource inputs, ongoing transformation activities, and final outputs simultaneously. This approach gives the manager the capability to determine (1) whether current output is in accordance with standards, and (2) whether there are any impending problems looming on the horizon.

The McDonald's restaurant chain provides a familiar example of a company that uses control mechanisms that are focused on inputs, transformation processes, and outputs in its attempts to maintain consistency in its french fried potatoes. McDonald's utilizes feedforward control with a stringent set of standards for purchased raw potatoes. It utilizes concurrent control by monitoring the oil temperature and frying time used in the cooking process and the amount of salt used in seasoning the french fries. Finally, it utilizes feedback control when the output (cooked french fries) is examined. If examination reveals improper color, it may be necessary to change the cooking oil, the temperature of the cooking oil, the cooking time, or perhaps some combination of all three to attain the desired results. Multiple focal points are important here, for if only the finished product were monitored, potential problems caused by a bad batch of raw potatoes or a defective fryer thermostat would not be revealed until defective french fries were produced.

Not only are control systems focused on inputs, transformations, or outputs, they are also implemented in all functional specialty areas of the organ-

▼ The control process for Mc-
Donald's french fries extends from
the raw potato state right through to
the finished product stage.

ization. Today's business organizations incorporate many highly interrelated
and overlapping functional specialties. Management, marketing, finance, and
accounting activities all play a critical role in the success of the organization,
and as such, each will have many aspects that require control mechanisms.
Noted management theorist Peter Drucker has identified eight areas in which
performance objectives should be set and results measured. These areas—
marketing, financial resources, productivity, physical resources, human organization, profit requirements, social responsibility, and innovation—extend
through all of the interrelated functional specialties of the business.[18]

MANAGERIAL CONTROL PHILOSOPHIES

Instituting a control system requires that managers do more than simply select
the appropriate focal points. It is also necessary to make a choice between
two philosophical control styles: (1) bureaucratic control and (2) organic control (often referred to as clan control).

BUREAUCRATIC CONTROL

Bureaucratic control
Use of formal mechanisms to influence behavior, assess performance,
and correct unacceptable deviations
from standards.

Bureaucratic control involves the use of rules, procedures, policies, hierarchy of authority, written documents, reward systems, and other formal mechanisms to influence behavior, assess performance, and correct unacceptable
deviations from standards.[19] This type of control is typical of the bureaucratic
style of management introduced in Chapter 2 and described elsewhere in this
book. In this method of control, standard operating procedures and policies
prescribe acceptable employee behavior and standards for employee performance. There is a rigid hierarchy of authority that extends from the top down
through the organization. Formal authority for the control process lies at the
supervisor level, and lower-level employees are not expected to participate in
the control process. Bureaucratic control relies on highly formalized mechanisms for selecting and training workers, and it emphasizes the use of monetary
rewards for controlling employee performance. Formal quantitative tools such
as budgets or financial reports and ratios are frequently used to monitor and
evaluate performance in bureaucratic control systems.

As we discussed in Chapter 2, the bureacratic style often has a negative connotation due to its very formal structure and perceived lack of flexibility. However, this method of control should not be viewed as a mechanism to restrain, force, coerce, or manipulate workers. Instead, it should be viewed as an effective, although rigid, mechanism to ensure that performance standards are met.

ORGANIC CONTROL

Organic control, often called **clan control,** is quite different from bureaucratic control. It relies upon social values, traditions, shared beliefs, flexible authority, looser job descriptions, and trust to assess performance and correct unacceptable deviations. The philosophy behind organic control is that employees are to be trusted and that they are willing to perform correctly without extensive rules and supervision. This type of control is particularly appropriate when there is a strong corporate culture and the values are shared by all employees. When cohesive peer groups exist, less top-down bureaucratic control is necessary because employees are likely to pressure co-workers into adhering to group norms. When employees exercise self-discipline and self-control and believe in doing a fair day's work for their pay, managers can take advantage of this self-discipline and use fewer bureaucratic control methods.

Such cohesiveness and self-discipline are characteristic of self-managed teams (SMTs), as you will recall from earlier chapters.[20] Organic control is a very appropriate style to use in conjucntion with SMTs. Although organic control is less rigid than bureaucratic control, it would be a mistake to assume that it is a better method. Both the bureaucratic and organic approaches can be useful for organizational control, and most organizations use some aspects of both in their control mechanisms. Table 16.2 provides a brief comparison of the bureaucratic and organic methods of control.

Before selecting one of these two control styles, managers must first evaluate several factors of their organization. The next sections describe the factors that help determine an appropriate choice of control style.

SELECTING A CONTROL STYLE IN TODAY'S DIVERSE AND MULTINATIONAL ORGANIZATIONS

The bureaucrtatic and organic approaches present two distinctly opposite control philosophies. Top management is often faced with a dilemma in choosing a style for their organization. This decision can be made more easily if managers first evaluate these four factors: (1) individual management style, (2) corporate culture, (3) employee professionalism, and (4) performance measures.[21]

Individual management style refers to whether the manager has a task-oriented or a people-oriented leadership style. These concepts were described earlier in Chapter 12, where we discussed behavioral approaches to understanding leadership. If a manager uses more relationship-oriented behaviors when interacting with subordinates, then an organic control style would tend to be more compatible with his leadership style. Examples of relationship-oriented behaviors include extending a high degree of trust, friendship, and respect to subordinates. In contrast, if a manager displays more task-oriented behaviors when interacting with subordinates, then a bureaucratic control style would tend to be more compatible with her leadership style. Task-oriented behavior occurs when the leader assumes the responsibility for planning, directing, providing job information, and maintaining standards of performance for subordinates. The key is that the control style needs to be consistent with the manager's leadership style.

Organic (clan) control
Reliance upon social values, traditions, shared beliefs, flexible authority, and trust to assess performance and correct unacceptable deviations.

▼ **Table 16.2**   Bureaucratic and Organic Methods of Control

	BUREAUCRATIC	ORGANIC
Purpose	Employee compliance	Employee commitment
Technique	Rigid rules and policies, strict hierarchy, formalized selection and training	Corporate culture, individual self-discipline, cohesive peer groups, selection and socialization
Performance expectation	Clearly defined standards of individual performance	Emphasizes group or system performance
Organizational structure	Tall structure, top-down controls	Flat structure, mutual influence
	Rules and procedures for coordination and control	Shared values, goals, and traditions for coordination and control
	Authority resides in position	Authority resides with knowledge and expertise
Rewards	Based upon individual employee achievements	Based upon group achievements and equity across employees
Participation	Formalized and narrow	Informal and broad

SOURCE: Based upon R. E. Walton, "From Control to Commitment in the Workplace," *Harvard Business Review* (March/April 1985): 76–85.

The second factor that determines a control style is corporate culture. If the corporate culture encourages employees to participate in decision making and rewards them for this participation and loyalty, then an organic control style is more appropriate. If the culture of the organization favors decision making at the top and avoids employee participation, then a bureaucratic control style will be the better choice. As we will see in the resolution to the opening Managerial Incident, Motorola created a common culture and a common language before adopting its targets for quality improvement.

Employee professionalism can also influence the control style an organization uses. Employees who are highly educated, highly trained, and professional are more likely to want to participate in decision making and are more likely to accept the high standards of behavior displayed in the group's norms. These employees will be good candidates for an organic control style. Employees who lack experience, training, or the desire to participate would be better candidates for a bureaucratic control style.

Finally, performance measures influence the choice of control style. If performance can be quantified and explicitly measured, then a bureaucratic control style would work well. If task performance is difficult to measure or quantify, however, then an organic control style would be more appropriate.

You should recognize from the preceding discussion that achieving quality in the control process requires a good fit between the situation and the control system. Care must be taken to accurately assess management style, corporate culture, employee professionalism, and types of performance measures before selecting a philosophical approach to control. The choice of a control style is contingent upon all of these situational factors.

The selection of a control style for a multinational organization presents some unique challenges. Although most multinational organizations develop control systems that are a blend of bureaucratic and organic control, the high level of standardization in many multinational organizations permits a heavier use of bureaucratic control as company manuals and specific rules, procedures, and policies may be applicable across certain subgroups of operating units. For example, since General Motors maintains a number of subsidiaries around the globe that manufacture the same types of engines, it has the potential to utilize bureaucratic controls in these units. Nevertheless, organic control mechanisms may also play an important part in the control process for multinational firms, for it is critical that each organizational subunit understands the role it plays in the network of subsidiaries. Strong shared values and philosophies help to ensure that behaviors and output at the subsidiary level are compatible with corporate-wide initiatives.[22]

MECHANISMS FOR FINANCIAL CONTROL ■■■■■■■■■■

One of the most important areas where control must be exercised is in the finances of an organization. At times financial performance may not be meeting standards, or it may fall short of expectations. If such situations go undetected and corrective actions are not taken, the company's survival might be at stake. We will only briefly examine some of the more important techniques and methods for establishing financial control. More thorough coverage of these topics is left to your accounting and finance classes.

FINANCIAL STATEMENTS

Two financial statements provide much of the information needed to calculate ratios that are used to assess an organization's financial health. These statements are the balance sheet and the income statement.

Balance Sheet

The **balance sheet** provides a picture of an organization's financial position at a given point in time. It usually shows the financial status at the end of a fiscal year or a calendar year, although the time interval can certainly be shorter (for example, at the end of each quarter). The balance sheet summarizes three types of information: assets, liabilities, and owner's equity.

Assets are the things of value that the company owns; they are usually divided into current assets and fixed assets. **Current assets** are those items that can be converted into cash in a short time period; they include such items as accounts receivable, inventory, and, of course, cash. **Fixed assets** are longer term in nature and include such items as buildings, land, and equipment.

Liabilities include the firm's debts and obligations. They can be divided into current liabilities and long-term liabilities. **Current liabilities** are the debts that must be paid in the near future; they include such obligations as accounts payable and not yet paid salaries earned by workers. **Long-term liabilities** are the debts payable over a long time span and include such obligations as payment on bonds and bank loans and mortgages for buildings and land.

Owner's equity is the difference between the assets and liabilities. It represents the company's net worth and consists of common stock and retained earnings. Table 16.3 shows an example of a balance sheet. Note that the totals on both sides of the balance sheet are equal; this must always be the case.

Income Statement

The **income statement** summarizes the organization's financial performance over a given time interval, typically one year. It shows the revenues that have come into the organization, the expenses that have been incurred, and the bottom-line profit or loss realized by the firm for the given time interval. For this reason, the income statement is often called a profit-and-loss statement. Table 16.4 shows the general structure of an income statement.

Balance sheet
Summary of an organization's financial position at a given point in time, showing assets, liabilities, and owner's equity.

Assets
The things of value that an individual or organization owns.

Current assets
Items that can be converted into cash in a short time period.

Fixed assets
Assets that are long-term in nature, and cannot be converted quickly into cash.

Liabilities
The firm's debts and obligations.

Current liabilities
Debts that must be paid in the near future.

Long-term liabilities
Debts payable over a long time span.

Owner's equity
The difference between the assets and liabilities.

Income statement
Summary of an organization's financial performance over a given time interval, showing revenues, expenses, and bottom-line profit or loss.

▼ **Table 16.3**   Balance Sheet

CESTARO MANUFACTURING COMPANY BALANCE SHEET DECEMBER 31, 1995				
ASSETS			**LIABILITIES AND OWNER'S EQUITY**	
Current assets:			Current liabilities:	
Cash	$ 30,000		Accounts payable	$ 20,000
Accounts receivable	50,000		Accrued expenses	10,000
Inventory	200,000		Income tax payable	40,000
Total current assets		$280,000	Total current liabilities	$ 70,000
Fixed assets:			Long-term liabilities	
Land	150,000		Mortgages	300,000
Buildings & Equipment	400,000		Bonds	100,000
Total fixed assets		550,000	Total long-term liabilities	400,000
Total assets		830,000	Owner's Equity	
			Common Stock	300,000
			Retained earnings	60,000
			Total Owner's equity	360,000
			Total liabilities & equity	$830,000

FINANCIAL RATIOS

Several financial ratios can be used to interpret company performance. Each ratio is simply a comparison of a few pieces of financial data. These ratios can be used to compare a company's current performance with its past performance, or they can be used to compare the company's performance with the performance of other companies in the same industry.

Liquidity Ratios

Liquidity ratios
Indicators of the firm's ability to meet its short-term debts and obligations.

Liquidity ratios indicate the firm's ability to meet its short-term debts and obligations. The most commonly used liquidity ratio is the current ratio, which is determined by dividing current assets by current liabilities. The current ratio for the Cestaro Manufacturing Company illustrated in Tables 16.3 and 16.4 is 280,000/70,000, or 4. This ratio indicates that Cestaro has four dollars of liquid assets for each dollar of short-term debt. Another liquidity ratio is the quick ratio, which is calculated by dividing current assets less inventory by the current liabilities. This ratio assesses how well a firm can expect to meet short-term obligations without having to dispose of inventories. For the Cestaro Company, the quick ratio is (280,000 − 200,000)/70,000, or 1.14.

Profitability Ratios

Profitability ratios
Indicators of the relative effectiveness, or profitability, of the organization.

Profitability ratios indicate the relative effectiveness of the organization. One important profitability ratio is the profit margin on sales, which is calculated as net income divided by sales. For the Cestaro Company this ratio is 230,000/ 2,300,000, or .1 (i.e., 10 percent). Another profitability measure is return on total assets (ROA), which is calculated by dividing the net income by total assets. For Cestaro this ratio is 230,000/830,000, or .28 (i.e., 28 percent). ROA is a valuable yardstick for potential investors, for its tells them how effective management is in using its assets to earn additional profits.

Debt Ratios

Debt ratios
Indicators of the firm's ability to handle long-term debt.

Debt ratios indicate the firms's ability to handle long-term debt. The most common debt ratio is calculated by dividing total liabilities by total assets. The

▼ **Table 16.4**   Income Statement

CESTARO MANUFACTURING COMPANY INCOME STATEMENT FOR THE YEAR ENDING DECEMBER 31, 1995		
Gross sales	$2,400,000	
Less sales returns	100,000	
Net sales		$2,300,000
Less expenses and cost of goods sold:		
Cost of goods sold	1,600,000	
Depreciation	50,000	
Sales expense	150,000	
Administrative expense	80,000	1,880,000
Operating profit		420,000
Other income		10,000
Gross income		430,000
Less interest expense	40,000	
Taxable income		390,000
Less taxes	160,000	
Net income		230,000

debt ratio for Cestaro is 470,000/830,000, or .57 (i.e., 57 percent). This indicates that the firm has 57 cents in debt for each dollar of assets. The lower the debt ratio, the better the financial health of the organization.

Activity Ratios

Activity ratios measure performance with respect to key activities defined by management. For example, the total cost of goods sold divided by the average daily inventory indicates how efficiently the firm is forecasting sales and ordering merchandise. When total sales are divided by average inventory, an inventory turnover ratio of calculated. This ratio indicates the number of times inventory is turned over to meet the total sales. A low figure means that inventory sits too long, and money is wasted.[23]

These and other similar ratios should be used to gain insights into a company's financial relationships and to identify areas that are out of control so that corrective action can be taken. When a ratio is out of line with either past company performance or the performance of comparable companies within the industry, managers must carefully probe through the numbers to determine the cause of the problem and devise a solution. Many of the numbers on the balance sheet and income statement are interrelated, and making a change to improve one ratio may have an undesirable impact on another. Therefore, managers must be very familiar with company operations in order to arrive at a proper remedy when using financial controls.

Activity ratios
Indicators of performance with respect to key activities defined by management.

ETHICAL ISSUES IN THE CONTROL OF A DIVERSE WORK FORCE ▬▬▬

Organizations are increasingly employing controversial mechanisms to control the behavior of individuals and groups within the organization. Sometimes these control mechanisms are known to the individuals, and sometimes the individuals are totally oblivious to their existence. There is considerable controversy over the ethics of using such control methods as drug testing, surveillance, and computer monitoring. The next sections briefly review the debates over these practices.

▼ Pre-employment drug testing: signs at the entrances to Home Depot stores advise prospective employees that all applicants are tested for drugs.

DRUG TESTING

It has been estimated that the use of illegal drugs is costing U.S. organizations close to $100 billion per year.[24] Drug abuse results in increases in defective output, absenteeism, workplace accidents, health care costs, and insurance claims. To combat the costs associated with these drug-related problems, organizations have increasingly turned to drug testing. One type of drug testing is pre-employment testing.[25] As the name suggests, organizations that use this approach require job applicants to submit to a drug detection test. In the Ethics: Take a Stand at the end of this chapter, you will see how the Home Depot Corporation uses drug testing on job applicants.

Another type of drug testing focuses on testing current employees. Organizations that test existing employees can follow any of three policies. Random testing subjects employees to unannounced and unscheduled examination. Testing can also be based upon probable cause. If an employee exhibits suspicious or erratic behavior, or if drug paraphernalia are found in an employee's locker, there may be probable cause for testing. Finally, testing may be prescribed after an accident. Since it is conceivable that impaired motor skills may be the cause of the accident, this is a reasonable time for a drug test. The Motorola Corporation described in the opening Managerial Incident began screening all employees for illegal drugs in 1990. Motorola estimates that lost productivity and absenteeism costs could be reduced by $190 million annually if drug addicts were removed from the workplace.[26]

The ethical issue posed by drug testing hinges on whether it constitutes an invasion of privacy. Do individuals have the right to do as they please with regard to drugs while on their own time, or do organizations have the right to test for drugs in an effort to reduce medical costs, lost productivity costs, absenteeism costs, and accidents in the workplace?[27] There is no easy answer to this question. The debate over drug testing continues and will undoubtedly continue for quite some time.

UNDERCOVER SURVEILLANCE

Businesses are constantly subjected to a variety of illegal activities that add to operating costs and decrease the bottom-line profit. Therefore, they are constantly looking for ways to control such activities. These activities include theft (pilferage, shoplifting, embezzlement, burglary), fraud (credit card, check, insurance), and malicious destruction of property (vandalism, arson).[28] Businesses often resort to a variety of surveillance techniques in order to control these illicit activities. Surveillance may be conducted by undercover internal security staffs, external security firms, or electronic devices. For example, General Electric uses tiny cameras hidden behind walls and ceilings to watch employees suspected of crimes, DuPont uses hidden cameras to monitor its loading docks, and Las Vegas casinos use ceiling-mounted cameras to observe activities on the gaming floors.[29]

Few would find fault when surveillance attempts to detect illegal activities being performed by individuals who are not part of the organization. However, undercover surveillance becomes a rather delicate issue when an organization's own employees are the subject of the scrutiny.[30] Again, the issue of invasion of privacy often surfaces in such instances, as does the concern that management has a low regard for and little trust in its own employees.

COMPUTER MONITORING

In many businesses, employees spend much of their time working at computer terminals and other similar electronic devices. Among these employees are data processors, word processors, airline reservation clerks, insurance claims workers, telemarketers, communications network personnel, and workers in many other occupations. Technology has evolved to the point where the work of these employees can be monitored electronically without their knowledge through the computers with which they interface.[31]

Although it is a form of undercover surveillance, computer monitoring is concerned with measuring employee performance rather than detecting illegal activities. This form of surveillance raises serious questions as to whether it violates a worker's right to privacy.[32] Many would question the appropriateness of the organization "electronically peeking over the workers' shoulders" to monitor their actions. They might argue that it is more appropriate to judge the net output of employees' efforts periodically (daily, weekly, monthly) rather than to constantly monitor their every action and/or decision.[33] There are no easy answers to the ethical questions raised by these control methods.

MANAGERIAL IMPLICATIONS

Throughout this book, we have been continually stressing that the successful organizations in the 1990s and beyond will be those that achieve quality in all aspects of their operations. Successful managers in these organizations will be those who can ensure that once plans have been set into place, all activities will be directed toward successfully carrying out those plans. The most effective device managers have for assessing the success of the organizational activities is a basic control system. In a sense, control systems help managers to chart a course, or set a direction, when standards of behavior or performance are established. Control systems also help to tell them whether they are on course by providing a way to monitor performance. Managers monitor their behavior or performance by measuring what has been done and comparing it to what should have been done. Finally, when organizations stray off course, control systems help to guide them back onto the right path by forcing managers to consider corrective actions to remove undesirable deviations from standards.

Successful managers of the future will be those who:

- Develop a control system for each important product, service, process, or activity within the organization.
- Incorporate sufficient variety, sensitivity, anticipation capability, and feedback into the control system.
- Gauge the control system's effectiveness by considering its relationship to corporate strategy, its completeness, the degree to which it incorporates objective and subjective performance measures, its timeliness, and its acceptability to individuals within the organization.
- Determine the appropriate points within the organization where control systems should be focused.

- Understand the intricacies of the financial data contained in the organization's financial statements, and can use various financial control techniques to assess the firm's financial health.
- Adopt a philosophy of control that is consistent with the management style, corporate culture, employee professionalism, and performance measures present within the organization.

The checklist shown earlier in Meeting the Challenge can be helpful in determining whether a control system has been designed effectively.

In short, the concepts of control presented in this chapter provide us with a mechanism for determining whether our plans and actions have turned out as we had expected or hoped they would. If they haven't, we would be alerted to that fact, allowing us to take the appropriate corrective action to keep matters on their proper course. By remaining on course, we stand a better chance of being successful in our organizational activities.

MANAGERIAL INCIDENT RESOLUTION

MOTOROLA, INC.—SURVIVAL THROUGH CONTROLS

Although Motorola was number one in the industry with a 50 percent market share at the time, one of the officers proclaimed in a 1979 meeting that "our quality stinks." Customers were not satisfied with delivery time, product reliability, and scores of other factors. So, the company launched a crusade to put in a wide range of control techniques to improve quality and reliability and stem the tide of Japanese competition.

Previously, each division had its own performance measures. These dissimilar systems made it virtually impossible for top management to assess and compare performance across the corporation, much less work toward common objectives. Motorola began by creating a common culture and a common language. A single measure for quality, total defects per unit of work, was chosen. The company then adopted a goal for a 10-fold improvement in all products and service by 1986, an additional 10-fold improvement by 1989, and then a 100-fold improvement by 1991. By 1989 Motorola had reduced its defects from 3,000 per million to less than 200 per million. In the mid-1990s the company was continuing to push toward its renowned "six sigma" goal, which would mean only 3.4 defects per million.[34] ▼

SUMMARY

- Organizational control is the systematic process through which managers regulate organizational activities to make them consistent with the expectations established in plans, targets, and standards of performance. Control is an extremely important managerial function because it ensures that all of the planning, organizing, and leading has gone as we hoped it would. If things have not gone as planned, this situation can result in a variety of negative consequences to the organization.
- An organized system for control would require that (1) standards of performance be established, (2) actual performance be measured, (3) comparisons be made between standards and actual performance, and (4) corrective action be taken when there are unacceptable deviations of the actual performance from the standards.

- When designing a control system, one should consider the amount of variety to include in the system, its ability to anticipate problems before they occur, the amount of sensitivity needed in the measuring instruments, and the type of data and information to be included in the feedback report.

- To be effective, the control system should be related to the organizational strategy, incorporate all the steps in the control process, blend both objective and subjective performance measures, provide feedback in a timely fashion, and be accepted by members of the organization.

- To determine the proper amount of control to be exercised in a given situation, several factors must be examined. The costs and benefits of the control effort must be assessed. The amount of control can also be affected by the reliability of the system being controlled or the importance of the item being controlled.

- Feedforward (or preventive) control systems focus on the inputs to the transformation process. Concurrent control systems focus on the ongoing activities of the transformation process. Feedback (or corrective) control systems focus on the outputs of the transformation process.

- Bureaucratic control is a more rigid philosophy of control that relies on prescribed rules, policies, a hierarchy of authority, written documents, and other formal mechanisms to influence behavior, assess performance, and correct unacceptable deviations from standards. Organic control is a more flexible philosophy that relies upon social values, traditions, flexible authority, and trust to assess performance and correct unacceptable deviations.

- Several financial control devices are available to assess on organization's financial health. The balance sheet and income statement are two important financial statements. In addition, there are several financial ratios that can be used to interpret company performance.

- It is becoming more common for organizations to test their employees for drug use, conduct undercover surveillance of their employees, and engage in computer monitoring. Such control procedures raise ethical questions of invasion of privacy and lack of confidence and trust in the employees.

KEY TERMS

Organizational control (p. 529)
Law of requisite variety (p. 536)
Variance reporting (p. 537)
Management by exception (p. 537)
Feedforward (preventive) control
  (p. 544)
Concurrent control (p. 544)
Feedback (corrective) control
  (p. 545)

Bureaucratic control (p. 546)
Organic (clan) control (p. 547)
Balance sheet (p. 549)
Assets (p. 549)
Current assets (p. 549)
Fixed assets (p. 549)
Liabilities (p. 549)
Current liabilities (p. 549)

Long-term liabilities (p. 549)
Owner's equity (p. 549)
Income statement (p. 549)
Liquidity ratios (p. 550)
Profitability ratios (p. 550)
Debt ratios (p. 550)
Activity ratios (p. 551)

REVIEW QUESTIONS

1. Why is control such a critical managerial function?
2. Discuss each of the steps in the control process.
3. Explain the difference between feedforward, concurrent, and feedback control.

4. Describe the difference between bureaucratic and organic control.
5. Discuss the factors that should be considered in selecting a control style.

6. Describe the factors that help determine the proper amount of control to be exercised.

7. Discuss the factors that should be considered in designing a control system.

8. Discuss the various criteria for effective control.

9. Discuss some of the organizational control practices that raise ethical dilemmas.

10. Describe the cost tradeoffs in a control system.

DISCUSSION QUESTIONS

Improving Critical Thinking

1. Through your personal observations, identify a situation in which bureaucratic control is being used and one in which organic control is being used. Discuss the reasons you feel each situation exhibits the type of control you have said it displays.

2. Identify some situations that you have encountered where electronic or undercover surveillance was being performed. Discuss how you felt about those practices.

Enhancing Communication Skills

3. Select some aspect of your life (some activity you engage in) and then design a system by which you could control that activity. Be specific in describing the activity, how you would perform each of the steps in the control process, and the potential corrective actions you could take if your performance was not up to your standards. To enhance your written communication skills, write a short (1–2 page) essay in which you describe the aspect of your life being controlled and the design of the control system.

4. The chapter cited two brief examples (air traffic controller and tree farm manager) in which the response times for control feedback were quite different. Identify several situations with varying response time requirements. Try to come up with examples having response times in seconds, minutes, hours, days, and months. To enhance your oral communication skills, prepare a short (10–15 minute) presentation for the class in which you describe your examples for each of these categories of response time.

Building Teamwork Skills

5. Identify two situations that you have observed where you think the sensitivity of the measuring device is inappropriate. One of those situations should have a device that is too sensitive and the other a device that is not sensitive enough. Thoroughly describe what is being measured and the device that is being used to measure it. Indicate why you feel that the sensitivity of the devices is inappropriate. To refine your teamwork skills, meet with a small group of students who have been given this same assignment. Compare and discuss your selections, and then reach a consensus agreement on the two best choices (one overly sensitive and one insufficiently sensitive device). Select a spokesperson to present your choices to the rest of the class.

6. Try to identify two situations in which the costs would suggest very different levels of control. In one situation, the cost tradeoffs should suggest high levels of control are warranted, and in the other they should suggest that low levels of control are appropriate. To refine your teamwork skills, meet with a small group of students who have been given this same assignment. Compare and discuss your selections, and then reach a consensus agreement on the two best choices (one requiring low levels of control and one requiring high levels of control). Sketch the cost tradeoff graphs for each situation. Then select a spokesperson to present your team's choices and graphs to the rest of the class.

ETHICS: TAKE A STAND

As this chapter mentioned, the use of illegal drugs is costing U.S. organizations close to $100 billion per year. Home Depot Corporation, a large chain of stores that specializes in the sale of home construction, home repair, home decorating, household, and gardening items, has a very strict policy on drugs. Anyone who approaches the front entrance of a Home Depot store is greeted by a sign in the window proclaiming that "We test all applicants for illegal drug use. If you use drugs, don't bother to apply!"

For Discussion
1. Discuss the ethical issues associated with this control mechanism for individual behavior.
2. Do you feel that pre-employment, or even post-employment, drug screening constitutes ethical behavior on the organization's part, or is it an invasion of personal privacy?

BUREAUCRATIC VERSUS ORGANIC CONTROL

THINKING CRITICALLY
Debate the Issue

Form teams of four to five students as directed by your instructor. Half of the teams should prepare to argue the benefits of bureaucratic control. The other half of the teams should prepare to argue the benefits of organic control. Where possible, identify companies that use these methods of control and assess their relative effectiveness. Two teams will be selected by the instructor to present their findings to the class in a debate format.

VIDEO CASE

Steelcase

 Steelcase has long been the world's leading designer and manufacturer of office furniture. For most of its history Steelcase specialized in the manufacture of desks, files, and chairs. Recently, the company instituted some radical changes in its operations. These changes were not made in response to any competitive threats. Instead, as customers began to ask for more specialized and customized products, Steelcase realized that it would have to change its manufacturing processes to meet its customers' requirements. According to Jerry Myers, president and CEO of Steelcase, "the biggest obstacle to change was overcoming the enormous success that we had in the past."

One of the biggest changes Steelcase instituted was in its manufacturing philosophy. Originally, the company had tried to achieve task simplicity. Processes were designed so that workers did the same thing all day and every day. The huge support systems needed to allow people to perform just one task resulted in complex processes and large amounts of inventory. In contrast, the new philosophy advocated flexible, well-trained workers who could perform a multitude of tasks. A focused factory concept was adopted. Each focused factory is comprised of work cells run by teams of employees. The teams are expected to handle the day-to-day business of the cells. These teams are self-managing—they do not wait to

be told what to do. Instead, they schedule their own shifts so that production requirements are met, and they solve routine problems that arise. Production workers also help design the cells and the manufacturing process, and they take the responsibility for the quality of their work. Workers view their production output as the input for other customers (usually internal to the firm) and strive to provide their customers with defect free input.

In short, decision making has been pushed down to the lower levels of the organization, layers of management have been removed, and processes have been simplified. Steelcase has benefited by seeing happier, more involved, and more dedicated workers, higher-quality products, and dramatically lower levels of inventory.[35]

For Discussion
1. Discuss what you feel were Steelcase's control styles before and after its change in manufacturing philosophy.
2. Given that the old style at Steelcase led to complex processes while the new style simplified processes, how do you feel the control system design factor "variety" has been affected?
3. With less inventory to fall back on when problems occur, how do you think the control system design factor "ability to anticipate problems" has been affected?

CASE

Minco Technology Labs

At Minco Technology Labs, Inc., of Austin, Texas, internal errors were frequent, delivery performance was poor, the rate of returns was unacceptable, and overhead was soaring. "In a nutshell, we were in trouble," says Elizabeth Coker, owner and CEO of the company, which tests semiconductors and assembles hybrid microcircuits, primarily for the military electronics market. She had located the company in Austin because the area had a number of semiconductor companies, an educated workforce, and modest housing and tax costs. It was equidistant from customers on both coasts and near a principal supplier ally, Texas Instruments.

When Coker realized that internal problems threatened Minco's existence, her first step was to simplify. She focused the company on its principal business—servicing the microcircuit processing market—and spun off services for customers in the custom packaging market. As changes proceeded, the overriding aim was "to ensure that any product going to our customers was correct and on time." The company established quality-control gates throughout its process to prevent any questionable product from being shipped. Each step from order taking to shipping was analyzed, through statistical process controls, to determine critical errors and their causes. Quality status reports identified problems. Company-wide training began.

Management was reduced to a single layer, with 12 managers and supervisors replacing 31. Responsibilities were shifted to teams of production-line workers. The number of meetings was cut. Quality, production, management visibility, team member suggestion, document review, and material review board meetings were combined into a single, one-hour daily meeting.

Team members met monthly. The CEO personally began teaching accounting principles and regularly provided every team member with full financial budget details. Nonmanagement teams reviewed scrap and rework materials. A team would research a problem, resolve it, record it, and dissolve upon achievement of the goal.[36]

For Discussion

1. Describe how and where Minco used a structured control process to try to improve its performance.
2. Discuss the various focal points for control that Minco employed.
3. What types of performance improvements might you expect or predict Minco would experience after implementing these changes?

EXPERIENTIAL EXERCISE 16.1

Assessing Timeliness of Control Systems

Purpose: To gain a greater awareness of the importance of timely feedback in control systems.

Procedure: Make a list of all the offices, departments, and officials that you have interacted with and received feedback from at your university. Then construct a table using the following column headings:

Encounter	Actual Response Time	Ideal Response Time	Problems and Difficulties

In the first column (Encounter), list all of the areas of interaction. In the second column (Actual Response Time), indicate the amount of time that elapsed before you received the feedback that you desired. In the third column (Ideal Response Time), list what you feel would have been an appropriate amount of time to receive the feedback. Finally, in the fourth column (Problems and Difficulties), note any problems or difficulties that you encountered because you did not receive the feedback in what you considered to be a timely fashion.

EXPERIENTIAL EXERCISE 16.2

Detecting Devices to Control Human Behavior

Purpose: To gain a greater awareness of the extent to which various devices are used to control individual behavior.

Procedure: Visit a shopping mall in your vicinity. Browse through several departments in a large department store and also visit several of the small speciality shops in the mall. See how many devices you can discover for controlling individual behavior. Compare and contrast the types of devices being used in the large department stores with those in small speciality stores. What factors seem to influence the use or nonuse of such devices?

NOTES

1. Adapted from M. M. Steeples, *The Corporate Guide to the Malcolm Baldrige National Quality Award* (New York: Business One Irwin, 1993), 242-49; S. Thomas, "Six Sigma: Motorola's Quest for Zero Defects," *APICS—The Performance Advantage*, July 1991, 36-41; B. Smith, "Six Sigma Quality: A Must Not a Myth," *Machine Design*, February 12, 1993, 63-66; and J. Morkes, "How Motorola Keeps Beating the Competition," *R & D Magazine*, December 1993, 30-32.

2. K. A. Merchant, *Control in Business Organizations* (Marshfield, Mass.: Pitman, 1985).

3. T. Lowe and J. L. Machin, *New Perspectives on Management Control* (New York: Macmillan, 1987).

4. B. Stratton, "Four to Receive 1990 Baldrige Awards," *Quality Progress*, December 1990, 9-21.

5. "Photronics," in *Real-World Lessons for America's Small Businesses: Insights from the Blue Chip Initiative* (*Nation's Business* on behalf of Connecticut Mutual Life Insurance Company and the U.S. Chamber of Commerce, 1993), 86-87.

6. Adapted from "Fullwood Foods," in *Real-World Lessons for America's Small Businesses: Insights from the Blue Chip Enterprise Initiative* (*Nation's Business* on behalf of Connecticut Mutual Life Insurance Company and the U.S. Chamber of Commerce, 1992), 97-98.

7. W. R. Ashby, *Introduction to Cybernetics* (New York: John Wiley & Sons, 1963).

8. S. Beer, *Cybernetics and Management* (New York: John Wiley & Sons, 1959), 44.

9. M. Goold and J. Quinn, "The Paradox of Strategic Controls," *Strategic Management Journal* (1990): 43-57.

10. D. Cray, "Control and Coordination in Multinational Corporations," *Journal of International Business Studies* (Fall 1984): 85-98.

11. P. Lorange and D. Murphy, Considerations in Implementing Strategic Control," *Journal of Business Strategy* 4 (Spring 1984): 27-35.

12. P. P. Schoderbek, R. A. Cosier and J. C. Aplin, *Management* (San Diego: Harcourt Brace Jovanovich, 1991).

13. J. R. Evans and W. M. Lindsay, *The Management and Control of Quality* (St. Paul, Minn.: West Publishing Co., 1993).

14. J. Young, "The Quality Focus at Hewlett-Packard," *Journal of Business Strategy* (Winter 1985): 6-9; and "The Push for Quality," *Business Week*, June 8, 1987, 130-44.

15. L. Krajewski and L. Ritzman, *Operations Management: Strategy and Analysis* (Reading, Mass.: Addison-Wesley, 1993), 516.

16. W. H. Newman, *Construction Control* (Englewood Cliffs, N.J.: Prentice-Hall, 1975).

17. P. Lorange, M. F. Scott Morton and G. Sumantra, *Strategic Control* (St. Paul, Minn.: West Publishing Co., 1986).

18. P. F. Drucker, *Management: Tasks, Responsibilities, Practices* (New York: Harper & Row, 1973), 100.

19. W. G. Ouchi, "Markets, Bureaucracies, and Clans," *Administrative Science Quarterly* 25 (1980): 128-41.

20. H. P. Sims, Jr. and C. C. Manz, *SuperLeadership: Leading Others to Lead Themselves* (New York: Simon & Schuster, 1989).

21. C. Cortland and D. A. Nadler, "Fit Control Systems to Your Managerial Style," *Harvard Business Review* (January/February 1976): 65-72.

22. B. R. Baliga and A. M. Jaeger, "Multinational Corporations: Control Systems and Delegation Issues," *Journal of International Business Studies* (Fall 1984): 25-40.

23. E. Brigham *Financial Management: Theory and Practice* 4th ed. (Chicago: Dryden Press, 1985).

24. F. J. Tasco and A. J. Gajda, "Substance Abuse in the Workplace," *Compensation and Benefits Management* (Winter 1990): 140-44.

25. M. A. McDaniel, "Does Pre-Employment Drug Use Predict on-the-Job Suitability?" *Personnel Psychology* (1988): 717-30.

26. T. W. Ferguson, "Motorola Aims High, So Motorolans Won't Be Getting High," *Wall Street Journal*, June 26, 1990, A19.

27. Tasco and Gajda, "Substance Abuse in the Workplace."

28. "Preventing Crime on the Job," *Nation's Business*, July 1990, 36-37.

29. J. Rothfeder, M. Galen and L. Driscoll, "Is Your Boss Spying on You?" *Business Week*, January 15, 1990, 74-75.

30. N.H. Snyder and K. E. Blair, "Dealing with Employee Theft," *Business Horizons*, May/June 1989, 27-34.

31. B. Dumaine, "Corporate Spies Snoop to Conquer," *Fortune*, November 7, 1988, 68-76.

32. M. McDonald, "They've Got Your Number," *Dallas Morning News*, April 7, 1991, F1.

33. H. J. Chalykoff, and T. A. Kochan, "Computer-Aided Monitoring: Its Influence on Employee Job Satisfaction and Turnover," *Personnel Psychology* (1989): 807-34.

34. Adapted from Steeples, *The Corporate Guide to the Malcolm Baldrige National Quality Award*; Tomas, "Six Sigma: Motorola's Quest for Zero Defects"; Smith, "Six Sigma Quality: A Must Not a Myth"; and Morkes, "How Motorola Keeps Beating the Competition."

35. Adapted from "We're Getting Closer," *Association for Manufacturing Excellence Videotape #6*, 1991.

36. Adapted from "Minco Technology Labs," in *Real-World Lessons for America's Small Businesses: Insights from the Blue Chip Enterprise Initiative* (*Nation's Business* on behalf of Connecticut Mutual Life Insurance Company and the U.S. Chamber of Commerce, 1993), 84-85.

Productivity and Quality in Operations

CHAPTER 17

▼ CHAPTER OVERVIEW

All business organizations engage in operations that transform inputs into outputs. Regardless of whether their organization manufactures a product or provides a service, operations managers have one very fundamental concern—that is, to provide the customers what they want, when they want it. As simple as this concept sounds, operations managers must make many decisions prior to delivering the product or service. To achieve quality in operations, managers must (1) understand the nature of the various decisions they will face and (2) understand the various tools, techniques, and approaches that can help them to make these decisions. How managers should approach these decisions depends to a large extent upon whether their organization is predominantly product or service oriented and upon the structural characteristics of the operating system.

In this chapter we first examine the differences between manufacturing and service organizations and review the basic system configurations that these organizations may exhibit. We then briefly examine some of the more important managerial decision areas for the long-term design of these systems, as well as some of the important decisions for their short-term operation and control. Since productivity and quality have a major impact upon the efficiency and effectiveness of operations decisions, ways to measure and improve them are examined. We also present some contributions of the most prominent, contemporary quality philosophers. We finish by discussing the roles that productivity and quality play in achieving excellence in operations.

▼ LEARNING OBJECTIVES

When you have finished studying this chapter, you should be able to:

- Identify the major differences between manufacturing and service organizations.
- Describe the volume/variety continuum for identifying different operating system configurations and identify the different types of manufacturing and service organizations that might exist, as well as their locations on the volume/variety continuum.
- Identify the two broad categories of decision-making areas within operating systems and describe some of the important decisions in each category.

- Define the concept of productivity and identify the three approaches to improving productivity.
- Provide definitions of quality from both a consumer perspective and a producer perspective.
- Describe the four categories of quality-related costs.
- Identify the various areas of concentration and commitment for a program of total quality management.
- Describe the major contributions of the most prominent, contemporary quality philosophers.

MANAGERIAL INCIDENT

FORD MOTOR COMPANY: REVERSING THE DECLINE

During the last few decades, a growing number of core industries in the once mighty U.S. manufacturing sector began to suffer at the hands of foreign competitors. Earlier domination of world markets had led to complacency, arrogance, and even sloppiness. This opened the door for foreign competitors, who boasted of products with higher quality and lower prices. This trend was probably most evident in the automotive industry, where foreign imports captured an increasingly large market share throughout the 1970s and 1980s.

The Ford Motor Company, one of the Big Three U.S. automakers, experienced financial difficulties during much of this period. In fact, with losses of $1.5 billion in 1980, $1.1 billion in 1981, and $658 million in 1982, Ford had little cash in reserve and was in danger of becoming bankrupt. Even when there was a profit, it represented a much lower percentage of total sales than in the earlier "good times." For example, in the early 1960s Ford's return on sales had never fallen below 5 percent. In 1970 it dropped to 3.5 percent, perhaps foretelling the huge losses that were to come in the early 1980s. Contributing to this problem was Ford's low labor productivity—the foreign competitors' automobile output per worker exceeded Ford's capabilities. It was clear that Ford would have to improve its labor productivity and find ways to regain some of its lost market share if the firm was to prosper again.[1] ▼

INTRODUCTION

The Ford Motor Company was facing a very serious problem. Because Ford's productivity and quality were below the levels being achieved by its foreign competitors, its market share was slipping and losses were mounting. Unless it could reverse this trend, Ford faced a distinct possibility of bankruptcy. Achieving excellence in its operations would require changes to correct its quality and productivity problems. As we will see as the chapter unfolds and in the closing resolution to this Managerial Incident, changes would eventually pervade many aspects of Ford's operations.

In this chapter we will focus on issues of productivity and quality in operations. Recall that in Chapter 16 we presented a simple model for operations. It described a process in which inputs are subjected to a transformation process that converts them into the product or service outputs of the organization. We will see that operations management has a strong decision-making orientation and contains several design and operating decision areas. How managers should approach these decisions depends upon the structural characteristics of their own operating systems and whether their organizations are predominantly engaged in manufacturing products or providing services.

We begin by examining the differences between manufacturing and service organizations and the structural differences between various operating systems. Some of the more important system design and operating decisions are then described. We conclude the chapter by discussing the roles that productivity and quality play in achieving excellence in operations and examining ways organizations can improve productivity and quality.

WHAT IS OPERATIONS MANAGEMENT?

Operations management is concerned with the design, planning, and control of the factors that enable us to provide the product or service outputs of the organization. Decision making is central to operations management. Operations managers must make decisions to ensure that the product or service output of the firm is provided (1) in the amount demanded, (2) at the appropriate time, (3) with the appropriate quality level, and (4) in a manner that is compatible with the goals of the organization.

The first three aspects of the operations manager's function are fairly straightforward: provide what the customers want, when they want it, and with a quality level that is acceptable to them. The last aspect can be a bit trickier. As we saw earlier in Chapter 4, organizations often have multiple goals, and some may be in conflict with one another. When this happens, operations management decisions cannot simultaneously satisfy all organizational goals. Consider, for example, the dilemma you would face if you were in charge of operations in a steel mill. Suppose that two of your organization's many goals were to (1) maximize bottom-line profits and (2) reduce the amount of pollutants that the mill discharges into the atmosphere. Installing scrubbers in the mill's smokestacks would reduce pollution, but the expense of these scrubbers would detract from your organization's bottom-line profits.

The decisions faced by operations managers can be conveniently separated into two broad categories. The first set of decisions relates to the design of the operating system. After the system has been designed and built, operations managers must then make the operating and control decisions necessary to keep the system running in a smooth and efficient manner. Managers can draw on many tools, techniques, and models to help them make these decisions. For many operations decisions, the proper decision-making tools depend upon whether the system is a manufacturing or service system. We will see later in the chapter that the manufacturing versus service distinction also impacts upon how quality and productivity are measured. Decision making tool selection also depends upon the structural characteristics of the operating system. Consequently, before we explore the important operations management decision areas, we first examine the differences between manufacturing and service organizations and the structural differences among various manufacturing and service organizations.

MANUFACTURING VERSUS SERVICE OPERATING SYSTEMS

Although manufacturing and service organizations both display the same input-to-output transformation process, a fundamental output characteristic distinguishes manufacturing organizations from most service organizations. The output of manufacturing will always be a physical product—something that can be touched, measured, weighed, or otherwise examined. For example,

IBM makes computers, General Motors makes automobiles, RCA makes audio and video equipment, and Nike makes athletic apparel.

Outputs of service organizations often lack physical properties. For example, H&R Block processes income tax returns, hospitals treat sick and injured people, and your college professors deliver lectures and convey knowledge to you. Sometimes, however, the outputs of service organizations do possess physical properties. When you eat in a fast-food restaurant, your lunch selection certainly has physical properties associated with it. Does this make the fast-food restaurant a manufacturing organization? Not really. The physical characteristic of outputs is not the only feature that distinguishes manufacturing from service organizations. As we take a closer look at other differences, continue to think about fast-food restaurants. You should have a definite opinion as to whether they are manufacturing or service organizations by the time we get to the end of the discussion.

Several of the differences between manufacturing and service stem from the physical nature of the output. Manufacturing can stockpile inventories of finished products in advance of customer demand.[2] Service organizations usually cannot. For example, a barbershop cannot stockpile a supply of haircuts prior to the Saturday morning peak demand period, and H&R Block cannot stockpile an inventory of completed income tax returns prior to April's peak demand. Service capacity is often described as being time perishable.[3] This means that if a service organization has excess capacity that goes unused, that service capability has been lost forever. On the other hand, a manufacturing organization with excess capacity can use the surplus capacity to produce additional product for later consumption.

Another difference is that production and consumption usually occur simultaneously in service organizations. In addition, the customer is normally a participant in the service process.[4] For example, you must show up at the barbershop or beauty salon to receive a haircut, and it will be performed while you sit in the barber's or hairdresser's chair. These two characteristics also impact on another difference between manufacturing and service—the system location considerations. Service systems, such as barbershops, restaurants, income tax preparation firms, and hospitals, need to be located close to their customers, while manufacturing systems would not consider this to be of prime importance.[5] Most adult Americans own an automobile, but few live within walking distance or an easy drive to an automobile manufacturing plant. However, most would like to have reasonable access to an automobile repair shop, for none of us would want to take our automobile back to Detroit (or Japan!) for repair service.

A final difference between manufacturing and service relates to the measurement of quality and productivity. The quality of a product is usually much easier to assess than the quality of a service.[6] Physical products are designed to meet various specifications that involve physical traits such as weight, dimensions, color, durability, and so forth. After manufacture, precise objective measurements of these characteristics can be made to determine the degree to which the product meets the quality standards. For example, once manufactured, an Apple Macintosh computer can be put through a variety of tests to ensure that it operates exactly as it was designed. Such precision is usually more difficult when assessing the quality of a service output. In many instances only subjective assessments can be made of the quality of the service output. Precise standards usually do not exist to determine how good the haircut is, how accurately the income tax return was prepared, or how tasty the hamburger was. Productivity, which gauges the relationship between inputs and outputs, is also easier to assess in manufacturing situations, where the physical nature of the inputs and outputs allows them to be precisely measured.[7] Meet-

CHECKLIST FOR MANUFACTURING/SERVICE CLASSIFICATION

To determine whether a business firm is a manufacturing organization or a service organization, answer the following questions with a zero (0) for no and a one (1) for yes:

1. Does the firm provide a tangible, physical output?
2. Can the output be stored in inventory for future use or consumption?
3. Can the output be transported to distant locations?
4. Can excess capacity be put to productive use?
5. Can the output be produced well in advance of its consumption?
6. Can the system operate without having the consumer of the output as an active participant?
7. Is it reasonable to have the system located a great distance from the consumer of the output?
8. Is productivity relatively easy to measure?
9. Is quality relatively easy to assess?

Total the value of your responses. The closer the total is to 9, the more inclined we would be to classify the system as a manufacturing organization. The closer the total is to 0, the more inclined we would be to classify the system as a service organization.

ing the Challenge presents a checklist for determining whether an organization is predominantly a manufacturing organization or a service organization. Apply the checklist to Ford Motor Company as described in the opening Managerial Incident. Into which category (manufacturing or service) does Ford fall?

Now let's think again about fast-food chains and the checklist in Meeting the Challenge. The service capacity of the fast-food outlets is usually time perishable. Excess capacity early in the day will go unused; it cannot be used to satisfy the needs of the lunch hour crowd. Using that early morning excess capacity to stockpile inventory in advance of the lunch hour rush is of limited practicality. Hamburgers and french fries cannot be cooked early in the day and then stored until the noon rush. In these situations, production and consumption must occur almost simultaneously, and the customer is an active participant in the process. The vast multitude of locations also points to a service orientation. One centralized McDonald's will not suffice. There must be plenty of outlets, scattered about so that they are near the customers in order to facilitate direct interaction between the customer and the service system. Thus, when all the tests are applied, a service classification proves to be more appropriate for fast-food restaurants.

Let's now turn our attention to an examination of the structural differences that can exist among manufacturing and service organizations.

STRUCTURAL DIFFERENCES AMONG OPERATING SYSTEMS

Individual operating systems can be categorized along a volume/variety continuum, as illustrated in Figure 17.1. Companies can differ in the variety of outputs produced, as well as in the volume of each item that is provided. As you move toward the left extreme of low variety and high volume, you encounter systems that provide very few different types of output, but deliver a

▼ **FIGURE 17.1**
Classification Scheme for Different
Operating Systems

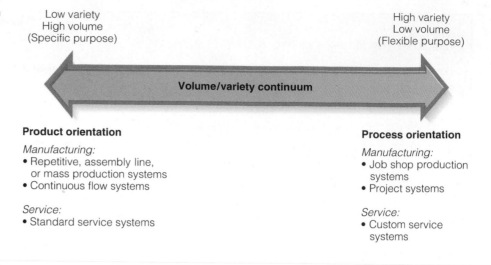

Low variety
High volume
(Specific purpose)

High variety
Low volume
(Flexible purpose)

Volume/variety continuum

Product orientation

Manufacturing:
• Repetitive, assembly line,
  or mass production systems
• Continuous flow systems

Service:
• Standard service systems

Process orientation

Manufacturing:
• Job shop production
  systems
• Project systems

Service:
• Custom service
  systems

large quantity of each. Toward the right extreme of high variety and low volume, you encounter systems that provide a very wide variety of different types of output, but deliver a small number of each. The endpoints of this line represent two extremes in both manufacturing and service organizations. Let's take a closer look at these configurations, first in manufacturing organizations and then in service organizations.

Types of Manufacturing Systems

The left portion of the continuum represents systems that have a specific purpose.[8] The extreme left reflects companies that make only one product, but produce it in large quantities. In such a system, operations can be standardized. When the product being made takes the form of discrete, individual units, the system is called a **repetitive production system, assembly line system,** or **mass production system.** For example, a company that makes only yellow #2 pencils with an eraser would be at the left end of the continuum. When a product is made in a continuous stream, and not in discrete units, the system is called a **continuous flow system.** Examples here would include an Exxon oil refinery, a Coors brewery, or perhaps a USX steel mill that produces long, continuous rolls of sheet steel.

At the right end of the continuum are systems that have a flexible purpose. The extreme right reflects companies that make many different types of items, but produce only one of each. This would be a custom manufacturing situation. In such a system, operations cannot be standardized, but instead must be flexible enough to accommodate the wide variety of items that will be manufactured. When the items to be made require small to moderate amounts of resources and time (hours or days), the systems are referred to as **job shop systems.** The term unit production is often used to signify systems that manufacture only a single unit of a particular item. A sign shop that custom fabricates neon advertising signs for small businesses would be an example of a company near the right extreme of this continuum. Sometimes flexible-purpose systems produce items that consume massive amounts of resources and require large amounts of time to complete (months or years). Such systems are referred to as **project systems.** Examples here would include construction companies that develop shopping centers, build roads and bridges, and so forth.[9]

Although the endpoints have been neatly defined for the continuum of Figure 17.1, it is very unusual to find an organization that lies at either extreme. While Eberhard-Faber is a large pencil manufacturer, this company makes more

Repetitive, assembly line, or mass production system
Produces high volume of discrete items.

Continuous flow production system
Produces high volume of output that flows in a continuous stream.

Job shop production system
Produces small quantities of a wide variety of specialized items.

Project production system
Produces large scale, unique items.

▼ This rolling hot mill producing sheet steel exemplifies continuous flow manufacturing systems.

than just yellow #2 pencils with erasers. It turns out pencils in a variety of colors with different types of lead. In addition to writing pencils, it also manufactures a variety of pens and marking pencils. All of these different writing instruments are produced in very large quantities. Consequently, Eberhard-Faber exhibits mass production characteristics and would certainly be close to the left extreme of the volume/variety continuum. Since Ford manufactures several models of automobiles and trucks, it is also near, but not quite at, the left extreme of the continuum. If the neon sign shop described earlier made a small number of several different signs, it would move slightly away from the right extreme. Even so, this system would still exhibit the basic characteristics of the job shop system.

Types of Service Systems

The continuum of Figure 17.1 also applies to different types of service systems. The left extreme reflects organizations that provide standard services, while the right extreme reflects organizations that provide custom services. Consider, for example, a college dormitory cafeteria line. It has all of the characteristics of an assembly line, since each customer moving through the line is serviced in exactly the same manner at each serving station. In contrast, a walk-in emergency clinic might exhibit all the characteristics of a custom job shop, since most patients are likely to have different types of injuries and illnesses and consequently will require different services.

As in the case of manufacturing, service organizations can easily lie somewhere between the extremes. The cafeteria line might have a la carte selections, in which case some customers might receive slightly different service. Likewise, the emergency clinic might have a few patients with broken arms whose service requirements are virtually identical. The wound will be cleaned and dressed, X-rays taken, and a cast applied for each of them.[10]

Whether an organization is a manufacturing or a service entity and wherever it fits on the volume/variety continuum, its operations managers will have to make decisions. The next section examines the many decisions that must be made for both the design and the operation of manufacturing and service organizations.

OPERATIONS MANAGEMENT DECISION AREAS

When you operate any business organization, a number of decisions must be made. Based upon the time frame involved, these decisions can be conveniently categorized as long-term system design decisions or as short-term operating and control decisions.[11] It is not our intention to present a thorough description of each of the operations management decision areas. That level of detail is best left to separate operations management courses with their specialized textbooks. Instead, we provide you with a brief, introductory overview of some of the more important operations management decision areas.

Long-Term System Design Decisions

Long-term system design decisions require substantial investments of time, energy, money, and resources. As the name implies, they commit the decision maker to a particular system configuration (i.e., arrangement of buildings and equipment) that will exist for many years, if not the entire life of the organization. Once these decisions are made and implemented, changing them would be costly. Although a thorough treatment of these various decisions would require several chapters, the following brief overview will provide a basic understanding.

Choice of a Product or Service   Prior to the development and start-up of any business, a fundamental decision must be made about what product or service will be provided. This decision is directly linked to the corporate strategy, for it answers the question "What business are we in?" The choice of product or service will ultimately dictate what inputs will be necessary and what type of transformation will be performed. To make a viable product/service selection decision, considerable interaction with the marketing function will be needed. This interaction will help the decision maker accurately assess the wants and needs of the marketplace as well as the strength of the competition, so that the product or service selected has a reasonable chance of success.

Product or Service Design   From a manufacturing standpoint, the development of a product involves a sequence of steps, as illustrated in Figure 17.2.[12] These steps might also be applied in certain service situations that involve physical output. The sequence of design steps requires (1) development of a concept,

▼ Computer-aided design (CAD) helps this General Motors engineer test the aerodynamics of a new automobile design.

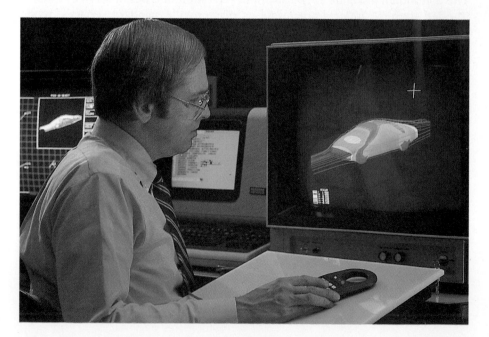

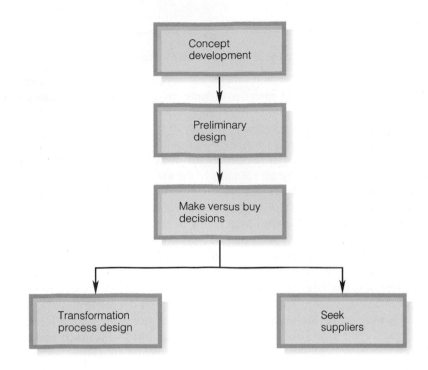

(2) development of a preliminary design or prototype, (3) development of make versus buy choices, and (4) selection of production methods, equipment, and suppliers.

Although each step in the design process is usually carried out by a different unit of the organization, design quality is facilitated when all participants from marketing, engineering, production, purchasing, and any other relevant areas work together as a design team. The instant feedback and enhanced interactions within the team help to achieve more rapid product development. The design process can also be facilitated by such recent high-tech developments as computer-aided design (CAD), computer-aided engineering (CAE), and computer-aided manufacturing (CAM).

System Capacity   Another decision to be made involves the capacity of the system.[13] This decision will determine the level of product or service output that the system will be able to provide. It is here that the firm will make its major investment decisions. The number of facilities to be built, the size of each facility, their individual capabilities, and the amount and type of equipment to be purchased must all be determined. In order to make high-quality decisions in this area, the decision maker must forecast the market demand for the product or service to be offered and assess the competition so that the organization's market share potential can be estimated. Next, the amount of labor and equipment needed to meet these market share projections must be calculated. Marketing will play a key role here, for accurate projections of market demand and competition will help to establish the size of the system being developed.

Process Selection   The selection of a framework for the transformation process will depend upon how the firm is likely to be categorized. Recall our classification scheme that categorized manufacturing and service organizations along a volume/variety continuum. An organization's self-assessment of the volume, variety, and type of product or service output likely to be generated will help to indicate the type of process to be selected. In a manufacturing setting, answers to these questions will indicate the types of material flow that can be

MANAGING FOR EXCELLENCE

GENERAL MILLS RUNS ITS RESTAURANTS AS IF THEY WERE FACTORIES

Minneapolis-based General Mills has seen its Olive Garden and Red Lobster restaurant chains thrive and grow in a time when other restaurants are struggling to remain afloat. The General Mills approach to success has been to utilize economies of scale and automation to bring down costs. Even a tiny cost savings on a meal will translate into significant annual savings when the number of meals served is factored into the calculations. To this end General Mills views its restaurants as simply the end of a long assembly line. Raw materials enter at the beginning of the line. In the case of Red Lobster, the raw materials consist primarily of assorted seafood items obtained worldwide and processed at a General Mills plant in St. Petersburg, Florida. For the Olive Garden chain, raw materials are even simpler, to a large degree consisting of semolina flour and water. Restaurant computers predict demand on a daily basis, enabling managers to plan each day's production accordingly. Kitchen equipment has been designed to prepare meals to precise specifications. At Red Lobster, for example, a 450-degree grill will cook a swordfish steak for no more than five minutes per side, and a lobster steamer will cook a one-pound lobster for ten minutes—no more and no less. Economies of scale and waste reduction achieved by taking an automated view of assembly and scheduling have allowed General Mills to deliver good value to its customers and at the same time provide excellent returns to its shareholders.

expected through the system. This in turn will determine the process configuration to be selected; that is, will the organization be configured as a continuous flow, a repetitive flow, a job shop, or a project system? In a service setting, the self-assessment of volume, variety, and type of service will determine whether the system process will provide custom or standard services. Once the process configuration has been selected, machinery and equipment compatible with that process can be obtained. Managing for Excellence, which describes the operations of Red Lobster and Olive Garden Restaurants, shows how this concept of assembly line process and equipment selection is just as applicable to service organizations as it is to manufacturing organizations.[14]

Facility Location   The facility location decision involves the selection of a geographic site on which to establish the organization's operations. This decision is extremely important, for once the physical structure has been built, its high cost usually dictates that the location decision will remain in effect for a considerable amount of time. Manufacturing and service organizations emphasize very different factors in making this decision. Consider what would be important to a hospital, a gasoline service station, a fast-food restaurant, an automobile manufacturing plant, a cement processing plant, and a ballpoint pen manufacturing plant. Some factors might be common to all, while other factors might be important for only certain types of systems. Survey data show that manufacturing location decisions are dominated by five factors: (1) favorable labor climate, (2) proximity to markets, (3) quality of life, (4) proximity to suppliers and resources, and (5) proximity to the parent company's facilities.[15] Table 17.1 describes these factors further.

In service organizations, proximity to customers is often the primary location factor to be considered. Since customers must usually interact directly with the service organizations, convenient locations are crucial. Barbershops,

▼ TABLE 17.1　Major Factors in Manufacturing Location Decisions

1. *Favorable labor climate.* Management's assessment of the labor climate would be based on such parameters as union activity, wage rates, available labor skill levels, required labor training, worker attitudes, and worker productivity.
2. *Proximity to markets.* Consideration would be given to both the actual distance to the markets and the modes of transportation available to deliver the products.
3. *Quality of life.* Attention would be paid to the quality and availability of schools, housing, shopping, recreation facilities, and other lifestyle indicators that reflect the quality of life.
4. *Proximity to suppliers and resources.* When companies rely on bulky or heavy raw materials and supplies, this factor is of prime concern. Distance and transportation modes would influence this factor.
5. *Proximity to the parent company's facilities.* This factor is important for companies with multiplant configurations. When parts and materials must be transferred between operating facilities, frequent interactions, communication, and coordination will be necessary. Additionally, the time and cost of material transfers must be minimized. All of this can be facilitated by geographical proximity between the facilities.

dry cleaners, supermarkets, and gasoline filling stations would do very little business if they are were situated in remote, inaccessible areas. Traffic volumes, residential population density, competition, and income levels all play an important part in the location decision for service organizations. The location criteria mentioned here should not be interpreted as an exhaustive list. Notice how the AVX Corporation described in Global Perspective also considered such factors as the availability of a skilled workforce and financial incentives offered by the government when it decided to build a manufacturing plant in Northern Ireland.[16]

Facility Layout　The primary objective of the facility layout decision is to arrange the work areas and equipment so that inputs progress through the transformation process in as orderly a fashion as possible. This will result in a smooth flow of materials or customers through the system. The precise configuration for a given system will depend on where the system fits into the volume/variety continuum. Systems at the flexible-purpose extreme, which must be able to handle a wide variety of product or customer service demands, will use a **process layout.** Conversely, systems at the specific-purpose extreme, in which all products or services are essentially the same, will use a **product layout.** Lying between these extremes are a variety of systems that need layouts combining aspects of each of the extreme cases. These systems would incorporate a **hybrid layout.** Finally, a system that produces extremely large or bulky items may use a **fixed position layout,** in which the item remains stationary while workers and equipment move to the item to provide processing.

Some of these long-term system design decisions present unique managerial challenges to multinational organizations. For example, before selecting and designing a product or service, the sociocultural and economic environments of the global markets in which the organization will operate must be assessed. In addition, it would be unwise to select international locations for operating units of the organization without first considering the political-legal climate, economic conditions, state of technological development, and cultural values

Process layout
Configuration flexible enough to accommodate a wide diversity of products or customers.

Product layout
Configuration set for a specific purpose, with all product or service demands essentially identical.

Hybrid layout
Configuration containing some degree of flexibility, lying between the extremes of process and product layouts.

Fixed position layout
Configuration used for large or bulky items that remain stationary in the manufacturing process.

AVX GOES GLOBAL IN ITS LOCATION

AVX Corporation, headquartered in New York, is a manufacturer of specialized electronic components. In selecting a site for a new plant, AVX considered all of the usual location factors. It examined labor climates and measured proximity to markets for each alternative site, as well as proximity to suppliers and resources and to the New York headquarters. The company also subjectively assessed the quality of life at each possible site.

In the final analysis, the firm decided to locate its new manufacturing plant in Northern Ireland. One of the overriding factors that influenced AVX's decision is not on the standard list. AVX's decision to select this foreign location was based in part on financial incentives provided by the Irish government. This advantage, coupled with the availability of a skilled workforce, had enabled AVX to compete successfully against several strong international players in the industry.

of the workforce in the potential locations. Success will come more easily to multinational organizations that thoroughly research all of these parameters in their long-term system design decisions.

Short-Term Operating and Control Decisions

After the long-term system design decisions have been made and the system is operational, it is time to begin making the short-term operating and control decisions. These decisions are made frequently (daily, weekly, or perhaps monthly), are quite capable of being changed, and in many cases are directly involved with the scheduling of work activities. In today's organizations, managers face new challenges as they schedule, lead, and control labor in the increasingly diverse workforce. Ethnic, racial, and gender differences often lead to different individual values and expectations. Hence, standards of individual behavior, performance, and productivity are sometimes more difficult to set and enforce.

Aggregate Planning   Before initiating any day-to-day or week-to-week detailed scheduling activities in a manufacturing firm, management must first make a series of decisions designed to set the overall level of operations for a planning horizon that generally spans the upcoming year. At this point, management makes rough production and labor scheduling decisions that will set the tone for the overall level of operations during the year. The goal is to ensure that customer demand can be satisfied, the firm's resources won't be overtaxed, and the relevant costs will be held to a minimum. These decisions constitute what is known as **aggregate planning.** This set of planning decisions represents the link between the more general business planning activities and the more specific master plans for short-range operation and control aspects of the firm.

In aggregate planning, management formulates a plan that involves such factors as production scheduling, workforce-level adjusting, inventory scheduling, production subcontracting, and employment scheduling so that enough product or service will be available to satisfy customer demands.[17] By their very nature, aggregate plans are rather rough. They are usually stated in terms of product families rather than individual products. Further, their monthly or quarterly time periods are incapable of directing the day-to-day scheduling of operations. The main purpose of aggregate plans is to provide broad produc-

Aggregate planning
Link between the more general business planning activities and the more specific master planning activities.

▼ This highly automated line for the assembly of washing machines, with its high-tech control room, provides an example of a product layout.

tion scheduling, inventory scheduling, and human resource scheduling guidelines within which more detailed scheduling decisions will eventually be made.

Master Production Scheduling   Although the rough schedule provided by aggregate planning will be quite useful for projecting the overall levels of production and labor requirements over an intermediate planning horizon, it will not contain enough detail and information for scheduling the various production activities. Another schedule is needed that not only contains detailed information about individual product identities but also divides the planning horizon into finer increments of time. Such a schedule, which is known as the master production schedule, will be used to drive all of the ensuing production scheduling activities within the system.

The **master production schedule** is a detailed statement of projected production quantities for each item in each time period.[18] Time periods are typically weekly intervals. The master production schedule is often thought of as an anticipated build schedule for finished products. A major constraint in the development of the master production schedule is that the total number of units scheduled for production must be compatible with the aggregate plan. Since the master production schedule is simply a more detailed breakdown of the aggregate plan, the sum of the parts (the master production schedule units) must equal the whole (the aggregate plan).

Inventory Management   One of the most studied of the short-term decisions deals with the control of inventories. Items in inventory may exist in any of four forms: (1) raw materials, (2) work-in-process, (3) finished goods, and (4) supplies. Raw materials are the basic inputs that have not yet been subjected to any processing transactions. Work-in-process represents semifinished items that are in various stages of completion. Finished goods are items that have had all processing transactions performed and are ready for delivery to the customer. Supplies represent purchased items that facilitate the completion of some production or service activity.[19] Two fundamental decisions must be made with respect to the replenishment of any item maintained in inventory: (1) how many should be ordered, and (2) when should they be ordered? These decisions are referred to as the lot-sizing and lot-timing decisions. The

Master production schedule
Detailed statement of projected production quantities for each item in each time period.

objective of inventory management is to make those decisions in a manner that minimizes the total of inventory-related costs. Many models have been developed to aid in making the lot-sizing and lot-timing decisions under varying conditions. The earliest and perhaps best-known of these models is the classic Economic Order Quantity (EOQ) model. Table 17.2 provides a brief overview of the specifics of this model.

Material Requirements Planning   Excellence in inventory control requires that the lot-sizing and lot-timing decisions be made correctly for all items used to construct a product. EOQ models of the type described above are quite capable of making the proper sizing and timing decisions for finished products. Unfortunately, they do a poor job of controlling the various raw materials, parts, and components that are assembled into those finished products. Material Requirements Planning (MRP) is a simple methodology devised for controlling these lower-level items.

The basic approach of MRP requires that the lot-sizing and timing decisions be made first for the finished product so that sufficient finished product will be available to support the master production schedule. These timing and sizing decisions for the finished product will determine the needs for the various components that combine directly into the finished product (i.e., those components one level of production removed from the finished product). The timing and sizing decisions can then be made for these components so that

▼ **TABLE 17.2**   Economic Order Quantity Model

• Relevant costs: Annual ordering cost and annual carrying cost
• Symbols used: D = annual demand or usage
S = cost per order (setup cost or purchase order cost)
H = carrying cost per unit per year
Q = order size (which is to be determined)

MODEL STRUCTURE

The total annual carrying cost is the average inventory level multiplied by the cost to carry a unit in inventory for a year. In symbolic form, the average inventory level is Q/2; therefore,

Total annual carrying cost $= (Q/2)(H)$

The total annual ordering cost is equal to the number of orders placed during the year times the cost per order. In symbolic form, the number of orders placed per year is D/Q; therefore,

Total annual ordering cost $= (D/Q)(S)$

Combining these two costs yields a total cost of

$TC = (Q/2)(H) + (D/Q)(S)$

DETERMINATION OF EOQ

Take the derivative of TC with respect to Q and set equal to zero, then solve for Q:

$H/2 - DS/Q^2 = 0$

An algebraic rearrangement of terms yields the following:

$Q^2 = 2DS/H$

and

$Q = \sqrt{2DS/H}$ (Also called the EOQ)

This is called the EOQ since this is the most economic order quantity.

sufficient amounts will be available to support the planned production of the finished product. Once this has been done, attention is focused on the next lower level of manufacture. By continually linking the successive levels of manufacture, lot-sizing and timing decisions for all raw materials, parts, and components used in making the finished product will be coordinated to ensure that the master production schedule will be met.[20] Since most multistage manufacturing systems have products that consist of hundreds or even thousands of individual raw materials, parts, components, subassemblies, and assemblies spanning dozens of levels of manufacture, a computerized system is necessary to perform the massive data handling and manipulation chores of the MRP process.

Just-in-Time Inventory Management   A recent phenomenon in the area of inventory control is a philosophy known as just-in-time (JIT) inventory management. This concept initially received considerable attention and refinement within the Japanese industrial community and is now quickly spreading worldwide. Despite its concern with inventory, JIT is more than just a technique for dealing with inventory. **Just-in-time inventory management** is an overall manufacturing philosophy that advocates eliminating waste, solving problems, and striving for continual improvement in operations.[21]

JIT attempts to reduce inventory because inventory can be costly and can hide problems. For example, problems like machine breakdowns, high levels of defective output, and worker absenteeism may not cause noticeable disruptions to flow when high levels of inventory exist to "ride over" those problems. Inventory reductions can be achieved quite simply. Regardless of whether we are dealing with a manufacturing or service organization, whenever any item is to be replenished, the replenishment lot size can be made smaller. Raw materials and supplies can be ordered in smaller batches from suppliers. Parts and components can be manufactured in smaller batches, just as finished goods can be assembled in smaller batches. Because the ultimate goal is the almost total elimination of inventory, JIT systems are often referred to as zero inventory systems, or stockless production systems. To economically justify reductions in lot size, JIT users must attempt to reduce the setup cost or ordering cost as much as possible. Return for the moment to the EOQ formula in Table 17.2, where you can see that a reduction in the setup or ordering cost will lead to a smaller lot size. Setup cost can be reduced by studying and redesigning setup procedures to make them as short as possible, training workers in the proper setup procedure, redesigning tools and equipment, and perhaps even replacing equipment. All of these efforts are aimed at achieving quicker setups.[22]

Since there is little inventory in a JIT system, there can be little tolerance for problems because these will inevitably disrupt flow and perhaps stop system output. This is why JIT is regarded as a broader philosophy of problem solving, waste elimination, and continual improvement. In addition to the zero inventory ideal, JIT also seeks to attain zero defects (perfect quality), zero breakdowns, and, in general, zero problems. In such systems, workers play an important role in attaining these goals. In addition to being responsible for their own manufacturing efforts, workers must also be responsible for such things as quality control, equipment maintenance, housekeeping duties in the work area, and general problem solving in the workplace.[23]

Recall the Managerial Incident at the beginning of Chapter 2 that told the story of Harley-Davidson. It was the successful use of the JIT philosophy by Japanese manufacturers that put Harley at such a severe competitive disadvantage. Harley's adoption of a JIT philosophy played a large role in the company's remarkable turnaround.

Just-in-time (JIT) inventory management
Philosophy that advocates eliminating waste, solving problems, and striving for continual improvement in operations.

Today most organizations face challenges and opportunities brought about by the continually shrinking world and our global marketplace. Multinational organizations with operating units in different countries may have to set different productivity goals to accommodate differences in work attitudes across national boundaries. In addition, the level of technological development may differ among nations, resulting in significant differences in attainable productivity rates. Political factors may also impact upon the way the organization can operate in foreign countries.

Even organizations that view themselves as purely domestic are not untouched by aspects of our global marketplace. Raw material inputs, purchased parts, and supplies needed in their transformation processes often originate in foreign countries. In these instances purchasing agreements must cut across national boundaries. Consequently, these "domestic" companies must be sensitive to the sociocultural, political-legal, technological, and economic environments of the supplying countries.

Thus far, we have seen that operations managers face a wide variety of decisions. To improve the quality of their operations, managers must make these decisions in a way that supports the goals of the organization. We have already noted that organizations can have a variety of goals. When this is the case, managers can move toward achieving excellence in operations by focusing on productivity and quality.

THE ROLE OF PRODUCTIVITY AND QUALITY IN OPERATIONS

Organizational goals can be many and varied. In firms operating on a for-profit basis, bottom-line profit will always have a high priority, while not-for-profit organizations will be more inclined to view service and customer satisfaction as the prime goals. But any of these firms might also strive to achieve other goals such as market share, improved satisfaction and welfare of its workforce, heightened social and environmental responsibility, and so forth. Operations managers rarely find it easy to relate their decisions directly to these system goals. Fortunately, there are two measures of operations efficiency and effectiveness that indirectly relate to these system goals. In the next section, we will see that productivity is a measure of operations efficiency and quality is a measure of operations effectiveness. Every decision that an operations manager makes—whether a long-term design decision or a short-term operating and control decision—has an impact on productivity and quality. Let's turn our attention to the fundamentals of productivity and examine the ways in which productivity can be improved.

FUNDAMENTALS OF PRODUCTIVITY

Productivity
Measure of the efficiency with which a firm transforms inputs into outputs.

In Chapter 16 we saw a diagram that showed how all operating systems engage in the transformation of inputs into outputs. **Productivity** is a measure of the efficiency with which a firm performs that transformation process. In the broadest sense, productivity can be defined as the ratio of system outputs to system inputs, or

$$\text{Productivity} = \frac{\text{system outputs}}{\text{system inputs}}$$

Measuring productivity is often easier said than done, for outputs can be quite varied and inputs quite diverse. Table 17.3 shows some of the various inputs and outputs for a few manufacturing and nonmanufacturing examples.

▼ **TABLE 17.3**   Examples of Inputs and Outputs for Productivity Measurement

OUTPUT	INPUT
Number of refrigerators manufactured	Direct labor hours, raw materials, machinery, supervisory hours, capital
Number of patients treated	Doctor hours, nurse hours, lab technician hours, hospital beds, medical equipment, medicine and drugs, surgical supplies
Number of income tax returns prepared	Staff accounting hours, desktop computers, printers, calculators, typewriters, supplies

Interest in productivity has increased during recent years in the United States, in large part because of the alarming decline in international competitiveness suffered by U.S. companies. Between 1960 and 1990, the United States had one of the lowest annual productivity increases of any of the industrialized nations. Our average annual increase of 3 percent was less than half of Japan's.[24] A lower level of productivity can result because less output is being produced from a given level of input or because more input is needed to achieve a given level of output. In either case, the cost per unit incurred to produce the goods or services will be higher, as will the purchase cost for the customers. This leads to a decline in sales volume, which results in decreased revenues. With less operating revenue, business and industry are likely to lower employment levels, which leads to idle capacity. This is likely to reduce productivity even further, resulting in a snowball effect. Many of these symptoms were creeping into Ford's system, as described in the opening Managerial Incident. Fortunately, most U.S. industries have recognized this phenomenon. Many firms are attempting to break this vicious cycle by instituting productivity improvement programs. Ford has done this quite successfully, as you will see in the resolution to the Managerial Incident.

Improving Productivity

Any increase in the numerator or decrease in the denominator of the productivity equation will result in a productivity increase. Simply stated, to increase productivity, all this is needed is an increase in output, a decrease in input, or a combination of both. Such changes can be achieved in several ways. We can categorize the productivity-enhancing tactics as being related to technology, people, or design.[25]

Productivity Improvement through Technology   Productivity can be improved through the use of new technology. If, for example, old office equipment and computers are replaced with newer, faster versions, the number of tax returns prepared per labor hour might be expected to increase. Or, in the case of manufacturing, if faster equipment replaces slower equipment, more units might be produced per labor hour.

Another technological approach to improving productivity is to substitute capital for labor. For example, certain operations that are performed manually may be done by a machine or robot. If the machine has a lower hourly operating cost, higher output rate, and greater precision than a human operator, then the substitution should be considered as a possible means to improve productivity. Ford relied heavily on the use of technology to improve productivity, as will be seen in the resolution to the Managerial Incident.

Productivity Improvement through a Diverse Workforce   One of the most important inputs to the productivity equation is the human resource element. We

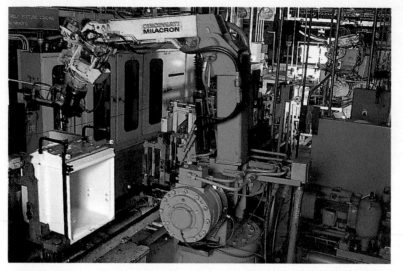

▼ Industrial robots, such as this one engaged in the manufacture of washing machines, can increase productivity with their higher output rates and greater precision than human operators.

have seen repeatedly throughout this book that the workforce is becoming increasingly more racially, ethnically, and gender diverse. These groups of individuals all have their own unique sets of values, expectations, motivations, and skills. Their interaction often has a synergistic effect on the work team, enabling the team to achieve results that exceed previous norms.

Effective management of people can often result in significant increases in output without an appreciable increase in the labor cost. This feat can be accomplished through the use of employee compensation programs and employee teams. Many companies have found that compensation can encourage higher productivity. For example, the practice of paying employees bonuses based upon productivity and company profitability has become more popular in recent years.

The most common form of employee team in current practice is the quality circle, which is described more fully later in this chapter. Various companies have given their employee teams different names, but they all have the general objective of increasing employee satisfaction and productivity by providing them with more autonomy and a greater degree of involvement in the decision-making and problem-solving process. As the resolution to the opening Managerial Incident explains, Ford has made use of this "people involvement" concept to improve both productivity and quality.

Productivity Improvement through Design   Several system design issues were described earlier in this chapter. These design decisions can have a direct bearing on productivity. If a product is designed in a way that makes it easier to produce, less time will be spent producing the item, fewer defective units will be produced, and less scrap will result. These improvements will ultimately lead to an increase in productivity.

Process design can also have a significant impact on productivity. If the process has been designed poorly, material flow may be restricted by bottlenecks. Inappropriate placement of work areas and tools can lead to inefficient material flows through the system. These inefficiencies will ultimately lead to greater production time per unit and reduced productivity. The resolution to the Managerial Incident provides a few rather dramatic examples of how simplified designs helped to improve Ford's productivity.

As we discussed in Chapter 8, job design is the third design area that can impact on productivity. If a worker's assigned job has been so narrowly defined that there is no job fulfillment, boredom and disinterest are likely to result. In such a situation, the quality of work can be expected to suffer. The resulting defects, scrap, and rework will diminish the level of productivity. To avoid these problems associated with excessive job specialization, many companies adopt philosophies of job enrichment, job enlargement, and job rotation.

As we continue through this chapter, we will encounter more and more evidence suggesting that productivity and quality are intertwined. Improvements in quality are likely to result in improved productivity. Later in this chapter, we will see more specifically how this occurs when we examine the five-step chain reaction of the late W. Edwards Deming, one of the world's foremost authorities on quality. But first, let's examine the fundamentals of quality.

FUNDAMENTALS OF QUALITY

People sometimes have an inaccurate perception about quality. Too often they assume that quality implies a high degree of luxury or expense. Grandeur, luxuriousness, shininess, and expense are not the prime determinants of quality, however. A more appropriate definition of quality can be approached from two different perspectives. From a consumer perspective, quality can be defined as the degree to which the product or service meets the expectations of the customer. From a producer perspective, quality can be defined as the degree to which the product or service conforms to design specifications. The more effective the organization is in meeting customer expectations and design specifications, the higher the implied quality level of its output.[26]

The Mercedes Benz and Honda Accord are two automobiles with very different prices and quite different features and accessories. However, this does not automatically mean that the more expensive and more elaborate Mercedes has a higher level of quality than the Honda. As the consumer perspective indicates, the test of quality is based upon user expectations. Each automobile has as its function the conveyance of passengers in a particular style, and those styles are different by design.

A similar observation could be made for service organizations. Ritz-Carlton Hotels and Holiday Inns both provide overnight lodging for guests. Ritz-Carlton Hotels feature larger, more elaborately decorated rooms with more amenities than Holiday Inns provide. But one fact remains—they both provide overnight sleeping and bathing accommodations for travelers. Ultimately, it is the individual guest who must determine the level of quality associated with these accommodations.

Once an organization selects the product or service that it will provide, design decisions are made that ultimately shape the product or service design characteristics. If the completed product or service output meets those design characteristics, the output would be viewed as high quality from the production perspective. If this output fails to meet customer expectations, however, then the initial design was probably inadequate, for the customer is not likely to purchase it regardless of the quality level that production perceives. Businesses are increasingly adopting this consumer perspective on quality. For example, if an Eckerd Photolab fails to have a customer's film developed by its promise date, there is no charge to the customer. Phar-Mor Drugs will pay customers $10 if its prescription price is not the lowest in town. Southtrust Bank of Orlando will pay customers $1 if they have to wait more than one minute for service, $5 if they are not treated courteously, and $10 if a mistake is made on a customer's bank statement. This list could go on and on. Think about the service encounters that you have had. Do you know any companies that make similar provisions in their attempts to deliver quality service?

Although the terms quality control, quality assurance, and total quality management (or total quality control) are often used interchangeably, these concepts are not identical. **Quality control** (QC) has the narrowest focus; it refers to the actual measurement and assessment of output to determine whether the specifications are being met. The responsibility for taking corrective actions when standards are not being met is also in the domain of quality control. Statistical procedures are useful in quality control. **Quality assurance** (QA) concerns itself with any activity that impacts upon the maintenance of quality at the desired level. It refers to the entire system of policies, procedures, and guidelines that the organization has established to achieve and maintain quality. Quality assurance extends from the design of products and processes through to the quality assessment of the system outputs. **Total quality management** (TQM) has an even broader focus than quality assurance,

Quality control
Focuses on the actual measurement of output to see if specifications have been met.

Quality assurance
Focuses on any activity that impacts upon the maintenance of quality at the desired level.

Total quality management
Focuses on managing the entire organization in a manner that allows it to excel in the delivery of a product or service that meets customer needs.

for its goal is to manage the entire organization in a manner that allows it to excel in the delivery of a product or service that meets customer needs. Before we look at TQM in more detail, it will be helpful to examine the factors for assessing quality.

Factors for Assessing Quality

A customer might evaluate many aspects of a product or service to determine whether it meets expectations. These aspects differ slightly for products and services.

Product Factors   When evaluating the quality of a product, a customer will probably first notice aesthetic characteristics, which are usually perceived by sensory reactions. Here the customer will observe how the product looks, sounds, feels, smells, or tastes. A product's features, are also likely to be judged early. If you were about to purchase an automobile, for example, you might look for such features as a stereo system, air bags, and power seats. Performance is another aspect that helps determine whether the product meets the customer's needs and expectations. If you do a lot of highway driving, acceleration and passing power are probably important to you, so you would check these performance characteristics before making your purchase decision. Another important aspect of quality is reliability, which refers to the likelihood that the product will continue to perform satisfactorily through its guarantee period. You might ascertain this through product warranty information or by referring to a consumer magazine such as *Consumer Reports.*

The serviceability aspect refers to the difficulty, time, and expense of getting repairs. In the case of your automobile purchase, you might assess this by considering the location and business hours of the dealer's automobile service center. The durability aspect refers to the length of time the product is likely to last. Both the manufacturer and independent consumer agencies might be a source of data here. Conformance reflects the degree to which the product meets the specifications set by the designers. For example, you will undoubtedly check to be sure that the automobile possesses all the accessories that the advertising suggests it will have. A final aspect is perceived quality, which has been described as an overall feeling of confidence based upon observations of the potential purchase, the reputation of the company, and any past experiences with purchases of this type.[27]

Service Factors   The product quality factors can be relevant to a service encounter if some physical commodity is delivered to the customer. For example, when you dine at a restaurant, the meal can be judged according to most of those characteristics. Unfortunately, service quality is sometimes more difficult to assess with quantitative measures. Suppose you visit a dentist for emergency treatment of a broken tooth. In this case you would use other attributes to measure your satisfaction with service quality. Responsiveness reflects the willingness and speed with which the service personnel (i.e., dentist, nurse, and receptionist) attend to you. Reliability is a measure of the dependability and accuracy of the service performed. Assurance refers to a feeling of trust and confidence you have in the service personnel. Empathy reflects the degree of attention and caring that the service personnel provide to you. Finally, tangibles are an assessment of such factors as the appearance of the service personnel, cleanliness of the equipment and physical system, and comfort of the surroundings.[28]

Cost of Quality

Any costs that a company incurs because it has produced less than perfect quality output, or costs that it incurs to prevent less than perfect quality output, are referred to as the cost of quality. The cost of quality can be organized into the following four major categories:[29]

1. *Prevention costs.* Prior to the production of the product or the delivery of the service, several activities are performed in an attempt to prevent defective output from occurring. These activities include designing products, processes, and jobs for quality; reviewing designs; educating and training workers in quality concepts; and working with suppliers. The costs of these activities are the prevention costs.

2. *Appraisal costs.* Appraisal costs are incurred to assess the quality of the product that has been manufactured or the service that has been provided. They include the costs of testing equipment and instruments, the costs of maintaining that equipment, and the labor costs associated with performing the inspections.

3. *Internal failure costs.* Defective output that is detected before it leaves the system will either be scrapped (discarded) or reworked (repaired). If it is scrapped, the company incurs the cost of all materials and labor that went into the production of that output. If it is reworked, a cost is incurred for the material and labor that went into the defective portion that was replaced or repaired. In addition, more material and labor costs are incurred for the rework activities. These costs all contribute to the internal failure costs.

4. *External failure costs.* Defective output that is not detected before being delivered to the customer incurs external failure costs. This category consists of the costs associated with customer complaints, returns, warranty claims, product recalls, or product liability suits.

The current popular view holds that prevention costs do not have to be increased substantially to reduce the number of defective units. Furthermore, this view suggests that as prevention costs increase, appraisal costs will decrease since less testing and inspection will be necessary due to inherently lower levels of defective units. Meanwhile, failure costs will also decrease with the reduced number of defective units.[30] Figure 17.3 displays these cost relationships and suggests that the most cost effective way of doing business is close to, if not at, the zero defect level.

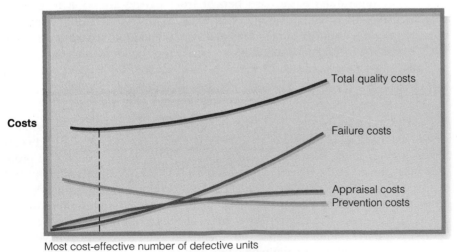

▼ FIGURE 17.3
Quality Costs

SERVICE CHALLENGE

SUPERVAN—A SHUTTLE SERVICE'S BUMPY ROAD

San Antonio, Texas, was introduced to a world-class concept in transportation in 1987 when SuperVan, Inc., began offering an alternative to both buses and taxis. Donald S. Rullo started the company in 1975 to provide shared-ride, door-to-door shuttle service to personnel at nearby Lackland Air Force Base. By 1983 revenue had grown to $160,000, but the company had no opportunity for expansion in this area for by then it controlled 100 percent of the air base market. Rullo then began planning to offer van services to the entire city of San Antonio, which was becoming an international tourist destination. He felt that demand for transportation services would grow as the city became a popular convention site and tourist center. Rullo was committed not only to helping meet the demand, but also to providing top-quality service. Since a visitor's first contact with a community is often through a transportation service, Rullo set strict quality controls that project a highly favorable image of the city. SuperVan vehicles are shiny outside and immaculate inside. Training of the uniformed drivers extends beyond operating a vehicle to include such areas as appearance and personal hygiene. The company looks for "people who like people" when it screens job applicants. Rullo has been able to offer this quality service at fares that are half those charged by local taxis.

SuperVan's competition includes taxis and vehicles operated by the local transit authority. Essentially, SuperVan introduced the concept of privatization and total quality management to compete with established public transportation services. While privatization offers many opportunities to entrepreneurs, it also comes with risks and obstacles. Since SuperVan posed a threat to established modes of public transportation, many struggles ensued and many disputes had to be resolved. But SuperVan's persistence is paying off. Between 1989 and 1992, the company's revenue increased fivefold to $3.2 million. SuperVan has dramatically demonstrated the contribution that quality service can bring to a city striving for world-class status.

Although these concepts of quality-related costs may seem to apply only to the physical products of manufacturing systems, Service Challenge shows that service organizations can also benefit from paying attention to quality-related costs.[31] Here we see how an emphasis on quality enabled a company offering passenger shuttle service to achieve a dramatic increase in revenue while becoming formidable competition to taxis and the local transit authority.

TOTAL QUALITY MANAGEMENT AS A TOOL FOR GLOBAL COMPETITIVENESS

Emphasis on quality is a key to achieving excellence in operations in today's global economy. This emphasis on quality is crucial for two reasons: (1) customers are becoming increasingly conscious of quality in their choice of products and services, and (2) increased quality leads to increased productivity and its associated benefits. It is no secret that in recent years U.S. manufacturers have struggled with the loss of market share to foreign competitors in the global marketplace. These losses have been attributed to the notion (in some cases real and in some cases perceived) that the foreign competitors have been able to supply products of higher quality and at a lower price. People who are trying to get the most from their disposable income have understandably been attracted to these products. These shifts to foreign manufacturers are evidence that consumers do consider the product factors discussed above prior to making purchase decisions. Any manufacturer who hopes to reverse this declining market share can begin to do so by focusing on the quality aspects of the product. A program of total quality management is one of the most effective ways to enhance an organization's competitive position. Ford's commitment to quality ("Quality Is Job One") helped the company reverse the life-threatening trends described in the opening Managerial Incident. A total quality management program involves several areas of concentration, commitment, and improvement.

Customer-Driven Standards

Since one definition of quality centers on meeting customer expectations, the **external customer** should play a central role in establishing product or service standards. Marketing will be instrumental in assessing the wants and needs of the external customers. These wants and needs can then be conveyed to design engineers who will make the product and service design decisions. Process design decisions will then follow. Ultimately, the products or services will be easier to sell if customers recognize that the products and services have been designed to satisfy their needs.

In some cases customers may be **internal customers** as opposed to external end users. For example, the customer might be the next worker or next department in the production process. Internal customers also have quality requirements that must be considered in the product or service design stage. In essence, everybody in the organization is a supplier to some customer, and these supplier-customer links represent a major area of concern in total quality management.

External customer
Consumer who purchases the product or service output of the organization.

Internal customer
In the sequence of stages that extend from purchasing raw materials through to final delivery of the product or service, an internal customer is any individual or department that uses the output of a prior stage.

Management and Labor Commitment

Recall from Chapter 11 the concepts of organizational culture and organizational change. If total quality management is to pervade all levels of an organization successfully, management must develop an organizational culture in which all workers are committed to the philosophy. This requires a strong commitment from top management, where the values to be shared by the organization originate. If all parts of the organization are to coordinate toward a common goal, then this goal must be embraced at the top. Top management must not only communicate this goal, but must also demonstrate a commitment to the goal through its actions, policies, and decisions. Management must back up slogans and catchy phrases with a willingness to institute changes, a receptiveness to employee suggestions, and recognition and reward for improvements. Ford demonstrated total commitment in this area. Management asked assembly line workers for advice before the design of the Taurus model was complete, and many of the suggestions were implemented. For example, all the bolt heads were made the same size so workers would not have to reach repeatedly for a new tool. Also, doors were designed with fewer pieces in order to improve assembly. Other such improvements are described in the Managerial Incident Resolution at the end of this chapter.

Organization and Coordination of Efforts

We have already seen that total quality management will result in a wide variety of diverse personnel interactions. Marketing serves as an intermediary between external customers and design engineers who in turn interact with production personnel. The internal supplier-customer linkages lead to many interactions among production personnel. Purchasing must interact with external suppliers. If total quality management is to be successful, communication linkages must be established between all of these internal and external entities to achieve proper coordination. As we saw in Chapter 9, such coordination efforts lead to a teamwork philosophy among all participants in the organization. Ford brought suppliers into the design process for the Taurus and started a program of supplier selection and evaluation. To improve the quality of materials from outside suppliers, Ford initiated a supplier certification process in its Total Quality Excellence (TQE) program.[32]

Employee Participation

A central theme of the total quality management approach is that all employees should be brought into the decision-making and problem-solving process. After all, those who are doing the work are closest to the action and will probably have valuable opinions about methods for quality improvement. By providing the workers with an opportunity to express those opinions, worker morale and motivation are enhanced. Workers develop more of a sense of responsibility and connection to their jobs. Worker participation and teamwork are further enhanced by the use of teams. The Motorola Corporation has been quite successful with teams at its microprocessor assembly plant in Austin, Texas. Management decided to build cross-functional teams (composed of representatives from management, first-line supervisors, line operators, internal vendors, and internal customers) in an effort to increase motivation, provide more creative problem solving, and stimulate ideas. Two of the more popular types of groups are quality circles and special-purpose teams.

Quality circle
Work team that meets regularly to identify, analyze, and solve problems related to its work area.

Quality Circles   A **quality circle** is a small group of supervisors and employees from the same work area.[33] Most quality circles have between 6 and 12 members, and membership is voluntary. Quality circles meet on a regular basis (usually weekly) to identify, analyze, and solve production and quality problems related to the work done in their part of the company. Many benefits accrue from quality circles. When workers are allowed to help shape their work, they usually take more pride and interest in it. Furthermore, quality circles have the potential to uncover and solve many problems or suggest ways to achieve improvements in operations. Even though some of these improvements may be very minor, collectively they can result in substantial cost savings, quality improvements, and productivity increases in the organization.

Special purpose team
Temporary team formed to solve a special or nonrecurring problem.

Special-Purpose Teams   On occasion **special-purpose teams** may have to be formed to solve a special or nonrecurring problem.[34] Unlike quality circles, special-purpose teams are likely to draw their members from many depart-

▼ Quality circles do not occur only in manufacturing. Here we see quality circle activities being conducted in a legal firm.

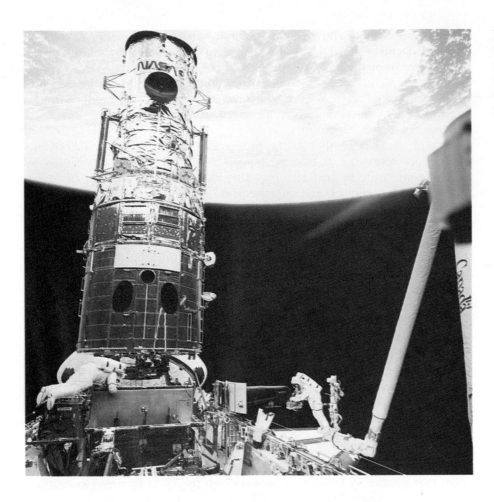

▼ The $750 million cost of the 1993 Space Shuttle *Endeavour* mission to repair the Hubble Space Telescope might have been avoided if a simple test had been performed prior to placing the telescope into orbit.

ments or work areas and bring together people from different functional specialties. For example, if some characteristic of a product no longer conforms to customer needs, marketing personnel will need to be on the team to explain the wants and needs of the customers. Design engineers would be needed to help translate those needs into new product design specifications. Production personnel would also be needed to determine if and how the redesigned product could be manufactured. Special-purpose teams also differ from quality circles in longevity. Quality circles are standing teams that continue in existence over time. Special-purpose teams are ad hoc groups that disband after the problem has been resolved.

PROMINENT QUALITY MANAGEMENT PHILOSOPHERS

Many of today's business organizations are placing more and more emphasis on quality because they are aware of how much it has helped their competition. It is safe to say that, in general, U.S. business organizations were a step behind many of their foreign competitors. Those competitors were able to get a head start in quality by taking the advice of some of the noted quality philosophers and consultants long before U.S. organizations did.

Perhaps the most prominent quality philosopher was W. Edwards Deming, an American who was considered the father of quality control in Japan. Deming emphasized the importance of improving quality through his five-step chain reaction: (1) costs decrease because of less rework, fewer mistakes, fewer delays, and better use of time and materials, (2) productivity improves, (3) market share increases with better quality and prices, (4) the company increases profitability and stays in business, and (5) the number of jobs increases.[35] Deming devised a 14-point plan to summarize his philosophy on quality improvement. Table 17.4 lists Deming's 14 points.

An example of the Deming chain reaction at work appears in Entrepreneurial Approach.[36] Here we see how a quality emphasis led to reduced costs, improved quality and productivity, increased markets, and eventually increased employment at S. B. Electronics.

Joseph Juran is another of the pioneers in quality management. Juran's experiences revealed that over 80 percent of quality defects are caused by factors controllable by management. This led Juran to develop a trilogy of quality planning, control, and improvement.[37] Quality planning involves linking product and service design with process design to achieve the quality characteristics desired. Quality control involves comparing products or services to standards and then correcting undesirable deviations. (This part of the trilogy relates directly to what we learned about control in Chapter 16). The final part of the trilogy involves getting into the habit of making significant improvements every year. An area with chronic quality problems is selected and analyzed, and an alternative is selected and implemented.

Other notable names in the area of quality are Armand Feigenbaum, Kaoru Ishikawa, and Phillip Crosby. Feigenbaum is credited with introducing the concept of total quality control and developing the quality cost categories described earlier in this chapter.[38] Ishikawa is credited with introducing quality-control circles, and he also developed the fishbone diagram (or cause and effect diagram), which helps to identify the causes of quality problems.[39] Crosby introduced the philosophy that "quality is free."[40] In his opinion, the most cost-effective level of defects is zero defects. Crosby contends that with no defects, rework costs are saved, scrap is eliminated, labor and machine time costs are reduced, and product failure costs are eliminated. Crosby believes that these cost reductions far outweigh the costs incurred in creating

▼ **TABLE 17.4**   Deming's 14 Points

1. Create constancy of purpose for improvement of product and service, and communicate this aim to all employees.
2. Learn and adopt the new philosophy throughout all levels within the organization.
3. Understand that inspection only measures problems but does not correct them; quality comes from improving processes.
4. Reduce the number of suppliers, and do not award business on the basis of price tag alone.
5. Constantly improve processes, products, and services while reducing waste.
6. Institute modern aids to training on the job.
7. Improve supervision.
8. Drive out fear of expressing ideas and reporting problems.
9. Break down barriers between departments and get people working toward the goals of the organization as a team.
10. Eliminate slogans, exhortations, and targets for the work force.
11. Eliminate numerical quotas for production; concentrate on quality, not quantity.
12. Remove barriers that rob people of pride of workmanship.
13. Institute a program of education and self-improvement for everyone.
14. Put everyone in the organization to work to accomplish the transformation.

S. B. ELECTRONICS—FROM EXECUTIVE TO ENTREPRENEUR

For 10 years Perry W. Browning was general manager of a Sprague Electric plant in Barre, Vermont. The plant manufactured three lines of film capacitors and had a workforce as high as 700. In 1985 Sprague decided to shut the plant down. It told Browning to transfer one line to a sister plant in Florida, sell the other two, and look for a buyer for the building. After that he would be transferred to another facility.

Browning completed his assignment with one twist—he sold the last of the three lines to himself in a leveraged buyout. The line was a 25-year-old design, and the market for it was shrinking, particularly in the television industry. But Browning wanted the challenge of being an entrepreneur, hoped to save a few jobs in the Barre area, and had ideas on how to make the venture work. "I knew I could run an operation that was more cost-effective," he says. "I knew I could reduce the overhead, from rent to janitorial supplies. I knew I could watch all of the cost items, down to the paper clips. And I knew that the team that I could put together could provide our customers with outstanding delivery performance, something many of our competitors were not doing."

In January 1986, the new company, S. B. Electronics, opened its doors and within a few weeks was in full production with 19 employees, including Browning, all of whom had been with Sprague. The new team was well trained and highly motivated, and everyone took a pay reduction so the company could make a go of it. Employees were asked to treat the company's equipment and tools as if they had bought them with their own funds.

Despite the shrinking market, SBE maintained a sales level of about $1.5 million for three years by emphasizing product reliability and outstanding customer service. Despite its old equipment, the company adopted a zero-defects policy and earned a reputation as a high-quality supplier. Efficiencies generated cost savings that could be passed on to customers. Employees have shared in the company's success through improved pay, profit sharing, and a retirement plan. In the past three years, SBE has doubled sales and now has 51 employees.

an environment that promotes the achievement of high quality. Crosby's philosophy is very much like the old adage, "An ounce of prevention is worth a pound of cure."

NASA's experience with the ill-fated Hubble Space Telescope illustrates this point. In April 1990, this $1.5 billion orbiting laboratory was launched for the purpose of viewing outer space. Not long after the launch, astronomers discovered that the telescope's view of the stars was somewhat blurred due to the incorrect grinding and polishing of its primary mirror. A relatively simple test costing a few hundred thousand dollars could have detected this flaw. As it turned out, repairs didn't come this easily or cheaply to NASA. To correct this defect and make a variety of other repairs, the space shuttle *Endeavour* embarked upon an 11-day mission in early December 1993. The repairs required five separate space walks by astronauts spaced over five days. The mission cost $750 million—$250 million for replacement parts and $500 million for the shuttle flight.[41]

NASA continues to provide one of the most visible examples of increasing diversity in the workforce. Astronaut crews on shuttle missions have become more diverse in race, nationality, and gender over the years. Kathy Thornton was one of the four astronauts who spent more than 35 space-walking hours repairing the ailing Hubble Telescope.[42]

In this chapter we have seen that operations management has a strong decision-making orientation in both manufacturing and service organizations. We have also learned that the concepts of productivity and quality are extremely important for assessing the efficiency and effectiveness of operations decisions. Let's conclude the chapter by considering the implications of these concepts for tomorrow's manager.

MANAGERIAL IMPLICATIONS

Excellence in operations can only be achieved if management strives to achieve perfection in all of the decision-making areas related to operations. Particular attention should be paid to the long-term system design decisions. Because of the difficulty in reversing decisions in this area, management may get only one chance at them. If a poor decision is made, operations may have to suffer the negative consequences for quite some time. Once the design decisions are behind them, managers must shift their attention to the short-term operating and control decisions. These decisions will continue to recur throughout the life of the organization, so managers should strive for continual improvement in this decision-making focus. In short, tomorrow's manager must:

- Be prepared to make the tough decisions that commit to a long-term design for the operating system.
- Strive for perfection in making the recurring short-term operating and control decisions.
- Focus on achieving continuous improvement as these operating and control decisions are made repeatedly throughout the life of the organization.
- Be aware of the importance of productivity to organizational success, and understand the ways in which productivity can be improved.
- Recognize the linkages between productivity and quality.
- Focus on improving the quality of the product or service provided.

The quality-productivity linkage is best illustrated by the Deming five-step chain reaction, which states that improved quality leads to lower labor and material costs, which lead to an improvement in productivity, which results in higher-quality and lower-cost items (and an associated increase in market share), which lead to increased profitability and an increase in the number of jobs. Emphasis on quality will enable tomorrow's manager to reap the benefits of this quality-productivity chain reaction.

MANAGERIAL INCIDENT RESOLUTION

FORD MOTOR COMPANY: REVERSING THE DECLINE

In recent years, the Ford Motor Company has achieved stunning improvements in productivity and quality, and it is now regarded as the most effective U.S. automaker. Its cars are acknowledged to be as good as, or better than, those of its European and Japanese competitors. Ford emerged from the 1980s with the greatest productivity increase among the U.S. Big Three automakers. General Motors experienced a 5 percent gain, Chrysler showed a 17 percent increase, and Ford achieved a whopping 31 percent improvement. By 1992 Ford was able to produce as many vehicles as it did in the 1970s with half the number of workers.

Ford's dramatic productivity improvements were accomplished by focusing on the workforce, technology, and product design. Ford promoted increased participation by its workforce. Front-line workers were given more control over how they did their jobs. In addition, they were made directly responsible for monitoring the quality of their work and correcting defects. Finally, they were encouraged to contribute ideas and make suggestions for improving job methodologies.

Ford also made a concerted effort to use state-of-the-art technologies. For example, many manual tasks are now performed by robots. Such technology provides the benefit of more consistent output, since robots do not suffer from fatigue, nor do they need periodic breaks. Furthermore, robots are advantageous for tasks that may be too dangerous or strenuous for humans.

A new focus on product design also contributed to the productivity improvements. Ford adopted a team concept in developing and designing new models. Team members come from a variety of departments, including accounting, engineering, marketing, personnel, and production. One of the things Ford learned was that simpler is better. For example, an instrument console for the Escort was redesigned with 6 parts instead of the 22 parts in an earlier model. The bumper on the Taurus has only 10 parts compared with more than 100 bumper parts on GM's competing Pontiac Grand Prix. Improvements such as these have enabled Ford to build its cars with one-third fewer labor hours than GM, giving Ford a cost advantage of almost $800 per vehicle.[43] ▼

SUMMARY

- Manufacturing organizations produce a physical product that can be stored in inventory and transported to different locations. Productivity and quality of this physical output are usually easy to measure. Service organizations differ in that their capacity is time perishable, customers are typically active participants in the service process, and their locations must be close to the customers.

- Operating systems can lie anywhere along a volume/variety continuum that extends from high volume and low variety on one extreme to low volume and high variety on the other extreme. Manufacturing organizations can be classified as repetitive manufacturing systems or continuous flow systems at the high volume/low variety extreme and job shop systems or project systems at the low volume/high variety extreme. Service organizations can be classified as standard service systems at the high volume/low variety extreme and custom service systems at the low volume/high variety extreme.

- Most operations management decisions can be classified as either long-term system design decisions or short-term operating and control decisions. Important long-term system design decisions include choice of a product or service, product or service design, system capacity, process selection, facility location, and facility layout. Important short-term operating and control decisions include aggregate planning, master production scheduling, inventory management, material requirements planning, and just-in-time inventory management.

- Productivity is a measure of the efficiency with which an organization converts inputs to outputs. It is measured as a ratio of system outputs to system inputs. Productivity can be improved through technology, people, or design.

- From a consumer perspective, quality can be defined as the degree to which the product or service meets the expectations of the customer. From a producer perspective, quality can be defined as the degree to which the product or service conforms to design specifications.

- There are four categories of quality-related costs. Prevention costs are incurred to prevent defective output from occurring. Appraisal costs are incurred to assess the quality of the output. Internal failure costs are associated with defective units that are detected before they reach the customers. External failure costs are associated with defective units that are not detected before they reach the customers.

- To achieve a successful total quality management program, concentration, commitment, and improvement should be focused on meeting customer expectations, attaining commitment to the philosophy and participation from every individual within the organization, and achieving coordination between all departments and functional specialties within the organization.

- W. Edwards Deming proposed a five-step chain reaction in which excellence in quality eventually leads to improved productivity, increased market share, increased profitability, and more jobs. Joseph Juran developed a trilogy of quality planning, control, and improvement. Armand Feigenbaum is credited with originating the concept of total quality control, Kaoru Ishikawa introduced the idea of quality circles, and Phillip Crosby developed the philosophy that quality is free.

KEY TERMS

Repetitive, assembly line, or mass production system (p. 566)
Continuous flow production system (p. 566)
Job shop production system (p. 566)
Project production system (p. 566)
Process layout (p. 571)

Product layout (p. 571)
Hybrid layout (p. 571)
Fixed position layout (p. 571)
Aggregate planning (p. 572)
Master production schedule (p. 573)
Just-in-time (JIT) inventory management (p. 575)
Productivity (p. 576)

Quality control (p. 579)
Quality assurance (p. 579)
Total quality management (p. 579)
External customer (p. 583)
Internal customer (p. 583)
Quality circle (p. 584)
Special purpose team (p. 584)

REVIEW QUESTIONS

1. Discuss the differences between manufacturing and service organizations.

2. Discuss the volume/variety continuum for categorizing operating systems. Provide several examples of both manufacturing and service organizations for each of the major categories.

3. What are the two major categories for classifying the decisions faced by the operations function?

4. List and briefly discuss several of the long-term system design decisions faced by the operations function.

5. List and briefly discuss several of the short-term operating and control decisions faced by the operations function.

6. In addition to reduced inventory, what does the just-in-time philosophy advocate?

7. List and briefly describe the three categories of tactics that might be used to enhance productivity.

8. Provide a definition of quality from a consumer perspective and a definition from a producer perspective.

9. List and briefly describe the different aspects of a product that might be judged in an attempt to assess its quality.

10. List and briefly describe the different aspects of a service encounter that might be judged in an attempt to assess its quality.

11. Briefly describe the areas of concentration and commitment for a program of total quality management.

12. Describe the major contributions of several prominent quality philosophers.

DISCUSSION QUESTIONS

Improving Critical Thinking

1. JIT advocates a holistic view of workers that takes advantage of all their skills, knowledge, and experiences and gives them added duties and responsibilities. Discuss these added duties and responsibilities, and compare this view with the traditional manufacturing view of workers. How do you feel these enhanced responsibilities might affect worker motivation and dedication to the job?

2. It has often been said that poor quality and poor productivity will detract from a company's competitiveness. Discuss the chain of events that you think would lead from poor quality and poor productivity to the eventual loss of competitiveness.

Enhancing Communication Skills

3. Imagine the way material would flow through a custom machine shop that fabricates metal parts for customers. Then imagine the way patients would flow through a walk-in emergency clinic. Discuss the similarities between the flows in these two systems. To enhance your oral communication skills, prepare a short (10–15 minute) presentation for the class in which you describe the flow similarities in these two systems.

4. Consider the aggregate planning problem in which the demand for a product or service is seasonal. List as many strategies as you can that could be used to cope with the fluctuating demand pattern. Try to identify strategies that you might use from an operations standpoint, and also try to envision strategies that you might use from a marketing standpoint (in an attempt to induce changes in the demand pattern). Finally, indicate which of your strategies might not be viable in a service organization. To enhance your written communication skills, prepare a short (1–2 page) essay in which you describe the strategies in each category and explain which strategies probably aren't appropriate for service organizations.

Building Teamwork Skills

5. The Crosby "quality is free" philosophy suggests that the only acceptable level of behavior is zero defects. Try to think of examples that might contradict this philosophy. That is, identify situations where the cost of totally eliminating defects might be higher than the failure cost incurred with a moderate level of defects. To refine your teamwork skills, meet with a small group of students who have been given the same assignment. Compare and discuss your selections, and then reach a consensus on the two best choices. Select a spokesperson to present your choices to the rest of the class.

6. Meet with a small group of students as directed by your instructor. To refine your teamwork skills, this group will operate as a quality circle. Discuss with one another some of the problems you have encountered in conjunction with your college education. These problems can cover any aspect of your education, and may relate to interactions with administration, faculty, or support services (for example, library, computer center, etc.). Reach a consensus on the most important or urgent problem, then conduct a brainstorming session to develop potential solutions to this problem. Select a spokesperson to present your problem and potential solutions to the rest of the class.

ETHICS: TAKE A STAND

When the demand for a product or service is seasonal, aggregate planning suggests several strategies for coping with the seasonal variations. One strategy calls for adjusting the size of the workforce by hiring and firing workers as demand fluctuates. This approach is often referred to as a chase strategy, since the organization is constantly varying its capacity to "chase" the contour of the fluctuating demand. The agricultural industry's need for people to harvest crops is highly seasonal. The industry typically follows a chase approach, hiring and firing migrant workers as the need arises.

For Discussion

1. Discuss the social and ethical implications of such a strategy. What alternative strategy or strategies might you suggest for such a situation?

2. Discuss the economic implications of your suggested strategies to agricultural firms and to you personally.

THINKING CRITICALLY
Debate the Issue

IS ZERO DEFECTS THE MOST COST-EFFECTIVE WAY?

Form teams of four or five students as directed by your instructor. Research the topic of quality costs and how they behave as one strives for higher levels of quality (i.e., higher levels of conformance to standards or lower levels of defective output). You will find that one theory holds that total quality costs will continually decrease and be at their lowest at a zero-defects level. (This is the current popular theory described in this chapter). Another theory, however, holds that total quality costs will initially decrease, but then begin to increase as defective output is further reduced. (This is the classical theory on quality costs). Prepare to provide arguments in support of both of these theories. When it is time to debate this issue in front of the class, your instructor will tell you which position to take.

VIDEO CASE

Lanier Worldwide, Inc.

Lanier Worldwide, Inc. is an organization whose entire market focus is reflected in a clear, unifying mission statement: *To be recognized worldwide as the preferred provider of office solutions dedicated to total customer satisfaction.* Lanier operates in more than 80 countries, and covers every county in the United States. The company has five main business areas: (1) copying, (2) facsimile systems, (3) information management systems, (4) dictation systems, and (5) presentation systems (overhead projectors, multimedia systems, etc.). Lanier's mission statement translates directly into its quest for customers to first think Lanier when they are in the market for these types of products and services.

Lanier's two core competencies are sourcing and distribution. Although it still manufactures dictation equipment and configures imaging equipment for its electronic filing systems for information management, it sources products for the other three product lines—copying, facsimile, and presentation systems. To ensure the utmost quality in these sourced products, Lanier's Product and Quality Assurance Engineers work closely with its manufacturing partners. Distribution is handled through 184 branches in 113 locations and 44 dealers in 110 locations, for a total of more than 200 outlets. This dual-distribution system works quite well, for it facilitates national coverage both within and outside of metropolitan areas, and at the same time enhances major account coverage.

Lanier has put several programs into place to ensure that it will achieve its mission. These include: (1) Customer Vision, (2) The Performance Promise, (3) 100 Percent Sold, and (4) The Lanier Team Management Process. The premise behind the Customer Vi-

sion program is that Lanier must see its business through the eyes of its customers and must respond to their needs as a team, at or above customer expectations. Lanier attempts to offer more than the competition through The Performance Promise, which offers guaranteed product satisfaction or replacement at no charge, guarantees on product up-time, free loaners, a 24-hour toll-free helpline, and a 10-year guarantee on availability of service, parts, and supplies. The 100 Percent Sold program has the ultimate goal of having every Lanier customer buy every one of its needed office solutions products from Lanier. Finally, The Lanier Team Management Process is a quality program that stresses a never-ending process of continuous improvement in quality, reliability, and performance in all things Lanier does at all levels of the company.

Industry analysts believe that Lanier is ready for the future. It has recognized what it is good at—sourcing and distribution. It has reorganized the company to be more streamlined, to take advantage of synergism among the product groups, and to serve the customer better. The driving force behind the company is to look at the business through the eyes of the customers. Lanier appears to be well on its way to achieving its vision—to be recognized worldwide as the preferred provider of office solutions, dedicated to total customer satisfaction.[44]

For Discussion

1. Do you think external customers should have an impact when Lanier develops or refines products, and if so, how?

2. To what degree do you feel teamwork and employee involvement are important to the

quality of Lanier's products?

3. What steps do you think Lanier's Product Quality Assurance Engineers should undertake when working with its manufacturing partners in order to ensure that Lanier products will be of utmost quality and meet customer needs?

CASE

Oregon Cutting Systems

Cutting technology is the science of designing and manufacturing cutting tools for various applications. This is the business of Oregon Cutting Systems (OCS). Each day OCS converts cold rolled steel into over 20 miles of cutting chain. Output varies from one-quarter-inch pitch chain for consumer markets to three-quarter-inch pitch chain used in mechanized forestry harvesters. OCS also manufactures related products, such as chain saw bars. It is the industry leader with more than one half the world's saw chain market. OCS is also an original equipment manufacturer, supplying the world's best-known brands of chain saws through its own network of distributors and dealers.

In the early 1980s, it became apparent that business as usual was no longer going to be good enough for OCS. According to Noel Hingley, division vice president for manufacturing, "the initial impetus for changing things came from a discomfort with quality problems that were too large, and problem solving that took too long and resulted in problems that weren't permanently solved." Self-inspection revealed an operation that was ripe with opportunities for improvement. Jim Osterman, president of OCS, noted that "when somebody came in with a problem or a complaint we were certain that it had to be their problem and not our product problem. As a consequence, we earned the reputation in the field of not covering our products." According to Charlie Nicholson, division vice president for quality, "we felt we knew so much about the market and the needs of our customers (our end users) that we could pretty well design for them and we made a lot of assumptions regarding their needs and expectations. We did develop chains without direct data from them for a while and we did design chains for large market segments. We've learned since that there are a lot of different market segments out there that demand different types of products."

OCS began its improvement program by implementing a just-in-time (JIT) approach to inventory management. This was not without problems, though. OCS found that it could go only so far with JIT before it encountered obstacles in the form of machinery that wasn't reliable enough to maintain consistent production and interruptions in production because of quality defects. OCS found that it couldn't maintain as low a level of inventory as it wanted or make further gains. Then the company shifted its focus to quality and continuous improvement. A strong emphasis on statistical process control was adopted. Production workers were trained in its procedures and were given the authority to make decisions and solve problems. At that point, operations improved dramatically. Work in process was reduced to 30 percent of pre-change levels, and new goals for an additional 50 percent cut in inventory and a 20 percent reduction in costs. A major element in OCS's success is its effort to translate customer requirements into product characteristics. In a process it calls Strategic Product Development, OCS starts with customer inputs and designs products to meet those customer needs. As a result of these changes, OCS now delivers value that is far above what it previously delivered. Customer problems that were chronic in the past are now nonexistent. At the same time, OCS production workers have become happier and more fulfilled on the job and are proud of their accomplishments.

In retrospect, President Osterman says, "I think what I would have done differently is understood the ramifications of total quality commitment a little better and started on the quality side before starting on the just-in-time side."[45]

For Discussion

1. Review the concepts of a consumer perspective on quality and a producer perspective on quality. Discuss how and when in the chronology of events each of these perspectives dominated the operating philosophy of Oregon Cutting Systems.

2. Discuss what you feel are the reasons that OCS met with limited success with JIT before it addressed the quality issue, and why such dramatic improvements were possible after the focus on quality and continuous improvement.

EXPERIENTIAL EXERCISE 17.1

Manufacturing versus Service Organizations

Purpose: To gain a better understanding of the characteristics of manufacturing and service organizations.

Procedure: Visit a local strip mall and a local industrial park in your town. Focus on five businesses in each location. Use the checklist in Meeting the Challenge to classify each of these 10 businesses as either a manufacturing or a service organization.

EXPERIENTIAL EXERCISE 17.2

Assessing Quality

Purpose: To gain a better understanding of the aspects of a product and a service that might be used to assess its quality.

Procedure: Think of a product and a service that you recently purchased that did not totally meet your expectations. First, list the various factors for rating a product's quality, then give your product a rating from 1 to 10 (1 is the lowest rating, 10 the highest) for each of the factors. Jot down reasons for each of the ratings that you assigned to the product. Finally, calculate an overall average rating for the product to see where it falls on your 1-10 scale. Perform similar ratings and calculations for the service you chose.

NOTES

1. Adapted from N. Templin, "Team Spirit: A Decisive Response to Crisis Brought Ford Enhanced Productivity," *Wall Street Journal,* December 15, 1992, A1; E. L. Hennessy Jr., "Back to the Basics: To Regain Greatness, U.S. Manufacturer Must Retool Its Thinking," *Industry Week,* November 20, 1989; A. Taylor III, "U.S. Cars Come Back," *Fortune,* November 16, 1992, 52-85; J. Main, "How to Steal the Best Ideas Around," *Fortune,* October 19, 1992, 102-6; A. Taylor III, "Ford's $6 Billion Baby," *Fortune,* June 28, 1993, 76-81; "Smart Design," *Business Week,* April 11, 1988, 102-8; and "How Ford Hit the Bull's Eye with Taurus," *Business Week,* June 30, 1986, 69-70.

2. L. J. Krajewski and L. P. Ritzman, *Operations Management: Strategy and Analysis,* 3d ed. (Reading, Mass.: Addison-Wesley, 1993).

3. J. R. Evans, D. R. Anderson, D. J. Sweeny, and T. A. Williams, *Applied Production and Operations Management,* 3d ed. (St. Paul, Minn.: West Publishing Co., 1990).

4. R. B. Chase and N. J. Acquilano, *Production and Operations Management: A Life Cycle Approach,* 6th ed. (Homewood, Ill.: Irwin, 1992).

5. Krajewski and Ritzman, *Operations Management: Strategy and Analysis.*

6. M. A. Vonderembse and G. P. White, *Operations Management: Concepts, Methods, and Strategies,* 2d ed. (St. Paul, Minn.: West Publishing Co., 1992).

7. Krajewski and Ritzman, *Operations Management: Strategy and Analysis.*

8. Vonderembse and White, *Operations Management: Concepts, Methods, and Strategies.*

9. R. J. Schonberger and E. M. Knod Jr., *Operations Management: Improving Customer Service,* 4th ed. (Homewood, Ill.: Irwin, 1991).

10. Chase and Acquilano, *Production and Operations Management: A Life Cycle Approach.*

11. Krajewski and Ritzman, *Operations Management: Strategy and Analysis.*

12. Vonderembse and White, *Operations and Management: Concepts, Methods, and Strategies.*

13. Ibid.

14. "Dinnerhouse Technology," *Forbes,* July 8, 1991, 98-99.

15. R. W. Schmenner, *Making Business Decisions* (Englewood Cliffs, N.J.: Prentice-Hall, 1982).

16. "Business in a Nation in Turmoil," *New York Times,* April 18, 1988.

17. Krajewski and Ritzman, *Operations Management: Strategy and Analysis.*

18. J. Heizer and B. Render, *Production and Operations Management* (Boston: Allyn & Bacon, 1988).

19. Evans, Anderson, Sweeny, and Williams, *Applied Production and Operations Management.*

20. Krajewski and Ritzman, *Operations Management: Strategy and Analysis.*

21. N. Gaither, *Production and Operations Management,* 5th ed. (Fort Worth, Tex.: Dryden Press, 1992).

22. Vonderembse and White, *Operations Management: Concepts, Methods, and Strategies.*

23. Evans, Anderson, Sweeny, and Williams, *Applied Production and Operations Management.*

24. Vonderembse and White, *Operations Management: Concepts, Methods, and Strategies.*

25. Evans, Anderson, Sweeny, and Williams, *Applied Production and Operations Management.*

26. Krajewski and Ritzman, *Operations Management: Strategy and Analysis.*

27. J. R. Evans and W. M. Lindsay, *The Management and Control of Quality,* 2d ed. (St. Paul, Minn.: West Publishing Co., 1993).

28. Ibid.

29. Evans, Anderson, Sweeny, and Williams, *Applied Production and Operations Management.*

30. Vonderembse and White, *Operations Management: Concepts, Methods, and Strategies.*

31. Adapted from "SuperVan," in *Real-World Lessons for America's Small Businesses: Insights from the Blue Chip Enterprise Initiative* (*Nation's Business* on behalf of Connecticut Mutual Life Insurance Company and the U.S. Chamber of Commerce, 1992), 166–67.

32. J. Welch, L. Cook, and J. Blackburn, "The Bridge to Competitiveness: Building Supplier-Customer Linkages," *Target,* November/December 1992, 17–29; *Total Quality Excellence Award Program Orientation Guide* (Plymouth, Mich.: Ford Quality Related Publications, 1990); and *Total Quality Excellence Award Program Assessment Manual* (Plymouth, Mich.: Ford Quality Related Publications, 1990).

33. Evans, Anderson, Sweeny, and Williams, *Applied Production and Operations Management.*

34. Krajewski and Ritzman, *Operations Management: Strategy and Analysis.*

35. W. E. Deming, "Improvement of Quality and Productivity through Action by Management," *National Productivity Review* (Winter 1981–1982): 12–22.

36. Adapted from "S. B. Electronics," in *Real-World Lessons for America's Small Businesses: Insights from the Blue Chip Enterprise Initiative* (*Nation's Business* on behalf of Connecticut Mutual Life Insurance Company and the

U.S. Chamber of Commerce, 1992), 67–68.

37. J. M. Juran and F. Gryna Jr., *Quality Planning and Analysis,* 2d ed. (New York: McGraw-Hill, 1980).

38. A. V. Feigenbaum, *Total Quality Control,* 3d ed. (New York: McGraw-Hill, 1983).

39. K. Ishikawa, *Guide to Quality Control* (Tokyo: Asian Productivity Organization, 1972).

40. P. B. Crosby, *Quality Is Free* (New York: McGraw-Hill, 1979).

41. S. Date, "No Gazing Off into Space on This Trip," *Orlando Sentinel,* December 4, 1993, A1+.

42. S. Date, "Endeavour Opens Some Eyes as Hubble Mission Ends at KSC," *Orlando Sentinel,* December 13, 1993, A1+.

43. Adapted from Templin, "Team Spirit: A Decisive Response to Crisis Brought Ford Enhanced Productivity"; Hennessy, "Back to the Basics: To Regain Greatness, U.S. Manufacturer Must Retool Its Thinking"; Taylor, "U.S. Cars Come Back"; Main, "How to Steal the Best Ideas Around"; Taylor, "Ford's $6 Billion Baby"; "Smart Design"; and "How Ford Hit the Bull's Eye with Taurus."

44. Ritter, Lynn, "Lanier Reorganizes for the Future," *Dataquest Perspective,* December 27, 1993, 1–10.

45. Adapted from "We're Getting Closer," Oregon Cutting Systems Segment, *Association for Manufacturing Excellence Videotape #6,* 1991.

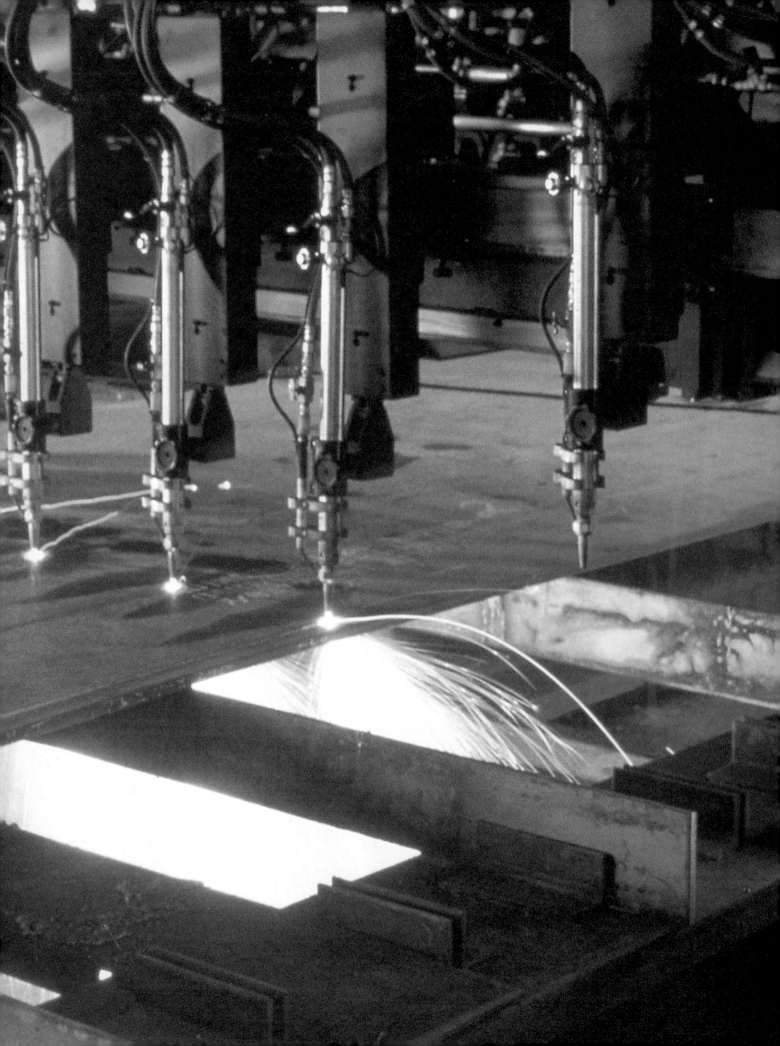

Information Technology and Control

CHAPTER 18

▼ CHAPTER OVERVIEW

Consider all of the information that is available to assist organizational decision makers. Good information is necessary for good decision making.

Information provides knowledge about past and current conditions in the organization and, if used carefully, can provide insights into possible future conditions. Ultimately, information provides a means of understanding the organization and its activities and making decisions on how to control the organizational system. The process of acquiring, processing, maintaining, and distributing this information increasingly involves information systems and information technology.

This chapter introduces the basic concepts of information and the information systems and technology that can be used to collect and distribute the information. First, we explore the differences between data and information and examine some characteristics of good information. We then introduce a basic model of an information system and the systems development process. Next, we look at the role of information technology in the organization and discuss several important categories of information technology. Finally, we look at the impact of technology on the organization and some of the limitations of computer-based information systems.

▼ LEARNING OBJECTIVES

When you have finished studying this chapter,
you should be able to:

- Explain the differences between data and information.
- Discuss the characteristics of useful information.
- Describe the various components in an information system.
- Illustrate the steps in the development of an information system.
- Explore the various roles of information technology in organizations.
- Describe a variety of types of technology that are changing the way we work.
- Discuss the impact of information technology on the organization.
- Explain the limitations of information technology.

MANAGERIAL INCIDENT

AETNA REENGINEERS USING INFORMATION TECHNOLOGY

Aetna Life and Casualty, an insurance company that has been in existence since before the Civil War, is a huge organization with over $90 billion in assets. Yet, in the early 1990s, the company was in deep trouble. Increasing competitive pressures, the worsening economy, and expanding regulations were all contributing to shrinking profits. Net income for 1992 was $56 million, down significantly from $560 million the year before. Aetna had almost $3 billion in underperforming or troubled real estate loans, accounting for almost 20 percent of its real estate holdings. Its workforce, at 50,000 employees, was bloated. Other insurance companies had been taken over during the late 1980s and early 1990s, and Aetna wanted to avoid a similar outcome. Industry analysts were not hopeful for Aetna's future.

Aetna's problems were immense. Mother-Aetna, as it was often called, was a bureaucratic, tradition-bound company. Employment was typically for life. Most claims processing and record keeping were accomplished via paper-based files. Aetna had 40 claims offices around the country. Mail might sit for a week or more before it was opened and processing started. Although Aetna had the best industry performance, a customer might have to wait several weeks for questions to be answered or a claim to be settled while paperwork and files were located and examined. Many of the customer service representatives at the various service centers used different and incompatible software systems that had been custom-built over the years. The personal and commercial claim systems also existed on separate and incompatible computer systems.

Since 1990, under CEO Ronald E. Compton's direction, Aetna has been undergoing a massive reengineering process that includes eliminating decades-old business practices and replacing them with concepts and methods that are driven by and built around technology. Although the initial costs are significant and the change in work methods has caused some disruption and turmoil, Compton suggests that this organizational reengineering, with its focus on information technology, is necessary for the company to survive.[1] ▼

INTRODUCTION

Aetna has realized that a major reengineering effort is needed if the company is to survive. Much of this effort is focused on regaining control of and better managing its biggest resource—information—through the development and use of information technology. How can the work methods be redesigned, incorporating technology where appropriate, to give workers the ability to manage their work more effectively and allow the organization to better meet customer needs and address customer concerns and complaints? How much will this reengineering cost? What are the benefits? Even if these changes are implemented, it is not clear whether they will be sufficient to ensure Aetna's survival. The problems facing Aetna are not uncommon.

Information technology in the world of business is barely 40 years old. It holds great promise for improving and even changing the way we manage and run our organizations. Yet, according to a recent special issue of *Fortune*, information technology has been described as "one of the most effective ways ever devised to squander corporate assets."[2] Investments in telecommunications, computer hardware and software, and technology-related equipment for the average large business can be as much as 8 percent of revenue every year. In 1992, information technology accounted for over 14 percent of capital investment in the United States, up from 8 percent in 1980. Worldwide, investment in technology totals over $350 billion a year. Yet, for the typical organization, productivity has barely improved. Still, a number of organizations are beginning to see results that can be directly linked to their investments in and better use of information technology.[3] Aetna is staking its future on the opportunities technology presents and the capabilities it offers.

The fundamental purpose of information technology is to monitor, process, and disseminate information to assist in managing, decision making, and controlling the organization. In this chapter we explore the basic issues related to information technology and controlling information. We will examine the basic concepts of information systems and look at some of the roles that information technology can play in organizations. Finally, we will illustrate some of the limitations of information technology that must be managed.

INFORMATION AND MANAGEMENT ━━━━━━━━━━━━━

Before inspecting the specifics of information technology, we need to know what information is and how it differs from data. Also important is understanding the characteristics of information that are useful in making decisions.

INFORMATION VERSUS DATA

The words *data* and *information* are often used interchangeably. In the organizational context, however, there can be a significant difference in meaning. **Data** are the raw facts or details that represent some type of transaction or activity within an organization. For example, the sale of items at a grocery store or the sale of an automobile creates a great deal of data representing that event. Data, therefore, are the objective measurements of the characteristics of the objects or transactions that are occurring in an organization.

Information is the end result of the process of transforming data into a meaningful and useful form for a specific purpose. In other words, data go through a process where meaning is added, yielding information. In data processing the data are aggregated and organized, manipulated through analysis, and placed in a proper context for evaluation and use by the end user. In a grocery store, the price and inventory amount for a particular product are examples of raw data. As sales occur, the inventory changes. The changes in inventory for this product, as well as the broader inventory changes that occur for all items available in the store, are examples of information. Each individual transaction is not that important in isolation; once combined, however, the transaction and sales figures provide useful information.

Other aspects of the data-information relationship also add complexity to organizational decision making and control. Information for one person may be data to another. For example, as customers make their purchases at the grocery store, the store's inventory is altered. If the store has automated cash registers, it can update the inventory immediately. If the store does not have automated registers, the inventory will have to be updated and reconciled manually at the end of the day. The transaction data, generated by and representing details of customer purchases, are important to the store manager. From these raw data, the manager derives information on the store's sales, the success or failure of specific specials, and inventories that need to be restocked, among other things. The regional manager for this chain of stores, however, is not as interested in the details of specific transactions. Instead, the regional manager is concerned with broader issues of how the stores as a whole are doing. Is one store in the region performing better than another? Do different specials or different store layouts generate better sales? Because

Data
Raw facts or details that represent some type of transaction or activity within an organization.

Information
End result of the process of transforming data into meaningful facts useful for a specific purpose.

the regional manager is interested in several stores as a unit, rather than in one store or individual customers, the information needs are different. In summary, the information for the store managers is data for the regional manager.

EVALUATING INFORMATION

Currently, many organizations are not taking advantage of all their opportunities to collect data and use the information that can be produced. Collecting and manipulating data entails costs, however, which must be weighed against the benefits that can be obtained from using the information. This process is called cost-benefit analysis.

Cost-Benefit Analysis

The opportunity presented by the collection, analysis, and use of data within an organization has both a positive side (benefits) and negative side (costs). The purpose of collecting data is to obtain useful information to improve decision making and control as managers strive to attain the organization's goals. Let's first examine the costs associated with data collection and information production.

These costs can be broken into tangible and intangible components. The **tangible costs** can be accurately quantified. For example, the costs of the hardware and software for a data-collection system are tangible costs. They include the costs of maintaining and updating the system, as well as the cost of compensation and related expenses for personnel to run and monitor the system. **Intangible costs,** on the other other hand, are hard to quantify, either due to the difficulty of precisely anticipating outcomes or the impossibility of predicting ultimate consequences. Examples of intangible costs include the loss of customer goodwill due to poor organizational performance, lower employee morale, and even work disruption due to changes in work procedures. As described in the Managerial Incident, Aetna is undergoing a massive reengineering process. The company must determine how to consolidate its claim centers, consolidate its various computer systems and databases, and restructure its methods of handling customer claims and requests. Once the redesign has been finalized, some specific costs for computer hardware and software can be explicitly defined, but many of these costs will remain unknown, in other words intangible, until the transition is actually made.

Benefits also consist of tangible and intangible components. Tangible benefits include increases in sales, reduction in inventory costs, and identifiable improvements in worker productivity. Intangible benefits might include improvements in information availability, better employee morale, and improved customer service. Aetna hopes that its reengineering process will improve its customer service, enabling it to guide customers through the labyrinth of insurance options, make suggestions on ways to deal with medical situations, and provide information about doctors, hospitals, and health maintenance organizations. Aetna has estimated that it will realize significant benefits in its operations due to improved productivity and a reduction in the number of employees. These benefits are projected to save the company more than $120 million a year. But until the transition is completed, the true costs and benefits will remain only estimates.

The decision on whether to collect more data so as to produce more and better information is difficult. As in many situations, identifying the probable costs is easier than predicting the potential benefits because the additional information has not been used before. In fact, often the most important benefits of new information were not anticipated, but simply emerged as employees became more familiar with the new information. Many organizations have

Tangible costs
Costs that can be accurately quantified.

Intangible costs
Costs that are difficult or impossible to quantify.

experienced this problem when they incorporated information technology. Not only were the anticipated benefits unrealistic, but the true benefits were often not foreseeable and, therefore, could not be quantified.

CHARACTERISTICS OF USEFUL INFORMATION

Information that is useful to decision makers in the organization has several characteristics. First, its quality must be very high. Second, it must be available to decision makers in a timely fashion. Finally, the information must be complete and relevant. Figure 18.1 shows the relationship among these three primary components of information.

Thus, in deciding whether to collect additional data and process it into information, the organization should consider the costs and the benefits. In a wholly rational decision-making environment, the costs and benefits will be known and can be carefully weighed against each other. As we discovered in Chapter 6, however, sometimes the decision-making environment is not entirely rational, and decision makers must weigh intangible benefits that are, at best, imperfectly known against known, tangible costs. As we saw, conclusions based on inaccurate or incomplete information often yield poor decisions. Nevertheless, decision makers must recognize that the decision of whether to incorporate information technology may have to be based on incomplete and imperfect information, especially about the potential benefits. Certain characteristics, however, make some information more useful than others, and we will examine those characteristics in the next section.

Quality

Quality is, perhaps, the single most important characteristic of information. Without high quality, the information is of little use. Quality consists of several components. First, quality information must be accurate. If the details do not accurately reflect current conditions, then any decision made using the information may be adversely affected. Clarity is another characteristic of quality information. The meaning and intent of the information must be clear to the decision maker. Quality information has an orderly arrangement and is presented in a form that assists the decision maker. Finally, the medium through which the information is communicated is important. For example, providing the decision maker with a massive computer printout instead of several pages of summary information is an inappropriate means of communication.

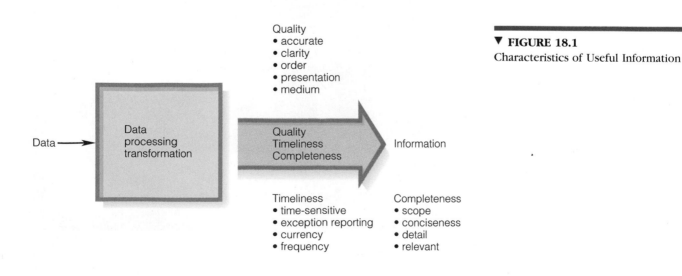

▼ **FIGURE 18.1**
Characteristics of Useful Information

Timeliness

Most organizational decision making requires timely information. Many day-to-day decisions are time-sensitive. In other words, decisions on how to respond to situations in an organization must be made quickly. Timely information has several ingredients.

First, information should be provided when and as it is needed, so that the decision maker has the information when it is needed to support making a decision. For example, a decision maker might ask for exception reports, which are reports that are generated when things fall outside a normal range of activity within the organization. Thus, if production on an assembly line falls below a certain threshold due to a malfunction, an exception report is generated to inform those who need to know so they can make appropriate repairs and adjustments. Another key ingredient of timely information is currency. Information should be up-do-date when it is provided to the decision maker. A final characteristic of timely information is frequency. Information should be provided as often as needed. For example, reports should be generated and provided to the decision maker on a regular reporting schedule, such as daily, weekly, monthly, or quarterly. Managing for Excellence describes how timely feedback of information on package location is critical to Federal Express's successful monitoring of packages in the delivery process.[4]

Completeness

If information is to contribute to making good decisions, it must be complete. Information completeness consists of several primary components. The scope of the information must be sufficient to allow the decision maker to make an accurate assessment of the situation and to arrive at a suitable decision. Where appropriate, decision makers should have access not only to current information, but also to past history and to future plans for the organization. Conciseness and detail are two additional aspects of completeness. Information should be presented to the decision maker in as concise a form as possible, but there should be sufficient detail to provide the decision maker with enough depth and breadth for the current situation. Too much detail, however, can overwhelm the decision maker, causing information overload, distracting from

▼ These air-traffic controllers at New Orleans International Airport require high-quality, timely, and complete information to guide aircraft in and out of the airport safely.

FEDERAL EXPRESS

Federal Express is an overnight package delivery service. In less than 15 years, it has grown into an organization with more than 400 planes, 30,000 vehicles, and 90,000 workers who handle close to one million packages a day. From the beginning, the company's goal has been to deliver every package on time—the next day—with no lost or misplaced packages. FedEx has been so successful that other companies have also entered the business, creating a very competitive environment. Yet, FedEx remains the number one overnight delivery company through constant monitoring of its work procedures, timing, scheduling, and careful tracking of each and every package.

How does FedEx keep track of every package? When a package is to be picked up, the customer calls FedEx, and the office schedules a person to pick up the package. When the package is picked up, the employee scans the bar codes on the destination form that has been filled out by the customer and enters the zip code for the destination. Each package has a specific identifier. At any time during the package's travel, the customer can request status information on the package.

When the driver unloads the truck at the FedEx terminal, each package is scanned again. The packages are placed in shipping containers for the trip to the sorting facility and are again scanned. Upon arrival at the sorting terminal, the packages are scanned once more as they are unloaded; as they are sorted, they are routed based on their destination zip code and are directed to appropriate shipping areas for unloading into containers. As each package is placed in a container, it is scanned again; then the container is placed on the aircraft for shipment to the destination city. Each package is scanned three more times: when the container is unloaded, when the package is placed on a truck for delivery, and finally when it is delivered. The delivery person also enters the time and collects the signature of the person receiving the package. Throughout this process, the scanning is done with bar code scanners that are placed in receptacles that communicate with a central computer. Consequently, the computer system can maintain an up-to-date record of the status and location of each package.

Currently, customers who send 5 to 10 packages a day have software provided by FedEx that allows them to query the tracking system for the status of any of their packages. FedEx has recently announced that the same capabilities will soon be available for all individuals, even those who only periodically send packages.

the decision, or making it virtually impossible to focus on the important information. Finally, only information that is relevant to the decision at hand needs to be provided. Once again, too much information may do more harm than good.

Some examples of these concepts might be helpful. Imagine the job of air-traffic controllers, who must manage a number of aircraft flying through a certain airspace. The relevant information consists of aircraft identification, speed, direction, planned flight path, weather, other aircraft in the area, and so on. Clearly, high-quality, timely, and complete information are necessary if the controllers are to guide all the aircraft into and out of airports and airspace safely. Another example might be a stockbroker. Can you image the problems brokers would face if their information was more than an hour old? Or, what if the most timely information the brokers had was yesterday's stock market results in the newspaper?

In October 1993 Bell Atlantic, a regional telephone company, announced that it would acquire Tele-Communications, Inc., often called TCI. Although this merger was not successfully completed, the stock market activity surrounding this announcement provides another example of what may happen when decisions are made with incomplete information. The day after the announcement, the stock with the ticker symbol TCI on the New York Stock Exchange quickly experienced 56 trades involving 55,000 shares; the price rose 15 percent.[5] Unfortunately, TCI is the NYSE symbol for Transcontinental Reality Investors, Inc., not TeleCommunications, Inc., which has the symbol TCOMA. Managers of the NYSE recognized the error after only a short time and halted trading in TCI before any major problems occurred. In this situation, intervention by the NYSE prevented investors from suffering serious financial damage as a result of their incomplete information.

In any business organization, the timeliness, quality, and completeness of information are important. Consider the manager of a manufacturing plant that practices just-in-time manufacturing. As we saw in Chapter 17, this means that raw materials inventory must arrive in a timely fashion in order for production to continue, since the company maintains little excess, or spare, inventory. The manufacturing machinery must also be running according to schedule so raw material inventory does not stack up. Scheduling of workers is also important, for the assembly line must have workers in order to run. Any deviation from plans—an exception—would be important to the facility's management, since they will have to adjust to current problems and conditions.

Finally, as the Managerial Incident described, Aetna is attempting to redesign the way it manages, processes, and distributes information throughout the organization. All three of the characteristics of useful information—quality, timeliness, and completeness—are important to the ultimate success or failure of the organization.

INFORMATION SYSTEMS FOR MANAGEMENT

The fundamental idea behind information systems is that they provide a systematic approach to collecting, manipulating, maintaining, and distributing information throughout an organization. Despite the common misconception, an information system does *not* require a computer. Systems of managing information existed long before computers. And even with the rapid increase in computers in recent years, many organizations still maintain systems for managing information that are not computerized. Nevertheless, computer systems and other advances in information technology are providing organizations and their workers with virtually unlimited opportunities to collect, explore, and manage information, opportunities that were not available just a few years ago.

INFORMATION SYSTEM COMPONENTS

A general system consists of five basic components: inputs, the processing or transformation area, outputs, procedures for providing feedback to the system, and a means of controlling the system. As Figure 18.2 shows, this general system model closely resembles the traditional computer-based information system except that the latter also includes hardware, software, and a database. The next paragraphs discuss the components of a computer-based system.

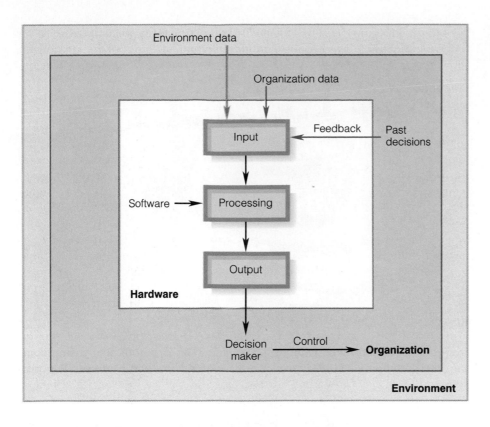

Input

The input portion of a computer-based information system consists of any type of computer input device that can provide data to the system. For example, the scanner cash registers in stores, often called point-of-sale terminals, provide input to the information system. Sensors and monitoring equipment in a manufacturing or production facility can provide input. Input can also come via telephone lines, satellite transmission, and archival data stored on computer disks and tapes. Input data can also be directly entered into the system by a user at a terminal or microcomputer, through a bar-code reader, and now even through pen-based computer systems that recognize handwriting.

Processing

The processing component of an information system—what we typically think of as the "brains" of the computer—is often called the central processing unit (CPU). When we think of a computer, we usually mean the CPU. This is the portion of the system where the raw data are manipulated and transformed into meaningful and useful information that can then be distributed to the relevant decision makers.

Output

The output portion of the system is the actual distribution of the information that is the end result of processing. Output can take a variety of forms, including paper printouts, electronic transmissions through telephone systems or via satellite, computer disks or tape, displays on computer monitors, and sounds or synthetic voices made available through speakers for audio use. It can even become available through the control and manipulation of computer-controlled machinery.

In the general systems model, the output process provides information to the decision makers, who can then manage and control the larger organizational system. Feedback occurs when the decision makers interpret the infor-

▼ Bar code scanning devices like this allow retailers to maintain up to the minute inventory status, for transactions automatically alter inventory records.

mation to determine what should occur next. The decisions that result from the interpretation and use of the information are a means of controlling the system.

Hardware

The physical components of the information system—the computer, terminals, monitors, printers, and so on—are the hardware. The storage devices, such as hard disks, floppy disk drives, and tape drives, are also hardware components. An infinite variety of hardware components are available and can be combined as needed to meet organizational information processing needs.

Software

The software portion of an information system consists of the various types of programs that are used to tell the hardware how to function. Software controls how the data are processed. Examples of software include word processing, spreadsheet, and accounting packages; other business applications; and even the games we commonly play. Ultimately, software governs how the information is stored and distributed.

Database

A database is the archived data and information that the organization uses. A database typically contains a vast amount of related information on company operations, financial records, employee data, customers, and so on. In the past, much of this information was maintained in separate files, which were often paper based. As a result, the data were often inconsistent and hard to locate and retrieve. Even early computerized systems often maintained data in separate files, leading to similar problems. A computerized database typically makes it easier for the organization to manage and use its data and information in decision making.

STEPS IN THE DEVELOPMENT OF HIGH-QUALITY MANAGEMENT INFORMATION SYSTEMS

End users
Those who will use and interact with the information system.

Most information systems are developed through a systematic process, in which system design specialists and programmers collaborate with the end users. **End users** are all the people who will use and interact with the information system, particularly the decision makers in the organization. This process, which is depicted in Figure 18.3, is often called systems analysis and design.

Investigation

The initial phase in the development of an information system is systems investigation. During this phase, the organization determines whether a problem or opportunity exists that can be addressed by an information system. In addition, a feasibility study is performed to determine whether a new information system is attainable. Once an organization ascertains that an information system is both appropriate and feasible, the organization develops a plan for managing the project and obtaining management approval. Aetna, for example, conducted an initial investigation of its needs and found that information technology could provide a great deal of assistance in its attempts to redesign its work methods.

Systems Analysis

Once the plan has been devised and management's approval has been obtained, the second phase, called systems analysis, begins. The purpose of this phase is to develop the functional requirements for the information system. In other words, this phase concentrates on what needs to be done to provide the desired information. This phase begins with an examination and analysis of the current systems in use, an assessment of the organizational environment, and a detailed assessment of the information needs of the end users. The organizational environment consists of both internal factors, such as the organization's structure, people, and activities, and external factors, such as industry considerations and the competition.

After studying these components, the system designers develop a set of functional requirements, or a detailed description of the necessary functional performance capabilities of the information system. These requirements focus on the type of information that decision makers require, the response times the users will need, and the format, frequency, and volume of information that should be produced and distributed. The specific hardware, software, and personnel that will ultimately be needed are not addressed in this stage. Aetna, for example, realized that the variety and incompatibility of the information systems used throughout the organization created a significant problem that needed to be addressed.

System Design

Phase three is the system design phase. This is the first phase where the system's technological capabilities are addressed. The designers identify the hardware, software, people, and data resources that will be needed and describe the information products that will be produced to satisfy the functional requirements specified in the previous phase. More specifically, the user interface, or the point of interaction between the people and the information, is designed. The data, their attributes and structures, and the relationships among the various data elements are created. These data will ultimately become the input for the database. Finally, the software system—the various computer programs and procedures—is designed. For Aetna, this part of the process was extremely important and complex, for it involved reconciling the company's many inconsistent and incompatible systems.

Computer-aided software engineering (CASE) tools are increasingly being used in this phase of the development process. CASE tools allow the system developers, or even the users themselves, to rapidly and easily develop prototype screens and report generators from a library of generic samples. In addition, once the prototypes have been designed, the CASE tools will generate the actual computer code that needs to be included in the larger system for those screens and reports. CASE tools are also more broadly used in business

Computer-aided software engineering (CASE)
Tools that allow system developers to create prototype screens and report generators rapidly and easily.

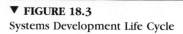

▼ **FIGURE 18.3**
Systems Development Life Cycle

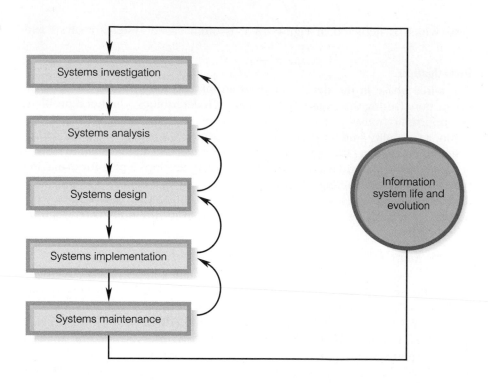

process planning, project management, database design, and software interface design.[6]

Systems Implementation

Once the analysis and design phases have been completed, systems implementation can begin. The outcome from this phase will be a system that is operational. The hardware and software that will be incorporated into the new information system are developed or acquired. As the system is put together, extensive testing is necessary to ensure that the system will meet all specified requirements. Any problems can be more easily corrected at this phase than at any later phase.

Documentation of the new system, or the relationship among the various pieces of hardware and software, should also be emphasized. The information system will not work perfectly, and the individuals who designed and developed it will not always be around to maintain it. Therefore, detailed and accurate descriptions of what was done, why it was done, and how it all works together are needed to assist in managing and maintaining the system.

Once the testing is completed, the system is ready for use, and the organization can switch from its old procedures to the new information system. This transition process may require operating both the new and the old system for a time in parallel. Operating the systems in parallel givens people time to learn and become comfortable with the new system and an opportunity to identify and correct most system bugs. Bringing the new system into operation on a trial basis, one location at a time, is called using a pilot system. Another alternative is the immediate cutover, where the old system is halted and the new system is started with no overlap in operations. All these transition methods have positive and negative aspects. The organization should carefully assess the benefits and potential costs before selecting an approach.[7]

Systems Maintenance

The final phase in the development of an information system is systems maintenance. Like an automobile, a house, or any piece of machinery, an information system will need to be maintained to keep it in top shape and to ensure that it will not encounter problems that could have been prevented. New hardware may be added to the system to address new needs or to replace older equipment. Software updates—new versions with added capabilities— are commonly available. In spite of extensive testing, most systems will contain errors, or bugs, some of them quite major. In addition, as the users work with the information system, they will discover additional things that need to be added, better ways of doing some things, and possibly areas that can be removed from the system.

The **systems development life cycle (SDLC)** is the recognition that the process of investigating, analyzing, designing, implementing, and maintaining an information system is ongoing. All of the activities in the life cycle of an information system are highly interrelated and are very interdependent. For example, the design process is directly affected by the outcome of the analysis phase. Any issues that are missed or are not completely addressed during the analysis will not be a part of the functional analysis and, therefore, will not be effectively handled during the design phase. Obviously, if issues are not addressed during the design, there will be nothing to implement. So, as shown in Figure 18.3, as each new phase is entered, it may be necessary at times to go back to the previous phase, or even an earlier one, to address any deficiencies that are identified.

But the SDLC goes beyond even this level of interrelationship. It recognizes that any system, no matter how well designed and maintained, will ultimately become obsolete and need to be replaced or will effectively be replaced as the organization and its information system evolve over time.[8] Aetna has discovered that new initiatives are added weekly to the already overwhelming change process underway. And each initiative adds complexity and cost to an already complex and expensive process.

One final aspect of any new information system is user training. The success of an information system depends on more than just thorough analysis, design, and implementation. Success is also, and perhaps ultimately, dependent upon the people who will use the system on a daily basis to assist in making decisions. To facilitate their use of the system, the users need to be trained in what the system can and cannot do and in how to accomplish the needed tasks. Training may be for simple tasks such as data entry or for very complex monitoring and operations of critical machinery within the organization. In larger organizations, the training role is commonly fulfilled by an information center.[9] As cultural diversity increases in the workplace, the training process can become more difficult due to language barriers and communication problems. In addition, as with any type of change, the process can be slower and more tedious, when cultural backgrounds cause resistance to change.

PITFALLS IN SYSTEM DESIGN

Several types of pitfalls can affect the system design process. These pitfalls involve the project's feasibility, the system's ability to meet user needs, and user expectations of the system.

Feasibility

An assessment of the system's feasibility focuses on evaluating alternative systems that will best meet the needs of the organization and its workers. Feasibility has several dimensions.[10] **Organizational feasibility** examines how well the proposed system supports the strategic objectives of the organization as a whole. Systems that do not directly contribute to the short-range and long-

Systems development life cycle (SDLC)
Recognition that investigating, analyzing, designing, implementing, and maintaining an information system is an ongoing process.

Organizational feasibility
Focuses on how well the proposed system supports the strategic objectives of the organization.

Economic feasibility
Focuses on whether the expected benefits of an information system will be able to cover the anticipated costs.

Technical feasibility
Focuses on the hardware and software capabilities of the proposed information system.

Operational feasibility
Focuses on the willingness and ability of all concerned parties to operate, use, and support the information system.

range goals of the organization should be rejected. **Economic feasibility** focuses on whether the expected benefits will be able to cover the anticipated costs. A system whose benefits do not match or exceed the costs will not be approved unless mandated by other considerations, such as government regulations. The economic feasibility includes the cost-benefit analysis discussed earlier in the chapter.

Technical feasibility addresses the hardware and software capabilities of the proposed system. Is the system, as proposed, capable of reliably providing the needed information to the appropriate people? Can the decision makers get the right kinds and amounts of data to support the desired decision making? And will the information be available when needed? The last type is **operational feasibility,** which focuses on the willingness and ability of all concerned parties to operate, use, and support the information system as it is proposed and implemented. If any one of the relevant constituencies, such as management, employees, customers, and suppliers, does not support or use the system, it is doomed to ultimate failure. For example, if the system is too difficult for the employees to use successfully, they will reject it and use other approaches to do their work. Others who depend on the employees' use of the system for information will be unable to get what they need, leading to a further loss of opportunity.

Ability to Meet Needs of Diverse Users

A second concern in the system design process is whether the system will ultimately meet the users' needs. The investigation, analysis, and design process is time-consuming and can be very costly. Time and cost often put pressure on designers to take shortcuts that may lead to an inferior or flawed system that does not meet users' needs. Systems that do not meet the users' needs can also occur because users often have difficulty describing their information needs adequately. This problem is exacerbated when, as is often the case, the systems specialists have little or no previous experience with the types of problems currently under consideration. Therefore, if care is not taken, the resulting system may not live up to the expectations of the users. In addition, as the users become more familiar with the system, their demands and expectations may increase.[11]

Another potential pitfall is that the users may resist the new system. This situation is especially common when workers are afraid that the new information technology may make some of the currently existing jobs unnecessary. Resistance is also more likely when the people who must work with the information systems are excluded from participating in its design and development. Not only does this lead to an incomplete analysis and design process, but it can also generate resentment toward the new system.[12]

User Expectations

Finally, in many instances the expectations of the users and the organization are too high. As we suggested earlier in the chapter, information technology has been touted as the savior of organizations, whereas in most cases the results have been minimal. In reality, however, the technology is not the key issue. Ultimately, the success or failure of the technology is dependent on how the organization and its employees align the capabilities of the technology with the needs of the organization.[13] The next section examines several aspects of this new realization.

Since management information systems frequently fail to do the job they were supposed to do, system designers can use the checksheet in Meeting the Challenge to improve their chances of achieving a successful information system design.

CHECKSHEET FOR SUCCESSFUL INFORMATION SYSTEM DESIGN

Frequently, management information systems fail to do the job they were supposed to do because they were inadequately designed or poorly thought out. Before, during, and after the design of the information system, system designers should see if they can provide a positive response to the questions on the following checksheet:

_____ Is the information that is provided to the decision maker accurate and clear?
_____ Is the information that is provided to the decision maker current?
_____ Is the information provided to the decision maker in a timely fashion?
_____ Is the information provided to the decision maker frequently enough?
_____ Is the information that is provided to the decision maker complete?
_____ Have all of the steps in the information system development process been completely performed?
_____ Does the information system support the strategic objectives of the organization?
_____ Do the benefits of the information system outweigh the costs?
_____ Are the hardware and software capable of providing the needed information to the appropriate people?
_____ Does the information system meet the users' need and expectations?

APPLICATIONS OF COMPUTER-BASED INFORMATION SYSTEMS

The traditional role of information systems has been to process data in order to assist the organization in maintaining control and in monitoring operations. That role still exists today, but it has become much broader as well. Organizations now depend much more heavily on information systems to manage their various functional areas, as well as to provide greater integration and sharing of information than were previously possible. And, in the last 10 years, information systems have even moved into the executive levels of organizations to provide support for strategic planning and decision making.

Managerial decision making is typically depicted as a pyramid, with operational control as the foundation, tactical or functional control as the middle, and strategic planning and control as the pinnacle. Note that the type of information, its focus, and the degree of detail will differ depending on the type of management decision making and control appropriate for that level of the organization. The use of information technology originated in the operational areas of the organization and is moving increasingly into the middle and upper levels of management.

ELECTRONIC DATA PROCESSING AND OPERATIONAL CONTROL

Computing in organizations usually originated at the operational levels of the organization, where it took care of basic data processing needs such as payroll operations, general accounting functions, and tracking transactions. These data are still important, for they provide a detailed picture of the activities taking place within the organization. These detailed data are the foundation for the information that is generated and used for management decision making.

Operational control also includes what is commonly referred to as process control. In some industries, such as manufacturing and refining, information technology can be used to monitor and report on operations. Automated monitors of an oil refinery, for example, provide detailed status reports on the refining process and equipment. Additionally, an automated process control system can assist in automatically updating inventory, reordering materials when certain thresholds are reached or adjusting material flow as production warrants.

Finally, office automation systems, which are discussed in more detail later in the chapter, provide for systematic approaches to handling and controlling business-related documents and communication.

MANAGEMENT INFORMATION SYSTEMS AND FUNCTIONAL CONTROL

Management information system (MIS)
Focuses on the routine, structured, regular reporting and information requirements of the organization.

Management information systems (MISs) are typically focused on the routine, structured, regular reporting and information requirements of the organization. Regularly scheduled reports, delivered daily, weekly, monthly, or quarterly, are generated by MISs. These systems support the day-to-day decision-making needs that have been incorporated as part of normal operations. They also often contain information about conditions external to the organization, such as industry and economic trends and the performance of competitors.

In many MISs, information is available on demand to facilitate monitoring exception conditions and to monitor moment-by-moment activities if desired. These reporting capabilities typically support the tactical or functional decision making in the organization. However, unanticipated reporting requirements and unusual operating conditions are not typically well supported by the systematic, structured nature of a traditional MIS.

DECISION SUPPORT SYSTEMS AND STRATEGIC PLANNING

Decision support system (DSS)
Focuses on assisting decision makers in analyzing and solving semi-structured problems.

Decision support systems (DSSs) are an important type of computer-based information system that is becoming increasingly prominent in organizational decision making. A DSS helps decision makers formulate quality decisions for ad hoc, semistructured problems—situations in which procedures can be only partially prespecified. Because the situations occur infrequently, the organization does not have routine procedures for dealing with them. This lack of routine means there are limited rules to guide decision behavior; therefore, outcomes are less predictable or obvious. These types of decision situations commonly arise at the middle and upper levels of the organization.

A DSS consists of several separate pieces, as shown in Figure 18.4. The user works with the DSS in an interactive, real-time basis. The DSS contains analytical models that can be used to examine and understand the situation, as well as specialized databases. The DSS allows users to combine their own insights and judgment with the analytical models and information from the database to examine alternative approaches and solutions to the situation. In particular, "what-if" analysis can be performed using the DSS. In other words, the decision maker can assess a variety of decision choices by modeling the expected outcomes of those decisions with the information that is currently available.

Think of a DSS as a tool for simulating a situation. Just as an airline pilot in a flight simulator can experience a variety of scenarios that might be en-

▼ These airline pilots training in a Boeing 747 flight simulator are actually using a form of decision support systems (DSS) to experience a variety of flight scenarios that they might encounter.

countered, a manager using a DSS can use data from a database and analytical models to simulate what might happen if different decisions are made. American Airlines has developed a DSS called An Analytical Information Management System (AAIMS) that is used by a variety of airlines, airline financial analysts, and aircraft manufacturers. AAIMS can be used to analyze aircraft utilization and operations as well as traffic statistics. The analysis allows decision makers to assess forecasts of airline market share, revenue, and profitability. From these forecasts, users can decide on ticket pricing, aircraft assignments and maintenance, alternative route requests, and other complex scheduling issues.

The most common DSS-type of software tool is a spreadsheet program, which allows the user to quickly update data within the spreadsheet to see the effects on other variables. However, other specialized DSS tools also exist. For example, RCA has developed a DSS called Industrial Relations Information System (IRIS) to assist with personnel problems, labor negotiations, and other types of employee-related situations that cannot be anticipated. The National Audubon Society has developed a DSS called EPLAN (Energy Plan) to evaluate the impact of government energy policy on the environment. A DSS called Quality Decision Management has been developed by Hewlett-Packard to aid in raw material inspection, statistical analysis, and product inspection.[14]

A more specialized type of DSS that has recently become popular is called an executive information system (EIS) or executive support system (ESS). Al-

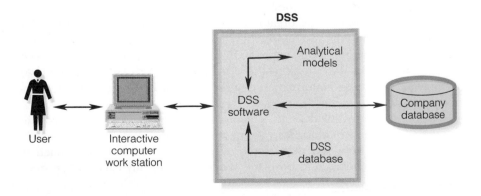

▼ FIGURE 18.4
Decision Support System (DSS)

▼ **Table 18.1**   Executive Information and Support Systems

EXECUTIVE INFORMATION SYSTEM (EIS)
• Tailored to individual user • Allows user to filter, expand, compress, and track critical information • Provide an up-to-date status report • Access to broad range of internal and external information and data • User-friendly and easily learned
EXECUTIVE SUPPORT SYSTEM (ESS)
An ESS is an EIS with additional capabilities: • Supports electronic communications • Provides a variety of data analysis tools (e.g., spreadsheets, DSS, expert system support, database access) • Often includes tools for personal productivity (e.g., electronic calendars and tickler files, rolodex)

though there is some distinction between the two, for our purposes they can be viewed as essentially the same. An EIS is a general information system combined with a DSS for use primarily by upper-level management and executive decision makers to support strategic decision making in the organization. As we discussed at the beginning of the chapter, decision makers at different levels of the organization have different information needs. An EIS provides the executives with the type of summary information they need and also gives them the opportunity to obtain additional details, that is, the data behind the information, if desired. Table 18.1 summarizes many of the characteristics of an EIS and an ESS.[15]

OTHER INFORMATION TECHNOLOGIES

In addition to the information systems we have just described, organizations may use several other types of information technology. Many of these are used at all levels of the organization to assist in communication, information transmission, and decision making.

TELECOMMUNICATIONS AND NETWORKING

Telecommunications is the transmission of information in any form from one location to another using electronic or optical means. This definition applies to all types of telecommunications, including the ordinary telephone call. Generally, however, the term implies that computer systems, and the people who use them, can communicate from almost any location.

The global integration of organizations is rapidly increasing the need for international phone calls and information transmission. For example, the number of international calls made annually to or from the United States has risen from 500 million in 1981 to almost 2.5 billion in 1991.[16] These numbers do not include the data and information that are transmitted through private communication systems.

The more advanced ideas in telecommunications typically concern the connection of multiple computer systems and multiple users in what is usually called a network. Networks that stretch over a wide geographic area, such as cities, regions, countries, and even the world, are typically called **wide area**

Wide area network (WAN)
Information system that extends over a broad geographic area, such as cities, regions, countries, or the world.

networks (WANs). For example, Wal-Mart and Sears, as well as many other companies, can easily communicate with their stores through a WAN. Network arrangements are becoming increasingly common in organizations that need to transmit and receive day-to-day information on business operations from their employees, customers, suppliers, and other organizations. A **local area network (LAN)** connects information systems and users within a much smaller area, such as a building, an office, or a manufacturing plant. The computer network on a college campus is usually a LAN or may contain several LANs.[17]

Many activities are now possible due to the ease of access and relatively low cost of telecommunications. **Electronic data interchange (EDI)** is the electronic transmission of transaction data using telecommunications. These data can include sales invoices, purchase orders, shipping notices, and so on. EDI provides an almost immediate transmission of the data and allows for a significant savings in printing, mailing, and labor costs as well as in time. In addition, since the orders and information are electronically transferred, fewer people have to handle the data, thereby reducing the chances for data entry and mishandling errors. Some companies have reported decreases of 25 to 50 percent in the amount of time it takes to receive and fill customer orders since adopting EDI. RCA has estimated that the cost to fill an order will drop from $50 to around $4 due to labor-saving use of EDI. General Motors has required all of its suppliers to use EDI, leading to estimated savings of about $200 per automobile produced. And the U.S. Department of Defense is moving toward a similar requirement for its suppliers.[18] Global Perspective describes how Ford Motor Company used telecommunications to transmit information to various units around the world when it designed the new version of the classic Mustang and prepared it for production.[19]

But EDI is not just for giant manufacturers and government. For example, InterDesign, of Solon, Ohio, makes plastic clocks, refrigerator magnets, soap dishes, and the like. Under pressure from a large retailer, the company adopted EDI. Now over half of the orders to InterDesign arrive via modem connected to its computer system instead of by mail or through a phone call. Virtually all order entry and shipping errors have been eliminated. Now employees who used to staff phones taking orders spend their time collecting valuable information the company couldn't afford to collect before. Sales are tracked by product, color, customer, region, and so on.[20] According to some predictions, by 1995 as many as one-third of all business documents will be transmitted by EDI.

The banking and retail industries are moving increasingly toward an environment of **electronic funds transfer (EFT),** where all financial transactions are done electronically. Many of us already depend on EFT for our banking and financial transactions. The automatic teller machine is an example of EFT. Being able to pay our bills over the phone is another example. And many of the point-of-sale terminals in retail stores, where our credit cards are checked, our checks are cleared, or our debit cards are used, depend upon EFT. Unlike a credit card, which it resembles, a debit card allows the money to be transferred from your account directly to the retailer's account upon completion of a transaction.

▼ Satellite transmitting and receiving dishes such as these are just one of the many types of modern-day telecommunications devices.

Local area network (LAN)
Information system that connects users in a small area, such as a building, an office, or a manufacturing plant.

Electronic data interchange (EDI)
Electronic transmission of transaction data using telecommunications.

Electronic funds transfer (EFT)
Electronic manipulation of financial transactions.

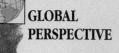

GLOBAL PERSPECTIVE

FORD MOTOR COMPANY: GLOBAL INTEGRATION THROUGH TECHNOLOGY

In October 1993, Ford announced the new version of the classic Mustang. The design process for the Mustang and the many people around the world who contributed to it are a good example of the opportunity provided by advances in information technology. Ford, using its $35 million a year telecommunications network, sends data to facilities around the world during the design and development of a new car or model update.

The sketches of an automobile designer in Dearborn, Michigan, are converted to digitized mathematical models using advanced computer workstations. This digitized data can be used for a variety of tasks in the design, development, and marketing of a new model.

Numerically controlled milling machines are used to create detailed styrofoam or clay models of the design. Each clay model costs approximately $100,000. Although Ford designers still feel they must have real, physical models, the computer technology has allowed them to make fewer than in the past. Any design changes made to the physical model can be captured by the computer technology, and the design is instantly updated.

Ford transmits the precise details of the car's shape to a facility in Duton, England. Here exacting three-dimensional models of the cars are created on computer screens to be used in simulated crash testing. These same data are used to estimate and analyze the weight and aerodynamic properties of the new design. An evaluation is made to determine whether Ford's metal-stamping machines can produce the required body panels.

The data from England are sent to Turin, Italy, for the production of physical models at Ford's Ghia studio. High-quality, computer-generated images, which are difficult to distinguish from actual photographs, are used by marketers to test interest in the proposed model design. The images created from these data can be used to create on-screen displays of a car from all conceivable angles, with authentic-looking reflections, surroundings, and light sources.

Ford plans to convert all of its design studios to the computer technology at an estimated cost of $50 million. But Ford anticipates a return on its investment of at least 50 percent, primarily through savings in labor and engineering costs. Ultimately, Ford anticipates that the entire product-development process will evolve in a similar manner.

Telecommuting
Situation in which a worker operates from a remote location, and interacts with the office via telecommunications.

Telecommuting, another facet of telecommunications, is a relatively new way to work. When workers telecommute, they operate from a remote location, such as a branch office or their home, and communicate with the office via telecommunications. Many jobs do not require an individual to be at the main office all of the time. In fact, some people find working from a remote site, such as their home, provides some big benefits.

American Express Travel Services has been experimenting with telecommuting for some of its employees. These jobs are oriented around providing customer service and information by telephone. Many employees located in the Houston area had a 60- to 90-minute commute to and from work each day. By telecommuting from their home, the workers found they had more time to spend with their families and were not stressed by the chore of driving in heavy traffic or bad weather. American Express has also seen some significant benefits. Thus far, workers have been able to handle 26 percent more calls with no reduction in the quality of service. In addition, the rent that would normally have been spent for office space for these employees could be saved. In New York, American Express estimates that it can save about $4,400 annually for every travel counselor who telecommutes. And, with advances in technology, managers can still monitor the employees' work performance in responding to customer phone calls.[21]

Recently, California instituted laws to encourage telecommuting to help reduce pollution caused by automobiles.[22] And the January 1994 earthquake near Los Angles did so much damage to the interstate highway system in the area that commuting times were significantly lengthened, sometimes by as much as two or three hours each way.[23] Telecommuting may be a way for companies to alleviate difficulties such as this.

Another advance that has grown out of telecommunications is electronic mail (E-mail) networks and bulletin board systems. E-mail systems, which are often a part of office automation systems, discussed below, are changing the way we work and communicate. You can think of E-mail as being like the postal system except that the messages and information are transmitted electronically through computer networks instead of being sent through the mail. Many companies, such as GTE, MCI, and TELENET, now offer E-mail services, and a number of personal computer networks, such as Prodigy, CompuServe, and Genie, are available for subscribers. Communication speeds are very fast. Whenever the people receiving messages are ready, they can read their mail.

In fact, E-mail received a lot of publicity immediately after the January 1994 earthquake near Los Angeles. The telephone companies purposely disabled long-distance telephone service into and out of the southern California area to allow for emergency communications. But this prevented many people from contacting and checking up on family and friends. For the most part, however, the local phone system remained in working order. Subscription E-mail is typically available to users through local phone service. So, in much the same way that ham radio operators often step to the fore after natural disasters, informal methods of sending and receiving messages and contacting family and friends via E-mail quickly and spontaneously developed. In the future E-mail is expected to be able to handle audio and video messages as well.

▼ Automatic teller machines (ATM) like this represent just one of the ways that the banking industry is moving increasingly toward an electronic funds transfer (EFT) environment.

ARTIFICIAL INTELLIGENCE

Artificial intelligence (AI) has the goal of developing computers and computer systems that can behave intelligently. Work in this area is derived from research in a variety of disciplines, including computer science, psychology, linguistics, mathematics, and engineering. Probably the most widely known application of artificial intelligence is in computer programs that play chess, some at or near the level of a grand master. But artificial intelligence applications go well beyond this. Two primary areas of research that have had some success in recent years are expert systems and robotics.

Expert Systems

An **expert system** is a knowledge-based information system. In other words, it is a computer-based system that contains and can use knowledge about a specific, relatively narrow, complex application. The knowledge the expert system contains and the way it is programmed to use this knowledge allow it to behave as an expert consultant to end users.

Fundamentally, an expert system is a type of software in which expert knowledge has been programmed to assist decision makers in a complex decision environment. The knowledge in an expert system has been painstakingly acquired from one or more experts in the knowledge domain of interest. Knowledge engineers, the expert system specialists, take this knowledge and carefully construct a knowledge base and the software that can use it. Users can then tap into this knowledge through the expert system and use it to provide expertise in difficult decision situations. Texas Instruments has developed an expert system, called IEFCARES (Information Engineering Facility Customer Response Expert System), to assist in providing service and support for their CASE product called IEF. Like many other credit companies, both ITT Commercial Finance Corporation and American Express have expert systems to assist in managing and monitoring credit requests and approvals. Expert systems are also commonly used for tasks such as loan portfolio analysis, diagnostic troubleshooting, design and layout configuration, and process monitoring and control.[24]

Robotics

The technology of building and using machines with humanlike characteristics, such as dexterity, movement, vision, and strength, is called **robotics.** A robot contains computer intelligence and uses research knowledge from AI, engineering, and physiology. Robots, often called "steel-collar" workers because they are used to perform manufacturing tasks that were previously performed by blue-collar workers, are programmed to do specific, repetitive tasks in exactly the same way each time. These automated machines offer significant benefits. They can be programmed to do very complex tasks that require a variety of movements and strength over and over again with precision. Robots don't have some of the faults of human workers, such as illness, fatigue, and absenteeism. In addition, robots can be very valuable in hazardous work areas and with tasks that are dangerous for humans.[25]

OFFICE AUTOMATION

One final area where information technology is having a major impact is in office automation. Systems for office automation are typically computer-based information systems that assist the organization in the processing, storage, collection, and transmission of electronic documents and messages among individuals, work groups, and organizations. Figure 18.5 shows the major cat-

Expert system
Computer-based system that contains and can use knowledge about a specific, relatively narrow and complex application.

Robotics
Use of machines with human-like characteristics, such as dexterity, movement, vision, and strength.

▼ This computer-controlled robot is engaged in electric arc welding the internal pipework of a car exhaust. It can be programmed for many industrial uses, including component assembly, micro-precision work, and welding.

egories of components in office automation systems. Many of these systems are important on their own merits, but when combined, they create an overall environment that supports all document and message processing.[26]

IMPACT OF INFORMATION TECHNOLOGY ON DYNAMIC ORGANIZATIONS

An organization is a sociotechnical system that consists of people and their tasks, as well as the organization's culture, structure, and environment. All of these things are affected by and will affect technology. As Service Challenge illustrates, advances in technology can provide benefits to people with severe physical limitations as well as to illiterate workers.[27]

MANAGEMENT EFFICIENCY

Information systems must produce useful and relevant information for management. Many of the areas that have been computerized have not yet resulted in the desired or expected gains. In part, this is because many organizations

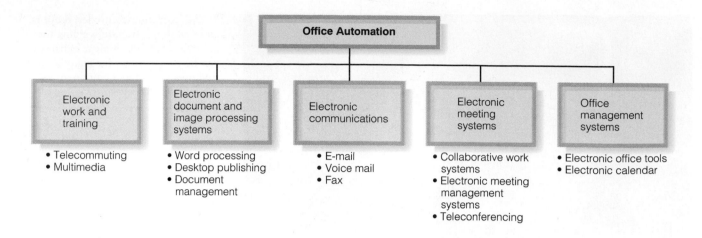

Office Automation

| Electronic work and training | Electronic document and image processing systems | Electronic communications | Electronic meeting systems | Office management systems |

- Telecommuting
- Multimedia

- Word processing
- Desktop publishing
- Document management

- E-mail
- Voice mail
- Fax

- Collaborative work systems
- Electronic meeting management systems
- Teleconferencing

- Electronic office tools
- Electronic calendar

▼ **FIGURE 18.5**
Components of Office Automation Systems

have used these new systems simply to replace traditional business practices instead of reassessing and redesigning the organization and the decision-making process to take advantage of the new technology's capabilities. Viewed another way, the primary, or first-order, effect of initial investments in information technology was simply to improve efficiency. Organizations still have a lot of room for improving the design and management of their information systems. Furthermore, we are discovering that the second-order effects, which are unintended and impossible to predict, are often more interesting and provide greater opportunities.[28] These unintended and unanticipated effects lead to a second area of impact.

SOCIAL RELATIONSHIPS

If information systems were used only by isolated individuals, the systems would have minimal impact on the social relationships among people. Currently, however, the very essence of the use of information technology within organizations is to enhance communication between people. Therefore, whenever information systems are used in this manner, they have a social component and potential social effects.

For example, what are the new technologies doing to power relationships within the organization? Does the technology change the dimensions and directions of determining priorities? If the use of the technology has negative consequences, who is accountable for the results? And the expanding use and dependence on information technology have created an interesting paradox. Information technology, like globalization, can extend an organization, making it less personal and less social. Yet, the effect of the technology often rewards intimacy.[29] These social implications suggest other, broader effects of information technology.

ORGANIZATIONAL STRUCTURE

In the early years of computer-based information systems, the technology was so limited that it was difficult to computerize even one division of the organization. As a result, data processing services tended to be decentralized. During the 1960s and 1970s, computer systems became much more powerful, and large systems were often able to handle many of the computing needs for the whole organization. This led to greater centralization of control over computer resources. The advent of the microcomputer in the late 1970s and the 1980s led to increased demands for computing access and power, creating a great

MAKING WORK EASIER FOR THOSE WITH CHALLENGES

Some have feared that the rapid advances in technology may soon make the workplace a forbidding and overwhelming environment for those who are illiterate or who can't read English. People who can't read, it has been thought, won't be able to function in an environment requiring workers to measure, record, and analyze everything using the computer.

But some companies have realized that in some cases at least, it is easier to use the technology to contend with illiteracy in workers than to eliminate illiteracy. Forklift operators, for example, can receive directions from talking computers on their belts. Other workers can use icons to make selections among various options on computer systems. Despite these successes, some commentators worry that overreliance on the technology will produce workers who are unable to think for themselves.

Many people with physical handicaps are also taking advantage of the capabilities of information technology. Voice recognition allows people with limited movement to work with a computer. Many people, who have found working for others to be difficult or unsatisfying, have even been able to run their own businesses. For some, doing this without the aid of technology would have been very difficult or impossible.

Computer-controlled environments are also allowing individuals with severe physical limitations some additional freedom and privacy. The technology can assist in the provision of many basic needs while also acting as a monitor and warning device in case of emergencies.

deal of confusion and conflict within organizations as they struggled to manage the rapid proliferation of varieties of hardware and software.

Neither centralization nor decentralization alone is the appropriate response. Instead, organizations should examine their specific computing needs and try to align their information technology to those needs. Some aspects of information processing in an organization may require greater centralization of computing resources, while others may lend themselves to greater decentralization.

Many note that information technology can help managers control the interdependencies of their organizations. In particular, as the competitive environment has become more complex, so too have the information needs of the decision makers. Information technology can help managers respond to this competitive environment. For example, unlike the situation during the Industrial Revolution, when the goal was to simplify, routinize, and separate tasks, current trends in information technology and data communications are to flatten the organization, fuse departments, create cross-functional teams, and increase and improve communications among employees, suppliers, and customers.[30] The structure of the organization can then be adjusted to take advantage of the varying needs. But despite its great promise, information technology also has limitations. We turn to them in the next section.

LIMITATIONS OF COMPUTER-BASED INFORMATION SYSTEMS

As we have seen, although investments in computer-based information systems have been substantial, the improvements that can be directly traced to the investment in technology have been minimal. Several factors may explain this low return on investments in technology.

First, the technology has been changing so rapidly in the last 10 years that organizations have had difficulty keeping up. In 1981 IBM produced its first microcomputer, marking for many the beginning of the rapid proliferation of computers in organizations and homes. Apple introduced its Macintosh system in 1984 as an easier-to-use alternative to the DOS (disk operating system) environment of IBM and IBM-compatible machines. In 1986 the Intel 386 microchip became the norm for microcomputer systems. The Intel 486 was released in 1991, and in 1993 the Intel 586 microchip began to show up in microcomputers. All of these versions of microchips and the microcomputers that use them have increased computing speed at a very low cost; they have also allowed larger and more sophisticated programs to be developed and have enabled almost all users to do types of computing that could be done only on mainframe computers just a few years ago. As computers have become more powerful, so have software programs. But this vast array of new hardware and software systems has made it difficult for organizations to maintain consistency throughout the organization. Furthermore, many people are reluctant to change their way of working to take full advantage of the capabilities of the technology.

The cost of computer systems and the time involved in switching from one method of managing and processing information to another is significant. As indicated in the opening Managerial Incident, Aetna will have to spend many millions of dollars over several years just to get to what it regards as the starting point.

MANAGERIAL IMPLICATIONS

Most organizations are only now coming to realize that the ways they incorporate technology into the workplace has a significant impact on their success or failure. A recent survey asked senior information system executives to name the 10 issues that are most important for the management and organizational use of information technology as we move into the twenty-first century.[31] Their responses are listed in Table 18.2.

Successful managers of the future will be those who:

- Understand the importance of quality information that is obtained in a timely fashion.
- Employ information systems capable of providing quality information that is both timely and complete.
- Are able to use that information to their advantage in the organizational decision-making process.
- Are well versed in the latest technological innovations for information gathering, processing, and disseminating.
- Are aware of the impact of information technology on management efficiency, organizational social relationships, and organizational structure.
- Are aware of the limitations of computer-based information systems.

As we have seen throughout this chapter, the ultimate success or failure of information technology is not always immediately clear. Technology is not the solution for all organization problems, and technology will not, in and of itself, provide relief from poor organizational practices. The benefits that can be gained from technology are many. But the ultimate benefits from technology are the vast amounts of information that can be more easily processed and

▼ **Table 18.2**   Twenty-First-Century Issues in the Use of Information Technology

1. Information architecture—creating a high-level map of the information requirements of the organization.
2. Data resources—data are now viewed as the important factor of production.
3. Strategic planning—considered the most important issue of the 1980s, it involves the close alignment of technology with business plans.
4. Human resources—recognition of the limited number of information systems professionals available to develop and maintain increasingly technical and complex organizational computing environments.
5. Organizational learning—learning how to make appropriate use of information technology.
6. Technology infrastructure—a new issue for this survey, it involves building an infrastructure that will support current operations while remaining flexible enough to adapt to changing technology and evolving organizational needs.
7. Information system organization alignment—effectiveness of support for organizational activities and operations without constraining either the technology or the organization.
8. Competitive advantage—technology is no longer the sole arbiter of competitive advantage, but is becoming the necessary, but not sufficient condition. Competitive advantage comes from the proper role of information technology in streamlining internal business processes, forging electronic links with suppliers and customers, and shaping the organization's design.
9. Software development—developing new tools and techniques to facilitate the rapid and error-free development of needed software systems.
10. Telecommunications system planning—can be used to reduce structural, time, and spatial limits on organizational relationships.

distributed. Management success—and, on a larger scale, organizational success—is still based primarily on the skills and insightful decisions of the managers. Still, it is up to the organization and its decision makers to take advantage of and properly use the information that becomes available.

AETNA REENGINEERS USING INFORMATION TECHNOLOGY

MANAGERIAL INCIDENT RESOLUTION

Heading into the 1990s, the management of Aetna Life and Casualty realized that the company faced severe financial difficulties. A large percentage of its real estate holdings were underperforming, the workforce was too large and inefficient, and industry competition was increasing. Coordination among the various claims offices was difficult due to outdated and inefficient business practices, and many of the computer systems in the company were incompatible. To address these problems, in 1990 CEO Ronald E. Compton instituted a massive reengineering process that was built around information technology.

To start the process, Aetna created 15 strategic business units by reorganizing its three major divisions. The workforce was reduced by 5,000. Then management began the process of convincing the remaining 43,000 workers of the need to change by redesigning work processes and giving them greater responsibility and control over their jobs. Aetna created a computer-based system that allowed employees to use their desktop computers to order supplies without having to get approval from purchasing. This produced savings of $20 million in 1992. Laptop computers were incorporated in the small business market group to allow the salespeople to enroll prospective members at the customer's site and instantly print out ID cards. The new process usually takes about half a day; the previous process required mailing handwritten applications to the central office and often took two months to complete. The new system saves as much as $700,000 annually in productivity costs. Aetna has also developed a computer-based training program to assist workers in the transition from the old work methods.

At the organizational level, Aetna consolidated the personal and commercial lines of property and casualty insurance by merging two huge databases that had been built in two different decades using different programming methods and user interfaces. Using the new database, Aetna has been able to consolidate 65 claim centers into 22 regional centers. By 1995, Aetna expects to save $100 million from streamlining these operations. Aetna is also installing an image-processing system to manage and process claims, alleviating the paper shuffling. Above all, Aetna is trying to become more than just a basic claims-dispensing insurance company. Its goal is to develop an enhanced role as a patient advocate, providing advice about doctors, hospitals, treatment alternatives, and coverage options.

Two of "Compton's 10 Commandments" summarize his intent and perspective: "Technology is never really the problem. The problem is how to use it effectively." "The weak link in reengineering is will. It is a huge job and it is agonizingly, heartbreakingly tough." Thus far, some tangible benefits have occurred, but the ultimate success of Aetna's reengineering is still an unanswered question.[32] ▼

SUMMARY

- Data are the raw facts, details, or objective measures that represent some type of transaction or activity within an organization. Data processing is the process where the data are aggregated and organized, manipulated through analysis, and placed in a proper context for evaluation and use by the end user. Information is the end result of the process of transforming data into a meaningful form for a specific purpose.

- To facilitate good decision making, the people making decisions must have useful information. Useful information has three primary characteristics. The quality of the information produced and distributed to decision makers must be very high. The information must be available in a timely fashion. Finally, the information must be complete in its scope.

- In general, the components of an information system consist of hardware, software, and data. The hardware consists of the input, processing, output, storage, and data transmission devices. The software consists of the various programs, which are the instructions that tell the hardware components what to do and how to do it. Data, which are often stored and maintained in a database, are the objective measures of an organization's activities.

- The development of an information system is a systematic process of examining and analyzing the current activities needed to maintain organizational operations. The systems design process involves several steps including: (1) investigation, (2) systems analysis, (3) systems design, (4) systems implementation, and (5) systems maintenance. The systems development life cycle (SDLC) is a common model for how information systems evolve over time with an organization.

- Information technology has moved throughout the organization to assist at all levels of the organization. Information technology supports first-line managers in operational control activities; these include basic data processing activities such as payroll processing and general accounting. The mid-level functional aspects of managing an organization, such as routine, structured, and regularly required reports, are often processed using information technology. Even many strategic decisions and operations are now aided by technology, such as decision support systems (DSSs) and executive support systems (ESSs).

- Various types of information technology are changing the way we work. Telecommunications and networking are especially important. Electronic data interchange (EDI), and electronic funds transfer (EFT) are allowing organizations to establish and maintain business relationships without direct person-to-person contact. Telecommuting is allowing more workers to conduct business activities at home or on the road with the customer. Applications of artificial intelligence, such as expert systems and robotics, are enabling technology to do tasks that were previously done by workers. Office automation is creating a technology-supported office environment to assist in the management and processing of office work and information.

- Information technology will have an impact on management efficiency, social relationships, and the structure within an organization. Efficiency will improve only when the organization and the decision making process are reassessed and redesigned to take advantage of the capabilities of the technology. When information systems are used to enhance communication between people in the organization, there is a social impact. Finally, as more aspects of an organization become integrated into the information system, more centralization of control over computer resources may occur.

- Among the limitations of information technology are (1) the difficulty in keeping up with technological advances, (2) the potentially high cost and time involved in changing technologies, and (3) the failure of many people to take advantage of the technology because of their reluctance to change the way they work.

KEY TERMS

Data (p. 599)
Information (p. 599)
Tangible costs (p. 600)
Intangible costs (p. 600)
End users (p. 606)
Computer-aided software engineering (CASE) (p. 607)
Systems development life cycle (SDLC) (p. 609)

Organizational feasibility (p. 609)
Economic feasibility (p. 610)
Technical feasibility (p. 610)
Operational feasibility (p. 610)
Management information system (MIS) (p. 612)
Decision support system (DSS) (p. 612)
Wide area network (WAN) (p. 614)

Local area network (LAN) (p. 615)
Electronic data interchange (EDI) (p. 615)
Electronic funds transfer (EFT) (p. 615)
Telecommuting (p. 616)
Expert system (p. 618)
Robotics (p. 618)

REVIEW QUESTIONS

1. How do data and information differ? Why is this distinction important?

2. Define and explain the characteristics of useful information.

3. What are the hardware and software components of an information system?

4. List and illustrate the steps in development of an information system. Is the process linear, or is it sometimes necessary to repeat previous steps? Explain.

5. List and briefly explain the various roles information technology can have in an organization.

6. What are four types of technology that are changing the way we work? What is the anticipated long-term effect of these technologies on the organization?

7. Identify and discuss the various effects information technology can have on an organization.

8. What are some of the limitations of information technology? Briefly discuss the causes and outcomes of each type of limitation.

DISCUSSION QUESTIONS

Improving Critical Thinking

1. Assume that the library at your school wishes to install an information system. Identify the major tasks necessary for each phase of a systems design process for the library. What difficulties in design and development might you expect to encounter in each phase?

2. Explain the concept of expert systems. If it is possible to capture the knowledge of an expert and place it in a expert system, one can argue that there is no longer a need for an expert. Furthermore, if the data are in a database, the knowledge of the expert becomes permanent. It can be transferred to different settings and even reproduced through copying processes. Can an expert system produce more consistent, reproducible results than the human expert on which it is based? Why or why not? Is it desirable to seek this result. Explain.

3. What can you do to ensure that you will have the technical knowledge and skills related to information technology that are necessary to compete effectively in the job market?

Enhancing Communication Skills

4. Examine the library at your school. What major types of activities must the library support as part of its mission? Which of these activities could be computerized? Can these various activities be integrated into one larger information system? Explain. Identify additional library functions that could be computerized. To enhance your oral communication skills,

prepare a short (10–15 minute) presentation of your answer for the class.

5. What news stories dealing with information technology have appeared in the news lately? What impact do you think these new technologies will have on organizations and management? To enhance your written communication skills, write a short (1–2 page) essay in which you discuss these impacts.

Building Teamwork Skills

6. What do you think the office or organization of the future will be like? What technology do you think the office of the future will use? To refine your teamwork skills, meet with a small group of students who have been given this same assignment. Compare your visions of the office of the future, then reach a consensus about how this office will look. Select a spokesperson to present your team's vision to the rest of the class.

7. Identify several types of data that might be collected in an organization. Think about how the information that can be derived from the data would differ for each level of management. In other words, how might the various levels of management in the organization make different uses of the same basic data? To refine your teamwork skills, meet with a small group of students who have been given this same assignment. Compare your lists and then, by consensus, consolidate your lists into a single list of the best four types of data. Select a spokesperson to present your team's findings to the rest of the class.

ETHICS: TAKE A STAND

What kind of privacy rights do workers have? The rapid proliferation of information technology within many organizations is putting this question to the test.

Many organizations use electronic mail (E-mail) to communicate rapidly and easily among offices, suppliers, customers, and remote sites. Most of the computer systems that support E-mail automatically create archives of all messages that are sent. These archives are accessible to anyone with the administrative right to view the files or the technical skill to break into the system. Many organizations reserve the right to monitor the E-mail transmissions of their employees, telling new employees up front that they will be monitoring the employee's E-mail messages.

The privacy issues go well beyond monitoring E-mail messages. Employee activities can also be monitored and recorded by computer monitoring technology. For example, technology can allow a manager, even one who is miles away, to monitor employees' phone calls, read their E-mail messages, and even count the number of keystrokes an employee types in an hour or a day. The employee's activities provide a profile from which mangers, or the automated system, can draw inferences about employee performance and effectiveness.

Additional privacy issues revolve around electronically stored information concerning employees, customers, clients, and suppliers. One issue is what the company that owns that information can do with it. For example, in 1991 Lotus Development Corporation announced it would publish and sell its Marketplace: Households compact disk. This database, which was to be updated quarterly, contained names, addresses, estimated incomes, and buying habits of 120 million Americans. After this announcement, more than 30,000 letters were sent to the firm in protest. Lotus stopped the product.

The Computer Professionals for Social Responsibility (CPSR) suggest that all companies should have a policy on privacy and should inform their employees and customers of the policy. The American Civil Liberties Union opposes companies reading an employee's electronic communications. Unfortunately, the laws dealing with these issues at both the federal and state levels are confusing, inconsistent, and badly out-of-date. Alan Westin, professor of public law and government at Columbia University, suggests: "The new office calls for us to redefine the reasonable expectations of privacy—what's fair and just to do."

For Discussion

1. Should organizations have the right to view an employee's E-mail messages without the employee's permission? Explain.

2. When might it be appropriate for an organization to examine an employee's E-mail messages without first receiving the employee's permission?

3. Justify the use of technology to monitor employee activities and productivity. What are the problems that can occur with this type of monitoring?

ROBOTICS—OPPORTUNITY OR THREAT TO BLUE-COLLAR WORKERS?

**THINKING CRITICALLY
Debate the Issue**

Form teams of four or five students as directed by your instructor. Research the topic of robotics in manufacturing, identifying aspects of their use that might be viewed as opportunities for blue-collar workers and aspects that might be viewed as threats. When it is time to debate this issue in front of the class, your instructor will tell your team which position (opportunity or threat) you will be assigned.

VIDEO CASE

First Bank Systems of Minneapolis

As recently as 1990, First Bank Systems (FBS) of Minneapolis was a constant topic of conversation in the banking community. Many executives had left the bank, and newspaper stories frequently questioned the bank's ability to survive, while speculating that it might be bought out. One of FBS's biggest problems was its antiquated information systems which had been developed in a piecemeal fashion in the early 1970s. The code and the file structures in some of the data bases were home-grown and did not even conform to the industry standard. The systems for check processing and savings processing were very old, and customer records were barely capable of identifying what products FBS customers had. As an illustration of how antiquated the system was, at one point in time customers actually had to go to the bank where they were signed up if they wanted to make a deposit! Customer service agents had a particularly difficult time responding to customer inquiries. For example, if a customer called with a question about her credit card account, the customer service agent had to access the credit card system. This system was developed with its own unique mode of entry, its own format for the layout of data, and its own idiosyncracies. If that same customer were to inquire about her checking account, then another system would have to be accessed, and it too had its own unique mode of entry and unique screens. And, if there was a savings account inquiry, yet another system would be accessed.

FBS established a mission that in part could be achieved via a goal of growth through acquisition. This seemed reasonable, for the market was right for the purchase and sale of banks at that time. But, in order to acquire these banks and the new customers that would come with them, FBS's challenge was to put an information system in place that would be able to handle the additional volume. Any newly acquired banks would then be converted over to this new information system. FBS's new information system was to be a totally integrated system, having centralized customer records with a lot of knowledge about customers, their households, and the amount of business each does with FBS as a household. Six major systems would have to be replaced by this centralized system.

This would pose a formidable challenge, for there are accounts of other banks that set out to replace only their checking systems and ended up spending up to three years and $40 million on the project. FBS decided that the information system changeover should be accomplished by buying and implementing packaged software. FBS thinking was that vendor support of the software after installation would be assured if they didn't alter the packaged software.

FBS was quite efficient in their information system changeover; it replaced the six major systems in about a year and a half. In addition to the customer service advantages that accrue from its centralized information system, FBS has been able to streamline the bank acquisition process. It can convert a major bank in 21 weeks, and often needs only 13 weeks to convert smaller community banks. The FBS "cookbook" process for acquisitions greatly facilitates the growth objective of its mission.

For Discussion

1. Discuss what you feel were the levels of quality, timeliness, and completeness for the information that FBS's old information systems could provide.

2. List and describe as many areas as you can think of where you would like the new information system to be able to provide you, an FBS customer, with information on your accounts, transactions, or interactions with the bank.

3. Do you feel it was a good idea or a bad idea for FBS to restrict itself to buying and implementing packaged software? Why? (Where possible, tie the rationale for your answer to the steps in the development of a management information system.)

CASE

WCB Enterprises

Lisa Fisher is in charge of marketing, sales, and purchasing for WCB Enterprises, a small company that manufactures a number of products that are sold primarily in retail stores. Lisa loves her job because of the variety and challenge involved. She is very good with people—customers, suppliers, and co-workers alike. As part of her job, Lisa has to travel to industry and sales conferences. These trips usually last no longer than two days, so she rarely falls more than a day or so behind company activities. This last trip, however, lasted a week because of a business-related

side trip. On her return, Lisa found that she was facing more problems than usual.

Late this past Thursday, after Lisa left for her trip, one of the primary suppliers for WCB lost its main manufacturing facility due to a fire. Lisa did not find out about this until very late on Friday evening while she was still traveling. This past Monday, while making a sales call, Lisa heard on the radio that one of WCB's other suppliers had just shut down because of a strike. Other unions were honoring the strike, so deliveries from the supplier had essentially stopped.

Today, a Thursday, was Lisa's first day back in the office. Usually, after a trip of this length, Lisa would find a few phone messages and some correspondence to catch up on. This time, however, she found a stack of phone messages from concerned customers that had accumulated while she was gone. WCB, a relatively small operation, had never really faced a crisis before. WCB had only an informal answering service, with no specific mechanism for relaying phone messages to employees away from the office; thus, its procedures were not well organized for communicating with an employee who was out of town.

Lisa spent the whole morning trying to respond to the phone messages. In many cases, she had to contact others at WCB to find out about supplies, shipping, and so forth. Sometimes she was successful in reaching her co-workers; other times no one answered. To compound her problems, Lisa realized that WCB was heading into its busiest time of the year—the months leading up to Christmas, the busiest time of the year for retailers.

As Lisa picked up the phone once again, she realized that she really had very little information at her disposal. She was good at her job, but because of her absence from the office for a business trip, she was behind on her information. The problems of the suppliers made the situation even worse. Lisa realized that she would have to obtain a great deal of information from others before she would be able to respond to the questions of her callers and of those who would call in the coming days. She could solve this problem, but she wanted to make sure it never happened again. Before leaving late Thursday night, she made a note to herself to encourage WCB to reexamine its system of providing information within the company.

For Discussion

1. What problems did Lisa have in getting the information she needed to make decisions and answer questions from customers? What, if anything, do you think Lisa could have done to avoid these problems?

2. How could information technology be used to support Lisa in her job? How would your suggestions affect her relationships with her customers? Her suppliers? Her co-workers?

3. If you were Lisa, what kind of approach would you make to your superiors to help them understand your need for better technology support? What would you ask for?

EXPERIENTIAL EXERCISE 18.1

What Technology Do You Need?

The purpose of this exercise is to explore the variety of options available to support you as a traveling businessperson.

Step 1. Assume you are a mid-level manager for a moderate-sized organization. A significant portion of your job is to travel to meet with clients. You travel more than 100,000 miles a year, with trips ranging from a day to 10 to 14 days for important contracts. Since your office is on the road as much as it is at headquarters, you need to be able to accomplish your job while traveling.

Step 2. Your task is to identify your hardware and software needs. Then investigate your options as if you were really going to purchase the required equipment. Remember that system compatibility and reliability are important. In addition, remember that you will be carrying this equipment with you along with your luggage. Therefore, weight is also an important factor. You may also be using this equipment to assist you in presentations to potential clients and current customers. Therefore, a quality system display is also a factor to consider.

Step 3. Discuss your conclusion with others in your class.

For Discussion

1. What kind of tradeoffs did you find yourself making in order to make your final selection of hardware and software? What hardware and software did you select?

2. What assumptions did you make about your job in the initial stages of working on this situation? What additional information would have been useful?

3. What maximum weight and cost limits, if any, did you use?

4. How did your decisions differ from those of others?

EXPERIENTIAL EXERCISE 18.2

Learning about E-Mail

If you have not done so before this time, see if you can acquire an account on your school's computer. Once this has been accomplished, learn about and try to use the E-mail system. With several of your classmates, explore the benefits, limitations, and difficulties of working via E-mail.

Step 1. Acquire a computer account and learn how to use the E-mail facility.

Step 2. Conduct a discussion/debate with several of your classmates using the E-mail facilities. As the discussion progresses, be aware of the problems of using E-mail to communicate

about and coordinate activities. Keep a list of your comments and observations.

Step 3. Discuss how E-mail can enhance and limit organizational communication. Develop a list of suggestions for an organization that is attempting to use E-mail to improve organizational effectiveness.

For Discussion

1. How difficult was it to become comfortable with E-mail?

2. How effective was the E-mail in supporting your discussion? What were the benefits? What were the limiting factors?

NOTES

1. "Reengineering Aetna," *Forbes ASAP*, A Technology Supplement to Forbes Magazine, June 7, 1993, 78–86.

2. "Information Technology, Special Report," *Fortune*, Autumn 1993, 15.

3. "Welcome to the Revolution," *Fortune*, December 13, 1993, 66–78.

4. L. M. Grossman, "Federal Express, UPS Face Off On Computers," *Wall Street Journal*, September 17, 1993, p. B1 +; *Blueprints for Service Quality: Federal Express Approach*, AMA Management Briefing, American Management Association, New York, 1991; R. A. Sigafoos, *Absolutely Positively Overnight!: Wall Street's Darling Inside and Up Close* (Memphis, St. Luke's Press), 1983.

5. "Can Bell Atlantic and TCI Pull It Off?" *Business Communications Review* 23 (November 1993): 8–10; and "Bell-Ringer," *Business Week*, October 25, 1993, 32–36.

6. J. L. Whitten, L. D. Bentley, and V. M. Barlow, *Systems Analysis and Design Methods*, 2d ed. (Homewood, Ill.: Irwin, 1989).

7. E. W. Martin, D. DeHayes, J. Hoffer, and W. Perkins, *Managing Information Technology: What Managers Need to Know* (New York: Macmillian, 1991), 299.

8. R. J. Benjamin, *Control of the Information Systems Development Cycle* (New York: Wiley-Interscience, 1971.)

9. D. Amoroso and P. Cheney, "Testing a Causal Model of End User Applications Effectiveness," *Journal of Management Information Systems* (Summer 1991); and K. Christoff, *Managing the Information Center* (Glenview, Ill.: Scott, Foresman/Little Brown, 1990.)

10. J. A. O'Brien, *Management Information Systems: A Managerial End User Perspective*, 2d ed. (Homewood, Ill.: Irwin, 1993.)

11. R. R. Panko, *End User Computing: Management, Applications, and Technology* (New York: John Wiley, 1988).

12. L. Fried, "A Blueprint for Change," *Computerworld*, December 2, 1991.

13. H. R. Shrednick, R. J. Shutt, and M. Weiss, "Empowerment: Key to IS World-Class Quality," *MIS Quarterly* 16 (1992): 491–505.

14. E. Turban, *Decision Support and Expert Systems: Management Support Systems*, 3d ed. (New York: Macmillan, 1993).

15. J. Rockart and D. DeLong, *Executive Support Systems: The Emergence of Top Management Computer Use* (Homewood, Ill.: Dow-Jones-Irwin, 1988).

16. "Welcome to the Revolution."

17. W. Stallings and R. Van Slyke, *Business Data Communications*, 2d ed. (New York: Macmillan, 1994).

18. "The Strategic Value of EDI," *I/S Analyzer*, August 1989.

19. S. Sherman, "How to Bolster the Bottom Line," *Fortune Information Technology Special Report*, Autumn 1993, pp. 15–28.

20. "Welcome to the Revolution."

21. "Information Technology, Special Report."

22. "The Race to Rewire," *Fortune*, April 19, 1993, 42–61.

23. "Buildings, Roads Fall in Tremblers Onslaught," *Orlando Sentinel*, January 18, 1994, A1 +.

24. Turban, *Decision Support and Expert Systems*.

25. O'Brien, *Management Information Systems*.

26. Ibid.

27. "Computer use by Illiterates Grows at Work," *Wall Street Journal*, June 9, 1992, B1, B5; and T. L. O'Brien, "A PC Revolution: Aided by Computers, Many of the Disabled Form Own Businesses," *Wall Street Journal*, October 8, 1993, A1, A9.

28. "Welcome to the Revolution."

29. D. Schuler, guest editor, "Social Computing," *Communi-*

cations of the ACM, Special Issue, January 1994.

30. "Welcome to the Revolution."

31. F. Niederman, J. C. Brancheau, and J. C. Wetherbe, "In-

formation Systems Management Issues for the 1990s," *MIS Quarterly* (December 1991): 475–500.

32. "Reengineering Aetna."

IBAX: Ensuring Quality and Financial Performance Through Controls

As you know, we have been following the progress of IBAX throughout the book. Recall that IBAX, a partnership between IBM and Baxter, had experienced significant performance problems since its inception in 1989. Jeff Goodman, who was appointed CEO of IBAX in early 1991, was charged with turning the company around. As we saw in the cohesion cases at the close of Parts II, III, and IV of the book, the turnaround required significant changes in the strategy of the company, the way it was organized, and the ways the people of the organization were managed. In this cohesion case, we will examine how the managerial function of control was affected by the retrenchment strategy. As we will see, the implementation of the retrenchment strategy required changes in quality and productivity controls, as well as financial and budgetary controls. Each of these controls first required the establishment of standards against which current performance could be compared.

ESTABLISHMENT OF STANDARDS

In the case at the close of Part II, we briefly noted that the development and implementation of clear performance standards were crucial to the success of the IBAX retrenchment strategy. PMOs (Performance Management Objectives) were established in four main areas: profitability, customer satisfaction, product commitments and delivery to customers, and human resource management. To help establish standards in some of these critical areas, IBAX relied heavily on benchmarking, a process by which a company reviews the performance of other companies in the same industry (or comparable industries) to help establish its own performance standards. IBAX developed comparisons on such measures as revenue per employee, return on assets, asset turnover, and a variety of other financial ratios. In the human resource area, IBAX examined what other companies were achieving in employee turnover, compensation levels, award programs, and other areas that contributed to the overall atmosphere and motivation within the company. To help get a better feel for appropriate quality and customer satisfaction levels, IBAX looked at other software vendors to see how they handled installations, support, incoming call rates, and so forth. In short, IBAX had a benchmarking perspective that was geared not just toward financial performance itself, but toward several operational variables that made financial performance effective.

QUALITY CONTROL

One of IBAX's most significant problems was in the area of product quality. The company did not deliver products that met the expectations and needs of its customers. As a result, customer satisfaction was extremely low. In fact, the relationship between the company and its customers had been described by some as "adversarial." Goodman learned just how serious product quality and customer problems were when he attended IBAX's first users group meeting. Not only was attendance at the meeting poor, but those who did attend were hostile toward the company and its employees.

To address quality control at IBAX, Goodman began with a thorough assessment of the product quality and customer satisfaction problems. The assessment indicated that most of the problems were a function of inaccurate base code, ineffective product training for customers, a general lack of understanding on the part of customers, and/or the company's failure to meet commitments for product delivery. Once the problems had been identified, intervention strategies to correct the problems were developed. Measurement systems were designed to ensure that the intervention strategies were effective. For example, customer satisfaction was measured by monitoring the calls coming into the company's client support center and assessing their nature. The time it took to resolve customer's problems was also measured. On the development side, time schedules and delivery dates were very carefully monitored. These kinds of specific, quantifiable measures were put in place around the quality improvement effort.

As product quality improved, so did productivity and financial performance. The time that was formerly spent correcting problems and dealing with customer complaints was redirected toward much more productive efforts. As customer satisfaction improved, revenues increased. Improving quality control had a tremendous effect on the overall performance of the company.

FINANCIAL CONTROLS

As we know, prior to Jeff Goodman, financial information was open only to the senior management of the company. The budgeting process was top down. The chief financial officer (CFO) distributed budgets to functional areas. There was very little interaction between the CFO and the department leaders, and as a result, the departments felt little ownership of the budget. Further, very little thought was given to the allocation of resources between departments. Budgets were based largely on previous-year allocations.

Goodman changed all that. First, he implemented his "open book" philosophy of financial management and provided employees with access to all critical financial information. Then he changed the top-down budgeting approach to a fully integrated, bottom-up budgeting process in which everyone who had any opportunity to touch either expenses or revenues was involved in the budgeting process.

Goodman started by decentralizing the finance function to the business unit level. This required the development of new positions—Business Unit Control Analysts. These individuals played both an advisory role for the business unit teams and a liaison role between the business units and the central finance group. With the help of the Business Unit Control Analysts, the business unit teams developed their own budgets and budgetary controls. In doing so, they sought to understand exactly what was driving revenues and expenses. They knew they would be held accountable for delivery against these preestablished measures of revenues and expenses, so they kept their focus on the drivers—not just on a quarterly or semiannual basis, but on a day-to-day basis. The development of these measurement systems was invaluable in getting the teams to focus on the things that really affected the performance of the business.

THE RESULTS

As we have seen, Goodman put the focus on metrics—ways to measure product quality, customer satisfaction, and financial performance. Benchmarking was used to establish appropriate standards of performance in these areas. Although the IBAX benchmarking efforts revealed that the company's performance measures were poor by any standards, the benchmarks did have a beneficial effect. Seeing how good they could be helped to energize and motivate people to strive for improvement.

Goodman established that employees would be responsible and accountable for delivering revenue and expense numbers that were compatible with standards, and that they would be empowered to make decisions to achieve the company's objectives. It was then that employees really began to pay attention to their contribution margins and the things that drove the revenue and expense components. They began to manage them on a day-to-day basis rather than on a quarterly or semiannual basis. Budgets improved once managers more thoroughly understood the cost and revenue components. Now these managers do the planning up front going into the fiscal year, since they will be held accountable for the dollars they spend throughout the year.

IBAX has also learned that quality and productivity are inextricably linked—improvements in quality lead directly to improvements in productivity. Real productivity improvements do not come by asking employees to work faster and produce more. Instead, IBAX found that the keys to improving quality were doing things better (not faster), ensuring that employees understood what they were trying to do, and delivering products that work. Delivering things on time and having them work have improved customer satisfaction and enabled IBAX to get new products on the market more quickly. Meanwhile, the corresponding reduction in human resource hours expended to correct problems and fix things that did not work correctly has resulted in productivity improvements for IBAX.

For Discussion:

1. Discuss the extent to which IBAX appears to have incorporated the various steps in the control process (presented in Chapter 16) in its attempts to improve both its financial position and the quality of its products and services.

2. Do you feel that it was important for IBAX to engage in benchmarking? Discuss the reasoning behind your response.

3. What potential benefits are associated with IBAX's improved quality? Indicate which benefits might enhance productivity, and discuss how they would lead to such a productivity increase. Also, discuss additional potential benefits that might occur as a result of these quality and productivity enhancements.

IBAX: A New Beginning

When Jeff Goodman joined IBAX in 1991, the future of the organization looked very bleak. The company had lost millions of dollars, product quality was poor, customer satisfaction was devastatingly low, and employee commitment was non-existent. But by the close of 1993, things had changed—dramatically. The company posted a profit of $2.1 million and financial projections for 1994 were favorable; product quality and customer service were greatly enhanced; productivity had been improved significantly; and the employees of IBAX were dedicated to making it a profitable and prosperous organization. What happened to cause such a turnaround? Many say it was strong leadership and a focus on using contemporary management practices to achieve success.

When Goodman and the IBAX partners (IBM and Baxter) realized that the company was no longer in danger of total collapse, they turned their attention to the long-term future. The company, though successful, was only the sixth largest player in an industry where economies of size and scope are critical. Consequently, IBAX appeared to have only two choices—become a larger company through the acquisition of competitors in the industry or be acquired by a bigger company that was large enough to compete effectively within the industry.

After much deliberation, it was determined that IBAX would be more successful as part of a larger organization. On June 1, 1994, IBAX was acquired by HBOC, an Atlanta-based company that is the market leader in the health care information systems industry. Although HBOC would not have been interested in acquiring IBAX in 1991, the company had become an attractive acquisition candidate by 1993. Goodman met his management challenge—he turned IBAX into a viable and prosperous organization.

APPENDIX

Career Development and Management

This appendix is designed to provide an overview of some important issues for you to consider as you begin thinking about entering a profession and developing plans for your lifetime of employment. Career development and management can help you take a proactive approach to planning and managing your career and can also help managers and organizations understand the experiences of their employees.

Since your job will be a major part of your life, you need to like what you are doing. According to Malcolm Forbes, former publisher of *Forbes* magazine, the foremost quality in selecting a career is to really love what you are doing. If you love it, you will do it well.[1]

But what exactly is meant by a career? We will suggest some answers and then examine the traditional career stages approach to career development and management. It is also possible to take alternative approaches to careers, and we will explore some of these before discussing a few current career management strategies. Finally, we conclude with some tactics and advice on achieving career success.

WHAT IS A CAREER?

A **career** is the individually perceived sequence of attitudes and behaviors associated with work-related experiences, activities, and positions over the span of a person's life.[2] As such, a career involves movement within an organization (such as moving up the organizational ladder) and between organizations, as well as the attitudes and behaviors that are associated with ongoing work-related activities and experiences. People build careers by moving among various jobs in different fields and organizations.

CAREER STAGES

The traditional and most common way to discuss career development and management is to view a career as a series of stages as shown in Figure 1. Regardless of the type of work or occupation, individuals typically move through four distinct career stages during their working lives: exploration and testing, establishment and advancement, maintenance, and withdrawal.[3]

EXPLORATION AND TESTING

The exploration and testing stage usually corresponds to the early years of an individual's career. During this period, the individual explores talents, inter-

▼ **FIGURE 1**
Career Stages

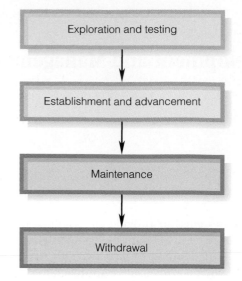

ests, and values; tries to find a good fit or match between career and self-image; makes an initial choice of an occupation; and attempts to become established. Once the individual joins an organization, the orientation and socialization process by the organization and his or her peers is extremely important. **Socialization** is the process by which the newcomer is transformed from an outsider into an effective member of the organization.[4] For example, most organizations conduct an orientation program that introduces the new employee to the requirements of the job, the social environment in which he or she will work, and the organization's policies, rules, and procedures, as well as to key individuals, norms, and culture. Though orientation programs vary widely depending on the organization, the process itself is vital at this career stage.

During this career stage, the individual is often expected to follow directions and to play the role of a helper or a learner. A good supervisor provides a coaching relationship, feedback, guidance, and opportunities that will increase levels of understanding.

ESTABLISHMENT AND ADVANCEMENT

During the establishment and advancement stage, the individual first establishes career goals and strives to achieve them and then is heavily oriented toward building a record of significant accomplishments that relate to success.[5] The individual depends on her or his supervisor to provide challenging assignments and furnish feedback about performance. Many individuals begin to form a specific career strategy in this stage and ideally will find a mentor to assist them. They are likely to be involved in special assignments, transfers, and promotions and to become more visible to higher management. They often become specialized, develop an expertise in one area, acquire professional standing, and take on greater organizational responsibilities. Key relationships are now with peers and peer groups. The major personal issue at this time is the conflict that may develop between the career and the individual's personal life—spouse, family, and other nonwork interests.

MAINTENANCE

Movement into the maintenance stage is often associated with professional accomplishments, progress up the organizational hierarchy, high involvement in the job, and the responsibility for training and directing others. This is also a time when most managers review their careers and may become concerned because they have not achieved all the personal and work goals they had planned. They may reaffirm or modify earlier career goals and attempt to cope with unfulfilled dreams, a sense of lost youth, or prospects of mortality. For other managers, this stage is a time for finding ways to continue growing rather than stagnating or allowing their skills to become obsolete.

WITHDRAWAL

The main tasks during the withdrawal stage involve remaining a productive contributor with a strong sense of self-worth, developing and training possible successors, and completing major long-term projects and assignments. Supervisors should provide a lot of freedom and autonomy to complete these tasks. An individual in this career stage must develop a self-image that does not include work and is based on his or her life and activities outside work.

These four stages are simply general guidelines to the major career phases that individuals are likely to encounter. It is important to note that individuals pass through these stages at various ages. Rather than comprising a rigid progression, the stages simply provide some basic notions about the ways careers are likely to unfold and the means by which individuals address career issues at different stages in their lives.[6]

Individuals may make major changes in direction during the course of their careers and revert to earlier stages as they pursue alternative goals, accept new jobs, join other organizations, and progress through adult developmental stages that provide unique challenges. Because work and personal life are inseparable, a person's career experiences cannot be understood without also examining her or his personal experiences.[7]

CAREER SUCCESS

Career success is subjective because ultimately it is the individual who must decide whether he or she has been successful. Though success sometimes is framed in terms of advancement, career specialists increasingly emphasize that individuals should establish their own criteria for success and that those criteria can be as diverse as pay, adventure, challenges, or helping others.

In recent years, relatively slow growth in the economy has combined with the large number of baby boomers entering mid-career to limit severely the opportunities for promotion into upper-level management. As a result, success, which formerly was based solely on upward mobility in the organization, has been redefined. Four alternative career concepts that serve as models for the "ideal career" have been identified:[8]

1. *Linear career:* An individual decides on a field early in life, develops a plan for upward mobility, and executes it. The linear career is often linked to a need for achievement and power.
2. *Steady-state career:* An individual selects a specific field of work and may continue to improve professionally and financially within that field. The steady-state career-driven person does not necessarily strive to move up the corporate hierarchy, but may remain at the same level of the organization indefinitely. This career concept is motivated by a need for security and the desire to maintain a role in society.
3. *Spiral career:* An individual views a career as a series of infrequent but major shifts into different fields of work. Within each occupation the per-

son works hard and excels in status and rank before moving on to new opportunities and challenges. Individuals are motivated by a need for personal growth.

4. *Transitory career:* The individual explores alternatives while seeking to find a career identity. Transitory career individuals are often troubleshooters who are driven by the novelty and challenge of problem solving. These individuals are motivated by a need for independence and identity and often drift from one occupation to another with no particular pattern.

STRATEGIES FOR CAREER MANAGEMENT

Career management is a lifelong process of learning about yourself as well as about various jobs and orgnaizations. Career management involves setting personal goals, developing strategies for achieving goals, and revising goals based on work and life experiences.[9] Most career experts suggest that individuals are primarily responsible for their own career management. One of the most important trends in American society is the new determination of many people to control their own career destinies and take full responsibility for their careers.[10]

Nevertheless, organizations also need to be involved in career management. Why would an organization be interested in careers or spend time on the career management of its employees? Effective career management results in a long-term fit between the individual and the organization. As we observed earlier, an individual's career is a process or sequence of work-related experiences. The organization has an important stake in the individual's career process, and its needs must be matched with the employee's needs and career goals. To the extent that the matching is done well, the organization is more effective and productive, and the individual is better satisfied, happier, and more successful.

Individuals can engage in career development and management on their own or in conjunction with career development programs sponsored by their organizations. Most organizations use informal career planning by human resource staff members. Career counseling may be a useful addition to an individual's efforts.

Significant reductions in the layers of middle management, restructuring, and rightsizing are common trends in many organizations. As a consequence, many individuals have been thrown off their career tracks. With more people competing for fewer promotions, individuals are likely to find themselves plateaued, at least periodically. A **career plateau** is a point in an individual's career where the likelihood of future promotion to a higher-level position is very low. Many professionals are attempting to overcome plateaus by: (1) using career counseling, (2) developing a strong network of other professionals, (3) becoming adaptable and less specialized, and (4) learning to be a team player.[11]

USING CAREER COUNSELING

Using personality and aptitude tests, career counselors help clients assess their skills and character traits. These are combined into a vocational profile that is matched with job options. Next, counselors help their clients target a field or job and determine how to transfer their skills, based on how much risk they can accept. The final step is a plan of action to get a new job. If the client does not want to change companies or professions, a counselor may recommend creating a special project to enhance the individual's value to the company or networking with other departments to make a lateral move.

Career counselors may charge $50 to $150 an hour and usually recommend 4 to 10 sessions. Some specialize in a field such as business or law, most counselors handle a broad range of professions. You can find career counselors through the yellow pages, personal contacts, university continuing educational programs, or the National Association for Career Development.

DEVELOP A STRONG PROFESSIONAL NETWORK

Networking is a determined effort to meet other professionals with the goal of building a valuable resource of professional experience, knowledge, and friendship.[12] It involves developing collegial relationships with others because you need to know them and they need to know you. Networking can be described as congeniality at work. Successful professionals develop and nurture active friendships with a large and varied group of professionals. They make it a point to maintain periodic contact with each other and to share information.

Networking is most often conducted by telephone, fax, and computer networks. It is a two-way professional friendship that is focused on an exchange of ideas, new information, and new contacts. It is being genuinely interested in what others do and know.

Professional networks are vast interconnections that provide a huge intellectual resource. They are assets that provide access to talent, skills, experiences, innovations, and progressive action.

Most professionals devote a large portion of their workday to interacting with coworkers and a broad spectrum of other people. Every active professional has compiled a substantial list of phone numbers. Each of these phone numbers represents access to a potential networkee—a prospective adjunct to your network.

Building a network is a valuable and necessary strategy in career management. The following points may help you build your own network:[13]

- Join national organizations in your field and related areas. Become active in local and national organizations by attending meetings and conferences. Join committees, volunteer, and get involved.
- When you attend meetings, go up to people and introduce yourself. Show an interest in them and what they do.
- Exchange business cards with everyone you meet.
- Ask questions and learn to be an effective listener. Reinforce discussions and questions with your comments, opinions, and related experience.
- Develop strong relationships within your own company. Walk around and talk to people at their work stations. Show interest in their work. Be friendly, assertive, and congenial.
- Keep notes on the people you meet and talk to on the phone to remind you of the encounter.

As you build your professional network contacts, look down as well as up. Offering to help less powerful people is a highly effective career management and advancement strategy.

BECOME ADAPTABLE AND LESS SPECIALIZED

According to a recent article in *Fortune*, workers will be rewarded in the future for knowledge and adaptability. That notion translates to less emphasis on career specialization and more on generalization. A key career management strategy is to be flexible and willing to move from one function to another by integrating diverse disciplines and perspectives. Individuals who can operate comfortably in a variety of environments will fare better than those locked into the mind-set of a particular corporate or even national culture. People will need the ability not only to learn fundamental new skills but also to un-learn outdated ways.

LEARN TO BE A TEAM PLAYER

With teamwork predicted to become a dominant form of organizational design, a critical career management strategy is to learn to become an effective team player. Team designs require managers to share more power with people they once regarded as subordaintes, and employees of lower rank are now experiencing increased responsibility. This means people skills have become extremely important, and even leaders will have to learn how to follow. As the paired forces of globalization and information technology increase the likelihood that teams will be working together across great distances, strong interpersonal and team player skills will be in demand.

TACTICS FOR CAREER SUCCESS

Regardless of how a career is defined, the following five tactics have been identified as important for career success:[14]

1. *Do excellent work.* High-quality performance and excellent work are the basics of a successful career. Though political savvy can sometimes give an average performer an advantage, politics can backfire. As a rule, the better the work, the greater are the chances of being promoted and given greater authority and responsibility.

2. *Increase your visibility.* To be rewarded for your performance, you have to be sure your superiors know about it. Some specific strategies for becoming visible are listed in Table 1. You can increase your visibility by taking or seeking a job with high visibility. A visible job has these characteristics:

   - Few rules and regulations.
   - Many rewards for unusual and/or innovative performance.
   - Many contacts with senior management; opportunities for participation in conferences and problem-solving task forces.
   - Relationships that cross departmental lines.

3. *Be mobile.* Mobility includes being flexible as well as being prepared to move. Experience in different functional departments (accounting, marketing, production, engineering, human resources) will help you develop a variety of skills needed to become a general manager. Take on new jobs or tasks and work with a variety of people. Experience at different geographical locations within the company can lead to an understanding

▼ TABLE 1   Strategies for Being Visible

1. Send memos to your superiors when projects have been completed.
2. Submit periodic progress reports.
3. Actively solicit and use feedback.
4. Get assigned to special high-impact projects and task forces.
5. Pay honest compliments to people.
6. Volunteer for a variety of assignments.

of the organization as a whole and may attract the attention of top management. Keep in mind that mobility usually has some costs, especially personal ones.

4. *Find a mentor.* A higher-level manager can be a powerful mentor. Most successful managers have had several mentors and have learned valuable lessons from each. Having more than one mentor also minimizes the danger that you will be identified too closely with a single mentor. Keep in mind that having a single mentor is one reason why some executives fail to advance. Having a variety of mentors can help you learn how to motivate various types of people and develop a sensitivity to their needs. Notably, managers most often learn what *not* to do from their mentors.

5. *Avoid deadwood.* Incompetent supervisors can hinder a career because they may not appreciate your abilities. Furthermore, their recommendations will not be taken seriously, because they themselves have been bypassed. Asking for a transfer to escape deadwood can be ineffective in some companies because it is considered a sign of disloyalty. A better method is to make sure a superior in another department knows of your work and availability and let that manager arrange the transfer.

Developing a successful career doesn't happen by accident. It takes planning and hard work to become a successful professional. Those who are willing to put forth the effort needed to develop their careers will be the successful managers of the future.

NOTES

1. For more specific information about how to choose the career that is right for you, see R. N. Bolles, *What Color Is Your Parachute?* (Berkeley, Calif.: Ten Speed Press, 1993); and C. Carter, *Majoring in the Rest of Your Life* (New York: Noonday Press, 1992.)

2. D. T. Hall, *Careers in Organizations* (Santa Monica, Calif.: Goodyear, 1976).

3. D. E. Super and D. T. Hall, "Career Development: Exploration and Planning," in M. R. Rosenzweig and L. W. Porter, eds., *Annual Review of Psychology, 29* (Palo Alto, Calif.: Annual Reviews, 1978); and D. T. Hall and Associates, *Career Development in Organizations* (San Francisco: Jossey-Bass, 1986).

4. D. C. Feldman, "The Multiple Socialization of Organizational Members," *Academy of Management Review* 6 (1981): 309–18.

5. J. Zahrly and H. Tosi, "The Differential Effect of Organizational Induction Process on Early Work Role Adjustment," *Journal of Organizational Behavior* 10 (1989): 59–74.

6. L. Baird and K. Kram, "Career Dynamics: Managing the Superior/Subordinate Relationship," *Organizational Dynamics* 11 (1983): 3–13.

7. For more specific information about the relationship between stages of adult development and career issues, see the variety of books and articles of D. J. Levinson and G. Sheehy.

8. M. J. Driver, "Career Concepts and Career Management in Organizations," in C. L. Cooper, ed., *Behavioral Problems in Organizations* (Englewood Cliffs, N.J.: Prentice-Hall, 1979).

9. J. H. Greenhaus, *Career Management* (Hinsdale, Ill.: CBS College Press, 1987).

10. S. Sherman, "A Brave New Darwinian Workplace," *Fortune*, January 25, 1993, 50–56.

11. "Getting Ahead: Jump-Starts for Stalled Careers," *Business Weekly*, July 1, 1992, 92; and Sherman, "A Brave New Darwinian Workplace."

12. W. E. Baker, *Networking Smart, How to Build Relationships for Personal and Organizational Success* (New York: McGraw-Hill, 1994).

13. A. Barber, and L. Waymon, *Great Connections: Small Talk and Networking for Business People* (New York: Impact Publications, 1992); L. Harrisberger, *Succeeding: How to Become an Outstanding Professional* (New York: Macmillan, 1994); O. Edwards, *Upward Nobility: How to Rise High in Business without Losing Your Soul* (New York: Crown Publishing, 1994); and Baker, *Networking Smart.*

14. K. C. Green and D. T. Seymour, *Who's Going to Run General Motors?* (Princeton, N.J.: Peterson's Guides, 1991).

GLOSSARY

Accountability   Employees must justify their decisions and actions with regard to the task they have been assigned.

Achievement-oriented leadership   Setting challenging goals, seeking performance improvements, emphasizing excellence in performance, and showing confidence.

Activity ratios   Indicators of performance with respect to key activities defined by management.

Adaptive organizations (horizontal corporation)   Organizations that eliminate bureaucracy that limits employee creativity and brings the decision makers of the organization closer to the customer.

Administrative management   Focuses on the managers and the functions they perform.

Affiliation need   The desire for friendship, love, and a feeling of belonging.

Aggregate planning   Link between the more general business planning activities and the more specific master planning activities.

Alternative courses of action   Strategies that might be implemented in a decision-making situation.

Artifacts   Cultural routines that form the substance of public functions and events staged by the organization.

Assessment center   A controlled environment used to predict the probable success of job applicants based on their behaviors in simulated situations.

Assets   The things of value that an individual or organization owns.

Attitudes   Relatively lasting beliefs, feelings, and behavioral tendencies held by a person about specific objects, events, groups, issues, or persons.

Authoritarianism   The tendency to adhere rigidly to conventional values, readily obey recognized authority, be concerned with toughness and power, and oppose the use of feelings.

Authority   The formal right of an employee to marshall resources and make decisions necessary to fulfill work responsibilities.

Autonomy   The degree to which job holders have freedom, independence, and decision making authority.

Balance sheet   Summary of an organization's financial position at a given point in time, showing assets, liabilities, and owner's equity.

BCG matrix   Business portfolio matrix that uses market growth rate and relative market share as the indicators of the firm's strategic position.

Behavior modification   The application of reinforcement theory that managers can use to motivate employees.

Behavioral approach   What the leader does is the primary variable that determines effectiveness.

Behavioral decision model   A descriptive framework for understanding that a person's cognitive ability to process information is limited.

Boundary-spanning roles   Lateral relationships that help to integrate and coordinate the activities of the organization (i.e., liaisons, committees, task forces, integrating positions, and interfunctional work teams).

Bounded rationality   Recognizes that people are limited by such organizational constraints as time, information, resources and their own mental capacities.

Brainstorming   A technique used to enhance creativity that encourages group members to generate as many novel ideas as possible on a given topic without evaluating them.

Breakeven analysis   A graphic display of the relationship between volume of output and revenue and costs.

Budgets   Single-use plans that specify how financial resources should be allocated.

Bureaucratic control   Use of formal mechanisms to influence behavior, assess performance, and correct unacceptable deviations from standards.

Bureaucratic management   Focuses on the overall organizational system.

Business ethics   The application of general ethics to business behavior.

Business portfolio matrix   Two-dimensional grid that compares the strategic positions of each of the organization's businesses.

Business strategy   Defines how each business unit in the firm's corporate portfolio will operate in its market arena.

Cash cows   Businesses that fall into the low market growth/high market share cell of a BCG matrix.

Centralized communication network   Communication that flows through a centralized group member.

Chain of command   The line of authority and responsibility that flows throughout the organization.

Changing   The second step in the change process focusing on learning new required behaviors.

Charismatic authority   Subordinates voluntarily comply with a leader because of her special personal qualities or abilities.

Classical perspective   The oldest formal viewpoints of management, it includes the scientific management approach, the administrative management approach, and the bureaucratic management approach.

Closed systems   Systems that do not interact with the environment.

Code of ethics   The general value system, principles, and specific rules that a company follows.

Coercive power   The power to discipline, punish, and withhold rewards.

Cohesiveness   The strength of the members' desires to remain in the group.

Communication   A process in which one person or group transmits some type of information to another person or group.

Communication network   A pattern of information flow

among task group members.

Compensation   Wages paid directly for time worked (base pay), incentives for better performance, and indirect benefits that employees receive as part of their employment relationship with the organization.

Competitive advantage   Any aspect of an organization that distinguishes it from its competitors in a positive way.

Computer-aided software engineering (CASE)   Tools that allow system developers to create prototype screens and report generators rapidly and easily.

Conceptual skills   The ability to analyze complex situations and respond effectively to the challenges faced by the organization.

Concurrent control   Focuses on the transformation process to ensure that it is functioning properly.

Consideration   The degree of trust, friendship, and respect extended to subordinates.

Constraints   Algebraic statements, in equation form, that reflect any restrictions on the decision maker's flexibility in making decision choices.

Contingency perspective   A view that proposes that there is no one best approach to management for all situations.

Contingency planning   Development of two or more plans based on different strategic operating conditions.

Contingency theories   Examine the fit between the leader's behavior and the situations in which they manage.

Continuous flow production system   Produces high volume of output that flows in a continuous stream.

Continuous schedule of reinforcement   Rewarding a desired behavior each time it occurs.

Controlling   Monitoring the performance of the organization, identifying deviations between planned and actual results, and taking corrective action when necessary.

Controls   The mechanisms used to monitor the organization's performance relative to its goals and plans.

Corporate social responsibility   The interaction between business and the social enviornment in which it exists.

Corporate strategy   Decisions and actions that define the portfolio of business units that an organization maintains.

Cost leadership strategy   A strategy for competing on the basis of price.

Current assets   Items that can be converted into cash in a short time period.

Current liabilities   Debts that must be paid in the near future.

Customer divisional structure   A structure in which the tasks of the organization are grouped according to customer segments.

Data   Raw facts or details that represent some type of transaction or activity within an organization.

Debt ratios   Indicators of the firm's ability to handle long-term debt.

Decentralized communication network   Communication that flows to all group members equally.

Decision making   The process through which managers identify and resolve problems and capitalize on opportunities.

Decision support system (DSS)   Focuses on assisting decision makers in analyzing and solving semi-structured problems.

Decision tree   A branching diagram that illustrates the alternatives and states of nature for a decision situation.

Decision variables   The factors that the decision maker can manipulate.

Decisional roles   The manager's responsibility for processing information and reaching conclusions.

Decoding   The translation of received messages into interpreted meanings.

Delegation   The process of transferring the responsibility for a specific activity or task to another member of the organization and empowering that individual to accomplish the task effectively.

Delphi technique   Uses experts to make predictions and forecasts about future events without meeting face-to-face.

Devil's advocacy   An individual or subgroup appointed to critique a proposed course of action and identify problems to consider before the decision is final.

Dialectical inquiry   Approaches a decision from two opposite points and structures a debate between conflicting views.

Differentiation strategy   A strategy for competing by offering products or services that are differentiated from those of competitors.

Directive leadership   Letting subordinates know what they are expected to do, giving specific guidance, asking subordinates to follow rules and procedures, scheduling and coordinating work.

Diversity   The heterogeneity of the work force in terms of gender, race, nationality, and ethnicity.

Divisional structure   Members of the organization are grouped on the basis of common products, geographic markets, or customers served.

Dogmatism   The tendency to be closed-minded, see the world as a threatening place, regard legitimate authority as absolute, and accept or reject others according to agreement with the accepted authority.

Dogs   Businesses that fall into the low market growth/low market share cell of a BCG matrix.

Downward communication   Flows from individuals in higher levels of the organization to those in lower levels.

Dynamic network   A network structure that makes extensive use of outsourcing through alliances with outside organizations.

Economic feasibility   Focuses on whether the expected benefits of an information system will be able to cover the anticipated costs.

Effectiveness   Pursuing the appropriate goals—doing the right things.

Efficiency   Using the fewest inputs to generate a given output—doing things right.

Electronic data interchange (EDI)   Electronic transmission of transaction data using telecommunications.

Electronic funds transfer (EFT)   Electronic manipulation of financial transactions.

Electronic mail (E-mail)   A computer-based system that allows individuals to exchange and store messages through computerized text-processing and communication networks.

Employee assistance programs   Designed to help employees cope with physical, personal, and emotional problems including substance abuse, alcoholism, stress, emotional illness, and family disturbances.

Employee-centered work redesign   An approach whereby employees design their work roles to benefit the organization and satisfy their individual goals.

Employment tests   Any instrument, device, or information used to make an employment decision is considered a test by the EEOC's Uniform Guidelines of Employee Selection.

Empowering employees   To increase the amount of control and discretion employees have over their job as a means of motivating behavior.

Encoding   Translating the sender's ideas into a systematic set of symbols or a language expressing the communicator's purpose.

End users   Those who will use and interact with the information system.

Entropy   The tendency for systems to decay over time.

Escalation of commitment   The tendency to increase commitment to a previously selected course of action beyond the level that would be expected if the manager followed an effective decision-making process.

Esteem needs   Personal feelings of achievement, self-worth, recognition, respect, and prestige from others.

Ethical audits   Methods by which compliance with ethical standards is measured.

Ethical behavior   Behavior which is morally accepted as good or right as opposed to bad or wrong.

Ethical dilemma   A situation in which a person must decide whether or not to do something that, although benefiting oneself or the organization, may be considered unethical and perhaps illegal.

Ethics   The established customs, morals, and fundamental human relationships that exist throughout the world.

Expectancy   The belief that a particular level of effort will be followed by a particular level of performance.

Expected monetary value (EMV)   The sum of each expected value for an alternative.

Expected value   The product of a payoff and its probability of occurrence.

Expert power   The power to influence because of expert knowledge and competence.

Expert system   Computer-based system that contains and can use knowledge about a specific, relatively narrow and complex application.

External customer   Consumer who purchases the product or service output of the organization.

External forces   Environmental factors that are fundamentally beyond the control of management.

Extinction   The withdrawal of the positive reward or reinforcing consequences for an undesirable behavior.

Feedback   Information about the status and performance of a given effort or system.

Feedback controls   Controls that compare the actual performance of the organization to its planned performance.

Feedback (corrective) control   Focuses on discovering undesirable output and implementing corrective action.

Feedforward controls   Controls designed to identify changes in the external environment or the internal operations of the organization that may affect its ability to fulfill its mission and achieve its strategic goals.

Feedforward (preventive) control   Focuses on detecting undesirable material, financial, or human resources that serve as inputs to the transformation process.

Fiedler's LPC model   A contingency model that predicts workgroup effectiveness based on a match between the leader's style and the demands of the situation.

Fixed assets   Assets that are long-term in nature, and cannot be converted quickly into cash.

Fixed interval schedule   Rewards at specific time intervals, assuming that the desired behavior has continued at an appropriate level.

Fixed position layout   Configuration used for large or bulky items that remain stationary in the manufacturing process.

Fixed ratio schedule   Provides a reinforcement after a fixed number of occurrences of the desired behavior.

Focus strategy   A strategy for competing by targeting a specific and narrow segment of the market.

Force-field analysis   A systematic process for examining the pressures that are likely to support or resist a proposed change.

Formal groups   Deliberately created to accomplish goals and serve the needs of the organization.

Functional managers   Managers who are responsible for managing a work unit that is grouped based on function served.

Functional strategy   Specifies the operations, research and development, financial, human resource management, and marketing activities necessary to implement the organization's corporate and business strategies.

Functional structure   Members of the organization are grouped according to the function they perform within the organization.

GE matrix   Business portfolio matrix that uses industry attractiveness and business strength as the indicators of the firm's strategic position.

General environment   Those environmental forces that are beyond a firm's influence and over which it has no control.

General managers   Managers who are responsible for managing several different departments that are responsible for different tasks.

Generic strategies   The fundamental way in which an organization competes in the marketplace.

Geographic divisional structure   A structure in which the activities of the organization are grouped according to the geographic markets served.

Global strategy   A strategy for competing in multiple international markets with a standard line of products and services.

Goal setting   A process intended to increase efficiency and effectiveness by specifying the desired outcomes toward which individuals, groups, departments, and organizations work.

Goals   The results that an organization seeks to achieve.

Grand strategy   A comprehensive, general approach for achieving the strategic goals of an organization.

Grapevine   The informal flow of messages throughout the organization.

Group   Two or more interdependent individuals who interact with and influence one another to accomplish a common purpose.

Groupthink   An agreement-at-any-cost mentality that results in ineffective group decision making.

Halo and horn effect   The process in which we evaluate and form an overall impression of an individual based solely on a specific trait or dimension.

Hawthorne effect   Phenomenon where individual or group performance is influenced by human behavior factors.

Horizontal communication   The lateral information flows that occur both within and between departments for the purpose of coordination.

Human Resource Management (HRM)   The management of the employees of the organization consisting of all the activities required to enhance the effectiveness of an organization's work force and to achieve organizational goals and objectives.

Human resource planning   The process of determining future human resource needs relative to an organization's strategic plan and taking the actions necessary to meet those needs in a timely manner.

Human rights approach   A situation in which decisions are made in light of the moral entitlements of human beings.

Human skills   The ability to work effectively with others.

Hybrid layout   Configuration containing some degree of flexibility, lying between the extremes of process and product layouts.

Hygiene factors   Associated with the job context or environment in which the job is performed.

Hyperchange   A condition of rapid, dramatic, complex, and unpredictable change that has a significant effect on the ways in which organizations are managed.

Income Statement   Summary of an organization's financial performance over a given time interval, showing revenues, expenses, and bottom-line profit or less.

Informal groups   Self-created groups that evolve out of the formal organization based on proximity, common interests, or needs of individuals.

Information   End result of the process of transforming data into meaningful facts useful for a specific purpose.

Information overload   Occurs whenever the capacity of a communication medium to process information is exceeded.

Information power   Control over information that involves the leader's power to access and distribute information that is either desired or vital to others.

Information technology   A broad category of communication techniques that includes videotape recorders, telephone-answering devices and services, closed-circuit television systems, and facsimile machines.

Informational roles   The manager's responsibility for gathering and disseminating information to the stakeholders of the organization.

Initiating structure   The degree to which a leader defines and structures his or her own role and the roles of subordinates toward the attainment of the group's formal goals.

Inputs   Such diverse items as materials, workers, capital, land, equipment, customers, and information used in creating products and services.

Instrumental values   Standards of conduct or methods for attaining an end.

Instrumentality   The probability assigned by the individual that a specific level of achieved task performance will lead to various work outcomes.

Intangible costs   Costs that are difficult or impossible to quantify.

Integrating mechanisms   Methods for managing the flow of information, resources, and tasks within the organization.

Interdependence   The degree to which work groups are interrelated.

Internal customer   In the sequence of stages that extend from purchasing raw materials through to final delivery of the product or service, an internal customer is any individual or department that uses the output of a prior stage.

Internal forces   Inside factors that are generally within the control of management.

Internal network   A network structure that relies on internally developed units to provide services to a core organizational unit.

Interpersonal roles   The manager's responsibility for managing relationships with organizational members and other constituents.

Intuition   An unconscious analysis based on past experience.

Jargon   Pretentious terminology or language specific to a particular profession or group.

Job analysis   Assimilating all of the information about a particular job including job descriptions and job specifications.

Job depth   The degree of control given to a job holder to perform their job.

Job description   An outline of the responsibilities and tasks associated with a given job.

Job design   The set of tasks and activities that are grouped together to define a particular job.

Job enlargement   Programs designed to broaden job scope.

Job enrichment   Programs designed to increase job depth.

Job involvement   The job's importance in the employee's life or to the employee's self-concept.

Job rotation   Assigning individuals to a variety of job positions.

Job satisfaction   The degree to which individuals feel positively or negatively about their jobs.

Job scope   The number of different activities required in a job and the frequency with which each activity is performed.

Job shop production system   Produces small quantities of a wide variety of specialized items.

Job specifications   The identification of the knowledge, skills, abilities, and other employee characteristics needed to perform the job.

Justice approach   A situation in which decisions are based on an equitable, fair, and impartial distribution of benefits and costs among individuals and groups.

Just-in-time (JIT) inventory management   Philosophy

that advocates eliminating waste, solving problems, and striving for continual improvement in operations.

Labor-management relations　　The formal process through which employees and unions negotiate terms and conditions of employment including pay, hours of work, benefits, and other important aspects of the working environment.

Language systems and metaphors　　The way that organizational members typically express themselves and communicate with each other.

Law of effect　　Determines if a behavior will be repeated or not, depending on whether the consequence is positive or negative.

Law of requisite variety　　Control systems must have enough variety to cope with the variety in the systems they are trying to control.

Leadership　　A social influence process that involves determining the group's objectives, motivating behavior in pursuit of these objectives, and influencing group maintenance and culture.

Leadership substitutes　　Situational variables that tend to outweigh the leader's ability to affect subordinate satisfaction and performance.

Leading　　Motivating and directing the members of the organization so that they contribute to the achievement of goals of the organization.

Least preferred coworker scale (LPC)　　Designed to measure relationship-oriented versus task-oriented behaviors according to a leader's choice of descriptive terms.

Legitimate power　　Power stemming from formal authority based on the particular positions in an organization or social system.

Liabilities　　The firm's debts and obligations.

Line personnel　　Those organizational members that are directly involved in delivering the products and services of the organization.

Liquidity ratios　　Indicators of the firm's ability to meet its short-term debts and obligations.

Local area network (LAN)　　Information system that connects users in a small area, such as a building, an office, or a manufacturing plant.

Locus of control　　The extent to which individuals believe that they can control events affecting them. Those with an internal locus of control believe that events are primarily the result of one's own behavior and actions. Those with an external locus of control believe that much of what happens is uncontrolled and determined by outside forces.

Locus of decision making　　The degree to which decision making is centralized versus decentralized.

Long-term liabilities　　Debts payable over a long time span.

Machiavellian personality　　Someone who vies for and manipulates others purely for personal gain and feels that any behavior is acceptable if it achieves one's goals.

Management　　The process of administering and coordinating resources effectively and efficiently and in an effort to achieve the goals of the organization.

Management by exception　　Focusing on the elements that are not meeting the standards.

Management by objectives (MBO)　　A method for developing individualized plans which guide the activities of individual members of an organization.

Management information system (MIS)　　Focuses on the routine, structured, regular reporting and information requirements of the organization.

Managers　　Organizational members who are responsible for planning, organizing, leading, and controlling the activities of the organization so that its goals can be achieved.

Market growth rate　　A measure of the annual growth percentage of the market in which the business operates.

Master production schedule　　Detailed statement of projected production quantities for each item in each time period.

Matrix structure　　A structure in which the tasks of the organization are grouped along to organizing dimensions simultaneously (e.g., product/geographic market, product/function).

Mechanistic systems　　Highly centralized organizations in which decision-making authority rests with top management.

Medium　　The carrier of the message or the means by which the message is sent.

Messages　　The tangible forms of coded symbols that are intended to give a particular meaning to the data.

Moral agent　　A business' obligation to act honorably and to reflect and enforce values that are consistent with those of society.

Motivation　　The forces acting on or within a person that causes the person to behave in a specific, goal-directed manner.

Motivator factors　　Related to job content or what people actually do in their work.

Multidomestic strategy　　A strategy for competing in multiple international markets by tailoring products and services to meet the specific needs of each host country market.

Myths　　Unproven beliefs that are accepted uncritically and used to justify current actions by communicating the practical benefits of certain techniques and behaviors.

Need for achievement　　The drive to excel, to accomplish challenging tasks, and achieve a standard of excellence.

Need for affiliation　　The desire for friendly and close interpersonal relationships.

Need for power　　The desire to influence and control one's environment.

Negative reinforcement　　The removal of negative consequences following a desired behavior.

Network structure　　A contemporary organizational structure that is founded on a set of alliances with other organizations that serve a wide variety of functions.

Noise　　Any internal or external interference or distraction with the intended message that can cause distortion in the sending and receiving of messages.

Nominal group technique (NGT)　　A structured process designed to stimulate creative group decision making where agreement is lacking or the members have incomplete knowledge concerning the nature of the problem.

Nonprogrammed decisions　　Decisions made in response to situations that are unique, unstructured, or poorly defined.

Nonverbal communication   All messages that are nonlanguage responses.

Norms   Unwritten and often informal rules and shared beliefs about what behavior is appropriate and expected of group members.

Objective function   A symbolic, quantitative representation of the primary goal that the decision maker is seeking to optimize.

Objectives   The desired results to be attained.

Open systems   Systems that must interact with the external environment to survive.

Operational feasibility   Focuses on the willingness and ability of all concerned parties to operate, use, and support the information system.

Operational planning   The process of determining the day to day activities that are necessary to achieve the long-term goals of the organization.

Operational plans   An outline of the tactical activities necessary to support and implement the strategic plans of the organization.

Opportunity   Situation which has the potential to provide additional beneficial outcomes.

Oral communication   All forms of spoken information.

Organic (clan) control   Reliance upon social values, traditions, shared beliefs, flexible authority, and trust to assess performance and correct unacceptable deviations.

Organic systems   Decentralized organizations that push decision making to the lowest levels of the organization in an effort to respond more effectively to environmental change.

Organization   A group of individuals who work together toward common goals.

Organizational change   Any alteration of activities in an organization that can be in the structure of the organization, the transfer of work tasks, introduction of a new product, or in attitudes among members.

Organizational commitment   The degree to which the employee is committed to the organization's values and goals, has a desire to remain a part of the organization, and is willing to expend considerable efforts for the organization.

Organizational control   Process through which managers regulate organizational activities to make them consistent with the expectations and help them achieve predetermined standards of performance.

Organizational culture   The system of shared beliefs and values that develops with an organization. In simple terms, organizational culture is the personality of the organization.

Organizational design   The way in which the activities of an organization are arranged and coordinated so that its mission can be fulfilled and its goals achieved.

Organizational Development (OD)   A process of planning change in organizations that use behavioral science knowledge, theory, and technology to help an organization improve its capacity for effective change.

Organizational feasibility   Focuses on how well the proposed system supports the strategic objectives of the organization.

Organizational mission   The reasons for which the organization exists; and provides strategic direction for the members of the organization.

Organizational structure   The primary reporting relationships that exist within an organization.

Organizing   The process of determining the tasks to be done, who will do them, and how those tasks will be managed and coordinated.

Orientation   The process of familiarizing new employees with the organization, their job, and their work unit, that enables them to become productive members of the organization.

Outputs   The physical commodity, or intangible service or information that is desired by the customers or users of the system.

Owner's equity   The portion of a business that is owned by the shareholders. The difference between the assets of an organization and its liabilities.

Partial schedule of reinforcement   Rewarding the desired behavior intermittently.

Participative leadership   Consulting with subordinates and taking their opinions and suggestions into account.

Participative management   Encompasses varied activities of high involvement where subordinates share a significant degree of decision-making power with their immediate superiors.

Path-goal model   Used because of its emphasis on how a leader influences subordinates' perception of work goals and personal goals, and the links or paths found between these two sets of goals.

Payoff table   A matrix which organizes the alternative courses of action, states of nature, and payoffs for a decision situation.

Payoffs   The outcomes of decision situations.

PERT (Program Evaluation and Review Technique)   A network approach for scheduling project activities.

Performance appraisal   A systematic process of evaluating employee job-related achievements, strengths, weaknesses, as well as determining ways to improve performance.

Personality   The enduring, organized, and distinctive pattern of behavior that characterizes an individual's adaptation to a situation.

Physiological needs   Food, water, air, and shelter are physiological needs.

Planning   Setting goals and defining the actions necessary to achieve those goals.

Plans   Blueprints for action that prescribes the activities necessary for the organization to realize its goals.

Policies   General guidelines for decision making within the organization.

Pooled interdependence   Occurs when organizational units have a common resource but no interrelationship with one another.

Positive reinforcement   The administration of positive and rewarding consequences following a desired behavior.

Power   The ability to marshal human, informational, or material resources to get something done.

Problem   Situation where some aspect of organizational performance is less than desirable.

Procedures   Instructions on how to complete recurring tasks.

Process consultation   Involves structured activities directed toward key "processes" through which members of a group work with one another on specific issues and activities.

Process layout   Configuration flexible enough to accommodate a wide diversity of products or customers.

Product divisional structure   A structure in which the activities of the organization are grouped according to specific products or product lines.

Product layout   Configuration set for a specific purpose, with all product or service demands essentially identical.

Productivity   Measure of the efficiency with which a firm transforms inputs into outputs.

Profitability ratios   Indicators of the relative effectiveness, or profitability, of the organization.

Programmed decisions   Decisions made in response to routine situations that have occurred in the past.

Programs   Single-use plans that govern a comprehensive set of activities designed to accomplish a particular set of goals.

Project production system   Produces large scale, unique items.

Projects   Single-use plans that direct the efforts of individuals or work groups toward the achievement of a specific goal.

Protected class   Composed of individuals who fall within a group identified for protection under equal employment laws and regulations.

Punishment   The administration of negative consequences following undesirable behavior.

Quality assurance   Focuses on any activity that impacts upon the maintenance of quality at the desired level.

Quality circle   Work team that meets regularly to identify, analyze, and solve problems related to its work area.

Quality control   Focuses on the actual measurement of output to see if specifications have been met.

Quality management   A formal approach to management where the overriding priority of the organization is to deliver a quality product or service and to work toward excellence and continuous improvement in all areas of the organization.

Quality-of-work-life (QWL) programs   Programs undertaken by an organization for the purpose of (1) improving the quality of employee's work life, or (2) improving group or organizational productivity.

Question marks   Businesses that fall into the high market growth/low market share cell of a BCG matrix.

Rational-economic model   A prescriptive framework of how a decision should be made that assumes managers have completely accurate information.

Rational-legal authority   Subordinates comply with a leader because of a set of impersonal rules and regulations that apply to all employees.

Reciprocal interdependence   Occurs when information, resources, and tasks must be passed back and forth between work groups.

Recruitment   The process of finding and attracting job candidates who are qualified to fill job vacancies.

Reengineering   Radically changing the organizational processes for delivering products and services.

Referent power   The ability to influence based on personal liking, charisma, and reputation.

Refreezing   The third step in the change process, centers on reinforcing new behaviors, usually by positive results, feelings of accomplishment, or rewards from others.

Relationship-oriented roles   Behaviors that cultivate the well-being, continuity, and development of the group.

Relative market share   The firm's market share divided by the market share of its largest competitor.

Repetitive, assembly line, or mass production system   Produces high volume of discrete items.

Responsibility   An obligation on the part of an employee to complete assigned activities.

Restraining forces   Promote organizational stability or the status quo and resist change.

Reward power   Derived from control over tangible benefits, such as promotion, a better job, a better work schedule, a larger operating budget, an increased expense account, and formal recognition of accomplishments.

Rites   A relatively dramatic, planned set of recurring activities used at special times to influence the behavior and understanding of organizational members.

Robotics   Use of machines with human-like characteristics, such as dexterity, movement, vision, and strength.

Roles   Shared expectations of how group members will fulfill the requirements of their positions.

Rules   Detailed and specific regulations for action.

Satisficing   The search and acceptance of something that is satisfactory rather than perfect or optimal.

Scalar principle   A clear line of authority must run throughout the organization.

Schedules of reinforcement   Specify the basis for and timing of reinforcement.

Scientific management   Focuses on the productivity of the individual worker.

Security need   The desire to have a safe physical and emotional environment.

Selection   The process of evaluating and choosing the best qualified candidate from the pool of applicants recruited for the position.

Selective perception   The tendency to screen out information with which we aren't comfortable or do not consider relevant.

Self-actualization needs   Self-fulfillment and the opportunity to achieve one's potential.

Self-esteem   The extent to which people believe they are capable, significant, successful, and worthwhile.

Self-managed teams   Groups of employees who design their jobs and work responsibilities to achieve the self-determined goals and objectives of the team.

Self-oriented roles   Behaviors that meet some personal need or goal of an individual without regard to the group's problems.

Sequential interdependence   Occurs when organizational units must coordinate the flow of information, resources, and tasks from one unit to another.

Sexual harassment   Actions that are sexually directed, unwanted, and subject a worker to adverse employment conditions.

Single-use plans   Plans which address specific organizational situations that typically do not recur.

Situational favorability   A combination of leader-member relations, task structure, and position power that determines the control needed by a leader in a specific situation.

Skill variety   The degree to which a job challenges the job holder to use various skills and abilities.

SLT model   States that effective leader behavior depends on the situational contingency of readiness and the appropriate behavior-readiness match.

Social context   The setting in which a communication takes place.

Social contract   An implied set of rights and obligations that are inherent in social policy and assumed by business.

Span of control   The number of employees reporting to a particular manager.

Special purpose team   Temporary team formed to solve a special or nonrecurring problem.

Stable environments   Environments which experience little change.

Stable network   A network structure that utilizes external alliances selectively as a mechanism for gaining strategic flexibility.

Staff personnel   Those organizational members that are not directly involved in delivering the products and services of the organization, but provide support for line personnel.

Staffing   Bringing in or placing people into the organization and making sure they serve as productive members of the workforce.

Stakeholders   People who are affected by or can affect the activities of the firm.

Standing plans   Plans that deal with organizational issues and problems that recur frequently.

Stars   Businesses that fall into the high market growth/high market share cell of a BCG matrix.

States of nature   Conditions over which the decision maker has little or no control.

Status   The perceived social ranking of one member relative to other members of the group.

Stereotyping   The tendency to assign attributes to someone, not on individual characteristics, but solely on the basis of a category or group to which that person belongs.

Stories   Accounts based on true events; they often contain both truth and fiction.

Strategic analysis   An assessment of the internal and external conditions of the firm.

Strategic control   The methods by which the performance of the organization is monitored.

Strategic decision-making matrix   Two-dimensional grid used to select the best strategic alternative in light of multiple organizational objectives.

Strategic goals   The results that an organization seeks to achieve in the long-term.

Strategic planning   The process by which an organization makes decisions and takes actions to enhance its long-run performance.

Strategic plan   A plan that identifies the markets in which an organization competes, as well as the ways in which it competes in those markets.

Strategy formulation   The establishment of strategic goals for the organization and the development of corporate and business level strategies.

Strategy implementation   The actions required to ensure that the corporate and business level strategy of the organization is put into place.

Supportive leadership   Giving consideration to the needs of subordinates, displaying concern for their welfare, and creating a friendly climate in the work unit.

Survey feedback   A method of improving relationships among members of groups or departments that gather information, perceptions, and attitudes through a customized survey questionnaire and present the information to participants to discuss.

Synergy   Phenomenon where an organization can accomplish more when its subsystems work together than it can accomplish when they work independently.

Systems analysis   An approach to problem solving that is closely aligned with the quantitative perspective on management.

Systems development life cycle (SDLC)   Recognition that investigating, analyzing, designing, implementing, and maintaining an information system is an ongoing process.

Tangible costs   Costs that can be accurately quantified.

Task environment   Those environmental forces that are within the firm's operating environment and over which the firm has some degree of control.

Task identity   The degree to which a job requires the completion of an identifiable piece of work.

Task-oriented roles   Behaviors directly related to establishing and achieving the goals of the group or getting the task done.

Task significance   The degree to which a job contributes to the overall efforts of the organization.

Team building   A process by which members of a work group diagnose how they work together and plan changes to improve their effectiveness.

Technical feasibility   Focuses on the hardware and software capabilities of the proposed information system.

Technical skills   The ability to utilize tools, techniques, and procedures that are specific to a particular field.

Telecommuting   The practice of working at a remote site by using a computer linked to a central office or other employment location.

Terminal values   Goals an individual will ultimately strive to achieve.

Theory X   Managers perceive that subordinates have an inherent dislike of work, and will avoid it if possible.

Theory Y   Managers perceive that subordinates enjoy work, and will gain satisfaction from their jobs.

Theory Z   Advocates that managers place trust in the employees and make them feel like an intimate part of the organization.

Total quality management (TQM)   A systematic approach for enhancing products, services, processes, and operational quality control.

Traditional authority   Subordinates comply with a leader because of custom or tradition.

Training   A planned effort to assist employees in learning job-related behaviors in order to improve performance.

Trait approach   The assumption that some people are "natural leaders," and are endowed with certain traits not possessed by other individuals.

Transformation process   The mechanism by which inputs are converted to outputs.

Transformational leadership   The process of influencing the attitudes and assumptions of organizational members and building commitment to the organization's mission and objectives.

Turbulent environments   Environments which are characterized by rapid and significant change.

Type A Orientation   Characterized by impatience, a desire for achievement, aggressiveness, irritability, and perfectionism.

Type B Orientation   Characterized as easy-going, relaxed, patient, able to listen carefully, and communicate more precisely than Type A individuals.

Unfreezing   Developing an initial awareness of the need for change and the forces supporting and resisting change.

Unity of command   A principle that each employee in the organization is accountable to one, and only one, supervisor.

Upward communication   Information to managers from their subordinates.

Utility approach   A situation in which decisions are based on an evaluation of the overall amount of good that will result.

Valence   The value or importance that the individual attaches to various outcomes.

Validity   A relationship between what a test proposes to measure and what is actually measured.

Values   Relatively permanent and deeply held preferences upon which individuals form attitudes and personal choices.

Variable interval schedule   When reinforcement is administered at random or varying times that cannot be predicted by the employee.

Variable ratio schedules   Reinforcement administered randomly.

Variance reporting   Highlighting only those things that fail to meet the established standards.

Videoconferencing   The technologies that use live video to unite widely dispersed company operations.

Vigilance   The concern for and attention to the process of making a decision that occurs when the decision maker considers seven critical procedures.

Whistleblower   Someone who exposes organizational misconduct or wrongdoing to the public.

Wide area network (WAN)   Information system that extends over a broad geographic area, such as cities, regions, countries, or the world.

Written communication   Letters, memos, policy manuals, reports, forms, and other documentation used to share information in the organization.

NAME INDEX

A

Aaker, D. A., 120, 142
Abell, Derek F., 218, 219, 240
Abernathy, W., 305, 314
Abramson, M. A., 440, 454
Acohido, B., 458, 482, 487, 488
Acquilano, N. J., 564, 567, 594
Adams, J. S., 371, 502, 520
Adler, A., 210, 235, 240, 241
Adler, N. J., 187, 206, 400, 419, 511, 512, 521
Adorno, T. W., 463, 487
Agor, W. H., 189
Akers, John, 22, 118, 284
Albert, Sam, 307
Albrecht, K., 136, 143
Alexander, L., 80, 105, 120, 142
Allaire, Paul, 362, 380
Altany, D. R., 577
Altier, W. J., 300, 314
Amabile, T. M., 498
Amoroso, D., 609, 630
Ancona, D. G., 371, 381
Anderson, Bob, 211
Anderson, D. R., 564, 573, 577, 581, 584, 594, 595
Anderson, Jon, 450
Andrews, K., 87, 106
Ansoff, H., 122, 142
Aplin, J. C., 541, 559
Aries, E., 404, 419
Artzt, Edwin L., 430–431
Ash, Mary Kay, 17, 356, 450, 495, 496, 520
Ashby, W. R., 536, 559
Augustine, Norman, 99
Austin, J. A., 393
Austin, L., 54, 69
Axline, L. L., 125, 142

B

Bacharach, M., 222, 240
Baird, J., 391, 419
Baldwin, S. R., 124, 142, 148, 175
Baliga, B. R., 549, 559
Barlow, V. M., 608, 630
Barnard, Chester, 52–53, 63, 69
Barnes, Thomas, 223
Barnes-Farrell, J. L., 196
Barnett, C., 362, 380
Baron, R. A., 52, 69, 486
Barrier, M., 125, 142
Barry, David, 22, 23, 35, 443, 454
Bartlett, C., 166, 176
Bass, B. M., 442, 454
Bassin, M., 263, 280
Bazerman, M. H., 190, 206
Beach, L. R., 197, 200, 207, 355, 380
Beall, Donald, 24

Beals, Vaughn, 38
Beam, H. H., 214, 240
Beamer, L., 400
Beatty, R. W., 330, 349
Becker, H., 91, 106
Beer, S., 536, 559
Behling, O., 189, 206
Bell, C. H., 371, 380
Benjamin, R. J., 609, 630
Benne, K. J., 476, 488
Bennett, J. V., Sr., 567
Bennis, Warren, 425, 441, 454
Bentley, L. D., 608, 630
Berelson, B., 474, 488
Berkowitz, L., 432, 454, 502, 520
Bernstein, A., 332, 339, 349, 350
Bernstein, P., 458, 487
Berry, B. H., 210, 235, 240, 241
Berss, M., 157
Bertalanffy, Ludwig von, 55
Bertrand, K., 19, 35, 125, 142
Bertsch, T. M., 163
Bettenhausen, K. L., 477, 488
Betts, K. S., 83, 106
Beyer, J. M., 355, 380
Bhide, A., 147
Bihler, D., 80, 81, 105
Birch, David, 354
Bishop, J., 464, 487
Blackburn, J., 584, 595
Blair, K. E., 553, 559
Blake, Robert R., 431, 454
Blanchard, K. H., 188, 206, 391, 419, 434, 435, 454, 471, 505, 521
Boccialetti, G., 373, 381
Bolman, L. G., 161
Borisoff, D., 404, 419
Boroski, J., 322
Borucki, C., 362, 380
Boulding, K., 54, 69
Boulian, P. V., 460, 487
Bowen, H. R., 75, 105
Bowers, Claude G., 43
Bracker, J., 149, 150, 176
Brady, F. N., 187, 206
Brancheau, J. C., 622, 631
Brass, D. J., 408, 420
Braun, D. J., 163
Braunstein, D.N., 498, 520
Brett, J. M., 194, 207, 339, 350
Brickner, W. H., 118, 142
Bridwell, L. G., 494, 520
Brigham, E., 551, 559
Brocka, B., 42, 68
Brocka, M. S., 42, 68
Brockhaus, R. H., Sr., 463, 487
Brooks, S. L., 210, 235, 240, 241
Brown, Bennett A., 137
Brown, Russ, 213

Brownell, J., 398, 404, 419
Browning, Perry W., 587
Bulkeley, W., 393, 419
Burke, W. W., 370, 380
Burnham, H., 500, 520
Burns, J., 54, 69
Burns, Stanley, 328, 329, 349
Burns, Tom, 304, 312, 314
Bush, J. B., 294, 314
Bush, President George, 398
Bush, Vannevar, 51
Bushardt, S. C., 270, 280
Butterfield, R. W., 564
Buzzell, R. D., 147, 175
Byrne, John A., 22, 24, 35, 94, 106, 292, 305, 314, 361, 364, 366, 380, 458, 487, 510, 511, 521

C

Cady, S., 401, 419, 478, 488, 512, 513, 521
Calfee, D. L., 155, 156, 176
Calingo, L.M. R., 147, 175
Calloway, Wayne, 354, 359, 374, 375, 379, 381
Campion, M. A., 251, 279
Cantoni, C., 397, 419
Carlzon, Jan, 389
Carnevale, A. P., 284, 292, 313, 314
Carroll, A. B., 73, 75, 79, 105
Carson, K. D., 509
Carson, P. P., 509
Carson, T., 258, 280
Carter, J. H., 272, 280
Cartwright, D., 426, 454
Cascio, W. F., 333, 349
Case, Thomas, 25, 35
Caudill, L. M., 304, 314
Cavanaugh, G. F., 86, 88, 106
Certo, S. C., 221, 240
Chalykoff, H. J., 553, 559
Champy, J., 354, 375, 380, 381, 388, 413, 418, 420, 424, 447, 453, 455, 510, 521
Chance, Paul, 23, 35, 262, 280
Chandler, Alfred D., 120, 142, 165, 166, 176
Charan, R., 294, 314
Chase, R. B., 564, 567, 594
Chatwal, Sant Singh, 190
Chen, Winston, 332
Chency, J. L., 295, 314
Cheney, P., 609, 630
Christoff, K., 609, 630
Churback, C., 394, 419
Ciampa, D., 191, 206
Circle, K., 220
Clement, R. W., 354
Clinton, President Bill, 84, 398
Cochran, P. L., 75, 76, 105

COMPANY INDEX

SUBJECT INDEX

TEXT CREDITS

CHAPTER 1

More Bang for Less Bucks at Gateway Computer   16
Source: Andrew Kupfer, "The Champ of Cheap Clones," 115-20. © 1991 Time Inc. All rights reserved.

Jubilations, Inc.: It Hasn't Been a Piece of Cake   18
Source: Jubilations, Inc., Real World Lessons for America's Small Businesses: Insights from the Blue Chip Initiative, 1991, 22.

American Express: The World Over   21
Source: Robert Tittleman, "Image vs. Reality at American Express," *Institutional Investor,* February 1992, 36-47, copyright Institutional Investor, reprinted with permission; and Kate Bertrand, "In Service, Perception Counts," *Business Marketing,* April 1989, 44.

CHAPTER 2

Denny's Embraces Diversity   59
Source: Denny's Advocates Diversity. *Orlando Sentinel,* October 12, 1993, C-5; Denny's, Blacks Settle Suits. Orlando Sentinel, May 25, 1994, A1+; Denny's Settles Bias Case. U.S.A Today, May 25, 1994, B2.

Ferco Tech   60
Source: Adapted from Ferco Tech, *Strengthening America's Competitiveness: The Blue Chip Initiative* (Warner Books on behalf of Connecticut Mutual Life Insurance Company and the U.S. Chamber of Commerce, 1991), 68-69.

Veit, Inc.: A Phenomenal Turn for the Better   50
Source: Adapted from Veit, Inc., *Real-World Lessons for America's Small Businesses: Insights from the Blue Chip Initiative* (Published by *Nation's Business* on behalf of Connecticut Mutual Life Insurance Company and the U.S. Chamber of Commerce, 1993), 74-75.

CHAPTER 3

Partnerships for Environmental Solutions   84
Source: Kellyn S. Betts, "The Coming Green Computers," The Environmental Magazine, April 1994, 28-35.

Gray Matters: *Ethics Becomes a Game to Play*   97
Source: "Gray Matters: The Ethics Game," Martin Marietta Corporations, 1992.

Nynex Corporation: Doing the Right Thing   94
Source: "Crime Stoppers: Tougher Penalties Put Ethics on the Front Burner at Nynex," *Business Ethics,* March/April 1992, 18; B. Hager, "What's behind Business' Sudden Fervor for Ethics," *Business Week,* September 23, 1991, 65.

CHAPTER 4

The Euro Disneyland Plan to Hire 12,000 Cast Members   127
Source: Vicki Vaughn, "Disney Begins Massive Task," *Orlando Sentinel,* D-1.

Kmart Versus W. T. Grant: Strategic Focus Versus Strategic Chaos   121
Source: J. Little and L. Alexander, "Kmart Stores: Where America Shops and Saves," *Selected Cases in Strategic Management,* ed. S. Certo and J. P. Peter (New York: McGraw-Hill, 1990), 227-31; "Investigating the Collapse of W. T. Grant," *Business Week,* July 19, 1976, 60-62; and "How W. T. Grant Lost $175 Million Last Year," *Business Week,* February 24, 1975, 74-76.

Friendly: A Mismatched Strategic and Operational Strategy   134
Source: H. Dawley, Friendly Makeover Completed: Company Moves Ailing Chain in New Direction—Maybe," *Restaurant Business,* April 10, 1992, 36; and C. Donahue and A. Snyder, "Hershey Kisses Off the Friendly Restaurant Chain," *Ad-Week's Marketing Week,* August 22, 1988, 3-4.

Forte Industries: Catching Up with Yourself   117
Source: "Forte Industries," *Strengthening America's Competitiveness: The Blue Chip Enterprise Initiative* (published by Warner Books on behalf of Connecticut Mutual Life Insurance Company and the U.S. Chamber of Commerce, 1991), 171.

CHAPTER 5

A Strategy for Vision of Dreamz   147
Source: N. J. Perry, "Vision of Dreamz: Big Returns from the Basics," *Fortune,* 90. © 1993 Time Inc. All rights reserved.

KAO Corporation: Total Flexibility   153
T. A. Stewart, "Brace for Japan's Hot New Strategy," *Fortune,* 62-74. © 1994 Time Inc. All rights reserved.

CHAPTER 6

Spurling Fire & Burglar Alarm: Managing by Committee   196
Source: Adapted from "Spurling Fire & Burglar Alarm: Managing by Committee," in *Real World Lessons for America's Small Businesses: Insights from the Blue Chip Enterprise Initiative* (published by Warner Books on behalf of Connecticut Mutual Life Insurance Company and the U.S. Chamber of Commerce, 1992), 143-44.

Assessing Your Decision-Making Skills   182
Source: Adapted from P. Fandt, *Management Skills: Practice and Experience* (St. Paul, Minn.: West Publishing Company, 1994), 320-21.

Chatwal's Satisficing Behavior Leads to Problems   190
Source: P. Gupte, "Merge in Haste, Repent in Leisure," *Forbes,* August 22, 1988, 85.

Decision Making in Other Cultures   188
Sources: N. J. Adler *International Dimensions of Organizational Behavior,* 2nd ed. (Boston: PWS-Kent Publishing Company, 1991); and P. Sethi, N. Maniki, and C. Swanson, *The False Promise of the Japanese Miracle* (Marshfield, Mass: Pitman, 1984).

New York Life's Gravediggers Deliver Quality and Service 194
  Source: "Gravedigging at New York Life," *Fortune,* September 21, 1992, 160. Reprinted with permission of New York Life Insurance Company.

CHAPTER 7

Agsco, Inc. 213
  Source: Adapted from "Agsco, Inc." *Real World Lessons for America's Small Businesses: Insights from the Blue Chip Initiative (Nation's Business* on behalf of Connecticut Mutual Life Insurance Company and the U.S. Chamber of Commerce, 1992), 36-37.
Computer Service Supply Corporation: When the Market Vanishes 223
  Source: Adapted from "Computer Service Supply Corporation," in *Real World Lessons for America's Small Businesses: Insights from the Blue Chip Initiative (Nation's Business* on behalf of Connecticut Mutual Life Insurance Company and the U.S. Chamber of Commerce, 1993), 139-40.
Coca-Cola's Bold New Decision 212
  Source: "How Coke Decided a New Taste Was It," *Fortune,* May 27, 1985, 80. © 1985 Time Inc. All rights reserved. And "Coke's Brand-Loyalty Lesson," *Fortune,* August 5, 1985, 44-46. © 1985 Time Inc. All rights reserved.

CHAPTER 8

Alcoa: Work Redesign as a Means of Meeting World Leader Standards 261
  Source: R. Jacob, "Thriving in a Lame Economy," *Fortune,* October 5, 1992, 44-54. © 1992 Time Inc. All rights reserved.
Shelby Die Casting: Investing in People 265
  Source: Adapted from "Shelby Die Casting," in *Real World Lessons for America's Small Businesses: Insights from the Blue Chip Initiative (Nation's Business* on behalf of Connecticut Mutual Life Insurance Company and the U.S. Chamber of Commerce, 1993), 58-59.

CHAPTER 9

Mearthane Products: Topping Japanese Quality 303
  Source: Adapted from "Mearthane Products," in *Real World Lessons for America's Small Businesses: Insights from the Blue Chip Initiative (Nation's Business* on behalf of Connecticut Mutual Life Insurance Company and the U.S. Chamber of Commerce, 1993), 52-53.
Lewis Galoop: A Dynamic Network 294
  Source: C. Snow, R. E. Miles, and H. Coleman, Jr., "Managing 21st Century Network Organizations," *Organizational Dynamics 10* (February 1992): 5-20.
Using Information Technology for International Business 300
  Source: F. V. Guterl, "Goodbye, Old Matrix," 35. Reprinted with permission, *Business Month* magazine, February, 1989. Copyright © 1989 by Goldhirsh Group, Inc., 38 Commercial Wharf, Boston, MA 02110.

CHAPTER 10

Avon Calling: Affirmative Action from the Bottom Up 321
  Sources: H. Keets, "Avon Calling—On Its Troops," *Business Week,* July 8, 1991, 53; S. B. Garland, "How to Keep Women Managers on the Corporate Ladder," *Business Week,* September 2, 1991, 64; and N. J. Perry, "If You Can't Join 'Em, Beat 'Em," *Fortune,* September 21, 1992, 58-59.
How Aware Are You of the Changing Workforce? 322
  Sources: G. Graham "Companies Forced to Become More Sensitive as Work Force Diversifies," *Orlando Sentinel,* July 2, 1992, B-1; *Monthly Labor Review* (June, 1992); and T. Cox, Jr., "Managing Cultural Diversity: Implications for Organizational Competitiveness," *Academy of Management Executive,* 3 (1991): 45-56.
An Entrepreneurial Spirit Inspires a Diverse Workforce 332
  Source: A. T. Demaree, "Oh, the Glory of a Baldrige Award," *Fortune,* March 9, 1992, 152-53. © 1992 Time Inc. All rights reserved.

CHAPTER 11

Never Kill a New Product Idea at 3M 358
  Source: T. J. Peters and R. H. Waterman, *In Search of Excellence* (New York: Harper & Row, 1983), 224-34; J. Galbraith, "The Innovating Organization," *Organizational Dynamics* (Winter 1982): 5-25 B. Dumaine, "Ability to Innovate," *Fortune,* January 29, 1190, 43-46; and C. Knowlton, "What America Makes Best," *Fortune,* March 28, 1988, 40-54.
Changes at American Express: Focusing on Service Rather than Growth 360
  Source: L. N. Spiro, "What's in the Cards for Harvey Golup?" *Business Week,* June 15, 1992, 112-24; and R. Wells, "American Express CEO Charges into Problems," *Orlando Sentinel,* September 20, 1993, F-1, F-7.
How Much Change are You Experiencing 366
  Source: Reprinted with permission from *Journal of Psychosomatic Research* 11, T. H. Holmes and R. H. Rahe, "Social Readjustment Rating Scale," 1967, Elsevier Science Ltd., Pergamon Imprint, Oxford, England.
Rejection Leads to Change and Success 370
  Source: L. Kraar, "Iron Butterflies," *Fortune,* October 7, 1991, 143-54. © 1991 Time Inc. All rights reserved.

CHAPTER 12

A Communication Self-Assessment 392
  Source: A. J. Dubrin, *Contemporary Applied Management: Skills for Managers* (Buur Ridge, Ill.: Irwin, 1994), 165. Used with permission.
Computer Networking: The Key to Productive Meetings 394
  Source: W. Bulkeley, "Computerizing Dull Meetings Is Touted as an Antidote to the Mouth That Bored," *Wall Street Journal,* January 28, 1992, B1. Reprinted by permission of The Wall Street Journal, © 1992 Dow Jones & Company, Inc. All rights reserved worldwide.
Using Feedback to Improve Your Writing Skills 396
  Source: Adapted from P. Fandt, *Management Skills: Practice*

and Experience (St. Paul, Minn.: West Publishing Company, 1994), 135.

Gegs: Listens to Employees   408
Source: Quality and Teamwork: Keys to Success (Cherry Hill, N. J.: General Electric Government Services, 1988) R. D. Prichard, P. L. Roth, S. D. Jones, P. J. Galgay, and M. D. Watson, "Designing a Goal-Setting System to Enhance Performance: A Practical Guide," *Organizational Dynamics* 17, (1988): 69-79; and M. Whitmire and P. R. Nienstedt, "Lead Leaders into the 90's" *Personnel Journal* (May 1991): 80-85.

CHAPTER 13

What Is Leadership   425
Source: Adapted from J. B. Lau and A. B. Shani, *Behavior in Organizations: An Experiential Approach,* 5th ed. (Boston: Irwin, 1992), 39.

Steven Jobs: Inspiring Others Through the Language of Leadership   441
Source: Adapted from J. A. Conger, "Inspiring Others: The Language of Leadership," *Academy of Management Executive,* 5 (1991): 31-45.

CHAPTER 14

Accidental Entrepreneurs: Controlling Their Efforts and Fate   464
Source: D. Young, "Accidental Entrepreneurs Break All Business School Rules," *Orlando Sentinel,* February 9, 1992, D1, D2.

Corning—Teaching Workers a New Way to Work   469
Source: J. Hoerr, "Sharpening Minds for a Competitive Edge," *Business Week,* December 17, 1990, 72-78; T. A. Steward, "New Ways to Exercise Power," *Fortune,* November 6, 1989, 52-64; and K. H. Hammonds, "Corning's Class Act," *Business Week,* May 13, 1991, 68-76.

CHAPTER 15

Recognition at Mary Kay Cosmetics   496
Source: M. K. Ash, *Mary Kay* (New York: Harper & Row, 1981) T. J. Peter, and R. H. Waterman, *In Search of Excellence* (New York: Harper & Row, 1982) and W. Zellner "Mary Kay Is Singing I Feel Pretty," *Business Week,* December 2, 1991, 102.

Acquired Needs Motivation Survey   499
Source: Adapted from R. M. Steers and D. N. Braunstein, "A Behaviorally-Based Measure of Manifest Needs in Work Settings," *Journal of Vocational Behavior 9* (1976): 251-61.

Hilton: Performance for Excellence Program   504
Source: As discussed in J. M. Kouzes and B. Z. Posner, *The Leadership Challenge: How to Get Extraordinary Things Done in Organizations* (San Francisco: Jossey-Bass 1987).

CHAPTER 16

Federal Express Corporation   531
Source: B. Stratton, "Four to Receive 1990 Baldrige Awards," *Quality Progress,* December 1990, 19-21. © 1990 American Society for Quality Control. Reprinted with permission.

Yokogawa-Hewlett-Packard: Problems with Quality   542
Source: J. Young, "The Quality Focus at Hewlett-Packard," *Journal of Business Strategy,* (Winter 1985): 6-9; and "The Push for Quality," *Business Week,* June 8, 1987, 130-44.

Fullwood Foods   534
Source: Adapted from "Fullwood Foods," in *Strengthening America's Competitiveness: The Blue Chip Initiative* (Warner Books on behalf of Connecticut Mutual Life Insurance Company and the U.S. Chamber of Commerce, 1991), 97-98.

CHAPTER 17

AVX Goes Global in its Location   572
Source: "Business in a Nation in Turmoil," *New York Times,* April 18, 1988.

General Mills Runs Its Restaurants as if They Were Factories   570
Source: "Dinnerhouse Technology," *Forbes,* July 8, 1991, 98-99.

SuperVan—A Shuttle Service's Bumpy Road   582
Source: Adapted from "SuperVan," in *Real-World Lessons for America's Small Businesses: Insights from the Blue Chip Enterprise Initiative* (*Nation's Business* on behalf of Connecticut Mutual Life Insurance Company and the U.S. Chamber of Commerce, 1992), 166-67.

S. B. Electronics—From Executive to Entrepreneur   587
Source: Adapted from "S. B. Electronics," in *Strengthening America's Competitiveness: The Blue Chip Initiative* (Warner Books on behalf of Connecticut Mutual Life Insurance Company and the U.S. Chamber of Commerce, 1991), 67-68.

CHAPTER 18

Federal Express   603
Source: Videotape accompanying Raymond McLeod, Jr., *Management Information Systems: A Study of Computer Based Information Systems,* 5th ed. (MacMillan Publishing Company, 1993).

Ford Motor Company: Global Integration Through Technology   616
Source: Stratford Sherman, "How to Bolster the Bottom Line," *Fortune,* Autumn, 1993, 14-28.

Making Work Easier for Those With Challenges   621
Sources: 'Computer Use by Illiterates Grows at Work," *Wall Street Journal,* June 9, 1992, B1, B5; and T. L. O'Brien, "A PC Revolution: Aided by Computers, Many of the Disabled Form Own Businesses," *Wall Street Journal,* October 8, 1993, A1, A9.

PHOTO CREDITS